THE BLACKWELL ENCYCLOPEDIA OF MANAGEMENT

MARKETING

T0368009

THE BLACKWELL ENCYCLOPEDIA OF MANAGEMENT

SECOND EDITION

Encyclopedia Editor: Cary L. Cooper
Advisory Editors: Chris Argyris and William H. Starbuck

Blackwell Encyclopedia of Management, Second Edition: Marketing
Edited by Dale Littler

The first edition of the *Encyclopedia of Marketing* has been revised and updated, with new content on aspects of cross cultural marketing, research in marketing methodologies, societal marketing and marketing strategy. The implications of developments in information and communications technologies are assessed while retailing has been extensively revised to embrace contemporary trends.

(b)

About the Editors

Editor in Chief
Cary L. Cooper is based at Lancaster University as Professor of Organizational Psychology. He is the author of over 80 books, is past editor of the *Journal of Organizational Behavior*, and Founding President of the British Academy of Management.

Advisory Editors
Chris Argyris is James Bryant Conant Professor of Education and Organizational Behavior at Harvard Business School.

William Haynes Starbuck is Professor of Management and Organizational Behavior at the Stern School of Business, New York University.

Volume Editor
Professor Dale Littler of Manchester Business School, University of Manchester, has held a number of senior positions at the Manchester School of Management, including Head of the Manchester School of Management and Dean of Management. He established the Customer Research Academy and the Center for Applied Management Research.

Dale Littler has been a visiting professor at major European business and management schools and departments. He has had several grants from the ESRC and was a principal investigator for around eight years on the ESRC-funded Programme of Information and Communication Technologies. He has also had research grants from the European Commission, the Chartered Institute of Management Accountants, the Department of Trade and Industry, the Council for Scientific Policy, the Teaching Company Secretariat, and from the private sector. He is on the editorial board of many marketing and technology management journals and has undertaken consultancies with a wide range of companies.

He has been a member of the Research Grants Board of the ESRC and is currently on the Academic Senate of the Chartered Institute of Marketing, the Executive of the Academy of Marketing, and is Chair of the national research committee of the Academy of Marketing.

THE BLACKWELL ENCYCLOPEDIA OF MANAGEMENT

SECOND EDITION

MARKETING

Edited by
Dale Littler
Manchester Business School,
University of Manchester

Blackwell
Publishing

BLACKWELL PUBLISHING
350 Main Street, Malden, MA 02148-5020, USA
9600 Garsington Road, Oxford OX4 2DQ, UK
550 Swanston Street, Carlton, Victoria 3053, Australia

First published 1997 by Blackwell Publishers Ltd
Published in paperback in 1999 by Blackwell Publishers Ltd
Second edition published 2005 by Blackwell Publishing Ltd

2   2006

Library of Congress Cataloging-in-Publication Data

The Blackwell encyclopedia of management. Marketing / edited by Dale Littler.
p. cm. — (The Blackwell encyclopedia of management ; v. 9)
Rev. ed. of: The Blackwell encyclopedic dictionary of marketing /
edited by Barbara R. Lewis and Dale Littler. 1997.
Includes bibliographical references and index.
ISBN 1-4051-0254-3 (hardcover : alk. paper)
1. Marketing—Dictionaries. I. Littler, Dale. II. Blackwell Publishing Ltd.
III. Blackwell encyclopedic dictionary of marketing. IV. Series.
HD30.15 .B455 2005 vol. 9
[HF5415]
658'.003 s—dc22
[658.8'003]
2004018071

ISBN-13: 978-1-4051-0254-4 (hardcover : alk. paper)

ISBN for 12-volume set 0-631-23317-2

A catalogue record for this title is available from the British Library.

Set in 9.5 on 11pt Ehrhardt
by Kolam Information Services Pvt. Ltd, Pondicherry, India

For further information on
Blackwell Publishing, visit our website:
www.blackwellpublishing.com

Contents

Preface

The contribution of marketing to economic welfare has been clearly identified in many studies on, *inter alia*, the development and adoption of innovations. Yet marketing continues to be viewed ambiguously: its status, both by practitioners and more especially by non-marketing academics, is not unreservedly acknowledged. It is often seen as lacking a clear paradigmatic framework and robust research methodological tradition, although this perception applies also to business and management studies in general. Even if true, this may not necessarily be an unhealthy state regarding serious treatment: knowledge diversity promotes discussion, dissension, even conflict, all of which can promote further exploration, thought, and analysis.

Nevertheless, marketing as a core body of knowledge has a generally accepted defined structure: it remains, as it should be, informed by practice; but it also draws on an eclectic mix of knowledge from other disciplines and is unconfined within an epistemological straightjacket. Differing philosophical perspectives can of course enrich our understanding. Marketing has in recent years broadened its scope, and its accommodation of different traditions and its acknowledgment of ethical and other concerns are reflections of its increasing confidence.

The second edition has embraced some recent developments – the importance of cross-cultural research, the developments in information and communications technology, the increasing sophistication of qualitative research. New entries and the updating of entries where appropriate have taken account of one or more of these areas.

As with the first edition, there was a large number of possible entries, and arbitrary decisions had to be taken on where to draw the boundaries of what constitutes an acceptable range of entries that will somehow provide information and insights on key areas of marketing. In some cases the encyclopedia is the beginning of further explorations, in others the end point, and in yet others a means of confirmation.

I am extremely grateful to all the contributors, all of whom are valued colleagues. They are, in alphabetical order: Dr Emma Banister, Dr Liz Barnes, Professor Margaret Bruce, Dr Charles C. Cui, Professor Gary Davies, Dr Jim Freeman, Mr Michael Greatorex, Dr Steve Greenland, Professor Phil Harris, Mr Mark P. Healey, Professor Margaret K. Hogg, Professor Nigel Holden, Dr Gillian C. Hopkinson, Dr Kalipso Karantinou, Professor Philip J. Kitchen, Dr Fiona Leverick, Professor Barbara R. Lewis, Dr Andrew Lindridge, Dr David Marsden, Professor Vincent-Wayne Mitchell, Dr Andrew Newman, Dr Rudolf Sinkovics, Professor Trevor Watkins, Professor Dominic Wilson, Dr Steve Worrall, Dr Mohammed Yamin, Mr David Yorke, Dr Judy Zolkiewski. I am especially indebted to Mark Healey, who reviewed the first edition, and to Miss Deborah A. Lee of Manchester Business School, University of Manchester, who provided invaluable, and very patient, assistance throughout the long and arduous process of bringing all the disparate parts into some form of whole.

Dale Littler

About the Editors

Editor in Chief
Cary Cooper is based at Lancaster University as Professor of Organizational Psychology. He is the author of over 80 books, past editor of the *Journal of Organizational Behavior*, and Founding President of the British Academy of Management.

Advisory Editors
Chris Argyris is James Bryant Conant Professor of Education and Organizational Behavior at Harvard Business School.
William Haynes Starbuck is Professor of Management and Organizational Behavior at the Stern School of Business, New York University.

Volume Editor
Professor Dale Littler of Manchester Business School, University of Manchester, has held a number of senior positions at the Manchester School of Management, including Head of the Manchester School of Management and Dean of Management. He established the Customer Research Academy and the Center for Applied Management Research.

Dale Littler has been a visiting professor at major European business and management schools and departments. He has had several grants from the ESRC and was a principal investigator for around eight years on the ESRC-funded Programme of Information and Communication Technologies. He has also had research grants from the European Commission, the Chartered Institute of Management Accountants, the Department of Trade and Industry, the Council for Scientific Policy, the Teaching Company Secretariat, and from the private sector. He is on the editorial board of many marketing and technology management journals and has undertaken consultancies with a wide range of companies.

He has been a member of the Research Grants Board of the ESRC and is currently on the Academic Senate of the Chartered Institute of Marketing, the Executive of the Academy of Marketing, and is Chair of the national research committee of the Academy of Marketing.

Contributors

Emma Banister
Lancaster University Management School,
Lancaster University

Liz Barnes
Faculty of Food, Clothing, and Hospitality
Management, Manchester Metropolitan
University

Margaret Bruce
Manchester Business School, University of
Manchester

Charles C. Cui
Manchester Business School, University of
Manchester

Gary Davies
Professor of Corporate Reputation, Manchester
Business School, University of Manchester

Jim Freeman
Manchester Business School, University of
Manchester

Michael Greatorex
Formerly of Manchester School of
Management, University of Manchester

Steve Greenland
London Metropolitan University

Phil Harris
University of Otago

Mark P. Healey
Manchester Business School, University of
Manchester

Margaret K. Hogg
Professor of Marketing, Lancaster University
Management School, Lancaster University

Nigel Holden
Kassel International Management School

Gillian C. Hopkinson
Lancaster University Management School,
Lancaster University

Kalipso Karantinou
Manchester Business School, University of
Manchester

Philip J. Kitchen
Chair in Strategic Marketing, Hull University
Business School, University of Hull

Fiona Leverick
School of Law, University of Aberdeen

Barbara R. Lewis
Professor of Marketing, Manchester Business
School, University of Manchester

Andrew Lindridge
Manchester Business School, University of
Manchester

Dale Littler
Professor of Strategic Management,
Manchester Business School,
University of Manchester

David Marsden
School of Marketing and Tourism, Napier
University Business School

Vincent-Wayne Mitchell
Professor of Consumer Marketing, Cass
Business School, City of London

Andrew Newman
Manchester Business School, University of
Manchester

Rudolph Sinkovics
Manchester Business School, University of
Manchester

Trevor Watkins
Formerly of London South Bank University

Dominic Wilson
Professor of Strategic Management, Associate
Dean (Postgraduate and Professional Programs),
University of Wolverhampton Business School,
University of Wolverhampton

Steve Worrall
Formerly of Manchester School of
Management, University of Manchester

Mohammed Yamin
Manchester Business School, University of
Manchester

David Yorke
Formerly of Manchester Business School,
University of Manchester

Judy Zolkiewski
Manchester Business School, University of
Manchester

A

above-the-line

Dale Littler

Traditionally, MARKETING COMMUNICA-
TIONS were divided into above- and below-
the-line, with ADVERTISING being in the former
category and all other marketing communications being categorized as below-the-line. PER-
SONAL SELLING was generally not placed in
either category. This demarcation placed a high
value on media advertising, which today still
accounts for the major proportion of the
marketing communications budget. Often,
below-the-line activities are viewed as providing
support for the media advertising campaign,
which may today still be given the greater attention even in advertising agencies that provide a
full range of services, including SALES PROMO-
TION, DIRECT MARKETING, PUBLICITY, and
so on. Increasingly, the development of effective
marketing communications is seen as involving a
thorough analysis of target audience behavior and
is not necessarily predicated on the basis that
advertising is the prime means of addressing it.

account manager

Dale Littler

The account manager has responsibility for
managing major customers (*see* PARETO'S
RULE). This may involve being the point of
contact between the selling organization and
the customer and acting as coordinator of all
the activities within the selling organization
aimed at delivering optimum value to the customer. Often, important personal relationships
are built between the account manager and his/
her counterpart(s) in the customer organization.

See also *key account*

acculturation

Andrew Lindridge

The term acculturation describes the process of
CULTURE change between two different cultural groups who come in contact with each
other (Sayegh and Lasry, 1993). The Social Science Research Council (1954: 974) definition of
acculturation, although nearly 50 years old, is
still recognized as perhaps the best: it describes
acculturation as arising from the interactions of
two separate, autonomous, cultural systems.
The origins of this interaction arise as a "consequence of direct cultural transmission" being
derived "from non-cultural causes, such as ecological or demographic modification induced by
an impinging culture; it may be delayed, as with
internal adjustments following upon the acceptance of alien traits or patterns; or it may be a
reactive adaptation of traditional modes of life."
Ultimately, the outcome of the acculturation
process is both culture's selecting and adapting
those cultural values that allow the individual
and his/her group's culture to continue to
exist, and maintaining varying levels of group
and individual differentiation and integration.

Ward and Kennedy (1993a, b) add that acculturation can be distinguished further between
the group and the individual attitudes and behaviors, separating acculturation into two distinct outcomes: psychological and sociocultural.
The former refers to a set of internal psychological outcomes, such as good mental health,
psychological wellbeing, and the individual
being ultimately satisfied with his/her new culture. The latter refers to external psychological

outcomes that relate individuals to their new cultural environment, for example, "white" society, and represents the acquisition of social skills and behaviors appropriate to engage with the new society on a daily basis. Acculturation then determines the individual's sense of self-identity (*see* ACCULTURATION MODELS; SELF-CONCEPT) and ultimately affects his/her consumer behaviors (*see* CONSUMER ACCULTURATION).

Bibliography

Sayegh, L. and Lasry, J.-C. (1993). Immigrants' adaptation in Canada: Assimilation, acculturation, and orthogonal cultural identification. *Canadian Psychology*, 34 (1), 98–109.

Social Science Research Council (1954). Acculturation: An exploratory formulation. *American Anthropologist*, 56 (6), 973–1002.

Ward, C. and Kennedy, A. (1993a). Where's the culture in cross-cultural transition? Comparative studies of sojourner adjustment. *Journal of Cross-Cultural Psychology*, 24 (2), 221–49.

Ward, C. and Kennedy, A. (1993b). Psychological and socio-cultural adjustment during cross-cultural transitions: A comparison of secondary students overseas and at home. *International Journal of Psychology*, 28, 129–47.

acculturation models

Andrew Lindridge

ACCULTURATION has been identified as an interaction between two cultures and the resulting CULTURE change that arises. How an ethnic minority group or individual negotiates the acculturation process has predominantly focused on whether the dominant culture takes precedence for the ethnic minority group/individual (unidirectional) or whether acculturation represents a continued long period of interaction between the two cultures (bidirectional).

A unidirectional assimilation model describing the cultural changes undergone by individuals of a minority group was first proposed by Gordon (1964). In this model the ethnic minority relinquishes its cultural attitudes, beliefs, behaviors, customs, and values in favor of the dominant culture (Garcia and Lega, 1979). This process is called the straight-line theory of acculturation representing the eventual absorption of the ethnic group by the dominant ethnic population. An underlying assumption of this model is that the ethnic minority group/individual loses their original cultural identity and acquires an identity based upon the dominant new culture (LaFromboise, Coleman, and Gerton, 1993). This model stresses that acculturation problems encountered by immigrants are due to their own failure in assimilating into the dominant culture (Bourhis et al., 1997).

A criticism of the unidirectional model is its underlying assumption of ethnic minority group/individual's desire to lose their native culture and identity. Mendoza (1984) also critiques this approach for its assumption that acculturation can be identified using a single dimension, for example, language usage. Taking this approach, an Indian Punjabi Sikh living in Britain who spoke fluent English would be identified as acculturated to British white society, regardless of his identifying with his religion, speaking Punjabi, and not wishing to engage with white cultural values. This mode of acculturation may not be true for all ethnic minorities, a point recognized by the bidirectional acculturation process models.

The bidirectional model of acculturation arose from criticisms of the unidirectional models by Szapocznik, Kurtines, and Fernandez (1980) and Szapocznik and Kurtines (1993). These models identify acculturation in terms of the individual's behavior and values and her identification with both her ethnic and dominant culture. Unlike the unidirectional model, these models recognize that ethnic minority and dominant cultural identities are not evident on either side of a bipolar scale but as dimensions are independent of and orthogonal to each other (Zak, 1973, 1976; Der-Karabetian, 1980). Zak (1973, 1976) proposed that an ethnic minority group/individual may identify themselves negatively or positively regarding both their cultures, or positively toward one culture while remaining negative to the other. This identification process gives rise to four acculturation outcomes:

1   the bicultural individual, where the individual has a high level of involvement in both cultures;

2 the monocultural individual, with a high level of involvement in either his/her own ethnic minority or the dominant culture;

3 the marginal monocultural individual, identified as having a low involvement in either his/her own ethnic minority or the dominant culture; and

4 the marginal bicultural individual, where the individual shows low levels of interest in either his/her own ethnic minority culture or the dominant culture (Der-Karabetian, 1980).

However, the bidirectional models of acculturation have also been criticized for their inherent assumption that as interactions with the host society increase, the ethnic minority individual's interactions with his/her own ethnic minority culture will decrease (Laroche, Kim, and Hui, 1997; Laroche et al., 1998). This is a criticism that may not be resolvable owing to cultural and societal variables combined with the unique nature of all human beings.

In response to criticisms of the unidirectional model and in developing Der-Karabetian's (1980) and Zak's (1973, 1976) research, Berry (1990, 1992, 1997) elaborated a bidirectional acculturation model drawing upon a two-dimensional acculturation strategy, i.e., ethnic cultural maintenance and contact with the dominant host group. In this model the existence of environmental influences, such as the degree of multiculturalism in the host society, is recognized as having an effect on the ethnic minority individual. Berry (1997) argues that his proposed framework should be used to identify acculturative stress amongst ethnic minority individuals by categorizing them according to four distinct acculturation strategies:

1 integration (an equal interest in engaging with both their ethnic and dominant culture);

2 separation (retention of ethnic identity and rejection of dominant cultural identity);

3 assimilation (rejection of their ethnic minority culture in favor of accepting the dominant culture); and

4 marginalization (rejection in both their ethnic minority culture and the dominant culture).

Hence, these four acculturation categories can be identified with Der-Karabetian's earlier acculturation categories.

The interactive acculturation model (IAM) arose from criticism of Berry's bidirectional acculturation model for the lack of importance regarding the host society's influence on the acculturation preferences of minority-group members (Bourhis et al., 1997). IAM argues that acculturation strategies of ethnic minority members are interlinked with the acculturation orientations of host-majority members. The latter group, due to its influence and power in society, exerts a stronger influence on the acculturation preferences of ethnic minorities.

In assessing acculturation amongst ethnic minority groups or individuals, IAM asks both the host community and ethnic minority members two questions (the latter group's are shown in italics):

1 Do you find it acceptable that (*should we as*) immigrants maintain their cultural identity?

2 Do you accept that (*should we as*) immigrants adopt the cultural identity of the host community?

Four acculturation outcomes can then be derived:

1 A "yes" to both questions indicates the minority group wishing to integrate into society.

2 A "no" to the first and "yes" to the second question indicates that the minority group expects to assimilate into the host society.

3 A "yes" to the first and "no" to the second question indicates that the minority group expects to remain separate from the host society.

4 A "no" to both questions indicates that the ethnic minority group views itself as being excluded from both its own ethnic group and society.

According to the IAM, concordance occurs when the host society and the ethnic minority group share virtually similar acculturation orientations, attitudes, and behaviors. Discordance between the host community and the minority group occurs when the acculturation orientation

4 acculturation models

profiles for the host society and for the minority group reflect little or no commonality (Bourhis et al., 1997).

In criticizing the uni- and bidirectional acculturation models, Turner et al. (1994: 456) state, "Self categories do not represent fixed, absolute properties... but relative, varying, context-dependent properties." Rohner (1984) adds that incompatible mixed values often stand side by side within an individual, each being employed successfully in different situations. An alternative acculturation model that addresses Turner et al.'s criticisms is the dialogical acculturation model. This model draws upon the philosophical assumptions of social constructionism and represents a dynamic, flexible, and holistic approach to viewing acculturation in an ethnic minority group or individual (Bhatia, 2002).

Bhatia (2002) argues that the dialogical process involves the ethnic minority group/individuals moving continuously between opposing cultural positions, while simultaneously holding positions of being assimilated, separated, and marginalized. (Hence, Bhatia's argument develops the acculturation categories in Berry's bidirectional acculturation model and addresses Turner et al.'s criticisms of uni- and bidirectional acculturation models.) The dialogical acculturation model implies that acculturation and identity are both dynamic, with the ethnic minority individual creating multiple presentations of the self depending on other individuals and situations encountered (Phinney, 1996). Bhatia's dialogical acculturation model draws upon Oswald's (1999) argument that ethnic minority individuals conduct a code-switching process. This process of code switching allows an ethnic minority individual to draw upon appropriate ethnic minority or host cultural values in appropriate situations. Hence, acculturation becomes the enactment of a variety of codes, representing the creation of multiple identities amongst ethnic minority individuals (Lindridge, Hogg, and Shah, 2004).

Central to the code-switching approach is language, with language being a central aspect of the cognitive system of culture. In examining the acculturation process, Giles and Johnson (1981), Liebkind (1992), Noels, Pon, and Clément (1996), and Sachev and Bourhis (1990) found that the extent to which individuals en-

dorse their ethnic identities was directly related to their choice of language. An ethnic minority individual's choice of language ultimately then influences the formation of an ethnic identity, with ethnic identity influencing language attitudes and usage (Sachev and Bourhis, 1990). This provides useful criteria for marketers to assess individuals' sense of engagement with culture and their sense of ethnic and self-identity, culminating in their effects on their consumer behavior (*see* CONSUMER ACCULTURATION).

Bibliography

Berry, J. W. (1990). Psychology of acculturation. In J. Berman (ed.), Nebraska symposium on motivation, 1989: Cross-cultural perspectives. *Current Theory and Research in Motivation*, 37. Lincoln: University of Nebraska Press, pp. 201–34.

Berry, J. W. (1992). Acculturation and adaptation in a new society. *International Migration*, 30, 69–85.

Berry, J. W. (1997). Immigration, acculturation, and adaptation. *Applied Psychology: An International Review*, 46 (1), 5–34.

Bhatia, S. (2002). Acculturation, dialogical voices and the construction of the diasporic self. *Theory and Psychology*, 12 (1), 55–77.

Bourhis, R. Y., Moïse, L. C., Perreault, S., and Senécal, S. (1997). Toward an interactive acculturation model: A social-psychological approach. *International Journal of Psychology*, 32 (6), 369–86.

Der-Karabetian, A. (1980). Relation of two cultural identities of Armenian-Americans. *Psychological Reports*, 47, 123–8.

Garcia, M. and Lega, L. I. (1979). Development of a Cuban ethnic identity questionnaire. *Hispanic Journal of Behavioral Sciences*, 1, 247–61.

Giles, H. and Johnson, P. (1981). The role of language in ethnic group. In J. C. Turner and H. Giles (eds.), *Intergroup Behavior*. Oxford: Blackwell, pp. 199–272.

Gordon, M. M. (1964). *Assimilation in American Life*. New York: Oxford University Press.

LaFromboise, T., Coleman, H. L. K., and Gerton, J. (1993). Psychological impact of biculturalism: Evidence and theory. *Psychological Bulletin*, 114 (3), 395–412.

Laroche, M., Kim, C., and Hui, M. K. (1997). A comparative investigation of dimensional structures of acculturation for Italian Canadians and Greek Canadians. *Journal of Social Psychology*, 137 (3), 317–31.

Laroche, M., Kim, C., Hui, M. K., and Tomiuk, M. A. (1998). Test of a non-linear relationship between linguistic acculturation and ethnic identification. *Journal of Cross-Cultural Psychology*, 29 (3), 418–33.

Liebkind, K. (1992). Ethnic identity: Challenging the boundaries of social psychology. In G. M. Breakwell (ed.), *Social Psychology of Identity and the Self-Concept.* London: Surrey University Press, pp. 147–85.

Lindridge, A. M., Hogg, M., and Shah, M. (2004). Imagined multiple worlds: How British South Asian women navigate the "border crossings" between household and societal contexts. Paper accepted for the *Journal of Consumption, Marketing and Culture.*

Mendoza, R. H. (1984). Acculturation and socio-cultural variability. In J. L. Martinez, Jr. and R. H. Mendoza (eds.), *Chicano Psychology.* New York: Praeger.

Noels, K. A., Pon, G., and Clément, R. (1996). Language, identity, and adjustment: The role of linguistic self-confidence in the acculturation process. *Journal of Language and Social Psychology*, **15** (3), 246–64.

Oswald, L. (1999). Culture swapping: Consumption and the ethno genesis of middle-class Haitian immigrants. *Journal of Consumer Research*, **25**, 303–18.

Phinney, J. S. (1996). When we talk about American ethnic groups, what do we mean? *American Psychologist*, **51** (9), 918–27.

Rohner, R. P. (1984). Toward a conception of culture for cross-cultural psychology. *Journal of Cross-Cultural Psychology*, **15** (2), 111–38.

Sachev, I. and Bourhis, R. Y. (1990). Language and social identification. In D. Abrams and M. A. Hogg (eds.), *Social Identity Theory: Constructive and Critical Advances.* New York: Western Wheatsheaf, pp. 211–29.

Szapocznik, J. and Kurtines, W. M. (1993). Family psychology and cultural diversity, opportunities for theory, research and application. *American Psychologist*, **48** (4), 400–7.

Szapocznik, J., Kurtines, W. M., and Fernandez, T. (1980). Bicultural involvement and adjustment in Hispanic-American youths. *International Journal of Intercultural Relations*, **4**, 353–65.

Turner, J., Oakes, P., Haslam, S. A., and McGarty, C. (1994). Self and collective: Cognition and social context. *Personality and Social Psychology Bulletin*, **20**, 454–63.

Zak, I. (1973). Dimensions of Jewish-American identity. *Psychological Reports*, **33**, 891–900.

Zak, I. (1976). Structure of ethnic identity of Arab-Israeli students. *Psychological Reports*, **38**, 239–46.

action

David Yorke and Dale Littler

The term "action" appears at the CONATIVE (or behavioral) STAGE of models of the hierarchy of effects of MARKETING COMMUNICATIONS, among the best known being AIDA, which stands for the four stages of attention, interest, desire, and action (*see* AIDA MODEL). Although it is widely recognized that the CONSUMER DECISION-MAKING PROCESS is more complex than represented in such models, they are still useful in providing an indication of the purposes and process of a communications campaign. The action phase can involve several different activities and refers to positive acts of the buyer/customer/consumer such as seeking further information from the supplying organization, TRIAL of the product or service, together with the first (and, ultimately, repeat) purchase of the product or service. Triggering desired forms of "action" is best achieved by specific communication techniques such as ADVERTISING (for seeking further information) and PERSONAL SELLING (for trial and purchase), although more recent developments in DIRECT MARKETING such as DIRECT MAIL, OFF THE PAGE selling, and TELEMARKETING are now being used to generate a complete range of actions. The action stage can stretch over a significant time and may be repeated each time the customer engages in the acquisition of the specific product or service.

Bibliography

Puth, G. (2000). Marketing communications. In K. Blois (ed.), *The Oxford Textbook of Marketing.* Oxford: Oxford University Press, ch. 12.

adaptive strategy

Dale Littler

This is one of three original strategic styles, the others being the entrepreneurial and planning (*see* ENTREPRENEURIAL STRATEGY; PLANNING STYLE), suggested by Mintzberg (1973). Several other strategic styles have since been identified, now termed "schools," by Mintzberg, Ahlstrand, and Lampel (1998). The adaptive mode is suited to large, often non-profit-oriented, organizations that will tend to be in the public sector. They have ambiguous goals and there are many different interest groups within the organization, each with its own objectives and agenda. Consequently, strategy often emerges (*see* EMERGENT STRATEGY) through a process of bargaining and consensus seeking, similar to that identified by Cyert and March (1963). This approach to strategy formation can be contrasted with the entrepreneurial style of bold decision-making. This is generally a feature of small organizations dominated by the owner-manager. However, such a perspective ignores research (e.g., Golby and Johns, 1971), suggesting that many small firms tend to be rather conservative, with their owners preferring to insure continued control rather than engaging in taking significant risks with a view to securing major growth. Large firms, particularly those with a dominant chief executive, may also engage in entrepreneurial strategy formation. Finally, the planning mode is the traditional approach to STRATEGIC PLANNING and tends to be suited to large, bureaucratic organizations operating in relatively stable environments with the resources to afford the detailed analysis such an approach requires. It is generally recognized that all strategy development evolves through a process of adaptation to changing knowledge about the context within which the strategy will be applied, and that the original intentions and assumptions about, *inter alia*, the environment will be modified or changed, in light of greater information and awareness.

Bibliography

Cyert, R. M. and March, J. G. (1963). *A Behavioral Theory of the Firm*. Englewood Cliffs, NJ: Prentice-Hall.

Golby, C. W. and Johns, G. (1971). *Attitude and Motivation*. Bolton Committee Research Report No. 7.

Mintzberg, H. (1973). Strategy making in three modes. *California Management Review*, 16, 2 (Winter), 44–53.

Mintzberg, H., Ahlstrand, B., and Lampel, J. (1998). *Strategy Safari*. London: Prentice-Hall.

adoption process

Dale Littler

The consumer adoption process for an innovation is typically represented as a number of stages consisting of, in the order through which they are passed: awareness, when the consumer first becomes knowledgeable about an innovation either passively or through an active search; information search, when the consumer is stimulated to acquire more details about the innovation; evaluation, when the consumer assesses whether or not the innovation satisfies his/her requirements, often against competing possibilities; TRIAL, when either physically or vicariously the consumer tries out the innovation in a way that minimizes the risk; and finally adoption or rejection. The process may not end there, however, because the consumer may go through a process of reevaluation that may lead to satisfaction or dissatisfaction with the decision to adopt, or it may lead the consumer for various reasons, including changed circumstances, to adopt an innovation previously tentatively rejected (*see* COGNITIVE DISSONANCE; CUSTOMER SATISFACTION).

The relative importance of each stage may vary according to the "newness" of the innovation, cultural influences, and personal factors, such as risk averseness (*see* PERCEIVED RISK). An alternative paradigm of the adoption decision process consists of: knowledge; persuasion; decision; and confirmation (Rogers and Shoemaker, 1991), and different communications channels may have different importance at different stages. Thus, impersonal channels, such as MASS MEDIA, may be important in the "knowledge" phase, whereas personal forms of communication, such as WORD-OF-MOUTH COMMUNICATIONS, are likely to assume a greater significance in the later, more evaluative phases.

Individuals differ in their propensity to adopt an innovation. Rogers (1995) developed a categorization based on the normal distribution curve using the mean and standard deviation. There are five categories of adopters: innovators (2.5 percent); early adopters (13.5 percent); early majority (34 percent); late majority (34 percent); and laggards (16 percent). There has been substantial research on the demographic and psychographic features of each innovator type. The original classification of ideal types still prevails, with the salient values of each being as follows: innovators – venturesome; early adopters – respectable; early majority – deliberate; late majority – skeptical; and laggards – traditional. Research on the various socioeconomic differences of each category has been largely inconclusive. There has been increasing questioning of whether or not there is a general trait of innovativeness (*see* INNOVATORS), and individuals' reactions to innovation may be significantly affected by their INVOLVEMENT or the particular intensity of their interests and requirements.

It has been argued that features of the product also affect the innovation process. Rogers (1995) initially identified these as: relative advantage; observability; complexity; trialability; and compatibility.

See also *diffusion process*

Bibliography

Engel, J. F., Blackwell, R. D., and Miniard, P. W. (1995). *Consumer Behavior*, 8th edn. Fort Worth, TX: Dryden Press.

Rogers, E. M. (1995). *Diffusion of Innovations*, 4th edn. New York: Free Press.

Rogers, E. M. and Shoemaker, F. F. (1991). *Communication of Innovations: A Cross-Cultural Approach*. London: Collier Macmillan.

Soloman, M., Bamossy, G., and Askegard, S. (1999). *Consumer Behavior: A European Perspective*. London: Prentice-Hall.

advertisement

see ADVERTISING

advertising

Barbara R. Lewis

Advertising is a paid form of non-personal presentation and communication about an organization and/or its goods and services, by an identified sponsor, that is transmitted to a target audience through a mass medium.

Advertising is a one-way communication from an organization to a customer and is subject to the consumer selective processes of: exposure, perception, selection, distortion, and retention (*see* CONSUMER PERCEPTIONS; SELECTIVE EXPOSURE; SELECTIVE RETENTION), i.e., the audience is not obligated to be attentive or respond, which in turn depends on: consumer attributes, needs and values, predispositions, characteristics of the company and its messages, and channels of communications. Key features of advertising are: its public presentation, which confers a legitimacy; its persuasive nature, which is possible through repetition; and its expressive nature in so far as it dramatizes a company and its products or services.

Advertising is an integral element of an organization's MARKETING COMMUNICATIONS (*see* COMMUNICATIONS MIX). It may be planned and executed within an organization or handed over to specialists, i.e., advertising agencies (*see* AGENCY). Advertising is an industry in its own right although it employs relatively few people, the major expenditures being for media time and space.

The major stages in the development of an organization's advertising are: setting advertising objectives; deciding on the budget; planning messages; selecting the media; and evaluating advertising effectiveness.

Advertising objectives flow from prior decisions on an organization's target market (or segments) (*see* MARKET SEGMENTATION; MARKETING MIX) and are various (e.g., Colley 1961 lists 52 possible objectives). They are concerned with informing, persuading, and reminding current and potential buyers/customers/consumers, including other organizations in the distribution chain, with respect to products and organizations/institutions (*see* COMMUNICATIONS OBJECTIVES). Product and brand advertising is typically focused on generating or defending sales, whereas institutional advertising is usually concerned with promoting an organization's image or reputation, developing goodwill, or improving a company's relationships with various groups to include customers, channels (of distribution) members, suppliers, shareholders, employees, and the general public. In setting the advertising budget, organizations may take account of factors such as stage in the PRODUCT LIFE CYCLE, market share and customer base, competition, advertising frequency, and product substitutability. These and other variables are built into advertising expenditure models which, as a result of developing computer technology, are becoming increasingly complex. The advertising budget can be established on the basis of what is affordable, as a percentage of sales, on the basis of competitors' expenditures, or on the basis of objectives and tasks.

Advertising messages represent the creative aspect of advertising (see MESSAGE) and organizations are concerned with developing messages, evaluating and selecting among them, and executing them effectively.

In deciding on advertising media, it is necessary to take account of the desired REACH, FREQUENCY, and IMPACT; choose among the major media types and vehicles; and decide on media timing.

The choice of media types is influenced by considerations such as the product/service being advertised, target audience media habits, the advantages and limitations of the media, and their costs. Advertising media comprise: TELEVISION, RADIO, NEWSPAPERS, MAGAZINES, TRADE JOURNALS, posters (billboards), and DIRECT MAIL. They are distinguished from other forms of communication, e.g., PUBLICITY, because the time and/or space has to be paid for.

Developing of advertising messages and choice of media are influenced, in part, by product sensitivity and advertising controls. For example, companies need to be aware of the sensitive nature of advertising alcohol and tobacco, the misuse of which may contribute to health and social problems. Advertising controls embrace government (legal) regulations and self-regulation. Various legal statutes impinge on advertising, e.g., the Trades Descriptions Act, the Medicines Act, food and drug labeling requirements, consumer credit regulations, together with restrictions with respect to the advertising of alcohol, tobacco, medicines, professional services, etc. Examples of industry self-regulation may be seen in various CODES OF PRACTICE, the Advertising Standards Authority, and the television advertising standards authorities.

The effectiveness of advertisements may be assessed in two major ways: pre-testing adverts (e.g., copy testing) and post-evaluating their effectiveness (e.g., recall and recognition tests). Advertisers also try to measure the communications effects on awareness, knowledge, preferences, and sales, although it is accepted that relationships between advertising and sales are not necessarily causal due to: the influence of other variables in the marketing mix; competitors' activities; and sales effects over time, e.g., adverts may not be seen immediately, impact may be later, there may be carry-over effects, or sales may be brought forward at the expense of future sales. The development of the Internet has created a new market for advertising with its incorporation in, for example, search engine sites (see INTERNET MARKETING); while the emergence of more television channels mainly from satellite broadcasting is leading to an increasing fragmentation of the market for television and therefore television advertising.

Bibliography

Colley, R. H. (1961). *Defining Advertising Goals for Measured Advertising Results*. New York: Association of National Advertisers.

Jobber, D. (2004). *Principles and Practices of Marketing*, 4th edn. London: McGraw-Hill.

advertising agency

see AGENCY

affect

Mark P. Healey

Affect is some degree of positive or negative subjective feeling. In the marketing field, it typically refers to feelings such as emotions and moods that result from interaction with consumption stimuli. The advertisements (see ADVERTISING), products, and brands encountered in the marketplace frequently stimulate feelings and sensations in consumers, such as surprise, happiness, desire, and sadness. Feeling excitement viewing an advertisement for a forthcoming film, or experiencing anger during a long wait for assistance using an automated telephone service, are both examples of affective reactions. An affective reaction is a valenced (positive or negative) mental sensation which diverges from an equilibrious or existing phenomenal state to bring about a certain mental and/or behavioral inclination. For example, feelings of regret following the purchase of a disliked brand can leave consumers with the intention of avoiding future purchases of this brand. Affect entails some degree of arousal or excitation and a sense of pleasure or displeasure, which combine to produce affective feeling.

An affective response is distinguished from other valenced psychological responses to consumption on the basis that it is characterized by a subjectively experienced feeling state, such as happiness or sadness, pleasure or pain. Non-affective cognitions, including remembering and evaluation, often induce specific feelings, but in themselves are affectively barren mental processes and can thus be differentiated from actual feeling states. However, in the kind of higher mental processes generally analyzed in studies of marketplace behavior, affect (feeling) and cognition (thinking) are often intertwined in their order and experiencing. Thinking about one's possessions or purchases can engender certain feelings, and current feelings and emotions can influence the way customers think about and react to the products they encounter.

Subtle differences in the usage of the term affect are evident throughout the marketing literature. Affect has been used as a generic term to describe all valenced mental processes, including emotions, moods, and attitudes. In contrast, affect has also been used to describe only valenced feeling states such as emotions and moods, with ATTITUDES differentiated as evaluative cognitions or thoughts rather than as feelings (Cohen and Areni, 1991). Affect is sometimes used to refer to feelings of lesser intensity, where emotions are viewed as more intense. Oliver (1997) differentiates affect, emotion, and mood, conceptualizing each as a discrete response. Primary affect is feeling, including pleasure and displeasure, coupled with visceral sensations from neural and physiological arousal. Emotion includes arousal, different feelings, and cognitive interpretations of feelings. Moods are distinguished via their relatively extended duration and lesser intensity. Some studies make meaningful conceptual and empirical distinctions between the constructs of affect, emotion, and moods, whilst others use these and other related terms interchangeably. Despite this vacillation, affect is predominantly conceptualized in terms of subjective feeling states, and contrasted with cold (unfeeling) cognition; tripartite models of attitudes distinguish between the affective (feeling) and cognitive (knowing) components of attitudes, for instance.

Several influential theories of consumption-related affect have been drawn from the psychology literature into the marketing domain. Russell's (1980) circumplex model conceives affect as consisting of two main dimensions, corresponding to pleasure and arousal. This has been particularly useful in understanding consumers' feelings toward consumption experiences (see Wirtz, Mattila, and Tan, 2000). Various theories consider three constructs and their interactions as components of affect: physiological arousal, psychological pleasure, and cognitive interpretation. Arousal states, such as surprise or excitement, may be viewed as distinct affects. However, others argue that since physiological arousal is neutral in that it can be interpreted in a positive or negative manner, arousal combines with valenced feelings to produce emotions of different intensities. For example, psychological pleasure combined with high physiological arousal results in feelings of joy, whereas pleasure allied to low arousal results only in feelings of contentment. In a different conceptualization, appraisal theories of emotion (see Bagozzi, Gopinath, and Nyer, 1999) hold that emotions result from cognitive evaluations or judgments of a product or a consumption experience in terms of its significance for a consumer's goals or personal wellbeing. Different appraisals result in different emotional reactions. For instance, anger may be felt where one attributes product failure to the manufacturer, regret where it is attributed to one's own misuse. Research has shown that positive and negative affect may be experienced simultaneously and contribute independently to customers' feelings following a consumption experience (Mano and Oliver, 1993).

Following a period in which marketing researchers focused primarily on the non-feeling, cognitive determinants of marketplace behaviors, affect is now viewed as a key influence on customers' psychological processes and behavior. Physiological arousal can influence how consumers form brand attitudes when viewing advertisements, for example. Consumers may use their feelings toward a product or advertisement as a guide for judgments, decisions, and behaviors (see Pham et al., 2001). The feelings associated with using a product can also shape CUSTOMER SATISFACTION, and remembering a happy product experience can enhance customers' positive feelings. Furthermore, various works have demonstrated that mood influences different consumption behaviors. A customer in a positive mood may evaluate brands more favorably and be more inclined to make immediate purchases than a customer in a negative or neutral mood.

Bibliography

Bagozzi, R. P., Gopinath, M., and Nyer, P. U. (1999). The role of emotions in marketing. *Journal of the Academy of Marketing Science*, **27** (2), 184–206.

Baumgartner, H., Sujan, M., and Bettman, J. R. (1992). Autobiographical memories, affect, and consumer information processing. *Journal of Consumer Psychology*, **1** (1), 53–82.

Cohen, J. B. and Areni, C. S. (1991). Affect and consumer behavior. In T. S. Robertson and H. H. Kassarjian (eds.), *Handbook of Consumer Theory and Research*. Englewood Cliffs, NJ: Prentice-Hall, pp. 188–240.

Gardner, M. P. (1985). Mood states and consumer behavior: A critical review. *Journal of Consumer Research*, **12** (December), 281–300.

Mano, H. and Oliver, R. L. (1993). Assessing the dimensionality and structure of the consumption experience: Evaluation, feeling, and satisfaction. *Journal of Consumer Research*, **20**, 3 (December), 451–66.

Miniard, P. W., Bhatla, S., and Sirdeshmukh, D. (1992). Mood as a determinant of postconsumption product evaluations: Mood effects and their dependency on the affective intensity of the consumption experience. *Journal of Consumer Psychology*, **1** (2), 173–95.

Oliver, R. L. (1997). *Satisfaction: A Behavioral Perspective on the Consumer*, international edn. New York: McGraw-Hill.

Pham, M. T., Cohen, J. B., Pracejus, J. W., and Hughes, G. D. (2001). Affect monitoring and the primacy of feelings in judgment. *Journal of Consumer Research*, **28**, 2 (September), 167–88.

Russell, J. A. (1980). A circumplex model of affect. *Journal of Personality and Social Psychology*, **39** (December), 1161–78.

Wirtz, J., Mattila, A. S., and Tan, R. L. P. (2000). The moderating role of target-arousal on the impact of affect on satisfaction: An examination in the context of service experiences. *Journal of Retailing*, **76**, 3 (Fall), 347–65.

affective stage

David Yorke

MARKETING COMMUNICATIONS models, which state that a target buyer or customer moves along a spectrum from a state of ignorance or unawareness of an organization and/or its products or services to ultimately making a purchase, comprise three principal stages, namely, the COGNITIVE, affective, and CONATIVE (or behavioral).

The affective stage is that which attempts to create a preference for one product, brand, or service in the target buyer's or customer's mind, in relation to all others. In other words, communications at the affective stage are designed to develop, maintain, and reinforce positive ATTITUDES in the mind of the target buyer, customer, or consumer. Investment of resources of time and money in attaining such an objective can be huge, but there is plenty of research evidence to support the notion that it can be achieved, e.g., Volvo is synonymous in many people's minds with security or safety, after spending millions of financial resources and many man-hours both on developing and testing safety features in its cars and on telling potential customers that it has effectively done so. Currently, major organizations are seemingly attempting to show that they are "environmentally conscious," i.e., that their concern for reducing the erosion of the earth's resources is reflected in their product or service offerings.

agency

David Yorke

An organization can develop its own ADVERTISING and promotional (*see* PRICE PROMOTIONS; SALES PROMOTION) skills or use those of an agency, either in-house, which is owned and controlled by the parent company, or one that is independent. Cost is a major consideration but other factors, such as generating an external perspective and the facility to offer a complete range of services from market research to distribution, may play a role in the client–agency relationship.

Advertising agencies vary, both in size and in expertise. The full service agency will be concerned with the creation of the advertisement, involving the development of copy (for print advertisements) or scripts (for television and cinema advertisements), and the overall visual design of the advertisement. It will also have responsibility for the selection of the media, the scheduling of the advertisements, and the purchasing of the relevant media space. It will be involved in negotiating with media owners over price. The agency will manage the account with the advertiser through an ACCOUNT MANAGER or director, who is responsible for managing the relationship with the advertiser. Large agencies will also have the facility for undertaking research, for example on how consumers think and feel about the advertiser's products, the current advertising, and so on, that will feed into the development of the advertising campaign. Agencies can be international, taking on advertising responsibility in several geographic markets; others are more local. Some specialize, such as in, for example, BUSINESS-TO-BUSINESS MARKETING, RETAILING, fashion, or finance; others handle a variety of accounts.

A substantial proportion of the income earned by the agency is from commission secured from the media owners. For example, where the published charge rate for a 30-second TV advertisement is, say, 5,000, the agency charges its client this full rate-card cost (the published standard amount), but pays the TV company this amount less, e.g., 15 percent, thus earning 750. Production charges and creative costs are often invoiced to the advertiser directly to cover such high costs.

AIDA model

David Yorke and Dale Littler

The AIDA model is an acronym for: attention → interest → desire → action. It is one of a number of models of MARKETING COMMUNICATIONS based on a hierarchy of effects because, simplistically, it is assumed that learning about a product will lead to feelings about the product that result in the purchase of the product. It is a LEARN-FEEL-BUY MODEL of consumer reactions to communications.

The first term relates to the COGNITIVE STAGE of the process, indicating a need for the marketing communicator to gain the receiver's attention before attempting to do anything else. Developing INTEREST and desire (to purchase) are elements in the AFFECTIVE STAGE, i.e., where positive ATTITUDES toward and preference for the product or service are sought. Action is the CONATIVE STAGE (the purchase).

Measures taken before and after a form of communication is used will enable objective(s) to be set and the success of it to be analyzed. Progression logically through the stages is not always possible – indeed, much depends on the product or service being offered and the target groups of receivers (*see* COMMUNICATIONS OBJECTIVES). The model assumes that the buyer will develop a strong desire prior to purchase; yet there is little evidence to support that this arises in the case of at least inexpensive products. It also focuses on the conversion of a non-buyer to a buyer whereas, certainly in mature markets, repeat purchasing dominates. The major objective in such markets is to retain buyers by reinforcing their favorable perceptions.

Recognizing that consumers may not be familiar with many innovative offerings, and that often they engage in IMPULSE PURCHASING, the communications may for example exhort the consumer to try out a new product to find out if s/he likes it (*see* BUY-FEEL-LEARN MODEL). Other communications might employ strong images to evoke an emotional response aimed at generating positive feelings (*see* FEEL-BUY-LEARN MODEL).

Bibliography

Cox, K. K. and Enis, B. M. (1972). *The Marketing Research Process*. Pacific Palisades, CA: Goodyear.
Dickson, P. R. (1997). *Marketing Management*, 2nd edn. London: Dryden Press/Harcourt Brace College Publishers, pp. 569–71.
Jobber, D. (2004). *Principles and Practices of Marketing*, 4th edn. London: McGraw-Hill.
Strong, E. K. (1925). *The Psychology of Selling*. New York: McGraw-Hill.

AIO (activities, interests, and opinions)

Vincent-Wayne Mitchell

Whereas values and PERSONALITY represent internal characteristics, lifestyle represents external consumer patterns of behavior which are often categorized into a consumer's activities (e.g., work, hobbies, holidays), interests (e.g., family, fashion, food), and opinions (e.g., social issues, politics, and the future) (Plummer, 1994). Consumers who have different activities, opinions, and interests may in fact represent distinct lifestyle segments.

Bibliography

Plummer, J. T. (1994). The concept and application of lifestyle segmentation. *Journal of Marketing*, January, 32–3.

alliances

see INTERNATIONAL STRATEGIC ALLIANCES

atmospherics

Steve Greenland and Andrew Newman

"Atmospherics is the tailoring of the designed (sometimes referred to as 'built' – see Mehrabian and Russell, 1974) environment to enhance the likelihood of desired effects or outcomes in users" (Greenland and McGoldrick, 1994). Other definitions focus upon the more subtle design effects that influence consumers at an almost subconscious level: "Atmospherics – the design of an environment via visual communications, lighting, colors, music and scent to stimulate customers' perceptual and emotional responses and ultimately affect their purchase behavior" (Levy and Weitz, 1998). A wider definition of atmospherics would encompass a range of lifestyle and image-related signage, to guide and inform consumers in retail stores (Newman and Cullen, 2002).

The term atmospherics was coined by Kotler (1973) in relation to a retail environment's contribution to its buyers' or customers' purchasing propensity. It is, however, relevant to a broad spectrum of product RETAILING and service environments and is an important consideration in both staff and customer management. This testifies to the importance of the social as well as the environmental influences that shape the atmospherics of any given place. Hence, the presence of staff and customers as well as the inanimate objects imbue atmospheric qualities, in a variety of consumer settings. Effective use of atmospherics can enhance a retail outlet's designed environment, improving staff satisfaction and performance levels, as well as stimulating favorable reactions and behavior in customers. Such favorable outcomes might include a propensity for customers to spend more time in the store and improvements in levels of IMPULSE PURCHASING, store patronage, and image. Research has established clear links between atmospherics and retail or store image, thus demonstrating the importance of this dimension of the customer experience (Newman, 2003).

See also *store design*

Bibliography

Greenland, S. J. (1994). The branch environment. In P. J. McGoldrick and S. J. Greenland (eds.), *Retailing of Financial Services*. Maidenhead: McGraw-Hill, pp. 163–96.

Greenland, S. J. and McGoldrick, P. J. (1994). Atmospherics, attitudes and behavior: Modeling the impact of designed space. *International Review of Retail, Distribution and Consumer Research*, 411–16.

Kotler, P. (1973). Atmospherics as a marketing tool. *Journal of Marketing Research*, **49** (4), 48–64.

Levy, M. and Weitz, B. A. (1998). *Retailing Management*, 3rd edn. Boston: McGraw-Hill.

Mehrabian, A. and Russell, J. A. (1974). *An Approach to Environmental Psychology*. Cambridge, MA: MIT Press.

Newman, A. J. (2003). Some manipulable elements of the service setting and their impact on company image and reputation. *International Journal of New Product Development and Innovation Management*, **4** (3), 287–304.

Newman, A. J. and Cullen, P. (2002). *Retailing: Environment and Operations*. London: Thomson Learning.

Spangeberg, E. R., Crowley, A. E., and Henderson, P. W. (1996). Improving the store environment: Do olfactory cues affect evaluations and behaviors? *Journal of Marketing*, **60**, 67–80.

attention

David Yorke

Attention is the first stage in the AIDA MODEL of MARKETING COMMUNICATIONS. Depending upon the channel of communication employed, various stimuli may be used to gain attention; for example, in the broadcast media, the first five seconds may need something emotionally appealing; in print media, the use of a dramatic headline or color may have a positive effect; in PERSONAL SELLING, appearance; or in TELEMARKETING, the initial verbal contact may be important.

Cost-effectiveness is vital in gaining attention. Broadly, less personal forms of communication such as media ADVERTISING are more cost-effective at this stage, although personal selling and telemarketing may be of use with higher-value products or services.

Bibliography

Strong, E. K. (1925). *The Psychology of Selling*. New York: McGraw-Hill.

attitudes

Margaret K. Hogg and Barbara R. Lewis

Attitude has been classically defined as "affect for or against a psychological object" (Thurstone 1931 cited in Ajzen 2001: 29). In many cases consumer attitudes are considered as mental states of readiness, organized through experience, exerting a directive or dynamic influence upon a customer's response to all objects and situations with which he/she is related. However, attitudes can also be seen as having evaluative components: "Attitude is a psychological tendency that is expressed by evaluating a particular entity with some degree of favor or disfavor" (Eagly and Chaiken 1993: 1).

Attitudes structure the way customers perceive their environment and guide the ways in which they respond to it, i.e., attitudes are characterized by a predisposition or state-of-readiness to act or react in a particular way to certain stimuli. They are relatively enduring and are useful guidelines as to what consumers may do in certain circumstances.

Attitudes have three components. The cognitive component refers to beliefs, i.e., the knowledge or descriptive thoughts one has, for example, about a product or brand, which is a function of available information. The affective component refers to the emotional content of attitudes and arouses either like or dislike; such feelings derive from PERSONALITY, motives, social norms, and previous experience. The conative component or action tendency concerns the disposition to take action of some kind, e.g., a purchase; a consumer may have favorable attitudes without making purchases or even intending to purchase.

A number of sources of influences are important in the formation of attitudes, including: information exposure – the cognitive content is largely built up from information from other people and from the media; group membership – the attitudes and opinions of people one interacts with have an impact on the individual; the environment, to include economic factors; and present levels of need satisfaction.

Attitudes are held toward many aspects of buying and consuming, e.g., toward products and services, brands, companies, stores, product appearance and packaging, promotion and price, and levels of service. Attitudes vary along various dimensions: direction, e.g., positive or negative, favorable or unfavorable; intensity, i.e., how positive or negative; complexity, i.e., toward one or more aspects of a product or brand; and fixity, i.e., will they change? With regard to complexity, one can refer to overall or general attitudes, e.g., toward a model of car; and to particular or specific attitudes, e.g., the individual features of a car such as its design, performance, or service provided. Further, one can consider "determinant" buying attitudes (see Myers and Alpert, 1968; Alpert, 1971), which refer to the features/aspects of a product that are critical in the decision to purchase a specific item or brand/model, e.g., cars and safety. Fishbein's model of attitude-toward-the-object identified three factors that predicted attitudes: salient beliefs (about attributes of the object); strength of beliefs about the object; and evaluation of the salient attributes.

However, a major question for marketers is the extent to which attitudes *predict* subsequent purchase behavior. This has been considered by Fishbein (1967) and others (Sheth, 1974; Fishbein and Ajzen, 1975; Ajzen and Fishbein, 1980; Wells, 1985). Ajzen and Fishbein (1980) present the theory-of-reasoned-action model in which a consumer moves from beliefs to attitudes to purchase intention to purchase. Ajzen and Fishbein's suggestion is that purchase intention may be a better predictor of behavior than merely having favorable attitudes. Even so, one has to take account of "intervening" variables that may prevail between the stages of intention to buy and purchase: these include economic factors, availability, price, and promotional activities.

Attitude change also needs to be taken into account to include changes in direction, intensity, and complexity. Factors that affect attitude change are: the attitudes themselves, e.g., extreme attitudes are harder to change; individual factors, e.g. personality and product needs; MARKETING COMMUNICATIONS, both the MASS MEDIA and INTERPERSONAL COMMUNICATIONS; and the MARKETING ENVIRONMENT, in particular economic variables and financial considerations.

Bibliography

Ajzen, I. (2001). Nature and operation of attitudes. *Annual Review of Psychology*, **52**, 27–58.

Ajzen, I. (2004). Attitude assessment. In R. Fernandez Ballesteros (ed.), *Encyclopedia of Psychological Assessment*. London: Sage.

Ajzen, I. and Fishbein, M. (1980). *Understanding Attitudes and Predicting Social Behavior*. Englewood Cliffs, NJ: Prentice-Hall.

Alpert, M. I. (1971). Identification of determinant attributes: A comparison of methods. *Journal of Marketing Research*, 8 (May), 184–91.

Arnould, E., Price, L., and Zinkhan, G. (2004). *Consumers*, 2nd edn. Boston: McGraw-Hill Irwin, ch. 15.

Bagozzi, R. P. and Warshaw, P. R. (1990). Trying to consume. *Journal of Consumer Research*, 17, 127–40.

Eagly, A. H. and Chaiken, S. (1993). *The Psychology of Attitudes*. Orlando, FL: Harcourt Brace Jovanovich.

Engel, J. F., Blackwell, R. D., and Miniard, P. W. (1995). *Consumer Behavior*, 8th edn. Fort Worth, TX: Dryden Press, ch. 11.

Fishbein, M. (1967). Attitudes and prediction of behavior. In M. Fishbein (ed.), *Readings in Attitude Theory Measurement*. New York: John Wiley, pp. 477–92.

Fishbein, M. and Ajzen, I. (1975). *Belief, Attitude, Intention and Behavior*. Reading, MA: Addison-Wesley.

Foxall, G. R., Goldsmith, R. E., and Brown, S. (1998). *Consumer Psychology for Marketing*, 2nd edn. London: International Thomson Business Press, ch. 5.

Hawkins, D. I., Best, R. J., and Coney, K. A. (1992). *Consumer Behavior: Implications for Marketing Strategy*, 5th edn. Homewood, IL: Irwin, ch. 12.

Hoyer, W. D. and MacInnis, D. J. (2001). *Consumer Behavior*, 2nd edn. Boston and New York: Houghton Mifflin, chs. 6, 7.

Loudon, D. L. and Della Bitta, A. J. (1993). *Consumer Behavior*, 4th edn. New York: McGraw-Hill, chs. 12, 13.

Mowen, J. C. and Minor, M. (1998). *Consumer Behavior*, 5th edn. Upper Saddle River, NJ: Prentice-Hall, chs. 8, 9.

Mowen, J. C. and Minor, M. (2001). *Consumer Behavior: A Framework*. Upper Saddle River, NJ: Prentice-Hall, ch. 7.

Myers, J. H. and Alpert, M. I. (1968). Determinant buying attitudes: Meaning and measurement. *Journal of Marketing*, 32 (October), 14.

Schiffman, L. G. and Kanuk, L. Z. (2004). *Consumer Behavior*, 8th edn. Upper Saddle River, NJ: Prentice-Hall, ch. 8.

Shaw, D., Shiu, E., and Clarke, I. (2000). The contribution of ethical obligation and self-identity to the theory of planned behavior: An exploration of ethical consumers. *Journal of Marketing Management*, 16, 879–94.

Sheth, J. N. (1974). An investigation of relationships among evaluative beliefs, affect, behavioral intention and behavior. In J. U. Farley, J. A. Howard, and L. W. Ring (eds.), *Consumer Behavior, Theory and Application*. Boston: Allyn and Bacon, pp. 89–114.

Solomon, M. R. (2002). *Consumer Behavior: Buying, Having, Being*, 5th edn. Upper Saddle River, NJ: Prentice-Hall, ch. 7.

Solomon, M. R., Bamossy, G., and Askegaard, S. (2002). *Consumer Behavior: A European Perspective*, 2nd edn. Upper Saddle River, NJ: Prentice-Hall, ch. 5.

Thurstone, L. L. (1931). The measurement of social attitudes. *Journal of Abnormal Psychology*, 26, 249–69.

Wells, W. D. (1985). Attitudes and behavior. *Journal of Advertising Research*, March, 40–4.

Wells, W. D. and Prensky, D. (1996). *Consumer Behavior*. New York: John Wiley, ch. 11.

awareness

David Yorke

Awareness is the first step in the DAGMAR, HIERARCHY OF EFFECTS, and INNOVATION-ADOPTION models of MARKETING COMMUNICATIONS which focus on the consumer purchasing process. At this initial stage in the buying process, the potential customer/buyer is made aware of the existence of the product, service, or organization supplying it. Various stimuli may be used to create awareness in the buyer's or customer's mind, depending on the channels of communication used (*see* COMMUNICATIONS MIX). Awareness is sometimes difficult to achieve due to the consumer's "selective" processes (*see* CONSUMER PERCEPTIONS; SELECTIVE EXPOSURE).

Bibliography

Colley, R. H. (1961). *Defining Advertising Goals for Measured Advertising Results*. New York: Association of National Advertisers.

Kotler, P., Armstrong, G., Saunders, J., and Wong, V. (2001). *Principles of Marketing*, 3rd European edn. Harlow: Prentice-Hall, ch. 18.

Lavidge, R. J. and Steiner, G. A. (1961). A model for predictive measurements of advertising effectiveness. *Journal of Marketing*, **25** (October), 61.

Rogers, E. M. (1995). *Diffusion of Innovations*, 4th edn. New York: Free Press.

B

BCG matrix

Dale Littler

The BCG matrix, as its name implies, is the eponymous technique developed by the Boston Consulting Group that gained popularity in the 1970s. It may be referred to as the growth-share matrix or the business portfolio matrix. It was advanced as a technique for assisting companies to analyze their diverse business or product portfolios. It is based on two major premises. The first relates to what the BCG terms the EXPERIENCE CURVE effect by which the total costs involved in manufacturing, distributing, and selling a product decline with increased experience in production. The experience is a composite of economies of scale and specialization; the modifications to or redesign of products to obtain lower costs; productivity improvements from technological change and/or learning effects leading to the adoption of new production methods; and the displacement of less efficient factors of production. The effects of experience can be depicted by plotting real unit cost against cumulative production volume as a measure of accumulated experience. If logarithmic scales are used, a straight line is normally obtained. In fact, the Boston Consulting Group argued that real unit costs fall by 20 to 30 percent for each doubling of cumulative experience. The implication, then, is that businesses should focus on securing high volume, and therefore high market share (reflecting greater experience), through aggressive pricing. The second premise is that the consumption of resources, in particular cash, is a direct function of market growth. BCG developed a four-box matrix (see figure 1) with market growth and market share relative to that of the next largest competitor (since this is the true indicator of competitive advantage) as the two parameters.

Each is measured as "high" or "low." Businesses (or products) can then be categorized according to whether or not they are "stars" (high market growth, low relative market share); "cash cows" (low growth, high share); "problem children" (high growth, low share); or "dogs" (low growth, low share). The cash cows should have lower costs than their rivals and demand comparatively lower investment. They therefore generate cash, which can be employed to convert some of the "question marks" into "stars" which are essentially cash neutral. The stars of today should become the cash cows of the future. Generally, it is argued that the deletion of the "dogs" should be seriously considered.

Businesses (or products) can be plotted in the matrix as circles representing their relative size (based, for example, on the sales revenue). From such a pictorial representation the decision-maker is able to gauge how balanced is the business or product portfolio.

The technique has been extensively reviewed and there have been many criticisms. There may be problems in defining "market" and hence "market share": for example, is a manufacturer of chocolate bars in the market for snack foods, confectionery, or chocolate bars (with it being possible to subdivide the latter in itself into

Relative market share

Market Growth	High	Low
High	Stars	Problem Children
Low	Cash cows	Dogs

Figure 1   The BGC matrix

various submarkets)? The measures of "high" and "low" are subjective and easily manipulable; the possibilities of external financing are excluded from the analysis; the assumption that cash flow is determined by a business's position in the matrix is questionable (some "stars" may in fact have a high cash flow); the use of market growth as a measure of market attractiveness ignores many other factors that can affect market attractiveness, including regulatory influences, the intensity of the competition; and the influence of NON-PRICE FACTORS on demand tends to be ignored. Moreover, the approach is overly deterministic and the acceptance of its prescriptions could lead to suboptimum and even significantly dysfunctional decisions. For example, so-called "dog" businesses might have cost and demand interrelationships with other businesses, and to delete these, as the analysis implies, could have adverse consequences for businesses at present in more attractive quadrants. Despite its prescriptive nature, the BCG matrix does not provide guidance on the criteria for deciding on which problem children are to receive investment, be deleted from the portfolio, or harvested.

In general, the analysis rests on the assumption that businesses' products have a life cycle (see PRODUCT LIFE CYCLE), of which, in particular, the "mature" stage is of sufficient duration to enable the company to reap the benefits of its previous investments in current "cash cows." The industry might, however, witness the introduction of a new technology, which might give a "groin kick" to the technology of the future cash cow, thereby undermining its future market position. The emphasis on market share can blinker decision-makers to such a possibility and perhaps further the dependence on a vulnerable industry, while rivals may leapfrog the firm by acquiring experience through the purchase of plant and equipment that embody state-of-the-art technology. Finally, cash cows may require considerable investment in order to protect their competitiveness, a fact that the analysis seems to overlook somewhat.

See also directional matrix; portfolio analysis

Bibliography

Hedley, B. (1976a). A fundamental approach to strategy development. Long Range Planning, 9 (6), 2–11.

Hedley, B. (1976b). Strategy and the "business portfolio." Long Range Planning, 10 (1), 9–15.
Wensley, R. (1981). Strategic marketing: Betas, boxes or basics. Journal of Marketing, 45, 173–82.

behavior theories

Margaret K. Hogg and Barbara R. Lewis

As the discipline of consumer behavior has developed, various theories have contributed to understanding behavior. These include economic theory. Economists were the first academic group to offer a theory of buyer behavior (see BUYER BEHAVIOR THEORIES). The Marshallian theory holds that consumer purchasing decisions are largely the result of "rational" and conscious economic calculations, i.e., the individual seeks to spend his/her income on goods that will deliver the most likely utility (satisfaction) according to his/her tastes and relative prices.

This model assumes that consumers derive satisfaction from consumption (probably not the case with expenditure on insurance, dental treatment, etc.) and seek to maximize satisfaction within the limits of income. The model also assumes that consumers have complete information with respect to supply, demand, and prices; complete mobility, i.e., can reach any market offer at any time; and that there is pure competition. In practice, consumers typically are not aware of and cannot judge all product offerings and may have restricted access. Consequently, consumers may well be "satisficing" rather than "maximizing" their utility.

Economic theory does have a role to play in understanding consumer behavior, in so far as people may be "problem solvers," trying to make rational and efficient spending decisions. However, economics is only one of the many disciplines that now inform consumer behavior research, which is an increasingly interdisciplinary field. The *Journal of Consumer Research* is the major journal that represents the range of debates (e.g., positivist versus non positivist) about different ways of understanding consumer behavior, drawing on such disciplines as psychology, social psychology, sociology, and anthropology. The annual conference of the

Association for Consumer Research (whose proceedings are available online at www.acrweb. org) also represents the range of ongoing debates about different theories of buyer behavior, and the associated ontological and epistemological issues. This means that it is necessary to consider and understand the impact that marketing and other stimuli have on buyer behavior (see CONSUMER BUYER BEHAVIOR), together with buyers' individual characteristics (e.g., ATTITUDES, perception, knowledge, values), in order to take account of various social and psychological influences on buying behavior. Some of the latest theories center around the meanings which consumers invest in the products and brands that they buy (e.g., SYMBOLIC CONSUMPTION). For an excellent overview of the debates see Belk (1995).

See also *behavioral perspective*

Bibliography

Arnould, E., Price, L., and Zinkhan, G. (2004). *Consumers*, 2nd edn. Boston: McGraw-Hill Irwin, ch. 1.

Belk, R. W. (1988). Possessions and the extended self. *Journal of Consumer Research*, 15 (September), 139–68.

Belk, R. W. (1995). Studies in the new consumer behavior. In Daniel Miller (ed.), *Acknowledging Consumption*. London: Routledge, pp. 58–95.

Cote, J. A., Siew, M. L., and Cote, J. (1991). Assessing the influence of *Journal of Consumer Research*: A citation analysis. *Journal of Consumer Research*, 18 (December), 402–10.

Foxall, G. R. (1999). The behavioral perspective model: Consensibility and consensuality. *European Journal of Marketing*, 33 (5/6), 570–96.

Hoffman, D. L. and Holbrook, M. B. (1993). The intellectual structure of consumer research: A bibliometric study of author co-citations in the first 15 years. *Journal of Consumer Research*, 19 (March), 505–17.

Hoyer, W. D. and MacInnis, D. J. (2001). *Consumer Behavior*, 2nd edn. Boston and New York: Houghton-Mifflin, ch. 1.

Hudson, L. A. and Ozanne, J. L. (1988). Alternative ways of seeking knowledge in consumer research. *Journal of Consumer Research*, 14 (March), 508–21.

Katona, G. (1953). Rational behavior and economic behavior. *Psychological Review*, September, 307–18.

Kotler, P. (1965). Behavioral models for analyzing buyers. *Journal of Marketing*, 29 (November), 37–45.

Levy, S. J. (1992). Constructing consumer behavior: A grand template (Presidential address). *Advances in Consumer Research*, 19, 1–6; www.acrweb.org.

Loudon, D. L. and Della Bitta, A. J. (1993). *Consumer Behavior*, 4th edn. New York: McGraw-Hill, ch. 19.

Mowen, J. C. and Minor, M. (1998). *Consumer Behavior*, 5th edn. Upper Saddle River, NJ: Prentice-Hall, ch. 1.

Mowen, J. C. and Minor, M. (2001). *Consumer Behavior: A Framework*. Upper Saddle River, NJ: Prentice-Hall, ch. 1.

Nicosia, F. M. and Mayer, R. N. (1976). Toward a sociology of consumption. *Journal of Consumer Research*, 3 (September), 65–75.

Richins, M. L. (2001). Consumer behavior as a social science (Presidential address). *Advances in Consumer Research*, 28, 1–5. Valdosta, GA: Association for Consumer Research.

Schewe, C. D. (1973). Selected social psychological models for analyzing buyers. *Journal of Marketing*, 37 (July), 31–9.

Solomon, M. R. (1983). The role of products as social stimuli: A symbolic interactionism perspective. *Journal of Consumer Research*, 10 (March), 319–29.

Solomon, M. R. (2002). *Consumer Behavior: Buying, Having, Being*, 5th edn. Upper Saddle River, NJ: Prentice-Hall, ch. 1.

Solomon, M. R., Bamossy, G., and Askegaard, S. (2002). *Consumer Behavior: A European Perspective*, 2nd edn. Upper Saddle River, NJ: Prentice-Hall, ch. 1.

Wells, W. D. (1993). Discovery-oriented consumer research. *Journal of Consumer Research*, 19 (March), 489–504.

Wells, W. D. and Prensky, D. (1996). *Consumer Behavior*. New York: John Wiley, ch. 1.

Zinkhan, G. M., Roth, M. S., and Saxton, M. J. (1992). Knowledge development and scientific status in consumer behavior research: A social exchange perspective. *Journal of Consumer Research*, 19 (September), 282–91.

behavioral perspective

Mark P. Healey

The behavioral perspective views the actions of CUSTOMERS as determined by the setting or situation in which consumption takes place, rather than by internal mental processes such as ATTITUDES or intentions (see CONSUMER BUYER BEHAVIOR). Consequently, the task for marketers is to shape customer behavior by controlling the immediate environment (see MARKETING ENVIRONMENT) in which consumption takes place. According to the behavioral perspective model (Foxall, 1990, 1999), behaviors such as product or brand choice (*see* BRAND) are determined by two situational factors: the consumption or purchase setting and the reinforcement indicated by features of the setting as determined by the consumer's learning history. The interaction between these two factors explains consumer behavior.

The consumption setting is comprised of physical, social, and temporal dimensions. A specific retail store occupied by certain individuals at a particular time of day would be one discrete setting, for example. The products and brands within a setting signal positive or negative usage consequences to a customer based on his/her previous experiences with them. When a consumer experiences a positive consequence as a result of a purchase, such as the pleasant taste of a food brand bought, this is said to operate as a reinforcer. A reinforcer will increase the likelihood that the behavior that produced it, namely the purchase, will be repeated in future similar situations. Experiencing aversive consequences, such as social disapproval of a brand purchased, decreases this likelihood. In this sense, the past behavior of a consumer dictates his/her future responses.

The positive consequences of an act of consumption can produce either utilitarian reinforcement, the pleasurable or functional benefit from purchase or use, or informational reinforcement, denoting the symbolic or social status gained from ownership. Both types of reinforcement often result from an act of consumption (Foxall, 2002). Managers should seek to find the combination of rewards in a product which produces emotional responses that will encourage repeated purchase. Information about the consequences of purchasing and possessing may be communicated by situational features other than the product itself, such as advertisements (*see* ADVERTISING) and marketplace promises, salespersons' descriptions, or situational norms. These discriminative stimuli, in addition to direct contact with the products themselves, may also encourage or discourage an act of consumption (Foxall, 1995).

Consumers' learning history, their past experiences with products and their consequences, determines which features of the current situation act as reinforcers or punishers. This history is activated only by the consumption setting, and shapes the actions of the customer within the setting. Acts of purchase and consumption are not compelled by the features of a product or brand *per se*, but by the usage consequences suggested by the product and other situational indicators. A consumer's learning history transforms otherwise neutral features of the situation into indicators of positive or negative consequences contingent upon a specific purchase action. The learning history and setting are thus said to combine to produce the consumer situation.

Behavioral interpretations are most adept at explaining the actions of consumers in closed consumption settings in which they exercise little control over the situation. However, most purchase acts take place in relatively open settings, where consumers are free to choose amongst stores, products, and brands. Behavioral interpretations may therefore be disadvantaged when explaining complex behaviors in open settings.

Focusing on the observable features of the setting as determinants of consumer choice behavior, without recourse to private pre-behavioral cognitions or psychological traits, positions behavioral interpretations as an alternative to cognitive models of consumer behavior (*see* CONSUMER DECISION-MAKING PROCESS). Proponents of behaviorist construals argue that relying on a single cognitivist paradigm to understand complex marketplace behavior limits the explanatory power of marketing theories. Thus calls are often made for theories that embrace the environmental and situational determinants of consumption to augment marketing's capacity for explanation and prediction. However, encouraging a pluralism of perspectives may be considered more productive than marginalizing cognitive explanations of behavior, which may appear unrealistic.

Bibliography

Foxall, G. R. (1990). *Consumer Psychology in Behavioral Perspective*. London: Routledge.
Foxall, G. R. (1995). Science and interpretation in consumer research: A radical behaviorist perspective. *European Journal of Marketing*, 29 (9), 3–99.
Foxall, G. R. (1999). The behavioral perspective model: Consensibility and consensuality. *European Journal of Marketing*, 33 (5/6), 570–96.

Foxall, G. R. (2002). Marketing's attitude problem – and how to solve it. *Journal of Customer Behavior*, 1, 1 (Spring), 19–48.

Hantula, D. A., DiClemente, D. F., and Rajala, A. K. (2001). Outside the box: The analysis of consumer behavior. In L. Hayes, J. Austin, and R. Flemming (eds.), *Organizational Change*. Reno, NV: Context, pp. 203–33.

Peter, J. P. and Nord, W. R. (1982). A clarification and extension of operant conditioning principles in marketing. *Journal of Marketing*, 46 (Summer), 102–7.

below-the-line

see ABOVE-THE-LINE

benefit segmentation

Vincent-Wayne Mitchell

Benefit segmentation is the division of a market according to the benefits consumers want from a product. For example, the benefits sought in the soft drinks market may be: energy; vitamins; low in calories; or low cost. One of the earliest attempts at benefit segmentation was made by Yankelovich (1964), who identified three main benefit segments for watches. These were: a price-sensitive segment, a durability and general product-quality segment, and a segment buying watches as symbols or gifts for some important occasion. Problems are sometimes encountered with benefit segmentation in terms of determining the size of the resultant benefit group and differences in the semantic variations of the stated benefits. Nonetheless, it remains one of the most conceptually valid approaches to take.

Bibliography

Yankelovich, D. (1964). New criteria for market segmentation. *Harvard Business Review*, 42 (March/April), 83–90.

bidding

Dominic Wilson and Mark P. Healey

Bidding or tendering is a process in which potential suppliers are invited to submit bids or tenders in which they set out their specifications, terms, and prices in response to a stated customer requirement. How to decide the price aspect of a bid or tender is made even more awkward by the UNCERTAINTY surrounding rival bids and the need to balance the wish to make a profit (or even just to cover costs) against the wish to secure the contract. Because price is only one aspect (if often the most important) of the bid or tender, the successful bidder will not always be that offering the lowest price, though evidence of a lower bid may be used to renegotiate the price offered by the eventual contractor. In organizational markets (*see* ORGANIZATIONAL MARKETING), where suppliers often seek to build advantageous long-term relationships (*see* RELATIONSHIP MARKETING) with their customers, a tendering organization may submit a bid that is priced suboptimally in terms of its profit-making potential in order to win an initial contract and help secure subsequent contracts. In pursuing such a bidding strategy, when preparing and pricing a competitive bid an organization should consider the balance between completing an unprofitable initial contract and the probability of winning subsequent follow-on contracts, and the benefits, financial and otherwise, of winning those contracts.

Bidding may be *closed*, whereby bidding is restricted to an approved list of suppliers, or *open*, where bids are invited from potential suppliers without restriction. Also, in *open bidding*, details of bids, particularly the price or amount, may be made public (Dibb et al., 2001: 629). Furthermore, in *negotiated bidding*, an organization selects the most competitive bid(s) and enters negotiation with the relevant bidders to amend or enhance the details of the bid until a favorable agreement is reached between the contracting parties.

There are variants of tendering, especially auction bidding and sealed-bid pricing, which is used in organizational markets (and Scottish real estate markets). These techniques for soliciting prices have the effect of orienting price decisions more toward competitive issues than toward issues of cost or demand.

There are several advantages to competitive bidding or tendering for the customer: it can help to remove many possibilities for corrupt or unethical practices; it provides important competitive information where this might otherwise be difficult to gather; it helps to insure value for money and cost minimization; and it provides insight to the costs associated with differences in the terms of the contract (e.g., in delivery arrangements, quality levels, service provision). Because of its apparent efficiency and probity, competitive bidding or tendering is increasingly being used in large-scale tenders where price is a major purchase constraint and/or where it is important to insure that processes are seen to be equitable and "above board" (e.g., in central and local government purchasing, and in OUTSOURCING).

Bibliography

Brooks, D. G. (1978). Bidding for the sake of follow-on contracts. *Journal of Marketing*, **42** (January), 35–8.

Dibb, S., Simkin, L., Pride, W. M., and Ferrell, O. C. (2001). *Marketing: Concepts and Strategies*, 4th European edn. Boston: Houghton-Mifflin, ch. 20.

Ford, D. (ed.) (1997). *Understanding Business Markets: Interaction, Relationships and Networks*, 2nd edn. London: Dryden Press.

bidirectional acculturation model

see ACCULTURATION MODELS

billboards

see POSTERS

bivariate analysis

Charles C. Cui and Michael Greatorex

Bivariate analysis refers to a group of statistical methods for analyzing the relationship between two variables. Such analyses reveal whether or not there exists an association, the strength of the association, or whether or not there are differences between two variables. For example, marketers may want to know whether a linear or straight-line relationship exists between consumers' perceptions of service quality and their satisfaction with the service. In such a case, the relationship indicates the degree to which the variation in one variable (perceptions of SERVICE QUALITY) is related to the variation in another variable (CUSTOMER SATISFACTION). Such a relationship is analyzed and statistically summarized by a bivariate analysis "product moment correlation" (or Pearson correlation coefficient, also referred to as simple correlation, bivariate correlation). There are other types of bivariate analysis for analyzing different kinds of relationships between two variables. The type of analysis conducted on pairs of variables varies in accordance with the nature of the variables of interest (e.g., nominal/categorical, ordinal, interval/ratio).

If both variables are measured on nominal (categorical) scales, CROSS-TABULATIONS (cross-tabs) can be used (known as bivariate cross-tabulations when two variables are involved). A cross-tab is a table (also called contingency table) with the categories (or values) for the two variables listed on the two axes and the counts of the number of times each pair of values occurs recorded in the cells of the table. The row and column totals are usually calculated and percentages across the rows and/or down the columns are also computed to aid in the interpretation, description, and discussion of the relationship between the two variables. In principle, cross-tabs can be formed in more than two dimensions when data for more than two categorical variables are analyzed, but interpretation becomes difficult because the increased number of cells often leaves empty cells or a number of cells with small counts. The observed association is of interest only if the association is statistically significant. The statistical significance of the observed association between two variables from the cross-tab is commonly assessed by the chi-square statistic.

If both variables are interval, the relationship between them can be studied, visually, using a scatter diagram and, numerically, using simple correlation and regression (*see* REGRESSION AND CORRELATION). The product-moment correlation coefficient measures the strength of a linear relationship between the variables: a value close to zero means no relationship or a very weak relationship; a value close to $+1$ means a very strong positive relationship; while a figure close to −1 means a very strong negative relationship. The regression analysis tells the form of the relationship, i.e., the way one variable affects the other is indicated by the straight-line equation estimated using regression techniques.

If both variables are measured on ordinal scales, cross-tabs may be used to summarize the data. Alternatively, correlation coefficients such as Kendall's tau or Spearman's rank correlation coefficient indicate the strength of any relationship between the variables.

When the variables are measured on scales of different types, a range of possibilities arises. For instance, when one variable is measured on an interval scale and the other on a categorical scale, the sample can be broken down into subsamples using the categorical variable and the data for the interval variable can be summarized for each subsample using a frequency distribution, histogram, and/or measures of average and variation. Subsamples can be compared by looking at, for example, the histograms or measures of average of the interval variable to see if and how they change with different values of the categorical variable.

A range of HYPOTHESIS TESTING is available to see if there are any significant relationships between the variables. The appropriate test depends upon the type of measurement used for each variable. For instance, if both variables are measured on categorical scales, either the chi-square test or an exact test using the hypergeometric distribution is likely to be used depending, among other things, on the size of the sample and the number of categories for each variable. If both variables are interval, the t-test and F-test are two examples involved in testing hypotheses related to simple correlation and regression. When one variable is interval and the other categorical, the t-test is used to test for the equality of arithmetic means of the interval variable when comparing just two subsamples defined by the categorical variable, and the F-test is used when there are two or more subsamples. If one variable is measured on an ordinal scale and the other on a categorical scale, then tests such as the Mann-Whitney U test, the Wilcoxon test, the runs-of-signs test, the Kolmogorov-Smirnov two-sample test, the Kruskal-Wallis one-way ANOVA (analysis of variance) test, and the Friedman two-way

ANOVA test are used, depending upon the circumstances. Many other tests are available for different sets of situations.

In addition to analyzing relationships, bivariate analysis of difference can also be conducted to determine if the variation in the distribution of one variable is statistically significant between two or more groups. Common analyses of this type include the scrutiny of differences between males and females or ethnic groups (comparison/independent variable) on a variable of interest such as sales volume (dependent/criterion variable), where a significant difference between groups may be noteworthy in both statistical and marketing terms.

Bibliography

Bryman, A. and Cramer, D. (2001). *Quantitative Data Analysis: A Guide for Social Scientists.* Hove: Routledge, chs. 7–8.

Malhorta, N. K. and Birks, D. (2000). *Marketing Research: An Applied Orientation,* European edn. London: Prentice-Hall, chs. 17, 19.

boundary spanning

Gillian C. Hopkinson and Judy Zolkiewski

Boundary spanning describes the location and activities of those organizational members who have contact, on behalf of the firm, with external actors. Such external actors may include customers, suppliers, investors, alliance partners, policy bodies, and service agencies. The concept relies upon an implicit notion of the firm as a bounded organization so that boundary spanners are those who relate to people both internally and externally. However, recent theoretic developments (*see* NETWORK; RELATIONSHIP MARKETING) argue that the firm is interpenetrated with its environment so that the organizational boundary is blurred and permeable. These developments have heightened interest in how boundary spanning activities can be performed, and by whom, to best link the organization to its environment and support the achievement of organizational objectives.

Boundary spanners perform many critical functions beyond the transacting of inputs and outputs. They represent the organization to outsiders, scan (*see* ENVIRONMENTAL SCAN-NING) and monitor aspects of the firm's environment, and link and coordinate activities with external actors. Additionally, boundary spanners are critical to bidirectional flows of information, so that with respect to some issues they may be required to protect organizational information and act as GATEKEEPERS whilst being required to enable the flow of other information. Intervention in flows of information also occurs as boundary spanners analyze and synthesize knowledge and disseminate it according to their perceptions of its relevance to particular internal actors. This can be seen as involving the "translation" of ideas between arenas with diverse interests and cultures.

Given the range of these activities, it is clear that many organizational members are involved in boundary spanning, and this is not limited to those in formally designated boundary spanning roles (e.g., sales and purchasing). Indeed, effective boundary spanning relies as much upon internal links so that it is associated with the degree to which an organizational member is perceived as being competent and has internal influence. This is critical to enable the dissemination of knowledge and ideas to facilitate innovation and adaptation (see Tushman and Scanlan, 1981).

An important area of inquiry has investigated the problems associated with boundary spanning for the individual. This has been explored particularly in the context of sales people and more recently key account managers (*see* ACCOUNT MANAGER; KEY ACCOUNT) or global account managers. Problems center particularly upon role conflicts and role ambiguity that emerge from the diverse pressures arising from multiple audiences and multiple organizational cultures. Loyalties and sympathies may be divided. Wilson and Millman (2003) argue that the boundary spanner may be a "self-server," "renegade," "partisan," or, ideally, an "arbiter" depending upon the extent to which he/she identifies with internal or external audiences. The important effects that identification with other organizations has upon the individual's work behavior are discussed by Hopkinson (2003).

Several factors have been found to promote effective boundary spanning activities. Some in-dividual competencies and styles of behavior are important (e.g., communication skills, management styles that rely upon influence and negotiation, and an ability to manage complexity) and therefore should be a focus in recruitment and training (Williams, 2002). The organizational factors that support these behaviors are also critical and the degree of role autonomy allowed amongst boundary spanners is associated with higher levels of TRUST across organizations (Perrone, Zaheer, and McEvily, 2003).

Bibliography

Aldrich, H. and Herker, D. (1977). Boundary spanning roles and organizational structure. *Academy of Management Review*, **2** (2), 217–31.

Hopkinson, G. C. (2003). Stories from the front-line: How they construct the organization. *Journal of Management Studies*, **40** (8), 1043–69.

Perrone, V., Zaheer, A., and McEvily, B. (2003). Free to be trusted? Organizational constraints on trust in boundary spanners. *Organization Science*, **14** (4), 422–39.

Tushman, M. L. and Scanlan, T. J. (1981). Characteristics and external orientations of boundary spanning individuals. *Academy of Management Journal*, **21** (1), 83–99.

Williams, P. (2002). The competent boundary spanner. *Public Administration*, **80** (1), 103–24.

Wilson, K. and Millman, T. (2003). The global account manager as political entrepreneur. *Industrial Marketing Management*, **32** (2), 151–8.

brand

Margaret Bruce and Liz Barnes

The original thinking behind branding was to take a commodity and endow it with special characteristics through imaginative use of name, PACKAGING, and ADVERTISING. Aaker (1991) defines a brand as: "a distinguishing name and/or symbol (such as a logo, trademark, or package design) intended to identify the goods or services of either a seller or a group of sellers and to distinguish those goods or services from those of its competitors." Essentially, the underlying purpose of branding is to differentiate a product or service from competitor offerings, and to achieve effective positioning (*see* PRODUCT POSITIONING). By stressing particular aspects, such as quality, consistency, and reliability, brands may influence what consumers wear, what they eat, where they shop, where and how they travel, and so on. Indeed, de Chernatony (1993) maintains that brands "ultimately reside in consumers' minds." Central to the value or equity of the brand (*see* BRAND EQUITY) is a set of assets, including BRAND LOYALTY, brand awareness, perceived quality, and brand associations. Allen (2000) defines a brand in terms of reputation = brand = behavior. If reputation is diminished, then the brand is damaged too and the associations of TRUST and loyalty may be irreparably altered. Feldwick (1996) refers to "brand strength" as an indicator of the degree of a consumer's attachment to a brand. Klein (2001) powerfully challenges the hegemonic nature of global brands by questioning the ethics of their production (e.g., impact on the environment, use of sweat-shops in production processes, etc.).

A manufacturer brand is initiated by a producer, such as Coca-Cola, and a private or "own-label" brand is initiated by a retailer, such as Tesco's "Value" product line (*see* PRODUCT). McGoldrick (2002) identifies five different types of retailer brands ranging from retailer name brands to generic brands to exclusive brands. In doing so, he is demonstrating the complex nature of "retailer own brands," which can be regarded as major brands in their own right and may no longer be sold exclusively through the retailers' own outlets; for example, Tesco exports its own brands to non-competing retailers in Europe. The benefits to the retailer can be evaluated in terms of store image/customer loyalty; competitive edge; and higher profits/better margins.

It should be noted that branding can emphasize the development of the identity of a manufacturer's "parent" brand (e.g., Ford, Cadbury, Heinz) in addition to, or in conjunction with, the product-level brand (e.g., Ford Mondeo, Cadbury's Caramel, Heinz tomato ketchup). The latter is termed overall family branding, and a strategy that places the company name as the dominant identity across its products is termed a corporate brand strategy. Other organizations seek to develop differentiated brand identities for multiple products, as Procter and Gamble does with its Daz and Fairy detergent brands, which have an established brand identity independent of their manufacturer. This is known as individual branding as part of a multi-brand strategy and enables organizations to target more precise segments within a market where each individual brand connotes differentiated benefits designed to appeal to consumers in specific segments.

Kotler et al. (2001) contend that the brand communicates four key types of message to customers: attributes, benefits, values, and personality. Product attributes are the characteristics readily associated with a brand, and benefits relate to the utility the consumer seeks from a brand, which may be functional or emotional. Brand values are associated with the values of a brand's buyers. For instance, Volvo buyers may value safety, reliability, and assurance. The notion of brand personality acknowledges that consumers may be attracted to brands that are congruent with their own self-image/concept. It is generally accepted that the most integral components of a brand are its "core values," the basic essence of the symbol, such as Intel's hi-tech innovative stance.

In addition to its role in consumer goods markets, branding has a part to play in organizational/industrial markets (*see* INDUSTRIAL MARKETING; ORGANIZATIONAL MARKETING). Organizations in industrial markets often seek to develop brand identity in order to stimulate demand for their products in consumer markets, thus pulling demand through the supply chain. Also, it is appropriate to note the upsurge in corporate branding practice in the services sector as a means of defining new service offerings and communicating their benefits to potential consumers. Branding serves to differentiate service offerings and to position them competitively in the market. Typically, service brands are derived from the company name, such as British Airways and America Online (AOL).

"Corporate rebranding" has also been markedly prevalent in recent years. Organizations operating in a number of sectors have sought to redefine or redevelop their corporate image through a process of corporate rebranding, which often involves renaming a business in addition to redesigning logos, symbols, decor, color schemes, and company livery, and remodeling public relations and advertising exercises in an attempt to establish a new corporate identity. Examples include Andersen Consulting's enforced change to Accenture.

See also *brand extension; brand image*

Bibliography

Aaker, D. A. (1991). *Managing Brand Equity: Capitalizing on the Value of a Brand Name.* New York: Free Press, ch. 1.

Allen, D. (2000). Living the brand. *Design Management Journal*, Winter, 35–40.

De Chernatony, L. (1993). Categorizing brands: Evolutionary processes underpinned by two key dimensions. *Journal of Marketing Management*, **32** (11/12), 1074–90.

Dibb, S., Simkin, L., Pride, W., and Ferrell, O. C. (2000). *Marketing: Concepts and Strategies*, European edn. Boston: Houghton Mifflin.

Doyle, P. (1993). Building successful brands: The strategic options. *Journal of Consumer Marketing*, 7 (2), 5–20.

Feldwick, P. (1996). What is brand equity anyway and how do you measure it? *Journal of the Market Research Society*, 38 (2), 85–104.

Harris, F. and de Chernatony, L. (2001). Corporate branding and corporate brand performance. *European Journal of Marketing*, Special edition on Corporate Marketing, 35 (3/4), 441–56.

Klein, N. (2001). *No Logo.* London: Flamingo.

Kotler, P., Armstrong, G., Saunders, J., and Wong, V. (2001). *Principles of Marketing*, 3rd European edn. Harlow: Prentice-Hall.

Low, G. S. and Fullerton, R. A. (1994). Brands, brand management and the brand manager system: A critical historical evaluation. *Journal of Marketing Research*, 31 (2), 173–90.

McGoldrick, P. J. (2002). *Retail Marketing*, 2nd edn. Maidenhead: McGraw-Hill.

Macrae, C. (1991). *World Class Brands.* Reading, MA: Addison-Wesley.

brand equity

Dale Littler

There has been increasing contemporary consideration of brand value or equity. This can be regarded as "the net present value of the future cash flow attributable to the brand name" (Doyle, 2000: 221). Successful brands generally have a set of powerful associations attributed to them by customers that act to differentiate them clearly from competing products. These qualities embrace intangible factors which collectively form the image of the brand, as well as other aspects of the product, such as performance, which generally reinforce this general BRAND IMAGE.

Aaker (2001) suggests that brand equity has four major components: brand awareness; brand associations; BRAND LOYALTY; and perceived quality. *Brand awareness* can generate a number of advantages including familiarity, giving preference to the brand against those less familiar, and spontaneous recall at significant points in the decision process. *Brand associations* are those attributes that are linked to the brand by the customer which assist in differentiating it from its competitors. Thus, the Virgin brand, for example, is clearly associated with Richard Branson who personifies a set of widely appealing values that enable the brand to be stretched across a range of products. *Brand loyalty* means that its existing customer base is unlikely to switch to rival brands and is especially important given the costs of replacing lost customers, and the additional revenues that can be obtained over the brand's lifetime from existing customers through, for example, cross-selling of other products. *Perceived quality* relates to the perception of the brand in terms of performance, durability, reliability, and other qualities that may be reinforced by, *inter alia*, ADVERTISING and promotion. It is argued that there has to be continued investment in the brand through advertising and product development (*see* NEW PRODUCT DEVELOPMENT) to project and support the brand's values. The returns are in the form of higher margins that customers are prepared to pay for the particular benefits attributed to the brand.

Some companies have attempted to value their brands but to date there has been no agreed methodology for including these values in companies' balance sheets. Firms often seem prepared to pay significant amounts to acquire brands, as the Nestlé takeover of Rowntree seemed to indicate. There continues to be prolonged debate about the inclusion of brand values on the balance sheet and the valuation of brand equity is a focus for research, especially in the US. The International Accounting Standards Committee has recommended that acquired brands, but not those developed internally, can be included on the balance sheet. However, they have to be amortized over 20 years on a straight-line basis.

Many distribution intermediaries have developed their own-label brands which may or may not be manufactured by the manufacturers of other brands (*see* OWN BRANDING). This means that the power of manufacturers to influence the channel of distribution through their own brands which have influential customer franchises is being eroded and more manufacturers, in order to insure continued volume of output, are being compelled to supply retailer-branded merchandise.

See also *brand; brand extension*

Bibliography

Aaker, D. A. (2001). *Strategic Market Management*, 6th edn. Chichester: John Wiley, pp. 165–9.
Doyle, P. (2000). *Value-Based Marketing*. Chichester: John Wiley, ch. 7.

brand extension

Mark P. Healey

A brand extension is a new or modified product or service that is marketed and promoted with strong associations with a preexisting brand, in order to infer the positive associations customers hold for the existing brand upon the new or modified offering. A brand extension strategy involves the introduction of a new or enhanced product either to the same product category in which the brand principally operates or, more often, to a new category. The Virgin organization, for example, has consistently used its rebellious brand connotations to launch new products and services in new categories, from airline and rail transport to mobile telecommunications.

Brand extension strategies afford considerable benefit to both organizations and consumers. Brand extensions may facilitate greater promotional efficiency than individual brands and enable a new product to enter a market with an established identity, aiding recognition and acceptance, and capitalizing on brand associations and existing loyalties. Depending upon its

BRAND IMAGE and higher-order associations (e.g., security, excitement), a product may demonstrate high or low extension elasticity. Where a brand becomes closely linked with particular concrete or functional attributes, the potential for brand extension may be low (inelastic) in that the benefits associated with the brand will not be applicable in a new category. High elasticity brands such as Disney successfully offer branded products across diverse categories due to their brand values of family-oriented entertainment and associations with secure enjoyment. However, brand extensions may not be effective where the existing brand associations conferred upon the new symbiont are incompatible with the new product category. Further, where a brand is applied excessively to numerous extensions without coordination of image and association, its positioning (*see* PRODUCT POSITIONING) may become ineffectual and brand dilution may result, leaving a weakened brand.

See also *brand; brand equity; brand loyalty*

Bibliography

Broniarczyk, S. M. and Alba, J. W. (1994). The importance of brand in brand extension. *Journal of Marketing Research*, **31** (May), 214–18.
Smith, D. C. and Park, C. W. (1992). The effects of brand extensions on market share and advertising efficiency. *Journal of Marketing Research*, **29** (August), 296–313.

brand image

Dale Littler

The consumer builds up associations with the brand based on personal experience, word-of-mouth (*see* WORD-OF-MOUTH COMMUNICATIONS), ADVERTISING, and promotion. The consumer therefore constructs an image of the brand which may or may not correspond to the identity that the brand owner wishes to project by means of its product form, name, visual signs, advertising, and so on. Brands may be purchased because they may be widely regarded as possessing particular values that are bestowed on their owner. For example, high-priced and visible brands, such as Burberry, may be seen as offering status.

Doyle (2000) argues that a successful brand image has three components: a "good" product, which is one that offers clear values (e.g., has functionality, good physical appearance); a distinctive identity, which means that "customers can recognize it and ask for it by name"; and added values "that elicit confidence in consumers that it is of higher quality or is more desirable than similar products" (p. 232).

See also *brand; brand equity; brand extension; brand loyalty*

Bibliography

Doyle, P. (2000). *Value-Based Marketing*. Chichester: John Wiley, pp. 232–3.

brand loyalty

Barbara R. Lewis and Mark P. Healey

Consideration of CONSUMER BUYER BEHAVIOR over a period involves an understanding of brand loyalty which follows from the formation of brand images and brand preferences.

BRAND IMAGE is a set of associations or perceptions that consumers have for a brand; it is awareness or recognition. It also implies attitudes toward a brand, either positive or negative, which are learned over time.

Brand preference is a definite expression of positive attitude. One would normally expect people to buy a preferred brand or brands, assuming that they are in the market for the product. However, there are occasions when the product may not be needed or the consumer cannot afford the preferred brand, or the preferred brand may not be available.

Brand loyalty implies purchasing the same brand more than once, again assuming that this is the preferred brand, although this may not necessarily be the case. Brand preference and brand loyalty may exist in relation to manufacturers' brands (e.g., Heinz) and distributors' brands (e.g., Tesco), and loyalty may prevail with respect to stores.

Definitions of brand loyalty have evolved and are typically concerned with a degree of consistency in the preference for each brand by a consumer, over a specified period of time. Some definitions also refer to "biased choice behavior" with respect to branded merchandise, or "consistent" purchasing of one brand, or the proportion of purchases a consumer (or household) devotes to the brand most often bought. There are inherent dangers in looking at sequences of purchases to define and measure loyalty as individuals and households may be buying more than one brand on a regular basis (e.g., toothpaste, breakfast cereals). Further, Day (1970) offers a two-dimensional concept of brand loyalty, bringing together attitudes and behavior. He asks, "Can behavior patterns be equated with preferences to infer loyalty?" and distinguishes between spurious and intentional loyalty. Spurious loyalty may just be habit or consistent purchase of one brand due to non-availability of others, continuous price deals, better shelf space, etc. (*see* HABITUAL BUYING BEHAVIOR). Intentional loyalty occurs when consumers buy a preferred brand, as would be evidenced by some attitude measurement. When a consumer is intentionally loyal and insists on a particular brand, he/she will be prepared to shop around for this brand, or defer purchase if the brand is unavailable, rather than accept a substitute.

The complexity of brand loyalty phenomena is illustrated by evidence that shows varying levels of allegiance to brands across product categories and within individuals. Consumption in some product categories appears to be more brand loyal than in others: petrol and tinned goods have been found to inspire little brand loyalty, whilst cigarettes and coffee have been noted as more likely to engender customer loyalty to the brand. Distinctions have also been made between brand loyalty in the markets for consumable goods, durable goods, and services. Furthermore, research suggests that brand loyalty is not unique to certain individuals. Consumers may be loyal to a particular brand in one product category, and may demonstrate considerable switching behavior in others.

Research has been unable to pinpoint particular determinants of brand loyalty, though a number of empirical investigations have suggested and looked for relationships between brand loyalty and: personal attributes, e.g., socioeconomic variables; group influence; levels of demand; sensitivity to promotion; and store factors. Nevertheless, manufacturers and distributors are concerned to encourage loyalty to their brands and switching away from other brands. Consumers switch brands for reasons of: curiosity with respect to new/different brands; disappointment with present brand; reassurance with respect to a favored brand; chance; inducement; and availability. Additionally, consumers may be multi-brand buyers for reasons of: indifference; perception that brands are perfect substitutes; for variety's sake; several preferences within a household; and as a response to availability and promotions.

The "double jeopardy" phenomenon, discovered by sociologist William McPhee in the 1960s, predicts that brands with large market share benefit from increased rates of repeat purchase in comparison to smaller brands. This effect has been demonstrated empirically in several product categories in varying countries over the past three decades, although the opinions of marketers as to the strategic implications of this effect remain equivocal.

See also *brand; brand equity; brand extension*

Bibliography

Carmen, J. M. (1970). Correlates of brand loyalty: Some positive results. *Journal of Marketing Research*, 7 (February), 67–76.

Day, G. S. (1970). *Buyer Attitudes and Brand Choice Behavior*. Chicago: Free Press.

Ehrenberg, A. S. C. (1972). *Repeat Buying: Theory and Applications*. New York: North Holland.

Ehrenberg, A. S. C., Goodhardt, G. J., and Barwise, P. T. (1990). Double jeopardy revisited. *Journal of Marketing*, 54 (July), 82–92.

Jacoby, J. and Chestnut, R. (1978). *Brand Loyalty: Measurement and Management*. New York: Ronald/John Wiley.

brand managers

see MARKETING ORGANIZATION

brand preference

see BRAND LOYALTY

branding

see BRAND

break-even analysis

Dominic Wilson

A break-even analysis is meant to identify the break-even point, i.e., the point in time at which the sum of fixed (or "indirect") costs and variable (or "direct") costs involved in the production and distribution of a good or service is matched by the sum of its accumulated sales. Beyond this break-even point the profitability of the good or service will be a function of the excess of sales revenues over variable costs. Break-even analysis is an important aspect of pricing calculations in that it can help to show the profitability of a product over time according to different assumptions about price, demand, and the allocation of costs (many costs, especially fixed costs, will be shared by several products and allocation can be problematic). The difficulty of anticipating demand response to different pricing policies emphasizes the importance of undertaking extensive break-even analysis for different assumptions.

business-to-business marketing

Fiona Leverick

Business-to-business marketing refers to the marketing of products and services to organizations rather than to households or ultimate consumers. The implied alternative is CONSUMER MARKETING, although the distinction between the two areas is not entirely clear-cut. Business-to-business marketing has also been termed variously: industrial marketing, commercial marketing, institutional marketing, and ORGANIZATIONAL MARKETING.

Although many of the same products will be bought by both business and consumers, it is possible to identify a number of ways in which the emphasis of business-to-business marketing differs from that of consumer marketing and this is reflected in the large volume of literature and research programs devoted exclusively to the business-to-business marketing area (Chisnall, 1989; Gross et al., 1993; Reeder, Brierty, and Reeder, 1991; Webster, 1991). These differences are seen to have considerable implications for the manner in which business-to-business marketing is undertaken.

Market structure is the first of these, with business markets tending to have a greater concentration of both buyers and sellers in comparison to consumer markets. DERIVED DEMAND is another feature, with the demand for business products and services said to be dependent to an extent on the level of activity the buying organization generates in its own markets, although this will clearly not always be the case. The scale of business purchases is often seen as greater than that for consumers and products are generally held to be more technologically complex, although both of these factors are relative and something of broad generalizations (Chisnall, 1989).

The manner in which purchase decisions are made is another area in which businesses are said to differ from consumers. Many organizations employ professional purchasers, or have a purchasing department, although it has been noted that the purchasing department is often not the most powerful influence on supplier choice (Webster and Wind, 1972). Purchases are generally made not for self-gratification but to achieve organizational objectives and are therefore often held to be based more on "rational," "economic," or "task" considerations, such as price, quality, and delivery criteria, than the purchases of individual consumers. Some authors assert that the "rational" nature of business buying behavior has been overemphasized. Chisnall (1989), for instance, refers to the influence of "non-task" factors such as motivation, personal values, or political, social, and cultural influences as important in business purchase decisions, since such decisions are necessarily made by personally motivated employees in a social-interactive context. However, it is widely recognized that business buying is more likely than consumer buying to be guided at least by formalized rules, evaluation criteria, or procedures.

Business purchase decisions are also typically seen as a more complex process than those of consumers, involving several people, frequently from different departments. A pioneer study in 1958, for example, showed that in 106 industrial firms three or more persons influenced buying processes in over 75 percent of companies studied (see Alexander, Cross, and Cunningham, 1961). A number of researchers have studied the concept of the BUYING CENTER, i.e., all organizational members involved in the buying decision, and have noted that this is likely to vary considerably according to the purchasing situation (see, e.g., Robinson, Faris, and Wind, 1967; Johnston and Bonoma, 1981). Various different organizational purchasing roles have been identified by Webster and Wind (1972), some or all of which may be played by individuals in the buying center. These include USERS of the product or service in question; GATEKEEPERS, who control information to be received by other members of the buying center; DECIDERS, who actually make the purchase decision, whether or not they have the formal authority to do so; and BUYERS, those who do have formal authority for supplier selection but whose influence is often usurped by more powerful members of the buying center (see ORGANIZATIONAL BUYING BEHAVIOR).

Finally, and perhaps most importantly, the importance of long-term, relatively stable relationships between buyers and sellers has been emphasized, with extensive work conducted by researchers involved in the International Marketing and Purchasing (IMP) Group (Håkansson, 1982, 1987; Ford, 1997). This recognition has led to the development of the NETWORK and interaction approaches to business-to-business marketing (see INTERACTION APPROACH), where the role of MARKETING MANAGEMENT is seen in terms of the management of a range of individual buyer–seller relationships in the context of a broader network of interconnected supplier, buyer, and competitor organizations.

The various differences in emphasis between business-to-business marketing and consumer marketing have led to attempts to develop the scope of the MARKETING CONCEPT and to reappraise such marketing tools as the MARKETING MIX, which is seen as inappropriate in its traditional form.

Improvements in, and increased adoption of, information technology have exerted considerable influence on business-to-business marketing, and the exchange of, for example, information via the Internet is now a common feature of many business-to-business relationships. Organizations have developed systems that enable them to share technical and product data with customers, receive and process orders and payments, and provide customer service support facilities via interactive commercial websites and Internet-based exchange systems.

Bibliography

Alexander, R. S., Cross, J. S., and Cunningham, R. M. (1961). *Industrial Marketing*. Homewood, IL: Irwin.

Chisnall, P. M. (1989). *Strategic Industrial Marketing*, 2nd edn. Englewood Cliffs, NJ: Prentice-Hall.

Ford, D. (ed.) (1997). *Understanding Business Markets: Interaction, Relationships and Networks*, 2nd edn. London: Dryden Press.

Gross, A. C., Banting, P. M., Meredith, L. N., and Ford, I. D. (1993). *Business Marketing*. Boston: Houghton Mifflin.

Håkansson, H. (ed.) (1982). *International Marketing and Purchasing of Industrial Goods: An Interaction Approach*. Chichester: John Wiley.

Håkansson, H. (ed.) (1987). *Industrial Technological Development: A Network Approach*. London: Croom Helm.

Johnston, W. J. and Bonoma, T. V. (1981). The buying center: Structure and interaction patterns. *Journal of Marketing*, 45 (Summer), 143–56.

Reeder, R. R., Brierty, E. G., and Reeder, B. H. (1991). *Industrial Marketing*, 2nd edn. Englewood Cliffs, NJ: Prentice-Hall.

Robinson, P. J., Faris, C. W., and Wind, Y. (1967). *Industrial Buying and Creative Marketing*. Boston: Allyn and Bacon.

Webster, F. E., Jr. (1991). *Industrial Marketing Strategy*, 3rd edn. New York: John Wiley.

Webster, F. E., Jr. and Wind, Y. (1972). *Organizational Buying Behavior*. Englewood Cliffs, NJ: Prentice-Hall.

buy-feel-learn model

David Yorke

The buy-feel-learn (BFL) model in MARKETING COMMUNICATIONS suggests that in some situations buyers/customers do not follow the logical learn-feel-buy sequence. The BFL model typically applies to IMPULSE PURCHASING and/or for new brands, where attitudes, know-ledge, and liking/preference are developed after purchase rather than prior to it.

See also *AIDA model; feel-buy-learn model; learn-feel-buy model*

Bibliography

Dickson, P. R. (1997). *Marketing Management*, 2nd edn. London: Dryden Press/Harcourt Brace College Publishers, pp. 571, 572.

buy grid model

see PURCHASING PROCESS

buyer behavior models

Barbara R. Lewis and Mark P. Healey

Parallel to the development of thought about the variables that are important in understanding CONSUMER BUYER BEHAVIOR have been attempts to organize the variables into models of the buying process and consumer behavior. The purpose of such models is to try to understand the buying process and aid market research. Models serve to simplify, organize, and formalize the range of influences that affect purchase decisions, and try to show the extent of interaction between influencing variables. Some models are descriptive and others decision models.

Descriptive models are designed to communicate, explain, and predict. They may postulate at a macro level some variables and the relationships between them (e.g., sales, income, price, ADVERTISING); or, at a micro level, consider more detailed links between a variable and its determinants (e.g., the effect of advertising on sales). In addition, a model at a micro-behavioral level may create hypothetical consumers and dealers who interact – with resulting behavior patterns being investigated. The well-known available models of consumer buyer behavior are descriptive and include those of Howard and Sheth (1969), Nicosia (1966), Andreasen (1965), Engel, Kollat, and Blackwell (see Blackwell, Miniard, and Engel, 2001).

The Howard and Sheth model is concerned with individual decision-making and has its roots in stimulus-response learning theory (*see* CONSUMER LEARNING). The focus is on repeat buying, and therefore the model incorporates the dynamics of purchase behavior over time. The model has four central parts: inputs or stimulus variables to include products and social factors; perceptual and learning constructs; output response variables; and exogenous variables to include environment, financial status, and culture. From these elements, it is possible to consider the impact of decision mediators in consumer motivations and brand choice decisions.

Nicosia's model is also focused on individual consumers' decision-making and considers the relation between a firm and its potential customers with respect to a new product. He used computer simulation techniques to explain the structure of consumer decision-making. The consumer starts off with no experience of the product, and from exposure to the environment and the company's marketing effort forms predispositions, attitudes, and motivations which lead, via information search and evaluation, to purchase.

Andreasen's model is a general one based on specific conceptions about attitude formation and change, the key to change being exposure to information, either voluntary or involuntary.

Engel, Kollat, and Blackwell focus on motivation, perception, and learning in the buying decision process and their model has elements such as a central control unit, information processing, decision process, and environmental influences.

In addition to these descriptive models are others which are also predictive, e.g., stochastic learning models and queuing models. Stochastic learning models contain probabilistic elements and consider buying over time, usually purchases of brands in a product category. The basic approach is that an individual consumer learns from past behavior and the degree of satisfaction will influence future purchases. Also, more recent buying experiences with a particular brand/product will have greater effect than those which took place at a more distant time. These models analyze the relative purchase frequencies of brands in a product category and

estimate the probabilities of switching brands on the next purchase. If such probabilities are assumed to be constant, then market shares for the future can be computed.

Finally, decision models have been designed to evaluate the outcomes from different decisions, and they include optimization models to find a best solution, and heuristic ones which use rules of thumb to find reasonably good solutions. They incorporate differential calculus, mathematical programming, statistical decision theory, and game theory.

The dominant buyer behavior models of the mid-twentieth century (e.g., Nicosia, 1966; Howard and Sheth, 1969) no longer wholly dictate theoretic and applied research in the discipline; that is not to say that the influence of the early models is not felt in approaches to the study of consumer behavior. Simonson et al. (2001) contend that two main factors contributed to the decline in emphasis on comprehensive buyer behavior models: the realization that buyer behavior is too complex to be captured in a single model, since it represents most of the elements of human psychology, and the difficulty inherent in empirically testing the generic models. Subsequent models of buyer behavior that have received widespread attention include Bettman's (1979) information-processing model of consumer choice and Foxall's (1990) behavioral perspective model.

The advent and rising popularity of information processing and cognitive research on consumer decision-making and buying behavior has led to an increasing appreciation of models which eschew theories of rational choice in favor of models that proffer bounded rationality (the theory that decision-making may be "imperfect" due to cognitive limitations) as a more realistic perspective on how consumers actually make purchase decisions. Bettman, Luce, and Payne (1998) suggest that consumer decision-making is constructive in nature: consumers have limited processing capacity (e.g., for memory and computation), may not have well-established preferences for all stimuli, and when required to make a choice or purchase decision for a product/service may compute preferences ad hoc. The model thus appreciates that consumer preferences may be context dependent, not derived from a predefined set of values,

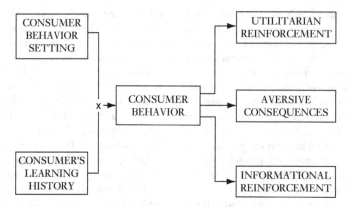

Figure 1   Behavioral perspective model of consumer choice (Foxall, 1999: 573)

and looks to intrapersonal cognitive phenomena such as memory and choice goals to model, explain, and predict buyer behavior.

Foxall's (1990, 1999) behavioral perspective model (BPM) of consumer choice proposes that the determinants of buyer behavior should be sought in the consumption environment rather than explaining buyer behavior merely by reference to intrapersonal information processing (see figure 1). Specifically, the BPM suggests that certain dimensions of buyer behavior can be predicted based on the contextual consumption setting and customers' reinforcement history in similar settings.

Bibliography

Andreasen, A. R. (1965). Attitudes and consumer behavior: A decision model. In L. Preston (ed.), *New Research in Marketing*. Berkeley Institute for Business and Economic Research, University of California, pp. 1–16.

Bettman, J. R. (1979). *An Information Processing Theory of Consumer Choice*. Reading, MA: Addison-Wesley.

Bettman, J. R., Luce, M. F., and Payne, J. W. (1998). Constructive consumer choice processes. *Journal of Consumer Research*, 25 (3), 187–217.

Blackwell, R. D., Miniard, P. W., and Engel, J. F. (2001). *Consumer Behavior*, 9th edn. New York: Dryden Press.

Foxall, G. R. (1990). *Consumer Psychology in Behavioral Perspective*. New York: Routledge.

Foxall, G. R. (1999). The behavioral perspective model: Consensibility and consensuality. *European Journal of Marketing*, 33 (5/6), 570–96.

Howard, J. A. and Sheth, J. N. (1969). *The Theory of Buyer Behavior*. New York: John Wiley.

Loudon, D. L. and Della Bitta, A. J. (1993). *Consumer Behavior*, 4th edn. New York: McGraw-Hill, ch. 19.

Nicosia, F. M. (1966). *Consumer Decision Processes*. Englewood Cliffs, NJ: Prentice-Hall.

Schiffman, L. G. and Kanuk, L. Z. (1991). *Consumer Behavior*, 4th edn. Englewood Cliffs, NJ: Prentice-Hall, ch. 20.

Sheth, J. N. (ed.) (1974). *Models of Consumer Behavior*. New York: Harper and Row.

Simonson, I., Carmon, Z., Dhar, R., Drolet, A., and Nowlis, S. M. (2001). Consumer research: In search of identity. *Annual Review of Psychology*, 52, 249–75.

buyer behavior theories

Barbara R. Lewis

As the discipline of consumer behavior has developed, various theories have contributed to understanding behavior. These include economic theory. Economists were the first professional group to offer a theory of buyer behavior. The Marshallian theory holds that consumer purchasing decisions are largely the result of "rational" and conscious economic calculations, i.e., the individual seeks to spend his/her income on goods that will deliver the most likely utility (satisfaction) according to his/her tastes and relative prices.

This model assumes that consumers derive satisfaction from consumption (probably not the case with expenditure on insurances, dental treatment, etc.) and seek to maximize satisfaction within the limits of income. The model also assumes that consumers have complete information with respect to supply, demand, and prices; complete mobility, i.e., can reach any market offer at any time; and that there is pure competition. In practice, consumers typically are not aware of and cannot judge all product offerings and may have restricted access. Consequently, consumers may well be "satisficing" rather than "maximizing" their utility.

Economic theory does have a role to play in understanding consumer behavior, in so far as people may be "problem solvers," trying to make rational and efficient spending decisions. However, it is also necessary to consider and understand the marketing and other stimuli that impact on buyer behavior (see CONSUMER BUYER BEHAVIOR), together with buyers' individual characteristics, i.e., to take account of various social and psychological influences on buying behavior.

See also buyer behavior models

Bibliography

Katona, G. (1953). Rational behavior and economic behavior. *Psychological Review*, September, 307–18.
Kotler, P. (1965). Behavioral models for analyzing buyers. *Journal of Marketing*, **29** (November), 37–45.
Schewe, C. D. (1973). Selected social psychological models for analyzing buyers. *Journal of Marketing*, **37** (July), 31–9.

buyers

Kalipso Karantinou

Buyers are those individuals with formal responsibility and authority for contracting with suppliers and ordering products or services, in the context of ORGANIZATIONAL BUYING BEHAVIOR (Cova and Salle, 2000; Turnbull and Leek, 2003). In many cases, however, they are not the only ones involved in decision-making. Industrial marketers have long been aware that some buying decisions are not made by the purchasing agent alone, but occur with the involvement of other members of the customer's organization (Cova and Salle, 2000), from different functions and organizational levels (Turnbull and Leek, 2003). USERS, initiators,

INFLUENCERS, DECIDERS, and GATEKEEPERS are other roles that have been identified (Cova and Salle, 2000) within the decision-making unit or BUYING CENTER.

The buyer's role within the buying center can range from a clerical officer, filling in forms and placing the order, to being the purchasing team leader, responsible for making the final recommendation to senior management. The importance of the buyer can vary depending on the organization's philosophy and attitude toward the purchase function and the level of risk associated with the purchase (McDonald and Christopher, 2003). A considerable amount of research has been conducted on the importance of the purchasing agent (the buyer) in influencing buying decisions (Turnbull and Leek, 2003).

The buying function of an organization has a significant strategic role, due to its key position as an intermediary between the organization and the supply market (Cova and Salle, 2000). Buyers in business-to-business markets (see BUSINESS-TO-BUSINESS MARKETING) are not passive, but actively search out and interact with suppliers, requiring customized products and services (Turnbull and Leek, 2003). Business markets are characterized by interaction, mutual dependency, and TRUST (ibid.), and the relationships that develop between buyers and the supplier organizations constitute an important aspect of the buying process (Dibb et al., 2001). In that respect, a crucial, and often overlooked, role of buyers is managing relationships with suppliers, as relationships between companies need substantial effort, active management, and investments from both parties (Turnbull and Leek, 2003; see INTERACTION APPROACH; ORGANIZATIONAL MARKETING).

The organizational buyer is influenced by a wide variety of factors, both from outside and within the organization. Understanding these factors and their interrelationships is critical to the development of appropriate business-to-business marketing strategy (Turnbull and Leek, 2003). Draper (1994) contends that organizational buyers are controlled, and it is the way in which they are controlled (through personal, bureaucratic, output, or cultural control) that provides the key to understanding their behavior.

Buyers in organizational markets have traditionally been assumed to be rational, unbiased, and optimization-oriented decision-makers, unaffected by personal factors, aiming to make efficient purchase decisions and maximize organizational benefits. However, the individual characteristics of buyers, such as age, education, personality, position in the organization, and income level can in fact influence decision-making (Dibb et al., 2001). Furthermore, buyers also can have personal goals that may influence their buying behavior (ibid.) and they tend to employ not only rational but also emotional criteria in decision-making (Dexter, 2002). It is now recognized that internal politics, power balances, and a desire for intra-organizational political gain can significantly affect buyers and the buying function within an organization. Farrell and Schroder (1999) demonstrated that members of buying centers use influence strategies to influence others and ultimately the purchasing decision (such as pressurizing, offering rewards, legitimating, using inspirational appeals, using rational persuasion) that are in general congruent with their respective power base (e.g., reinforcement, referent, legitimate, expert, or information power). They recommend, as a result, that marketers not only pay attention to the formal or informal types of power held by individuals, but also consider the way such power is exercised. In that respect, influential individuals within the purchasing organization should be targeted with appropriate information that is relevant to both their power bases and the corresponding influence strategy.

Bibliography

Cova, B. and Salle, R. (2000). Organizational buying behavior. In K. Blois (ed.), *The Oxford Textbook of Marketing*. Oxford: Oxford University Press, pp. 131–49.

Dexter, A. (2002). Egotists, idealists and corporate animals: Segmenting business markets. *International Journal of Market Research*, 44 (1), 31–51.

Dibb, S., Simkin, L., Pride, W. M., and Ferrell, O. C. (2001). *Marketing: Concepts and Strategies*, 4th European edn. Boston: Houghton Mifflin, ch. 5.

Draper, A. (1994). Organizational buyers as workers: The key to their behavior? *European Journal of Marketing*, 28 (11), 50–62.

Farrell, M. and Schroder, B. (1999). Power and influence in the buying center. *European Journal of Marketing*, 33 (11/12), 1161–70.

McDonald, M. and Christopher, M. (2003). *Marketing: A Complete Guide*. Basingstoke: Palgrave Macmillan, ch. 2.

Turnbull, P. W. and Leek, S. (2003). Business-to-business marketing: Organizational buying behavior, relationships and networks. In M. J. Baker (ed.), *The Marketing Book*, 5th edn. London: Butterworth-Heinemann, pp. 142–70.

buying center

Judy Zolkiewski

In business-to-business markets (*see* BUSINESS-TO-BUSINESS MARKETING) buying decisions tend to be made by a group of people in the organization (the decision-making unit, DMU) rather than by an individual, as is often the case in consumer purchasing (*see* CONSUMER BUYER BEHAVIOR). The people in the organization who are involved in the buying process are collectively known as the buying center.

Research into the composition, roles, and influences in the buying center can be traced back to the 1960s (Wind and Thomas, 1980). It is argued that the buying center includes players with different roles, such as USERS, INFLUENCERS, DECIDERS, and GATEKEEPERS (Webster and Wind, 1972), or policy-makers, purchasers, users, technologists, influencers, gatekeepers, and deciders (Turnbull, 1999), and that its composition varies by organization and also according to the buying situation (Johnston and Bonoma, 1981). Johnston and Bonoma (1981) also point out the need to consider both lateral and vertical involvement in the buying center, i.e., the different levels of the organizational hierarchy and the different functional departments involved. It should also be noted that the buying center may include members from outside organizations such as customers, consultants, and suppliers (Hill and Hillier, 1977) and that members of the buying center may have more than one role.

Much of the research into the operation of the buying center has taken the buy grid model (Robinson, Faris, and Wind, 1967) (*see* PURCHASING PROCESS) as the basis for investigation. For example, McWilliams, Naumann, and

Scott (1992) found that the buying center consisted of fewer members when it was undertaking a STRAIGHT REBUY and that the number of members increased as it moved through modified rebuy situations to new buy situations (*see* MODIFIED REBUY; NEW TASK). This finding is supported by the work of Johnston and Lewin (1996), who consider the influence of the PERCEIVED RISK of the buying decision on the buying center. These authors suggest that as the purchase gets riskier, the buying center will become larger and more complex, members will be more experienced, proven suppliers will be favored, information search will be more intensive, and interfirm (buyer–seller) relationships and communication networks become increasingly important. Ronchetto, Hutt, and Reingen (1989) also remind us that the role of the internal social network within a firm needs to be considered when the buying center is being investigated.

McWilliams et al. (1992) also found that the membership of the buying center changed as the purchase phases changed, for example, the number of members was lower for the supplier selection phase than for the need identification phase. They also speculate that the trend toward RELATIONSHIP MARKETING may result in buying center membership expanding as firms develop wider sets of inter-organizational linkages.

It is important for business-to-business marketers to be aware of the interactions and power dynamics within the buying center. However, they must also insure that these roles are not taken to be prescriptive.

See also *organizational buying behavior*

Bibliography

Hill, R. W. and Hillier, T. J. (1977). *Organizational Buying Behavior*. London: Macmillan.
Johnston, W. J. and Bonoma, T. V. (1981). The buying center: Structure and interaction patterns. *Journal of Marketing*, 45 (Summer), 143–56.
Johnston, W. J. and Lewin, J. E. (1996). Organizational buying behavior: Toward an integrative framework. *Journal of Business Research*, 35, 1–15.
McWilliams, R. D., Naumann, E., and Scott, S. (1992). Determining buying center size. *Industrial Marketing Management*, 21, 43–9.
Robinson, P. J., Faris, C. W., and Wind, Y. (1967). *Industrial Buying and Creative Marketing*. Boston: Allyn and Bacon.
Ronchetto, J. R., Jr., Hutt, M. D., and Reingen, P. H. (1989). Embedded influence patterns in organizational buying systems. *Journal of Marketing*, 53 (October), 51–62.
Turnbull, P. W. (1999). Business-to-business marketing: Organizational buying behavior, relationships and networks. In Michael J. Baker (ed.), *The Marketing Book*, 4th edn. Oxford: Butterworth-Heinemann.
Webster, F. E., Jr. and Wind, Y. (1972). *Organizational Buying Behavior*. Englewood Cliffs, NJ: Prentice-Hall.
Wind, Y. and Thomas, R. J. (1980). Conceptual and methodological issues in organizational buying behavior. *European Journal of Marketing*, 14 (5/6), 239–63.

buying operations

see CONSUMER DECISION-MAKING PROCESS

buying process

see PURCHASING PROCESS

calibration equivalence

see CONSTRUCT EQUIVALENCE

call planning

David Yorke and Mark P. Healey

PERSONAL SELLING (by representatives from supplier organizations to customers) is considered a vital element in the marketing COMMUNICATIONS MIX. However, it is extremely expensive and increasingly so. Cost-effectiveness of the personal selling effort, i.e., making more productive use of salespersons' time, will be enhanced if the schedule for calling on customers, both actual and potential, can be planned. Call planning therefore involves defining the effort (the number of visits per planning period and the amount of time to be directed to servicing each) each salesperson is to allocate. Clearly, four factors are of importance, namely, the time available to the salesperson, the requirements of the customer, the strategic significance of the customer, and the level and importance (in terms of sales volume or profitability). Some companies may classify accounts into A, B, and C accounts according to, for example, their sales volume and specify the frequency of calls per period for each of these accounts, the bigger accounts having more frequent calls. However, some customers may need more frequent contact with salespersons and may even specify the frequency and the times to meet. The objective of call planning, therefore, is to use the resource of personal selling as efficiently as possible with no unnecessary or duplicated calls. However, time should be set aside for possible emergency calls as requested by customers.

Bibliography

Baker, M. J. (ed.) (1998). *Macmillan Dictionary of Marketing and Advertising*. London: Macmillan.

Kotler, P., Armstrong, G., Saunders, J., and Wong, V. (2001). *Principles of Marketing*, 3rd European edn. Harlow: Prentice-Hall.

category equivalence

see CONSTRUCT EQUIVALENCE

causal research/causation

Charles C. Cui

Causal research is a research design that uses sample data and statistical methods to obtain evidence of cause–effect relationships (causation or causality) between the variables of interest. In marketing, causal research is often used to infer causation or causality, i.e., which variables are the cause (called independent variables) and which variables are the consequence or effect (called dependent variables). In other words, causation means that an independent variable is expected to produce a change in the dependent variable in the direction and of the magnitude specified by the theory (e.g., hypotheses). For example, the marketing manager may want to understand whether the reduction of ADVERTISING efforts (the independent variable) has caused consumers to switch to the competitor's mobile phone (the consequence, the dependent variable). The scientific notion of causation holds that causality cannot be proven but can only be inferred.

Three conditions should be satisfied if we want to draw causal inferences: concomitant variation, time order of occurrence of variables, and absence of other possible causal factors. Concomitant variation requires that a cause (X) and an effect (Y) occur or vary together (called covariation) as predicted by the hypothesis. Evidence of concomitant variation (or covariation) can be obtained by identifying correlation between phenomena. Time order of occurrence of variables requires that the causing event occur either before or simultaneously with the effect. The absence of other possible causal factors refers to the fact that the variable being investigated should be the only possible causal explanation. In other words, a relation between two variables cannot be explained by a third variable (also called nonspurious relation or nonspuriousness).

Causal research is conducted by means of causal modeling and HYPOTHESIS TESTING through EXPERIMENTATION (experimental research). Among many other techniques, structural equation modeling (see STRUCTURAL EQUATION MODELS) is most widely used for causal research in marketing.

Bibliography

Aaker, D. A., Kumar, V., and Day, G. S. (1998). *Marketing Research*, 6th edn. New York: John Wiley, ch. 13.

Bagozzi, R. P. (1980). *Causal Models in Marketing*. New York: John Wiley.

Malhorta, N. K. and Birks, D. (2000). *Marketing Research: An Applied Orientation*, European edn. London: Prentice-Hall, chs. 3, 9.

channel conflict

Gillian C. Hopkinson

Channel conflict refers to any conflict amongst members of a retail channel of distribution (see RETAIL DISTRIBUTION CHANNELS). Conflict has been widely defined as the perception of one person that his/her interests and goals are impeded by another (Gaski, 1984). The interdependence of actors in a marketing channel, their likely divergence of goals, and the dependence of each upon the effective running of the system form the conditions in which there is a high potential for conflict. The forms in which conflict appears are complex, making this a difficult phenomenon to identify and analyze. Pondy (1966) suggests a model of conflict stages comprising latent, perceived, felt, and manifest conflict as well as conflict aftermath. This suggests that what we would commonly recognize as conflict is only a restricted part of a phenomenon that, present in some form, is influential to many interactions.

Several fundamental causes of conflict in marketing channels have been identified. These include role incongruities (the defining of appropriate behavior for any member), differences of perception, domain disagreements relating to which parties should be able to make particular decisions, differences of expectation, goal incompatibilities, communication difficulties, and resource scarcities (Berman, 1996). These give rise to conflicts with respect to many issues that vary somewhat according to channel structure and industry. Of particular importance are conflicts regarding PRICING and retailer margins (see MARGIN), the quantity of supply of products, the supply to competing outlets, and the use of cooperative ADVERTISING. In contractual channels, such as in the case of FRANCHISING, where the channel leader is more formally designated, there are additional conflicts associated with, amongst other issues, retailer territory, style of premises, provision of training, the introduction of bureaucratic tasks, and the use of incentives.

The factors that are associated with high levels of channel conflict are held to differ according to the governance form of the channel because of the ways in which power structures vary with governance. Where power is relatively formalized, as it is held to be in a franchise context, research has explored the association between levels of conflict and power bases, or the use of power of the more powerful channel member (assumed to be the franchisor). Of five widely recognized power bases (coercive, reward, legitimate, expert, and referent; see French and Raven, 1959), it has been shown that the possession of coercive power is associated with high conflict levels. Reward power may also lead to high conflict, since to have the ability to reward is to have the ability to withhold reward and may therefore be seen as a form of coercion. The association between conflict and coercion is broadly supported by work that has related styles of management to channel conflict. Where channel leaders use managerial styles that emphasize participation and promote a favorable channel climate, there is less conflict and better means of conflict resolution (Schul, Pride, and Little, 1983; Strutton, Pelton, and Lumpkin, 1995). A climate that encourages solidarity, mutuality, and flexibility is likely to be found where less coercive influence strategies are used, for example where threats and legal pleas are less used and communication involves higher levels of requests and information exchange (Boyle et al., 1992). The work relating conflict and power was mostly carried out in the 1970s and 1980s and Gaski (1984) provides a thorough and useful summary of much of it. This work was conducted largely in contractual channels in which there is a relatively formalized power structure and a recognized channel leader. Since the focus is upon how the channel leader may influence conflict, its findings can only tentatively be applied to independent channel contexts.

There has recently been a decline in studies of conflict in channel contexts. Several factors have contributed to this. Firstly, although there is now some understanding of how conflict can be reduced, no strong, consistent relationship has been found between conflict and performance. The link between the two is likely to be complex and not linear (Duarte and Davies, 2003). Alternatively, performance may be adversely affected by dysfunctional conflict but enhanced by functional conflict. Since Frazier and Rody (1991) find that manifest conflict can be functional, Frazier (1999) argues that we require a more complex understanding of the conflict processes and stages in order to make the important link to performance. The functionality of manifest conflict is supported by Bradach (1998), who argues that the franchisees' argument with franchisors can lead to more questioning of ideas and, ultimately, better solutions to business problems.

A movement of interest toward RELATIONSHIP MARKETING amongst both marketers and academics has also contributed toward a decreased emphasis upon conflict in research. Relationship marketing draws upon more healthy-sounding concepts such as TRUST, commit-

ment, and cooperation (see INTERNATIONAL STRATEGIC ALLIANCES) that seem to sit uneasily alongside conflict. However, it has been argued that conflict can coexist with cooperation. The combination of ostensibly opposed phenomena within any one business relationship has gained greater attention through recent introduction of the notion of co-opetition (Nalebuff and Brandenburger, 1996). Dapiran and Hogarth-Scott (2003) examine category management amongst food retailers and key suppliers and find this model of close and committed retail relationships to be underscored by a continued presence of conflict and imbalanced power. The UK Competition Commission reported "a climate of apprehension" among many suppliers in their relationships with large retailers (Competition Commission Report 2000 on supermarkets, available online at www.competition-commission.org.uk/rep_pub/reports/index.htm. Theories of conflict are not, then, made redundant by the more relational orientation that pervades current marketing theory, but an understanding of channel behavior calls for theories that integrate conflict with cooperation and trust. In some retail channel situations, the costs of establishing and maintaining committed and trusting relationships may outweigh the benefits that such relationships can offer (Frazier, 1999; Hopkinson and Hogarth-Scott, 1999). Conflictual relationships may therefore remain appropriate according to the particular goals and strategies of channel members.

The key focus of research and comment with respect to channel conflict has been vertical conflict (between members at different levels in the channel) and has considered the dyad (e.g., the relationship between one retailer and one supplier). This focus has led to a lack of attention to both horizontal conflict (between channel members at the same level) and inter-type conflict in dual distribution systems or multiple channels. Such channels where, for example, a manufacturer sells both directly and through independent channels or through channels with different types of intermediaries (e.g., category killers and independent specialists) are now becoming "the rule rather than the exception" (Frazier, 1999). The growth of dual distribution systems is likely to be fueled by the introduction of Internet retailing, which offers new routes to the consumer (*see* INTERNET MARKETING). The ample trade press evidence of the conflicts that arise because of dual channels of distribution is illustrated by Bucklin, Thomas-Graham, and Webster (1997). These authors argue that such conflict is sometimes harmless, sometimes positive since it forces channel members to adapt to changing environments, and sometimes dangerous as it threatens the economics of the channel. The relative absence of knowledge with respect to inter-type conflict is a shortcoming of the literature and calls for a greater understanding of retail systems as networks (*see* NETWORK) whereby activities in different areas of the system are interdependent.

Bibliography

Berman, B. (1996). *Marketing Channels*. New York: John Wiley.

Boyle, B., Dwyer, F. R., Robicheaux, R. A., and Simpson, J. T. (1992). Influence strategies in marketing channels: Measures and use in different relationship structures. *Journal of Marketing Research*, 29 (4), 462–73.

Bradach, J. L. (1998). Using the plural form in the management of restaurant chains. *Administrative Science Quarterly*, 42 (2), 276–303.

Bucklin, C. B., Thomas-Graham, P. A., and Webster, E. A. (1997). Channel conflict: When is it dangerous? *McKinsey Quarterly*, 36–44.

Dapiran, G. P. and Hogarth-Scott, S. (2003). Are cooperation and trust being confused with power? An analysis of food retailing in Australia and the UK. *International Journal of Retail and Distribution Management*, 31 (4), 256.

Duarte, M. and Davies, G. (2003). Testing the conflict-performance assumption in business-to-business relationships. *Industrial Marketing Management*, 32 (2), 91–138.

Frazier, G. L. (1999). Organizing and managing channels of distribution. *Academy of Marketing Science Journal*, 27 (2), 226–41.

Frazier, G. L. and Rody, R. C. (1991). The use of influence strategies in interfirm relationships in industrial product channels. *Journal of Marketing*, 55 (1), 52–70.

French, J. and Raven, B. (1959). The bases of social power. In D. Cartwright (ed.), *Studies in Social Power*. Ann Arbor: University of Michigan Press, pp. 150–67.

Gaski, J. F. (1984). The theory of power and conflict in channels of distribution. *Journal of Marketing*, 48 (3), 9–30.

Hopkinson, G. C. and Hogarth-Scott, S. (1999). Franchise relationship quality: Micro-economic explanations. *European Journal of Marketing*, 33 (9), 827–43.

Nalebuff, B. J. and Brandenburger, A. M. (1996). *Co-opetition*. London: HarperCollins.

Pondy, L. R. (1966). A systems theory of organizational conflict. *Academy of Management Journal*, 9 (3), 246–57.

Schul, P. L., Pride, W. M., and Little, T. L. (1983). The impact of channel leadership behavior on intrachannel conflict. *Journal of Marketing*, 47 (3), 21–35.

Strutton, D., Pelton, L. E., and Lumpkin, J. R. (1995). The influence of psychological climate on conflict resolution strategies in franchise relationships. *Journal of the Academy of Marketing Science*, 21 (3), 207–16.

channels of distribution

Dale Littler

Products and services are moved from their source of production to the customer by means of a channel of distribution. The channel may be simple when the producer sells direct to customers (through, e.g., DIRECT MAIL) or it can consist of one or more intermediaries, such as agents, WHOLESALERS, and retailers (*see* RETAILING). The form and complexity of the distribution channel employed depend on the product (its perishability, bulk, frequency of purchase, whether or not it is an industrial or consumer product), the customers for the product, and their geographic dispersion.

A producer may employ an intermediary because it is the traditional practice of the industry, although often significant competitive advantages can be gained from innovating. Selling direct (*see* DIRECT MARKETING) can be employed by firms selling particular categories of industrial products, such as expensive capital goods or bulk raw materials. Such sales involve high-value dispatches, relatively infrequent purchases, and special pre-sale NEGOTIATION on price and technical specifications. However, direct selling is employed widely in consumer markets and is gaining more widespread appeal, partly because of the often considerably lower costs.

In both organizational and consumer markets, the development of information and communications technologies, particularly in the form of the Internet, has led to a widespread and substantial increase in direct selling, giving rise to what has been termed DISINTERMEDIARIZATION. This is posing a particular challenge for many consumer industries: for instance, the ability to download music may have significant repercussions for traditional record retailers as well as the chain of companies involved with the preparation of traditional music CDs.

Where independent intermediaries are used, a distinction can be drawn between those who act merely on behalf of the manufacturer (e.g., selling and distributing the product) without purchasing the product (i.e., they do not take title), and those who take title and undertake all further responsibility for distribution and perhaps other aspects of marketing. Intermediaries who do not take title include brokers and manufacturers' sales agents. A broker will attempt to find possible purchasers of the product and bring the manufacturer and these potential customers together. Manufacturers' sales agents fulfill similar functions, although they will often employ their own sales staff, carry stock on consignment, and provide ancillary services.such as financing, installation, and so on. Both brokers and agents receive a commission on any sales.

Intermediaries who do take title include wholesalers and retailers. These both buy and sell. Wholesalers will collect a range of goods from various manufacturers and usually sell them to other intermediaries (e.g., small retailers). Wholesalers are used when, for example, the amount sold per customer is relatively small, or when customers are widely scattered geographically. Generally, wholesalers sell to other companies or to retailers. Retailers, which carry out a similar function, mostly sell to the final customer. Large retailers will generally take delivery direct from manufacturers.

There are various transfers between the different elements of the distribution chain. Five types of transfer can be identified:

- *Physical goods transfers*: The movement of goods, ranging from the initial raw materials, through components and subassemblies, to the final product.
- *Ownership transfer*: As the product passes through the chain, the ownership of the physical goods can change.
- *Payment transfer*: The movement of money for the payment of goods and services.
- *Information transfer*: The flow of information between different stages in the chain.
- *Influence transfer*: The way in which different elements in the chain attempt to promote themselves and thereby influence other elements in the chain.

See also *electronic commerce; electronic data interchange; retail distribution channels*

Bibliography

Jobber, D. (2004). *Principles and Practices of Marketing*, 3rd edn. London: McGraw-Hill.

cluster analysis

Michael Greatorex

Cluster analysis refers to a body of techniques used to identify objects or individuals that are similar. Using measurements on several variables for a number of cases, a small number of exclusive and exhaustive groups or clusters are formed. Each cluster has high within-cluster homogeneity and high between-cluster heterogeneity. Usually a measure of the distance between individuals is used to build up clusters. When the number of cases is small, the clustering can be observed, but with larger numbers of cases faster clustering is used and less detailed output is provided by computer packages, e.g., the STATISTICAL PACKAGE FOR THE SOCIAL SCIENCES (SPSS), which are necessary for cluster analysis. Once the sample has been partitioned and the clusters have been identified using some of the variables in the analysis, the remaining variables can be investigated to obtain profiles of the clusters and to see if and where there are differences between clusters.

Cluster analysis differs from DISCRIMINANT ANALYSIS in that there is no external means of grouping the cases.

The usefulness of cluster analysis in marketing to help in segmenting populations (*see* MARKET SEGMENTATION) should be obvious. The variables used to define the clusters could be the needs and LIFESTYLES of individuals and the subsequent profiling may involve demographic, socioeconomic, and other variables to see where the clusters differ and to see if the clusters can be named. If the researcher has a large sample, a cluster analysis may precede the application of other statistical methods, including other multivariate techniques (*see* MULTIVARIATE METHODS (ANALYSIS)), to each cluster in turn.

Bibliography

Johnson, R. A. and Wichern, D. W. (1998). *Applied Multivariate Statistical Analysis*, 4th edn. Englewood Cliffs, NJ: Prentice-Hall.

codes of practice

David Yorke

It is desirable that industries conform to certain rules or regulations in the conduct of their business. Broadly, such regulations may be imposed by external organizations (e.g., by law) or they may be self-imposed (e.g., codes of practice such as advertising industry standards and those enforced by professional service firms). The advantages claimed for codes of practice are: they can help to raise the standards of an industry; organizations within the industry are often happy to accept restrictions imposed by voluntary codes of practice rather than be subject to the law, over which they have little control or influence; and codes may offer a cheaper and quicker means of resolving grievances than using more formal legal channels.

Trade or industry associations are encouraged to adopt codes of practice and to update them constantly as the MARKETING ENVIRONMENT changes. For example, in the UK the Advertising Standards Authority is responsible for implementing the British Code of Advertising Practice that requires that ADVERTISING should be "legal, decent, honest and truthful." In the case of market research, there are comprehensive codes that have been developed by ICC/ESOMAR, the UK Market Research Society, the Council of American Survey Research Organizations, and others.

cognitive dissonance

Margaret K. Hogg and Barbara R. Lewis

Consistency theory in the psychology of ATTITUDES "refers to the idea that people's mental representations of their beliefs, attitudes and attitudinally significant behaviors, decisions and commitments tend to exist in harmony with one another, and that *disharmony motivates cognitive changes designed to restore harmony*" (Eagly and Chaiken, 1993: 469, emphasis added). Central to Festinger's (1957) theory of cognitive dissonance "is the assumption that the presence of dissonance gives rise to pressures to eliminate or at least reduce it" (Eagly and Chaiken, 1993: 472). Individual consumers' cognitions for products which are expressed in terms of values, beliefs, opinions, and attitudes tend to exist in clusters that are generally both internally consistent and consistent with behavior; and an individual strives for consistency within his or her self.

However, any two cognitive elements or attitudes may or may not be consonant with each other. If such an inconsistency exists in a pre-purchase situation, a consumer has a state of conflict which makes it difficult to make a choice. If, after a purchase, there is inconsistency between cognitive elements, then cognitive dissonance is said to exist, i.e., it is a post-purchase state of mind.

When making choices between alternatives, consumers invariably experience cognitive dissonance as on few occasions do they make a completely "right" decision; consumers may remain aware of positive features of rejected alternatives, and negative features of a selected alternative, which are inconsistent/dissonant with the action taken. Thus cognitive dissonance relates to the sense of loss associated with the choices that have been forgone.

Cognitive dissonance will be high when: the buying decision is important, either psychologically or in terms of financial outlay; when a number of desirable alternatives are available; when the alternatives are dissimilar with little cognitive overlap, e.g., the choice between a television or a washing machine; when decision choice is a result of free will with no help or applied pressure from others; when the purchase is a high-involvement purchase (*see* INVOLVEMENT); and when the individual has dissonance tendency.

The existence of cognitive dissonance is psychologically uncomfortable and so consumers develop strategies to reduce/eliminate it in order to reachieve consistency or consonance. These strategies include: eliminating responsibility for the decision, e.g., returning the product; changing attitudes toward the product to increase cognitive overlap; reevaluating the desirability of the chosen product favorably and/or the alternative product negatively; denying, distorting, or forgetting information (e.g., cigarette smokers and health warnings); seeking new information to confirm one's choice; or reducing the importance of the decision. For marketing managers, one important commercially salient strategy for reducing or lowering dissonance is to provide consumers with positive information that confirms their purchase decision.

Bibliography

Arnould, E., Price, L., and Zinkhan, G. (2004). *Consumers*, 2nd edn. Boston: McGraw-Hill Irwin, ch. 15.
Aronson, E. (1978). The theory of cognitive dissonance: A current perspective. In L. Berkowitz (ed.), *Cognitive Theories: Social Psychology*. London: Academic Press, 215–20.
Cummings, W. H. and Venkatesan, M. (1976). Cognitive dissonance and consumer behavior: A review of the evidence. *Journal of Marketing Research*, August, 303–8.
Eagly, A. H. and Chaiken, S. (1993). *The Psychology of Attitudes*. Orlando, FL: Harcourt Brace Jovanovich, ch. 10, pp. 427–98, and esp. pp. 469–79.
Festinger, L. (1957). *A Theory of Cognitive Dissonance*. Stanford, CA: Stanford University Press.
Heider, F. (1958). *The Psychology of Interpersonal Relations*. New York: John Wiley.
Loudon, D. L. and Della Bitta, A. J. (1993). *Consumer Behavior*, 4th edn. New York: McGraw-Hill, ch. 18.
Mowen, J. C. and Minor, M. (1998). *Consumer Behavior*, 5th edn. Upper Saddle River, NJ: Prentice-Hall, ch. 9.
Schiffman, L. G. and Kanuk, L. Z. (2004). *Consumer Behavior*, 8th edn. Upper Saddle River, NJ: Prentice-Hall, ch. 8.
Solomon, M. R. (2002). *Consumer Behavior: Buying, Having, Being*, 5th edn. Upper Saddle River, NJ: Prentice-Hall, ch. 7.
Solomon, M. R., Bamossy, G., and Askegaard, S. (2002). *Consumer Behavior: A European Perspective*, 2nd edn. Upper Saddle River, NJ: Prentice-Hall, chs. 4, 5.
Venkatesan, M. (1973). Cognitive consistency and novelty seeking. In S. Ward and T. S. Robertson (eds.), *Consumer Behavior: Theoretical Sources*. Englewood Cliffs, NJ: Prentice-Hall, pp. 355–84.
Wells, W. D. and Prensky, D. (1996). *Consumer Behavior*. New York: John Wiley, ch. 11.

cognitive stage

David Yorke

Models of the MARKETING COMMUNICATIONS process suggest that a target buyer or customer moves from a state of ignorance or unawareness of an organization and/or its products or services to ultimately making a purchase. This process comprises three principal stages: cognitive, AFFECTIVE, and CONATIVE. It is, however, widely recognized that buyers may not necessarily proceed through the predetermined sequence of the cognitive, affective, and behavioral stages in that order (*see* AIDA MODEL).

The cognitive stage is that which draws the ATTENTION of the buyer or customer to an organization, its products, service, or brands, creates an AWARENESS of their existence, and develops a clear understanding of what is being offered. The cost-effectiveness of achieving this is determined largely by the media used (*see* MASS MEDIA), and the size and type of the target group(s). For example, PERSONAL SELLING is less cost-effective when the number in the target group is large, although TELEMARKETING and DIRECT MAIL can reduce the cost; and ADVERTISING is considered to be relatively successful at the cognitive stage providing there are media appropriate for reaching only the target group.

Bibliography

Solomon, M. R. (2002). *Consumer Behavior*, 5th edn., NJ: Prentice-Hall.

collective self

see CULTURE AND SOCIAL IDENTITY

communications mix

David Yorke

The marketing communications mix is a subset of the MARKETING MIX. It includes all the techniques available to the marketer which may be "mixed" in order to deliver a message to the target group of buyers, customers, or consumers.

Generally, techniques may be classified using two dimensions: first, whether they are delivered personally (e.g., PERSONAL SELLING, TELE-MARKETING) or whether the medium used is impersonal (e.g., ADVERTISING, PACKAGING, SALES PROMOTION, PUBLIC RELATIONS); and secondly, whether or not the technique involves a payment by the sponsor. All of the first group are thus "commercial." Examples of "non-commercial" techniques are PUBLICITY and opinion leaders (see INTERPERSONAL COMMUNICATIONS). The use of information and communication technologies is affecting the means by which marketers strive to communicate with their different audiences, with, for example, the use of targeted emails and text messages.

Different techniques have different strengths (and, conversely, weaknesses). There is a need for the marketer to define the target groups, to set objectives for each, and to evaluate the most cost-effective means of reaching the target(s) and attaining the objectives. A different mix, for example, would be employed at different stages of the PRODUCT LIFE CYCLE. A similar situation exists for products or services of high or low value (where the degree of PERCEIVED RISK in the target's mind will vary) and depending on whether the target group is concentrated or dispersed.

See also *marketing communications*

Bibliography

Doyle, P. (1998). *Marketing Management and Strategy*, 2nd edn. London: Prentice-Hall.

Kitchen, P. J. (1999). *Marketing Communications: Principles and Practice*. London: International Thomson.

communications objectives

Barbara R. Lewis

The objectives of MARKETING COMMUNICA-TIONS are concerned primarily with information and education about companies and their products and services, and ultimately with consumer purchase and satisfaction, together with achievement of corporate goals such as profits, return on investment, growth, and market shares (see MARKET SHARE).

However, "purchase" behavior is typically the end result of the CONSUMER DECISION-MAKING PROCESS and the marketing communicator wishes to move the target audience (e.g., buyer/consumer) through several stages of readiness to buy, i.e., through the COGNITIVE, AFFECTIVE, and CONATIVE (or behavioral response) STAGES, although not necessarily in that sequence.

Specific objectives might be to: provide information about a new PRODUCT or BRAND and create awareness of the product/brand; generate interest in the product or brand from a target market (or segment; see MARKET SEGMENTA-TION); encourage sales from new customers; increase sales among existing customers; increase market share; introduce price concessions; provide information on product changes and availability; and educate customers or the general public about features/benefits of the product. Communication objectives might also be concerned with providing information and generating attitudes and responses from other organizations in the distribution chain, e.g., encouraging new distributors or improving dealer relationships; or they may relate to consumers' ATTITUDES and responses toward organizations, e.g., generating goodwill and creating a corporate image.

Marketing communications objectives that are concerned with consumers' responses to products/brands are reflected in various response-hierarchy models that have been offered, e.g., AIDA MODEL, DAGMAR MODEL, HIERARCHY OF EFFECTS MODEL, and INNOVATION-ADOPTION MODEL. These models assume that a buyer moves through the cognitive, affective, and behavioral stages in that order, i.e., the "learn-feel-buy" sequence (see LEARN-FEEL-BUY MODEL); alternative sequences, depending on the product category and consumer IN-VOLVEMENT, are buy-feel-learn and feel-buy-learn (see BUY-FEEL-LEARN MODEL; FEEL-BUY-LEARN MODEL).

As a consequence, communications objectives may be set depending on the product, consumer involvement, and stage in the consumer decision-making process.

Bibliography

Colley, R. H. (1961). *Defining Advertising Goals for Measured Advertising Results*. New York: Association of National Advertisers.

Doyle, P. (2000). *Value-Based Marketing*. Chichester: John Wiley, p. 306.

Lavidge, R. J. and Steiner, G. A. (1961). A model for predictive measurements of advertising effectiveness. *Journal of Marketing*, **25** (October), 61.

Rogers, E. M. (1995). *Diffusion of Innovation*, 4th edn. New York: Free Press, pp. 79–86.

communications research

Dale Littler

Communications research is aimed at optimizing the effectiveness of communications through pre-testing and post-testing of various aspects of the COMMUNICATIONS MIX. Pre-testing focuses on gathering information before the implementation of the communications. It may involve, for example, assessing the target audience's reactions to the possible content of the communications (the MESSAGE), and the manner in which this is to be communicated. Post-testing is concerned with the evaluation of the "effectiveness" of the MARKETING COMMUNICATIONS. ADVERTISING effectiveness tends to receive more emphasis because it usually commands much higher expenditures than other elements of the communications mix. Pre-testing (before the communication is used on the public at large) may be employed to assess reactions to different forms of the communication in order to identify the version that is likely to yield the most favorable response. A variety of research techniques may be employed, ranging from the gathering and analysis of ATTITUDES to laboratory tests using equipment to measure physiological responses such as pupil dilation, heartbeat, and blood pressure. Post-testing can include evaluating consumers' ability to recall or to recognize communications (generally advertisements).

The relationship between sales and expenditure on communications is much more difficult to ascertain. However, by the use of carefully designed experiments (*see* EXPERIMENTATION) it may be possible to measure the sales effect of, say, advertising. A classic study of advertising effectiveness using experimentation involved Du Pont's paint division. It divided its 56 sales areas into high, average, and low MARKET SHARE territories and allocated the usual amount to advertising in one third, two and a half times the amount in another third, and four times the usual amount in the final third. The experiment suggested that an increased spend on advertising increased sales at a diminishing rate, and that the sales increase was weaker in Du Pont's high market share territories (Buzzell, 1964). The increasing sophistication of information and communications technologies means that it is possible to collect data at the point of sale on specified products and relate these to changes in various communications stimuli in confined areas. Other research on effectiveness has attempted to identify a historical relationship between sales and, for example, the expenditure on advertising using advanced statistical techniques.

Generally, though, there are difficulties in assessing the impact of communications on sales. First, without carefully controlled experimentation, one cannot conclude that there is any direct link between the communication and the sales/profits secured; there are too many other variables involved. Even if all the extraneous variables are controlled, there might still be some external influence, unthought of by the experimenters, that may affect the results.

Secondly, the full impact of the communication may be spread over time. Taking the case of advertising, some people who are acquainted with the advertising in the early stages of the campaign may react quickly; others may, for various reasons, delay a response. A further group of people may not learn of the advertising for some time after it starts. In the same way, the full effects of reducing or stopping advertising may not become apparent for some time; there may well be a "carry-over" effect. Thus, when considering the impact of advertising at any given time, it is possible to have a distorted picture of its general effectiveness. It may well be that there is a steep rise in sales stemming from the advertising, but this may be because the advertising has *brought forward* sales that, in its absence, would have been made some time in the future; so the total sales may be unaffected. Of course, this may well be what the advertiser desired as he/she will have the advantage of obtaining, perhaps, a higher market share (and earlier); in addition, there will be resulting higher sales revenue in the early stages of the PRODUCT LIFE CYCLE concerned.

Thirdly, the creativity of the communication can be expected to influence its effectiveness. Thus, spending large amounts of money on advertising will not lead inevitably to substantial sales if the campaign itself leads to resentment, fails to stimulate interest, or lacks credibility. Similarly, of course, any communication will be ineffective, in the medium term, if the product is unreliable, of poor quality, or has undesirable side-effects. Because of the specificity of most of the marketing variables (i.e., the development of a specific campaign for a specific product), it becomes difficult to make general conclusions about the effectiveness of an additional dollar spent on advertising.

Bibliography

Buzzell, R. D. (1964). E. I. Du Pont de Nemours and Co.: Measurement of effects of advertising. In *Mathematical Models and Marketing Management*. Boston: Division of Research, Graduate School of Business Administration, Harvard University, pp. 157–79.

competitive advantage

Dale Littler

Competitive advantage may be secured through differentiation of the organization and/or its products and services in some way in order to gain preference by all or part of the market over its rivals. This may result in higher MARKET SHARE and/or margins (*see* MARGIN) than competitors. In general, competitive advantage will be obtained through offering higher customer value. Day and Wensley (1988) argue that there is no common meaning of "competitive advantage," it being used interchangeably with "distinctive competence" to mean relative superiority in skills and resources, or with "positional superiority in the market," as providing greater customer value yields high market share.

Resource-based theories argue that there are mainly two related sources of competitive advantage: assets, i.e., the resource endowments the business has accumulated (e.g., investments in the scale, scope, and efficiency of facilities and systems, BRAND EQUITY, etc.), and capabilities, which may also be referred to as "competencies" and "organizational routines." These are defined as "the glue that brings these assets together and enables them to be deployed advantageously" (Dierickx and Cool, 1989). Organizational routines/competencies involve assembling firm specific assets into "integrated clusters spanning individuals and groups so that they enable distinctive activities to be performed" (Teece, Pisano, and Shuen, 1997: 516). They may, for example, include the ability to coordinate all the activities involved in NEW PRODUCT DEVELOPMENT to produce innovative products effectively and efficiently.

Capabilities differ from assets in that they cannot be given a monetary value. They are, according to Dierickx and Cool, "so deeply embedded in the organizational routines and practices that they cannot be traded or imitated." They include skills and processes, and are often tacit. They have some similarity to the core competencies described by Prahalad and Hamel (1990) except that these are seen as the capabilities that support multiple businesses within an organization. Recently, Teece et al. (1997) have noted the importance of dynamic capabilities, defined as "the firm's ability to integrate, build, and reconfigure internal and external competencies to address rapidly changing environments. Dynamic capabilities thus reflect an organization's ability to achieve new and innovative forms of competitive advantage given path dependencies and market positions" (p. 516).

Day (1994) suggests that two capabilities are particularly critical to competitive advantage, namely, market sensing capability, which is the ability to detect changes in the market and to anticipate the possible responses to marketing actions that may be taken; and customer linking capability, which embraces the "skills, abilities and processes needed to achieve collaborative customer relationships so that individual customer needs are quickly apparent to all functions and well-defined procedures are in place for responding to them." Littler (2004) suggests that there are at least four dimensions to competitiveness, regarded as securing a relative advantage to competitors. These are: marginal differentiation, the ability to be perceived as different in valued ways by potential purchasers; efficiency, insuring that the customer-perceived values are delivered at a cost at least comparable to that of the nearest competitors; flexibility, or the capability to respond to the unexpected; and proprietariness, the scope for protecting the advantages that the business has.

As Porter (1980) argues, it is important to establish a competitive advantage that is sustainable, i.e., not easily eroded by environmental changes or imitated by existing or potential competitors. Barney (1991) suggests that there are four features of assets that provide a sustainable competitive advantage: they are valuable; rare; imperfectly imitable; and there are no strategically equivalent substitutes. Fahy and Hooley (2002) suggest that "value and inimitability are both essential elements of key resources and determine the sustainability of competitive advantage in a rapidly changing technological environment" (p. 250). However, the advantages that any organization has at one stage can be effectively challenged through technological innovation, rivals' exploitation of changes in customer preferences, new regulations that undermine the competitive advantage, or through the concerted efforts of competitors using different marketing and other strategies.

Bibliography

Barney, J. (1991). Firm resources and sustained competitive advantage. *Journal of Management*, 17 (1), 99–120.

Day, G. S. (1994). The capabilities of market-driven organizations. *Journal of Marketing*, 58 (October), 37–52.

Day, G. S. and Wensley, R. (1988). Assessing advantage: A framework for diagnosing competitive superiority. *Journal of Marketing*, 520–1.

Dierickx, I. and Cool, K. (1989). Asset stock and accumulation and sustainability of competitive advantage. *Management Science*, 35, 1504–11.

Fahy, J. and Hooley, G. (2002). Sustainable competitive advantage in electronic business: Toward a contingency perspective on the resource-based view. *Journal of Strategic Marketing*, 10, 241–53.

Littler, D. (2004). Innovation and sustainable competitive advantage. In P. J. Kitchen (ed.), *Marketing Mind Prints*. Basingstoke: Palgrave Macmillan.

Porter, M. E. (1980). *Competitive Strategy: Techniques for Analyzing Industries and Competitors*. New York: Free Press.

Prahalad, C. K. and Hamel, G. (1990). The core competence of the corporation. *Harvard Business Review*, 68, 3 (May/June), 79–91.

Teece, D. J., Pisano, G., and Shuen, A. (1997). Dynamic capabilities and strategic management. *Strategic Management Journal*, 18 (7), 509–33.

Wensley, R. (1995). Marketing strategy. In M. J. Baker (ed.), *Companion Encyclopaedia of Marketing*. London: Routledge, pp. 215–33.

competitive strategy

Dale Littler

Widely popularized by Michael Porter (e.g., Porter, 1980) during the 1980s, "competitive strategy" tended to be accepted as a new approach to organizational strategy (*see* CORPORATE STRATEGY). Its roots are within the traditional area of industrial economics, and particularly the structure-conduct-performance paradigm. Porter argues that there are five major forces that affect the attractiveness of an industry. These are: intra-industry rivalry; the threat of new entrants; the existence, or potential development, of substitutes; customers; and suppliers. New entrants pose a threat as they augment existing capacity and may be disruptive because they will have to secure a market position in order to justify the costs of entry. Substitutes place a ceiling on the price that can be charged. Supplier power can lead to higher input costs and is increased where suppliers are highly concentrated relative to the customer industries, have a unique product, and there are switching costs. The power of customers, which can result in downward pressure on margins (*see* MARGIN), is enhanced where they purchase in large volume, the product they purchase is standard or undifferentiated, and the product accounts for a significant proportion of the buyer's cost and, therefore, profits. Rivalry is likely to be intense where there are many firms of equal size, growth is slow, the product is undifferentiated, and there are high fixed costs presenting significant barriers to exit. Porter argues that it is these specific industry factors that are important since macroeconomic and other factors (*see* ENVIRONMENTAL ANALYSIS) will affect all industries equally. The major objective is, then, for organizations to position themselves favorably with regard to each of these five forces. Thus, they may strive to establish or reinforce barriers to entry; or build in switching costs; or develop alternative sources of supply through, for example, collaborative product development with other possible suppliers.

Porter assumes that industries evolve, with distinct phases to their life cycle (nascent, growth, maturity, decline), and he applies the five forces framework to each of these stages. He develops the concept of strategic groups based on the view that industries can be disaggregated into clusters of firms with each cluster pursuing different strategies. There may be mobility barriers inhibiting the movement of firms from one cluster to another. However, the approach is essentially descriptive and, it can be argued, lacks robustness since firms can be clustered in two or more ways depending on the criteria employed to define the clusters.

Porter argues that the major focus of competitive strategy is to provide customer value. This can be perceived in terms of lowering customer costs and/or allowing the customer to secure higher quality, for example. Firms can follow one of four generic competitive strategies (*see* GENERIC STRATEGIES). They can aim at the lowest cost position (*see* COST LEADERSHIP STRATEGY) or differentiation (*see* DIFFEREN-TIATION STRATEGY) within the market as a whole; or they can strive for one of these positions aimed at a particular segment/or segments of the market (*see* FOCUS STRATEGY; MARKET SEGMENTATION). Firms which aim neither at the lowest cost position nor at the differentiated position become, according to Porter, "stuck in the middle" with suboptimal returns. However, there is little empirical evidence to substantiate his thesis; indeed, there has been increasing evidence that high performers can follow high levels of efficiency as well as having a significantly differentiated market position (e.g., Hall, 1980; Cronshaw, Davis, and Kay, 1994).

Porter's work and that of his followers makes at least three important contributions: first, it provides a coherent framework for analyzing industries; second, it emphasizes the importance of exit barriers as an influence on corporate behavior; and third, it focuses on the means of providing customer value. In later work, Porter has noted the need to adopt a more dynamic approach to competitive strategy formation (Porter, 1991).

Commentators such as Ohmae (1988) believe that the focus on "competitive strategy" can lead to an emphasis on competitors *per se* rather than on the changing values and requirements of customers, and that this may lead to tit-for-tat competitive rivalry, perhaps at the expense of providing adequately satisfactory offerings to customers, thereby opening up opportunities to those, including new entrants, that do.

A firm's analysis of its competitive arena, however, is subjectively rooted and all forms of cognitive biases may affect how it perceives its environment. For example, there may be an inability to identify or acknowledge significant challenges to the firm's competitive position from, for example, technological developments or new entrants that have a different basis of competitiveness.

Bibliography

Cronshaw, M., Davis, E., and Kay, J. (1994). On being stuck in the middle or Good Food Costs Less at Sainsbury. *British Journal of Management*, 519–32.

Hall, W. K. (1980). Survival strategies in a hostile environment. *Harvard Business Review*, **58**, 5 (September/October), 75–85.

Ohmae, K. (1988). Getting back to strategy. *Harvard Business Review*, **66**, 6 (November/December), 149–56.

Porter, M. E. (1980). *Competitive Strategy: Techniques for Analyzing Industries and Competitors*. New York: Free Press.

Porter, M. E. (1991). Toward a dynamic theory of strategy. *Strategic Management Journal*, **12**, Special issue, "Fundamental Research Issues in Strategy and Economics," 95–117.

comprehension

Emma Banister

Comprehension refers to the point at which a consumer attaches meaning to a stimulus. Accurate comprehension indicates that the receiver has extracted the source's intended meanings from the communication (Jacoby and Hoyer, 1989). Comprehension can also specifically refer to the second step in the DAGMAR

48 computers in marketing

MODEL of communications. It describes the part of the COGNITIVE STAGE (*see* TARGET MARKET) when the target buyer or customer understands the product or service and what it is designed to achieve.

Bibliography

Colley, R. H. (1961). *Defining Advertising Goals for Measured Advertising Results*. New York: Association of National Advertisers.

Jacoby, J. and Hoyer, W. D. (1989). The comprehension/miscomprehension of print communication: Selected findings. *Journal of Consumer Research*, **15** (March), 434–41.

computers in marketing

Michael Greatorex

Computers have had far-reaching effects on MARKETING RESEARCH and MARKETING and their use stretches to all aspects of marketing.

Computers are being utilized increasingly for the storage and retrieval of data using databases (*see* DATABASE) and marketing information systems. These data can form the basis of the monitoring of an organization's external and internal environments, which permits the analysis of opportunities and threats (*see* SWOT ANALYSIS) facing the organization. Again, such data are useful in the preliminary problem identification stages of the marketing research process.

In PRIMARY RESEARCH, software is available to help in the design of questionnaires (*see* QUESTIONNAIRE DESIGN). A satisfactory questionnaire can be printed and used in postal surveys or personal interviews, but the use of the computer can be taken further in telephone interviewing when the questionnaire appears on a screen used by the interviewer as a prompt and a means of recording the answers given by the respondent. In computer interviewing, the respondent, using a keyboard, mouse, or touch screen, directly communicates answers to questions as they appear on the screen without the use of an interviewer. Computers can be used in telephone interviewing to select members of the sample using random digit dialing. The computer will dial numbers, make recalls if needed,

check on the productivity of the interviewers, and generally help in the management of the interviewing stage of a survey. Computers can be used to represent different consumption experiences (simulated shopping) or provide a range of visual product concepts. Data can be collected directly by the computer (Brooks, 1988; Burke et al., 1992; Campo, Gijsbrechts, and Guerra, 1999; Wirtz and Bateson, 1999).

Further examples of the use of computers to capture data occur in the use of electronic devices in observational research (*see* OBSERVATION). The use of scanners at the point of sale is revolutionizing marketing research by providing management with timely data on sales that help decisions on new products, styles, designs, and packaging, on sales promotions (*see* SALES PROMOTION), PRICING, point of sale ADVERTISING, and on such routine decisions as inventory control and production planning for established products.

An important use of computers is in the analysis of PRIMARY DATA collected using both qualitative and quantitative methods, especially the latter. The statistical analysis of surveys is carried out using computer packages such as the STATISTICAL PACKAGE FOR THE SOCIAL SCIENCES (SPSS) and MINITAB. Large samples need computers for data analysis even to obtain simple summaries for each variable such as tabulations of frequencies or DESCRIPTIVE STATISTICS such as measures of average and dispersion. In BIVARIATE ANALYSIS, analyses such as CROSS-TABULATIONS or comparisons of means are readily specified and obtainable using these packages. MULTIVARIATE METHODS (ANALYSIS) is only possible using computers. Such methods as multiple regression (*see* REGRESSION AND CORRELATION), DISCRIMINANT ANALYSIS, FACTOR ANALYSIS, CLUSTER ANALYSIS, STRUCTURAL EQUATION MODELS, and MULTIDIMENSIONAL SCALING including CONJOINT ANALYSIS are carried out using either general packages such as those mentioned above or specialist software available for some of the methods.

Multiple regression is useful in FORECASTING along with such time-series methods as exponential smoothing and autoregressive moving average methods. Computers are useful in the selection and development of a suitable forecasting procedure for a particular problem such as the demand for a specified product. Since organizations often require forecasts for many products, computers are also useful in the application of the chosen procedures for the different products.

MARKETING DECISION SUPPORT SYSTEMS involve databases, marketing models, and, crucially, computer hardware and software and a communication interface so that the user can interact directly with the databases and marketing models. Marketing decision support systems have been devised to help marketing decision-makers with a variety of problems, especially those concerning the elements of the MARKETING MIX.

Marketing decision support systems have been created using spreadsheets. Spreadsheets have also been used in marketing for forecasting, budgeting, and controlling.

There has been a significant growth in online (Internet-based) purchasing and consumption (*see* ELECTRONIC COMMERCE; ELECTRONIC DATA INTERCHANGE). Data can be collected at the point of sale to develop profiles of consumers and purchasing patterns for specific products (*see* EPOS).

Computers are also useful in teaching marketing and marketing research. Obvious examples include business games centered around marketing topics, computer-based marketing case studies, exercises, and computer-aided learning modules.

Bibliography

Brooks, M. (1988). Search monitor: An approach for computer-controlled experiments involving consumer information search. *Journal of Consumer Research*, 14, 117–21.

Burke, R., Harlam, B., Kahn, B., and Lodish, L. (1992). Comparing dynamic consumer choice in real and computer-simulated environments. *Journal of Consumer Research*, 19, 71–82.

Campo, K., Gijsbrechts, E., and Guerra, F. (1999). Computer-simulated shopping experiments for analyzing dynamic purchasing patterns: Validation and guidelines. *Journal of Empirical Generalizations in Marketing Science*, 4, 22–61.

Gosling, J. (2001). Avatars: Virtual incarnations and their implications for life and work on the web. Paper presented at Critical Management Studies Conference, Manchester, July.

Parkinson, L. K. and Parkinson, S. T. (1987). *Using the Microcomputer in Marketing*. Maidenhead: McGraw-Hill.

Wirtz, J. and Bateson, J. E. G. (1999). Introducing uncertain performance expectations in satisfaction models for services. *International Journal of Service Industry Management*, 10 (1), 82–99.

conative stage

David Yorke

Consumer decision-making models (*see* CONSUMER DECISION-MAKING PROCESS) which suggest that a target buyer or customer moves from a state of ignorance or unawareness of an organization and/or its products or services to ultimately making a purchase comprise three main stages: COGNITIVE, AFFECTIVE, and conative. The conative or behavioral stage is that which elicits some action on the part of the buyer or customer. Action is not necessarily a purchase, although this is, ultimately, what is desired by organizations; rather, it may be seeking further information about the product or service, or product TRIAL.

Of the MARKETING COMMUNICATIONS techniques available in the COMMUNICATIONS MIX, those which are more likely to initiate action in the conative stage are PERSONAL SELLING, SALES PROMOTION, and forms of DIRECT MARKETING such as TELEMARKETING, DIRECT MAIL, and OFF THE PAGE selling.

concept testing

Margaret Bruce and Liz Barnes

Concept testing is concerned with the evaluation of a new PRODUCT CONCEPT to: determine ways to improve the concept; ascertain the best target markets; and gauge potential customer acceptance to warrant further product development (*see* NEW PRODUCT DEVELOPMENT).

A product concept is "a printed or filmed representation of a product or service. It is simply a device to communicate the subject's benefits, strengths and reasons for being" (Schwartz, 1987). The concept is a description of the product that also includes the benefits it offers.

Concept tests identify: whether or not there is sufficient consumer appeal to warrant further development; the appropriate TARGET MARKET; and ways to improve the concept. They also provide an estimate of the percentage of people who may try the new product (Moore and Pressemier, 1993). Concept testing can also be used to help assess ADVERTISING or POSITIONING approaches by identifying which benefits should be offered. Another aspect of concept testing is that of pilot testing the concept amongst those with specialist knowledge with the intention of avoiding problems at a later stage, and helping to refine the concept/product specification. This may involve securing the perspectives of different parties, for example, members of different organizational functions, external experts suppliers, key customers, and so on, in the product development process. The concept may be subject to simulation testing, in order to refine the concept further. Suppliers of components and subsystems may be engaged in the process and their specialist knowledge could save costs and time in subsequent development and production.

Tidd, Bessant, and Pavitt (1997) note that environmental concerns have led to the "greening" of existing product ranges and firms may explore alternative and complementary concepts that provide an environmentally friendly dimension.

A variety of techniques are available for concept testing, for example, qualitative discussions with potential customers to assess their reaction to possible new product ideas, postal questionnaire surveys, telephone interviews, FOCUS GROUPS, product mapping, and personal interviews (see SURVEY RESEARCH).

Monadic tests, where respondents evaluate one concept, have yielded successful applications. Others argue that competitive tests, which involve presenting the new concept alongside a rival concept, are more realistic. Whilst some concept tests may involve buyer evaluation of a concept in a written or simple visual format (Ozer, 2002), Cooper (1993) argues that the most reliable results arise from a full-proposition concept test, i.e., a test designed to convey to the final customer what the final product will be and

do, for example, in-home research where products are tested where they will be used (Wilson, 2003). Objectives for the concept test include: a measure of the customer's interest in the proposed product, a measure of the liking of the product, a comparative measure with competing products/brands currently in use, the way the product is used, and an indication of the intention to purchase.

"Working with lead users," who are often the major customers in a particular sector and regarded as the most demanding, Tidd et al. (1997) argue could lead to "stretching the concept to meet their needs" and so insure that the needs of most other potential users are taken into account during concept testing.

It is important to note that concept tests are likely to overstate the realized market acceptance, so that a result of "30 percent of respondents would definitely buy" is not likely to translate into a MARKET SHARE of 30 percent. The respondent may well continue to buy competing products, potential buyers may lack information on the product because they may not be reached by ADVERTISING and promotion, and people may tend to respond positively to concept tests where money and commitment are not involved. Typical problems with concept tests include asking the "wrong" respondents, promising more than the product will actually deliver, and issues surrounding "leaking" of information on new products. It is considered that concept testing is particularly difficult for radical innovations as consumers have nothing with which to compare the concept (Duke, 1994). The product ADOPTION PROCESS can be longer than could be predicted in a concept test; for example, automated bank teller machines took years to become fully accepted.

A single exposure may not be a good predictor of eventual reaction to a product. Concept tests can only estimate the number of people who will try the product. The concept can change between the test and the market introduction (see TEST MARKETING), consumer ATTITUDES can change, and other new products may be introduced between the test and the market introduction. All of this can affect the accuracy of the predictions from concept tests.

Bibliography

Cooper, R. G. (1993). *Winning at New Products: Accelerating the Process from Idea to Launch*, 2nd edn. Reading, MA: Addison-Wesley, ch. 6, pp. 153–61.

Duke, C. R. (1994). Understanding customer abilities in product concept tests. *Journal of Product and Brand Management*, 3 (1), 48–57.

Moore, W. L. and Pressemier, E. A. (1993). *Product Planning and Management: Designing and Delivering Value*. New York: McGraw-Hill, ch. 8, pp. 253–65.

Ozer, M. (2002). Concept testing of Internet services. *European Journal of Innovation Management*, 5 (4), 208–13.

Schwartz, D. (1987). *Concept Testing: How to Test New Product Ideas Before You Go to Market*. New York: American Management Association.

Tidd, J., Bessant, J., and Pavitt, K. (1997). *Managing Innovation: Integrating Technological, Market and Organizational Change*. Chicester: John Wiley.

Wilson, A. (2003). *Marketing Research: An Integrated Approach*. London: Financial Times/Prentice-Hall, p. 136.

conceptual equivalence

see CONSTRUCT EQUIVALENCE

confidence intervals

Michael Greatorex

Estimates of population parameters, for example, the population mean, based upon data from a sample are often required. When a probability sample (*see* SAMPLING) has been taken, relatively simple methods and formulae are available to provide best single point estimates. For instance, the best estimate of the population mean based upon data collected by a simple random sample is the sample mean.

However, by the very nature of sampling, a single point estimate is unlikely to give an exactly true estimate. Therefore, as well as providing single point estimates, interval estimates are also calculated. Confidence interval estimation is a way of computing two points between which the population parameter will lie with a given level of probability. Thus, in addition to reporting that the best point estimate of the population average is 200, it can more realistic-

ally be said that there is a 95 percent chance that the population mean lies in the range 190 to 210.

Confidence intervals, which are calculable for data from probability samples, depend upon the variability of the data in the sample, the size of the sample, the appropriate sampling distribution, and the specified level of probability. The greater the variability, the smaller the sample and the greater the specified level of probability, the larger will be the confidence interval. The relevant sampling distribution is often the t-distribution or the standard normal distribution.

conjoint analysis

Michael Greatorex and Mark P. Healey

Conjoint analysis is a set of techniques that allows the researcher to derive indirectly the relative importance respondents place on different attributes and the utilities assigned to different values of each attribute when selecting from among several brands (*see* BRAND). It assumes that products are evaluated by purchasers as attribute bundles (Green and Wind, 1975).

The several attributes (and the levels they can take) that are used to characterize a product are identified. Thus, the attributes for a car may be style, color, country of origin, running costs, price, performance, etc., and, as an example, the values that the attribute style may take could be saloon, hatchback, estate car, and so on. Rather than ask the respondent to evaluate the attributes and their values directly, respondents are offered hypothetical combinations of levels of the attributes and asked to evaluate the overall offerings. If the numbers of attributes and levels are small, all possible combinations can be offered to the respondent for evaluation. In more typical circumstances a reduced set of combinations, chosen in a manner similar to the way experiments (*see* EXPERIMENTATION) are designed, is offered so that sufficient information is efficiently collected. The implied utility attached to each possible level of an attribute is calculated by the computer and the relative importance of each attribute can be identified. Combinations not evaluated by respondents can then be analyzed, trade-offs involving different levels of different attributes can be evaluated, and the utilities of potential new brands can be compared to those of brands on the market. Simulations can be used to estimate MARKET SHARE. Specialized software for PCs is available to help the researcher conduct conjoint analysis.

Conjoint analysis can be employed for determining consumers' perceptions of attribute importance in choice processing; estimating market share of products differing in attribute levels; analyzing the composition of preferred brands; and segmentation (*see* MARKET SEGMENTATION) based on homogeneous preference segments.

Bibliography

Green, P. E. and Wind, Y. (1975). New way to measure consumers' judgments. *Harvard Business Review*, July/August, 107–17.

Tull, D. S. and Hawkins, D. I. (1993). *Marketing Research: Measurement and Method*, 6th edn. New York: Macmillan, pp. 405–19.

construct equivalence

Andrew Lindridge

Construct equivalence aims to identify whether the constructs being measured in a cross-cultural/societal study hold the same meaning and value in the different cultures/societies being researched (*see* CULTURE). The methodological requirement for construct equivalence arose from Campbell's (1964) observation that a major cross-cultural/societal methodological problem was falsely attributing behavioral differences to cultural/societal causes. The application of construct equivalence, as a methodological application, therefore attempts to control influencing variables (Malhotra, Agarwal, and Peterson, 1996), insuring that any significant differences between the cultures/societies being studied arise from cultural/societal differences and not extraneous variables.

The concept of construct equivalence has been criticized, however. Sechrest, Fay, and Zaidi (1972) describe the concept of equivalence as misleading, arguing that the pursuit of construct equivalence may partially or wholly destroy the very cultural/societal differences that are being measured. Green and White (1976),

while recognizing the desirability and need for equivalence in cross-cultural/societal research in marketing, believe, however, that MARKETING RESEARCH has not yet reached the stage where equivalencies can be imposed onto hypotheses, owing to insufficient knowledge about consumer behaviors in different cultures/societies. Whether marketing research into differing cultures and societies since Green and White's (1976) comment has reached a stage where hypotheses can be imposed is unclear. However, the researcher in conducting cross-cultural research should recognize the importance of construct equivalence in cross-cultural/societal methodology.

Construct equivalence consists of a number of subequivalencies that need to be addressed during the cross-cultural/research design stage, summarized in figure 1.

Functional equivalence. Functional equivalence suggests that behavior in two separate cultures/societies is related through a common functional problem, resulting in similar behavioral goals (Bhallah and Lin, 1987; Yu, Keown, and Jacobs, 1993). For example, children's birthdays are celebrated throughout the world. To achieve functional equivalence, the research tool must have the same meaning for respondents in all the cultures/societies being studied. Van Raaij (1978) suggests that functional equivalence can be achieved through pilot studies to identify similar cultural/societal behaviors and their antecedents. The subsequent identification of commonly shared behaviors should then be used to form the basis of the marketing research design.

Conceptual equivalence. Conceptual equivalence holds that certain beliefs or values may be culture/society specific and should not be used in cross-cultural/societal research (Yu et al., 1993). This implies that the meaning of research concepts, materials, and stimuli should be equivalent across cultures/societies (Malhotra et al., 1996). Conceptual equivalence can be achieved through using the derived etic solution (*see* ETIC-EMIC DILEMMA), through identifying universal values from interviews, a literature search, interviews with representatives of the research sample group, and screening the research tool with representatives from the cul-

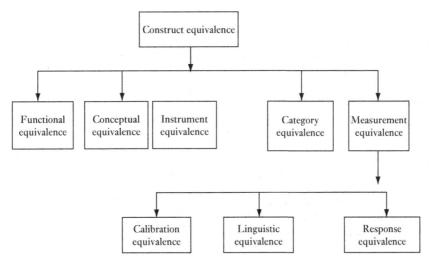

Figure 1   Construct equivalence

ture/society being measured (Triandis, Malpass, and Davidson, 1971, 1973).

Instrument equivalence.   Instrument equivalence insures that questionnaire stimuli (such as brands), response categories, and scale items are interpreted identically by different cultures/societies. This is particularly important in cross-cultural/societal studies where cultural differences may affect the RELIABILITY and the VALIDITY of the research data. For example, the use of a Likert scale (*see* RATING SCALES) in Far East Asian countries may be problematic, as research respondents may be unwilling to express an opinion categorized from "strongly agree" to "strongly disagree," instead choosing a middle score to avoid offending the researcher. Instrument equivalence would then be achieved through the use of a semantic differential scale, a scale suitable for a wide variety of cultures/societies.

Category equivalence.   Category equivalence requires sample groups to share similar socioeconomic backgrounds to minimize those variables that may adversely affect interpretation of the data analysis. For example, a female partner's influence in the CONSUMER DECISION-MAKING PROCESS may differ between Argentina and the US. Cross-cultural comparisons between two cultures/societies must recognize

and address these differences either through acknowledging that differences exist, or preferably through the research sample group satisfying a strict matched-sampling criterion (*see* MATCHED SAMPLING).

Measurement equivalence.   Measurement equivalence is based on the premise that the research tool should strive to measure underlying construct equivalencies. This is achieved through *calibration, linguistic,* and *response equivalence.*

- *Calibration equivalence* requires the research tool's measurement units to have the same value in the cultures/societies being investigated. For example, a car in Canada may be viewed as a necessity product but in China as a high-status luxury product. Cross-cultural/societal research regarding ATTITUDES and behaviors toward cars would not then be equivalent. Calibration equivalence, however, does not provide a resolution to this problem. The researcher must either decide to measure cross-cultural/societal attitudes and behaviors using a product that all cultures/societies can relate to in the same equal manner, or accept that calibration equivalence cannot be achieved. If calibration equivalence cannot be achieved, then the researcher should either not proceed with the research or recognize that this issue represents a severe limitation to his/her research.

- *Linguistic equivalence* argues that idiomatic issues, such as grammatical and syntax difficulties arising from translating a questionnaire into another language, are addressed. Linguistic equivalence is achieved using a back-translation method, where the original research tool is translated by an independent translator into the representative language of the country being studied. A second independent translator then translates the questionnaire back into the original language. The twice-translated questionnaire is then compared to the original questionnaire to identify idiomatic differences, such as grammatical and syntax difficulties. Where idiomatic differences exist, those questionnaire areas are rewritten to address these differences and resubmitted to the back-translation method. This process is continued repeatedly until there are no more idiomatic differences between the original questionnaire and the back-translated questionnaire.
- *Response equivalence* attempts to assess bias in respondents' answers. As individuals are not objective in their opinions there is a possibility that their responses may be (un)intentionally biased. For example, Bhallah and Lin (1987) indicated that British respondents' responses lay between understating and overstating their intentions. Asian respondents, however, may provide answers that they believe will please the researcher, i.e., hospitality bias (Douglas and Craig, 1983; Sekaran, 1983). Where bias may be evident in the data, the researcher can either attempt to weight the data accordingly or accept that the bias is a cultural response in itself, worthy of recognition within the research.

See also *Galton's problem*

Bibliography

Bhallah, G. and Lin, L. Y. S. (1987). Cross-cultural marketing research: A discussion of equivalence issues and measurement strategies. *Psychology and Marketing*, 4 (4), 275–85.

Campbell, D. (1964). Distinguishing differences of perceptions from failures of communication in cross-cultural studies. In *Epistemology in Anthropology*. New York: Harper and Row.

Douglas, S. P. and Craig, C. S. (1983). *International Marketing Research*. New York: Prentice-Hall.

Green, R. T. and White, P. D. (1976). Methodological considerations in cross-national consumer research. *Journal of International Business Studies*, 7 (3), 81–7.

Malhotra, N. K., Agarwal, J., and Peterson, M. (1996). Methodological issues in cross-cultural marketing research: A state of the art review. *International Marketing Review*, 13 (5), 7–43.

Sechrest, L., Fay, T. L., and Zaidi, S. M. H. (1972). Problems of translation in cross-cultural research. *Journal of Cross-Cultural Psychology*, 6 (March), 41–56.

Sekaran, U. (1983). Methodological and theoretical issues and advancements in cross-cultural research. *Journal of International Business*, 14 (Fall), 61–73.

Triandis, H. C., Malpass, R., and Davidson, A. (1971). Cross-cultural psychology. In B. Siegel (ed.), *Biennial Review of Anthropology*. Stanford, CA: Stanford University Press, pp. 1–84.

Triandis, H. C., Malpass, R., and Davidson, A. (1973). Psychology and culture. *Annual Review of Psychology*, 24, Palo Alto, CA: Annual Reviews, pp. 355–78.

Van Raaij, W. F. (1978). Cross-cultural research methodology as a case of construct validity. *Advances in Consumer Research*, 5, 693–701.

Yu, J. H., Keown, C. F., and Jacobs, L. W. (1993). Attitude scale methodology: Cross-cultural implications. *Journal of International Consumer Marketing*, 6 (2), 45–63.

consumer acculturation

Andrew Lindridge

Consumer acculturation is an aspect of the ACCULTURATION process. It describes an eclectic process of learning (*see* CONSUMER LEARNING) and demonstrating consumption behaviors, knowledge, and skills specific to a CULTURE, which occur at the group and individual levels (O'Guinn, Lee, and Faber, 1988; Penaloza, 1989; Jun, Ball, and Gentry, 1993). Penaloza (1989) argues that consumer acculturation is characterized by a number of stages encountered by ethnic minorities. Initially individuals, using consumption information they perceive as representative of their culture, may attempt to copy the consumption patterns of the host culture. However, the dominance of their native cultural values can cause dissonance in ethnic minorities' consumer behavior (*see* CONSUMER BUYER BEHAVIOR). To reduce this dissonance, individuals then resort to familiar products from their native country. Finally, after a period of time, the immigrants' consumer confidence and knowledge increase. This allows the individuals to adapt to their new consumer culture surroundings. Lindridge, Dhillon, and Shah (2002) argued that consumer acculturation can be identified with Berry's (1990, 1992, 1997) bidirectional acculturation categories (*see* ACCULTURATION MODELS). They concluded that SYMBOLIC CONSUMPTION was indicative of ethnic minorities publicly demonstrating both their chosen acculturation style to their own ethnic group and their relationship with the dominant culture.

Symbolic consumption being indicative of acculturation has also been noted to be situationally determined, with symbolic consumption among ethnic minorities often being determined by the dominant group with which the individual engages in differing situations. For example, Lindridge, Hogg, and Shah (2004) found that in Britain, South Asian women's choice of products was determined by their interactions with both British white and British South Asian society. Interactions with the former resulted in a desire to conform, and interactions with other South Asians resulted in a desire to demonstrate conformity, through consumption, to South Asian culture. This situationally determined consumer acculturation behavior was identified with the dialogical model of acculturation.

Bibliography

Berry, J. W. (1990). Psychology of acculturation. In J. Berman (ed.), Nebraska symposium on motivation, 1989: Cross-cultural perspectives. *Current Theory and Research in Motivation*, 37. Lincoln: University of Nebraska Press, pp. 201–34.

Berry, J. W. (1992). Acculturation and adaptation in a new society. *International Migration*, 30, 69–85.

Berry, J. W. (1997). Immigration, acculturation, and adaptation. *Applied Psychology: An International Review*, 46 (1), 5–34.

Jun, S., Ball, D. A., and Gentry, J. W. (1993). Modes of consumer acculturation. *Advances in Consumer Research*, 20, 76–82.

Lindridge, A. M., Dhillon, K., and Shah, M. (2002). The role of products in perpetuating cultural marginality:

The case of Punjabi Sikhs in Britain. Paper presented at the AMS Multicultural Marketing Conference, Valencia, Spain.

Lindridge, A. M., Hogg, M., and Shah, M. (2004). Imagined multiple worlds: How British South Asian women navigate the "border crossings" between household and societal contexts. Paper accepted for the *Journal of Consumption, Marketing and Culture*.

O'Guinn, T. C., Lee, W.-N., and Faber, R. J. (1988). Acculturation: The impact of divergent paths on buyer behavior. *Advances in Consumer Research*, 18, 579–83.

Penaloza, L. (1989). Immigrant consumer acculturation. *Advances in Consumer Research*, 16, 110–18.

consumer attitudes

see ATTITUDES

consumer buyer behavior

Margaret K. Hogg and Barbara R. Lewis

Consumer buyer behavior has developed, since the 1960s, as a separate discipline within MARKETING, for a number of reasons. The impact of the MARKETING CONCEPT throughout all industries, in both the public and private sectors, and on an international basis, has led to increasing consumer AWARENESS and sophistication. Consumers are better educated and informed and thus more discriminating in their selection of goods and services. Hence, it behoves manufacturers and distributors to research and understand their needs and preferences and to respond accordingly.

With the fast pace of product introductions, spurred by technological development, companies need to search for better information about what people are willing to buy. Product life cycles (*see* PRODUCT LIFE CYCLE) are shorter and so it is necessary to anticipate consumer LIFESTYLES and to develop products to satisfy future needs. The growth of MARKET SEGMENTATION as a MARKETING STRATEGY enables companies to better cater to the needs of specific homogeneous groups of consumers. Further, there is: increased interest in CONSUMER PROTECTION and the growth of private consumer groups; the setting of public policy to protect the interests and wellbeing of consumers (cf. the debates about genetically modified food-stuffs); increasing environmental concerns; and growing anxiety about consumer privacy with the growth of web-based marketing (*see* INTERNET MARKETING) and new opportunities to capture consumer information. Additionally, computer and statistical developments provide the tools and techniques to facilitate research into consumer behavior and develop customer databases (*see* DATABASE).

In consumer MARKETS, various market exchanges take place between companies and "consumers" who may be described as "consumers," "buyers," "customers," "purchasers," etc., as a function of their involvement in buying and consuming. This is better understood in terms of buying roles within a household or family. These roles are typically:

- *initiator*: someone who first suggests the idea of buying a particular good or service;
- *influencer(s)*: those who have implicit or explicit influence from within or outside the household;
- *decider(s)*: a person who decides on any component of a buying decision in relation to whether to buy, what to buy, where from, when, and how to pay;
- *purchaser*: the purchasing agent who goes into a shop; and
- *user(s)*: those who use or consume the product/service.

In addition, one can consider who pays for/funds the purchase, and the extent to which joint decision-making is evident, i.e., where two or more people fulfill buying role(s) (see, e.g., Davis and Rigaux, 1974; Davis, 1976; Filia-trault and Brent-Ritchie, 1980); this in turn may depend on stages in the CONSUMER DECISION-MAKING PROCESS.

Consumer buyer behavior is concerned with a series of processes in buying and consuming goods and services, which approximately cover pre-purchase, purchase, and post-purchase stages. One can also consider consumer shopping behavior, i.e., visiting the retail shopping environment, which is characterized by various personal and social motives (see Tauber, 1972). Personal motives include: role-playing, diversion, self-gratification, learning about new trends, physical activity, and sensory stimulation. Social motives include social experience outside the home, communication with others having a similar interest, peer group attraction, status and authority, and pleasure of bargaining.

Consumer buyer behavior is partly explained and understood in terms of economic theory (*see* BUYER BEHAVIOR THEORIES). However, it is also necessary to consider social and psychological explanations, together with other influences on consumers (see figure 1), to include marketing and other stimuli and buyer characteristics.

Marketing stimuli relate to the activities and inputs of manufacturers and distributors, in particular the components of their MARKETING MIX, namely, product, price, place, and promotion. Other stimuli include economic, political, and technological elements in the MARKETING ENVIRONMENT. These impact on buyers whose social and cultural background (*see* CULTURE AND SOCIAL IDENTITY), lifestyles, and group memberships influence their buying behavior.

In addition one needs to consider the makeup of consumer psychological characteristics (e.g.,

Consumer buyer behavior

Marketing Stimuli	Other Stimuli	Buyer's Characteristics	Buyer's Decision Process	Buyer's Decision
Product	Economic	Culture	Problem recognition	Product choice
Price	Technological	Social	Information search	Brand choice
Place	Political	Personal	Evaluation	Dealer choice
Promotion	Cultural	Psychological	Decisions	Purchase timing
			Post-purchase behavior	Purchase amount

Figure 1   Influences on consumers (Kotler, 1994: 174)

PERSONALITY, CONSUMER NEEDS AND MO-
TIVES, perception, and CONSUMER LEARN-
ING), together with an understanding of the
ways in which consumer ATTITUDES are
formed and developed (see COGNITIVE DIS-
SONANCE), and the ways in which consumers
perceive and handle risk in buying situations (see
PERCEIVED RISK).

In most buying situations, consumers progress through a decision-making process that
results in various buying decisions in relation
to PRODUCT and BRAND choice, store/dealer
choice, purchase time, methods of payment, and
so on. Buying decisions of special interest to
researchers and practitioners include those that
involve a time dimension, e.g. BRAND LOY-
ALTY and the ADOPTION PROCESS for product innovations (see PRODUCT INNOVATION).

However, there is increasing discussion about
how far consumers necessarily follow the "rational man" approach as embodied in many of
the complex models of consumer behavior. Debates in the *Journal of Consumer Research* and in
Advances in Consumer Research (available online
via www.acrweb.org) have centered around
ontological and epistemological issues that can
be divided *very roughly* into positivist and non-
positivist approaches to understanding consumer behavior, although both these approaches
encompass a variety of different philosophical
positions in terms of formulating and researching issues, and generating theory. Three perspectives have been identified in researching
consumer behavior: decision-making perspective; experiential perspective; and the behavioral
influence perspective (Mowen and Minor, 1998:
11). Recent studies have highlighted the importance of experiential and hedonic aspects of consumption which are not necessarily captured by
traditional models of consumer buyer behavior.
An analysis of "the intellectual structure of the
field of consumer research" (Hoffman and Holbrook, 1993) captured some, but not all, of the
variety of approaches and methods employed for
exploring consumer behavior research, many of
which only started to appear in the *Journal of
Consumer Research* in the 1990s, for example,
Thompson's key papers on phenomenology,
and implications for methods of data collection
and analysis; Linda Scott's work on advertisements; Mick's work on semiotics, and the semi-

otic interpretation of advertisements (Mick and
Buhl, 1992); McQuarrie and Mick's (1992, 1996)
studies on rhetoric in ADVERTISING, and their
1999 paper which combined three different
methods with different philosophical underpinnings.

Examining the presidential addresses in *Advances in Consumer Research* also shows the key
emergent issues in researching consumer behavior since 1990, for example, Hirschman (1991)
called for more attention to contemporary problems such as crime, prostitution, and addiction;
and Andreasen (1993) at the first European Association of Consumer Research conference in
Amsterdam called attention to public policy
issues and SOCIAL MARKETING. In addition,
successive postmodern issues have also been
raised about the interrelationship between consumer behavior and marketing (Brown, 1995).

Bibliography

Andreasen, A. R. (1993). The future of the Association for
Consumer Research: Backward to the past. In G.
Bamossy and W. F. van Raaij (eds.), *European Advances
in Consumer Research*, 1, 1–4.

Arnould, E. J. and Price, L. L. (1993). River magic: Extraordinary experience and the extended service encounter. *Journal of Consumer Research*, 20 (June), 24–45.

Arnould, E., Price, L., and Zinkhan, G. (2004). *Consumers*, 2nd edn. Boston: McGraw-Hill Irwin, chs. 1–3.

Belk, R. W., Sherry, J. F., and Wallendorf, M. (1988).
A naturalistic inquiry into buyer and seller behavior at a
swap meet. *Journal of Consumer Research*, 14 (March),
449–70.

Belk, R. W., Wallendorf, M., and Sherry, J. F. (1989).
The sacred and the profane in consumer behavior:
Theodicy on the odyssey. *Journal of Consumer Research*,
16 (June), 1–38.

Brown, S. (1995). *Postmodern Marketing*. London: Routledge, ch. 5.

Brown, S. (1998). *Postmodern Marketing 2: Telling Tales.*
London: International Thomson Business Press.

Catterall, M., Maclaran, P., and Stevens, L. (eds.) (2000).
Marketing and Feminism: Current Issues and Research.
London: Routledge.

Davis, H. L. (1976). Decision-making within the household. *Journal of Consumer Research*, 2 (March), 241–60.

Davis, H. L. and Rigaux, B. P. (1974). Perceptions of
marital roles in decision process. *Journal of Consumer
Research*, 1, 51–62.

Engel, J. F., Blackwell, R. D., and Miniard, P. W. (1995).
Consumer Behavior, 8th edn. Fort Worth, TX: Dryden
Press, chs. 4, 21, 23.

Filiatrault, P. and Brent-Ritchie, J. R. (1980). Joint purchase decisions: A comparison of influence structure in family and couple decision-making units. *Journal of Consumer Research*, 6 (September), 131–40.

Frank, R. E. (1974). The *Journal of Consumer Research*: An introduction. *Journal of Consumer Research*, 1 (June), i–ii.

Hirschman, E. C. (1991). Secular mortality and the dark side of consumer behavior: Or how semiotics saved my life. *Advances in Consumer Research*, 18, 1–4; www.acrweb.org.

Hoffman, D. L. and Holbrook, M. B. (1993). The intellectual structure of consumer research: A bibliometric study of author co-citations in the first 15 years of the *Journal of Consumer Research*. *Journal of Consumer Research*, 19 (March), 505–17.

Hogg, M. K., Bettany, S., and Long, G. (2000). Shifting the discourse: Feminist perspectives on consumer behavior research. In M. Catterall, P. Maclaran, and L. Stevens (eds.), *Marketing and Feminism: Current Issues and Research*. London: Routledge, pp. 112–28.

Holbrook, M. B. and Hirschman, E. C. (1982). The experiential aspects of consumption: Consumer fantasies, feelings and fun. *Journal of Consumer Research*, 9 (September), 132–40.

Hoyer, W. D. and MacInnis, D. J. (2001). *Consumer Behavior*, 2nd edn. Boston and New York: Houghton Mifflin, chs. 1, 18.

Katona, G. (1960). *The Powerful Consumer*. New York: McGraw-Hill.

Kotler, P. (1994). *Marketing Management: Analysis, Planning, Implementation and Control*, 8th edn. London: Prentice-Hall, p. 174.

Loudon, D. L. and Della Bitta, A. J. (1993). *Consumer Behavior*, 4th edn. New York: McGraw-Hill, chs. 17, 19.

McQuarrie, E. F. and Mick, D. G. (1992). On resonance: A critical pluralistic inquiry into advertising rhetoric. *Journal of Consumer Research*, 17, 180–97.

McQuarrie, E. F. and Mick, D. G. (1996). Figures of rhetoric in advertising language. *Journal of Consumer Research*, 22, (4), 424–39.

McQuarrie, E. F. and Mick, D. G. (1999). Visual rhetoric in advertising: Text-interpretive, experimental, and reader-response analyses. *Journal of Consumer Research*, 26, 1 (June), 37–65.

Mick, D. G. and Buhl, C. (1992). A meaning-based model of advertising experiences. *Journal of Consumer Research*, 19 (December), 317–38.

Mowen, J. C. and Minor, M. (1998). *Consumer Behavior*, 5th edn. Upper Saddle River, NJ: Prentice-Hall, chs. 1, 2, 16.

Mowen, J. C. and Minor, M. (2001). *Consumer Behavior: A Framework*. Upper Saddle River, NJ: Prentice-Hall, chs. 1, 2, 9.

Schiffman, L. G. and Kanuk, L. G. (2004). *Consumer Behavior*, 8th edn. Upper Saddle River, NJ: Prentice-Hall.

Schouten, J. W. and McAlexander, J. H. (1995). Subcultures of consumption: An ethnography of the new bikers. *Journal of Consumer Research*, 22 (June), 43–61.

Scott, L. M. (1994a). Images in advertising: The need for a theory of visual rhetoric. *Journal of Consumer Research*, 21, 2 (September), 252–74.

Scott, L. M. (1994b). The bridge from text to mind: Adapting reader-response theory to consumer research. *Journal of Consumer Research*, 21 (December), 461–80.

Simonson, I., Carmon, Z., Dhar, R., Drolet, A., and Nowlis, S. M. (2001). Consumer research: In search of identity. *Annual Review of Psychology*, 52, 249–75.

Stern, B. (ed.) (1998). *Representing Consumers: Voices, Views and Visions*. London: Routledge.

Solomon, M. R. (2002). *Consumer Behavior: Buying, Having, Being*, 5th edn. Upper Saddle River, NJ: Prentice-Hall, chs. 1, 12, 16.

Solomon, M. R., Bamossy, G., and Askegaard, S. (2002). *Consumer Behavior: A European Perspective*, 2nd edn. Upper Saddle River, NJ: Prentice-Hall, chs. 1, 11, 14, 17.

Tauber, E. M. (1972). Why do people shop? *Journal of Marketing*, 36 (October), 46–9.

Thompson, C. J., Locander, W. B., and Pollio, H. R. (1989). Putting consumer experience back into consumer research: The philosophy and method of existential phenomenology. *Journal of Consumer Research*, 16 (September), 133–46.

Thompson, C. J., Locander, W. B., and Pollio, H. R. (1990). The lived meaning of free choice: An existential-phenomenological description of everyday consumer experiences of contemporary married women. *Journal of Consumer Research*, 17 (December), 346–61.

Wells, W. D. and Prensky, D. (1996). *Consumer Behavior*. New York: John Wiley, chs. 2, 7.

consumer decision-making process

Margaret K. Hogg, Barbara R. Lewis,
and Mark P. Healey

The consumer decision-making process is concerned with buying operations and the stages in which a buyer (individual or household) may be involved when making purchases. These stages are usually referred to in complex models of CONSUMER BUYER BEHAVIOR (e.g., Engel, Blackwell, and Miniard, 1995) as problem recognition, information search, information evaluation, purchase decisions, and post-purchase evaluation.

PROBLEM RECOGNITION

Problem recognition occurs when a consumer recognizes a buying problem or goal, an unsatisfied or unfilled need. Sources of problems are various and include: assortment deficiency (e.g., the coffee jar is empty); exposure to new information; expanded desires for more or better products and services; expanded means (e.g., more resources available, such as finance, time, or opportunity); and changing expectations and needs (see CONSUMER NEEDS AND MOTIVES). Buying needs may relate to products, brands, stores, services, and so on, and a variety of needs will prevail at any one time which have to be prioritized (for an individual or household) as a function of time, money, urgency, role involvement, etc. A readiness to buy thus emerges.

INFORMATION SEARCH

Information search is the stage at which consumers attempt to match needs with market offerings to identify purchase alternatives and find out more about them. Information may come from: personal sources, such as friends, family, neighbors; commercial sources, e.g., ADVERTISING and promotion, displays, and salespeople; public sources, e.g., MASS MEDIA and consumer organizations; and from experience/use.

The amount of information sought will be a function of both PRODUCT and individual factors. Product factors include frequency of purchase, price, social conspicuousness, essentiality of the product, and intensity of need. Individual factors, or search styles, include values and aspirations, degree of INVOLVEMENT with the purchase, risk perceptions and risk-handling styles (see PERCEIVED RISK), availability of information without search, previous experience and knowledge of the product, time available, perceptions of the costs and value of information search, and satisfaction to be gained from searching.

INFORMATION EVALUATION

When considering consumers' evaluation of information with respect to product and BRAND alternatives, formal or informal organization of information may occur (see Bettman, 1979).

Formal organization might include detailed financial analysis, for example with respect to house or car purchase. Further, alternatives are evaluated with respect to various decision criteria. These are related to: costs, e.g., price, operating costs, repairs, servicing, extras; performance, e.g., durability, economy, efficiency, dependability; suitability, of brand, style, store image, appearance, etc.; and convenience, e.g., of store location, atmosphere, service.

Alternatives that are evaluated will be part of an AWARENESS set as the consumer does not necessarily have information with respect to all the alternatives available. Those which meet initial buying criteria fall into a consideration set, which leads to a choice set.

PURCHASE DECISIONS

At this point one can refer to consumer purchase intentions, i.e., those products/brands or other aspects of buying and consuming that a consumer (or household) is intending to carry out in the form of purchase decisions. However, one has to be aware that intervening variables may come into play between purchase intention and purchase decision. These include ATTITUDES of other consumers, availability, and unexpected situational factors (e.g., with respect to income and employment), and may delay purchase decisions or cause them not to take place at all. For example, plans for a holiday may be canceled owing to unforeseen financial circumstances or ill health, or an intention to purchase a satellite television may be postponed because a washing machine suddenly breaks down and has to be replaced.

Purchase decisions are made with respect to products and services, stores, and methods of payment. Product decisions include choice of brands (including distributors' versus manufacturers' brands), reaction to price deals, and impulse purchase decisions (see IMPULSE PURCHASING). Decisions also relate to choice of store (to include location, personnel, atmosphere, car parking, services, credit availability), home shopping, MAIL ORDER, and frequency of shopping.

POST-PURCHASE EVALUATION

After purchasing, consumers experience some levels of satisfaction or dissatisfaction with each of their decisions (*see* CUSTOMER SATISFAC-TION). With respect to product/brand choice, if perceived product performance meets consumer expectations then the customer is satisfied; if performance does not meet expectations (i.e., disconfirmed expectations), then dissatisfaction occurs. Dissatisfaction leads to one of several post-purchase activities, including returning the product, seeking information to confirm the choice made (*see* COGNITIVE DISSONANCE), or complaining (see Gilly and Hansen, 1985).

Further, results of purchasing activities can be evaluated either informally, among family and friends, or more formally, e.g., with respect to car performance and costs, by comparison with others. Post-purchase evaluations provide the consumer with an idea of how well he/she is doing in the market and add to his/her state of experience, knowledge, and information to be used in future purchasing decisions.

When considering models of the consumer decision-making process, it is important to note that not all the stages may be relevant, timing between stages varies, and feedback loops exist. Further, the extent to which a formal process does happen will depend on the extent of consumer involvement. One can consider a continuum of low–high involvement consumer decision-making. Products that are expensive, risky, reflect self-image, or have positive reference group influence (*see* INTERPERSONAL COMMUNICATIONS) may be referred to as high-involvement situations and subject to extensive problem solving, i.e., active information search and evaluation. At the other end of the continuum are routine, low-involvement (often repurchase) situations with no motivated search for information (the costs are likely to outweigh the benefits), and the consumer proceeds on the basis of what he/she already knows. This is further developed by Assael (1987), who identified four types of consumer buying behavior based on the degree of buyer involvement and the degree of difference among brands:

- complex buying behavior, when consumers are highly involved and there are significant differences between brands (e.g., personal computers);
- dissonance-reducing buying behavior, when consumers are highly involved in a purchase but see little difference between brands (e.g., carpets);
- habitual buying behavior, characterized by low consumer involvement and little difference between brands (e.g., petrol and commodities); and
- variety-seeking buying behavior, with low involvement but significant differences between brands (e.g., biscuits, soap powders).

However, there is decreasing reliance on complex models of consumer decision-making, firstly because of the growing realization that buyer behavior is too complex to be captured in a single model, since it represents most of the elements of human psychology, and secondly, because of the difficulty inherent in empirically testing the generic models (Simonson et al., 2001). Subsequent models of buyer behavior that have received widespread attention include Bettman's (1979) information-processing model of consumer choice and Foxall's (1990, 1999) BEHAVIORAL PERSPECTIVE model.

The advent and rising popularity of information processing and cognitive research on consumer decision-making and buying behavior have led to an increasing appreciation of models that eschew theories of rational choice in favor of models that proffer bounded rationality (the theory that decision-making may be "imperfect" due to cognitive limitations) as a more realistic perspective on how consumers actually make purchase decisions. Bettman, Luce, and Payne (1998) suggest that consumer decision-making is constructive in nature: consumers have limited processing capacity (e.g., for memory and computation), may not have well-established preferences for all stimuli, and when required to make a choice or purchase decision for a product/service may compute preferences ad hoc. Their model thus appreciates that consumer preferences may be context dependent, not derived from a predefined set of values, and looks to intrapersonal cognitive phenomena such as memory and choice goals to model, explain, and predict buyer behavior.

Foxall's (1990, 1999) behavioral perspective model (BPM) of consumer choice proposes that the determinants of buyer behavior and consumer decision-making should be sought in the consumption environment, rather than by explanations which refer to intrapersonal information processing. Specifically, the BPM suggests that certain dimensions of buyer behavior and decisions can be predicted based on the contextual consumption setting and customers' reinforcement history in similar settings.

Bibliography

Arnould, E., Price, L., and Zinkhan, G. (2004). *Consumers*, 2nd edn. Boston: McGraw-Hill Irwin, chs. 5, 15, 16.

Assael, H. (1987). *Consumer Behavior and Marketing Action*. Boston: Kent.

Bettman, J. R. (1979). *Information Processing Theory of Consumer Behavior*. Reading, MA: Addison-Wesley.

Bettman, J. R., Luce, M. F., and Payne, J. W. (1998). Constructive consumer choice processes. *Journal of Consumer Research*, **25** (3), 187–217.

Engel, J. F., Blackwell, R. D., and Miniard, P. W. (1995). *Consumer Behavior*, 8th edn. Fort Worth, TX: Dryden Press, chs. 4, 5, 6, 7, 8.

Foxall, G. R. (1990). *Consumer Psychology in Behavioral Perspective*. New York: Routledge.

Foxall, G. R. (1999). The behavioral perspective model: Consensibility and consensuality. *European Journal of Marketing*, **33** (5/6), 570–96.

Gilly, M. C. and Hansen, R. W. (1985). Consumer complaint handling as a strategic marketing tool. *Journal of Consumer Marketing*, Fall, 5–16.

Hawkins, D. I., Best, R. J., and Coney, K. A. (1995). *Consumer Behavior: Implications for Marketing Strategy*, 6th edn. Boston: Irwin.

Hoyer, W. D. and MacInnis, D. J. (2001). *Consumer Behavior*, 2nd edn. Boston and New York: Houghton Mifflin, part 3.

Kotler, P. (2003). *Marketing Management: Analysis, Planning, Implementation and Control*, 11th edn. Englewood Cliffs, NJ: Prentice-Hall.

Loudon, D. L. and Della Bitta, A. J. (1993). *Consumer Behavior*, 4th edn. New York: McGraw-Hill, chs. 15, 16, 17, 18.

Mowen, J. C. and Minor, M. (1998). *Consumer Behavior*, 5th edn. Upper Saddle River, NJ: Prentice-Hall, chs. 1, 11, 12, 13.

Mowen, J. C. and Minor, M. (2001). *Consumer Behavior: A Framework*. Upper Saddle River, NJ: Prentice-Hall, chs. 1, 7, 9.

Schiffman, L. G. and Kanuk, L. Z. (2004). *Consumer Behavior*, 8th edn. Upper Saddle River, NJ: Prentice-Hall, ch. 16.

Simonson, I., Carmon, Z., Dhar, R., Drolet, A., and Nowlis, S. M. (2001). Consumer research: In search of identity. *Annual Review of Psychology*, **52**, 249–75.

Solomon, M. R. (2002). *Consumer Behavior: Buying, Having, Being*, 5th edn. Upper Saddle River, NJ: Prentice-Hall, chs. 9, 10, 12.

Solomon, M. R., Bamossy, G., and Askegaard, S. (2002). *Consumer Behavior: A European Perspective*, 2nd edn. Upper Saddle River, NJ: Prentice-Hall, chs. 8, 9, 10, 11.

Wells, W. D. and Prensky, D. (1996). *Consumer Behavior*. New York: John Wiley, chs. 12, 14.

Wilkie, W. L. (1994). *Consumer Behavior*, 3rd edn. New York: John Wiley, chs. 17, 18, 19.

consumer knowledge structures

Mark P. Healey

One of the principal aims of basic or theoretical MARKETING RESEARCH is to understand how consumers think about and react to marketplace stimuli. Consequently, exploring the way in which information about these is represented in memory and cognition has become a major research objective. A knowledge structure is an abstract mental representation of known information about an object or group of objects such as a BRAND, a PRODUCT category, or a set of consumption experiences. A knowledge structure organizes information in memory and is activated when a relevant object is encountered, whereupon it influences cognitive processes such as perception, memory encoding, and the interpretation and judgment of new information. Knowledge structures are developed through direct and indirect experience and have specific organizational properties. For example, a knowledge structure developed through repeated consumption of soft drinks enables a customer to infer that these are typically carbonated, slightly sweet, and high in preservatives. Knowledge structures serve to organize in memory consumers' product and consumption-related knowledge, enabling them to make sense of the consumption environment and to process information effectively.

Two generic characteristics of knowledge structures can be distinguished: cognitive structure and content. Cognitive structure refers to the organizational properties of representations – how information is arranged, linked together, and specified by the configuration of the structure – and how this influences processes such as memory and judgment. Cognitive content refers to the nature of the information contained within a structure, whether this is verbal or visual, for example. Expert consumers are thought to possess product knowledge structures which differ from those of novices in complexity of both structure and content (Mitchell and Dacin, 1996).

Knowledge structures have proved particularly useful concepts for understanding various aspects of consumer psychology, including categorization, evaluation, judgment, goal formation, and memory. The way that new information is processed, what is perceived and stored, and how it is dealt with by consumers, depends on their existing knowledge structures, as does the way in which the past is remembered. The knowledge structures of managers, marketers, and contact employees have also been studied to elucidate the cognitive underpinnings of their behaviors and skills. The performance of effective salespersons has been linked to the complexity and abstractness of their knowledge structures, for example (see Leong, Busch, and Roeder, 1989; Sharma, Levy, and Kumar, 2000).

Market-related knowledge is represented in different types of structure, including categories and stereotypes, which hold different kinds of information, such as exemplar or prototype data (see Carlston and Smith, 1996). The nature of different knowledge structures varies according to their function and the type of knowledge stored within. Many of those studied in marketing have their conceptual origins in associative network and schema theories popularized in cognitive and social psychology in the 1970s and 1980s.

In associative network models, information is stored in nodes connected by links between related knowledge. Associative networks predict that, through a process of spreading activation, thinking of one concept in a networked structure will increase the likelihood that others related within the structure will also be activated. For example, thinking about hamburgers may bring to mind associations with the brands McDonald's or Burger King, depending on the nature of one's knowledge structures.

A schema is an organized representation of knowledge abstracted from experience, which specifies default values for product attributes; that calculators are rectangular, for example. Built up from repeated experience with a brand or product, schemata enable customers to make inferences about typical properties and attributes, knowledge that is often applied to encounters with both familiar and new products (see Gregan-Paxton, 2001). Schematic knowledge structures are frequently invoked to explain features of consumers' memory and evaluations (cf. Alba and Hasher, 1983). A new product may be evaluated based on an existing product schema, for example (see Meyers-Levy and Tybout, 1989).

A related type of knowledge structure is the cognitive script. Scripts contain knowledge pertaining to familiar consumption events and experiences, such as eating in restaurants or visiting the theater, and are structured hierarchically around the goals of an activity. Scripts specify the typical attributes of experiences, such as the behavior of airline employees, or the usual wait required at one's bank branch, and can thus be evoked to generate expectancies (*see* CUSTOMER EXPECTATIONS) and guide behavior in familiar contexts, and can influence memory for past experiences (Smith and Houston, 1985; Hubbert, Sehorn, and Brown, 1995). Young people develop shopping scripts, which enable them to operate effectively as consumers, by amalgamating the key events of individual experiences to form abstract cognitive structures containing central actions and behavioral contingencies. The notion of script has been particularly relevant to services research (see Solomon et al., 1985).

Marketing research has sporadically investigated the nature and influences of other types of consumer knowledge structures (see Lawson, 2002), including how price knowledge may be constructed from underlying frame structures (Lawson and Bhagat, 2002), the representation of product knowledge in category structures, the operation of category-based product evaluations (Sujan, 1985), and the role of associative networks in brand perception, preference, and choice (Henderson, Iacobucci, and Calder, 1998). Recent writings have taken a wider perspective on consumers' mental representations based on contemporary psychophysiological research. For example, Zaltman's (1997) work emphasizes the centrality of visual imagery, feelings, and non-conscious thoughts to the mental models consumers apply to understanding brands and advertisements.

Bibliography

Alba, J. W. and Hasher, L. (1983). Is memory schematic? *Psychological Bulletin*, 93 (2), 203–31.

Brown, T. J. (1992). Schemata in consumer research: A connectionist approach. In J. F. Sherry (ed.), *Advances in Consumer Research*, vol. 19. Ann Arbor, MI: Association for Consumer Research, pp. 787–94.

Carlston, D. E. and Smith, E. R. (1996). Principles of mental representation. In E. T. Higgins and A. W. Kruglanski (eds.), *Social Psychology: Handbook of Basic Principles*. New York: Guilford Press, pp. 184–210.

Fisk, R. P., Grove, S. J., and John, J. (2000). *Interactive Services Marketing*. Boston: Houghton Mifflin, chs. 5, 9.

Gregan-Paxton, J. (2001). The role of abstract and specific knowledge in the formation of product judgments: An analogical learning perspective. *Journal of Consumer Psychology*, 11 (3), 141–59.

Henderson, G. R., Iacobucci, D., and Calder, B. J. (1998). Brand diagnostics: Mapping branding effects using consumer associative networks. *European Journal of Operational Research*, 111, 2 (December 1), 306–27.

Hubbert, A. R., Sehorn, A. G., and Brown, S. W. (1995). Service expectations: The consumer versus the provider. *International Journal of Service Industry Management*, 6 (1), 6–21.

Lawson, R. (2002). Consumer knowledge structures: Background issues and introduction. *Psychology and Marketing*, 19, 6 (May), 447–55.

Lawson, R. and Bhagat, P. S. (2002). The role of price knowledge in consumer product knowledge structures. *Psychology and Marketing*, 19 (6), 551–68.

Leong, S. M. L., Busch, P. S., and Roeder, J. (1989). Knowledge bases and salesperson effectiveness: A script theoretic approach. *Journal of Marketing Research*, 26 (2), 164–79.

Meyers-Levy, J. and Tybout, A. M. (1989). Schema congruity as a basis for product evaluation. *Journal of Consumer Research*, 16, 39–54.

Mitchell, A. A. and Dacin, P. A. (1996). The assessment of alternative measures of consumer expertise. *Journal of Consumer Research*, 23, 219–39.

Sharma, A., Levy, M., and Kumar, A. (2000). Knowledge structures and retail sales performance: An empirical examination. *Journal of Retailing*, 76 (1), 53–69.

Smith, R. A. and Houston, M. J. (1985). A psychometric assessment of measures of scripts in consumer memory. *Journal of Consumer Research*, 12, 214–24.

Solomon, M. R., Surprenant, C., Czepiel, J. A., and Gutman, E. G. (1985). A role theory perspective on dyadic interactions: The service encounter. *Journal of Marketing*, 49, 99–111.

Sujan, M. (1985). Consumer knowledge: Effects of evaluation strategies mediating consumer judgments. *Journal of Consumer Research*, 12, 31–46.

Tansik, D. A. and Smith, W. L. (1991). Dimensions of job scripting in services organizations. *International Journal of Service Industry Management*, 2 (1), 35–49.

Zaltman, G. (1997). Rethinking marketing research: Putting people back in. *Journal of Marketing Research*, 34 (November), 424–37.

consumer learning

Margaret K. Hogg and Barbara R. Lewis

Most behavior of consumers is learned from experience and consumer learning may be defined as a trend, change, or modification of CONSUMER PERCEPTIONS, ATTITUDES, and behavior resulting from previous experience and behavior in similar situations. Learning is to do with acquiring information, and there are two major theories concerning learning and CONSUMER BUYER BEHAVIOR which are, together, relevant: behavioral and cognitive theories of learning.

Behavioral learning includes classical conditioning, operant conditioning, and observational learning. Classical conditioning includes stimulus-response theories which postulate that learning is the development of behavior (response) as a result of exposure to a set of stimuli, and that consumer behavior is conditioned by association (e.g., music can be played in retail outlets or restaurants either to speed up or slow down consumers' behavior). The suggestion is that consumers respond to marketing cues or stimuli as a function of the drives/needs that determine when, where, and how they respond. In another example a beer advertisement may stimulate a thirst drive, but response also depends on other cues, such as time of day and availability of beer and other thirst quenchers. Satisfaction leads to reinforcement and a tendency for repetition when the same drives and cues reappear. Operant conditioning is "a process in which the frequency of occurrence of a behavior is modified by the consequences of that behavior" (Mowen and Minor, 1998: 139). In the context of consumer behavior this could involve the likelihood of repurchase, if a product performs well. Observational learning or social learning is when people "develop 'patterns of behavior' by observing the actions of others" (Mowen and Minor, 1998: 147) and is very important in the consumer socialization of children (e.g., they learn to shop alongside their parents).

On the other hand, cognitive theories (e.g., insight learning, latent learning) view learning as a process of restructuring individual cognitions with respect to specific problems. The suggestion here is that individuals acquire habits not only from stimulus-response repetition but also by using their insight, thinking, and problem-solving techniques, i.e., using intellectual activities. Problem solving becomes the focus of consumer behavior, and to solve problems consumers need information about products and services, acquisition of which may be planned or incidental. Given the range of information available, consumers are receptive to and retain some information (*see* CONSUMER PERCEPTIONS), which in turn leads to knowledge about products/brands that may or may not lead to purchase or repurchase. Information will include that which is stored from previous experience to help form, change, or reinforce attitudes toward products/brands, which might encourage reinforcement of prevailing attitudes and stimulate repurchase, or lead to product/brand rejection.

Bibliography

Arnould, E., Price, L., and Zinkhan, G. (2004). *Consumers*, 2nd edn. Boston: McGraw-Hill Irwin, ch. 9.

Engel, J. F., Blackwell, R. D., and Miniard, P. W. (1995). *Consumer Behavior*, 8th edn. Fort Worth, TX: Dryden Press, ch. 15.

Foxall, G. R., Goldsmith, R. E., and Brown, S. (1998). *Consumer Psychology for Marketing*, 2nd edn. London: International Thomson Business Press, ch. 4.

Hawkins, D. I., Best, R. J., and Coney, K. A. (1995). *Consumer Behavior: Implications for Marketing Strategy*, 6th edn. Boston: Irwin.

Hoyer, W. D. and MacInnis, D. J. (2001). *Consumer Behavior*, 2nd edn. Boston and New York: Houghton Mifflin, chs. 7, 8.

Loudon, D. L. and Della Bitta, A. J. (1993). *Consumer Behavior*, 4th edn. New York: McGraw-Hill, ch. 12.

Mowen, J. C. and Minor, M. (1998). *Consumer Behavior*, 5th edn. Upper Saddle River, NJ: Prentice-Hall, chs. 4, 5.

Mowen, J. C. and Minor, M. (2001). *Consumer Behavior: A Framework*. Upper Saddle River, NJ: Prentice-Hall, chs. 3, 4.

Schiffman, L. G. and Kanuk, L. Z. (2004). *Consumer Behavior*, 8th edn. Upper Saddle River, NJ: Prentice-Hall, ch. 7.

Solomon, M. R. (2002). *Consumer Behavior: Buying, Having, Being*, 5th edn. Upper Saddle River, NJ: Prentice-Hall, ch. 3.

Solomon, M. R., Bamossy, G., and Askegaard, S. (2002). *Consumer Behavior: A European Perspective*, 2nd edn. Upper Saddle River, NJ: Prentice-Hall, ch. 3.

Wells, W. D. and Prensky, D. (1996). *Consumer Behavior*. New York: John Wiley, ch. 10.

Wilkie, W. L. (1994). *Consumer Behavior*, 3rd edn. New York: John Wiley, ch. 10.

consumer marketing

Fiona Leverick

Consumer marketing refers to the buying of products and services for personal or household use, as opposed to buying by organizations. The implied alternative is BUSINESS-TO-BUSINESS MARKETING, although the distinction between the two areas is not entirely clear cut. The techniques of consumer marketing management dominate most standard marketing textbooks, with the result that specialized textbooks tend not to be exclusively devoted to consumer marketing in the same way as for business-to-business marketing. Indeed, the view of MARKETING MANAGEMENT presented in standard texts such as Kotler (1994) or McCarthy and Perreault (1993) is often essentially synonymous with consumer, as opposed to business-to-business, marketing management. More recently, however, consumer marketing, especially for services, has developed somewhat in nature and scope to include, in particular, some of the techniques more traditionally found in business-to-business marketing, for example RELATIONSHIP MARKETING (*see* SERVICES MARKETING).

Consumer purchase decision-making is also generally held to be subject to the influence of "non-task" or "irrational" factors to a far greater extent than business-to-business marketing.

CONSUMER BUYER BEHAVIOR is a major area for research in marketing (*see* MARKETING RESEARCH) and has involved the investigation of such areas as: individual decision-making influences (such as PERSONALITY, CONSUMER PERCEPTIONS, and ATTITUDES); group decision-making influences (such as opinion leadership, reference groups, or lifestyle influences; *see* INTERPERSONAL COMMUNICATIONS; LIFESTYLES); and cultural influences on consumer behavior.

Bibliography

Kotler, P. (2003). *Marketing Management: Analysis, Planning, Implementation and Control*, 11th edn. Englewood Cliffs, NJ: Prentice-Hall.
McCarthy, E. J. and Perreault, R. (1993). *Basic Marketing*, 11th edn. Homewood, IL: Irwin.

consumer motivation

see CONSUMER NEEDS AND MOTIVES

consumer needs

see CONSUMER NEEDS AND MOTIVES

consumer needs and motives

Margaret K. Hogg and Barbara R. Lewis

It may be argued that MARKETING rests on the premise that consumer needs are the starting point from which business activity should be planned. Consumer needs are biological, relating to primary or physiological elements; or psychological, i.e., emotional. Primary needs are often modified by psychological needs, and are subject to social and other influences. Consumers have a sophisticated structure of needs relating to social, cultural, emotional, and intellectual interests, all affecting CONSUMER BUYER BEHAVIOR.

Maslow (1970) offered a hierarchy of needs from the level of physiological needs, i.e., primary needs for food and shelter, to: safety needs, e.g., for security, protection, education and training, assurance and insurance; belongingness and love needs, e.g., for affection, affiliation, sense of being part of a group; esteem needs, e.g., the desire for prestige, reputation, attention, recognition and appreciation, confidence, achievement and success; and the need for self-actualization, e.g., personal influence. The hierarchy suggests fulfillment at one level before progressing to the next; however, in reality, consumers may well be influenced by higher-level needs when lower needs have not been satisfied. Although a number of critiques have been offered of Maslow's hierarchy (e.g., inconsistent research findings), it is still widely used by marketing practitioners. Other lists of needs have been generated, for example by Murray (1938, cited in Mowen and Minor, 1998: 167): "abasement, achievement, affiliation, aggression, autonomy, counteraction, defendance, deference, dominance, exhibition, harm avoidance, nurturance, order, play, rejection, sentience, sex, succourance and understanding"; and by Foxall, Goldsmith, and Brown (1998: 151): physiological, social, symbolic, hedonic, cognitive, and experiential. McLelland's theory of learned needs has been well supported by research, and is another broad theory of motivation. McLelland identified three basic learned motivational needs: needs for achievement, affiliation, and power. More recently, the trend in consumer behavior research has been toward "midrange theories that explain the narrower facets of human behavior" (Mowen and Minor, 1998: 169ff.) and motivation, including: opponent process theory; maintaining optimum stimulation levels; motivation for hedonic experiences and experiential consumption; desire to maintain behavioral freedom; motivation to avoid risk; and motivation to attribute causality (see Mowen and Minor, 1998: 169–85).

Consumer motives activate and direct action to be taken in satisfaction of identified needs, i.e., they are an internal driving force or stimulus to purchase. They organize, sustain, and direct activities toward diverse objects and needs. A number of different motives are relevant for consumers, including rational buying motives that take account of economic factors such as price, product reliability, cash and credit facilities, and irrational buying motives that relate to higher-level consumer needs, in order to take account of the influence of other people. However, there are other important motives that are less obviously linked to the functional characteristics of products and brands, but rather relate to their symbolic characteristics, for example, what role the products play in our lives, in helping us establish our identity, in providing links with the past, or in eliciting strong emotional bonds linked to warmth, passion, and affiliation (Solomon, 2002: 12–13).

Bibliography

Arnould, E., Price, L., and Zinkhan, G. (2004). *Consumers*, 2nd edn. Boston: McGraw-Hill Irwin, ch. 7.

Bandura, A. (1997). *Self-Efficacy: The Exercise of Control.* New York: Freeman.

Belk, R. (1988). Possessions and the extended self. *Journal of Consumer Research*, 15 (2), 139–68.

Belk, R. and Guliz, G. (1996). Cross-cultural differences in materialism. *Journal of Economic Psychology*, 17 (1), 55–78.

Dichter, E. (1964). *The Handbook of Consumer Motivations.* New York: McGraw-Hill.

Foxall, G. R., Goldsmith, R. E., and Brown, S. (1998). *Consumer Psychology for Marketing*, 2nd edn. London: International Thomson Business Press, ch. 6.

Hawkins, D. I., Best, R. J., and Coney, K. A. (1995). *Consumer Behavior: Implications for Marketing Strategy*, 6th edn. Boston: Irwin.

Hoyer, W. D. and MacInnis, D. J. (2001). *Consumer Behavior*, 2nd edn. Boston and New York: Houghton Mifflin, ch. 3.

Loudon, D. L. and Della Bitta, A. J. (1993). *Consumer Behavior*, 4th edn. New York: McGraw-Hill, ch. 10.

Maslow, A. H. (1970). *Motivation and Personality*, 2nd edn. New York: Harper and Row.

Mowen, J. C. and Minor, M. (1998). *Consumer Behavior*, 5th edn. Upper Saddle River, NJ: Prentice-Hall, ch. 6.

Mowen, J. C. and Minor, M. (2001). *Consumer Behavior: A Framework.* Upper Saddle River, NJ: Prentice-Hall, ch. 5.

Schiffman, L. G. and Kanuk, L. Z. (2004). *Consumer Behavior*, 8th edn. Upper Saddle River, NJ: Prentice-Hall, ch. 4.

Sheldon, K. M., Elliot, A. J., Kim, Y., and Kasser, T. (2001). What is satisfying about satisfying events? Testing 10 candidate psychological needs. *Journal of Personality and Social Psychology*, 80 (2), 325–39.

Solomon, M. R. (2002). *Consumer Behavior: Buying, Having, Being*, 5th edn. Upper Saddle River, NJ: Prentice-Hall, ch. 4.

Solomon, M. R., Bamossy, G., and Askegaard, S. (2002). *Consumer Behavior: A European Perspective*, 2nd edn. Upper Saddle River, NJ: Prentice-Hall, ch. 4.

Wells, W. D. and Prensky, D. (1996). *Consumer Behavior.* New York: John Wiley, ch. 8.

Wilkie, W. L. (1994). *Consumer Behavior*, 3rd edn. New York: John Wiley, chs. 5, 6.

consumer panels

Vincent-Wayne Mitchell

In MARKETING RESEARCH, the same sample of individuals may be used over and over again, often asked questions on the same topic, indeed, asked the same questions at different points in time. Such a sample of consumers is called a panel and this type of continuous research is becoming more and more prevalent compared to "one-off" research. The need for benchmarks is less important in continuous research as comparisons with previous results provided by the same panel are integral to this research design.

Consumer panel data can be gathered at the point of sale using barcoding and related electronic systems, or in the home by means of: (1) home audits; (2) diaries; and, more recently, (3) electronic scanners used in panel households (computer-assisted panel research, CAPAR). Home audits involve research staff visiting panel members' homes and physically checking household stocks of specific products ("dustbin check"). In recent years Internet panels have grown in popularity. One variation, diary media panels, yields information helpful for establishing ADVERTISING rates by RADIO and TELEVISION networks, selecting appropriate programming, and profiling viewer or listener subgroups.

Some advantages of panels are that they allow the study of trends over time, allow changes to be identified, and thus facilitate the search for causes of changes. They place less reliance on recall and more reliance on recording behavior as it happens. The cost of recruiting the sample can also be spread over several pieces of research.

Panel research data are particularly useful in developing forecasts (see FORECASTING) for the long-term sales of new products that have been subject to TEST MARKETING, but it should be remembered that extrapolation assumes that market conditions remain relatively unchanged, which is problematic.

There are disadvantages of panels. First, it is harder to recruit individuals to the sample if they know that they will be expected to cooperate again and again. Second, some members of the panel will drop out and equivalent replacements will have to be found. There may be a policy of rolling replacement of a given proportion of the panel each period, partly to forestall fatigue. Third, respondents' behavior may be affected because they know that they are on the panel or because their behavior is conditioned by answering questions on a previous occasion. It can also be difficult to investigate ATTITUDES or motivations (*see* CONSUMER NEEDS AND MOTIVES) on a continuous or repetitive basis because the first questioning will have alerted respondents and caused them to develop different attitudes.

Bibliography

Malhotra, N. K. and Birks, D. F. (2003). *Marketing Research: An Applied Approach*, 2nd European edn. London: Financial Times/Prentice-Hall.

consumer perceptions

Barbara R. Lewis

Consumers are continually exposed to a multitude of stimuli from companies, the environment, and other people and endeavor to make sense of visual stimuli through the perceptive process, which may be defined as the result of interaction between stimuli and individual/personal factors.

The perceptive process is subjective and individuals tend to select, organize, and interpret stimuli and information according to existing beliefs and ATTITUDES, which in turn influence consumer reaction, attitudes, and behavior. Further, there are limits to the number of stimuli that consumers can pay attention to and comprehend at any one time and so the receptive process becomes selective. In fact, consumers have selective exposure to stimuli, selective perceptions (and sometimes distortion), and in turn selective retention and selective decision-making. In addition, perception changes as needs and motives (*see* CONSUMER NEEDS AND MOTIVES) change, more stimuli become available, and as a function of increasing experience as consumers.

Bibliography

Antonides, G. and van Raaij, W. F. (1998). *Consumer Behavior: A European Perspective*. New York: John Wiley, ch. 6.

Arnould, E., Price, L., and Zinkhan, G. (2004). *Consumers*, 2nd edn. Boston: McGraw-Hill Irwin, ch. 8.

Foxall, G. R., Goldsmith, R. E., and Brown, S. (1998). *Consumer Psychology for Marketing*, 2nd edn. London: International Thomson Business Press.

Schiffman, L. G. and Kanuk, L. Z. (2004). *Consumer Behavior*, 8th edn. Upper Saddle River, NJ: Prentice-Hall, ch. 6.

consumer protection

David Yorke

Despite the notion of caveat emptor (let the buyer beware), consumer protection is now a part of the legal framework of most developed countries. For example, in the UK, modern laws concerned with food and drink go back to 1860 and modern weights and measures legislation began in 1878. The regulations regarding the testing of new pharmaceutical products are especially rigorous. For example, Dickson (1997) notes that it took from 1967 to 1976 for the Federal Drug Administration (FDA) to approve beta-blockers that are used for the treatment of cardiovascular disease and hypertension. There is now a whole raft of consumer and environmental protection legislation that in Europe mainly emanates from the European Commission, driven, *inter alia*, by changes in consumer awareness and attitudes. The adverse consequences of, for example, the continued use over extended periods of particular products are, however, difficult to forecast and much of the legislation is often a response to effects realized after marketing.

Bibliography

Dickson, P. R. (1997). *Marketing Management*, 2nd edn. London: Dryden Press/Harcourt Brace College Publishers, p. 298.

consumerism

Vincent-Wayne Mitchell

Consumerism involves those activities of government, business, independent organizations, and consumers themselves which help protect consumers against unfair or unethical business practices.

The main era of development for the consumerist movement was in the US in the early 1960s when President John F. Kennedy presented his consumers' Bill of Rights to Congress in 1962. This Bill established the basic principles of consumerism, namely, the right to safety, to be protected against dangerous and unsafe products; the right to be informed and protected against fraudulent, deceitful, and misleading statements, advertisements, labels, and so on and to be educated on how to use financial resources wisely; the right to choose and be assured access to a variety of products and services at competitive prices – although when competition is not possible government regulation should be substituted; and the right to be heard by government and business regarding unsatisfactory or disappointing practices.

In addition, one of the most successful consumer groups was founded around this time. Ralph Nader's Public Citizen group lifted consumerism into a major social force, following publication of his book *Unsafe at Any Speed* (1965), which was a detailed examination of the automobile industry. Following similar investigations into meat processing and money lending, several laws were passed which established fairer practices. Consumer organizations have won battles for consumers in many other countries, e.g., in Scandinavia, the Netherlands, France, Germany, Japan, and the UK, in a number of areas of business activity. For example, the practice of inertia selling, which involved the sending of unsolicited goods to people, was curbed in the UK by laws passed in 1971 and 1975; and organizations such as the Better Business Bureau in the US and the Consumers' Association in the UK have fought for truth in ADVERTISING, adequate food labeling of nutrition and ingredients, and the use of "sell-by" and "open-by" dates. Germany has the strongest standards for truth where deception is defined as occurring when 10 to 15 percent of reasonable consumers,

even gullible ones, perceive a message as misleading, as determined by research (Petty, 1997). In Germany deception cases are tried in courts and even the words *best* or *better* are considered misleading (Jeannet and Hennessey, 1992). In addition to government and industry agencies, more than 100 national organizations look out for various consumer interests, e.g., National Consumers' League, Action for Children's Television.

Regulators have long been interested in MARKETING COMMUNICATIONS and the extent to which they violate consumer rights in areas such as: (1) deceptive advertising and labeling; (2) deceptive selling practices; and (3) advertising to children. The basic problem for consumer advocacy is that young children, particularly those under 7 years of age, have not yet developed the cognitive abilities to distinguish between the advertisment and the programme (Meringoof and Lesser, 1980). The doctrine of responsibility expects that companies should be able to anticipate normal risky uses of a product/service and can be held responsible for misuses that might occur from normal consumption of a product or service and that could have been prevented or at least minimized.

Consumerism can be seen as the ultimate expression of the MARKETING CONCEPT since it compels companies to think from the consumer's perspective. For example, environmental groups have raised consumer awareness of green issues and companies have responded to the opportunity by creating "green" products. One UK group, the Campaign for Real Ale (CAMRA), successfully insured the existence of naturally fermented beers, which were in danger of being phased out by the major breweries.

Several reasons have been given for the growth of consumerism in western economies, such as a more impersonal marketplace, increased product complexity, more intrusive advertising, MASS MEDIA which are quick to publicize unethical or questionable practices by marketers (*see* MARKETING ETHICS), and the emergence of less materialistic values in consumers (Hawkins, Best, and Coney, 1995). Recently, rights for US consumers in the information age have been suggested and include:

- The right to be educated about product strengths and weaknesses.
- The right to trust sources of product information.
- The right to a state-of-the-art information infrastructure that empowers consumers to efficiently use their time, money, and energy.
- The right of all Americans, whether urban or rural, rich or poor, to access the information infrastructure.
- The right to privacy, preventing sellers and others from abusing personal information gained in product transactions (Snider, 1993).

In one sense, there is a philosophical conflict between the existence of consumerism and the marketing concept, because if the marketing concept were operating properly, there should be no need for consumerism. However, the diversity of consumer needs means that it is virtually impossible to produce products that satisfy every individual's needs. Secondly, organizations must produce goods within certain cost parameters to insure profit. Thirdly, not all organizations have embraced or implemented the marketing concept fully.

Bibliography

Allport, G. (1937). *Personality: A Psychological Interpretation*. New York: Holt, Rinehart and Winston.
Bloom, P. N. and Greyser, G. A. (1981). The maturity of consumerism. *Harvard Business Review*, November/December, **59**, 130–9.
Fletcher, K. (1994). The evolution and use of information technology in marketing. In M. J. Baker (ed.), *The Marketing Book*, 3rd edn. Oxford: Butterworth-Heinemann, p. 352.
Hawkins, D. I., Best, R. J., and Coney, K. A. (1995). *Consumer Behavior: Implications for Marketing Strategy*, 6th edn. Boston: Irwin, ch. 21.
Hoyer, W. D. and Macinnis, D. J. (2001). *Consumer Behavior*, 2nd edn. Boston: Houghton Mifflin.
Jeannet, J.-P. and Hennessey, H. D. (1992). *Global Marketing Strategies*. Boston: Houghton Mifflin.
Meringoof, L. K. and Lesser, G. S. (1980). Children's ability to distinguish television commercials from program material. In R. P. Adler (ed.), *The Effect of Television Advertising on Children*. Lexington, MA: Lexington Books, pp. 29–42.
Morrison, L. J., Coleman, A. M., and Preston, C. C. (1995). Mystery customer research: Cognitive processes affecting accuracy. *Journal of the Market Research Society*, **37**, 4 (October).
Nader, R. (1965). *Unsafe at Any Speed*. Public Citizen Group.
Petty, R. D. (1997). Advertising law in the United States and European Union. *Journal of Public Policy and Marketing*, Spring, 2–13.
Snider, J. H. (1993). Consumers in the information age. *The Futurist*, January/February, 15–19.
t' Petros, S. L. and Petrella, F. (1982). Preschoolers' awareness of television advertising. *Child Development*, August, 933–7.
Ward, S. (1974). Consumer socialization. *Journal of Consumer Research*, September, 1–13.

contingency planning

Dale Littler

In stable environments, organizations should be able to devise and implement plans based on their analysis of the important variables likely to affect demand and supply. However, in general, organizations operate in environments where there is significant change and, therefore, some UNCERTAINTY about the possible future outcomes. Even in relatively stable environments there is always the probability of some unforeseen event that can affect the outcome. Organizations may, therefore, strive to forecast a possible range of future states or scenarios and to devise appropriate plans for each of these. This is contingency planning. As it becomes clearer which scenario is unfolding, the organization can draw on the appropriate contingency plan.

See also *scenario building*

continuous innovation

Dale Littler

It has been suggested that innovations, and in particular technological innovations, can be viewed along a continuum, ranging from incremental or continuous innovations to the more radical or discontinuous innovations (*see*

INNOVATION; DISCONTINUOUS INNOV-
ATION) according to the degree of technological
change involved. However, from a MARKETING
perspective, a more relevant criterion is the
extent to which innovations affect demand. An
innovation does not have to be radical to lead to
substantial changes in demand: relatively minor
changes in the features of an offering might have
significant implications for demand. Most consumers or buyers are concerned less about the
intrinsic aspects of the offering and more about
what values it provides in terms of functionality,
ease of use, and quality. It is how the customer/
buyer perceives the innovation that many regard
as the critical issue. Overall, though, continuous
innovation involves relatively little change in
such dimensions as technology, habits, motivations, and working practices.

See also *product innovation*

Bibliography

Littler, D. A. (1988). *Technological Development*. Oxford:
    Philip Allan, ch. 1.
Robertson, T. S. (1971). *Innovative Behavior and Commu-
    nication*. New York: Holt, Rinehart, and Winston.

contribution

Dominic Wilson

The contribution of a product or service is the
residual sum (after deducting variable costs) that
a product contributes toward profit and toward
the fixed costs of its production and distribution.
Thus, contribution is an internal measure used
to analyze the performance of a product in con-
tributing to the productivity and profitability of
an organization (Thomas, 1986). The concept of
contribution is particularly useful where fixed
costs may be difficult to assign to any specific
offering, perhaps because they are shared by
several product ranges and variants. Therefore,
a predetermined contribution MARGIN is sometimes assigned to a product for the purposes of
calculating price because it is not possible (or
practicable) to identify its contribution more
precisely, making it difficult to calculate price
on the basis of cost-plus methods (*see* PRICING
METHODS). Thus, products with low contribu-

tion will generally be low priorities for investment purposes and in strategic marketing
planning (*see* STRATEGIC PLANNING). It is
important to take into account interlinkages
among products whereby, for example, a product may have a low (or even negative) contribution while being a necessary prerequisite for
another more profitable offering (e.g., after-
sales warranty services). Equally, a product or
service may seem to be unproductive and unprofitable (e.g., a train with very few passengers)
and yet still earn a worthwhile contribution because the variable costs involved (e.g., the fuel to
run the train) are very low compared to the fixed
costs (e.g., the cost of the railway network, stations, engine, and rolling stock), which have
already been incurred.

Bibliography

Thomas, M. J. (1986). Marketing productivity analysis: A
    research report. *Marketing Intelligence and Planning*, 4
    (2), 3–71 (entire issue).

conviction

David Yorke

Conviction is the third step in the DAGMAR
MODEL of MARKETING COMMUNICATIONS.
It is part of the AFFECTIVE STAGE, i.e., the
buyer or customer is convinced that the product
or service will meet the need or specification.
Although it is the penultimate step before
ACTION, the link between conviction and a sub-
sequent purchase is difficult to measure.

Bibliography

Colley, R. H. (1961). *Defining Advertising Goals for
    Measured Advertising Results*. New York: Association
    of National Advertisers.

corporate reputation

Gary Davies

The reputation of an organization is the term used
to denote its standing, whether or not it has a
"good name" in the eyes of its various stakeholders. Definitions of reputation tend to emphasize

different aspects of the concept. Many emphasize the need to consider more than one stakeholder and the time a reputation takes to build, e.g., "The reputation of an organization is the accumulated impression that a stakeholder has of the organization" (Fombrun, 1996). Others focus on one particular stakeholder, the customer, where reputation is typically described as "not what the company believes, but what the customer believes or feels about the company from his experiences and observation" (Bernstein, 1984). The latter is close to definitions of "corporate image" used by marketing scholars, for example, the "attitudes and feelings consumers have about the nature and underlying reality of the company" (Pharoah, 1982: 243) or "the result of how consumers perceive the firm" (Grönroos, 1984). Other definitions of corporate reputation are similar to those used to define BRAND, as they emphasize the affective nature of the construct, as in "the net affective or emotional reaction . . . to the company's name" (Fombrun, 1996: 37).

Still more definitions emphasize that reputation is an intangible asset, capable of affecting the performance of the company in its various markets. A favorable reputation may cause desirable consequences such as the charging of premium prices to the customer and the attraction of more investors (Fombrun and Shanley, 1990). Reputation is seen from a strategic perspective as something that is difficult to imitate and which can therefore provide a sustainable COMPETITIVE ADVANTAGE (Fombrun, Gardberg, and Sever, 2000). A superior reputation will attract better employees and promote lower employee turnover (Markham, 1972; IOD, 1999), increase buying intention among corporate customers (Yoon, Guffey, and Kijewski, 1993), create higher credibility (Herbig, Milewicz, and Golden, 1994), and create more favorable media reputation (Deephouse, 1997). There is some confusion between the terms reputation and IMAGE, and this is compounded by the use of the term "identity" in a similar context. Some writers use the three words interchangeably. Others use the words to label very specific and quite different ideas, but what these ideas are varies from one source and from one academic discipline to another.

Whatever labels are used, there are two important questions that the management of corporate reputation seeks to address: "Who are you?," the question most likely to be asked by an external stakeholder, and "Who are we?," the question most likely to be asked by an internal stakeholder. The first is best understood as the company's *market reputation*. The second concerns the way employees view the organization they work for, best denoted by the term *organizational identity* (e.g., Albert and Whetten, 1985). *Corporate identity*, visual representation such as logos and the design of corporate notepaper, is also relevant to reputation but they are not one and the same thing (even though design companies often imply that they are).

Reputation management is often seen as the alignment or coordination of two or more elements, "How others (the customers) see us," "Who we really are," and "What we say we are" (e.g., Davies and Miles, 1998). One coordinating mechanism can be the "corporate story," a discourse about the company encapsulating many of its myths and legends (van Riel, 1997). Alternatively, the company mission and vision statement (*see* MISSION STATEMENT; VISION STATEMENT) can provide the "glue" that holds all aspects of reputation management together (Chun and Davies, 2001).

A common way of examining corporate reputation is through the lens of corporate branding (Balmer, 1995). In the same way that a product can become a brand, a company name can become a corporate brand. The point is that the corporate brand is more than what is tangibly offered by the firm and is something that has, like a consumer brand, an emotional appeal (Gardner and Levy, 1955). Corporate brands must, however, appeal to internal as well as external stakeholders (Upshaw, 1995; de Chernatony, 1999). They reflect the philosophy and culture of the organization, and, ideally, the internal values of the firm, which should be aligned with or even become its external brand values (Davies et al., 2003a, b). It has been claimed that reputation management commences with a company's employees, and how they perceive the company (Gray, 1986). How the company is seen internally transfers to the customer through the interactions the customer has with employees.

An image can be developed by external stakeholders depending on their image of the internal stakeholders they meet or see (King, 1973; Kennedy, 1977). If a customer-facing employee and the customer share the same positive view of the organization, then a positive interaction between them is more likely to occur. The view that customer-facing employees have of their organization is held to influence the impression that customers form of the organization (de Chernatony, 1999) because the contact between customers and employees can shape the image customers hold of it (Bettencourt, Meuter, and Gwinner, 2001). Customers catch the displayed emotions of employees through a process of "emotional contagion" and this affects their image of the service they receive (Pugh, 2001). If these links between the internal and external perspectives exist, then the potential is there to influence both simultaneously. For example, a corporate website can be used to communicate a company's mission and vision, and this can influence how various stakeholders perceive the organization (Chun and Davies, 2001). Managers should be cognizant of any differences between the content of communications that might affect employees and customers directly or indirectly and the current perceptions held by both.

There is a debate about what can be used to best shape reputation and the relative importance of CULTURE (Alvesson, 1990), DESIGN and other tangibles (Olins, 1978; Selame and Selame, 1988), ADVERTISING and PUBLIC RELATIONS (Meyers, 1984; Kitchen and Proctor, 1991; Wartick, 1992), and SOCIAL RESPONSIBILITY (McGuire, Sundgren, and Schneeweis, 1988). Van Riel and Balmer (1997) suggest that companies can manage their external reputation through the "corporate identity mix," which consists of three elements: the behaviors of (in particular customer-facing) employees, corporate communication (including but not only advertising), and symbolism. Corporate symbols will include tangibles such as buildings and intangibles such as design. Topalian (1984) cites tangibles such as the company size, its products and structure as influencing external image. To those coming at the area from a design perspective (Ind, 1992), tangibles include all that is to do with graphic and building design. Kotler and Barich (1991) provide a long list of attributes that might affect image. This includes all the elements of the MARKETING MIX (the 4Ps and 2Ss), plus corporate social conduct, conduct toward employees, and business performance.

The role of key individuals, particularly that of the CEO and his or her style, will influence the way both internal and external stakeholders see the firm (Dowling, 1993). Herbig, Milewicz, and Golden (1994) link external image/reputation (defined as the consistency of outcomes with market signals over time) with credibility (the belief that a company will do what it says it will). The idea of consistency is useful in that it emphasizes again the need for coherence between the many factors that can influence internal and external image.

The role of advertising in reputation management is a controversial one. Shostack (1977), a bank executive and an academic writer, was early in explaining that images for service companies, which provide intangibles, are created through tangibles (such as building design), while images for tangible products are created through the intangible imagery of media advertising. Many corporate names do not represent tangible products. Some claim that advertising can only be used to communicate a reputation and should not be used to try to create one. Advertising what you are not will raise expectations that will not be met by the experience the customer, employee, or supplier perceives is being delivered and will be at best a waste of time, and at worst actually damaging to reputation (Davies et al., 2003a).

The CEO can be thought of as the corporate brand manager responsible for managing the image of the firm, both internally and externally and to a multiplicity of stakeholders. Gerald Ratner's poor choice of joke in a speech in London's Albert Hall in the 1980s is an extreme example of how the actions of a CEO can influence the reputation of the company. Ratner compared the price of one of his products, a pair of gold earrings, to that of a prawn sandwich, quipping that the sandwich would probably last longer than the earrings. The resulting media comment in Britain's tabloid newspapers led to the collapse of his global jewelry retail business, as customers returned products but did not return themselves. Staff were disillusioned by both the jokes and the media coverage. In the case of such a crisis, the links between reputation and financial performance are clear. Adverse media comment creates a decline in confidence that can become a collapse if not well handled. The fall of Arthur Andersen globally has been ascribed to a loss of confidence in the firm following allegations of its involvement in the Enron saga. The BSE crisis in the 1980s had a long-term impact on beef sales in Britain. The British Ministry of Agriculture handled the crisis in a very logical way, waiting for hard facts before deciding finally to cull the beef herd. However, consumers were reacting emotionally, encouraged by media comment that will always be sensational rather than objective in such circumstances.

While the links between reputation and financial performance are brutally obvious in a crisis, a conviction that reputation and performance are more generally linked is not universally shared. In one survey of those responsible for reputation management, one view was that it is misleading to see them as linked in causality, because a good reputation is a given for all larger businesses. A different opinion was that reputation is a leading indicator of performance; but the two do not necessarily go hand in hand (Davies and Miles, 1998). Thus far, Fortune's annual America's Most Admired Companies survey has been a key data source for exploring linkages between reputation and financial performance, and a Fortune ranking correlates with superior financial returns (Roberts and Dowling, 1997; Vergin and Qoronfleh, 1998). However, since financial performance is a major input to the Fortune rankings, the measure is heavily influenced by a financial halo and such correlations are unlikely to offer proof of causality. Evidence for a link between reputation and performance is apparent in most service organizations (e.g., British Airways, McDonald's, Wal-Mart, Oxford University, the Catholic Church, KPMG) as, whether they exist for profit or not, they will depend for their success upon the associations the public makes with their corporate names. The ultimate sense of there being a link between reputation and performance is, then, difficult to deny. One problem in proving the link is the ephemeral nature of reputation and the difficulty in measuring it.

How reputation is measured will depend on how it is defined, and, as we have seen, there is more than one definition of the construct. While both frameworks and techniques are available for image measurement, there is no generally accepted method of measuring reputation. Business practice tends to rely upon measuring the amount and content of media comment, emphasizing the strong links between public relations and reputation management in companies. Similar approaches to that of Fortune can be seen in the UK's *Management Today* Britain's Most Admired Companies and *Asian Business* Asia's Most Admired Companies surveys. An improvement to the approach of Fortune has been that of Fombrun, Gardberg, and Sever (2000), whose dimensions include an emotional appeal factor (admire, respect, trust) that can assess how members of the public feel about a firm, rather than just how they perceive its performance financially. Other measures have been developed to assess reputation from the perspective of customers (e.g., van Riel and Balmer, 1997).

Corporate reputation is a complex construct. Metaphor is often useful to make what is complex accessible for researcher and respondent alike (Black, 1962). There has been a tradition of assessing the customer's view of retailers using the "organization as person" metaphor since Martineau (1958) first coined the expression "the personality of the retail store." Markham (1972) was early in suggesting the use of a generic "personality" scale to compare the customer's perception of any company with that of its competitors. What has been widely labeled as "brand personality" has been seen as being accessible for researchers more through qualitative than through quantitative means (Durgee, 1988; Hanby, 1999). However, more recent work has opened the door to quantification. Aaker (1997) validated a scale including five dimensions for "brand personality," each with a number of traits. The scale is used to assess the customers' view of a brand but has been found to be less valid in the context of corporate reputation where the views of other stakeholders must be considered (Chun and Davies, 2001). A similar approach in using the organization as person metaphor has been used to define a "corporate character scale" validated for both internal and external stakeholders (Davies et al., 2003b). The seven dimensions are labeled as: agreeableness (e.g., friendly, supportive, sincere), enterprise (e.g., trendy, innovative), competence (e.g., reliable, leading), chic (e.g., stylish, elitist), ruthlessness (e.g., arrogant, controlling), informality (casual, easygoing), and machismo (e.g., rugged, tough). Academic research exploring the links between reputation and performance using such measures may offer a useful way to test the various claims made for the management of reputation in practice.

Bibliography

Aaker, J. L. (1997). Dimensions of brand personality. *Journal of Marketing Research*, 34 (August), 347–56.

Albert, S. and Whetten, D. (1985). Organizational identity. In B. M. Staw (ed.), *Research in Organizational Behavior*. Greenwich, CT: JAI Press, pp. 263–95.

Alvesson, M. (1990). Organization: From substance to image? *Organization Studies*, 11 (3), 373–94.

Balmer, J. M. T. (1995). Corporate branding and connoisseurship. *Journal of Global Management*, 21 (1), 24–46.

Bernstein, D. (1984). *Company Image and Reality: A Critique of Corporate Communications*. London: Holt, Rinehart, and Winston.

Bettencourt, L. A., Meuter, M. L., and Gwinner, K. P. A. (2001). Comparison of attitude, personality, and knowledge predictors of service oriented firms. *Journal of Applied Psychology*, 86 (1), 29–41.

Black, M. (1962). *Models and Metaphors*. New York: Cornell University Press.

Chun, R. and Davies, G. (2001). E-reputation: The role of mission and vision statements in positioning strategy. *Journal of Brand Management*, 8 (4/5), 315–33.

Davies, G. and Miles, L. (1998). Reputation management: Theory versus practice. *Corporate Reputation Review*, 2, 16–27.

Davies, G., Chun, R., daSilva, R., and Roper, S. (2003a). *Corporate Reputation and Competitiveness*. London: Routledge.

Davies, G., Chun, R., daSilva, R., and Roper, S. (2003b). The personification metaphor as a measurement approach for corporate reputation. *Corporate Reputation Review*, 4 (2), 113–17.

De Chernatony, L. (1999). Brand management through narrowing the gap between brand identity and brand reputation. *Journal of Marketing Management*, 15, 157–79.

Deephouse, D. L. (1997). The effect of financial and media reputation on performance. *Corporate Reputation Review*, 1 (1/2), 68–72.

Dowling, G. R. (1993). Developing your company image into a corporate asset. *Long Range Planning*, 26 (2), 101–9.

Durgee, J. F. (1988). Understanding brand personality. *Journal of Consumer Marketing*, 5 (3), 21–5.

Fombrun, C. J. (1996). *Reputation: Realizing Value from the Corporate Image*. Cambridge, MA: Harvard Business School Press.

Fombrun, C. J., Gardberg, N. A., and Sever, J. M. (2000). The reputation quotient: A multi-stakeholder measure of corporate reputation. *Journal of Brand Management*, 7 (4), 241–55.

Fombrun, C. J. and Shanley, M. (1990). What's in a name? Reputation building and corporate strategy. *Academy of Management Journal*, 33 (2), 233–58.

Gardner, B. B. and Levy, S. J. (1955). The product and the brand. *Harvard Business Review*, March/April, 33–9.

Gray, J. (1986). *Managing the Corporate Image*. London: Quorum.

Grönroos, C. (1984). A service quality model and its marketing implications. *European Journal of Marketing*, 18, 36–44.

Hanby, T. (1999). Brands – dead or alive? Qualitative research for the 21st century: The changing conception of brands. *Journal of the Market Research Society*, 41 (1), 1–8.

Herbig, H., Milewicz, J., and Golden, J. (1994). A model of reputation building and destruction. *Journal of Business Research*, 31, 23–31.

Ind, N. (1992). *The Corporate Image*. London: Kogan Page.

Institute of Directors (IOD) (1999). *Reputation Management: Strategies for Protecting Companies, their Brands and their Directors*. Director's Guide Series, London: Director Publications.

Kennedy, S. H. (1977). Nurturing corporate image: Total communication or ego trip. *European Journal of Marketing*, 31 (1), 120–64.

King, S. (1973). *Developing New Brands*. London: Pitman.

Kitchen, P. and Proctor, T. (1991). The increasing importance of public relations in fast-moving consumer goods firms. *Journal of Marketing Management*, 7, 357–70.

Kotler, P. and Barich, H. (1991). Framework for marketing image management. *Sloan Management Review*, Winter, 94–104.

McGuire, J. B., Sundgren, A., and Schneeweis, T. (1988). Corporate social responsibility and firm financial performance. *Academy of Management Journal*, 31 (4), 854–72.

Markham, V. (1972). *Planning the Corporate Reputation*. London: George Allen and Unwin.

Martineau, P. (1958). The personality of the retail store. *Harvard Business Review*, 36 (January/February), 24–36.

Meyers, W. (1984). *The Image Makers*. London: Orbis.

Olins, W. (1978). *The Corporate Personality*. London: Design Council.

Pharoah, N. (1982). Corporate image research in brewing industry from red revolution to country goodness in ten years. *Journal of the Market Research Society*, **24** (3), 240–56.

Pugh, S. D. (2001). Service with a smile: Emotional contagion in the service encounter. *Academy of Management Journal*, **44** (5), 1018–27.

Roberts, P. W. and Dowling, G. R. (1997). The value of a firm's corporate reputation: How reputation helps sustain superior profitability. *Corporate Reputation Review*, **1** (1/2), 72–6.

Selame, E. and Selame, J. (1988). *The Company Image*. New York: John Wiley.

Shostack, G. L. (1977). Breaking free from product marketing. *Journal of Marketing*, April, 73–81.

Topalian, A. (1984). Beyond the visual overstatement. *International Journal of Advertising*, **3**, 55–62.

Upshaw, L. B. (1995). *Building Brand Identity: A Strategy for Success in a Hostile Marketplace*. New York: John Wiley.

Van Riel, C. B. M. (1997). Protecting the corporate brand by orchestrated communication. *Journal of Brand Management*, **4** (6), 409–18.

Van Riel, C. B. M. and Balmer, J. M. T. (1997). Corporate identity: The concept, its measurement and management. *European Journal of Marketing*, **31** (5/6), 340–55.

Vergin, R. C. and Qoronfleh, M. W. (1998). Corporate reputation and the stock market. *Business Horizon*, **41**, 19–26.

Wartick, S. (1992). The relationship between intense media exposure and change in corporate reputation. *Business and Society*, **31** (1), 33–49.

Yoon, E., Guffey, H. J., and Kijewski, V. (1993). The effects of information and company reputation on intentions to buy a business service. *Journal of Business Research*, **27**, 215–28.

corporate strategy

Dale Littler

Corporate strategy is regarded as encompassing the aims and objectives of the organization together with the means of how these are to be achieved. It is, by definition, holistic, i.e., it embraces all of the company's different businesses and functions. Andrews (1971) defined corporate strategy as: "the pattern of major objectives, purposes or goals and essential policies or plans for achieving those goals, stated in such a way as to define what business the company is in or is to be in and the kind of company it is or is to be" (p. 28). Chandler (1962) believed that it should also be concerned with "the allocation of resources necessary for carrying out these goals" (p. 13). It is viewed as being concerned with adding value to all of the constituent parts of the organization, the major purpose being, according to a dominant contemporary emphasis, to increase shareholder value.

Nevertheless, in defining its corporate strategy, the firm has to satisfy the sometimes contradictory expectations of several differing constituencies, or stakeholders, including, obviously, customers as well as suppliers, shareholders, and employees. Increasingly also, companies are aware of the need to demonstrate a wide societal commitment, and some even publish SOCIAL RESPONSIBILITY audits to demonstrate this. It has been suggested that in countries such as the UK, the short-term requirements of institutional shareholders prevent longer-term investments, often to the detriment of sustainable competitiveness (*see* COMPETITIVE ADVANTAGE; COMPETITIVE STRATEGY).

It is widely believed that corporate strategy should address the essentials of the organization, namely, the "what," "why," "how," and "when" of the organization. It is concerned with "what businesses is the company in or would like to be in?" This may involve the articulation of the organization's MISSION STATEMENT or definition of the vision (*see* VISION STATEMENT) or strategic intent, the desired future state, of the firm. Secondly, it embraces "why the company is in business," i.e., the specific sales, profit, rate of return, and growth targets it has or should have. Thirdly, the company needs to define "how" it aims to achieve those targets, such as the technologies it will use, the markets it is or should be operating in, and the products it markets or should market in order to achieve those objectives. Finally, the company needs to decide "when" it aims to achieve those goals and the period over which it defines its strategy.

Often, companies engage in formal STRATEGIC PLANNING as a means of developing a coherent corporate strategy, and the corporate strategy may be embodied in written strategic plans. In recent years, there has been much emphasis on competitive strategy with the focus on identifying the various structural determinants of performance and POSITIONING the company to exploit these advantageously. However, it has been convincingly argued that a sound corporate strategy will be informed by a close monitoring of the evolving requirements of the various constituencies that the organization has to satisfy, and in particular of its existing and potential customer targets.

In practice, environmental vicissitudes or sheer opportunism can mean that formal corporate strategies may need to be frequently reviewed and consequently modified or substantially revised.

Bibliography

Andrews, K. (1971). *The Concept of Corporate Strategy.* Homewood, IL: Irwin.

Chandler, A. D. (1962). *Strategy and Structure.* Cambridge, MA: MIT Press.

correlation

see REGRESSION AND CORRELATION

cost

Dominic Wilson

The production and distribution of any good or service involves costs, which will vary over the life cycle of the good/service. These costs can be divided into fixed costs and variable costs. Fixed costs are those that are incurred in order for production to take place and so are, broadly speaking, not directly related to the volume of actual production (e.g., costs of R&D, premises, production assets, basic workforce), whereas variable costs are those that vary directly in proportion to the level of actual production (e.g., costs of materials and energy). Investment in capital assets (and therefore the level of fixed costs) is generally higher at the start of a product's life cycle (*see* PRODUCT LIFE CYCLE) than toward the end. It can sometimes be very difficult to identify the costs of a product unambiguously, especially where fixed costs are shared by a wide range of products at different stages of their life cycles. Corporate accounting policies (e.g., in depreciation and asset valuation) can

also affect cost calculations. However, assessing costs is obviously a crucial part of assessing price, despite the many problems involved.

Bibliography

Shim, E. and Sudit, E. F. (1995). How manufacturers price products. *Management Accounting,* **76,** 8 (February), 37–9.

cost leadership strategy

Dale Littler

This is one of the GENERIC STRATEGIES proposed by Porter (1980) (*see* COMPETITIVE STRATEGY). Companies having the lowest costs should be in a strong position with regard to:

- competitors, because they will always be able to undercut them, while taking advantage of a higher MARGIN to invest in increasing MARKET SHARE, NEW PRODUCT DEVELOPMENT, and other corporate development policies;
- suppliers, because they can more easily absorb increases in costs;
- customers, because they are able to respond to demands for lower prices; and
- substitutes, because they will be better able to react to them in terms of cost.

In order to be a cost leader, the company must have low overheads, be highly efficient, and generally not direct resources to activities that are seen as being extraneous to achieving continued lowest cost. Companies may follow a focused cost leadership strategy aimed at particular customers or market segments (*see* MARKET SEGMENTATION), or a broad market cost leadership strategy. Apart from the fact that by definition there can only be one cost leader, there are risks to the emphasis on cost leadership, in particular the bases of customer choice may move toward NON-PRICE FACTORS and technological change may shift the COMPETITIVE ADVANTAGE to rivals, including late entrants. In general, it is probably problematic for a company in a developed country to secure a longer-term advantage from pursuing a cost leadership strategy because developing countries will generally be able to secure a cost advantage through access to lower-cost resources such as cheaper labor and natural resources; and through the purchase of more efficient versions of the technology as embodied in plant and equipment.

Bibliography

Porter, M. E. (1980). *Competitive Strategy: Techniques for Analyzing Industries and Competitors.* New York: Free Press, ch. 2.

cost per thousand

Dale Littler

Traditionally, media costs have been measured in terms of the cost per thousand of delivered audience. However, this fails to differentiate between different buying habits of members of the audience such as whether or not they are non-users, light users, or heavy users. For this reason advertisers are more interested in measuring the cost per thousand of the target audience delivered.

See also *reach*

coupons

David Yorke

Coupons are a SALES PROMOTION device which try to persuade buyers/customers to purchase. They may offer a discount on the first or subsequent purchase of a product/service, or they may need to be collected in order to be redeemed against a future purchase or to receive gifts or cash. Coupons are likely to appeal most to the price-conscious consumer. Redemption rates of coupons are traditionally low.

The use of retailer loyalty cards (*see* REWARD/ LOYALTY CARDS) means that retailers can capture data on customers' purchasing behavior that enable them to target their customers directly with coupons that are related to their demonstrated purchasing preferences.

creative content

Margaret Bruce and Liz Barnes

Creative content refers to the visuals and words or elements of the visual identity system of an organization. The creative content of these elements reinforces, for example, a hospital's IMAGE through the use of color, symbol, logotype, and typeface (Bruce and Greyser, 1995). The creative content of a brochure or an advertisement or a pack is a tangible expression of the organization and offers signals of its values which, in turn, influence the perceptions and opinions of its various publics. A Caterpillar corporate communications brochure (1994) points out that the visual elements cannot just show pictures of the products but "they have to show what we make possible for our customers, we have responsibility to show products being used by the types of people who actually use them." Similarly with the text, "we can't just say Caterpillar products and services are best. We have to demonstrate their superiority in terms people find meaningful and important.... To our many audiences, it's not what we make that counts; it's what we make possible." So, the creative content (e.g., the words and visuals) of an advertisement or brochure or other form of communication usually contains four elements: the principal benefit offered by the product or service; the characteristics of the product or service; the image of the product or service; and the uses of the product or service.

Bibliography

Aaker, D. A. and Myers, J. G. (1987). *Advertising Management,* 3rd edn. Englewood Cliffs, NJ: Prentice-Hall, ch. 15.
Bruce, M. and Greyser, S. (1995). *Changing Corporate Identity: The Case of a Regional Hospital.* Teaching case. Boston: Design Management Institute and Harvard Business School.
Caterpillar, Inc. (1994). *Communicating Caterpillar: One Voice.* Peoria, IL.

cross-tabulations

Michael Greatorex

Cross-tabulations are very popular in the analysis of survey data and they are concerned with the quantitative analysis of data where several variables are analyzed together, usually to see if there are any relationships between the variables.

If two of the variables are measured on nominal (categorical) scales, cross-tabulations (cross-tabs) can be used to summarize the sample data. A cross-tab is a table with the categories (or values) for the two variables set out on the two axes and the counts of the number of times each pair of values occurs recorded in the cells of the table. The row and column totals are usually calculated and percentages across the rows and/or down the columns are also computed to aid in the interpretation, description, and discussion of the results. Cross-tabs can be formed in more than two dimensions when data for more than two categorical variables are analyzed, but interpretation may become difficult as the increased number of cells often leaves empty cells or a number of cells with small counts.

The variables may be ordinal variables such as those measured on rating scales or interval variables where the data have been grouped into a few classes for each variable. Again, the cross-tab records the counts of the number of cases falling into each cell of the table.

HYPOTHESIS TESTING relating to cross-tabs often involves the chi-square test. Other tests and summary statistics are available depending on the type of data; for instance, if both variables are measured on ordinal scales, Spearman's rank correlation coefficient or Kendall's tau may be used.

As well as recording the number of cases in each cell, a cross-tab can be used to present summary statistics of other variables for the cases in each cell. For instance, while a basic cross-tab may count the sample numbers, broken down by gender and occupation, it is possible to present the average income (or the average of any similar variable) of the cases in each gender/occupation cell. Further analysis of such data may involve analysis of variance, but the cross-tab analysis described above is a convenient way to get a feel for these data and to present results in a convenient, descriptive manner.

Bibliography

Tull, D. S. and Hawkins, D. I. (1993). *Marketing Research: Measurement and Method*, 6th edn. New York: Macmillan, pp. 610–12.

cue

David Yorke

A cue is a non-verbal signal communicated by a person, PRODUCT, or service that serves to give direction to customer drives or motives (*see* CONSUMER NEEDS AND MOTIVES). An advertisement, for example, may provide a stimulus as to how to satisfy a salient motive. People draw inferences from visual interpersonal contact that gives access to the face, the hands, the posture, or the physical environment in which the interaction is taking place. Information is communicated via the aggregate of social cues provided by visual and physical presence. Similarly, products and services also communicate evaluative information via intrinsic and extrinsic stimuli such as physical attributes, or ADVERTISING messages. Thus, desired impressions, feelings, and ATTITUDES may be subtly encouraged by MARKETING COMMUNICATIONS techniques (e.g., PERSONAL SELLING, PACKAGING, TELEMARKETING).

Bibliography

Loudon, D. L. and Della Bitta, A. J. (1993). *Consumer Behavior*, 4th edn. New York: McGraw-Hill.
Rutter, D. R. (1994). *Looking and Seeing: The Role of Visual Communication in Social Interaction*. Chichester: John Wiley.

cultural environment

see CULTURE; CULTURE AND BEHAVIOR; CULTURE AND SOCIAL IDENTITY; CULTURE AND SOCIETAL BEHAVIOR

culture

Andrew Lindridge

Triandis et al. (1986) described culture as "a fuzzy, difficult to define construct," and LaFramboise, Coleman, and Gerton (1993) criticized definitions of culture for either omitting a salient aspect or generalizing beyond any real meaning. Although culture may ultimately be difficult to define, one of the most commonly cited and applicable definitions of culture is

Taylor's (1891: 1): "That complex whole which includes knowledge, beliefs, art, morals, law, customs and any other capabilities and habits acquired by man as a member of that society." To this we can add Sojka and Tansuhaj's (1995: 469) definition of culture as "a set of socially acquired behavior patterns and meanings common to the members of a particular society or human group." Venkatesh (1995) adds that the concept of a pure culture, one that remains independent of external influence, can only exist in the mind of the individual. Instead, culture changes through conflict, creativity, disagreement, democratization, INNOVATION, internal or external industrialization, and modernization (Rohner, 1984; Oyserman, 1993). Culture, then, represents an ongoing and evolving set of norms and values adhered to by a group of people.

Yet does an inability to reach a consensus definition of culture pose a problem for MARKETING RESEARCH? Whiting (1976) argues that culture should be kept as a packaged, unexamined variable, while Rohner (1984: 111) adds that "little attempt is made, as a rule, to determine what culture is, or to determine what about culture produces the claimed effects." Segall (1983) argues that this approach is acceptable as attempts to define culture are irrelevant. Instead, culture should be viewed as a complex bundle of independent variables, which are attributed to behavior. Problems in defining culture and whether it can be researched may be related to its ontological reality, typified by the contrasting arguments of the cultural nominalists and cultural realists.

Cultural nominalists argue that "Culture has no ontological reality; it is neither a superorganic reality external to the organism, nor is it an idea in the mind of the organism. Culture is a logical construct, abstracted from human behavior, and as such, it exists only in the mind of the investigator" (Spiro, 1951: 24). The belief of cultural nominalists that culture exists only in the mind of the investigator, typified by Segall's (1983) cultural definition, is problematic. Acceptance of this argument would imply that any marketing research investigating the role of culture might be attributable to the researcher's imagination.

Cultural realists' definition of culture offers a more acceptable approach for marketing research. They argue that culture represents a continuum of extrasomatic elements, moving "in accordance with its own principles, its own laws; it is a thing *sui generis*. Its elements interact with one another forming new combinations and syntheses.... Culture is not determined by man, by his wishes, will, hopes, fears, etc. Man is, of course, prerequisite to culture; he is, so to speak, the catalyst that makes the interactive process possible. But the culture process is culturally determined, not biologically or psychologically" (White, 1949: 374). If culture exists as an entity external to individuals, as the cultural realists believe, can culture then be measurable and observable for marketing research? Keesing's (1974) definition, drawing upon the cultural realists, identifies culture as a system of three ideational systems that can be identified with human behavior: cognitive, structuralist, and symbolic (*see* SELF-CONCEPT).

The cognitive system, drawing upon the Sapir–Whorf hypothesis, argues that individuals are cognitively dependent on the categories and distinctions within their language. If no words exist to express a concept, then that concept is not available to those people (Hayes, 1994). The language we are taught from birth intentionally shapes and structures both our social behavior and our vision of the world. Farb's (1974) research among bilingual Japanese women married to American servicemen supports this idea. When respondents were interviewed in both languages, attitudes expressed differed markedly depending on the language used. For example, written responses to the statement "When my wishes conflict with my family ..." in Japanese were, "It is a time of great unhappiness" (evidence of group sorrow), but in English were, "I do what I want" (evidence of individual strength). It was concluded that this was evidence of the women expressing attitudes relevant to that particular language world (Farb, 1974). Farb's research suggests that bilingual individuals may subconsciously alternate between differing cultures and subsequently demonstrate noticeably different behavior patterns.

The structuralist approach, drawing upon the work of Lévi-Strauss, focuses on the social organization, societal structures, and the manner in which they are learned and acted upon by individuals. Culture is viewed as a set of shared symbolic systems which are a construct of cumulative creations in the individual's mind, manifesting themselves in art, kinship, language, and myths (Keesing, 1974). Reber (1985) adds that the structuralist approach should also include religion, as religion exists as a societal structure. This structure provides a system of beliefs with either institutionalized or traditionally defined patterns of behavior and ceremony.

The third ideational theory views culture as a symbolic system manifesting itself through a system of shared meanings and symbols, which are recognized by individuals as part of their culture. The symbolic system can be categorized into objective and subjective culture (Rohner, 1984). Objective culture is defined as a physical object whose status or function is publicly verifiable and is not dependent upon internal mental processes. For example, a statue of the god "Ganesha" becomes a physical manifestation of Hindu religious beliefs. Subjective culture is defined as a group's characteristic way of perceiving and controlling its social environment through norms, roles, rules, and values (Triandis and Vassiliou, 1972). These values dictate desirable or prescribed behaviors for those holding positions in the social structure.

See also *acculturation; culture and behavior; culture and social identity; culture and societal behavior*

Bibliography

Farb, P. (1974). *Word Play: What Happens When People Talk*. New York: Bantam.

Hayes, N. (1994). *Foundations of Psychology*. London: Routledge.

Keesing, R. M. (1974). Theories of culture. *Annual Review of Anthropology*, 3, 73–97.

LaFramboise, T., Coleman, H. L. K., and Gerton, J. (1993). Psychological impact of biculturalism: Evidence and theory. *Psychological Bulletin*, 114 (3), 395–412.

Oyserman, D. (1993). The lens of personhood: Viewing the self and others in a multicultural society. *Journal of Personality and Social Psychology*, 65 (5), 993–1009.

Reber, A. S. (1985). *The Penguin Dictionary of Psychology*. London: Penguin.

Rohner, R. P. (1984). Toward a conception of culture for cross-cultural psychology. *Journal of Cross-Cultural Psychology*, 15 (2), 111–38.

Segall, M. H. (1983). On the search for the independent variable in cross-cultural psychology. In S. H. Irvine

and J. W. Berry (eds.), *Human Assessment and Cultural Factors*. New York: Plenum Press, pp. 127–37.

Sojka, J. Z. and Tansuhaj, P. S. (1995). Cross-cultural consumer research: A twenty-year review. *Advances in Consumer Research*, 22, 461–74.

Spiro, M. E. (1951). Culture and personality: The natural history of a false dichotomy. *Psychiatry*, 14 (1), 19–46.

Taylor, E. B. (1891). *Primitive Culture*. New York: John Murray.

Triandis, H. C., Bontempo, R., Betancourt, H., Bond, M., Leung, K., Brenes, A., Georgas, J., Hui, C. H., Marin, G., Setiadi, B., Sinha, J. B. P., Verma, J., Spangenberg, J., Touzard, H., and de Montmollin, G. (1986). The measurement of the etic aspects of individualism and collectivism across cultures. *Australian Journal of Psychology*, 38 (3), 257–67.

Triandis, H. C. and Vassiliou, V. (1972). A comparative analysis of subjective culture. In *The Analysis of Subjective Culture*. New York: John Wiley, pp. 395–415.

Venkatesh, A. (1995). Ethno-consumerism: A new paradigm to study cultural and cross-cultural consumer behavior. In *Marketing in a Multicultural World: Ethnicity, Nationalism and Cultural Identity*. Beverley Hills, CA: Sage, pp. 68–104.

White, L. (1949). Ethnological theory. In R. W. Sellars, V. J. McGill, and M. Farber (eds.), *Philosophy for the Future*. New York: Macmillan.

Whiting, B. B. (1976). The problem of the packaged variable. In *The Developing Individual in a Changing World*. Cited in Rohner, R. P. (1984). Toward a conception of culture for cross-cultural psychology. *Journal of Cross-Cultural Psychology*, 15 (2), 111–38.

culture and behavior

Andrew Lindridge

Culture's relationship with measurable human behaviors is problematic, reflecting wider cultural nominalist and realist arguments (*see* CULTURE). Segall (1983), arguing from a cultural nominalist perspective, notes that the concept of culture is so difficult to define and conceptualize that it is impossible to identify any relationship to behavior. Rohner (1984: 116–17) agrees with this, commenting that "the behavior of individuals in various work settings is never guided by culture *per se*. Rather, it is guided by the individual's own cognitive, affective, perceptual and motivational dispositions that may, in varying degrees, also be what the analyst ultimately comes to call culture."

If culture is a set of ideas, which bond together a group of people, then this implies a collective knowledge of their cultural values. Rohner (1984: 122) argues against this, as no single individual can know "the full range of meanings that define the culture of his or her people." Therefore, culture cannot, from a cultural nominalist perspective, be attributed to behavior.

Bond (1988) and Kim et al. (1994), drawing upon the arguments of cultural realists, maintain that culture and the individual are interrelated. This interrelationship is manifested in interactions between the beliefs, norms, organizations, and social structures of a culture and the individuals that belong to that culture (Giddens, 1984). Leung and Bond (1989) suggest that this interrelationship encourages interdependence, allowing individuals, society, and their culture to function. With each situation encountered by society or its members, cultural conventions are drawn upon, prompting behavior acceptable to the society. Kitayama et al. (1997) and Kim et al. (1994) add that individuals are aware of their cultural values but use them for guidance only, as in themselves they are self-directing. The individual can then accept, reject, or select any cultural value. Therefore, culture does affect human behavior.

See also *acculturation; culture and social identity; culture and societal behavior*

Bibliography

Bond, M. H. (1988). Finding universal dimensions of individual variation in multicultural studies of values: The rokeach and Chinese value surveys. *Journal of Personality and Social Psychology*, 55 (6), 1009–15.

Giddens, A. (1984). *The Constitution of Society: Outline of the Theory of Structuration*. Cambridge, MA: Polity.

Leung, K. and Bond, M. H. (1989). On the empirical identification of dimensions for cross-cultural comparisons. *Journal of Cross-Cultural Psychology*, 20 (5), 133–51.

Kim, U., Triandis, H. C., Kagitcibasi, C., Choi, S.-C., and Yoon, G. (1994). Introduction. In *Individualism and Collectivism: Theory, Method and Applications*. London: Sage, pp. 1–16.

Kitayama, S., Markus, H. R., Matsumoto, H., and Norasakkunit, V. (1997). Individual and collective processes in the construction of the self: Self-enhancement in the United States and self-criticism in Japan. *Journal of Personality and Social Psychology*, 72 (6), 1245–67.

Rohner, R. P. (1984). Toward a conception of culture for cross-cultural psychology. *Journal of Cross-Cultural Psychology*, 15 (2), 111–38.

Segall, M. H. (1983). On the search for the independent variable in cross-cultural psychology. In S. H. Irvine and J. W. Berry (eds.), *Human Assessment and Cultural Factors*. New York: Plenum Press, pp. 127–37.

culture and social identity

Andrew Lindridge

Hoare (1991) states that an individual exists within a society that anchors and sponsors identity, allowing the individual to engage with his/her cultural values. Douglas and Isherwood (1979) add that the self becomes a product of CULTURE, enabling "a person to act, live and function naturally and adaptively to the respective cultural context" (Kitayama et al., 1997: 1246). This interaction between culture and self-identity provides the individual with a means of self-identification with a group, for example, being a Mexican American.

How individuals' sense of identity is construed within collectivist and individualistic cultures/societies is dependent upon their sense of "self." Reber (1985: 676) describes the term "self" as an "inner agent or force with controlling and directing functions over motives, fears, needs, etc." Greenwald and Breckler (1984) and Greenwald and Pratkanis (1984) describe the individual's sense of self as consisting of three motivational facets: the collective, private, and public self.

The collective self is defined as a need "to gain a favorable evaluation from a reference group by fulfilling one's role in a reference group and achieving the group's goals" (Yamaguchi, Kuhlman, and Sugimori, 1995: 659). These groups are typically ones with which the individual has a strong affiliation and ultimately will help to define his/her identity (Wong and Ahuvia, 1995). Such behavior is typical of collectivist values where the individual's identity is construed through the expectations of significant others and social relationships, for example, the family (Ames, Dissanayake, and Kasulis, 1994; Kitayama et al., 1997). Individuals will then be motivated in their social relationships to follow those norms that reinforce and perpetuate a positive image of their family. The collective self relates to behaviors that are typical of collectivist cultures; for example, Mehta and Belk (1991) infer the collective self as being evident amongst Indians in Mumbai, India, where possessions were shown to visitors to demonstrate the family's success. Consumers with a collective self would then be motivated to purchase those publicly identifiable products that are synonymous with materialism and that represent an individual's family success.

Yamaguchi et al. (1995: 659) define the private self as the motivation "to act so that one can attain a positive self-evaluation according to internal standards." These internal standards are "based on the belief of the inherent separateness of distinct individuals," a belief inherent in many western cultures (Markus and Kitayama, 1991: 226). Johnson (1985) supports this view, noting that the western self is able to consider situations using analytic and inductive modes of thinking. Ultimately, this allows the individual to view reality as an aggregation of parts. Individuals can therefore observe events or objects as existing separately from themselves, reinforcing the belief in their unique self-identity. This behavior relates to the individualistic cultural values noted earlier. Lindridge (2004) argues that in western cultures the individual's sense of private self is a strong motivator in product purchasing, with products often purchased for the ability to satisfy inner needs and not arising from a desire to gain external approval, i.e., the collective or public self.

An individual with a public self strives "to gain a favorable evaluation from important others who are not necessary in one's reference group" (Yamaguchi et al., 1995: 659). For example, the comment that "People think I'm successful" demonstrates the public self (Triandis, 1989). Sinha (1985, cited in Triandis, 1989) argues that the public self is evident in both collectivist and individualistic societies. In collectivist societies the public self manifests itself as a need to achieve conformity with the norms of the individual's environment. This may be demonstrated in the consumption of products that signify the individual's social status and wealth; for example, Lindridge,

Dhillon, and Shah (2002) found that South Asians in Britain consumed products with the specific need to enhance their public self within their wider South Asian community. Within individualistic societies the public self is associated with individual autonomy, demonstrated through choice of dress, possessions, and speech patterns. Therefore, individuals may consume those products which enhance their sense of individuality. Sinha's distinction of differing public selves, based upon society's cultural values, may however be too simplistic as it infers that individuals in individualistic cultures do not conform to the norms of their environment. Individualistic individuals would therefore not be expected to seek external approval in achieving a sense of self-identity. This may be unrealistic, as demonstrations of individuality through choice of dress and so forth may still be motivated by a need for external recognition.

See also *acculturation; culture and behavior; culture and societal behavior*

Bibliography

Ames, P. T., Dissanayake, W., and Kasulis, T. P. (1994). *Self as a Person in Asian Theory and Practice.* Albany: State University of New York Press.

Douglas, M. and Isherwood, B. (1979). *The World of Goods: Toward an Anthropology of Consumption.* New York: Norton.

Greenwald, A. G. and Breckler, S. J. (1984). To whom is the self presented? In *The Self and Social Life.* New York: McGraw-Hill, pp. 126–45.

Greenwald, A. G. and Pratkanis, A. R. (1984). The self. In *The Handbook of Social Cognition,* vol. 3. Hillside, NJ: Lawrence Erlbaum, pp. 129–78.

Hoare, C. H. (1991). Psychological identity development and cultural others. *Journal of Counseling and Development,* 70 (September/October), pp. 45–53.

Johnson, F. (1985). Western concept of self. In *Culture and Self: Asian and Western Perspectives.* London: Tavistock, pp. 91–137.

Kitayama, S., Markus, H. R., Matsumoto, H., and Norasakkunit, V. (1997). Individual and collective processes in the construction of the self: Self-enhancement in the United States and self-criticism in Japan. *Journal of Personality and Social Psychology,* 72 (6), 1245–67.

Lindridge, A. M. (2004). Culture's manifestation in brown-good purchases: A cross-cultural comparison. *International Marketing Review Journal.*

Lindridge, A. M., Dhillon, K., and Shah, M. (2002). The role of products in perpetuating cultural marginality:

The case of Punjabi Sikhs in Britain. Paper presented at the AMS Multicultural Marketing Conference, Valencia, Spain.

Markus, H. R. and Kitayama, S. (1991). Culture and the self: Implications for cognition, emotion and motivation. *Psychological Review*, 98 (2), 224–53.

Mehta, R. and Belk, R. W. (1991). Artefacts, identity and transition: Favorite possessions of Indians and Indian immigrants to the United States. *Journal of Consumer Research*, 17 (March), 398–411.

Reber, A. S. (1985). *The Penguin Dictionary of Psychology*. London: Penguin.

Triandis, H. C. (1989). The self and social behavior in differing cultural contexts. *Psychological Review*, 96 (3), 506–20.

Wong, N. and Ahuvia, A. (1995). *Self-Concepts and Materialism: A Cross-Cultural Approach*. Winter Educators Conference, Chicago: American Marketing Association, pp. 112–19.

Yamaguchi, S., Kuhlman, D. M., and Sugimori, S. (1995). Personality correlates of allocentric tendencies in individualist and collectivist cultures. *Journal of Cross-Cultural Psychology*, 26, 6 (November), 658–72.

culture and societal behavior

Andrew Lindridge

Hofstede's (1980) research on cultural values in 53 countries applied a construct entitled "collectivism" and "individualism." Yamaguchi, Kuhlman, and Sugimori (1995: 744) describe these terms as "the degree by which a culture encourages, fosters and facilitates the needs, wishes, desires and values of an autonomous and unique self over those of a group." These two generic terms provide a classification of a country's CULTURE AND BEHAVIOR, which is relevant to MARKETING RESEARCH.

Collectivist cultures/societies emphasize the need for a collective identity derived from connectedness, mutual deference or compromise, and social interdependence (Hofstede, 1980; Triandis, 1989; Tafarodi and Swann, 1996). Individuals in these societies subordinate their own needs to suit the perceived wishes of those in their social milieu, i.e., in-group (Tafarodi and Swann, 1996). Individual subordination is then accepted in return for affiliation to the majority group (Triandis et al., 1988). Triandis (1990: 36) describes the consequences of individual subordination as "homogeneity of affect, if group

members are sad, one is sad. Pride is then taken in the group's successes and achievements rather than any one individual's contribution."

Individualistic societies can be categorized as either expressive or utilitarian. Expressive individualism emphasizes individual assertiveness, autonomy, creativity, emotional independence, and initiative. Furthermore, the individual has a right to behavior regulated by his/her own individual attitudes, primacy of personal goals over in-group goals, and privacy (Triandis et al., 1988; Triandis, 1989; Tafarodi and Swann, 1996). Markus and Kitayama (1991) argue that the individual is encouraged to view others in terms of autonomy (independent of specific others) and abstract dispositions (internal attributes that are invariant over time and context). Any attempt at conformity is shunned as a sign of weakness (Tafarodi and Swann, 1996).

Utilitarian individualism stresses "personal interest, material success, personal responsibility, accomplishment, property, work, earning and saving money" (Halman, 1996: 198). This is utilitarian because it "sees life as an effort by individuals to maximize their self-interest. ... Utilitarian individualism views societies as arising from a construct that individuals enter into only in order to advance their self-interest" (Bellah et al., 1986: 336).

Societal behaviors have been identified as being either collectivist or individualistic. This generic classification of societal behavior does not, however, identify individuals' roles within these societies. This is important as individuals are vassals of their respective cultures who will identify with that culture and behave accordingly. The individual's role and sense of identity within a culturally determined society and its subsequent effects is discussed in CULTURE AND SOCIAL IDENTITY.

See also *acculturation; culture; international marketing*

Bibliography

Bellah, R. N., Marsden, R., Sullivan, W. M., Swidler, A., and Tipton, S. M. (1986). *Habits of the Heart*. New York: Perennial Library.

Halman, L. (1996). Individualism in individualized society: Results from the European values surveys.

International Journal of Comparative Sociology, **37** (3/4), 195–214.

Hofstede, G. (1980). Motivation, leadership and organization: Do American theories apply abroad? *Organizational Dynamics*, **9** (Summer), 42–63.

Markus, H. R. and Kitayama, S. (1991). Culture and the self: Implications for cognition, emotion and motivation. *Psychological Review*, **98** (2), 224–53.

Tafarodi, R. W. and Swann, W. B., Jr. (1996). Individualism–collectivism and global self-esteem. *Journal of Cross-Cultural Psychology*, **27**, 6 (November), 651–72.

Triandis, H. C. (1989). The self and social behavior in differing cultural contexts. *Psychological Review*, **96** (3), 506–20.

Triandis, H. C. (1990). Cross-cultural studies of individualism–collectivism. *Nebraska Symposium on Motivation*, **35**, 33–41. Lincoln: University of Nebraska Press.

Triandis, H. C., Bontempo, R., Villareal, M. J., Asai, M., and Lucca, N. (1988). Individualism and collectivism: Cross-cultural perspectives on self in-group relationships. *Journal of Personality and Social Psychology*, **54** (2), 323–38.

Yamaguchi, S., Kuhlman, D. M., and Sugimori, S. (1995). Personality correlates of allocentric tendencies in individualist and collectivist cultures. *Journal of Cross-Cultural Psychology*, **26**, 6 (November), 658–72.

customer expectations

Mark P. Healey

Customer expectations are the future-oriented beliefs about a PRODUCT or act of consumption. They are brought to mind when a customer thinks about an object such as a BRAND, often in readiness for further contact with it. Conceived functionally, expectations are anticipations or predictions of the consequences of an impending action such as a product purchase or brand choice. In this sense, almost all acts of consumption are based on expectations that a product will meet certain needs or wants (*see* CONSUMER NEEDS AND MOTIVES). Consumers buy mobile telephones because they expect them to permit remote contact with friends, and purchase specific brands anticipating that these will possess the desirable attributes advertised, for example. Expectations are often based on previous experience, situational clues, or other external information.

Since expectations are used by consumers to anticipate the future from existing knowledge, they are often assumed to have certain defining characteristics. Firstly, expectancies have subjective probability; they are beliefs held with varying degrees of certainty of realization, ranging from possible to almost certain. Whilst the possible outcomes of a purchase are often known, the probability that they will occur is not. A customer will know that an airline flight might be delayed, for example, but anticipate this as unlikely. When forced to endure this with regularity, he/she may come to expect it with greater probability. Moreover, the consequences of a purchase may be unknowable in advance, such as a new product developing a fault the consumer did not know was possible (Oliver, 1997). The unknowable outcomes of purchase or patronage may be represented in customer expectations by apprehensions and anxiety (Oliver, 1997).

Secondly, where expectations function to guide behavior, they require evaluative meaning. That is, in anticipation of purchase, a product or service must be evaluated as potentially good or bad in terms of its likely benefit for the individual.

Thirdly, although consumers' salient expectations may often be consciously articulated, many expectations are held and processed implicitly or unconsciously (Olson, Roese, and Zanna, 1996). Purchasers of a CD player may choose a particular model based on the anticipation that it will provide superior sound quality, but they may also implicitly expect it to possess track search and programming facilities, for example, although this may not be explicitly expressed at the time of purchase. Oliver and Winer (1987) further argue that expectations may be active or passive, where passive expectations are not processed until disconfirmed.

Customers' expectations are drawn from a variety of sources. Perhaps chief amongst these is personal experience. Expectations may be generated based on direct experience with a focal product or brand, or may be generated from relevant experience with other product categories. The service one expects from healthcare providers may be influenced by the service one receives from one's bank, for example, or customers' experiences online may affect their expectations for offline transactions. Consumers may base expectancies on norms derived from the typical performance of a specific brand or product, or on norms based on the average performance of a group of brands or products within a product category (Cadotte, Woodruff, and Jenkins, 1987). Customers' expectations can further be influenced by ADVERTISING, PRICING and environmental cues, word-of-mouth (*see* WORD-OF-MOUTH COMMUNICATIONS), situational factors, personal values, needs, and desires, and internal factors such as availability in memory.

In MARKETING RESEARCH, expectation is a construct key to understanding both pre- and post-consumption phenomena. Expectancy value theory, for example, states that consumers' pre-purchase ATTITUDES are a function of their beliefs about product attributes and the evaluation of those beliefs (Fishbein and Ajzen, 1975). Perception of marketplace stimuli may also be influenced by expectancies. Consumers are known to afford significant attention to surprising advertisements that conflict with expectations, as well as to brands and other items that are expectancy consistent. Moreover, expectations can guide interpretations in a confirming direction, such that customers may often see what they expect to see. Brand-loyal customers may interpret ambiguous product or service attributes in a more favorable manner than those without firm expectations (*see* BRAND LOYALTY).

In satisfaction research expectancies are often viewed as pre-consumption predictions or anticipations of product performance. Customers are satisfied when a product meets their expectations. However, customer expectations may exist at different levels, encapsulating their hopes, desires, and fears, as well as their predictions. Customers may hold expectations of the desired, adequate, and predicted levels of service offered by an organization (Zeithaml, Berry, and Parasuraman, 1993), for example. Generic expectations of performance may encompass minimum and ideal performance levels, with multiple expectations being held simultaneously. A zone of tolerance represents a range of expectancy values (e.g., between adequate and desired) which, if product or service performance occurs within, customers will accept; if it occurs without, however, customers will respond negatively. The importance of expect-

ancies to consumer reactions, such as their perceptions of quality, has led to managerial concern with managing expectations. Some confusion exists over whether organizations should "under-promise and over-deliver" to optimize responses by engendering and then exceeding lowered expectations, as well as over the precise nature and role of expectations in determining consumers' evaluations (Parasuraman, Zeithaml, and Berry, 1994).

See also *customer satisfaction*

Bibliography

Cadotte, E. R., Woodruff, R. B., and Jenkins, R. L. (1987). Expectations and norms in models of consumer satisfaction. *Journal of Marketing Research*, 24, 305–14.
Fishbein, M. and Ajzen, I. (1975). *Belief, Attitude, Intention and Behavior: An Introduction to Theory and Research*. Reading, MA: Addison-Wesley.
Kardes, F. (2002). *Consumer Behavior and Managerial Decision-making*, 2nd edn. Upper Saddle River, NJ: Prentice-Hall, chs. 2, 7.
Oliver, R. L. (1980). A cognitive model of the antecedents and consequences of satisfaction decisions. *Journal of Marketing Research*, 17 (November), 460–9.
Oliver, R. L. (1997). *Satisfaction: A Behavioral Perspective on the Consumer*, international edn. New York: McGraw-Hill, ch. 3.
Oliver, R. L. and Winer, R. S. (1987). A framework for the formation and structure of consumer expectations: Review and propositions. *Journal of Economic Psychology*, 8, 469–99.
Olson, J. M., Roese, N. J., and Zanna, M. P. (1996). Expectancies. In E. T. Higgins and A. W. Kruglanski (eds.), *Social Psychology: Handbook of Basic Principles*. New York: Guilford Press, pp. 211–38.
Parasuraman, A., Zeithaml, V. A., and Berry, L. L. (1994). Reassessment of expectations as a comparison standard in measuring service quality: Implications for further research. *Journal of Marketing*, 58, 111–24.
Zeithaml, V. A., Berry, L. L., and Parasuraman, A. (1993). The nature and determinants of customer expectations of service. *Journal of the Academy of Marketing Science*, 21 (1), 1–12.

customer portfolios

Judy Zolkiewski

The application of portfolio theory (*see* PORTFOLIO ANALYSIS) to customer and/or supplier relationship analysis has essentially been "borrowed" from traditional corporate and marketing strategy theory (*see* CORPORATE STRATEGY; MARKETING STRATEGY): the analysis of strengths, weaknesses, opportunities, and threats (*see* SWOT ANALYSIS), BCG (*see* BCG MATRIX), and so on. Its application to customer/supplier analysis is still problematic, particularly in relation to the appropriate dimensions of analysis. To date, the development of customer and supplier portfolio planning has largely been related to business-to-business markets (*see* BUSINESS-TO-BUSINESS MARKETING). This is probably due to the relative power of a small number of players in such markets; it is common for a firm serving business markets to be highly dependent on a small number of customers and, therefore, the addition or loss of a major customer can have dramatic effects on the company's turnover, profitability, and indeed its viability. Hence the need to implement customer portfolio analysis.

During the last 15 years a number of one-step, two-step, and three-dimensional portfolio models have been specifically developed to address this situation. They have taken the relationship as the unit of analysis and can be assumed to be based upon an understanding that long-term interactive relationships are often the norm in this type of market structure. These models include those proposed by Cunningham and Homse (1982), Fiocca (1982), Campbell and Cunningham (1983), Yorke (1984), Shapiro et al. (1987), Krapfel, Salmond, and Spekman (1991), Rangan, Moriarty, and Swartz (1992), Yorke and Droussiotis (1994), Turnbull and Zolkiewski (1997), and Olsen and Ellram (1997). See figure 1 for an example of such a model.

The models have all used a variety of axes, the majority of which have taken into account customer profitability. The issues of customer profitability, relationship value, and the mix of objective and subjective values on the axes used, exacerbated by the difficulty in accurately collecting some of the more insightful data, mean that customer/supplier portfolios have not been as widely adopted as could be expected. However, the growing power of databases (*see* DATABASE) and the introduction of activity-based costing, along with an emphasis on CUS-

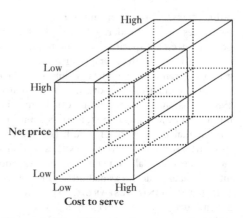

Figure 1 Three-dimensional customer classification matrix (Turnbull and Zolkiewski, 1997: 320)

TOMER RELATIONSHIP MANAGEMENT, seem to be leading to increased interest in their use.

Bibliography

Campbell, N. C. G. and Cunningham, M. T. (1983). Customer analysis for strategy development in industrial markets. *Strategic Management Journal*, 4, 369–80.

Cunningham, M. T. and Homse, E. (1982). An interaction approach to marketing strategy. In Håkan Håkansson (ed.), *International Marketing and Purchasing of Industrial Goods*. New York: John Wiley.

Fiocca, R. (1982). Account portfolio analysis for strategy development. *Industrial Marketing Management*, 11, 53–62.

Krapfel, R. E., Jr., Salmond, D., and Spekman, R. (1991). A strategic approach to managing buyer–seller relationships. *European Journal of Marketing*, 25 (9), 22–37.

Olsen, R. F. and Ellram, L. M. (1997). A portfolio approach to supplier relationships. *Industrial Marketing Management*, 26, 101–13.

Rangan, K. V., Moriarty, R. T., and Swartz, G. S. (1992). Segmenting customers in mature industrial markets. *Journal of Marketing*, 56 (October), 72–82.

Salle, R., Cova, B., and Pardo, C. (2000). Portfolios of supplier–customer relationships. In Arch Woodside (ed.), *Advances in Business Marketing and Purchasing*, vol. 9. Greenwich, CT: JAI Press.

Shapiro, B. P., Rangan, V. K., Moriarty, R. T., and Ross, E. B. (1987). Manage customers for profits (not just sales). *Harvard Business Review*, September/October, 101–8.

Turnbull, P. W. and Zolkiewski, J. M. (1997). Profitability in customer portfolio planning. In David Ford (ed.), *Understanding Business Markets*, 2nd edn. London: Dryden Press.

Yorke, D. A. (1984). An interaction approach to the management of a portfolio of customer opportunities. In Peter Turnbull and Stanley J. Paliwoda (eds.), *Proceedings of Research Developments in International Marketing*, September. Manchester: UMIST.

Yorke, D. A. and Droussiotis, G. (1994). The use of customer portfolio theory: An empirical survey. *Journal of Business and Industrial Marketing*, 9 (3), 6–18.

Zolkiewski, J. and Turnbull, P. W. (2002a). Do relationship portfolios and networks provide the key to successful relationship management? *Journal of Business and Industrial Marketing*, 17 (7), 575–97.

Zolkiewski, J. and Turnbull, P. W. (2002b). Relationship portfolios: Past, present and future. In David Ford (ed.), *Understanding Business Marketing and Purchasing*, 3rd edn. London: Thomson Learning.

customer relationship management

Kalipso Karantinou

According to one of the many definitions put forward for CRM, variously understood as customer relationship marketing and/or customer relationship management (O'Malley and Tynan, 2003), it comprises the organization, processes, and systems through which an organization manages its relationships with its customers (McDonald and Christopher, 2003). The reason there is no exact and widely accepted definition for CRM is because it is still in the formative stages of development and has yet to be given a universally agreed meaning. "As with many management fashions, relationship marketing, customer relationship marketing and relationship management are terms that many managers or marketers use but define in different ways" (Stone, Woodcock, and Macthynger, 2000: 1). Furthermore, as with relationship marketing, the confusion over the definition of the term also reflects the complexity of the concept.

CRM refers to the management of the lifetime relationship with the customer and is usually associated with the use of information technology (IT) in managing these relationships (Ryals, 2000). Although philosophically in line with RELATIONSHIP MARKETING, the focus in CRM is on technology, particularly the technology which attempts to manage all customer contact points and provide a single picture of the customer (O'Malley and Tynan, 2003) through combining the IT systems relating to the customer interface (McDonald and Christopher, 2003). The aim is to facilitate the efforts to build customer retention and profitability. Data warehouses, big databases that contain information about customers (*see* DATABASE), are particularly useful back-office tools for CRM (Ryals, 2000). The most usual interpretation of CRM is essentially as a type of data mining, used to identify profitable customers and classify customer segments (*see* MARKET SEGMENTATION) for differential targeting (Evans, 2003). Adopting a CRM approach to managing customer relationships promises to reduce unpredictable customer behavior to data that can be analyzed, plotted, planned, and categorized (McDonald and Christopher, 2003).

However, it must ultimately be remembered that the objective is to build relationships, not databases (O'Malley and Tynan, 2003); there is a danger that managers may allow the scope of their CRM software to dictate the scope of their CRM strategy (McDonald and Christopher, 2003). Rather than focusing solely on data mining, real relationship marketing should be characterized by more affective factors (Evans, 2003) and must be combined with a deep understanding of the market and the needs of customers within market segments (McDonald and Christopher, 2003). Along the same lines, Wilson, Daniel, and McDonald (2002) propose that, given the strategic implications of CRM, it is not sufficient to involve the technology manager alone. Rather, all departments should participate in the development of CRM systems, which have to be designed from a user point of view if they are to be acceptable by all relevant parties within the organization.

Stone et al. (2000) pinpoint four requirements necessary for CRM initiation and success: good operations and distribution; efficient inquiry/sales/complaint-handling processes and measurement systems; appropriate information technology systems, enabling company-wide distribution and availability of information on customers; and motivated, well-trained personnel. Human resource issues are central to the success of CRM (Harris and Ogbonna, 2000). Successful implementation of CRM relies heavily on internal markets (*see* INTERNAL MARKETING), both the cross-functional working between departments and the willingness of individual employees to work with new technologies (Ryals, 2000). These are the people who have to be "won over" if a CRM strategy is to be implemented and be successful. Nevertheless, employees in many organizations still tend not to be encouraged toward, or rewarded based upon, collecting data on customers or forming emotional bonds.

Ultimately, CRM is about achieving and sustaining a COMPETITIVE ADVANTAGE. However, whether CRM on its own can achieve this goal is questionable; customer relationship management needs to be based on three aspects in order to work: strategy, marketing, and IT (McDonald and Christopher, 2003).

Bibliography

Evans, M. (2003). Market segmentation. In M. J. Baker (ed.), *The Marketing Book*, 5th edn. London: Butterworth-Heinemann, pp. 246–83.

Harris, L. C. and Ogbonna, E. (2000). The responses of frontline employees to market-orientated culture change. *European Journal of Marketing*, 34 (3/4), 318–40.

McDonald, M. and Christopher, M. (2003). *Marketing: A Complete Guide*. Basingstoke: Palgrave Macmillan, ch. 13.

O'Malley, L. and Tynan, C. (2003). Relationship marketing. In M. J. Baker (ed.), *The Marketing Book*, 5th edn. London: Butterworth-Heinemann, pp. 32–52.

Ryals, L. (2000). Organizing for relationship marketing. In Cranfield School of Management, *Marketing Management: A Relationship Marketing Approach*. London: Macmillan, pp. 249–63.

Stone, M., Woodcock, N., and Macthynger, L. (2000). *Customer Relationship Marketing*. London: Kogan Page.

Wilson, H., Daniel, E., and McDonald, M. (2002). Factors for success in customer relationship management systems. *Journal of Marketing Management*, 18, 193–219.

customer satisfaction

Mark P. Healey

Customer satisfaction refers to the evaluations, judgments, and feelings that result from customers' interactions with objects of consumption, including brands (*see* BRAND), products (*see* PRODUCT), and services, and the organizations that produce them. It is an intrapersonal response to the various physiological, psychological, functional, and symbolic benefits that consumption confers upon an individual, group of individuals, or buying unit.

Satisfaction is generally held to comprise a post-consumption evaluation of a product or service that results in feelings of fulfillment. Customers' needs and desires are therefore central to satisfaction formation, since a customer seeks to fulfill these through some act of consumption. Satisfaction is, then, the psychological response to judgments of met needs, desires, expectations, and goals. Feelings of pleasurable contentment or gratification thus comprise this response. More specifically, satisfaction judgments entail the comparative evaluation of consumption stimuli and their performance referents, including product attributes and usage consequences. Customers compare the products and services they consume to various external and internal standards when evaluating them in terms of their benefit for the individual. Satisfaction is a key determinant of customers' subsequent behavior, since they will often repurchase positively evaluated products, and continue to patronize organizations whose services engender pleasurable feelings. It can thus be said to have three progressive facets: cognitive evaluation, affective reaction, and conative implication, or consequence for subsequent behavior (*see* AFFECTIVE STAGE; COGNITIVE STAGE; CONATIVE STAGE).

As a construct of interest to marketers and theoreticians, satisfaction provides an empirical and conceptual link between pre-purchase decision-making, the act of consuming, and the outcomes of consumption, including repurchase behavior and loyalty. Satisfaction completes the loop, uniting the three phases of consumption. It is generally held to occur after a choice, purchase, or experience, and is therefore often considered solely as a post-consumption reaction. However, since it is derived from evaluations that may take place at various stages of consumption, satisfaction may be determined at any time a salient evaluation takes place: prior to, during, or at any time after consumption. A distinction is often made between satisfaction with a specific product or transaction, and overall satisfaction, with a brand or an organization's total service, for example.

DEVELOPMENT OF INTEREST IN CUSTOMER
SATISFACTION

The modern origins of the satisfaction concept
can usefully be traced to the utilitarianism of
Jeremy Bentham. Bentham argued that human
behavior was governed by judgments of the potential of actions to produce pain or pleasure,
and distinguished the pleasures of acquisition
and possession of material wealth as one form
of simple pleasure. Similarly, some early
writings devoted to understanding consumer
behavior viewed the anticipated outcomes of
consumption as its drivers. Yet the genesis of
the contemporary notion of customer satisfaction, connoting the commercial focus on achieving corporate goals by insuring pleasurable
customer reactions and thus loyalty, perhaps
owes most to the "rediscovery" of the importance of the consumer in the mid-twentieth century. This apparent innovation in economic
thinking reasoned that a customer's satisfaction
with an organization's products would develop
into a favorable attitude toward the product,
brand, or organization, and thus insure the con-
tinuance of demand for its products.

The purported reconceptualization of the
MARKETING CONCEPT is evinced in the corpus
of the 1950s North American MARKETING
school expounding the emergence of customer
orientation as the distinguishing feature of the
marketing lens. The emphasis placed on the importance of customer satisfaction to organizational success by influential writers of this
period is typified by Drucker's (1961) view of
business as being "directed toward the satisfaction of a customer want" (p. vi). From this re-
emerged customer satisfaction as a direct concern
for marketers.

The notion of satisfying customers has continued to assume a privileged role in marketing
thought, reflected by its inclusion in several key
conceptual definitions of marketing. Kotler and
Levy (1969) suggested that marketing is a pervasive societal activity concerned with customer
satisfaction engineering. Moreover, the official
definitions of marketing constructed by the
Chartered Institute of Marketing and the American Marketing Association both embrace the
notion of marketing as a process designed to
satisfy customer requirements and objectives.

The contemporary emphasis on RELATION-
SHIP MARKETING further emphasizes the importance of customer satisfaction to firms, since
satisfaction is integral to relational success in
both consumer and organizational markets.

A similar focus can today be found in business
practice, where the rhetoric of both public and
private sector organizations often identifies satisfaction as a key concern. Motorola promulgates
the satisfaction of its customers as its very raison
d'être, whilst the MISSION STATEMENT of the
BBC stresses that the corporation's primary goal
is to satisfy all of its audiences. Perhaps more
indicative of the real import of satisfaction to
organizations is the explicit interest many companies demonstrate in the reactions of their customers. Organizations as diverse as the National
Health Service (NHS), British Airways, and
Ford regularly assess the success of their output
based on research showing levels of customer
satisfaction, whilst the Asda/Wal-Mart brand
guarantee promises buyers "complete satisfaction or your money back." In 2001 the Sony
Corporation established a customer satisfaction
charter, seeking to make satisfaction the cornerstone of its corporate culture. Its customer
satisfaction center includes a human interface
laboratory aimed at increasing satisfaction
through consumer-focused product DESIGN.
The degree to which organizations are directly
concerned with customer satisfaction varies
from tokenism to corporate permeation.

In addition to its importance to individual
companies, satisfaction is considered important
at the macroeconomic and societal levels as
"critical to improving a nation's economic performance, global competitiveness, and quality
of life" (Anderson and Fornell, 1994: 242).
Due to its commercial importance, marketers
in both academia and industry have been concerned with the nature and function of satisfaction's relationship with subsequent customer
activities.

CONSEQUENCES OF CUSTOMER
SATISFACTION

Perhaps the most elementary premise of the
marketing field is that satisfied customers will
make repeat purchases of a product, service, or
brand which satisfies them. Through such behavioral loyalty organizations will benefit in

terms of improved customer retention and positive word-of-mouth (see WORD-OF-MOUTH COMMUNICATIONS), enhanced MARKET SHARE, and increased revenue and profits (see Reichheld, 1996; Heskett, Sasser, and Schlesinger, 1997). These assumptions drive commercial interest in customer satisfaction; few organizations are interested in satisfaction per se, but rather in its behavioral consequences.

Early BUYER BEHAVIOR MODELS recognized that satisfaction influences post-purchase attitude (see ATTITUDES) and behavioral intentions to repurchase. The dominant cognitive perspective views as integral to satisfaction formation the evaluation of the product, service, or brand consumed (see Oliver, 1980). In what is often modeled as a four-stage linear causal chain (satisfaction–attitude–intention–behavior), the satisfaction evaluation is thought to influence the consumer's attitude toward the object evaluated (e.g., the product, service, or brand) or toward the act of buying or consuming that object. Resulting product attitudes, customers' memorized evaluations or likes and dislikes, then also play an important role in their future choices (see Lynch, Marmorstein, and Weigold, 1988). Post-purchase attitudes in turn impact upon behavioral intentions toward the object or act, although satisfaction can also influence intentions to repurchase directly. Finally, behavioral intentions are considered a major determinant of product approach or avoidance, although this relationship is mediated considerably by internal and situational factors such as social pressures.

Due to the role of such mediating variables, the correlation between satisfaction and behavioral intentions is consistently found stronger than the link between satisfaction and actual behaviors such as repurchasing and repatronage, complaining, or switching. Even where they are highly correlated when measured simultaneously, the impact of satisfaction on repurchase intentions can decay to insignificance after as little as two weeks (Mazursky and Geva, 1989). Furthermore, individual differences mediate the relationship, since customers are thought to hold different satisfaction thresholds for repurchase behavior. Consumers with low thresholds are more likely to make repurchases than those with high thresholds at the same level of satisfaction (Mittal and Kamakura, 2001).

The indirect relationship between customer satisfaction and future consuming behaviors has received much, if mixed, empirical support at micro and macro levels (see Rust and Zahoric, 1993; Szymanski and Henard, 2001). It is noteworthy, however, that the influence of post-consumption satisfaction on future behaviors is often obfuscated by more potent and direct determinants of consumer choice that become salient at the time of decision-making, including the desirability of competitive alternatives, switching costs, and situational forces. As a result, self-professed satisfied customers are found to engage in switching behavior and dissatisfied customers may exhibit considerable "loyalty" (Keaveney, 1995).

Customer loyalty is achieved in part through continued satisfaction. Loyalty is difficult to achieve, particularly in certain product categories, but is strong and beneficial once developed (see Oliver, 1999). Satisfaction also directly influences company profits by improving customer retention (see Anderson, Fornell, and Lehmann, 1994). Moreover, satisfied customers are more likely to increase their consumption rates, and will be more resistant to price changes and the advances of competitors.

Satisfaction is also influential in terms of more immediate post-consumption behaviors such as complaining. Complaining and word-of-mouth responses are most prevalent where dissatisfaction results from perceived inequity, and when customers directly attribute poor performance to the organization (see Oliver, 1997). Information provided by customer complaints can be used to diagnose and rectify performance problems, leading to improvements in satisfaction levels. In the event of a dissatisfying experience, the catharsis of complaining can actually improve a customer's satisfaction level, as can company recovery efforts.

CAUSES AND MODELS OF CUSTOMER SATISFACTION

Due to its significance, understanding, predicting, and modeling the causes of satisfaction has become an important research goal (for a review, see Yi, 1990). The principle at the core of most models is that satisfaction is the result of a comparative evaluation. That is, customers judge the positivity or negativity of a product or service, including its attributes or usage outcomes, in relation to an exogenous reference point, such as their expectations, other products, or some normative or ideal benchmark. The feelings and emotions that result from such evaluations constitute satisfaction's phenomenal basis and can be distinguished from the psychological evaluation process itself.

Perhaps the most prominent model of consumer satisfaction is the expectancy disconfirmation model (see Oliver, 1980, 1997). This model views satisfaction formation as a process in which consumers "form preconsumption expectancies, observe product (attribute) performance, compare performance with expectations, form disconfirmation perceptions, combine these perceptions with expectation levels, and form satisfaction judgments" (Oliver, 1993: 418). In simple form, the disconfirmation model predicts that performance below customers' expectancy levels results in negative disconfirmation and thus dissatisfaction. Performance consistent with expectations produces expectancy confirmation and moderate satisfaction, and better than expected performance generates positive disconfirmation and high satisfaction.

According to disconfirmation theory, expectations are predictions of attribute or product performance. Satisfaction judgments may be assimilated toward customers' prior expectations, or be contrasted with them (known as assimilation and contrast effects). Furthermore, a distinction is typically made between objective (calculated) and subjective (inferred) disconfirmation. Subjective disconfirmation judgments exert greater influence on satisfaction, since objective, quantifiable performance and expectancy referents are not always available to, or calculated by, consumers. The expectancy disconfirmation framework has been subjected to many modifications and criticisms (see Iacobucci, Grayson, and Ostrom, 1994).

According to the desires congruency model of satisfaction, the performance of products and services is evaluated based on the extent to which they fulfill existing desires (Spreng, MacKenzie, and Olshavsky, 1996). Desires exist at higher and lower levels connected in a means–end chain, such that higher-level desires (e.g., to protect oneself from harm) create lower-level desires (e.g., to buy products which are safe)

and ultimately attribute-level desires (e.g., antilock brakes installed in a car). In this view, when making satisfaction judgments customers make subjective comparisons between their performance perceptions and personal desires. The resulting judgment of desires congruency determines satisfaction with specific product attributes, which in turn influences overall satisfaction. Performance which closely matches consumers' desires will produce feelings of satisfaction, whereas unmet desires may result in dissatisfaction and all it entails.

A related conception postulates that satisfaction results from judgments of need gratification. The extent to which service or product performance meets customers' explicit needs (e.g., for a package to be delivered before a deadline) can exert greater influence on satisfaction than expectancy disconfirmation (Wirtz and Mattila, 2001). However, needs, desires, wants, and values are terms used interchangeably in the literature, and the distinction between their operation as satisfaction influencers is sometimes unclear.

Models based on equity theory assert that satisfaction can be influenced by customers' perceptions of justice, or judgments of the fairness of an exchange (Oliver and Desarbo, 1988). In deciding if they have received what they deserve, consumers may make comparisons of the relationship between their own inputs (e.g., price paid) and outputs (e.g., benefits gained) to a transaction, and the relationship between the inputs and outputs of other parties to the transaction (Oliver and Swan, 1989). Parties to which consumers may compare include the producing company, salespersons, and other customers. Satisfaction results where the customer perceives his/her input to output ratio to be at least proportionate to that of the comparative operator, or to fairness norms. Unfavorable comparisons result where an individual judges that other customers have received better treatment or prices from the same provider (interpersonal equity), or that a vendor has not provided what the customer considers is deserved or has profited unduly from the customer (merchant equity). Such invidious comparisons are likely to result in perceptions of inequity and therefore customer dissatisfaction.

The preceding models show that the standards to which consumers compare a product or service are multifarious, and will influence satisfaction indirectly through comparative evaluation. Many further models are variants on this theme. Research shows that satisfaction results where customers compare their perceptions of how a product has performed to experience-based norms, such as the typical performance of a category (Cadotte, Woodruff, and Jenkins, 1987), to ideal standards (Tse and Wilton, 1988), to the performance of forgone alternatives (Dröge, Halstead, and MacKoy, 1997), to conjectures of how performance might have been different (counterfactual standards: Tsiros and Mittal, 2000), and to brands and products from other categories (Gardial et al., 1994). Furthermore, several studies have shown that multiple comparison standards can simultaneously influence consumers' post-consumption evaluations (e.g., Boulding et al., 1993).

Whilst marketers may exercise little control over what a customer compares their goods or services to, they can shape the other main determinant of consumer satisfaction, the performance of a product. Although the importance of different performance referents to satisfaction judgments does vary between products and contexts, several dimensions of performance have been found to be influential across contexts. In service industries, the process or functional elements of performance (the way service is delivered), in addition to service outcomes, have been found to be key determinants of satisfaction, including waiting times, interpersonal dimensions such as the behavior of contact employees, and tangible dimensions such as the pleasantness of the physical SERVICE ENVIRONMENT. The quality of a product or service also has a considerable influence on satisfaction. Taxonomies of universally important elements of product performance necessarily operate at high levels of abstraction. For example, satisfaction may be influenced by utilitarian performance (the basic or core features of a product) or by hedonic outcomes (the intangible pleasures that result from consumption). Satisfaction with individual product attributes, such as the fuel economy of a car or the taste of a restaurant meal, contributes to overall satisfaction with the product, service, or brand. Since the performance attributes that determine satisfaction vary between products and services, marketers must

often establish which particular attributes determine satisfaction in a specific context. Consumers' performance attributions will also influence their satisfaction levels; poor performance attributed to personal misuse may be less dissatisfying than poor performance that is attributed to flawed product design, for example (Folkes, 1984).

Much research assumes that satisfaction formation requires complex and effortful psychological endeavor by the consumer. Another line of research shows, however, that consumers may often rely on heuristics, or mental short cuts, when making satisfaction judgments. These include basing satisfaction on previously formed judgments (Mattila, 1998) and inferring judgments from current moods (Bickart and Schwarz, 2001). The satisfaction formation process may also be different for high- and low-INVOLVEMENT products and situations; low-involvement satisfaction judgments may be based on the most available information, for example. Moreover, it is commonly assumed that customer satisfaction and dissatisfaction are the opposing extremes of a single bipolar construct. However, several researchers have sought to establish satisfaction and dissatisfaction as distinct response states that should be modeled and measured separately. Two-factor theory holds that satisfaction and dissatisfaction have different causes, for example (see Maddox, 1981). This is potentially important for marketers seeking to avoid dissatisfaction and boost satisfaction, since strategies for achieving each may need to be different.

AFFECTIVE DIMENSIONS OF CUSTOMER SATISFACTION

Recent research has sought to elucidate the emotional dimensions of satisfaction, traditionally viewed as a cognitive-evaluative response. Different perspectives exist which explain how emotions influence satisfaction, and these can be separated into two major approaches. The first, which one might term precursive theories of affective satisfaction, views emotions as causal antecedents of (dis)satisfaction judgments. Here, negative (e.g., anger, fear) and positive (e.g., joy, contentment) emotions and moods (see AFFECT) are viewed as distinct response states which influence satisfaction by being factored into its judgment (see Westbrook and Oliver, 1991). Emotions and moods provide information that is inputted into evaluative judgments. The second perspective conceptualizes satisfaction as an actual emotional response in itself, which results from consumers' evaluations. Here, the feeling of satisfaction is equated with emotions such as pleasure, happiness, and joy.

In different conditions, consumers may experience a variety of emotions resulting from product and service interactions, including frustration, anxiety, disgust, anger, excitement, pleasure, and relief. Such distinct states may reflect more accurately customers' specific reactions than the generic term satisfaction (Bagozzi, Gopinath, and Nyer, 1999). Such specific emotions, in addition to satisfaction, may be better predictors of customers' intentions than satisfaction alone (Nyer, 1997). Recent research has therefore examined the causes and implications of specific post-consumption reactions such as regret and delight. Emotional or affective post-consumption responses have been considered particularly significant components of consumers' reactions to service exchanges, since the act of consuming a service is a socioexperiential activity that may produce multitudinous emotional reactions.

The debate over whether satisfaction is best conceived as a cognitive or emotional response has somewhat clouded the truism that customers will inevitably experience emotions and feelings as a result of their consumption experiences *and* make various appraisals of their purchases and possessions, and that the interplay between the two is complex. The evaluative and affective dimensions of satisfaction will vary in their predominance and concatenation across different situations (see Oliver, 1997: 316). Some might argue that the cognitive evaluative core of satisfaction is more important for future product choices. However, satisfaction is an adaptive response, and both emotions and evaluations serve to facilitate consumers' subsequent behaviors.

Consistent with these notions, satisfaction has recently been described as a blend of cognitions, emotions, and meanings. These emerge and develop across repeated interactions with a product in complex social environments (Fournier and Mick, 1999). Viewed as a longitudinal construct, satisfaction with a product evolves dynamically as the benefits customers gain from product performance facilitate their current life themes and social roles.

Customer satisfaction is an important marketing concept because knowledge of its functioning allows managers some direct control over the future behavior of existing and potential customers. As satisfaction research broadens, marketers are likely to gain greater insight into the conduit between post-consumption reactions and customers' subsequent behaviors.

See also *customer expectations; service quality*

Bibliography

Anderson, E. W. and Fornell, C. (1994). A customer satisfaction research prospectus. In R. T. Rust and R. L. Oliver (eds.), *Service Quality: New Directions in Theory and Practice.* Thousand Oaks, CA: Sage, pp. 241–68.

Anderson, E. W., Fornell, C., and Lehmann, D. R. (1994). Customer satisfaction, market share, and profitability: Findings from Sweden. *Journal of Marketing*, **58** (July), 53–66.

Bagozzi, R. P., Gopinath, M., and Nyer, P. U. (1999). The role of emotions in marketing. *Journal of the Academy of Marketing Science*, **27** (2), 184–206.

Bickart, B. and Schwarz, N. (2001). Service experiences and satisfaction judgments: The use of affect and beliefs in judgment formation. *Journal of Consumer Psychology*, **11** (1), 29–42.

Boulding, W., Kalra, A., Staelin, R., and Zeithaml, V. A. (1993). A dynamic process model of service quality: From expectations to behavioral intentions. *Journal of Marketing Research*, **30**, 7–27.

Cadotte, E. R., Woodruff, R. B., and Jenkins, R. L. (1987). Expectations and norms in models of consumer satisfaction. *Journal of Marketing Research*, **24**, 305–14.

Dröge, C., Halstead, D., and MacKoy, R. D. (1997). The role of competitive alternatives in the postchoice satisfaction formation process. *Journal of the Academy of Marketing Science*, **25** (1), 18–30.

Drucker, P. F. (1961). Preface. In H. Lazo and A. Corbin (eds.), *Management in Marketing.* New York: McGraw-Hill.

Folkes, V. S. (1984). Consumer reactions to product failure: An attributional approach. *Journal of Consumer Research*, **10**, 398–409.

Fournier, S. and Mick, D. G. (1999). Rediscovering satisfaction. *Journal of Marketing*, **63** (October), 5–23.

Gardial, S. F., Clemons, D. S., Woodruff, R. B., Schumann, D. W., and Burns, M. J. (1994). Comparing consumers' recall of prepurchase and postpurchase product evaluation experiences. *Journal of Consumer Research*, **20** (March), 548–60.

Heskett, J. L., Sasser, W. E., and Schlesinger, L. A. (1997). *The Service Profit Chain*. New York: Free Press.

Iacobucci, D., Grayson, K. A., and Ostrom, A. L. (1994). The calculus of service quality and customer satisfaction: Theoretical and empirical differentiation and integration. In T. A. Swartz, D. E. Bowen, and S. W. Brown (eds.), *Advances in Services Marketing and Management*, vol. 3. Greenwich, CT: JAI Press, pp. 1–67.

Keaveney, S. M. (1995). Customer switching behavior in service industries: An exploratory study. *Journal of Marketing*, **59**, 71–82.

Kotler, P. and Levy, S. J. (1969). Broadening the concept of marketing. *Journal of Marketing*, **33** (January), 10–15.

Lynch, J. G. J., Marmorstein, H., and Weigold, M. F. (1988). Choice from sets including remembered brands: Use of recalled attributes and prior overall evaluations. *Journal of Consumer Research*, **15** (September), 169–84.

Maddox, R. N. (1981). Two-factor theory and consumer satisfaction: Replication and extension. *Journal of Consumer Research*, **8**, 97–102.

Mattila, A. (1998). An examination of consumers' use of heuristic cues in making satisfaction judgments. *Psychology and Marketing*, **15** (5), 477–501.

Mazursky, D. and Geva, A. (1989). Temporal decay in satisfaction–purchase intention relationship. *Psychology and Marketing*, **6** (3), 211–27.

Mittal, V. and Kamakura, W. (2001). Satisfaction, repurchase intent, and repurchase behavior: Investigating the moderating effect of customer characteristics. *Journal of Marketing Research*, **38** (1), 131–42.

Nyer, P. U. (1997). A study of the relationships between consumption appraisals and consumption emotions. *Journal of the Academy of Marketing Science*, **25** (4), 296–304.

Oliver, R. L. (1980). A cognitive model of the antecedents and consequences of satisfaction decisions. *Journal of Marketing Research*, **17** (November), 460–9.

Oliver, R. L. (1993). Cognitive, affective, and attribute bases of the satisfaction response. *Journal of Consumer Research*, **20**, 418–30.

Oliver, R. L. (1997). *Satisfaction: A Behavioral Perspective on the Consumer*, international edn. New York: McGraw-Hill.

Oliver, R. L. (1999). Whence consumer loyalty? *Journal of Marketing*, **63**, 33–44.

Oliver, R. L. and Desarbo, W. S. (1988). Response determinants in satisfaction judgments. *Journal of Consumer Research*, **14**, 495–507.

Oliver, R. L. and Swan, J. E. (1989). Equity and disconfirmation perceptions as influences on merchant and product satisfaction. *Journal of Consumer Research*, **16** (3), 372–84.

Reichheld, F. F. (1996). *The Loyalty Effect: The Hidden Force Behind Growth, Profits, and Lasting Value*. Boston: Harvard Business School Press.

Rust, R. T. and Zahoric, A. J. (1993). Customer satisfaction, customer retention, and market share. *Journal of Retailing*, **69** (2), 193–215.

Spreng, R. A., MacKenzie, S. B., and Olshavsky, R. W. (1996). A reexamination of the determinants of consumer satisfaction. *Journal of Marketing*, **60** (July), 15–32.

Szymanski, D. M. and Henard, D. H. (2001). Customer satisfaction: A meta-analysis of the empirical evidence. *Journal of the Academy of Marketing Science*, **29** (1), 16–35.

Tse, D. K. and Wilton, P. C. (1988). Models of consumer satisfaction formation: An extension. *Journal of Marketing Research*, 204–12.

Tsiros, M. and Mittal, V. (2000). Regret: A model of its antecedents and consequences in consumer decision-making. *Journal of Consumer Research*, **26**, 401–17.

Westbrook, R. A. and Oliver, R. L. (1991). The dimensionality of consumption emotion patterns and consumer satisfaction. *Journal of Consumer Research*, **18**, 84–91.

Wirtz, J. and Mattila, A. (2001). Exploring the role of alternative perceived performance measures and needs-congruency in the consumer satisfaction process. *Journal of Consumer Psychology*, **11** (3), 181–92.

Yi, Y. (1990). A critical review of consumer satisfaction. In V. A. Zeithaml (ed.), *Review of Marketing*. Chicago: American Marketing Association, pp. 68–123.

customer service

see SERVICE QUALITY

customers

Kalipso Karantinou

Customers can be defined as social actors (Bagozzi, 1975) – individuals or social units – involved in selecting, acquiring, consuming, and disposing of products, services, experiences, and ideas (Mowen and Minor, 1998; Solomon, 2002). Central to the concept of customer, and indeed to that of MARKETING, is the concept of EXCHANGE, which involves the transfer of resources between social actors. Money, goods, services, and information, but also status and feelings, can act as resources in the exchange process (Mowen and Minor, 1998). According to economists, customers engage in exchanges to increase the total utility of the assortment of goods they possess. The utilitarian exchange theory views customers as rational in their behavior, free from external influences and possessing complete information on alternatives available to them in exchanges (Bagozzi, 1975). Research into CONSUMER BUYER BEHAVIOR, however, has revealed other aspects that lead to a different overall picture. Customers are sometimes rational, sometimes irrational, motivated by tangible as well as intangible rewards, by internal as well as external forces, engaging in utilitarian as well as symbolic exchanges (*see* SYMBOLIC CONSUMPTION), more often than not basing their decisions on incomplete information and settling for less than optimum gains in their exchanges. Indeed, marketing exchanges are complicated, involving both utilitarian and symbolic aspects, which are often very difficult to separate (Bagozzi, 1975).

Social relationships are also characterized by the existence of complex exchanges (not in the simple *quid pro quo* notion characterizing most economic exchanges) (Bagozzi, 1975). Focusing on these broader exchanges rather than on products or services only has widened the relevance of marketing to other areas beyond business and thus expanded the notion of the customer, which led to the broadened concept of marketing (Kotler and Levy, 1969). Marketing is therefore concerned with satisfying customer needs (Kotler and Armstrong, 2004) and with facilitating exchanges, in a variety of different contexts.

Other developments in the scope of marketing expand the notion of customer even further. According to INTERNAL MARKETING theory, organizations should view their employees as customers and apply marketing internally within the company, with programs of communication targeted at internal audiences. This is considered to play a vital role in developing a customer-focused organization (Dibb et al., 2001). Satisfying the needs of internal customers is believed to upgrade the organization's capability to satisfy the needs of external customers (Lewis, 1995). Internal marketing therefore aims to develop internal and external customer AWARENESS and to remove functional or human barriers to organizational effectiveness. It centers on the notion that every member of the organization has a "supplier" and a "customer" (Dibb et al., 2001). This "internal customer" concept is often ascribed to the founder of Toyota, who was reported to have said in the 1950s: "the next process is your customer" (Gummesson, 2000).

Bibliography

Bagozzi, R. P. (1975). Marketing as exchange. *Journal of Marketing*, **39** (October), 32–9.

Dibb, S., Simkin, L., Pride, W. M., and Ferrell, O. C. (2001). *Marketing: Concepts and Strategies*, 4th European edn. Boston: Houghton Mifflin, ch. 23.

Gummesson, E. (2000). Internal marketing in the light of relationship marketing and network organizations. In R. J. Varey and Barbara R. Lewis (eds.), *Internal Marketing: Directions for Management*. London: Routledge, pp. 27–42.

Kotler, P. and Armstrong, G. (2004). *Principles of Marketing*, 10th edn. Upper Saddle River, NJ: Prentice-Hall, ch. 1.

Kotler, P. and Levy, S. J. (1969). Broadening the concept of marketing. *Journal of Marketing*, **33** (January), 10–15.

Lewis, B. R. (1995). Customer care in services. In W. J. Glynn and J. G. Barnes (eds.), *Understanding Services Management*. New York: John Wiley, pp. 55–88.

Mowen, J. C. and Minor, M. (1998). *Consumer Behavior*, 5th edn. Upper Saddle River, NJ: Prentice-Hall.

Solomon, M. R. (2002). *Consumer Behavior: Buying, Having, Being*, 5th edn. Upper Saddle River, NJ: Prentice-Hall.

D

DAGMAR model

David Yorke

The DAGMAR model (Defining Advertising Goals for Measured Advertising Results) is a model of MARKETING COMMUNICATIONS that was developed by Colley (1961) specifically for the measurement of ADVERTISING effectiveness. It postulates that the customer/buyer moves from a state of unawareness through AWARENESS of the product or service, COMPREHENSION (an understanding of what the product or service will do), CONVICTION that it will meet requirements, to ACTION (a purchase). A benchmark measure is first taken of the position along the spectrum to which members of the target group(s) have progressed. Objectives are then established, advertising is produced, and a further measure is taken to discover whether or not any effective shift has occurred (i.e., whether or not the objectives have been met). Precise measurement is impossible as so many other variables are present. Furthermore, such variables become more numerous the further one moves toward action. The principal contribution of the DAGMAR model is in acknowledging that the effectiveness of advertising can only be validly assessed where specified criteria for judging effectiveness are derived from explicit advertising objectives.

See also *communications objectives*

Bibliography

Colley, R. H. (1961). *Defining Advertising Goals for Measured Advertising Results*. New York: Association of National Advertisers.

database

Vincent-Wayne Mitchell

A database is a collection of related information which is capable of being organized and accessed by a computer. Depending on the software being used, information can be entered as numeric, text, voice, or image. Common numerical database systems such as spreadsheets allow a high degree of querying, analysis, sorting, and extraction of information. *Data warehousing* is a term that managers of information technology use to refer to the process that allows important data collected from day-to-day computer systems to be stored and organized into separate systems designed for simplified access.

The most common usage of databases in MARKETING is to develop a customer database that can help in the wider process of CUSTOMER RELATIONSHIP MANAGEMENT (CRM) (*see* RELATIONSHIP MARKETING). Typically, customer information such as purchase history, value and timing of orders, responses to previous offers, name, address, and demographic characteristics (*see* DEMOGRAPHICS) will be gathered as well as additional information from salespersons' reports and external sources such as geodemographic profiles (*see* GEODEMOGRAPHICS). Database marketing allows closer monitoring of a company's customers and can be used to: identify the most profitable/least profitable customers; allow cross-selling of goods; identify possible customer segments; and help in communicating individually with customers.

Database marketing has developed hand-in-hand with a more tailored approach to marketing goods and services, since more is known about customers as individuals and they can be reached through direct mail campaigns. "Shopping basket analysis" from data gathered from customers using loyalty cards (*see* REWARD/LOY-ALTY CARDS) can show what sets of products or brands are bought together among the different segments. Indeed, database marketing is a self-enhancing activity where every iteration and addition improves the total value of the database. So when consumers "hook up" to an online company, through their home computers, television, or even mobile phone, they help to develop the customer database. Data mining is the process of digging deeply into vast amounts of data to extract valuable and statistically valid patterns that cannot be obtained through queries.

Databases can also be useful for bibliographic searches, site location, media planning, market FORECASTING, MARKET POTENTIAL studies, and MARKET SEGMENTATION. Many commercial numeric databases exist which contain information on sales, population characteristics, the business environment, economic forecasts, specialized bibliographies, and other material. For example, ABI/Inform contains abstracts of articles in approximately 1,300 business publications worldwide. Predicasts (PTS) provides numerous online databases on products, markets, competitors, demand forecasts, annual reports, etc. PROFIT IMPACT OF MARKETING STRATEGIES (PIMS) is an ongoing program of research conducted by the Strategic Planning Institute (Cambridge, MA) into the impact of marketing strategies: over 250 companies provide data on over 2,000 businesses for at least four years' trading. Given the huge diversity of databases available, several networks have been established to allow users easier access to each. One of the largest of these host networks is DIALOG, which contains over 600 different databases. NEXIS is another large system as well as PROQUEST, INFOTRAC, and the Web of Science.

Bibliography

Zikmund, W. G. (2003). *Exploring Marketing Research*, 8th edn. Mason, OH: Thomson South-Western.

deciders

Dominic Wilson

Deciders are those members of the decision-making unit (DMU) who are responsible for the final purchase decision (though they do not always sign the purchase contract). For major purchase decisions the decider may be the chief executive, a director, or the chief procurement officer, but for relatively insignificant purchase decisions the decider may be a junior member of the purchasing staff.

See also *buying center; organizational buying behavior; purchasing process*

decision-making unit

see BUYING CENTER

demand

Dominic Wilson

At its simplest, demand for a product/service over a set period of time can be defined in monetary terms as the number of buyers in the market, multiplied by the volume of their purchase over the period in question, and multiplied by the average price at which they buy. However, each of these variables is problematic, with extensive potential variation in the volume purchased and in the price paid by each buyer, different patterns in different markets and over different time periods, and even variability in the actual product/service purchased by different buyers and at different times.

Some products tend to be regarded as essential (e.g., salt, televisions, insurance, water), with important implications for PRICING. The demand for most products tends to be variable ("elastic") with respect to price, whereas the demand for an "essential" product is said to be largely "inelastic" with respect to price. However, it is difficult to make use of this fundamental economic principle in making real pricing decisions because there are very few products that are "essentials" in contemporary global markets with multiple suppliers and a high rate of PRODUCT INNOVATION and rivalry. Closer examination suggests that such essential products are dependent on the cultures, economies, and even the segments in question. For example, rural consumers in developing economies are likely to have different "essential" products to those in affluent urban economies, while both contexts will also each comprise multiple segments with significantly different priorities (e.g., consider vegetarians, commuters, parents). The principle of elasticity may be more useful when applied to other influences on demand, such as ADVERTISING expenditure and disposable income, and has been subsumed to some extent within the broader notion of sensitivity between multiple variables (aided by spreadsheet analysis).

Nevertheless, and despite the difficulties involved, the assessment of demand is crucial to professional pricing analysis and decision-making. While simplistic formulae may be worthless in many cases, the accumulated experience and professional insight of the analysts and managers involved (too easily dismissed as "intuition") can be invaluable – so long as it is coupled with careful analysis of appropriate data (where "appropriate" is generally determined intuitively). These "appropriate data" should be analyzed in terms of extrapolated trends based on the evolution of demand (including changes in the broader socioeconomic environment, the patterns of use, rival offerings, and psychosocial product associations), rather than just a statistical extrapolation of historic sales records (as with the Ford Edsell motor car) or wishful guesswork propped up by selective data (as with the Sinclair C5 electric mini-car).

The demand for a product or service can be seen as historic, existing, latent, or potential (see LATENT DEMAND; MARKET POTENTIAL). Historic demand describes customers (individuals and organizations) who have purchased a particular product or service in the past, whereas existing demand describes customers who are currently purchasing the product or service. Potential demand describes those customers who might purchase the product or service in the foreseeable future given various changes in MARKETING STRATEGY or environmental circumstances (e.g., protectionism). Some authorities also use the term latent demand to refer, in effect, to demand that could be developed (so distinguishing latent demand from potential demand) with appropriate marketing strategies but which meanwhile remains dormant. The most easily adapted aspect of marketing strategies is pricing, and this is usually the quickest way to translate latent demand or potential demand into existing demand. Yet too much demand can be just as problematic for a supplier as too little demand and a responsible pricing policy will therefore depend crucially on careful assessment of demand.

Clearly there will often be similarities between these forms of demand, but there can also be important differences. For example, the product or service in question may well have changed significantly over time to the extent that historic demand is no longer a useful indication of potential demand. The characteristics of demand can also change over time (e.g., in DISPOSABLE INCOME, customer sophistication, and sensitivity to particular product aspects). In addition, there is usually sufficient environmental change and UNCERTAINTY about the data to mean that demand should generally be assessed cautiously. Demand is even more difficult to assess where a product or service is innovative, making historic reference points even more problematic. This caution is captured in the concept of REALIZABLE DEMAND, which refers to that fraction of potential demand which an organization considers it can achieve realistically with its chosen marketing strategy and pricing decisions.

See also price elasticity

demographic environment

Dominic Wilson

The demographic environment is one of the elements of the MARKETING ENVIRONMENT and includes such important aspects as population size and growth rates, age and sex profiles, family life-cycle stages, occupation patterns, levels of education, actuarial health and morbidity projections, etc. Every country produces basic demographic statistics, sometimes on a regional and local basis, most of which are readily available to the marketing analyst. Trends and dramatic shifts in demographic data are vital factors in determining marketing decisions, both to identify opportunities and to anticipate declining demand. An example of this is the postwar "baby boom," which has combined with trends of improving medical technology and individual affluence to generate a substantial increase in the size and wealth of the "gray market" (i.e., consumers over the age of 50), with a flood of new products and services targeted at this market. The opportunities are evident (e.g., cruise holidays, financial planning services), but there are also waning markets (e.g., funeral savings schemes).

See also *demographics; environmental analysis*

demographics

Barbara R. Lewis

Demographics comprise probably the most important variable in the MARKETING ENVIRONMENT of any organization. Demographics describe, and provide a statistical study of, a human population in terms of its size, structure, and distribution. Size is the number of individuals in a population and is determined by: fertility and birth rates; life expectancy and death rates; and migration between and within countries. Structure describes the population in terms of age, gender, education, and occupation, and distribution refers to the location of individuals in terms of geographic region or rural, urban, or suburban location.

Demographic data are developed, primarily, from population censuses and the study of demographics is concerned with understanding trends to include forecasts of future demographic size, structure, and distribution.

Demographics affect the behavior of consumers and contribute to the overall demand for goods and services. They are changing in a number of ways, influenced by social and cultural variables (*see* CULTURE). Such trends, in developed economies, include:

- increased life expectancy and an aging population;
- a slowing down of the birth rate and population growth;
- growing per capita income and DISCRETIONARY INCOME;
- changing mix of household expenditure;
- increasing participation of women in the workforce and their changing roles at home and at work;
- increasing proportion of white-collar workers;
- trends in literacy and education;
- geographic shifts in population, e.g., urban to rural and city to suburbs and new towns;
- changing ethnic and racial mixes;
- changing family and household structure, to take account of age profiles, later marriage and age of childbearing, fewer children in a family, divorce and single-parent families, increasing numbers of single-person households, and total number of households;
- increased home ownership and increased ownership of consumer durables;
- widespread availability of credit;
- fewer traditional shoppers and more home shopping;
- increased leisure time and participation in leisure activities;
- changing media habits;
- increases in crime and social problems;
- increased access to mobile communications and the Internet.

These changes/trends are of key interest to marketing organizations. For example, they may see opportunities arising as particular age groups increase, or threats occurring as some age groups decline. Demographic trends have implications for: product and service development; identification of target markets (*see* TARGET MARKET) and market segments (*see* MARKET SEGMENTATION), and other elements in the MARKETING MIX. These impact not only on manufacturers and distributors but also on those organizations that supply consumer good manufacturers, e.g., producers of commodities and capital equipment.

See also *lifestyles*

100 depth interviews

Bibliography

Blackwell, R. D., Miniard, P. W., and Engel, J. F. (2001). *Consumer Behavior*, 9th edn. London: Harcourt College Pubs., ch. 7

Central Statistical Office. *Annual Abstract of Statistics.* London: HMSO.

Hawkins, D. I., Best, R. J., and Coney, K. A. (1995). *Consumer Behavior: Implications for Marketing Strategy*, 6th international student edn. Boston: Chicago Irwin, ch. 3, pp. 78–88.

United States Bureau of the Census. *Statistical Abstract of the United States.* Austin Reference Press.

depth interviews

Kalipso Karantinou

A depth interview is a one-to-one interview that explores issues in depth (Parasuraman, Grewal, and Krishnan, 2004) and is considered to be a powerful research technique for interpretive research (see QUALITATIVE RESEARCH). It is a useful method for exploring new and under-researched topics, as it enables the researcher/interviewer to gather rich and meaningful data (Carson et al., 2001) and is one of the most commonly recognized forms of qualitative research method (Mason, 1996). The central difference of this form of interview from structured interviews (see SURVEY RESEARCH) is its open-ended character (May, 1997).

Although depth interviews vary in form and level of structure (Carson et al., 2001), the term *depth interview* or *qualitative interview* is usually intended to refer to in-depth, semi-structured or loosely structured forms of interviewing (Mason, 1996). The researcher/interviewer normally does not have a specific set of pre-specified questions that must be asked according to the order imposed by a questionnaire. Instead, there is freedom to create questions and to probe further those responses that appear relevant (Tull and Hawkins, 1993). This is believed to help challenge the preconceptions of the researcher/interviewer, as well as enable the interviewee to answer questions within his/her own frame of reference (May, 1997).

Depth interviews are considered to be the most revealing instrument of inquiry, allowing the researcher/interviewer to step into the mind of another person, to see and experience the world as he/she does (McCracken, 1988). Such interviews therefore yield rich insights into people's experiences, opinions, aspirations, ATTITUDES, and feelings (May, 1997). Structured interviews, on the contrary, are thought to allow very little room for people to express their own opinions in a manner of their choosing. They must fit into boxes or categories which the researcher/interviewer has predetermined (May, 1997).

Commonly, a tension is thought to exist between subjectivity and objectivity in the interviewing process (May, 1997). The personal interviewing process is characterized by the interaction of the following entities: the researcher/interviewer, the interviewee, and the interview environment. Collectively, these characteristics influence the interviewing process and, ultimately, the interview itself (Kumar, Aaker, and Day, 2002). Considerable bias can be introduced by the presence of the researcher/interviewer (Maxwell, 1996), as he/she can have an effect on the interviewee and hence the material collected (May, 1997), as well as by the overall way verbal and non-verbal communication is handled, the topics addressed, and the sequence of the questions. As a result, the researcher/interviewer should always be careful not to impose his/her own perspective on the respondent (Carson et al., 2001) and should very carefully manage the complex relationship between investigator and respondent (McCracken, 1988).

Although depth interviews can be particularly rewarding, generating rich data, they are intellectually, practically, socially, and ethically difficult (Mason, 1996) and require a great deal of planning. In the absence of a pre-designed set and sequence of questions, the researcher/interviewer has to be able to make on-the-spot decisions during the interview process about the content and sequence of the interview, quickly and in ways which are consistent with the research questions (Mason, 1996). Depth interviews are therefore time and effort consuming, both in preparation and in execution and analysis.

Bibliography

Carson, D., Gilmore, A., Perry, C., and Gronhaug, K. (2001). *Qualitative Marketing Research*. London: Sage.

Kumar, V., Aaker, D. A., and Day, G. S. (2002). *Essentials of Marketing Research*, 2nd edn. New York: John Wiley, ch. 8.

McCracken, G. D. (1988). *The Long Interview*. London: Sage.

Mason, J. (1996). *Qualitative Researching*. London: Sage.

Maxwell, J. A. (1996). *Qualitative Research Design*. Thousand Oaks, CA: Sage.

May, T. (1997). *Social Research: Issues, Methods and Process*, 2nd edn. Milton Keynes: Open University Press, ch. 6.

Parasuraman, A., Grewal, D., and Krishnan, R. (2004). *Marketing Research*. Boston: Houghton Mifflin, ch. 7.

Tull, D. S. and Hawkins, D. I. (1993). *Marketing Research: Measurement and Method*, 6th edn. Upper Saddle River, NJ: Prentice-Hall, ch. 13.

derived demand

Dale Littler

The demand for organizational goods and services is derived from the demand for the goods which they help to produce or in which they are incorporated and ultimately from consumer demand for the final product.

See also *demand*

derived etic

see ETIC–EMIC DILEMMA

descriptive statistics

Michael Greatorex and Jim Freeman

Unless the sample in a market research project is very small, the data will be tabulated and analyzed using a computer. The simplest kind of statistical analysis of data involves descriptive statistics where the object is to summarize the data and describe the results for the sample. The alternative kind of analysis involves statistical inference, covering such topics as estimation and HYPOTHESIS TESTING. Descriptive statistical analysis can be carried out on a univariate, bivariate, or multivariate basis (*see* BIVARIATE ANALYSIS; MULTIVARIATE METHODS (ANALYSIS); UNIVARIATE ANALYSIS).

Univariate analysis involves the quantitative analysis of data where each variable is analyzed in isolation and is often the first stage in the analysis of a survey. Without some form of aggregation it is unlikely the analyst will be able to make much sense of original (raw) data. This is true even for a single variable. Typically, one of the first steps in the summarization process is for sample values to be tabulated as a frequency distribution, using a convenient number of classes (or "bins" if the data are interval). A frequency distribution may be in actual counts or in percentages, in cumulative or non-cumulative form. Another stage may be to present the data in a graphical form, using a pie diagram, bar chart, histogram, ogive, etc., as required. A further stage in the summarization process is to calculate and present descriptive statistics such as measures of location (mean, median), variation (standard deviation, variance, range, interquartile range), skewness, and kurtosis for each variable. In this way, surveys yielding thousands of numbers on each variable can be summarized into a small number of diagnostic results for each variable. This enables comparisons to be made more easily between variables and with other surveys, and allows the researcher to report his/her results in a condensed form and to incorporate the results using the summary descriptive statistics into the text of the report. Exploratory data analysis (EDA) methods are increasingly used in descriptive analysis – graphical tools such as boxplots, stem and leaf plots, and dotplots enabling statistical comparisons to be made routinely and automatically.

Bivariate analysis is concerned with the quantitative analysis of data where pairs of variables are analyzed together, usually to see if there is any relationship between the variables. The analysis depends upon the types of measurements; CROSS-TABULATIONS can be used to compare variables measured on nominal scales or even variables measured on interval scales where the cases are grouped into classes. At the other extreme, correlation (in terms of the Pearson coefficient) and regression (*see* REGRESSION AND CORRELATION) is useful for data measured on interval scales. If one variable is measured on a nominal scale and the other on an interval scale, the nominal variable can be used to split the sample into subsamples, and arithmetic means for the other variable can be calculated to enable the subsamples to be compared. Graphical representations such as scatter diagrams, bar charts, etc. are useful aids in bivariate statistical description.

The methods of multivariate methods analysis, including those methods which require an understanding of statistical inference for maximum appreciation, can be used in a descriptive, explorative way. Methods such as multiple regression, DISCRIMINANT ANALYSIS, FACTOR ANALYSIS, CLUSTER ANALYSIS, CONJOINT ANALYSIS, and MULTIDIMENSIONAL SCALING are available in computer analysis packages to help the researcher analyze the quantitative data on many variables obtained in surveys.

Bibliography

Tull, D. S. and Hawkins, D. I. (1993). *Marketing Research: Measurement and Method*, 6th edn. New York: Macmillan.

design

Margaret Bruce and Liz Barnes

The term "design" covers a wide range of activities – architecture, interior design, graphic design, industrial design, and engineering design. Designers usually specialize in one of these disciplines. All design terms involve the creative visualization of concepts, plans, ideas, and the representation of those ideas (as sketches, blueprints, models, or prototypes) so as to enable the making of something that did not exist before, or not quite in that form. Marketing managers tend to regard design as a tool to differentiate products, to entice consumers to buy; and consumers want the design to satisfy a given need – fun, function, price, etc.

Also, design is referred to as "the process of seeking to optimize customer satisfaction and company profitability through the creative use of major design elements (performance, quality, durability, appearance and costs) in connection with products, environments, information and corporate identities" (Kotler and Rath, 1984). Design activities lead to the creation of new products or services, new packs, corporate identities, and advertisements. It is design that takes the values of the organization and the ideas about the product or service and transforms them into the desired artifacts. In order to communicate Body Shop's MISSION STATEMENT, "We will be the most honest cosmetic company," this has to be translated into a strategy for design in terms of: a corporate identity program, the product presentation, the labeling and container design, and the retail outlets.

Mounting evidence supports the case that investment in design expertise contributes to commercial performance (Lorenz, 1986; Walsh et al., 1992). Walsh et al. (1992) carried out an international study of different industries, ranging from electronics to furniture, to assess systematically the economic effect of design investment on business performance. The results of the study showed that design investment made a positive contribution to business performance, but only if the design resource was well managed and integrated with other corporate activities, notably MARKETING and production. Another study of over 200 British firms found that investment in design positively influenced project performance. Over 90 percent of products launched into the market achieved profitability and a return on investment within a short time frame (average 15 months). Critical factors affecting project outcome were top-level commitment to design investment and the ability of managers, particularly marketing, to liaise effectively with the design resource (Potter et al., 1991).

Bibliography

Kotler, P. and Rath, G. A. (1984). A powerful but neglected strategic tool. *Journal of Business Studies*, 5, 216–21.

Lorenz, C. (1986). *The Design Dimension*. Oxford: Blackwell.

Potter, S., Roy, R., Capon, C., Bruce, M., Walsh, V., and Lewis, J. (1991). *The Benefits and Costs of Investment in Design Expertise in Product and Graphics Projects*. Milton Keynes: Design Innovation Group, Open University.

Walsh, V., Roy, R., Bruce, M., and Potter, S. (1992). *Winning by Design: Technology, Product Design and International Competitiveness*. Oxford: Blackwell, ch. 1.

design management

Margaret Bruce and Liz Barnes

Design management refers to the process entailed in the generation, integration, coordination, and evaluation of corporate communication strategies. Von Stamm (2003) defines it succinctly as: "the conscious decision-making process by which information (an idea) is transformed into an outcome, be it tangible (product) or intangible (service)." Design management has the responsibilities of defining, in a visual way, the nature of the organization and insuring that this visual expression is reinforced throughout the organization. The physical manifestations of a service organization, for example, are planned to convey the nature and quality of the organization, such as the environment, company logo, and packaging. British Airways, for instance, has a distinctive identity which is conveyed throughout the organization by its logo, staff uniforms, brochures, and so on. For product companies, the functional and aesthetic elements of the product are supported by the presentation of the product, its PACKAGING, and ADVERTISING. For example, Volvo communicates its attention to safety in car design in its promotion and advertising; Citroën focuses on price and fun for a "youth" market.

The main activities undertaken by design managers are: conducting design audits; preparation of design briefs; sourcing of design expertise from within the organization and from external suppliers; and project management of the design process.

DESIGN AUDITS

This involves examining, periodically, the corporate use of design, through every aspect of product, environment, and communication. Oakley (1990) regards design audits as serving much the same function as financial audits – "basically to review the return (or potential return) being achieved on the resources employed, to check whether the level of resources is adequate for the tasks involved and to highlight the relative successes and failures." Cooper and Press (1995) suggest that a design audit covers a number of topics: firstly, environ-mental issues (such as legislation and market trends); secondly, corporate culture (e.g., an organization's values and vision); thirdly, "tactical" management of design projects and processes; and, finally, the physical manifestation of design (i.e., the offering and its communication by the organization).

DESIGN BRIEF

For the design function to have a good grasp of the project, objectives, and the work entailed, a design brief is prepared. The brief needs to indicate the TARGET MARKET, the intended price, and timescales and should include inputs from the functions involved in developing and implementing the end product, including marketing and production. If the brief is not fully prepared, then critical technical and other information may be missing that can delay project completion, or the design may be developed to a higher price than intended, e.g., more expensive materials may be used by the design function (Walsh et al., 1992).

DESIGN SOURCING

Organizations use a range of different skills from graphic, interior, engineering, and industrial design. These may have to be outsourced and, if so, design managers have to identify and liaise with external design professionals. Choice of external design suppliers is based on the competence of the designer to accomplish the objectives for a set fee, as well as more intangible considerations of the design–client relationship, such as TRUST and loyalty.

PROJECT MANAGEMENT

Regular contact between design and other functions, notably marketing, during the project is critical to insure that the concepts and prototypes are meeting their requirements and that the project is on time and to the appropriate cost (Bruce and Morris, 1994).

It is considered that design management provides benefits to a business through management of design activities, integration of the design function into all business processes, and integrating design methods and decisions into the design vision within the company's strategy (Sinah, 2002).

Bibliography

Bruce, M. and Bessant, J. (2002). *Design in Business: Strategic Innovation Through Design*. Harlow: Pearson Education.

Bruce, M. and Cooper, R. (1997). *Design Management and Marketing*. London: International Thomson.

Bruce, M. and Morris, B. (1994). Managing external design professionals in the product development. *Techno Vation*, **149**, 585–99.

Cooper, R. and Press, M. (1995). *The Design Agenda: A Guide to Successful Design Management*. Chichester: John Wiley, ch. 6.

Oakley, M. (1990). Assembling and managing a design team. In M. Oakley (ed.), *Design Management: A Handbook of Issues and Methods*. Oxford: Blackwell, ch. 34, p. 325.

Potter, S., Roy, R., Capon, C., Bruce, M., Walsh, V., and Lewis, J. (1991). *The Benefits and Costs of Investment in Design Expertise in Product and Graphics Projects*. Milton Keynes: Design Innovation Group, Open University.

Sinah, P. (2002). The mechanics of fashion. In M. Bruce and T. Hines (eds.), *Fashion Marketing*. Oxford: Butterworth-Heinemann.

Von Stamm, B. (2003). *Managing Innovation, Design and Creativity*. Chichester: John Wiley.

Walsh, V., Roy, R., Bruce, M., and Potter, S. (1992). *Winning by Design: Technology, Product Design and International Competitiveness*. Oxford: Blackwell, ch. 7.

dialogical acculturation model

see ACCULTURATION MODELS

differentiation strategy

Dale Littler

This is the alternative generic strategy (*see* GENERIC STRATEGIES) to the COST LEADERSHIP STRATEGY, as suggested by Porter (1980). Organizations strive to secure a COMPETITIVE ADVANTAGE by distinguishing themselves from their competitors using such means as DESIGN, customer service, IMAGE, PACKAGING, and additional functionality in ways which are perceived by customers as adding value. In effect, it embraces everything other than being the most efficient and demands in particular knowledge-based competencies such as design and research and development. The differentiation strategy can be focused on par-

ticular customers or market segment(s) (*see* MARKET SEGMENTATION) or devised for the general market. The risk of pursing the differentiation strategy is that an over-emphasis on producing additional features will add costs that result in a price that some customers/buyers find too high, while there may be macroeconomic changes that result in purchasers becoming price sensitive.

See also *competitive strategy*

Bibliography

Porter, M. E. (1980). *Competitive Strategy: Techniques for Analyzing Industries and Competitors*. New York: Free Press, ch. 2.

diffusion of innovation

see DIFFUSION PROCESS

diffusion process

Barbara R. Lewis

The diffusion process is concerned with how product innovations (*see* PRODUCT INNOVATION) are spread or assimilated within a market or industry. It is a macro process and may be defined as the process by which the acceptance of an innovation (product, service, or idea) is spread by communications (impersonal and interpersonal) to members of a social system (e.g., market or target segment) over a period of time. In other words, it is the spread of a new idea from its source of invention or creation to its ultimate users or adopters.

A number of product characteristics influence the diffusion of innovation and the rate of adoption by users (*see* ADOPTION PROCESS), i.e., some products may be an overnight success (e.g., video recorder), and some may be very slow to diffuse (e.g., dishwasher). These characteristics are:

- relative advantage with respect to ease of operations and reliability: the degree to which a new product appears superior to the buyer than previous products and existing substitutes;

- compatibility: the degree to which a potential customer feels that a new product is consistent with present needs, values, and behavior, i.e., with experiences in the social system, or complementary processes in the case of industrial innovations;
- complexity: the degree to which a new product is difficult to comprehend and use – more complex innovations take longer to diffuse;
- divisibility: the degree to which a new product may be tried on a limited basis – the more opportunities to try, the easier it is for a consumer or user to evaluate; and
- communicability: the degree to which results from product use and ownership are observable and describable to others, i.e., the ease of seeing a product's benefits and attributes – so that products with a high degree of social visibility (e.g., fashion) are more easily diffused.

Insuring a rapid diffusion of new products has become particularly important given the rapid rate of technological change and the increased intensity of competition, because the honeymoon period during which companies have a quasi-monopoly position, and can therefore charge premium prices that enable them to recover the often high costs of development and make an appropriate return on their investment, is consequently shorter.

Bibliography

Robertson, T. S. (1967). The process of innovation and the diffusion of innovation. *Journal of Marketing*, January, 14–19.

Rogers, E. M. (1962). *Diffusion of Innovations*. New York: Free Press.

Schiffman, L. G. and Kanuk, L. Z. (2004). *Consumer Behavior*, 8th edn. Upper Saddle River, NJ: Prentice-Hall.

direct mail

David Yorke

Direct mail is a part of DIRECT MARKETING and, specifically, is ADVERTISING that is sent directly to the mailing address of a target customer. Increasingly, material is being sent by email. Thus, direct mail offers the advertiser the opportunity for high audience selectivity and targeting, and wide-ranging geographic flexibility. Such specific targeting is enhanced by the use of customer information obtained from the use of, *inter alia*, loyalty cards (*see* REWARD/LOYALTY CARDS), company-held information, or data obtained from subscriptions that may be passed on to third parties (with the customer's permission). It can be personalized (via individual letters), but much direct marketing either lacks personalization or is personalized with computer fill-ins, leading to a "junk mail" appearance.

Evidence of the growth of direct mail is seen in the following:

- generation and sale/purchase of computer-based mailing lists, i.e., databases (*see* DATABASE), so that direct mail messages (*see* MESSAGE) may be carefully targeted to create consumer AWARENESS and/or to generate ACTION;
- the growth of specialized direct mail agencies; and
- the increasing marketing orientation of the postal services with various incentive discounts.

direct marketing

David Yorke

Direct marketing is sometimes confused with DIRECT MAIL. It is not a medium but a MARKETING technique, comprising an interactive system of marketing, which uses one or more communications media (direct mail, print, telephone, broadcast) for the purpose of soliciting a direct and measurable consumer response. Its objective is to make a sale or obtain a sales lead inquiry.

Computers are an indispensable tool in direct marketing, in particular in generating personalized direct mail sources. Indeed, the success of direct marketing depends on the acquisition and maintenance of a DATABASE of customers or potential customers.

The growth of direct marketing has been stimulated by socioeconomic changes (e.g., an aging population, single-person or single-parent households, and working women with less shopping time), the increasing use of credit, a consumer convenience orientation, rising DISCRETIONARY INCOME, and developing computer technology and communications media.

Kotler et al. (2001) note that direct marketing has undergone a dramatic transformation in light of technological developments used to complement (even replace) other approaches. For example, websites are being employed for direct marketing, while marketers are using online marketing to target, for instance, specific customer groups.

Bibliography

Kotler, P., Armstrong, G., Saunders, J., and Wong, V. (2001). *Principles of Marketing*, 3rd European edn. Harlow: Prentice-Hall, ch. 22.

Schiffman, L. G. and Kanuk, L. Z. (2004). *Consumer Behavior*, 8th edn. Upper Saddle River, NJ: Prentice-Hall, pp. 292–4.

directional matrix

Dale Littler

This summarizes the major growth strategies available to organizations. As defined by Ansoff (1965), it consists of two parameters: markets and technologies, subdivided according to whether or not they are "new" or "existing." The quadrants are: market penetration (existing markets and technologies), with the aim being to increase volume sales through, for instance, higher MARKET SHARE or greater per capita consumption from, for example, new uses for the product; NEW PRODUCT DEVELOPMENT, involving the introduction of products based on new technologies into existing markets; market development, which involves extending the geographic reach of existing products; and DIVERSIFICATION, the introduction of products based on new technology into new markets. It is obvious that the last strategy is the most risky option. Although overly simplistic and general, the framework may be useful for practitioners when formulating specific development strat-

egies. It does not draw the distinction between organic, or internal, development and external development through mergers and acquisitions.

See also *corporate strategy*

Bibliography

Ansoff, H. I. (1965). *Corporate Strategy: An Analytic Approach to Business Policy for Growth and Expansion.* New York: McGraw-Hill, ch. 6.

discontinuous innovation

Dale Littler

This can be viewed as being at the polar extreme of a continuum with CONTINUOUS INNOVATION at the other extreme. It is generally used with reference to technological innovation. It can be seen as involving radical changes in technologies and, consequently, it may result in the development of new demand schedules. A MARKETING perspective would suggest that discontinuous innovations require significant changes in behavior and are thus likely to have slower rates of diffusion (*see* DIFFUSION PROCESS; INNOVATION).

discount

Dominic Wilson

Discount is the term used to refer to any reduction in price offered to a customer. Discounts are offered to encourage customers to purchase where it is thought they may not otherwise do so. Discounting is widely practiced in organizational markets where price is more often a matter of negotiation than in consumer markets (Blois, 1994). The usual reasons for offering discounts include: to encourage purchase in greater quantity than normal (discount for volume); to respond to competitive developments (e.g., price wars, tendering); to accelerate sales of outdated stock (e.g., discontinued lines); to encourage purchase at "unpopular" times (e.g., end-of-season sales, off-peak electricity tariffs); to reduce a customer's PERCEIVED RISK (e.g., introductory discounts for new products); to provide incentives for another product (e.g., membership discounts); and, illegally, to drive out competition with a view to achieving a monopoly predatory price.

Bibliography

Blois, K. J. (1994). Discounts in business marketing management. *Industrial Marketing Management*, **23**, 2 (April), 93–100.

discourse analysis

Gillian C. Hopkinson

Discourse analysis is a qualitative and interpretive approach to social research that is increasingly being applied in the field of MARKETING. Although there is considerable diversity in the techniques employed, discourse analysts generally share a view of the social world as socially constructed and regard this as being accomplished through discourse.

Social constructionism holds that humans act in the world as they interpret that world to be and therefore refutes the notion of "given" or "natural" categories that define the world (for fuller explanations see Burr, 1995; Weick, 1995). Social constructionists are therefore concerned with the ways in which humans make sense of their world by, in effect, mapping the world through the categories that they produce. The notion of discourse draws particularly upon the work of Foucault (see, e.g., Foucault, 1979; for a fuller discussion see Mills, 1997) and is applied to the system of statements that can be made with respect to an object (or idea, concept, or person). Discourse refers, then, to how texts (speech, writings, advertisements, and so on) come to constitute the objects of which they speak.

A distinctive perspective that arises from discourse theory is the understanding of text as social practice, since in speaking of something we are producing a particular picture of that object. We also draw upon dominant and wider understandings and ideas associated with the objects of which we speak. Discourse is formed therefore in a particular social context, draws upon the ideas privileged in that context, and is both productive and reproductive. For this reason, discourse and power are held to be interpenetrated since discourses both gain credence according to who authorizes them and put forward visions of the world that produce particular patterns of social power.

The key concern of discourse analysts is, then, to generate an understanding of the interpretations of the world that are produced amongst the subjects or participants of their study. By understanding the world as other people see it, they aim to understand the features of the world that drive those people's actions. In many cases there is a particular emphasis upon the power structures that hold in those worlds, so that discourse analysis is a potentially useful interpretive approach amongst critical researchers of marketing (see Elliott's 1996 discussion of discourse analysis in marketing and Denzin's 2001 discussion of critical marketing and consumer research). In arguing for "critical discourse analysis," Fairclough (1989) demonstrates a robust analytic approach to critical discourse studies.

Discourse analysis can be applied to any form of text and a variety of techniques can be applied. Its diversity is discussed by Burr (1995), Mills (1997), Potter (1997), and Alvesson and Karreman (2000). Amongst the distinctions they draw is that between a fine-grained and linguistically based analysis that focuses upon individuality and a broader analysis that looks at how key themes are presented and maintained across a range of social texts. Approaches differ also with respect to the extent to which cultural discourses are seen as deterministic or as drawn upon in more fluid ways to produce an emergent understanding. These distinctions can be seen in the application of discourse analysis to marketing topics. Amongst other applications, discourse analysis has been applied to consumers' understanding of fashion and ADVERTISING (Elliott et al., 1995; Thompson and Haytko, 1997), to consumers' construction of the self on the Internet (Gould and Lerman, 1998), and to the construction of the self in retail managers' narratives (Hopkinson, 2001). The studies of consumers attach differing levels of importance to the conventional use of long-standing consumer narratives in the construction of the self. The narrative-based research (Hopkinson, 2001) provides an example of a linguistically based analysis that explores the personal meanings forged within a particular context.

Since the analyst's concern is with what is taken to be true, the approach has been seen as relativist and has been associated with postmodernism (*see* POSTMODERN MARKETING).

Bibliography

Alvesson, M. and Karreman, D. (2000). Varieties of discourse: On the study of organizations through discourse analysis. *Human Relations*, **53** (9), 1125–50.

Burr, V. (1995). *An Introduction to Social Constructionism*. London: Routledge.

Denzin, N. K. (2001). The seventh moment: Qualitative inquiry and the practices of a more radical consumer research. *Journal of Consumer Research*, **28** (2), 324–30.

Elliott, R. (1996). Discourse analysis: Exploring action, function and conflict in social texts. *Marketing Intelligence and Planning*, **14** (6), 65ff.

Elliott, R., Jones, A., Benfield, A., and Barlow, M. (1995). Overt sexuality in advertising: A discourse analysis of gender responses. *Journal of Consumer Policy*, **18** (2), 187–218.

Fairclough, N. (1989). *Language and Power*. London: Longman.

Foucault, M. (1979). *Discipline and Punish*. Harmondsworth: Penguin.

Gould, S. J. and Lerman, D. B. (1998). "Postmodern" versus "long-standing" cultural narratives in consumer behavior: An empirical study of NetGirl on line. *European Journal of Marketing*, **32** (7), 644–55.

Hopkinson, G. C. (2001). Influence in marketing channels: A sense-making investigation. *Psychology and Marketing*, **18** (5), 423–44.

Mills, S. (1997). *Discourse*. London: Routledge.

Potter, J. (1997). Discourse analysis as a way of analyzing naturally occurring talk. In David Silverman (ed.), *Qualitative Research: Theory, Method and Practice*. London: Sage.

Thompson, C. J. and Haytko, D. L. (1997). Speaking of fashion: Consumers' use of fashion discourses and the appropriation of countervailing cultural meanings. *Journal of Consumer Research*, **24** (1), 15–43.

Weick, K. (1995). *Sensemaking in Organizations*. London: Sage.

discretionary income

David Yorke

An element in the ECONOMIC ENVIRONMENT, discretionary income, i.e., that part of household net income which remains after fixed commitments such as mortgage and loan repayments have been made, is likely to vary from one market segment (*see* MARKET SEGMENTATION) to another. It represents a challenge for all organizations to be able to persuade buyers and customers to spend a greater proportion of their discretionary income than hitherto on a particular product or service. In theory, all providers of goods and services are competing with one another for a share of the consumer's discretionary income, which in affluent countries accounts for a significant proportion of total net (disposable) income. Changes in discretionary income not only affect those organizations selling directly to households, but also, ultimately, have repercussions on suppliers of capital equipment.

See also *disposable income*

discriminant analysis

Michael Greatorex

Discriminant analysis is used when there are observations from a sample of a population on many variables for cases which belong to two or more known groups. The groups may be owners and non-owners of a particular consumer durable, or good or bad credit risks, or buyers of three different brands of coffee, and the variables could be typical MARKETING RESEARCH variables, e.g., socioeconomic, demographic, or psychographic variables, for each respondent, or the respondent's opinions, perceptions, evaluations, etc. measured on a range of rating scales. The purpose of discriminant analysis is to use these data about individuals whose group membership is known to facilitate the classification of individuals whose group membership is unknown to one or another of the groups. In the situation where there are just two groups, a linear discriminant function of the variables is formed, the coefficients of the variables being chosen to best separate the two groups.

Discriminant scores can be calculated for each individual in the groups and a plot of these scores, indicating to which group each case belongs, will show, it is hoped, two non-intersecting histograms. Usually, however, the plots will be chosen so that cases will be classified by the discriminant function according to whether they are above or below the critical value. If there is overlap, some cases will be misclassified, even by the discriminant function whose fitting they contributed to. A classification table of "hits and misses" is one way of judging the usefulness of the discriminant analysis. Also used to judge the adequacy of a discriminant function are measures such as Wilks' lambda and the canonical correlation coefficient.

A satisfactory discriminant function can then use measurements on the variables for a previously unclassified case to predict to which of the groups the case belongs. For example, based on the data for an individual on the variables in a discriminant function on good and bad credit risks, the discriminant function should indicate whether or not the individual is a good credit risk.

Significance tests for coefficients are available. The discriminant function can be built up in a stepwise fashion. The method can be used in an analytical way. Thus, large coefficients identify variables that are important for discriminating between and describing the groups and therefore worthy of further attention by management.

The method can be extended to more than two groups when several discriminant functions will be estimated. Statistical packages, e.g., the STATISTICAL PACKAGE FOR THE SOCIAL SCIENCES (SPSS), that have discriminant analysis routines are essential.

Bibliography

Johnson, R. A. and Wichern, D. W. (1998). *Applied Multivariate Statistical Analysis*, 4th edn. Englewood Cliffs, NJ: Prentice-Hall.

disintermediarization

Dale Littler

Disintermediarization refers to the process whereby marketers bypass traditional intermediaries, such as retailers, to sell directly to the final customer/purchaser. The process has been stimulated by the development of the Internet whereby the REACH of, for example, producers could be extended into people's homes. The Internet also gave rise to changes in some people's buying behavior, with the greater avail-

ability of information it provided on marketers and rival products, and the enhanced awareness of possible price advantages and greater convenience of direct purchasing. However, there is still a significant role for intermediaries since they undertake responsibilities that enable producers to focus on activities where they can add the most value. In addition, many traditional retailers have established major Internet presences as a means of augmenting their traditional formats.

See also *retail distribution channels; retailing*

disposable income

David Yorke

Unlike DISCRETIONARY INCOME, total disposable income (household income after deduction of direct taxation and national insurance contributions) is not available for competition among all suppliers. Local taxes have to be paid and "essential" purchases (e.g., fuel for heating and energy) are likely to reduce the amount of total disposable income available for spending/saving.

distribution

see RETAIL DISTRIBUTION CHANNELS

distributors

see RETAIL DISTRIBUTION CHANNELS

diversification

Dale Littler

Diversification is regarded as the option involving the greatest risk in Ansoff's (1965) DIRECTIONAL MATRIX. It involves the organization introducing products based on new technologies into new markets. However, there are gradations in the degree of risk involved, depending on whether or not the diversification is related or unrelated (also referred to as concentric diversi-fication). Related diversification involves com-monalities with the firm's existing business, so that there is potential synergy between the new and the existing businesses based on a common facility, asset, channel, skill, or opportunity (Mintzberg, 1988). These commonalities may be either tangible or intangible (Porter, 1985), the latter involving tacit management skills. Un-related, or conglomerate, diversification involves the extension into new business areas which have no relationship with the company's existing technologies, markets, or products. Companies may also engage in horizontal diversification whereby the company may develop new prod-ucts aimed at its existing customers but which are unrelated to its existing technologies, al-though this does not accord with Ansoff's defin-ition of diversification.

Bibliography

Ansoff, H. I. (1965). *Corporate Strategy: An Analytic Approach to Business Policy for Growth and Expansion.* New York: McGraw-Hill, ch. 6.

Mintzberg, H. (1988). Generic strategies: Toward a com-prehensive framework. In *Advances in Strategic Man-agement*, vol. 5. Greenwich, CT: JAI Press, pp. 1–67.

Porter, M. E. (1985). *Competitive Advantage: Creating and Sustaining Superior Performance.* New York: Free Press.

E

economic environment

David Yorke

The economic environment is one of the elements in the MARKETING ENVIRONMENT in which an organization is operating. A national government, after taking account of international factors such as capital and currency movements, is responsible for creating and maintaining a favorable macroeconomic environment (*see* MACRO ENVIRONMENT). It achieves this by the use of monetary and fiscal policies aimed at manipulating the levels of inflation and employment and, hence, the levels of DISPOSABLE INCOME and DISCRETIONARY INCOME among various segments of the population. Thus, the level of economic activity will govern the possible success of all organizations. At any one time, the economic environment for different countries will vary widely. Thus, the ability to forecast changes from current base levels will be a major factor in the decision to invest or not.

EFTPOS

Andrew Newman and Steve Greenland

EFTPOS, or electronic funds transfer at point of sale, refers to debit or "plastic" card payment at the point of sale by direct funds transfer from the customer's account to the retailer's account. The method first evolved in the early to mid-1980s and has become a leading payment system for goods and services. Retailers such as supermarket and petrol chains have played a key role in helping the debit card to become a major payment mechanism. Most retailers offer the "cashback" facility as a customer service.

EFTPOS terminals reduce fraud through the acceptance of lower floor limits, above which debit card transactions must be checked "online" against the cardholder's account (Worthington, 1996). The online version of EFTPOS enables customers to make a credit card payment securely over the Internet. This facility allows users to enter the amount they wish to pay, so it is ideal for settling invoices of varying amounts. The payment web page has the same 128-bit encryption as banks, so this method of payment is very secure (Newman and Cullen, 2002). Transactions are processed in real time in the same way as an EFTPOS machine at the petrol station or supermarket.

Since 1995 the use of plastic payment has brought about a fundamental shift in payment methods in the UK (Worthington, 1996; Worthington and Edwards, 2000). EFTPOS has created the impetus for retailers to become financial service providers, and direct competitors to banks. By developing financial service relationships, retailers are able to generate closer relationships with their customers (Alexander and Colgate, 2000).

Bibliography

Alexander, N. and Colgate, M. (1998). The evolution of retailer, banker and customer relationships: A conceptual framework. *International Journal of Retail and Distribution Management*, **26** (6), 225–36.

Alexander, N. and Colgate, M. (2000). Retail financial services: Transaction to relationship marketing. *European Journal of Marketing*, **34** (8), 938–53.

McGoldrick, P. J. (2002). *Retail Marketing*, 2nd edn. Maidenhead: McGraw-Hill.

Newman, A. J. and Cullen, P. (2002). *Retailing: Environment and Operations*. London: Thomson Learning.

Penn, V. (1990). Retail EFTPOS 90: Paper holds out against plastic. *International Journal of Retail and Distribution*, **19** (1) 10–12.

Worthington, S. (1996). Smart cards and retailers – who stands to benefit? *International Journal of Retail and Distribution Management*, 24 (9), 27–34.

Worthington, S. and Edwards, V. (2000). Changes in payments markets, past, present and future: A comparison between Australia and the UK. *International Journal of Bank Marketing*, 18 (5), 212–21.

electronic commerce

Andrew Newman

This term has been widely used to describe various forms of electronic business interactions between two or more parties. Such activity usually involves some form of purchasing (EX-CHANGE), whether business to consumer (B2C) or business to business (B2B). McGoldrick (2002) draws the distinctions between B2B and B2C and other forms of e-commerce such as government to business (G2B) and consumer to business (C2B). A common factor to all these channels, however, is that communication takes place electronically and usually through the Internet, extranet, or other online systems. However, payments may or may not take place online when, for example, items are paid for using conventional paper-based bank transfers.

Online grocery shopping and entertainment purchases such as books and CDs typically form the bulk of consumer purchases. For business users, the increased capacity of Internet service connections and related technology has encouraged retailers to deal electronically with suppliers and manufacturers for procurement and other services. The push toward the creation of retail websites, some of which tend to be designed for non-transactional purposes, also stems from the actions of competitors and the need to compete on a like-for-like basis. There is strong evidence to suggest that the proliferation of email for business and personal communication has helped to foster the use of paperless channels for transactions of all kinds. Email has effectively revolutionized communication systems by replacing a vast portion of the physical mail in the past few years. Not only has it reduced the time in delivering the MESSAGE, but it is also virtually costless, and therefore an excellent method for businesses to communicate with customers (Smith, Speaker, and Thompson, 2000).

E-commerce merges suppliers, marketers, and consumers in a fully integrated and seamless operation. The system can convey accumulated data on consumer tastes and their preference for various merchandise, and its quality, price, and after-sales requirements, to suppliers and retailers in real time. Digital interaction thus reduces the cost and time of the necessary communications between producers, suppliers, and retailers, and so increases the chances of CUSTOMER SATISFACTION. This makes for a highly efficient online system of ordering that benefits all partners in the exchange process (De Kare-Silver, 2000).

Bibliography

De Kare-Silver, M. (2000). *E-shock 2000*. London: Macmillan, pp. 7–22.

McGoldrick, P. J. (2002). *Retail Marketing*. London: McGraw-Hill.

Smith, R., Speaker, M., and Thompson, M. (2000). *E-commerce UK*. London: Pearson Education.

electronic data interchange (EDI)

Andrew Newman and Margaret Bruce

Electronic data interchange (EDI) refers to computer-to-computer exchange of standard business documentation in machine processable form, between the retailer and the wholesaler and/or manufacturer. The object of this type of exchange is to simplify and streamline the transaction communication (Van Weele, 2002). EDI messages are highly structured so that information generated by one organization on one computer can be read by another computer in the same or a different organization. This means that generally the protocols or dialogues that computers use to talk to one another must be the same. In pre-1980 EDI systems this was more difficult to achieve due to the dissimilarity of company networks. As most communication in the 2000s use the Internet Protocol (IP) address such integration is relatively straightforward.

The prime applications of EDI have been for transactions, e.g., orders and invoices. The benefits of this have been found in speeding up trade communications and reducing labor costs. In the automotive industry, for example, EDI is used by component suppliers, manufacturers, and dealers to facilitate the trading processes involved in buying and selling components and cars. However, there are added benefits to be derived from the relationships that evolve as a result of the close partnerships needed to facilitate the EDI dialogues. In many cases cross-functional teams take responsibility for purchasing rather than single departments. The amalgamation with other functions, divisions, and suppliers leads to a fully integrated supply chain management approach. The cost savings and, above all, increased customer focus make this type of approach highly beneficial in sectors such as fashion and food retailing.

Bibliography

Holland, C., Lockett, G., and Blackman, I. (1992). Planning for electronic interchange. *Strategic Management Journal*, **13**, 359–550.

Van Weele, A. (2002). *Purchasing and Supply Chain Management: Analysis, Planning and Practice*. London: Thomson Learning.

Williams, L. R. (1994). Understanding distribution channels: An interorganizational study of EDI adoption. *Journal of Business Logistics*, **15** (2), 173–204.

emergent strategy

Dale Littler

In analyzing the process of strategy formation, a distinction has been made (e.g., Mintzberg and Waters, 1985) between deliberate and emergent strategies. The former embraces strategies that are devised and implemented as intended. Emergent strategy, as termed by Mintzberg (1987), is a strategy that is not carefully pre-planned; it is realized in the absence of intentions, or in an unexpected form. As Mintzberg notes: "strategies can form as well as be formulated. A realized strategy can emerge in response to an evolving situation, or it can be brought about deliberately, through a process of formulation followed by implementation." In the case of a planned strategy, the emergent strategy may be realized though not as intended, possibly as a result of changes in the environment; alterations in the personnel, who may have different perspectives and motives; and adjustments made by those involved in the implementation in order to take account of local conditions not anticipated by the planners of the strategy. Moreover, as strategy develops, those participating in the process will become acquainted with new knowledge, sometimes through a process of discovery involving active research, sometimes serendipitously, and sometimes through feedback from actions taken which suggests in some cases the need for adjustments to original assumptions and desired consequences. Given the uncertainties (*see* UNCERTAINTY) that surround organizational decision-making, it may be rare for there to be pure deliberate strategies: all strategies are likely to involve some blend of intention and adaptation.

Bibliography

Mintzberg, H. (1987). Five Ps for strategy. *California Management Review*, **30** (1), Fall.

Mintzberg, H. and Waters, J. A. (1985). Of strategies, deliberate and emergent. *Strategic Management Journal*.

emic

see ETIC–EMIC DILEMMA

end users

Dale Littler

End users are those who ultimately consume or use the product or service. They may or may not be the purchasers of products. In both organizational and consumer markets end users can have a significant influence on the purchasing decision (e.g., children in connection with certain household purchasing decisions).

See also *users*

entrepreneurial strategy

Dale Littler

Entrepreneurial strategy is one of Mintzberg's (1973) three STRATEGIC STYLES (*see*

ADAPTIVE STRATEGY; PLANNING STYLE). Mintzberg et al. (1998) have now proposed ten different schools relating to the formation of strategy.

The features of the entrepreneurial strategic style are likely to be bold decision-making by visionary individuals who are risk takers. Mintzberg suggests that it is likely to occur most in organizations that are under the personal control of one individual and are "located in a protected niche in the environment."

Such risk-taking behavior is not restricted to small organizations, as, for example, Littler and Leverick (1994) identified in their study of entrants into mobile communications markets. Indeed, many decisions to enter new markets, and especially, but not exclusively, those founded on advances in technology, are likely to have a degree of entrepreneurial behavior, if only because the uncertainties (see UNCERTAINTY) make calculation of the costs and benefits extremely problematic.

Bibliography

Littler, D. A. and Leverick, F. (1994). Market planning in new technology sectors. In J. Saunders (ed.), *The Marketing Initiative*. Englewood Cliffs, NJ: Prentice-Hall.

Mintzberg, H. (1973). Strategy making in three modes. *California Management Review*, **16**, 2 (Winter), 44–53.

Mintzberg, H., Ahlstrand, B., and Lampel, J. (1998). *Strategy Safari*. London: Prentice-Hall.

environmental analysis

Dominic Wilson

Organizations exist within a complex and dynamic environment which can be described as the MARKETING ENVIRONMENT. Understanding this environment, and its ensuing threats and opportunities, is one of the most important and difficult aspects of management and has traditionally been regarded as a marketing responsibility (see MARKETING AUDIT). Obviously, the number of variables influencing this marketing environment are many, so environmental analysis attempts to identify the most influential factors and trends affecting the organization and its offerings.

Kotler (2003) has suggested that it may be helpful to group these variables into two interdependent but distinguishable categories: the MICRO ENVIRONMENT and the MACRO ENVIRONMENT, together comprising the marketing environment. Analysis of the macro environment – sometimes referred to as the external marketing audit (see EXTERNAL AUDIT) – can usefully be considered under six headings: the DEMOGRAPHIC ENVIRONMENT, the ECONOMIC ENVIRONMENT, the NATURAL ENVIRONMENT, the TECHNOLOGICAL ENVIRONMENT, the POLITICAL ENVIRONMENT, and the cultural environment (see CULTURE; CULTURE AND BEHAVIOR; CULTURE AND SOCIETAL BEHAVIOR). Whereas all six of these aspects of the environment will be relevant to all markets, some aspects will, of course, be more applicable than others in specific markets. There can also be a danger of compartmentalization using this approach – for example, important issues of ecology or CONSUMERISM might seem less significant when split up among six headings. Perhaps the most notable limitation of this approach to environmental analysis is that it seems to give little priority to competitors *per se*, and it may therefore be appropriate to add a "competitive environment" to Kotler's six categories.

The level of effort and resources which any organization will invest in environmental analysis will depend on many factors, including: the availability and RELIABILITY of secondary data (e.g., census data, government statistics, published market analyses); the cost of PRIMARY DATA (e.g., commissioned market research, in-house surveys); the volatility of the environment (where analysis can be out of date even before it is finished); the competitiveness of markets (why should organizations invest in analysis when there is little threat of losing customers?); and what priority managers give to environmental analysis, in the context of other demands and rewards on their time.

It is often suggested that the environment is becoming increasingly complex and fast moving. This observation has, of course, been made of many earlier centuries also, but it does seem particularly true of the late twentieth and early twenty-first centuries, and this emphasizes the importance of environmental analysis while also highlighting the problems of analyzing such volatile dynamics. These problems have encouraged the development of different analytical techniques, such as scenario development (*see* SCENARIO BUILDING) (Schoemaker, 1993), delphi methods (Linstone and Turoff, 1975), and even the use of chaos theory (Stacey, 1995), in order to understand the marketing environment surrounding an organization.

Bibliography

Day, G. S. and Wensley, R. (1988). Assessing advantage: A framework for diagnosing competitive superiority. *Journal of Marketing*, **52** (April), 1–20.

Kotler, P. (2003). *Marketing Management: Analysis, Planning, Implementation and Control*, 11th edn. Englewood Cliffs, NJ: Prentice-Hall.

Linstone, H. A. and Turoff, M. (1975). *The Delphi Method: Techniques and Application*. Reading, MA: Addison-Wesley.

Porter, M. E. (1979). How competitive forces shape strategy. *Harvard Business Review*, **57** (March/April), 137–45.

Sanderson, S. M. and Luffman, G. A. (1988). Strategic planning and environmental analysis. *European Journal of Marketing*, **22**, 214–27.

Schoemaker, P. J. H. (1993). Multiple scenario development: Its conceptual and behavioral foundation. *Strategic Management Journal*, **14**, 193–213.

Shapiro, B. P. (1988). What the hell is market oriented. *Harvard Business Review*, **66** (6), 119–25.

Stacey, R. D. (1995). The science of complexity: An alternative perspective for strategic change processes. *Strategic Management Journal*, **16** (6), 477–95.

environmental scanning

Dominic Wilson

Environmental scanning is the process of monitoring and analyzing the MARKETING ENVIRONMENT, usually with the intention of identifying trends and developments in the environment that may require marketing strategies (*see* MARKETING STRATEGY) or tactics to be adjusted. Management has to make decisions on what to scan and the processes to be used for undertaking the scanning. The complexity, volatility, and potential strategic significance of environmental developments are becoming more apparent to many organizations and there is increasing attention to using information and communication technologies to cope with the rapidly growing volume of data concerning environmental developments. For example, there are now many commercially available MARKETING INFORMATION SYSTEMS (MkIS) and executive information systems (EIS) that claim to offer environmental scanning services. On closer examination, however, these systems can only scan those aspects of the environment at which they are "directed" (through programming) by the systems designers and managers involved, and so they risk perpetuating and legitimizing the very perceptual prejudices that they are meant to correct.

Computer systems do, of course, provide a valuable aid to coping with the sheer diversity and volume of environmental data, in terms of both scanning and analysis and manipulation. To insure that the appropriate information is suitably integrated in timely analyses designed to inform MARKETING PLANNING processes, a structured and systematic approach to this task (e.g., Brownlie, 1995) is essential, with some environmental aspects scanned continually (e.g., DEMAND), others regularly (e.g., technological developments), and unexpected developments (e.g., new market entries) generating special focused scans as necessary. However, even with the most sophisticated scanning systems providing a stream of information, there is no substitute for the human characteristics of alertness, curiosity, and openness to INNOVATION, which are essential in turning environmental "scanning" into environmental "understanding."

Bibliography

Brownlie, D. (1994). Environmental scanning. In M. J. Baker (ed.), *The Marketing Book*, 3rd edn. London: Heinemann, pp. 139–92.

Brownlie, D. (1995). Environmental analysis. In M. J. Baker (ed.), *Companion Encyclopedia of Marketing*. London: Routledge, ch. 18.

Calori, R. (1989). Designing a business scanning system. *Long Range Planning*, **22**, 113 (February), 69–82.

EPOS

Andrew Newman and Steve Greenland

EPOS or electronic point of sale systems record data, concerning goods sold, via highly efficient electronic scanning equipment reading product barcodes at the retailer checkout. Their introduction has radically improved distribution and merchandise management in the retail sector by providing detailed and accessible information concerning product movement through stores and purchasing behavior, dramatically reducing the paperwork associated with inventory control. In addition to this, barcode-scanning technology in supermarket checkouts and the subsequent introduction of customer loyalty cards (*see* REWARD/LOYALTY CARDS) has meant that retailers have had the IT facilities to construct and analyze huge amounts of data. This has made it possible to improve the efficiency of their product replenishment systems, and to analyze what products customers are placing in their trolleys and baskets. Hence, a new type of retail intelligence has emerged that draws on "real-time" information about customer preferences. Many "tie-ins" have emerged such as discount COUPONS offering reductions in item-specific areas, thus helping to manage waste and stockouts in the food and clothing sectors. This has naturally evolved into promotional offer and mailshots tied precisely to customer buying preferences.

With this type of refinement in data gathering two basic strategies emerged: new ways of understanding and dealing with consumer product categories, and the sharing of research findings to best serve consumers through these categories. The role of supplier/manufacturer and retailer has thus altered and embraces the development of a much closer relationship (*see* ELECTRONIC DATA INTERCHANGE). SUPPLIERS and retailers have the benefit of very disparate perspectives and knowledge regarding the consumer. Retailers have a broad understanding of their own customers, whilst manufacturers enjoy specialist knowledge of their product groups across the full range of consumers. The combining of such knowledge through cross-functional relationships and reciprocity creates a more synergistic arrangement. This is a departure from the traditional role of retailers as mere distributors of products, whereas manufacturers/suppliers tend to be viewed as guardians of consumer needs and rights.

Bibliography

Harris, D. and Walters, E. (1992). *Retail Operations Management*. Englewood Cliffs, NJ: Prentice-Hall.

McGoldrick, P. J. (2002). *Retail Marketing*. Maidenhead: McGraw-Hill.

Rosenbloom, B. (1991). *Marketing Channels*. Chicago: Dryden Press.

equivalence

Rudolph Sinkovics

With international research, marketers encounter special problems and conditions which make their tasks inherently more sophisticated than in a domestic research environment. In dealing with international markets (*see* INTERNATIONAL MARKETING), firms encounter markets that require a set of substantially different factors to be considered. They are confronted with proliferating competition and, especially in developing countries, a lack of research infrastructure may be present. However, despite these idiosyncrasies in the international market research environment, it must be insured that the data that are collected and subsequently subjected to rigorous cross-national analysis have the same meaning or interpretation, and conform to the same level of accuracy, precision of measurement, and RELIABILITY. This is where the term "equivalence" or data comparability comes into play.

Equivalence refers to the comparability of data at the measurement level. If cross-national or cross-cultural data that have been collected from various international market contexts are considered equivalent, their scores can be compared. To this end, equivalence refers to a situation where virtually no bias, which might challenge the VALIDITY of cross-cultural comparisons, exists (Poortinga, 1989). Van de Vijver and Poortinga (1982) identify three types of biases and common causes. Construct bias may arise from an incomplete overlap of definitions of the constructs across cultures, poor sampling of all relevant behaviors, or incomplete coverage of the construct. Method bias may arise due to differential social desirability, different response styles (extremity scoring and acquiescence bias), unfamiliarity with the stimulus, and differences in the physical conditions of administration and tester/interviewer effects. Finally, they identify item bias, which results from poor translation, inadequate formulation, or differences in the appropriateness of the item content.

The importance of generating data that are comparable from one country to another suggests that equivalence needs to be carefully monitored at all stages in the research process (Craig and Douglas, 2000). A discussion of the various aspects of equivalence is provided by Salzberger, Sinkovics, and Schlegelmilch (1999), who illustrate their arguments graphically (see figure 1).

Salzberger et al. (1999) address the issue of equivalence from a conceptual and empirical perspective. Conceptually (depicted in the lower section of the figure), they separate the cross-cultural research process into four stages, i.e., problem definition, data collection, data

preparation, and data analysis (see also Churchill and Iacobucci, 2002). In each stage, various equivalence issues have to be dealt with conceptually and resolved for successful implementation of cross-cultural comparisons.

At the problem definition stage, the equivalence of research topics represents the minimum requirement for cross-cultural research. In examining equivalence of research topics, the first issue to consider is that concepts, objects, or behaviors studied may not necessarily be functionally equivalent, that is, they may not hold the same role or function in all countries studied (Berry, 1969). The example of bicycles given by Craig and Douglas (2000) illustrates that while bicycles are predominantly used in the US for recreation, in the Netherlands or China they provide a basic mode of transportation.

Conceptual equivalence is concerned with the use of theoretical concepts and their applicability

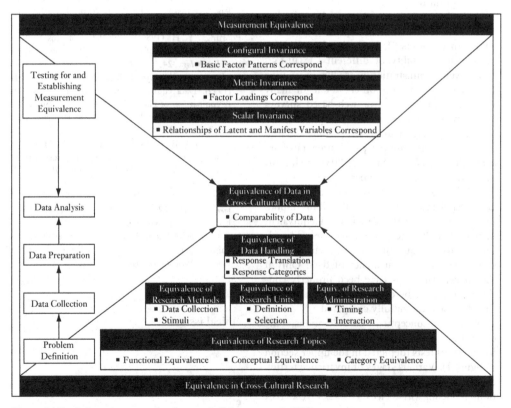

Figure 1 Equivalence in cross-cultural research (Salzberger et al., 1999)

in cross-cultural research. Many concepts are culture-bound (*see* CULTURE) and may therefore not be appropriate for research in other countries. The definition of "family values," for example, is likely to be different for European consumers from the definition in countries such as Korea, Vietnam, or China. Yet another type of equivalence to be considered at the problem definition stage relates to the category in which objects or other stimuli are placed. In the beverage market, for example, what is considered a soft drink, as well as forms of soft drinks such as canned or bottled sodas, mineral waters, fruit juices, iced tea, and powdered and liquid fruit concentrates, varies significantly from one culture to another (Craig and Douglas, 2000). In the US, for example, coffee is consumed with a variety of meals and to this end is similar to a soft drink, whereas in Italy and southern European countries it is primarily enjoyed as a social drink or a reinvigorating drink after meals.

Once the equivalence of research topics has been considered, the next step is to deal with equivalence aspects of data collection. For instance, the reliability of different SAMPLING and survey administration procedures may vary from one country to another. While in many western countries email or web-based surveys are demonstrating reasonable response rates among corporate managers, in some African countries, where Internet penetration rates are lower (Taylor Nelson Sofres, 2003), such sampling frames cannot be properly applied.

At the stage of data preparation, care has to be taken that data are equally handled. This implies that responses are translated in an equivalent manner as well as response categories. The ultimate goal of quantitative cross-cultural research lies in the equivalence of data. Only if the conceptual issues have been properly considered can data be considered equivalent and therefore be meaningfully compared.

Next to conceptual considerations, the equivalence of data can be further substantiated by statistical tests (depicted in the upper section of figure 1). Various stages of invariance testing can be undertaken by means of structural equations modeling (*see* STRUCTURAL EQUATION MODELS) or latent trait theory-based approaches (Mullen, 1995; Steenkamp and Baum-

gartner, 1998; Salzberger et al., 1999). The possible outcome of such analyses, namely, that the data do not justify comparability, might cause a reluctance among researchers to actively engage in rigorous testing of data equivalence. This is unfortunate, as non-equivalence should in itself be a highly valued research result with far-reaching consequences for subsequent studies (Salzberger et al., 1999).

See also *construct equivalence*

Bibliography

Berry, J. W. (1969). On cross-cultural comparability. *International Journal of Psychology*, 4 (2), 119–28.

Churchill, G. A. and Iacobucci, D. (2002). *Marketing Research: Methodological Foundations.* Mason, OH: South-Western.

Craig, C. S. and Douglas, S. P. (2000). *International Marketing Research*, 2nd edn. Chichester: John Wiley.

Mullen, M. R. (1995). Diagnosing measurement equivalence in cross-national research. *Journal of International Business Studies*, 26 (3), 573–96.

Poortinga, Y. H. (1989). Equivalence of cross-cultural data: An overview of basic issues. *International Journal of Psychology*, 24, 737–56.

Salzberger, T., Sinkovics, R. R., and Schlegelmilch, B. B. (1999). Data equivalence in cross-cultural research: A comparison of classical test theory and latent trait theory-based approaches. *Australasian Marketing Journal*, 7 (2), 23–38.

Steenkamp, J.-B. E. M. and Baumgartner, H. (1998). Assessing measurement invariance in cross-national consumer research. *Journal of Consumer Research*, 25 (1), 78–90.

Taylor Nelson Sofres (2003). *Interactive Global Ecommerce Report 2002*; www.tnsofres.com/ger2002/download/index.cfm (November 23).

Van de Vijver, F. J. R. and Poortinga, Y. H. (1982). Cross-cultural generalization and universality. *Journal of Cross-Cultural Psychology*, 13, 387–408.

ethical issues

see MARKETING ETHICS

etic

see ETIC–EMIC DILEMMA

etic-emic dilemma

Andrew Lindridge

The terms etic and emic are widely used methodological themes in cross-cultural research, describing how a cultural phenomenon can be assessed. How the researcher measures differing cultural behaviors ultimately has implications for the nature of the research gathered. Berry (1969) argues that cultural observations should be made via an external source using either an emic or etic approach. The emic approach measures behavior within a particular culture, using only concepts employed within that culture (Davidson et al., 1976). The etic approach observes behavior by imposing a set of universal values onto that CULTURE. Both these approaches are problematic. An emic approach may prevent cross-cultural research because its insular nature inhibits comparisons. An etic approach uses generalizations to describe observed behavior differences, which may not measure cultural differences. This problem is called the etic-emic dilemma (Berry, 1969).

Triandis, Malpass, and Davidson (1971, 1973) proposed two alternative methods for addressing the etic-emic dilemma: imposed and derived etic. The imposed etic approach uses emic measures that are assumed to be etic, for example, a belief in celebrating good fortune is a universal human behavior. This approach is criticized for being western-centric as the researcher, typically from the western world, incorrectly believes western cultural values are universally applicable. The researcher, by imposing these etic values onto the research tool, raises RELIABILITY and VALIDITY issues (Triandis, 1982; Albaum and Peterson, 1984; Sampson, 1985).

The derived etic approach accepts that the dilemma cannot be resolved. Instead etic values are amended until they resemble emic values applicable to the culture under investigation. If this process is conducted correctly and the new emic values are relatively similar to the original etic values, then cross-cultural behavioral comparisons can be made. For example, a cross-cultural study on the family's influence on the CONSUMER DECISION-MAKING PROCESS may investigate differences in parental roles between Asian Indian and North American white cultures. The biological relationship between a parent and his/her offspring is a universal etic value but the nurturing relationship in these cultures differs respectively (emic value). This cultural value can therefore be measured cross-culturally through a derived etic. For example, a researcher may measure parent–child relationships in the consumer decision-making process with the statement: "Parents' wishes should always take precedence in choosing a product." The statement measures a value that both countries could relate to but which only Indians would be expected to agree with, i.e., a derived etic has been achieved.

See also *construct equivalence; Galton's problem; matched sampling*

Bibliography

Albaum, G. and Peterson, R. A. (1984). Empirical research in international marketing. *Journal of International Business Studies*, 15 (1), 161–73.

Berry, J. W. (1969). On cross-cultural comparability. *International Journal of Psychology*, 4 (2), 119–28.

Davidson, A. R., Jaccard, J. J., Triandis, H. C., Morales, M. L., and Diaz-Guerrero, R. (1976). Cross-cultural model testing: Toward a solution of the etic-emic dilemma. *International Journal of Psychology*, 11 (1), 1–13.

Sampson, E. E. (1985). The decentralization of identity: Toward a revised concept of personal and social order. *American Psychologist*, 40 (11), 1203–11.

Triandis, H. C. (1982). Dimensions of cultural variation as parameters of organizational theories. *International Journal of Management and Organization*, 12 (4), 139–69.

Triandis, H. C., Malpass, R., and Davidson, A. (1971). Cross-cultural psychology. In B. Siegel (ed.), *Biennial Review of Anthropology*. Stanford, CA: Stanford University Press, pp. 1–84.

Triandis, H. C., Malpass, R., and Davidson, A. (1973). Psychology and culture. *Annual Review of Psychology*, 24. Palo Alto, CA: Annual Reviews, pp. 355–78.

evoked set

Emma Banister

The evoked set refers to the number of alternatives (e.g., products and brands) that are considered by customers during the problem-solving process. Sometimes known as the consideration set, this set tends to be small relative to the total number of options that are available (Hauser and Wernerfelt, 1990).

Bibliography

Hauser, J. R. and Wernerfelt, B. (1990). An evaluation cost model of consideration sets. *Journal of Consumer Research*, March, 393–408.

exchange

Fiona Leverick

While it is often seen as the central concept underpinning MARKETING, there is some debate over exactly what constitutes exchange. At the simplest level, exchange might be seen as the action of voluntarily transferring ownership of a PRODUCT or service to another in return for another object deemed to be equivalent in value. Wider definitions of the scope of exchange might not see payment as a necessary condition, or indeed might not restrict the scope of exchange to two parties or to products and services. The debate is paralleled by that on the nature and scope of marketing itself and is well summarized in Bagozzi (1975).

Bibliography

Bagozzi, R. P. (1975). Marketing as exchange. *Journal of Marketing*, 39, 4 (October), 32–9.

exhibitions

David Yorke

Exhibitions or trade shows are an element in the marketing COMMUNICATIONS MIX. They are used primarily for ORGANIZATIONAL MARKETING and are usually industry-specific. They are designed to promote supplier organizations and their products/services, identify prospective customers, and are integral to building relationships (*see* RELATIONSHIP MARKETING) with existing customers.

Their success is often evaluated in terms of "number of inquiries received" at the event. Other measures such as "orders placed" may

be implemented after the exhibition or trade show, and may be a reflection of other communication activities.

See also *marketing communications*

Bibliography

Bonoma, T. V. (1983). Get more out of your trade shows. *Harvard Business Review*, 61, 75–83.

existing demand

see DEMAND

experience curve

Dale Littler

The experience curve suggests that as a firm accumulates "experience," its real costs will decline at a predictable rate. It is a composite of several factors, including: learning, observed for example in the US aircraft industry in the 1930s, by which workers become more efficient with the number of times they repeat a task (leading to the notion of the learning curve); economies of scale; the substitution of more efficient factors of production; product redesign to lower costs of production; and the general use of technological advances. By plotting unit costs against cumulative production, a downward-sloping experience curve is produced. It is suggested (Hedley, 1976) that unit costs decline by 20 to 30 percent for each doubling of cumulative production, but only through organizations actively seeking to capitalize on experience curve effects by, for example, investing in labor-substituting technologies.

The experience curve underpins the BCG methodology for business PORTFOLIO ANALYSIS (*see* BCG MATRIX). It implies an emphasis on lowering costs in order to reduce prices to secure higher MARKET SHARE (since this could be regarded as a measure of greater cumulative experience) in order to be abreast, if not ahead, of competitors on the experience curve. Companies may even lower prices to reflect costs yet to be achieved on the experience curve in order to increase market share to a level when such costs can be obtained. However, the strategic implications of the experience curve can be questioned (see Porter, 1979). For instance, a firm's market share dominance, and therefore its alleged greater experience, can be undermined by superior innovative technology, while later entrants to an industry can purchase plant and equipment that embody accumulated experience in the form of, for example, latest versions of the technology. New entrants may therefore be able to secure lower costs and thus offer lower prices than industry incumbents. Moreover, price may not be a major determinant of market share in some markets (*see* NON-PRICE FACTORS).

Bibliography

Aaker, D. A. (2001). *Strategic Market Management*, 6th edn. New York: John Wiley, pp. 177–9.

Hedley, B. (1976). A fundamental approach to strategy development. *Long Range Planning*, 9 (6), 2–11.

Porter, M. E. (1979). How competitive forces shape strategy. *Harvard Business Review*, 57, 135–45.

experimentation

Michael Greatorex

Experimentation is a type of primary MARKETING RESEARCH (*see* PRIMARY RESEARCH) in which the experimenter systematically manipulates the values of one or more variables (the independent variables), while controlling the values of other variables, to measure the effect of the changes in the independent variables on one or more other variables (the dependent variables).

Experimentation is often used to infer causal relationships. Causation cannot be inferred unless there is evidence that (1) the change in the independent variable(s) occurs before or simultaneously with the change in the dependent variable(s); (2) the effects of other extraneous variables are measured or controlled; and (3) there is a strong association between the changes in independent and dependent variables in the way predicted by hypotheses. However, the scientific process is such that, even when these conditions are met, causation may not necessarily be proven, only a possible causal relationship inferred.

The need to rule out other causal factors in order to infer that the changes in the experimental variables cause the changes in the dependent variables is the reason behind the control of other possible causal factors. Control is obtained by devices such as: (1) use of a control group that receives no treatment; (2) randomization, where test units are assigned to different experimental and control groups at random; (3) matching, where test units are matched on background variables before being assigned to groups; (4) use of a laboratory where conditions are controllable; (5) use of specific experimental designs that control extraneous variables; and (6) measuring and accounting for the effect of extraneous variables using statistical techniques such as multiple regression (*see* REGRESSION AND CORRELATION) or analysis of covariance.

There are many types of experimental design. The simplest, the "after-only" design, involves changing the independent variable (the treatment) and following this with measurement of the dependent variable. Obvious weaknesses include the lack of a benchmark for comparison purposes and failure to control for the effect of extraneous variables. The "before-after" design, which takes measurements of the dependent variable both before and after the treatment, does allow effect of the treatment to be measured by the difference between the before and after measurement. However, this design too suffers from a lack of control of intervening variables.

The "before-after with control group" design (with cases assigned to groups at random) can help to overcome the problem of intervening variables in that changes to many intervening variables will affect both groups, and so the effect of the treatment can be measured when the before-after differences for the treatment group and the control group are compared.

Statistical designs permit the effect of changes to more than one independent variable to be measured. They allow the researcher to control for specific extraneous variables and an efficient design will allow several effects to be measured using as small a number of observations as possible. A randomized block design is useful when there is one major – or obvious – extraneous variable in addition to the dependent variable and treatment variable. The units being tested are assigned to groups or blocks defined by the extraneous variable, the experiment is carried out on the test units and the results analyzed to see if the treatment has an effect and to see if the effect is different in the various blocks. A Latin square design is similar to a randomized block design except that it enables the experimenter to specify blocks using two non-interacting external variables, thus allowing the experimenter to control for two extraneous variables. A Greco-Latin square allows the experimenter to control for a third non-interacting extraneous variable.

A factorial design is used to measure the effects of two or more independent variables. A particular value of factorial designs is that they allow interaction effects to be measured and investigated.

Data obtained from such experimental designs can be analyzed using analysis of variance (ANOVA) methods, including – where relevant – multiple range tests.

Experiments can take place in the field or in the laboratory. The advantage of field experiments is the high degree of realism that can be generated. Unfortunately, there is a lack of control, especially over intervening variables such as the weather, competitors, and the economy at large. What is worse is that the researcher may not be aware of changes to these variables. Field research is harder to conceal from competitors, who have an opportunity of early discovery of possible new developments. Field research often turns out to be time consuming and costly. However, for TEST MARKETING of new products or for measuring the effects of ADVERTISING, field experiments in actual market conditions may be necessary. Laboratory experiments allow the researcher more control over not only the possible extraneous variables, but also the measurement of the dependent variables and the changes to the independent variables. It is easier to use electronic/mechanical devices to measure dependent variables in the laboratory and the changes to the independent variables can be speeded up to reduce the time needed to conduct the experiment. However, because the experiment is conducted in an artificial environment, the generalizability of the results of laboratory experiments to the real world is reduced. Copy testing of television (or press) commercials is an example of experimentation often carried out in the laboratory.

Bibliography

Aaker, D. A., Kumar, V., and Day, G. S. (1995). *Marketing Research*, 5th edn. New York: John Wiley, ch. 12.
Tull, D. S. and Hawkins, D. I. (1993). *Marketing Research: Measurement and Method*, 6th edn. New York: Macmillan, ch. 7.

expert opinion

see INTERPERSONAL COMMUNICATIONS

expert systems

Margaret Bruce and Liz Barnes

A computer program that uses knowledge and inferencing to solve problems can be regarded as a knowledge-based system. When knowledge and inference procedures are modeled after human experts, then such a knowledge-based system is an expert system. In other words, an expert system is a computer program that uses expert knowledge to solve problems in a specific domain. Expert systems technology incorporates some "expertise," some knowledge in a program to enable a relatively inexperienced individual to make accurate decisions, or to provide a backup decision-support system perhaps to facilitate or check the stages in a decision-making process. Thus, an "expert's" knowledge can be decentralized and made more widely available.

Expert systems are advisory systems and can provide advice directly to the consumer, so generating a new PRODUCT. Main applications include fire-risk underwriting in financial services, flight scheduling in the travel industry, and generic marketing uses, e.g., the creation of customer profiles for DATABASE marketing and staff training. Examples of expert systems used in MARKETING include ADCAD (used for making ADVERTISING decisions) and SHANEX (a system for understanding changes in product MARKET SHARE) (Duan and Burrell, 1997). More "radical" potential uses, such as self-service holiday booking systems, may come into everyday use at some future stage.

Bibliography

Duan, Y. and Burrell, P. (1997). Some issues in developing expert marketing systems. *Journal of Business and Industrial Marketing*, **12** (2), 149–62.
Moutinho, L. and Rita, P. (1994). Expert systems. In S. Witt and L. Moutinho (eds.), *Tourism Marketing and Management Handbook*, 2nd edn. Hemel Hempstead: Prentice-Hall, pp. 554–8.

exporting

Nigel Holden

It is not easy to make a clear-cut distinction between exporting and INTERNATIONAL MARKETING, either for conceptual purposes or in terms of operational practices. However, it could be argued that, whereas exporting entails some elements of international marketing, international marketing can be understood as a business function quite independent of exporting. In international marketing, the emphasis is on: firms' strategy development; the management of marketing functions pertaining to firms' overall international position; and the degree and complexity of their involvements in foreign markets. Exporting may be seen, therefore, as one of the minimal stages of firms' involvements with foreign markets. The characterization of exporting as "selling in foreign markets" is only of limited value, implying that exporting is somewhat hit-and-miss or unfocused.

The point not to be overlooked is that a majority of all international firms, no matter how globally known and dominant today, were at one time small or at least substantially smaller international players. Exporting can then be seen to be an element of the growth path or learning curve of international business operations. In the 1970s and 1980s a substantial number of academic studies examined exporting firms, with the center of interest being how they became exporters. There were two dimensions of interest. The first was concerned with the motives that stimulated non-exporters to become exporters, the second with the stages of internationalization, in other words, forms or degrees of dependence on foreign business. With respect to the first dimension, the motives would be classified in terms of internal and external impulses, on the one hand, and proactive and reactive factors, on the other, as exemplified in table 1.

The second dimension, which attracted considerable scholarly attention, posited stages of internationalization of the firm through the increasing extension of its exporting activities and their sophistication. The 1970s and 1980s produced a number of models in Europe and the US, based on industry samples. The Swedish scholars Johanson and Vahlne (1977) proposed a four-stage model, according to which firms: export sporadically; export using an agent; export via a sales subsidiary; and manufacture in a foreign subsidiary. Other models have attempted to demonstrate a "natural" progression from passive or occasional exporting to a stage of making no distinction between home and foreign

Table 1 Motives for non-exporters to become exporters

	Internal stimuli	External stimuli
Proactive factors	• management decision • economies of scale • unique product or competence • perceived profitability • marketing competence	• identified foreign business opportunities • stimulation/incentives from government, chambers of commerce
Reactive factors	• risk diversification • excess capacity • retrenchment	• unsolicited foreign orders • small or shrinking home market

markets. But these characterizations have been criticized by subsequent scholars who, with some justification, find them "too logical" and therefore not consistent with actual experience. This has developed, in the US, to a keen interest in the managerial influences, including competencies, on export development; in Europe, studies of internationalization have led to extensive investigations of firms' international networking (see NETWORK) behavior.

The problem with these preoccupations with export motivations and stages of internationalization is that they deflect attention from exporting as an everyday business activity. It is in the exporters' task that we find a clear distinction between exporting and international marketing. First of all, exporting is a form of foreign market entry (see INTERNATIONAL MARKET ENTRY AND DEVELOPMENT STRATEGIES), the essential characteristic of which is that it involves direct selling to foreign customers. The selling can be completely direct in the sense that, even if the firm makes use of the services of an export house or a locally appointed agent or sets up an export department, the direct investment in the foreign market is small. In other words, exporting is selling into foreign markets with a permanent and (more or less) exclusive representation by a stock-holding market intermediary such as a distributor.

With respect to export departments, it should be emphasized that their prime purpose, generally, is not to support the foreign sales effort through undertaking market studies or assisting with export development plans, but to process the paperwork associated with the physical transfer of products into foreign markets. Such activity can include: the issuing and processing of invoices; the arranging of payments inward and outward in foreign currencies; the preparation of company brochures in foreign languages; and the supervision of transportation arrangements taking account of special requirements concerning customs procedures and goods certification in the target market.

As for the job of export managers, one of their main tasks is to forecast DEMAND in given for-

eign markets and to prepare the company accordingly to meet it. Evidence suggests that forecasts of demand are based on personal relationships (see RELATIONSHIP MARKETING) with customers that are particularly close. The export manager is unlikely to engage in the more sophisticated and expensive forms of INTERNATIONAL MARKETING RESEARCH, which seek to create coherent and systematic methodologies for identifying foreign customers and developing specific, culture-sensitive, business approaches. It would, however, be mistaken to assume that the export manager is perforce less adroit than the international marketing manager. The point to emphasize is that export managers represent different approaches to business development in foreign markets, the crucial difference residing in the scale of investment that the firm is willing to commit to foreign markets. In relative terms, selling industrial refrigerators to Saudi Arabia may be equally demanding as developing a MARKETING STRATEGY for the same products in China.

Bibliography

Johanson, J. and Vahlne, J.-E. (1977). The internationalization process of the firm: A model of knowledge development and increasing foreign market commitments. *Journal of International Business Studies*, **81** (Spring/Summer), 23–32.

external audit

David Yorke

This is one part of a MARKETING AUDIT (the other being INTERNAL AUDIT), and it consists of collecting and analyzing information on the different aspects (economic, social, legal, technological, political, etc.) of the environment (see MARKETING ENVIRONMENT) within which the organization is operating, with a view to identifying the threats to, and opportunities for, an organization.

See also *SWOT analysis*

F

factor analysis

Michael Greatorex

Factor analysis, a type of multivariate analysis (*see* MULTIVARIATE METHODS (ANALYSIS)), is concerned with the interrelationships within a set of variables and with reducing the variables required to represent a set of observations. The procedure involves the construction of a number of factors to explain the variation in the measured variables. The data reduction arises because the number of factors created is less than the number of variables. One example has 17 variables concerned with the usefulness of 17 risk relievers explained by three factors identified as clarifying, simplifying, and risk-sharing factors.

Factor analysis is empirical in that the computations are carried out on the data set, the number of factors being determined by a stopping rule. The factors may or may not be meaningfully interpreted to fit in with any theoretical ideas. If meaningful factors are obtained, factor scores for each case are computed for further use, e.g., to describe individuals or as variables in multiple regression (see REGRESSION AND CORRELATION) or in CLUSTER ANALYSIS.

Factor analysis is best carried out using a computer package such as the STATISTICAL PACKAGE FOR THE SOCIAL SCIENCES (SPSS). STRUCTURAL EQUATION MODELS have extended the ideas of factor analysis.

Bibliography

Johnson, R. A. and Wichern, D. W. (1998). *Applied Multivariate Statistical Analysis*, 4th edn. Englewood Cliffs, NJ: Prentice-Hall.

Tull, D. S. and Hawkins, D. I. (1993). *Marketing Research: Measurement and Method*, 6th edn. New York: Macmillan, pp. 422–4, 693–7.

factorial research design

Mark P. Healey

This is a type of experimental research design (*see* EXPERIMENTATION) for investigating causal relationships between MARKETING variables. It allows the marketer to investigate the effects of two or more different variables on a phenomenon of interest in a single study (termed main effects), and to examine the way these causes interact to influence the phenomenon being studied (termed interactions). In such a design, two or more causal or independent variables are simultaneously manipulated, resulting in a different treatment cell for each different combination of variables or factors. In a typical factorial design (see figure 1), the focal independent variables or factors (e.g., a, customer expectations; b, product performance), theorized to causally influence a dependent variable (e.g., customer satisfaction), are ascribed two or more levels (e.g., a_1, low, a_2, high expectations; b_1, low, b_2, moderate, b_3, high performance). The number of factors and factor levels thus determines the number of treatment cells since all levels of each factor are combined in the design (e.g., $a_{1,2} \times b_{1,2,3} = 2 \times 3 = 6$ cells). Participants are randomly assigned to one of the resulting treatment groups until the sample quota is reached, with treatment groups of equal size constituting a balanced factorial. Participants under each different treatment condition respond to identical measures of the dependent variable. The effects of each different treatment on the dependent variable can then be assessed based on treatment cell means using statistical analysis of variance.

Interaction between multiple causal variables reflects their joint influence on a dependent variable. Interaction is evident where the effect

Factor 2 Product performance (b)			
Factor 1 Customer expectations (a)	Low (b_1)	Moderate (b_2)	High (b_3)
Low (a_1)	Low expectations, low performance ($a_1 \times b_1$)	Low expectations, moderate performance, ($a_1 \times b_2$)	Low expectations, high performance, ($a_1 \times b_3$)
High (a_2)	High expectations, low performance ($a_2 \times b_1$)	High expectations, moderate performance ($a_1 \times b_2$)	High expectations, high performance ($a_2 \times b_3$)

(Customer satisfaction is the hypothetical dependent variable)

Figure 1   Example of a factorial research design

of one causal variable on the phenomenon of interest varies under different levels of another variable. For example, in one study consumers in a low-involvement state (*see* IN-VOLVEMENT) evaluated a BRAND EXTENSION more positively when it was congruent with the parent brand than when it was incongruent (Maoz and Tybout, 2002). The opposite effect was found under high-involvement conditions, thus providing evidence of interaction between the two variables of involvement and brand congruity. In a factorial design, the analysis of main effects can be achieved by averaging the effect of one variable across the different conditions of other study variables. The other independent variables are disregarded so that only differences in the phenomenon of interest arising from different levels of the main effect variable are focused upon (see Keppel, Saufley, and Tokunga, 1992).

The factorial design affords the researcher several notable advantages, both theoretical and practical. Analyzing the causal influence of multiple variables in the same study, at different levels, allows a better approximation of natural conditions than a single-factor design in which the influence of a lone variable is scrutinized, providing a more realistic appreciation of causation (Keppel et al., 1992). This is particularly important when studying inherently complex market behavior: theoretical explanations of marketplace phenomena are likely to

be more comprehensive where they incorporate multiple conceptual determinants and their interactions (Iacobucci, 1994). The study of interactions is perhaps the major benefit of factorial designs, since interactive effects often capture more adequately the complexity of causation, where the effect of one variable is mediated by another. Given the practical constraints of much MARKETING RESEARCH, factorial designs are also advantageous because they require fewer participants to test multiple main effects than would be necessary when conducting separate experiments to test these individually, yet maintain equivalent statistical power. However, where factorial designs incorporate several variables, each manipulated at multiple levels, the resulting number of different conditions or cells can quickly become unwieldy in terms of the total number of research participants required to fill all cells and complete the design.

In marketing research, the factorial design is typically used for basic or theory-testing purposes, including the study of decision-making, ATTITUDES, and persuasion, where the two-factor factorial is most common. Although primarily employed in laboratory studies in controlled settings, factorial designs are also used in field experiments, such as in TEST MARKETING.

See also *statistical tests*

Bibliography

Bryman, A. and Cramer, D. (2001). *Quantitative Data Analysis: A Guide for Social Scientists*. Hove: Routledge, ch. 9.

Iacobucci, D. (1994). Analysis of experimental data. In R. P. Bagozzi (ed.), *Principles of Marketing Research*. Cambridge, MA: Blackwell, pp. 224–78.

Keppel, G., Saufley, W. H., and Tokunga, H. (1992). *Introduction to Design and Analysis*, 2nd edn. New York: W. H. Freeman, ch. 9.

Maoz, E. and Tybout, A. M. (2002). The moderating role of involvement and differentiation in the evaluation of brand extensions. *Journal of Consumer Psychology*, **12** (2), 119–31.

family life cycle

Vincent-Wayne Mitchell

Wells and Gubar (1966) identified nine life-cycle stages, from bachelor to retired solitary survivor. The problems with their classification are that it takes no account of the number of single-parent families within many countries, or the increasing number of childless and same-sex couples. In addition, the cycles are distorted because more women are postponing having children until later in their lives and family size has declined. Murphy and Staples (1979) devised a more modern family life structure, as follows: (1) young, single; (2) young, married without children; (3a) young, divorced without children; (3b) young, married with children, infant, 4 to 12 years old, adolescent; (3c) young, divorced with children, infant, 4 to 12 years old, adolescent; (4a) middle-aged, married without children; (4b) middle-aged, divorced without children; (4c) middle-aged, married with children, young, adolescent; (4d) middle-aged, divorced with children, young, adolescent; (4e) middle-aged, married without dependent children; (4f) middle-aged, divorced without dependent children; (5a) older, married; (5b) older, unmarried, divorced, widowed; (6) others.

Bibliography

Murphy, P. E. and Staples, W. A. (1979). A modernized family life cycle. *Journal of Consumer Research*, June, 12–22.

Wells, W. C. and Gubar, G. (1966). Life cycle concept in marketing research. *Journal of Marketing Research*, **3** (November), 355–63.

feel-buy-learn model

David Yorke

The feel-buy-learn (FBL) model in MARKETING suggests that in particular situations buyers/customers do not follow the traditionally conceived learn-feel-buy sequence of communications (*see* AIDA MODEL; HIERARCHY OF EFFECTS MODEL; INNOVATION-ADOPTION MODEL). In the FBL situation, buyers/customers have images of and feelings toward products and services prior to purchase, but learning (*see* CONSUMER LEARNING) about the product (service) attributes does not occur until after purchase. This happens, for example, when it is not easy or possible to describe a product or service using words; instead pictures or images are used to invoke feelings in the potential buyers'/customers' minds in the hope that such feelings will lead to a purchase. Examples include perfume, travel, aspects of entertainment, and leisure activities.

See also *buy-feel-learn model; learn-feel-buy model*

Bibliography

Dickson, P. R. (1997). *Marketing Management*, 2nd edn. London: Dryden Press/Harcourt Brace College Publishers, pp. 569–71.

feminism

David Marsden

Feminism is the umbrella term for a number of different theories concerning the status and role of women in society, the main ones being: liberal, radical, Marxist, and black feminism (for other theories, see Bristor and Fischer, 1993; Stern, 1993; Catterall and Maclaran, 2000). They are united in the goal of eradicating all forms of exploitation and oppression directed against women – economic, political, social, and cultural. On this basic point there are no differences among feminists. However, a considerable divergence of views exists as to the root cause of women's exploitation and oppression and the best way to eradicate it.

At one pole is liberal feminism, which focuses on reform, particularly of the law, in order to promote equal opportunities and the assimilation of women into education and employment. As Bristor and Fischer (1993: 520) explain, liberal feminists "advocate eliminating laws that establish different rights for men and women, promoting legislation that prohibits various kinds of discrimination against women." In terms of MARKETING, liberal feminists are concerned with gender role stereotypes in ADVERTISING and the marketing professions. For example, the findings from a recent study found that whilst 22 percent of all sales managers in the US are women, only 4 per cent are in senior management positions (Lane and Crane, 2002).

At the other pole is radical feminism, which promotes separatism – the celebration of the unique identity and culture of women separate from men. From this perspective, men are viewed as women-haters, something that is innate to them. Radical feminists have been proactive in campaigning against the selling and use of pornography in the media. Revolutionary Marxist feminism, in contrast, contends that class is the cause of women's exploitation and oppression and that this will only be truly eradicated with the overthrow of capitalism. Using a Marxist-feminist framework, Hirschman (1993) has shown that many of the key words and concepts associated with marketing (e.g., rationality, technology, competition) reinforce sexist ideologies that seek to justify women's inferior status in capitalist societies and the marketing professions.

Finally, black feminism criticizes the whole white/middle-class bias of the feminist movement by emphasizing the colonial/imperialist origins of race and class, both in society at large and in the media (for studies on ethnic representation in the media, see van Zoonen, 1994; Hall, 1997). Black feminism raises a basic problem with feminist theory as a whole in that there is no single concept of a woman, as Woodruff (1996: 16) points out: "Women may be rich, poor, educated, white, black, lesbian, politically active or not politically active, voters, consumers, mothers, wives, daughters." Overall, feminist marketing theory seeks to offer insights and alternatives to current practice and marketing thought (Bristor and Fischer, 1993). Although each theory tends to give a totally different explanation of the cause of women's exploitation and oppression, and how to eradicate it, they are best considered in conjunction with one another because in all probability each one reflects a grain of truth.

Bibliography

Bristor, J. M. and Fischer, E. (1993). Feminist thought for consumer research. *Journal of Consumer Research*, 19 (4), 518–37.
Catterall, M. and Maclaran, P. (2000). *Marketing and Feminism: Current Issues and Research*. London: Routledge.
Hall, S. (1997). The spectacle of the "other." In S. Hall (ed.), *Representation: Cultural Representations and Signifying Practices*. London: Sage, pp. 223–80.
Hirschman, E. (1993). Ideology in consumer research, 1980 and 1990: A Marxist and feminist critique. *Journal of Consumer Research*, 19, 537–55.
Lane, N. and Crane, A. (2002). Revisiting gender role stereotyping in the sales profession. *Journal of Business Ethics*, 40 (2), 121–32.
Stern, B. (1993). Feminist literary criticism and the deconstruction of ads: A postmodern view of advertising and consumer responses. *Journal of Consumer Research*, 19 (4), 556–67.
Van Zoonen, L. (1994). *Feminist Media Studies*. London: Sage.
Woodruff, H. R. (1996). Methodological issues in consumer research: Toward a feminist perspective. *Marketing Intelligence and Planning*, 14 (2), 13–18.

financial planning for marketing communications

David Yorke

Expenditure on MARKETING COMMUNICATIONS activities must be monitored, evaluated, and controlled. Such control can only be undertaken against a plan, using one of the communication models. The plan should contain, both in total and for each target segment of buyers/customers (*see* MARKET SEGMENTATION), an analysis of the current situation, e.g., level of AWARENESS, number of product trials (see TRIAL), an objective, e.g., to increase the level of trial from X percent to Y percent in six months, and an allocation of financial resources over the chosen elements in the COMMUNICA-TIONS MIX, e.g., SALES PROMOTION, PERSONAL SELLING, EXHIBITIONS. Both during and after the period of time covered by the plan, performance can be monitored against objectives.

financial services marketing

see MARKETING FINANCIAL SERVICES

financial services retailing

Steve Greenland and Andrew Newman

Financial services retailing refers to the distribution of financial services via branch distribution networks. Within this sector the services offered are increasingly being viewed as products and the branches are being viewed as retail environments in which the staff members are salespersons rather than "bankers," practicing selling skills (Riley and Knott, 1992). The face of the high street bank has altered irrevocably to accommodate this new image. Concepts and techniques of retail marketing have been readily adopted by most types of financial institution that have direct interface with the consumer market. Since the late 1980s the major UK institutions, some with network sizes in excess of 2,000 branches, have without exception been conducting nationwide rationalization and refurbishment programs (Greenland, 1994).

A significant move by supermarkets and some discount stores into financial services throughout the 1990s introduced a major new element of competition in the sector. For consumers, this has meant a much wider range of products and service providers to choose from and, significantly, a reduction across the sector in the cost of many traditional financial services products. Food retailers are well placed to build long-term relationships with customers because of the regular customer interaction that takes place, as well as the popularity

of store card ownership and other loyalty schemes (*see* REWARD/LOYALTY CARDS). This break into financial services by the food giants essentially created a further dimension of long-term benefits for the customer in the form of a developed portfolio of financial services products.

Traditional financial service institutions (i.e., building societies and banks) are unable to differentiate by product alone, and thus see RETAIL IMAGE as a key to achieving COMPETITIVE ADVANTAGE. The branch, the front-line physical presence on the high street, is an important medium for image communication. Outlets have become far more customer oriented with key RETAIL MERCHANDISING concepts and principles being incorporated into modern branch designs. Traditional buildings of impressive appearance have been for the most part phased out and exchanged for modern glass-fronted stores. The modern financial service outlet is far more open plan, with reduced use of bandit screens and with placement of staff in the banking hall area, large glazed frontages, and much more of a shop-like appearance than traditional branches (*see* STORE DESIGN).

See also *marketing financial services*

Bibliography

Dawes, J. and Swailes, S. (1999). Retention sans frontières: Issues for financial service retailers. *International Journal of Bank Marketing*, 17 (1), 36–44.

Greenland, S. J. (1994). Rationalization and restructuring in the financial services sector. *International Journal of Retail and Distribution Management*, 22 (6), 21–8.

McGoldrick, P. J. and Greenland, S. J. (1994). *Retailing of Financial Services*. Maidenhead: McGraw-Hill.

Riley, D. and Knott, P. A. (1992). Through the eyes of the customer: Research into the new look and functioning of bank and building society branches. 155th ESOMAR Seminar on Banking and Insurance.

focus groups

Vincent-Wayne Mitchell

A focus group interview is an unstructured, free-flowing interview with a small group of people.

The participants may range from consumers talking about hair coloring, petroleum engineers talking about problems in the "oil patch," or children talking about toys. Numerous topics can be discussed and many insights can be gained, which is why focus groups are often used for concept screening and concept refinement. Also, focus groups are used in preliminary research to help in clarifying the research issues, in new product research and CONCEPT TESTING, in ADVERTISING and communications research, in studying ATTITUDES and behavior, and in designing questionnaires for use in subsequent research (*see* QUESTIONNAIRE DESIGN).

The ideal size of the focus group is six to ten relatively similar people. If the group is too small, one or two members may intimidate the others. Groups that are too large may not allow for adequate participation by each group member. Homogeneous groups seem to work best. The moderator's job is to develop a rapport with the group and to promote interaction among its members. The group session may take place at the research agency, the advertising agency (*see* AGENCY), a hotel, or one of the participants' homes. Commercial facilities often have videotape cameras in observation rooms behind one-way mirrors and microphone systems connected to tape recorders and speakers to allow observation by others who are not in the room. Streaming media consists of multimedia content such as audio or video that is made available in real time over the Internet or a corporate intranet, with no download wait and no file to take up space on a viewer's hard disk. This allows researchers to "broadcast" focus groups that can be viewed online. With such videoconferenced focus groups, marketing managers can be in a different location.

Variations on the standard group discussion format include the following:

- A *reconvened group* is one that is recruited to take part in at least two discussions, usually separated by about a week. Participants are briefed on a task that is to be completed in time for the next meeting, for example, "can you live without...?" The group reconvenes for the second discussion to impart their thoughts, feelings, and experiences.

- A *friendship group* consists of pairs or groups of friends or family members and is often used when researching children or teenagers.
- A *sensitivity panel* is a series of group discussions using the same group of people and making use of the psychodynamic processes within the group. The level of TRUST and rapport grows, allowing disclosure and "sharing" to take place.
- An *online focus* group refers to a QUALITATIVE RESEARCH effort in which a group of individuals provide unstructured comments by entering their remarks into a computer connected to the Internet. Online groups can be quick and cost effective. However, because there is less interaction between participants, group synergy and snowballing of ideas may be diminished.

Other variations of the standard procedure include:

- *Two-way focus group*: This allows one target group to listen to and learn from a related group, for example, physicians viewing a focus group of patients discussing the treatment they desired.
- *Dueling-moderator group*: This has two moderators who deliberately take opposite positions on the issues to be discussed.
- *Client-respondent group*: Client personnel are part of the discussion group and offer clarifications that will make the group process more effective.

Traditional brainstorming and industrial group discussions are two other variations.

Advertising material such as brochures, posters, or even video recordings of television or cinema adverts can be shown to focus groups and a response generated. One of the most frequently used forms of stimuli is the mood board, which is a collage created in a focus group setting. For example, focus group respondents may be asked to snip words and pictures from magazines that they see as representing the values a particular BRAND is perceived to have. In some circumstances, collages can also be made up from audio and video tapes. The mood board has two main functions: as a *reference point*, to reflect upon the discussion; and as an *enabling device* that gets respondents to loosen up and talk more freely.

Advantages of focus groups include the stimulation from interaction within the group that allows each individual to refine and expand his/her views in light of contributions from other members of the group. Furthermore, the ability to show the video tape of the discussion to executives provides them with almost direct contact with customers. Disadvantages include the possibility of respondents "lying" in order to conform to group pressures or, conversely, disagreeing with fellow participants to whom they take a dislike. The moderator can introduce biases, and interpreting and reporting the results of the discussions is subjective. Because the number of groups is usually small and the selected samples not random, generalizing the results to the population is not possible.

Bibliography

Zikmund, W. G. (2003). *Exploring Marketing Research*, 8th edn. Mason, OH: Thomson South-Western.

focus strategy

Dale Littler

The focus strategy is one of Porter's (1980) GENERIC STRATEGIES and involves concentrating on one or more niches or segments (*see* MARKET SEGMENTATION), as against aiming at securing broad market appeal. Companies adopting a focus strategy aim to secure a sustainable COMPETITIVE ADVANTAGE by being able to differentiate more effectively, or have lower costs, than their rivals for the particular customer cluster(s) they have targeted. Because they are concentrating on a more closely defined group of customers, they are able to develop more specifically defined offerings based on the target customers' particular requirements. However, there is the risk that competitors may adopt an even narrower focus or that, in the case of a differentiation focus strategy (*see* DIFFERENTIATION STRATEGY), the costs of the focus strategy make those pursuing it uncompetitive compared to those firms aiming at the broad market. Moreover, if such a niche strategy is

highly profitable, it will attract rivals which, in turn, will diminish profits.

See also *competitive strategy; cost leadership strategy*

Bibliography

Porter, M. E. (1980). *Competitive Strategy: Techniques for Analyzing Industries and Competitors.* New York: Free Press, ch. 2.

forecasting

Michael Greatorex and Jim Freeman

Forecasts, implicit or explicit, are used every time a MARKETING decision is made. Strategists need long-term forecasts of changes in the environment and of DEMAND for both current and potential products in different markets and segments (*see* MARKET SEGMENTATION). Marketing managers use medium-term forecasts to aid decision-making concerning PRICING and the allocation of resources such as ADVERTISING budgets and salesforce personnel to different products and markets. In addition, marketers are often called upon to provide short-term forecasts of sales to enable the production and distribution departments to plan production, inventories, and distribution. Further, marketers are required to provide forecasts of sales and revenues for the budgets that are the basis of management and control in every organization.

FORECASTING METHODS

Forecasting techniques divide into qualitative and quantitative methods. Quantitative methods further subdivide into causal and non-causal approaches.

Non-causal forecasting methods. Non-causal methods take a time series of past observations of the variable to be forecast and extrapolate the series into the future using graphical or, more usually, numerical methods.

The naive method uses a single observation, usually the latest, as the forecast of future values.

With the well-known decomposition method, a series is decomposed into its constituent parts, namely: trend, cycle, seasonality, and error. The constituent parts may be combined in additive or multiplicative fashions. Forecasts are prepared by estimating these individual components, which can then be recombined, once future trend values have been found by extrapolation, to provide forecasts for the original series. The classical decomposition method has been extended into an iterative form, together with an ability to take account of special events, in the Census II software currently available and in use today.

However, forecasting methods based on exponential smoothing are more popular than the classical decomposition and the Census II methods. Simple exponential smoothing uses a weighted average of past observations; the fact that the weights decline exponentially gives a simple formula that enables the computations to be made every time a new observation becomes available, thus making timely use of up-to-date data. Simple exponential smoothing is used for data that fluctuate about a set level (i.e., are "stationary"). Data with a trend require a slightly more complicated procedure, such as Holt's method, while data that also contain a seasonal cycle can be handled by Winters's method (see Bails and Pepper, 1993: ch. 8). Historically, it has been helpful for a control procedure to be used with exponential smoothing. Typical control procedures are based on cumulative sums of the errors in one-period-ahead forecasts or a tracking procedure such as Trigg's tracking signal. The main advantage of exponential smoothing methods is the simplicity of the computations and the potential flexibility and responsiveness of the methods.

Box and Jenkins (1976) developed a technique that explained the data series in terms of autoregressive and moving average processes. Potential models are identified by examining the autocorrelation and partial autocorrelation functions. The model is then estimated and a series of diagnostic checks tests the adequacy of the model. Given an acceptable model, forecasts then follow on.

Trend curve analysis attempts to fashion a relationship between the data series and time as the single explanatory variable. Various forms of relationship such as linear, polynomial, logarithmic, power, exponential, logistic, Gompertz, etc. are fitted using least squares or alternative procedures, where necessary.

Causal forecasting methods. Causal modeling attempts to identify the underlying determinants of demand. The relationship of these variables with demand is investigated with a view to using the relationship to obtain forecasts. Thus, as well as providing forecasts, causal methods can provide insights into underlying processes, in particular into identifying the variables that affect the variable being forecast. The methods include leading indicators, multiple regression (*see* REGRESSION AND CORRELATION), econometrics, and input–output methods. A leading indicator is a time series of data for another variable whose changes tend to lead changes in the variable of interest by a fixed period. There may be a reason for the relationship, e.g., sales of drainage pipes may precede sales of roofing tiles by a period equivalent to the difference between the laying of the foundations in a housing development and the building of the roofs. The main use of leading indicators (or diffusion indices) is to predict the overall level of the economy.

In multiple regression, the variation in a dependent variable is explained by the corresponding variation in a number of independent (or predictor) variables. Time-series data or, sometimes, cross-sectional data are used with the least squares method to estimate the relationship. A number of checks are carried out to test the applicability of the least squares method. If a suitable regression equation is found, forecasts of the dependent variable are forthcoming but are based on values of the independent variables which themselves may need forecasting. Although this may be a disadvantage of the regression method as far as forecasting is concerned, the insight into the underlying influences may be invaluable. Econometric models build upon multiple regression methods and usually involve specifying several (sometimes many depending on the problem) simultaneous relationships between the variables of interest. Special estimation techniques for econometric models are available. While econometric models are used at the company level, they are best known for their use in modeling and forecasting at the national macroeconomic level. Input–output methods are based mainly upon the transactions between industries as measured by government statisticians in input–output matrices. The focus is on inter-industry flows. Potentially, this should be a good basis for forecasting, especially for industrial markets. However, the collection of data upon which input–output matrices are built is so slow that by the time the tables are published the information is out of date for most practical forecasting purposes.

Qualitative forecasting methods. Qualitative methods rely on "soft" data based on the perceptions and subjective judgment of individuals. These may involve the subjective opinions of salespeople, sales managers, marketing managers, or subjective forecasters providing forecasts on sales for budgets, production, inventory control, and MARKETING MIX decisions. Aggregating the forecasts of individual sales representatives of sales of each product to each customer and potential customer (after adjustment for biases in previous forecasts) is a common procedure.

Forecasts can be point forecasts or interval forecasts or probability forecasts. A point forecast is a specific amount and is almost bound to be wrong. An interval forecast provides a range of values within which the actual value may fall with a given level of confidence. Sometimes minimum, most likely, and maximum values are estimated; other assessors are asked to provide pessimistic, most likely, and optimistic forecasts. A probability forecast attaches probabilities to given outcomes, e.g., that the variable being forecast will lie in several possible intervals, or uses a probability distribution to describe the subjective assessment. Long-range forecasts concerning technical innovations may be obtained from "experts" in the relevant field using, for instance, the delphi method. Surveys of buyers' intentions and consumer confidence are considered to provide soft data that may be useful for predicting discretionary purchases such as consumer durables.

COMBINING FORECASTS

Forecasts of the same variable obtained by different methods are often combined. In addition, forecasts obtained by exponential smoothing may be adjusted using the subjective estimates of a forecaster.

SELECTION OF FORECASTING METHOD

The selection of an appropriate forecasting technique is fraught with difficulty, depending as it does on forecasting horizon, the nature of the data, the accuracy required, and the ease and cost of use of different methods. Practitioners need to employ an appropriate technique for the specific situation. For instance, non-causal time-series methods such as exponential smoothing are particularly suitable for use by multiproduct organizations that need detailed and frequent short-term forecasts for the planning of production and inventories.

Bibliography

Bails, D. G. and Pepper, L. C. (1993). *Business Fluctuations: Forecasting Technique and Applications*, 2nd edn. Englewood Cliffs, NJ: Prentice-Hall.
Box, G. E. P. and Jenkins, G. M. (eds.) (1976). *Time Series Analysis: Forecasting and Control*. San Francisco: Holden Day.

franchises

see RETAIL FRANCHISES

franchising

Gillian C. Hopkinson

Franchising is a contractual business arrangement used especially in RETAIL DISTRIBUTION CHANNELS. The arrangement involves a BRAND owner (franchisor) and an independent businessperson (the franchisee). The franchisee invests in the business both by funding set-up costs such as premises and through an initial joining fee. The franchisee then makes ongoing payments that are usually calculated as a percentage of turnover. The franchisee receives the right to trade in the brand within a particular area and for a particular period.

Franchise contracts are usually long term (i.e., 20 to 30 years). The contract specifies, often in great detail, the manner in which the business is to be run and allows for the regulation of this by the franchisor. Additionally, the franchisor provides management support and training. A level of regulation across independent businesses is deemed necessary to protect the value of the brand and hence the value of the franchisee investments. The franchisee is the residual claimant (that is, owns all profits or losses) resulting from the business after payments to the franchisor (as outlined above) have been made.

Diverse forms of franchising exist but two categories are of particular importance. *Product franchising* occurs, for example, in the car industry where franchisees retail the branded product manufactured by the franchisor. *Business format franchising* involves the tighter specification of all aspects of the business by the franchisor and is thus suited to highly branded, "cloned" styles of business such as those found in the fast food, niche retailing, and hotel industries.

Several theoretic approaches help to explain why franchising has been adopted as a business model. As a contractual arrangement, franchising is considered as a hybrid system of governance. Williamson (1985) argues that a combination of elements of authority (the hierarchical control mechanism) with elements of the market mechanism provides for an efficient system. The contract is used to obtain an appropriate mixed mechanism. Others (see, e.g., Bradach and Eccles, 1989) argue that TRUST is associated with relationships and that this, therefore, also contributes to efficient transacting in franchise situations.

Several reasons may explain why a brand owner would choose to franchise instead of owning and directly operating the business units (Hopkinson and Hogarth-Scott, 1999). One reason may be the financing that franchisees make available, thus facilitating rapid growth so that franchising overcomes resource constraints. Franchising may also be seen as an efficient way to operate a unit that is some distance from head office: if the franchisee has invested in the business, he/she will make sure it is run well (the agency cost argument). Finally, it is argued that franchising brings on board local managers with local knowledge and therefore reduces the search costs associated with gaining localized information. Although some support for these arguments can be found, each problem may also be addressed by ways other than franchising so that these seem to be only partial explanations. A more precise understanding of franchise use is gained by considering its fit with the specific market conditions and strategic goals of the franchisor (Carney and Gedajlovic, 1991; Hoffman and Preble, 1991).

For franchisees, it has been argued that franchise systems offer a low-risk route to business ownership since the concept has been tested and the franchisor provides management support. However, this argument underestimates the risk associated with a franchisee (see Stanworth et al., 2001) and also relies on a picture of franchisees as small and lacking experience. Increasingly, franchise arrangements are entered into between very sizeable businesses (see Bradach, 1998).

Franchise systems pose some particular managerial and strategic challenges. Managerially, the franchisor seeks to "lead" an inter-organizational network. This involves gaining agreement, or at least compliance, from independent businesses. The problems associated with this account for the interest that has been shown in franchise CHANNEL CONFLICT. Strategic challenges include the introduction of new units within a territorial system, adaptation of the system to changing environments, and maintenance of a homogeneous operation. Adaptation may involve further franchisee investment and threaten homogeneity.

Generally, franchising occurs within a dual distribution system comprising both franchised and company-owned units. Although the two may have a symbiotic relationship (Bradach, 1998), dual distribution may introduce direct competition between franchisor and franchisees and therefore is associated with some tensions. This intra-channel but inter-organizational competition is likely to become more prevalent as electronic technologies facilitate new and more direct distribution channels between brand owner and consumer.

Bibliography

Bradach, J. L. (1998). Using the plural form in the management of restaurant chains. *Administrative Science Quarterly*, **42** (2), 276–303.

Bradach, J. L. and Eccles, R. G. (1989). Price, authority and trust: From ideal types to plural forms. *Annual Review of Sociology*, **15** (1), 97–119.

Carney, M. and Gedajlovic, E. (1991). Vertical integration in franchise systems: Agency theory and resource explanations. *Strategic Management Journal*, **12** (8), 607–25.

Hoffman, R. C. and Preble, J. F. (1991). Franchising: Selecting a strategy for rapid growth. *Long Range Planning*, **24** (2), 74–85.

Hopkinson, G. C. and Hogarth-Scott, S. (1999). Franchise relationship quality: Micro-economic explanations. *European Journal of Marketing*, **33** (9), 827–43.

Stanworth, J., Purdy, D., English, W., and Willems, J. (2001). Unravelling the evidence on franchise system survivability. *Enterprise and Innovation Management Studies*, **2** (1), 49–65.

Williamson, O. E. (1985). *The Economic Institutions of Capitalism*. New York: Free Press.

free sample

Dale Littler

The provision of a free sample, particularly of a new PRODUCT, is a means of encouraging TRIAL. Free samples may be distributed to households; provided with magazines or newspapers; or given with existing products that are purchased. Free samples are obviously a means of reducing PERCEIVED RISK and (generally) apply to fast-moving consumer goods.

See also *adoption process*

frequency

David Yorke

As part of their advertising programs, organizations have to decide which media (*see* MASS MEDIA) to use, and a major consideration here is the desired frequency, i.e., the number of times within a specified period that an average person, household, or organization is exposed to the advertising message. The requisite frequency to have the desired effect (e.g., purchase) will be contingent on several factors including the competitive POSITIONING of the BRAND, the content and creativity of the MESSAGE (*see* CREATIVE CONTENT), and various customer behavior characteristics.

See also *advertising*

functional equivalence

see CONSTRUCT EQUIVALENCE

G

Galton's problem

Andrew Lindridge

In sample group designs for cross-cultural/societal research, the issue of sample group independence arises, i.e., Galton's problem. Galton's problem recognizes how different cultures/societies develop and adopt similar behaviors and practices through a transfusion process (Sekaran, 1983). For example, Britain's economic and historical links with the US insure that neither country's population could be considered to be truly independent from the other in a comparative study. Sample group independence is therefore violated, potentially resulting in analysis that falsely infers causal relationships between a CULTURE/society and its population (Ember and Otterbien, 1991).

Whether sample group independence represents an issue to cross-cultural/societal research depends upon the extent that the population being studied needs to be an isolated one. Ember and Otterbien (1991) argue that cross-cultural sample group independence cannot be achieved, as few societies are truly isolated. The authors argue that societies' connections with others should simply be acknowledged and identified regarding how they potentially influence cultural/societal behavior and values being studied.

See also *construct equivalence; etic-emic dilemma; matched sampling*

Bibliography

Ember, M. and Otterbien, K. F. (1991). Sampling in cross-cultural research. *Behavior Science Research*, **25** (1–4), 217–33.

Sekaran, U. (1983). Methodological and theoretical issues and advancements in cross-cultural research. *Journal of International Business*, **14** (Fall), 61–73.

gatekeepers

Dominic Wilson and Dale Littler

Gatekeepers can have an important (if often unnoticed) informal influence on organizational purchasing (*see* ORGANIZATIONAL BUYING BEHAVIOR; PURCHASING PROCESS), although they are not members of the decision-making unit (*see* BUYING CENTER) in a formal sense. The term refers to key influencers who actively acquire and disseminate information from both external and internal sources. They often are identified within the organization as a source of informed intelligence and their opinions may be sought, particularly with regard to purchase decisions. Gatekeepers may influence the flow of information into an organization and identifying and targeting the gatekeepers with MARKETING COMMUNICATIONS can have a major influence on the effectiveness of the MARKETING STRATEGY in organizational markets.

generic strategies

Dale Littler

These are a menu of broad or general strategies which can be applied by different organizations in different contexts. Writers on strategy tend to have their own lists. For example, Ansoff (1965) presented the matrix of four "directional" strategies (*see* DIRECTIONAL MATRIX; GROWTH

VECTOR MATRIX). Michael Porter (1980) defined the widely known group of generic strategies: COST LEADERSHIP STRATEGY, DIFFERENTIATION STRATEGY, and FOCUS STRATEGY (*see* COMPETITIVE STRATEGY). Others have produced more extensive lists. Mintzberg (1988) developed what he argued is a comprehensive set of generic strategies, grouped into five clusters. There are those which are concerned with: locating the core business, i.e., defining what are the boundaries of the business, its essential processes, etc.; distinguishing the core business, i.e., identifying what is different about the business that can provide a COMPETITIVE ADVANTAGE, including how value is added and the core competitive strategies it has adopted; elaborating the core business, such as developing its product offering within the business and other strategies defined within the Ansoff matrix; extending the core business, such as through DIVERSIFICATION, VERTICAL INTEGRATION; and reconceiving the core business, such as through redefining the business in terms of broader needs, rather than from a narrow product or technology perspective, as Levitt (1960) argued.

The notion of generic strategies can be criticized along two fronts. First, they can only be presented in broad outline form since the specific features of the business, and the context within which the organization operates, will define the content of the strategy and influence the process of IMPLEMENTATION. Second, the competitive process involves rivalry between businesses seeking to secure some advantage from being different, so that the most appropriate competitive strategies are likely to be those which are innovative or at least different in some way from those of other firms, and do not follow some accepted strategic recipe. Generic strategies as such therefore can only at best offer an outline of the possible range of options, whereas the color and texture will have to be added for the company to be able to secure a differential advantage.

Bibliography

Ansoff, H. I. (1965). *Corporate Strategy: An Analytic Approach to Business Policy for Growth and Expansion.* New York: McGraw-Hill.

Levitt, T. (1960). Marketing myopia. *Harvard Business Review*, 38, 4 (July/August), 45–56.

Mintzberg, H. (1988). Generic strategies: Toward a comprehensive framework. In *Advances in Strategic Management*, vol. 5. Greenwich, CT: JAI Press, pp. 1–67.

Porter, M. E. (1980). *Competitive Strategy: Techniques for Analyzing Industries and Competitors.* New York: Free Press, ch. 2.

Rumelt, R. (1980). The evaluation of business strategy. In William F. Glueck (ed.), *Business Policy and Strategic Management*, 3rd edn. Maidenhead: McGraw-Hill.

geodemographics

Vincent-Wayne Mitchell

Geodemographic groups of consumers (i.e., identified by geographic and demographic variables), referred to as geodemographic classifications, are built on the premise that people who live in similar neighborhoods are likely to have similar purchasing and lifestyle habits. Most classifications are built by using data from the census of population such as employment type, age, marital status, family size, property type, etc. Other variables can be used and some classifications have adopted this approach, e.g., Mosaic, Finpin. Sometimes a preliminary process called principal component analysis is used on the raw variables to identify commonalities in the data. Either the raw variables or the principal components are then subject to CLUSTER ANALYSIS to identify similar types of geographic areas. (For details of the classifications and methods, see *Journal of the Market Research Society*, 1989.)

Some of the major classifications in the UK are: ACORN (A Classification Of Residential Neighborhoods); PIN (Pinpoint Identification Neighborhoods); Mosaic; and Superprofiles. As an example, ACORN classifications have been divided into six major categories: Thriving, Expanding, Rising, Settling, Aspiring, and Striving. These are further desegregated into 17 groups and 54 types. For example, the Thriving category includes groups of Wealthy Achievers in Suburban Areas, Affluent Grays in Rural Communities, and Prosperous Pensioners in Retirement Areas, and thus provides a means of locating where these types of individuals are likely to reside.

One question that has been raised in the literature is, does it really make sense to use one standard segmentation tool across all sorts of industry sectors, markets, products, and organizations? The answer appears to be that each general classification product does discriminate, but the degree of discrimination varies according to market sector and there is no single best standard geodemographic product for all situations from those available. Two of the first market-specific applications to be devised were Financial Mosaic and Finpin, which were designed specifically to segment the market for financial services. Sources of data used for Financial Mosaic include: the number of company directors, the level and value of share ownership, the level of application for various financial services, the proportion of mortgages and outright home owners, and the frequency and value of county court judgments. This has resulted in a classification of 36 Financial Mosaic types: for example, Young Entrepreneurs, Wealthy Businessmen, and Captains of Industry are three types grouped under Capital Accumulators.

The demand for, and supply of, tailored or bespoke segmentation classifications has risen recently, e.g., Investor ACORN incorporates data from the Investors' Register, a DATABASE of over 1 million investors, and Art ACORN combines demographic data with information from the box offices of arts venues throughout Great Britain. The extension of these more targeted classifications is to have a bespoke classification for each particular market. If organizations have sufficient information on their customers, this can be used to create bespoke classifications for any product market, e.g., cars, food, hi-fis, etc. ACORN Lifestyles UK is a new database of 44 million individuals who are rated 0–100 according to their propensity to have a product or service, e.g., a current account, credit card, types of holiday, listening to music. Lifestyles UK database can be linked to the full ACORN family classification system. People*UK is the first classification system of individual people in the UK; it is an individual-level ACORN. It is a mix of geodemographics, lifestyle (see LIFESTYLES), and life-stage data condensed in an easy-to-use format.

CCN has made major inroads into building classifications within many European countries. Euromosaic identifies ten major pan-European types that are consistent across the following European countries: Great Britain, the Netherlands, Germany, Spain, Ireland, Sweden, and Belgium. An example of a Euromosaic type is Elite Suburbs. These are well-established suburban neighborhoods in large and medium-sized cities, consisting of residential properties in large grounds. These people are wealthy, but live in restrained luxury. Finally, GLOBAL Mosaic is a single classification system encompassing the whole world.

The major advantages of geodemographics are: their multifaceted nature, i.e., they do not rely on unidimensional classification variables; their ease of use and actionability, being linked to the postcode system and covering all consumer addresses within the UK; their ability to link with different data sets that have been geodemographically coded for ABOVE-THE-LINE and below-the-line marketing activities, e.g., TV audience rating data and regional press; and their ability to describe the types of houses people live in which can help the marketer to understand his/her target segment. They are now an essential part of retail site analysis and branch/store assessment. For example, by knowing how many of a certain type of customer are within a branch/store catchment area, a more accurate assessment of alternative branch locations and of market and sales targets can be undertaken. They are useful in MEDIA PLANNING, since media data sources such as the National Readership Survey and Target Group Index are geodemographically coded. ADVERTISING and promotional messages can also be communicated to the target audience using DIRECT MAIL and door-to-door leaflet campaigns, which can be geodemographically targeted. Finally, they are extensively used in customer profiling, which involves geodemographically analyzing existing customers.

Geodemographic systems do have several weaknesses. First, because the census information is released at an aggregated level of about 150 households (enumeration district), classifications are not particularly good at targeting certain differences, e.g., age, at the household or postcode level. However, several products have been designed to overcome this problem. "Monica" from CACI attempts to use the Christian names of household dwellers to indicate their likely age band, e.g., Ethel and Arthur are names that have an older age profile than Simon and Amanda.

A second problem, known as the "ecological fallacy," refers to the assumption that the behavior of all individuals will be the same within a given geodemographic type. Since geodemographic classifications describe neighborhoods rather than people, it is fallacious to assume that all the people within a given neighborhood will purchase in the same way. Mosaic is one system that has attempted to address both the age and the aggregated data problem by incorporating many variables that are measured at the postcode, rather than at the enumeration district, level. This allows more precise targeting, since there are typically only 15 households per postcode. In addition, Persona from CCN is one of the first behavioral targeting systems. If in geodemographic terms "you are where you live," with Persona, "you are what you do." Developed from the National Shopping Survey, it divides UK households into distinctive behavioral types. These types range from so-called "Bonviveurs" to "New Teachers," "Craftsmen," and "Home Makers." Such data counter another of the weaknesses of traditional census-based classifications in that they give more information about people's income, assets, leisure activities, and purchasing behavior, which is not available from the census.

A final problem with census-based classifications is the age of the data on which they are based, resulting from the fact that the census is conducted only once every ten years in most countries including the UK. More than half of the data contained within Mosaic is non-census information and is updated regularly, although the Mosaic types themselves are only updated every two years. These non-census data sources allow the classification to be applied to newly built areas.

See also *market segmentation; segmentation variables*

Bibliography

Journal of the Market Research Society (1989). Special issue on geodemographics, 31, 4 (January).

Chisnall, P. (2001). *Marketing Research*, 6th edn. Maidenhead: McGraw-Hill.
Sleight, P. (1995). Explaining geodemographics. *APMAP*, January, No. 347, 48.

global strategy

Dale Littler

A global strategy can be considered as a coherent overarching strategy for the parts of the world in which an organization operates. Yip (1989) suggests that it emerges as part of a three-stage process: first, the development of a core strategy or a distinct COMPETITIVE ADVANTAGE, generally in the firm's domestic market; second, the extension of the firm's geographic REACH of the core strategy, which will be adapted to match local features; and third, GLOBALIZATION, viewed as the INTERNATIONAL MARKETING of standard offerings (*see* OFFERING) (Levitt, 1983), through the integration of these adapted strategies into a global strategy. This is an obvious simplification of the international development of organizations, which may not involve this sequence of stages.

A global strategy tends to be seen as synonymous with a standard strategy across international markets. Such a strategic approach can be regarded as yielding distinct advantages through, in particular, economies of scale, which may be the major driver to the adoption of a global strategy. As Hill (2001) notes, a global strategy is appropriate where there are pressures for low costs and where there are not significant specific local requirements, as would appear to be increasingly the case in many industrial goods industries, such as the semi-conductor industry. However, as several commentators have noted, there are many barriers to such a standard global strategy, especially in consumer goods industries, including differences in the physical environment and CULTURE, and they question the feasibility of a global standardized branding strategy, arguing that the differences, from language alone, far outweigh any similarities.

Adaptability and variation in marketing strategies (*see* MARKETING STRATEGY) across geographic markets are likely to be the norm. It may be an essential requirement to acknowledge dissimilarities between countries and adjust marketing strategies to suit specific regional requirements. Quelch and Hoff (1986) suggest that there is a spectrum of strategic possibilities with different elements (such as PRODUCT features, ADVERTISING, MESSAGE content) having greater or smaller degrees of homogeneity across markets.

It has been suggested (e.g., Littler and Schlieper, 1995) that many markets may be converging under the influences of more widespread communications, the market DIVERSIFICATION strategies of manufacturers and retailers, and the development of free trade areas, such as the European Union, although there are still evident significant elements of local variation. As Bartlett and Ghoshal (1989) have argued, there are such powerful competitive pressures that, in order to survive, companies are compelled to "exploit experience-based cost economies and location economies" and "transfer core competencies within the firm" while at the same time "paying attention to local responsiveness." They also note that in the modern multinational corporation the core competencies do not reside only in the "home" country but may be distributed throughout the organization. Therefore, companies should strive to capture these core competencies wherever they are situated. To do so, they need to encourage two-way flows between subsidiaries and the center of the organization.

See also *international product adaptation; international product standardization*

Bibliography

Bartlett, C. A. and Ghoshal, S. (1989). *Managing Across Borders: The Transnational Solution*. Boston: Harvard Business School Press.

Hill, C. W. L. (2001). *Global Business*, 2nd edn. Boston: Irwin McGraw-Hill.

Levitt, T. (1983). The globalization of markets. *Harvard Business Review*, **61**, 3 (May/June), 92–102.

Littler, D. and Schlieper, K. (1995). The development of the Eurobrand. *International Marketing Review*, **12** (2), 22–37.

Quelch, J. A. and Hoff, E. J. (1986). Customizing global markets. *Harvard Business Review*, **64** (May/June), 59–68.

Yip, G. S. (1989). Global strategy in a world of nations? *Sloan Management Review*, **30** (Fall), 29–41.

globalization

Mohammed Yamin

Globalization is best described as a process of deepening internationalization. The major actors in the global economy, firms and governments, are both impacted by this process and also have helped to shape its development. So far as firms are concerned, internationalization has been an uninterrupted process of increasing significance and intensity since the 1950s. Three aspects of this process are particularly noteworthy.

First, an increasing number of firms have been involved in international production. Leading firms from all major capitalist countries have followed the earlier example of their US and UK rivals and have become more and more international in their scope, utilizing not only international trade but also direct foreign investment, as well as other forms of international production such as LICENSING, INTERNATIONAL JOINT VENTURES, and subcontracting.

Second, there has been a sectoral widening of international production. Thus, while during the 1960s the most rapid growth of international production took place in manufacturing, since then it has been the service sector that has experienced the most rapid growth in internationalization. This tendency has been most prominent in banking and financial services. Other business-related services such as ADVERTISING and accountancy have also experienced growing internationalization.

Finally, it is important to note that international business activities have experienced qualitative as well as quantitative expansion. These qualitative changes relate to the increasing process of intra-firm integration of international business activities. Most firms have changed from being international to being more multinational or even global in their internal organization (Leong and Tan, 1993). An international firm is one for whom its domestic market is of predominant importance and which views international business as a way of further exploiting assets and capabilities developed for the domestic market. A multinational firm treats foreign markets as being equally important to the home market. A global firm makes little distinction between foreign and domestic markets. In business terms, globalization relates to the competitive REACH of the company. Thus according to Yip (2003: 7) "a global company does not have to be everywhere, but it has the capability to go anywhere, deploy any assets and access any resources and it maximizes profits on a global basis." Although direct participation in international production is still confined to a relatively small number of firms, all firms are nevertheless impacted by the process of internationalization. For one thing, firms in almost all industries face direct competition from international rivals. As an example, the majority of firms in the fast food industry are very small with only local marketing horizons; however, the fiercest competition faced by such firms comes from global firms such as McDonald's or Pizza Hut. Further, technological change is breaking down industry boundaries and, as a consequence, firms experience (unexpected) competition whose origin is often from outside their domestic market. For example, traditional postal businesses are increasingly being impacted by electronic mail and other computer network services.

Recent research has introduced a degree of skepticism as to the degree of globalization. For example, Rugman (2003) has argued forcefully that globalization is a "myth"; both aggregate and firm-level data point to a picture that is much more accurately described as "regionalization." Thus most trade and investment flows are intra-regional within each of the three key regions (the European Union, East Asia, and North America). Over the last 20 years trade and investment flows within each region have grown faster than between regions, and few companies are truly global in the sense of having significant presence in all three regions. In a somewhat similar vein, Chamewat (2003) has elaborated the concept of *semi-globalization* by showing that although most indicators of market integration have shown significant increase over recent years, it is far from the case that markets are fully integrated and many barriers to cross-country integration remain. The limited success of the World Trade Organization (WTO) in removing protectionist policies is a relevant consideration.

Taking a broader societal perspective, a debate is emerging as to the nature or meaning of globalization. The common "orthodox" view is that globalization is a process of growing homogenization in which national differences are inexorably being diluted by technological and economic forces (Hill, 2003). This view implies a sense of neutrality in the process in that *all* countries are held to be mutually converging. However, in some respects, reality is at odds with this view. For example, developments in transitional and emerging countries are more accurately described as a process of forced adaptation than a process of mutual convergence. Zander (2002), in fact, has defined globalization as a process in which the traditional patterns of economic, social, and cultural life are forced to adapt to the "modern." "Modernity" in this context refers to the economic and societal system in "western" countries (now including Japan). The institutions of modernity (market economy, minimal government, secularism, human rights, etc.) do diffuse to traditional societies, but this is a slow and incremental process even in the age of the Internet. However, a segment of the population in traditional societies will have modern aspirations (an aspiration fueled by the ease of information flow and greater awareness of life opportunities in modern countries). This segment will be likely to regard the pace of modernization in their own countries as too slow and will seek to migrate to the modern world, thus leaving their own countries increasingly populated by people who reject "modern" values. In this way, globalization generates polarization (between modern and traditional societies) rather than homogeneity. The implication of this view of globalization is that the business environment is frequently affected by underlying political and cultural tensions and by a pervading sense of insecurity.

Bibliography

Chamewat, P. (2003). Semi-globalization and international business strategy. *Journal of International Business Studies*, 34, 138–52.

Hill, C. (2003). *International Business*, 4th edn. New York: McGraw-Hill.

Leong, S. and Tan, C. (1993). Managing across borders: An empirical test of the Bartlett and Ghoshal organizational typology. *Journal of International Business Studies*, **24** (3), 449–64.

Rugman, A. (2003). Regional strategy and the demise of globalization. *Journal of International Management*, **9** (4), 409–17.

Yip, G. (2003). *Total Global Strategy II*. Upper Saddle River, NJ: Prentice-Hall.

Zander, U. (2002). When Mohammed goes to the mountain: Globalization, cathedrals of modernity and a new world order. In V. Havila, M. Forsgren, and H. Hakansson (eds.), *Critical Perspectives on Internationalization*. New York: Pergamon Press.

graphical representation

Michael Greatorex

The results of MARKETING RESEARCH can be presented in graphical form as part of the reporting procedure. Quantitative analysis, starting with the summarization procedures of the construction of frequency distributions or calculation of measures such as totals or measures of average and variation, is taken a stage further with the presentation of the results of quantitative research in the form of pie diagrams, line charts often showing graphs over time, bar charts, histograms, ogives, and scatter diagrams. Contemporary data analysis computer packages, e.g., the STATISTICAL PACKAGE FOR THE SOCIAL SCIENCES (SPSS), even Excel, provide facilities for summarizing data using automatically generated graphical representation.

A pie diagram is simply a circle divided into sections with each section representing portions of a total. For instance, the total sales in a market can be represented by the area of the circle with sections representing competitors' sales, thus permitting market shares (*see* MARKET SHARE) to be presented. Pie diagrams allow relative sizes at any moment to be presented. It is possible to present a few pie diagrams side by side to show shares in different situations, e.g., at two different times or in two different markets. In this case, the total area of the circles would vary to represent the totals in the different situations.

The line chart is useful for depicting results over many periods. It is the common time-series graph with time measured on the horizontal axis and the variable(s) of interest measured on the vertical axis. When more than one variable is presented, different colored lines or dashed and dotted lines can be used to identify the particular variables. A stacked line chart showing a total and its components stacked on each other shows how relative sizes or shares change over time and is similar, yet preferable, to a series of pie diagrams.

A bar chart has many variations. The magnitude of a variable is represented by a bar on a graph. The sales of each of several brands in a period can be represented in a bar chart by horizontal (or vertical) bars. Another simple version of a bar chart shows measures of a variable over time as a series of vertical bars as an alternative to a line chart as a means of depicting a time series. In pictograms, the bars are converted to pictorial representations of the variable. Thus, if the variable is sales of wine, a horizontal bar could be replaced by a number of bottles in a row. If several variables are to be represented over time, a simple bar chart can be replaced by a grouped bar chart, in which the values of the variables for each period are represented by groups of bars placed next to each other, one group for each period. Alternatively, if the several variables are components of a total, a stacked bar chart can be used.

One use of a bar chart is to depict the number of times each value occurs for a variable measured on a nominal scale, e.g., the numbers of males and females in a sample. If the variable is measured on an interval scale that is split into a number of contiguous classes, the numbers in the classes can be represented in a histogram by a series of adjacent vertical rectangles, the areas of which are proportional to the frequencies, and the bases of the rectangles are determined by the width of each class. This is the standard way of representing frequency distributions, e.g., the distribution of heights in a sample of first-year male college students. When the data are based on a sample, the histogram may be a series of rectangles that give a very rough approximation to the population distribution, which for some variables is the smooth bell-shaped curve known as the normal distribution.

If the frequencies are cumulated to show the number of cases below (or greater than) a series of values of the variable, then a cumulative frequency curve or ogive can be plotted. When the variable is normally distributed, the less than cumulative frequency curve will be S-shaped.

The relationship between two variables can also be represented on a scatter diagram. If one variable can be identified as the dependent variable, it will be represented on the vertical (or y) axis, with the independent variable on the horizontal (or x) axis. Each pair of values is represented on the graph and a scatter of points builds up. If the points are scattered all over the graph, then prima facie there is little or no relationship between the variables (a low correlation coefficient will confirm this). On the other hand, if there is a pattern to the points, then the analyst will be able to spot a possible relationship for further investigation using perhaps regression methods (*see* REGRESSION AND CORRELATION).

See also *types of measure*

Bibliography

Churchill, G. A. (1991). *Marketing Research: Methodological Foundations*, 5th edn. Chicago: Dryden Press, ch. 18.

green issues

see CONSUMERISM

gross margin

Dominic Wilson

Gross margin (usually expressed as a percentage of sales) is sales revenues minus the costs of production (e.g., raw materials, components, labor, energy). Calculating the gross margin of a product or service is an important stage in assessing its unique CONTRIBUTION and profitability since gross margin includes the variable costs incurred in production. The allocation of other costs (mostly fixed costs) is often heavily influenced by corporate accounting policy and so may not provide as good an indication of a product's individual profitability.

See also *margin*

group influences

see INTERPERSONAL COMMUNICATIONS

growth-share matrix

see BCG MATRIX

growth vector matrix

Dale Littler

Traditionally, this identifies two major parameters for defining growth (*see* GENERIC STRATEGIES): markets and products, each of which are categorized as "new" or "existing" (Ansoff, 1965). Four strategies can be identified: market penetration; market development; product development; and DIVERSIFICATION. Market penetration involves increasing MARKET SHARE and/or volume of existing products in existing markets by increasing the number of customers and/or the amount existing customers purchase. ADVERTISING, promotion, and other MARKETING approaches may be employed to persuade existing customers to purchase more of the product, switch customers from rival products, or even develop new customers for the product. Market development involves the targeting of new segments (*see* MARKET SEGMENTATION) or expanding into new geographic markets using existing products. Product development involves modifying existing products, or the development of new ones (*see* NEW PRODUCT DEVELOPMENT), for customers in existing markets. Diversification is considered the most risky of the options since it involves the development of both new markets and new products. Such diversification may be related to what the company currently does in some way, or it may be completely unrelated. Aaker (2001) adds VERTICAL INTEGRATION as a growth strategy. Growth may also be secured through HORIZONTAL INTEGRATION.

Bibliography

Aaker, D. A. (2001). *Strategic Market Management*, 6th edn. New York: John Wiley & Sons Inc., ch. 12.
Ansoff, I. (1965). *Corporate Strategy*. New York: McGraw-Hill.

guarantees

Mark P. Healey

Guarantees can be employed as a technique for reducing PERCEIVED RISK and thus increasing purchase intentions/likelihood. They are also a means of reducing post-purchase dissonance (*see* COGNITIVE DISSONANCE) and of influencing consumers' product and service evaluations (e.g., of quality), and thus influence repurchase/repatronage behavior. Generic guarantees, such as those offered by retailers such as the John Lewis Partnership, make an assurance that it is "Never knowingly undersold" and offer to "pay the difference" if purchasers can buy the identical product elsewhere. Many producers and retailers offer such guarantees because competitors often do so.

habitual buying behavior

Dale Littler

Purchasers will tend to engage in limited search and evaluation behavior where the purchase has little INVOLVEMENT for the buyer. For some repeat purchases the buyer simplifies the decision-making even further by making the purchase on the basis of what he/she has done before. This is likely to occur where there is considerable BRAND LOYALTY based on high CUSTOMER SATISFACTION with previous purchases of the BRAND, for example. Inertia may also play an important role where there is little perceived difference between available offerings (*see* OFFERING) and there is no other incentive, such as a considerably lower price or dissatisfaction with a previous purchase of the brand or product, to change behavior.

Bibliography

Dickson, P. R. and Sawyer, A. G. (1990). The price knowledge and search of supermarket shoppers. *Journal of Marketing*, 54, 42–53.

hierarchy of effects model

Margaret K. Hogg and David Yorke

This is a model of MARKETING COMMUNICATIONS developed by Lavidge and Steiner (1961) that proposes seven stages through which the buyer/customer passes from unawareness of a product or service to purchase: unawareness, AWARENESS, knowledge, liking, preference, conviction, and purchase. The COGNITIVE STAGE is denoted by awareness and knowledge, the AFFECTIVE STAGE by liking, preference, and conviction, and the CONATIVE (or behav-ioral) STAGE by a purchase. Measures taken before or after a form of communication is used will enable objective(s) to be set and the communication's success to be analyzed. Logical progression through the stages is not always possible – indeed, much depends on the product or service being offered and the target group of receivers. In addition to the standard high-involvement hierarchy (*see* INVOLVEMENT), the low-involvement hierarchy proposes that consumers move from thinking to acting to feeling; the attribution hierarchy proposes that consumers move from acting to feeling to thinking (Wells and Prensky, 1996: 482–4); the experiential/impulse hierarchy moves from feeling to acting to thinking; and the behavioral influence hierarchy moves from doing to thinking to feeling (Mowen and Minor, 1998: 256–7).

Also of importance is the consumer's level of involvement in relation to the information content and creative form (*see* CREATIVE CONTENT) of the marketing communication such as ADVERTISING. This is known as the elaboration likelihood model and describes two routes that the marketer can use for persuading consumers to respond to marketing messages (*see* MESSAGE). Where consumers are highly involved with products and prepared to devote significant effort to processing information, then advertising messages can be used to invoke a *central route to persuasion*. In this case consumers will be "motivated to integrate the new information into existing knowledge... and will use this integrated knowledge to develop new attitudes or strengthen existing attitudes" (Wells and Prensky, 1996: 446). However, if the product or service is linked with low involvement, then marketing messages will appeal to the *peripheral persuasion route*, and creative messages are often used in order to influence consumer

ATTITUDES in the short term rather than trying to get consumers to process the information into their long-term memory (Wells and Prensky, 1996: 447).

See also *buy-feel-learn model; feel-buy-learn model; learn-feel-buy model*

Bibliography

Hoyer, W. D. and MacInnis, D. J. (2001). *Consumer Behavior*, 2nd edn. Boston and New York: Houghton Mifflin, ch. 11.

Kotler, P. (2003). *Marketing Management: Analysis, Planning, Implementation and Control*, 11th edn. Englewood Cliffs, NJ: Prentice-Hall.

Lavidge, R. J. and Steiner, G. A. (1961). A model for predictive measurements of advertising effectiveness. *Journal of Marketing*, October, 61.

Mowen, J. C. and Minor, M. (1998). *Consumer Behavior*, 5th edn. Upper Saddle River, NJ: Prentice-Hall, ch. 8.

Mowen, J. C. and Minor, M. (2001). *Consumer Behavior: A Framework*. Upper Saddle River, NJ: Prentice-Hall, ch. 7.

Solomon, M. R. (2002). *Consumer Behavior: Buying, Having, Being*, 5th edn. Upper Saddle River, NJ: Prentice-Hall, ch. 7.

Solomon, M. R., Bamossy, G., and Askegaard, S. (2002). *Consumer Behavior: A European Perspective*, 2nd edn. Upper Saddle River, NJ: Prentice-Hall, ch. 5.

Wells, W. D. and Prensky, D. (1996). *Consumer Behavior*, New York: John Wiley, ch. 15.

hierarchy of needs

see CONSUMER NEEDS AND MOTIVES

high street retailing

Steve Greenland and Andrew Newman

High street retailing refers to retail activity in the traditional shopping areas of town, city, urban, and suburban locations. (Traditional shopping areas are described by Guy, 1994.) This type of shopping is frequently termed strip or ribbon centers by some US retailers (see, e.g., Levy and Weitz, 1998). Continued movement of major retailers to newly developed out-of-town, suburban locations and the growth of shopping malls and planned shopping centers has fueled debate concerning the future vitality and viability of high street retailing (e.g., Schiller, 1994). The 1990s was characterized by a resurgence of town center development and the gentrification of dilapidated districts. Despite this, many long-established high street shops disappeared to be replaced by estate agents, banks, and insurance brokers, as consumers gravitated toward large out-of-town supermarkets and one-stop shopping. Stores of this type are designed to provide a complete shopping service for a major part of the consumer's needs (Newman and Cullen, 2002: 18). The changes described reflect various economic and social changes in the UK and elsewhere that affect the relative ability of the small retailer to deliver the retail services expected by modern consumers (Newman and Cullen, 2002).

See also *shopping centers*

Bibliography

Guy, C. (1994). *The Retail Development Process*, 2nd edn. London: Routledge.

Howard, E. (1992). Evaluating the success of out-of-town regional shopping centers. *International Review of Retail, Distribution and Consumer Research*, 2 (1), 59–81.

Levy, M. and Weitz, B. A. (1998). *Retailing Management*, 3rd edn. Boston: McGraw-Hill.

Newman, A. J. and Cullen, P. (2002). *Retailing: Environment and Operations*. London: Thomson Learning.

Schiller, R. (1994). Vitality and viability: Challenge to the town center. *International Journal of Retail and Distribution Management*, 22 (6), 46–50.

historic demand

see DEMAND

horizontal integration

Dale Littler

This is regarded as an integrative growth strategy and involves acquiring or merging with competitors within the same industry, as opposed to a vertically integrative strategy, which involves the acquisition of SUPPLIERS (backward integration) or customers (forward integration).

Horizontal integration may not necessarily be undertaken as a means of growth; it might also be employed to rationalize an industry, which is maturing or declining, by removing capacity.

See also *competitive strategy; growth vector matrix; vertical integration*

hypothesis testing

Michael Greatorex

Hypothesis testing or statistical significance testing is important in MARKETING RESEARCH. A battery of significance tests is available to test hypotheses concerning population means, proportions, differences between means and proportions, correlation coefficients, etc. based on data from a probability sample (*see* SAMPLING; STATISTICAL TESTS).

Although there are many different tests depending upon the circumstances, the philosophy underlying the tests is the same. A null hypothesis is developed concerning a characteristic or parameter of the population. The null hypothesis is that the population parameter, e.g., a mean, a proportion, the difference between two means or two proportions, is equal to a particular specified value. This is the hypothesis that is tested and is assumed to be true for the purpose of the test. An alternative hypothesis is developed in relation to the null hypothesis. The alternative hypothesis can be a simple hypothesis, e.g., that the parameter is equal to a different specific value, or more usually that the parameter is not equal to (or sometimes either greater than or less than) the value specified in the null hypothesis. Where the null hypothesis typically assumes no difference in a parameter between two or more groups, the alternative hypothesis typically predicts differences between groups on the specified parameter. The null and alternative hypotheses are specified before sample data are examined.

The test chooses between the two hypotheses using a test statistic whose sampling distribution is known, assuming the null hypothesis to be true. In practice, the null hypothesis is not rejected when the chances of obtaining a particular value or a more extreme value of the test statistic are high; it is rejected if those chances are low. The question is, what is a high and what is a low chance? A probability level, the level of significance, say 5 percent or 1 percent or 10 percent, is fixed before the test statistic is calculated. This enables ranges of values for the test statistic to be worked out. If the test statistic, when calculated, falls in one range, it is not rejected; if it falls in other ranges, usually extreme ranges, it is rejected. Alternatively, when the calculations are being done using computer packages, the computer works out the probability (often called the p value) of obtaining a more extreme value of the test statistic than the one obtained; if this is less than the previously specified significance level, the null hypothesis is rejected, otherwise the null hypothesis is accepted.

Thus, when a null hypothesis is rejected, there is a small chance of rejecting a hypothesis that is true. It would, on the face of it, make sense to make the chances of this error, called a Type I error, as small as possible by using very low significance levels. However, there is another kind of error, a Type II error, which is the chance of not rejecting a false hypothesis, which, for a given sample size and test statistic, increases when the chance of a Type I error is reduced. Increasing the size of the sample is one way of improving the sensitivity of a test.

It is important to note that a statistically significant difference between the means of two groups may or may not say something about the practical or commercial difference between the two groups. For instance, the difference between the means of two groups may be statistically significant (because of large samples), but the actual difference between the sample means may be very small and of no practical significance whatever.

Bibliography

Chisnall, P. (2001). *Marketing Research*, 6th edn. Maidenhead: McGraw-Hill.

I

image

Margaret Bruce and Liz Barnes

Image is the perception of a service, BRAND, PRODUCT, or organization by its publics. For example, a Ford Escort may be perceived in different ways by Ford dealers, by the corporate buyer of a fleet of cars, by a family man, and by a single female buyer. A hospital's image includes all aspects of patient care, customer service, and the overall impression of the hospital by those who encounter the organization in a variety of forms as patient, employee, and local resident.

Images held by consumers are formed from a combination of factual and emotional material and are governed by past experiences, influential people who express their likes and dislikes, for example celebrities, and the perceived benefits. The image (or identity) of an organization is the sum of all the ways the organization chooses to present or define itself to the various publics. This includes the physical environment, stationery, publications, names, language style, signs, advertisements, uniforms, and so on. This results in the *corporate identity*, which is the impression, image, and personality projected by the organization (de Mooij, 2004).

McGoldrick (2002) notes the importance of image monitoring to the evaluation and formation of retail marketing strategies. He claims that retailers are increasingly aware that a poorly perceived image can result in low store patronage and ultimately in store failure. For retail chains, a clear differentiation is required; for example, the distinction in being perceived as "clean and white," "the store where you can see your friends," and the "store with helpful personnel." Creating the right image for a retailer, brand, or corporation is important as there are clear links between consumers' self-image and their choice of product or brand – consumers will tend to choose the product or brand that they regard as being a reflection of their own self-image (Hines and Bruce, 2002; de Mooij, 2004).

Bibliography

Aaker, D. A. and Myers, J. G. (1987). *Advertising Management*, 3rd edn. Englewood Cliffs, NJ: Prentice-Hall, ch. 5.

De Mooij, M. (2004). *Consumer Behavior and Culture*. Thousand Oaks, CA: Sage.

Hines, T. and Bruce, M. (2002). *Fashion Marketing*. London: Butterworth-Heinemann.

McGoldrick, P. (2002). *Retail Marketing*, 2nd edn. Maidenhead: McGraw-Hill.

impact

David Yorke

In the context of ADVERTISING and decisions relating to choice of media (*see* MASS MEDIA), organizations take account of the potential impact of advertisements. The impact is related to the CREATIVE CONTENT of the advertisement and the media scheduling (*see* MEDIA SCHEDULE). Impact is the qualitative value of an exposure through a given medium, e.g., an advertisement for kitchen appliances would have a higher impact in *Good Housekeeping* than in *Sports Illustrated*.

implementation

Dale Littler

The implementation of strategy is regarded as the third part of a four-stage process of STRA-

TEGIC PLANNING involving the stages of analysis, planning, implementation, and control. The process assumes that after analysis, plans are devised that act as blueprints for action. Appropriate feedback mechanisms should be in place to detect deviations from plans so that, where possible, actions can be taken to put the business back on course as specified in the planned strategy. In larger organizations based on, for example, a functional structure, the MARKETING function (or functions if it is a multidivisional company) will have responsibility for insuring that the appropriate aspects of the MARKETING MIX are carried out to make sure that the CORPORATE STRATEGY is effectively implemented. The organization has to insure that the requisite resources are in place to support the strategy.

The view of strategy development often presented depicts the devisers of plans as separate from those who implement them. Action, then, is regarded as divorced from the formulation of strategy, which, according to Bonoma and Crittenden (1988), has tended to receive the greater academic emphasis.

However, it might be expected that the implementation of strategy would itself be significant in shaping the way in which it emerges. Those at the interface with the market, for example, will be faced with issues on a day-to-day basis that the planners, remote from customers and the ebb and flow of the market, will not have a detailed grasp of; while, of course, the plan formulators cannot possibly anticipate all of the issues and changes that arise. These may demand pragmatic responses which, in turn, can affect the emerging strategy (see EMERGENT STRATEGY). Mintzberg (1990) criticized the view of what he termed the "design school," which portrays formulation and application as separate stages: "Our critique of the Design School revolves around one central theme: its promotion of thought independent of action, strategy formation above all as a process of *conception*, rather than as one of *learning*" (p. 182).

Because of the uncertainties (see UNCERTAINTY), it would be realistic to assume that organizations need to have the flexibility to adapt, adjust, and augment what may have been proposed in any original plans in response to newly emergent information, the conse-

quences of past actions, competitors' reactions, and other developments. Effective implementation may, as Piercy (1990) argues, be an iterative process which involves the major protagonists and which takes cognizance of the different power relationships in the organization. Organizations may revise their strategy and how it is implemented in light of the feedback from customers and others, and changes in the context within which they are operating. Strategy in some cases may be seen as emerging (Mintzberg, 1973; Hutt, Reingen, and Ronchetto, 1988), and the process of developing strategy may be intimately interwoven with the action of implementation.

Those involved with the implementation of the strategy in some way can influence the realized strategy through how they interpret what should be done, how they decide what should be done (e.g., to fit in with their own personal requirements), and, for those who interact with customers and other important stakeholders, what they communicate verbally or otherwise. Those at the interface with the customer have a particularly important role in strategy implementation in service industries.

Bibliography

Bonoma, T. V. and Crittenden, V. L. (1988). Managing marketing implementation. *Sloan Management Review*, **29** (Winter), 7–14.
Hutt, M. D., Reingen, P. H., and Ronchetto, J. R. (1988). Tracing emergent processes in marketing strategy formation. *Journal of Marketing*, **52** (January), 4–19.
Mintzberg, H. (1973). Strategy making in three modes. *California Management Review*, **16**, 2 (Winter), 44–53.
Mintzberg, H. (1990). The design school: Reconsidering the basic premises of strategic management. *Strategic Management Journal*, **11**, 3 (March/April), 171–95.
Piercy, N. (1990). Marketing concepts and actions: Implementing marketing-led strategic change. *European Journal of Marketing*, **24** (2), 24–42.

impulse purchasing

Andrew Newman

Impulse purchasing refers to the act of buying an item of merchandise without prior consideration or premeditation, but taking the decision to buy "on the spur of the moment." From a consumer behavior perspective (*see* CONSUMER BUYER BEHAVIOR), this type of purchasing involves generally little or no information gathering during the *search* stage of the CONSUMER DECISION-MAKING PROCESS. Often this is because the consumer experiences a sudden urge that he/she cannot resist (Solomon, Bamossy, and Askegaard, 2002: 286), and therefore provides immediate gratification and sense of satisfaction. Such behavior has therefore significant implications for retailers and the layout of stores, where the lure of the surroundings and merchandise on display can imbue consumers with the desire to consume (*see* STORE DESIGN). Former research in environmental psychology (Snodgrass and Russell, 1988) and MARKETING (Gardner, 1985; Rook and Gardner, 1986) suggests that some settings provide an important sense of emotional security. The implications of this are that the physical setting can, in some circumstances, regulate human emotional states. For example, consumers' moods may be heightened or lowered by the impact of the physical (retail) setting, and especially at the point of purchase, thereby impacting on the amount of money spent.

In general, retailers carefully position merchandise in stores to maximize the chance of customer purchase. Discount retailers in particular strategically target customers who buy on impulse. Here the accent is on impulse purchasing of a wide range of pick-up items, many at very low prices, particularly in the household and personal care product categories. Store interiors can be lit with strategically placed lighting that highlights racks of goods and tempts customers with attractive offers, leading to impulse purchasing (*see* ATMOSPHERICS). Strategic placing of accessories in close proximity to clothing and similar merchandise gives rise to associated sales, which consumers pick up "on impulse" (Newman and Cullen, 2002).

Bibliography

Gardner, M. P. (1985). Mood states and consumer behavior: A critical review. *Journal of Consumer Research*, 12, 281–300.

Newman, A. J. and Cullen, P. (2002). *Retailing: Environment and Operations*. London: Thomson Learning.

Rook, D. W. (1987). The buying impulse. *Journal of Consumer Research*, 14 (September), 189–99.

Rook, D. W. and Fisher, R. J. (1995). Normative influences on impulsive buying behavior. *Journal of Consumer Research*, 22 (December), 305–2.

Rook, D. W. and Gardner, M. P. (1986). Mood factors and impulsive buying behavior. Working paper, University of Southern California. In Ronald P. Hill and Meryl P. Gardner (1987), "The buying process: Effects of and on consumer mood states." *Journal of Consumer Research*, 14 (September), 189–99.

Snodgrass, J. and Russell, J. A. (1988). Planning, mood and place-liking. *Journal of Environmental Psychology*, 8, 209–22.

Solomon, M. R., Bamossy, G., and Askegaard, S. (2002). *Consumer Behavior: A European Perspective*, 2nd edn. Upper Saddle River, NJ: Prentice-Hall, p. 286.

inbound communications

David Yorke

Communications in DIRECT MARKETING may be either inbound or outbound (*see* OUTBOUND COMMUNICATIONS). The latter are initiated by the supplier organization directly to the buyer or customer, e.g., DIRECT MAIL and TELEMARKETING. Inbound communication occurs when a potential buyer or customer is stimulated to reply to a form of indirect communication that appears in the media, e.g., TELEVISION or RADIO advertisements or advertisements in NEWSPAPERS, MAGAZINES, or TRADE JOURNALS, which may invite a response from the receiver in person, in writing, by telephone, or through electronic mail. Evaluation of the cost effectiveness of the stimulus is relatively easy in terms of either the number of positive responses, e.g., requests for information, or, if possible, the value of sales generated.

Bibliography

Roberts, M. L. and Berger, P. D. (1989). *Direct Marketing Management*. Englewood Cliffs, NJ: Prentice-Hall.

indirect communications

David Yorke

MARKETING COMMUNICATIONS may be either direct, e.g., personal, face-to-face, verbal, or in writing with the targeted buyer, customer, or consumer; or indirect where it is intended that the target will receive a communications MESSAGE through an appropriate impersonal channel. Indirect communication channels comprise the MASS MEDIA (e.g., TELEVISION, RADIO, NEWSPAPERS, MAGAZINES, TRADE JOURNALS), PUBLICITY, SALES PROMOTION, or PACKAGING.

industrial marketing

Dominic Wilson

This is the term originally coined in the 1960s to describe the process of MARKETING between organizations. It referred implicitly to organizations engaged in industry (especially "smokestack" industries). During the 1980s it became accepted that the term was inadequate because it failed to reflect the full diversity of marketing activities between organizations, especially between commercial organizations such as banks, publishers, distributors, and retailers. The term BUSINESS-TO-BUSINESS MARKETING was then coined as an alternative, though nowadays the term ORGANIZATIONAL MARKETING is preferred by many authorities because it recognizes that the principles and practice of marketing between organizations are not confined to "businesses" but also extend to a vast range of organizations such as hospitals, orchestras, prisons, armed forces, schools, charities, governments, and unions.

influencers

Dominic Wilson

Influencers are actual or potential members of the decision-making unit (*see* BUYING CENTER) and are those individuals who may be influential in the PURCHASING PROCESS without necessarily being USERS, DECIDERS, or SPECIFIERS. This is an imprecise categorization but might include individuals who are affected by a purchasing decision without being directly involved. For example, security staff might suggest additional features (such as temporary electronic tagging) that would make it more dif-

ficult for personnel to steal components from a factory (e.g., theft of car radios from car factories).

See also *organizational buying behavior*

information systems

see MARKETING INFORMATION SYSTEMS

innovation

Dale Littler

Innovation is distinct from invention in that it involves the adoption of a new idea, product, service, technique, structure, or process as against the creation of something new. Schumpeter (1939) highlighted what he regarded as innovation's central role in economic development. He depicted this as a process of "creative destruction" caused by the introduction of innovations, which undermined existing forms and modes of doing things, and the responses of entrepreneurs to them. The upswing of a major economic cycle (the Kondratieff 50- to 60-year cycle) has been associated with investment in a major innovation by pioneering entrepreneurs. These are later followed by a host of imitators who temporarily glut the market so that price declines and profits collapse. Some firms are bankrupted and business confidence lost, only to be revived by the next innovation.

However, such innovations are likely to be radical or discontinuous (*see* DISCONTINUOUS INNOVATION), whereas the majority of innovations are continuous or incremental adjustments to existing procedures, products, structures, and processes (*see* CONTINUOUS INNOVATION).

Given the significant changes that can occur in the environment (*see* ENVIRONMENTAL ANALYSIS) of an organization, the importance of being alert to external innovations has been emphasized in the strategic management literature. Companies need to be prepared to be innovative, not only to respond to and preempt such external changes, but also to establish a strategic agenda of their own.

The diffusion of an innovation (*see* DIFFU-SION PROCESS) is, according to Rogers (1995), affected by five major features of the innovation: relative advantage; complexity; observability; divisibility; and compatibility. An innovation does not have to be absolutely new ("new to the world") to be regarded as an "innovation," but can be new only to the market or other context into which it has been introduced.

In MARKETING, an innovation may be a new product/service *per se* (*see* NEW PRODUCT DE-VELOPMENT), but it may also embrace a raft of other changes – new PACKAGING, new distribution channels, new modes of communication with customers – that can provide a COMPETI-TIVE ADVANTAGE if they are valued by customers and provide a sufficient degree of differentiation from competitors.

Bibliography

Rogers, E. M. (1995). *Diffusion of Innovations*, 4th edn. New York: Free Press.
Schumpeter, J. A. (1939). *Business Cycles*. New York: McGraw-Hill.

innovation-adoption model

David Yorke

The innovation-adoption model was developed by Rogers (1995), who postulated a number of stages through which a targeted buyer or customer passes, from a state of unawareness, through AWARENESS, INTEREST, TRIAL, to purchase/adoption. Awareness relates to the COGNITIVE STAGE of the process, interest and evaluation to the AFFECTIVE STAGE, and trial and adoption to the CONATIVE (or behavioral) STAGE.

Progression through the stages may or may not be logical and will depend on factors such as: the product or service being offered; stage in the PRODUCT LIFE CYCLE; and the buyers – their needs, socioeconomic position, present product ownership, PERSONALITY, perceptions of risk (*see* PERCEIVED RISK), media habits, and so on.

See also *adoption process; diffusion process; marketing communications*

Bibliography

Rogers, E. M. (1995). *Diffusion of Innovations*, 4th edn. New York: Free Press.

innovators

Dale Littler

Innovators are those who first adopt (*see* DIFFU-SION PROCESS) an INNOVATION. In consumer markets they are seen as being venturesome (Rogers, 1995), more outward looking, and less risk averse. In Rogers's categorization of adopters on the basis of innovativeness, using the standard distribution curve, innovators are identified as the first 2.5 percent of those who adopt an innovation. The degree of INVOLVEMENT with the product class may also be an important factor, so that innovators may, at least to some extent, be product-category specific.

Using the Kirton adaption-innovation (KAI) inventory, which is a measure of cognitive style, Foxall (1995) found that both adapters, "more controlled, systematic, consistent, steady, reliable, prudent, sensitive, realistic, efficient and orderly than Innovators" (Foxall and Goldsmith 1994: 136), and "innovators," who "tend to be more extrovert, less dogmatic, more tolerant of ambiguity, more radical, flexible, assertive, expedient, undisciplined and sensation seeking than Adapters" (ibid.), are among early purchasers of a range of products. Level of involvement is also found to be important, but here again adapters and innovators are present.

In summary, "In terms of Kirton's adaption-innovation theory, so-called consumer innovators might exhibit either adaptive or innovative cognitive styles. Personal involvement with the product field also emerged as a powerful explicator of 'innovative' consumer behavior" (Foxall, 1995: 285). Foxall suggests that a more appropriate term for those who first adopt an innovation is "market initiator."

Bibliography

Foxall, G. R. (1995). Cognitive styles of consumer initiators. *Technovation*, **15** (5), 269–88.
Foxall, G. R. and Goldsmith, R. E. (1994). *Consumer Psychology for Marketing*. New York: Routledge, pp. 133–45.

Rogers, E. M. (1995). *Diffusion of Innovations*, 4th edn. New York: Free Press.

instrument equivalence

see CONSTRUCT EQUIVALENCE

integrated marketing communications

Philip J. Kitchen

Integrated marketing communications (IMC) "is a strategic business process used to plan, develop, execute, and evaluate coordinated, measurable, persuasive brand communication programs over time with consumers, customers, prospects, and other targeted, relevant external and internal audiences" (Schultz and Kitchen, 2004: 65). This definition implies that IMC has moved beyond MARKETING COMMUNICATIONS as tactical output, to marketing communications as strategic partner. Arriving at IMC as a strategic business process implies business development, INNOVATION, and resource allocation. Such a process is not just a matter of labeling.

TOPIC SUMMARY

IMC extends well beyond the promotional mix. In this short summary, two related questions will be addressed:

1 What is IMC?
2 Can IMC be interpreted (understood) differently by academics and by practitioners?

WHAT IS IMC?

IMC is a product of the late twentieth century. Its birth can be traced to practitioner (ADVERTISING, DIRECT MARKETING, and PUBLIC RELATIONS) activities in the late 1980s, as witnessed by articles in the trade literature. Its growth can be traced directly to emergent academic interest, commencing in the early 1990s, spearheaded by work at the Medill School of Journalism, Northwestern University, led by Professor Don Schultz. Since that time, its growth has been meteoric. But, like so many

MARKETING developments, it has been driven by several factors:

- Market dynamics.
- Continued academic inputs in the trade and academic literature (see, e.g., the series of articles and papers in *Marketing News*, the main practitioner magazine for the American Marketing Association).
- The fact that from its earliest beginnings, the development was embraced and supported by "gurus" in the generic marketing discipline (e.g., the top-selling textbook in marketing is by Professor Philip Kotler, also from Northwestern University).
- The widespread adoption of IMC by advertising agencies (*see* AGENCY) around the world, who were themselves driven by organizational exigency. Thus, ad agencies are now integrated agencies.
- The apparent adoption of IMC by major companies around the world. Integrated approaches make sense to businesses, and to agencies who service their needs.
- The need to have "promotion" appear to be consumer oriented and consumer driven; previously, "promotion" had been internally driven by a philosophy of separatism, where each promotion mix element had its own foci and its own dynamics.
- The need to overcome the "silo mentality" associated with promotion mix singularity.

Yet IMC has a multiplicity of definitions and a multiplicity of understandings. Hence, there is potential and actual variability in terms of applications. Thus, IMC itself, conceptually and in terms of application, is not integrated (see above definition of IMC).

CAN IMC BE INTERPRETED (UNDERSTOOD) DIFFERENTLY BY ACADEMICS AND BY PRACTITIONERS?

The answer to this question is in the affirmative. Different definitions mean different interpretations, hence different applications. Businesses are also diverse. They are each exposed to different market dynamics. The stages theory of IMC as well as the reluctance of many companies to progress along a developmental path have been discussed elsewhere (see Kitchen,

2004). The reason for the apparent reluctance to move up a beneficial development path is simple – it costs money, time, and resources. It means relearning how to communicate. It means taking marketing itself seriously (see Kitchen, 2004), which most businesses do not. Instead, they adopt a simplistic, half-hearted approach to marketing and communications that is characterized in two words: "*inside-out.*" That is, all that is required for them to implement IMC is a rather straightforward bundling together of promotional mix elements so that all messages speak, sound, or look alike, at least to receivers. Thus, to implement IMC at stage 1 means no real attempt has to take place to understand consumer, customer, and prospect dynamics (after all, that is an investment, a cost, and it means communication has to change from inside-out to outside-in). No investment has to be made to build and maintain databases (*see* DATABASE) or to apply information technology rigorously. No attempt is made to measure marketing communications return on investment, nor to ally marketing more closely with financial criteria. Yet, understanding and interpretation of IMC lead directly to application. Furthering that understanding requires study and learning. Applying increased knowledge requires financial and technological resources, and management or executive time.

IMC is here to stay. It is indeed defined and practiced in various ways. In the latest text (Kitchen and de Pelsmacker, 2004), IMC is located in one stage, though the authors stretch beyond this in terms of critical comments and theoretical foundations. The text is designed to "prime" students to further studies in this emergent field of academic and practitioner endeavor.

See also *communications mix; communications objectives; communications research*

Bibliography

Goldenberg, J. (2004). Invisible forces: How consumer reactions make the difference. In P. J. Kitchen (ed.), *Marketing Mind Prints*. Basingstoke: Palgrave Macmillan, ch. 5.

Kitchen, P. J. (1999). *Marketing Communications: Principles and Practice*. London: International Thomson.

Kitchen, P. J. (ed.) (2004). *Marketing Mind Prints*. Basingstoke: Palgrave Macmillan.

Kitchen, P. J. and de Pelsmacker, P. (2004). *Integrated Marketing Communications: A Primer*. London: Routledge.

Schultz, D. E. and Kitchen, P. J. (2000). *Communicating Globally: An Integrated Marketing Approach*. Basingstoke: Palgrave Macmillan.

interaction approach

Judy Zolkiewski

The interaction model was first introduced in 1982 by the IMP Group. The group was made up of like-minded researchers from a number of European countries and included Håkansson, Kucschken, Johanson, Turnbull, Valla, Cunningham, and Ford. The group was involved in a joint research project, based in international markets, which saw the buyer/seller relationship as being central to the whole tenet of INDUS-TRIAL MARKETING. It marked an interesting and important development in the field of industrial marketing: no longer was the MARKETING MIX considered as central in this area, nor was the selling firm considered to be the only active partner in a relationship.

The theoretical framework of the interaction approach has its roots in inter-organizational theory and new institutional economic theory, as well as some earlier thinking in MARKETING and purchasing, which included studies that had a distribution system perspective and studies that realized the importance of inter-company relations. Ford (1997) outlines the motivation behind the development of the interaction approach. Firstly, the realization that much of the prevailing literature did not adequately describe what really happens in business markets, i.e., the fact that buyers were not passive, transactions were not isolated events, and there was not a homogeneous market, led to the realization that an interactive process was involved rather one of action and reaction. Secondly, there was the recognition that many business interactions are long term and enduring, i.e., they can be described as relationships rather than as individual transactions. Finally, there was the need for an emphasis on understanding and analyzing the relationship, which in turn provides the basis for understanding the management of such relationships (from a buyer's or seller's perspective).

The approach also emphasizes a number of other factors that need careful consideration when investigating industrial markets and that did not appear to have been considered in depth previously. These factors include the complexity of the patterns of interaction that take place in industrial markets, the observation that links between buyers and sellers can often become institutionalized and close links can exist between companies that only buy/sell infrequently, e.g., in the case of capital goods (Håkansson, 1982).

The IMP Group believe that the marketing and purchasing of industrial goods can be seen as an interactive process involving two parties inside a specific environment. They analyze the interaction by considering four elements:

1 The process.
2 The participants in that process.
3 The environment in which the interaction occurs.
4 The atmosphere, which both affects and is affected by the interaction.

They also recognize two levels of interaction: the organizational level, where technology, structure of the organization, and management strategy are important; and the individual level, where the aims and experience of the individuals involved are important (Håkansson, 1982).

THE INTERACTION PROCESS

There are two distinct constituents of the interaction process: the short-term episodes, such as placing an order or obtaining information, and the longer-term relationship, which develops as a result of the individual episodes (Håkansson, 1982).

Episodes involve exchange between two parties and Håkansson et al. identify four different elements that can be exchanged:

- *Products or services*: The characteristics of the product or service are important here – how much UNCERTAINTY is involved, how closely does it fit the buyer's requirements, etc.
- *Information*: Technical, financial, organizational, and social.

- *Finance (money)*: The economic importance of the relationship.
- *Social interaction*: This can reduce uncertainty and is particularly important when the distance between the parties is high – it is one of the important factors in developing mutual TRUST.

Håkansson (1982) believes that the individual episodes (especially social) are the building blocks for long-term relationships. As relationships develop they can become institutionalized, with both parties having clear expectations of the role of the other. Also, as the relationship develops, it is often common to find that adaptations are taking place, e.g., product changes may be introduced to meet a customer's requirements or modifications may be made to the way deliveries or payments are made. They suggest that although adaptation may take place unconsciously, it can also present a powerful strategic tool and should be carefully considered in decisions about MARKETING STRATEGY.

THE INTERACTING PARTIES

The IMP Group recognize that it is not simply the elements of the interaction that influence the process of interaction. They observe that the characteristics of the organizations (and the people that represent them) are also important. They identify the following features:

- *Technology*: Tying or linking technology between two parties is often seen as being a critical factor in the development of relationships.
- *Organizational size, structure, and strategy*: Size and power of the parties provide the starting point for any interaction. Is one party particularly dominant? Can it dominate the relationship?
- *Organizational experience*: Does the organization have experience of similar relationships? Such experience can help in coping with the environment of the interaction.
- *The individuals involved*: The reaction of these individuals to the individual episodes impacts on how the relationship develops – this facilitates individual and organizational learning (Håkansson, 1982).

ATMOSPHERE

The atmosphere of a relationship is described by Håkansson (1982) as a product of the relationship, which in turn is influenced by a group of variables internal to that relationship. These variables include:

- power/dependence;
- closeness/distance;
- cooperation/conflict;
- expectations.

They interact with one another to provide different atmospheres in different circumstances, and Håkansson (1982) suggests evaluating the atmosphere on two dimensions: economic and control. These variables have also attracted much research attention.

THE INTERACTION ENVIRONMENT

The interaction approach recognizes that the interaction between two organizations cannot be considered in isolation; the wider environment also needs to be considered. Such an environment encompasses factors such as:

- *Market structure*: What are the other relationships in the same market? Is the market concentrated? What are the alternatives? etc.
- *Dynamism*: Is the relationship close? Are there costs associated with relying on this relationship?
- *Internationalization*: How international is the market?
- *Position in the manufacturing channel*: Is the company at the bottom of the chain or in the middle? This impacts upon how relationships are related to one another.
- *The social system*: The characteristics of the wider environment surrounding the relationship. Do influences such as source of origin factors, exchange rate fluctuations, or the impact of the euro come into effect (Håkansson, 1982)?

Campbell (1985) points out that the concept of "environment" proposed in the interaction approach can be problematic because it is an aggregated environment and does not really give explicit consideration to the individual environ-

ments of the buyer and seller. Blois (1988) also raises this criticism of the approach and suggests that there is a need to understand the overall economic climate that prevailed during the individual studies to gain real insight into the workings of the relationships.

IMPLICATIONS FOR MANAGEMENT

The development of the interaction approach has had significant implications for the management of industrial marketing and purchasing situations, not least in its role as one of the antecedents of the RELATIONSHIP MARKETING paradigm (Christopher, Payne, and Ballantyne, 1991). Other management implications have been identified by Turnbull and Valla (1986), who discussed the need for relationship management and the results of adapting offerings (*see* OFFERING) to individual customers' needs. In this context customer portfolio management (*see* CUSTOMER PORTFOLIOS) and areas such as key account management (see KEY ACCOUNT) become important. Additionally, issues such as *joint* design, technology development, and new product or service development (*see* NEW PRODUCT DEVELOPMENT) are central issues for managers in the context of their strategic customer relationships. Consideration of the complexity of relationships was also highlighted by Håkansson and Snehota (1995), who reminded us that close relationships are not necessarily good. They point out that relationships do not always have a positive balance of outcomes and may become burdensome. This recognition of the complexity of the relationships in which a firm is involved has continued to provide a research focus and much of the more recent work of the group focuses on networks of relationships (*see* NETWORK).

Bibliography

Blois, K. J. (1988). *Buyer–Seller Relationships in Industrial Marketing (MRP 88/9)*. Oxford: Templeton College Management Research Papers.

Campbell, N. C. G. (1985). An interaction approach to organizational buying behavior. Reprinted in David Ford (ed.) (1990). *Understanding Business Markets*. San Diego, CA: Academic Press.

Christopher, M., Payne, A., and Ballantyne, D. (1991). *Relationship Marketing*. Oxford: Butterworth-Heinemann.

Ford, D. (ed.) (1997). *Understanding Business Markets: Interaction, Relationships and Networks*, 2nd edn. London: Dryden Press.

Ford, D. (ed.) (2002). *Understanding Business Marketing and Purchasing*, 3rd edn. London: Thomson Learning.

Håkansson, H. (ed.) (1982). *International Marketing and Purchasing of Industrial Goods*. Chichester: John Wiley.

Håkansson, H. and Snehota, I. (1995). The burden of relationships or who's next. In Peter Turnbull, David Yorke, and Peter Naudé (eds.), *IMP 11th International Conference Proceedings. Interaction, Relationships and Networks, Past, Present, Future*. Manchester: Manchester Federal School of Business and Management.

Möller, K. and Wilson, D. T. (eds.) (1995). *Business Marketing: An Interaction and Network Perspective*. Boston: Kluwer Academic.

Turnbull, P. W. and Valla, J.-P. (eds.) (1986). *Strategies for International Industrial Marketing*. London: Croom Helm.

interaction model

see INTERACTION APPROACH

interactive acculturation model

see ACCULTURATION MODELS

interest

David Yorke

Interest is a measure of a customer's state of mind in relation to a PRODUCT or service. It is a part of the AFFECTIVE STAGE in a number of models of MARKETING COMMUNICATIONS, i.e., the development of a positive attitude as a prerequisite to purchasing the product or service (*see* AIDA MODEL; INNOVATION–ADOPTION MODEL). Measures of evaluation are, as with most elements at the affective stage, difficult.

internal audit

Dominic Wilson

An internal audit is one part of the MARKETING AUDIT (the other being EXTERNAL AUDIT) and involves examination of the internal operations, strengths, and weaknesses of an organization. There are many ways to approach this audit, but all methods involve, in essence, the allocation of all internal operations and assets into various categories labeled judgmentally according to whether they are perceived as organizational advantages or disadvantages. Thus, one method recommends the identification of "strengths" and "weaknesses" (*see* SWOT ANALYSIS), while another method would be to identify "core" activities and "peripheral" activities (Prahalad and Hamel, 1990). Porter (1980) suggests that internal activities can be analyzed in terms of a "value added" (*see* VALUE CHAIN), with the implication that operations that add little "value" to the organization's output should be improved, or minimized (if they are unnecessary), or subcontracted (if they lie outside the organization's core competence). All these methods of identifying internal strengths and problems risk, through disaggregation, losing sight of the collective synergies arising from the operations of the organization as a whole. Thus, an activity such as an annual Christmas party or a weekly newsletter to customers may not seem to add significant value to the organization's offerings (*see* OFFERING), but cancelation could have important implications for the perception of an organization's commitment to its stakeholders.

Bibliography

Porter, M. E. (1980). *Competitive Strategy: Techniques for Analyzing Industries and Competitors*. New York: Free Press.

Prahalad, C. K. and Hamel, G. (1990). The core competence of the corporation. *Harvard Business Review*, 68, 3 (May/June), 79–91.

internal marketing

Barbara R. Lewis

The role of an organization's personnel in SERVICE QUALITY has come increasingly to the forefront, and investment in people becomes integral to the service–profit chain (see Heskett, Sasser, and Schlesinger, 1997):

internal service quality → employee satisfaction → employee retention → external service quality → customer satisfaction → customer retention → profit

Much of the attention given to personnel relates to the concept of internal marketing, which views employees as internal customers and jobs as internal products (Berry, 1980); and a company needs to sell the jobs to employees before selling its service(s) to external customers (Sasser and Arbeit, 1976). In other words, satisfying the needs of internal customers upgrades the capability to satisfy the needs of external customers. Grönroos (1981, 1985) referred to three objectives of internal marketing:

1 *Overall*: To achieve motivated, customer-conscious, and care-oriented personnel.
2 *Strategic*: To create an internal environment that supports customer-consciousness and sales-mindedness among personnel.
3 *Tactical*: To sell service campaigns and MARKETING efforts to employees – the first marketplace of the company – via staff training programs.

Internal marketing is primarily the province of human resource managers, who have responsibility for developing enlightened personnel policies to include recruitment, selection, and training, and also appraisal, rewards, and recognition.

Successful personnel policies include recruitment and selection of the "right" people. Key characteristics for employees to perform effectively may relate to: process and technical skills; interpersonal and communication skills; teamwork skills; flexibility and adaptability; and empathy with the external customers. In general, employees must be willing and able to deliver desired levels of service and so avoid Gap 3, referred to as the service performance gap (Zeithaml, Berry, and Parasuraman, 1988; *see* SERVICE QUALITY GAPS).

Training needs will, however, vary as a function of the amount of contact (visible and non-visible) with customers, the skills and equipment/technology required, and the extent of relationships with customers and with other employees. Training programs cover: product,

company, and systems knowledge; awareness of employees' role in assessing and meeting customer needs; and the economic impact of everyone working together to support company goals. Critical to this are SERVICE ENCOUNTERS within organizations, at all levels and between levels (Lewis and Entwistle, 1990), that contribute to the service delivered to external customers. These include relationships between customer contact and backroom staff, between operations and non-operations staff, and between staff and management at all levels and locations.

In addition to product/technical knowledge and relationship management, personal skills and interpersonal communication skill development allows organizations to empower employees to respond to customers' needs and problems (e.g., Bowen and Lawler, 1992; *see* SERVICE RECOVERY). Empowerment should lead to better job performance and improved morale. It is a form of job enrichment, evidenced by increased commitment to jobs and reflected in attitudes toward customers. Knowing that management has confidence in employees helps create positive attitudes in the workplace and good relationships between employees, and between employees and customers. Zeithaml et al. (1988) indicate that successful training programs lead to: teamwork, employee–job fit, technology–job fit, perceived control, supervisory control systems, avoidance of role conflict, and avoidance of role ambiguity.

REWARDS

Berry (1981) suggested that employee rewards, typically motivating factors, should be subject to market research and segmentation (*see* MARKET SEGMENTATION). Organizations can carry out research among employees to identify their needs, wants, and attitudes with respect to working conditions, benefits, and company policies. People are as different as employees as they are as customers and may be segmented in a number of ways, e.g., with respect to flexible working hours that lead to increased job satisfaction, increased productivity, and decreased absenteeism. In addition, "cafeteria benefits" could be appropriate with respect to health insurance, pensions, holidays, creche and nursery facilities, share options, and profit-sharing schemes. The notion is that employees use "credits" (as a function of salary, service, age, etc.) to choose their benefits, i.e., fringe benefits to embrace the heterogeneity of the labor force. Recent attention of service companies is focused on issues of supervision, appraisal, and performance evaluation together with performance-related pay, recognition, and rewards schemes for excellent employees. Customer service awards may be financial or not, and may involve career development.

Successful internal marketing requires human resource managers to develop relationships not only with employees, but also with marketing managers and operations management, and will lead to an appropriate service culture to support relationships with external customers.

The concept of internal marketing has further been researched by Varey and Lewis (1999, 2000), who considered how it might be developed to take greater account of the social and non-economic needs and interests of people working in an organized enterprise. They identified some limitations of the popular concept of internal marketing and offered a broader conception to include: marketing-oriented service employee management, the organization as an internal market, internal marketing as a social process, the individual person in an internal market, a relational perspective on communication, and empowerment.

Finally, Ahmed and Rafiq (2002) discuss the development and evolution of the internal marketing concept, models of internal marketing, and links with service quality, CUSTOMER SATISFACTION, customer loyalty, and profitability.

Bibliography

Ahmed, P. K. and Rafiq, M. (2002). *Internal Marketing: Tools and Concepts for Customer-Focused Management.* Oxford: Butterworth-Heinemann.

Berry, L. L. (1980). Services marketing is different. *Business*, **30**, 3 (May/June), 24–9.

Berry, L. L. (1981). The employee as customer. *Journal of Retail Banking*, **3** (1), 33–40.

Bowen, D. E. and Lawler, L. L. (1992). Empowerment: Why, what, how and when. *Sloan Management Review*, Spring, 31–9.

Bowen, D. E. and Lawler, L. L. (1995). Empowering service workers. *Sloan Management Review*, Summer, 73–84.

Gilmore, A. and Carson, D. (1995). Managing and marketing to internal customers. In W. J. Glynn and J. G. Barnes (eds.), *Understanding Service Management.* Chichester: John Wiley, pp. 295–321.

Grönroos, C. (1981). Internal marketing: An integral part of marketing theory. In J. H. Donnelly and W. E. George (eds.), *Marketing of Services.* Chicago: American Marketing Association, pp. 236–8.

Grönroos, C. (1985). Internal marketing: Theory and practice. In T. M. Bloch, G. D. Upah, and V. A. Zeithaml (eds.), *Services Marketing in a Changing Environment.* Chicago: American Marketing Association, pp. 41–7.

Grönroos, C. (2000). *Service Management and Marketing*, 2nd edn. Chichester: John Wiley, ch. 14.

Heskett, J. L., Sasser, W. E., and Schlesinger, L. A. (1997). *The Service Profit Chain.* New York: Free Press.

Lewis, B. R. and Entwistle, T. W. (1990). Managing the service encounter: Focus on the employee. *International Journal of Service Industry Management*, **1** (3), 41–52.

Lovelock, C., Vandermerwe, S., and Lewis, B. (1999). *Services Marketing: A European Perspective.* Upper Saddle River, NJ: Prentice-Hall, ch. 14.

Palmer, A. (2001). *Principles of Services Marketing*, 3rd edn. Maidenhead: McGraw-Hill, ch. 12.

Sasser, W. E., Jr. and Arbeit, S. P. (1976). Selling jobs in the service sector. *Business Horizons*, **19**, 61–5.

Varey, R. J. and Lewis, B. R. (1999). A broadened concept of internal marketing. *European Journal of Marketing*, **33** (9/10), 926–45.

Varey, R. J. and Lewis, B. R. (2000) (eds.). *Internal Marketing.* London: Routledge.

Wilkinson, A. and Brown, A. (2003). Managing human resources for quality management. In B. G. Dale (ed.), *Managing Quality*, 4th edn. Oxford: Blackwell Publishing, pp. 176–202.

Zeithaml, V. A., Berry, L. L., and Parasuraman, A. (1988). Communication and control processes in the delivery of service quality. *Journal of Marketing*, **52** (April), 35–48.

Zeithaml, V. A. and Bitner, M. J. (2003). *Services Marketing: Integrating Customer Focus Across the Firm*, 3rd edn. New York: McGraw-Hill, ch. 11.

international channel management

Rudolph Sinkovics

In MARKETING, the term distribution has two distinct yet interconnected meanings. The first refers to the physical movement of goods from the place of manufacture to a location in or close to points of purchase. A location in a point of purchase might be a supermarket; a location near a point of purchase might be a storage facility supplying, say, spare parts to industry in a given region. Distribution in this sense is called LO-GISTICS or physical distribution management. The second meaning refers to channel management. This will be discussed further here.

A marketing channel can be seen as a concatenation of individuals and organizations involved in the process of making goods or services available for use or consumption. Distribution arrangements for international markets are varied. The persons or organizations involved in the distribution process include agents, distributors, representatives who may be externally appointed (e.g., an export house), locally established sales offices, or franchisees (see FRAN-CHISING).

The precise choice of these channel partners is influenced by factors such as the nature of the product or service, the degree of day-to-day control that the marketing firm wishes to exercise from the outside, its knowledge and experience of given markets, its strategic remit, and its INTERNATIONAL MARKETING policy. Internationally operating firms need to address five strategic decisions in the selection and implementation of channel management schemes (Terpstra and Sarathy, 2000):

1   Should the firm extend its domestic distribution approach to foreign markets or adapt its distribution strategy to each national market?
2   Should the firm use direct or indirect channels in foreign markets?
3   Should the firm use selective or widespread distribution?
4   How can the firm manage the channel?
5   How can the firm keep its distribution strategy up to date?

One problem in international channel management is the geopolitical separation of (exporting) firm and channel intermediaries (agents or distributors). The exporter relies on intermediaries for its local knowledge and access to local customers. However, the intermediary – while a crucial facilitator of the exporter's market entry and consecutive market development activities – may potentially exploit the exporting firm's de-

pendence unilaterally. For the exporter this means that it is crucial to select the best channel partner for its requirements and, once a contractual agreement is signed, to manage the relationship successfully. Agency theory (Bergen, Dutta, and Walker, 1992) suggests that exporters need to enforce appropriate controls, otherwise there is a natural tendency for opportunism and non-conformism on the part of the channel partner. The literature also identifies cultural challenges between the distant parties and suggests a relational approach that combines transactional and moderate behavioral control measures for effective inter-organizational relationships (Heide, 1994; Bello and Gilliland, 1997).

See also *channels of distribution; retail distribution channels*

Bibliography

Bello, D. C. and Gilliland, D. I. (1997). The effect of output controls, process controls, and flexibility on export channel performance. *Journal of Marketing*, **61** (1), 22–38.

Bergen, M., Dutta, S., and Walker, O. C., Jr. (1992). Agency relationships in marketing: A review of the implications and applications of agency and related theories. *Journal of Marketing*, **56** (3), 1–24.

Heide, J. B. (1994). Interorganizational governance in marketing channels. *Journal of Marketing*, **58** (1), 71–85.

Terpstra, V. and Sarathy, R. (2000). *International Marketing*, 8th edn. Fort Worth, TX: Dryden Press.

international joint ventures

Charles C. Cui

An international joint venture (IJV) refers to a cooperative operation formed by two or more independent entities from different countries to achieve common or complementary objectives. Joint venture partners may be privately owned companies, government agencies, or government-owned companies. The media and practitioners often refer to an international joint venture as anything from a business collaboration or alliance (see INTERNATIONAL STRA-TEGIC ALLIANCES) on a contractual basis to an equity entity that is owned and controlled by two or more partners from different countries. The specific legal definition varies across countries. In business studies, an international joint venture is identified as either a contractual joint venture or an equity joint venture. A contractual joint venture refers to a partnership in which two or more partner organizations share the cost of an investment, the risks, and the long-term profits. An equity joint venture includes the sharing of assets, risks, and profits, and participation in the ownership (i.e., equity) of a particular enterprise or investment project by more than one partner organization or economic group. Equity joint ventures take the form of a limited liability company. The equity contributed by the partners may take the form of money, plant and equipment, and/or technology and other forms of assets.

The international joint venture is characterized by jointly controlled operations, jointly controlled assets, and jointly controlled entities, hence issues involved in cooperation and control are often the major concern. The IJV is a popular mode of market entry and expansion. Many nations have encouraged the use of IJVs as a means for local companies to acquire technology, management expertise, and NETWORK in the global market. Firms use IJV as a market entry form to achieve strategic purposes such as penetrating the international market, reducing the production cost, taking advantage of the local network for market expansion, gaining access to indigenous management talent, and knowledge of local legislation and market conditions (Young et al., 1989). In recent years an increasing number of global corporations and small firms have become involved in IJVs, covering many sectors, industries, and product groups. However, its cooperative and interdependent nature makes the IJV fragile and vulnerable to failure. It is known that the failure rate of IJVs is above 30 percent, which is markedly higher than other alternative forms of market entry and operation. Reasons for IJVs' instability include mismatch of objectives, inadequate market research and feasibility analysis, misfit of communications and managerial styles, forming an IJV when it may not have been the best form to be used, choosing the wrong partner, misunderstanding of managerial roles, failure in building TRUST and handling conflict, and so on.

In the 1970s and 1980s, studies on IJVs were mainly based on approaches of transaction cost economics, strategic behavior, and organizational behavior (Kogut, 1988). Since the 1990s scholars have focused on wider issues with new orientations, including how parent companies control IJVs through ownership structure and the integration of an IJV into parent company activities (Child, Yan, and Lu, 1997; Yan and Gray, 1994), the relationship between control and performance (Geringer and Hebert, 1991; Luo, Shenkar, and Nyaw, 2001), strategic choice of IJVs, the interaction of transaction cost and strategic option, agency costs and parent-firm performance, the longevity of IJVs based on organizational learning theory, relationship management (Madhok, 1995), partners' working relationship and managerial fit (Cui, Ball, and Coyne, 2002), cross-cultural differences and longevity (Hennart and Zeng, 2002), the impact of source-country factors on equity ownership (Pan, 2002), the relationship involving contract, cooperation, and performance (Luo, 2002), and trust (Currall and Inkpen, 2002; Boersma, Buckley, and Ghauri, 2003).

See also *international market entry and development strategies*

Bibliography

Boersma, M. F., Buckley, P. J., and Ghauri, P. N. (2003). Trust in international joint venture relationships. *Journal of Business Research*, **56** (12), 1031–42.

Child, J., Yan, Y., and Lu, Y. (1997). Ownership and control in Sino-foreign joint ventures. In P. W. Beamish and J. P. Killing (eds.), *Cooperative Strategies: Asian Pacific Perspectives*. San Francisco: New Lexington Press, pp. 181–225.

Cui, C. C., Ball, D., and Coyne, J. (2002). Working effectively in strategic alliances through managerial fit between partners: Some evidence from Sino-British joint ventures and the implications for R&D professionals. *R&D Management*, **32** (4), 343–57.

Currall, S. C. and Inkpen, A. C. (2002). A multilevel approach to trust in joint ventures. *Journal of International Business Studies*, **33** (3), 479–95.

Geringer, J. M. and Hebert, L. (1989). Control and performance of international joint ventures. *Journal of International Business Studies*, **20**, 235–54.

Geringer, J. M. and Hebert, L. (1991). Measuring performance of international joint ventures. *Journal of International Business Studies*, **22** (2), 249–63.

Hennart, J.-F. and Zeng, M. (2002). Cross-cultural differences and joint venture longevity. *Journal of International Business Studies*, 33 (4), 699–716.

Julian, C. and O'Cass, A. (2002). The effect of firm and marketplace characteristics on international joint venture (IJV) marketing performance. *Asia Pacific Journal of Marketing and Logistics*, 14 (1).

Kogut, B. (1988). A study of the life cycle of joint ventures. In Farok J. Contractor and Peter Lorange (eds.), *Cooperative Strategies in International Business*. Lexington, MA: D. C. Heath, pp. 169–85.

Lane, H. and Beamish, P. (1990). Cross-cultural cooperative behavior in joint ventures in LDCs. *Management International Review*, 30 (Special issue), 87–102.

Luo, Y. (2002). Contract, cooperation, and performance in international joint ventures. *Strategic Management Journal*, 23, 903–19.

Luo, Y., Shenkar, O., and Nyaw, M.-K. (2001). A dual parent perspective on control and performance in international joint ventures: Lessons from a developing economy. *Journal of International Business Studies*, 32 (1), 41–58.

Madhok, A. (1995). Opportunism and trust in joint venture relationships: An exploratory study and a model. *Scandinavian Journal of Management*, 11 (1), 57–74.

Pan, Y. (2002). Equity ownership in international joint ventures: The impact of source country factors. *Journal of International Business Studies*, 33 (2), 375–84.

Yan, A. and Gray, B. (1994). Bargaining power, management control, and performance in United States–China joint ventures. *Academy of Management Journal*, 37, 1478–1517.

Young, S., Hamill, J., Wheeler, C., and Davies, J. R. (1989). *International Market Entry and Development: Strategies and Management*. Hemel Hempstead: Harvester Wheatsheaf/Prentice-Hall.

international market entry and development strategies

Rudolph Sinkovics

International market entry decisions are often treated as if they were binary, comprising simple "entry/non-entry" options. In reality, however, international market entry decisions are complex and dynamic, entailing a continuum of varying levels of involvement in foreign target countries. Thus, the use of the term "market entry and development strategies" has

advantages over the term "market entry" (Young et al., 1989), in that the shorter expression focuses attention only on methods of entry, whereas the reality of INTERNATIONAL MARKETING is that the method of entry is a prelude to market penetration: the process of business development and consolidation within a foreign market over time. In other words, the selection of methods of market entry or combination of methods is directly connected to both the overall business strategy for the market in question and the scale of investment allocated to achieve the STRATEGIC OBJECTIVES.

Market entry and development strategies greatly differ in advantages and drawbacks and since the trade-offs are difficult to evaluate, various classifications have been developed. Anderson and Gatignon (1986), building on transactions cost analysis, have concluded that the most appropriate entry mode is a function of the trade-off between control and the cost of resource commitment. Further factors determining the appropriate entry choice include time, risk, flexibility, barriers to entry, financial commitment, and degree of autonomy and transfer of resources (see, e.g., Terpstra and Sarathy, 2000; Jeannet and Hennessey, 2004). Building on the control/resource commitment trade-off, figure 1 depicts the principal methods of market entry and development graphically. These include indirect and direct EXPORTING, LICENSING, FRANCHISING, INTERNATIONAL JOINT VENTURES, and acquisitions/wholly owned subsidiaries.

Another way of thinking about market entry and development strategies is to classify alternatives into direct and indirect methods (see table 1). It is possible to make a distinction between strategies that involve MARKETING only and those that involve marketing and production. This classification also comprises management contracts and turnkey contracts. Sometimes also cooperation agreements, of which so-called strategic alliances (*see* INTERNATIONAL STRATEGIC ALLIANCES) are a prime example, are listed.

Market entry decisions are among the most important that internationally operating firms must make. They depend on the quality and

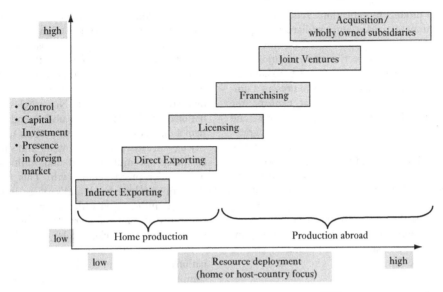

Figure 1   Market entry alternatives (adapted from Müller-Stewens and Lechner, 1997)

Table 1   Market entry and development strategies

	Indirect entry	*Direct entry*
Marketing only strategy (home production)	• Exporting • Direct mail (from outside) • Export management companies • Export trading companies	• Import houses • Wholesale or retail purchasing groups • Public trading agencies • Export departments • Foreign sales representatives or branch offices
Marketing and production abroad	• Licensing • Franchising • Production or management contracts	• Joint ventures • Direct foreign investment • Acquisitions

accuracy of information inputs obtained through INTERNATIONAL MARKETING RESEARCH. Furthermore, they have a direct bearing on the evolution of the main MARKETING STRATEGY for the selected foreign market. Any one particular method or combination of methods comes with operational implications: control issues (are key decisions affecting operations in the market taken by a firm's local representatives or by an independent center such as a firm's

international headquarters?); initial resource commitment; subsequent resource commitments; and definition of objectives. In the case of consumer products, decisions on market entry and development involve channel management issues (*see* INTERNATIONAL CHANNEL MANAGEMENT) or MARKETING COMMUNICATIONS including ADVERTISING. Miscalculations arising from wrong decisions can result in unforeseen and therefore unwelcome costs in the form of product modifications, redeployment or reselection of market intermediaries, or price increases.

A refreshing perspective on internationalization and market entry is offered by Malhotra, Agarwal, and Ulgado (2004), who present a unified theoretical framework that explains the internationalization process, entry modes, and timing strategies. Their framework integrates multiple theoretical work from the international product life cycle (IPLC) theory (see PRODUCT LIFE CYCLE), the market imperfection theory, strategic behavior theory, the resource-advantage theory of competition, transaction cost economics, the eclectic theory, the internationalization theory, and the network theory and includes large and small as well as manufacturing and service firms.

Bibliography

Anderson, E. and Gatignon, H. (1986). Modes of foreign entry: A transaction cost analysis and propositions. *Journal of International Business Studies*, **17** (3), 1–26.

Jeannet, J.-P. and Hennessey, H. D. (2004). *Global Marketing Strategies*, 6th edn. Boston: Houghton Mifflin.

Malhotra, N. K., Agarwal, J., and Ulgado, F. M. (2004). Internationalization and entry modes: A multitheoretical framework and research propositions. *Journal of International Marketing*, **11** (4), 1–31.

Müller-Stewens, G. and Lechner, C. (1997). Unternehmensindividuelle und Gastlandbezogene Einfluafaktoren der Markteintrittsformen. In Klaus Macharzina and Michael-Jörg Oesterle (eds.), *Handbuch Internationales Management*. Wiesbaden: Gabler, pp. 231–52.

Terpstra, V. and Sarathy, R. (2000). *International Marketing*, 8th edn. Fort Worth, TX: Dryden Press.

Young, S., Hamill, J., Wheeler, C., and Davies, J. R. (1989). *International Market Entry and Development: Strategies and Management*. Hemel Hempstead: Harvester Wheatsheaf/Prentice-Hall.

international marketing

Charles C. Cui

International marketing is generally known as MARKETING activities across borders. There is no universally agreed definition of international marketing. Continuous efforts are being made toward an unambiguous and consistent term. Marketing activities taking place in more than one country are often described as international marketing or global marketing. Other terms are also found in the literature, including multinational, multilocal, multiregional, multidomestic, transnational, and glocal marketing (Svensson, 2002). Nevertheless, international marketing can be understood as the firm's marketing management process for identifying and satisfying needs, wants, and values of customers in multinational and multicultural markets for profit and growth. This requires the firm to deliver goods and services and communicate information with customers of different industrial and commercial experience from different cultural backgrounds.

In contrast to domestic marketing, international marketing is characterized by the complexity and diversity in its marketing operations (Craig and Douglas, 2000). As a result of differences in national environments, organizational and management systems, strategies and approaches, and customer behaviors in different national and cultural markets, international marketing entails familiarity with foreign market environments, exchange rate dynamics, local business NETWORK and logic, and various geopolitical, economic, and sociocultural factors. International marketing operations involve different types (or a combination) of activities and management systems such as export (see EXPORTING), LICENSING, FRANCHISING, strategic alliances (see INTERNATIONAL STRATEGIC ALLIANCES), contractual arrangement or joint ventures (see INTERNATIONAL JOINT VENTURES), and direct investment through equity joint ventures or wholly owned subsidiaries.

The value of international marketing can be seen at two levels. For the interest of national economies, international marketing activities provide the opportunity to mobilize resources beyond national borders, accumulate foreign exchange reserves, improve national productivity, promote information and technology advancement, and enhance general quality of life. For individual firms, international marketing provides the firm with effective marketing processes and operational tools for facilitating corporate growth, improving financial performance, strengthening competitive edge, and sustaining corporate IMAGE and POSITIONING in the world market.

It was only in the late 1950s and early 1960s that scholars started to pay attention to the differences between domestic and foreign market environments (Bartels, 1988). The firm's increasing involvement in the global market and an emphasis on catering for customers within the context of the firm's market environment in the 1980s played a role in the development of international marketing as a discipline (Bradley, 1987). Although the discipline was criticized for not being ready to form many theories by the late 1980s (Bradley, 1987), since the 1990s it has evolved into an integrated and systematic field of study and has achieved a certain degree of scientific status (Li and Cavusgil, 1995), as evidenced by the efforts to apply vigorous research methods in the field and the resultant exponential growth of literature (Katsikeas, 2003).

As a growing body of knowledge and an established discipline, international marketing contains an increasing number of theories that deal with complex issues in cross-border and cross-cultural marketing activities and provide marketing tools for firms and practitioners engaged in the international marketing process. Studies of the phenomena of international marketing are seen in eight broad categories of research streams (Li and Cavusgil, 1995):

1   *Environmental studies of international marketing*, which investigate the impact of economic, cultural, political, and legal factors on international marketing activities.
2   *Comparative studies of market systems*, which examine similarities and differences among market systems and practices in different countries.
3   *International marketing management*, which focus on managerial issues of export and entry strategies, investment decisions, MARKET SEGMENTATION, product and PRICING policies, and channel distribution and service.
4   *Internationalization process perspectives*, which research on the behavioral and attitudinal changes experienced by firms in the process of internationalization.
5   *International marketing research* (*see* INTERNATIONAL MARKETING RESEARCH),

which involves the methodology of conducting research in the international context.
6   *Buyer behavior studies*, which explore buyer behavior (*see* BUYER BEHAVIOR MODELS; BUYER BEHAVIOR THEORIES) in international markets and foreign countries.
7   *Interaction approach* (*see* INTERACTION APPROACH), which examines relationships of networks, cooperative ventures, and alliances among international companies.
8   *Market globalization perspectives* (*see* GLOBALIZATION), a stream that views the world market and customer tastes as increasingly converging and investigates the impact of such change on firm strategies.

Bibliography

Bartels, R. (1988). *The History of Marketing Thought*. Columbus, OH: Publishing Horizons.
Bradley, M. F. (1987). Nature and significance of international marketing: A review. *Journal of Business Research*, **15**, 205–19.
Craig, C. S. and Douglas, S. P. (2000). *International Marketing Research*, 2nd edn. Chichester: John Wiley.
Katsikeas, C. S. (2003). Advances in international marketing theory and practice. *International Business Review*, **12**, 135–40.
Li, T. and Cavusgil, S. T. (1995). A classification and assessment of research streams in international marketing. *International Business Review*, 4 (3), 251–77.
Svensson, G. (2002). Beyond global marketing and the globalization of marketing activities. *Management Decision*, **40** (6), 574–83.

international marketing culture

Rudolph Sinkovics

Although MARKETING is primarily seen as an economic activity, involving the EXCHANGE of goods and services, it is important to appreciate that sociocultural factors have a tremendous influence on marketing behavior. Hence, marketing is a cultural as well as economic phenomenon. Particularly in the context of INTERNATIONAL MARKETING, we must acquire knowledge of diverse cultural environments in order to successfully integrate cultural dynamics in marketing decision-making.

The literatures of management, anthropology, and sociology are replete with definitions of "culture" and numerous scholars have analytically approached cultural factors and their implications for management. In a significant study of the impact of cultural difference on management performance and behavior, Hofstede (1984) defined culture as "the collective programming of the mind which distinguishes one human group from another.... Culture, in this sense, includes systems of values, and values are building blocks of culture." This definition implies that culture underpins values and, by extension, beliefs and attitudes that are particular to one group and not to others; that culture is learned and not innate; and that culture influences group behavior and attitudes in distinctive ways that are, within reason, predictable. Culture, looked at this way, is an implicit form of social life. However, culture can also be an explicit phenomenon, manifesting itself in material culture, aesthetic codes, belief systems such as religions, and conviction systems such as ideologies. Language is both an implicit and explicit manifestation, both a personal possession and a social influence (Hall, 1959). Hofstede (1983, 1984) contributed by offering four analytically derived cultural typologies (power distance, individualism/collectivism, masculinity/femininity, uncertainty avoidance), later extended to account for Confucian dynamism (Hofstede and Bond, 1988) and with direct relevance to international business and management (Hofstede, 1994). In a similar vein, Trompenaars and Hampden-Turner's *Riding the Waves of Culture* (1998) dispels the idea that there is only one way to manage and encourages us to understand our own culture in the workplace before managing or doing business with other national cultures. They reveal seven key dimensions of business behavior and how these combine to create four basic "types" of corporate culture.

In operational terms, the key distinction between domestic marketing and international marketing is that the latter deals with the diversity of cultural differences and the impact of these differences on company planning and performance. In international marketing studies, the treatment of culture both as an internationally variegated phenomenon and in relation to specific economic-cultural constructs (i.e., MARKETS) has frequently been found wanting. Virtually all writers of international marketing

texts devote a chapter to cultural elements of the international environment (*see* INTERNATIONAL MARKETING ENVIRONMENT), emphasizing how these elements act as a constraint on international marketing activity in a general way (e.g., language barriers) or on understanding the business mentality and associated behaviors in particular markets. Such insights enable marketers to acquire so-called cultural awareness, avoid marketing blunders (Ricks, 1999), and present their product offerings (*see* OFFERING) to markets in culture-sensitive ways.

Cultural issues have also been systematically investigated in relation to MARKETING MIX factors and to embrace factors that are strongly influenced by cultural background and exert a powerful influence over the quality and outcome of international business encounters. Such factors include business ethics and negotiation behavior (extending into conflict resolution) (Ghauri and Fang, 2001). Cultural issues have further contributed to the "perennial" debate over theories of customization versus standardization (Agrawal, 1995; Leonidou, 1996; Solberg, 2002; Theodosiou and Leonidou, 2003) and the European variation thereof, the "Euroconsumer" (Kale, 1995), who is the target of so-called "Euromarketing" (Schuh, 2000; Whitelock, Roberts, and Blakeley, 1995).

See also *culture*

Bibliography

Agrawal, M. (1995). Review of a 40-year debate in international advertising: Practitioner and academician perspectives to the standardization/adaptation issue. *International Marketing Review*, 12 (1), 26–48.

Ghauri, P. N. and Fang, T. (2001). Negotiating with the Chinese: A socio-cultural analysis. *Journal of World Business*, 36 (3), 303–25.

Hall, E. T. (1959). *The Silent Language*. Garden City, NY: Anchor Press/Doubleday.

Hofstede, G. (1983). The cultural relativity of organizational practices and theories. *Journal of International Business Studies*, 14 (2), 75–89.

Hofstede, G. (1984). *Culture's Consequences: International Differences in Work-Related Values*. Newbury Park, CA: Sage.

Hofstede, G. (1994). The business of international business is culture. *International Business Review*, 3 (1), 1–14.

Hofstede, G. and Bond, M. H. (1988). The Confucius connection: From cultural roots to economic growth. *Organizational Dynamics*, **16** (4), 4–21.

Kale, S. H. (1995). Grouping Euroconsumers: A culture-based clustering approach. *Journal of International Marketing*, **3** (3), 35–48.

Leonidou, L. C. (1996). Product standardization or adaptation: The Japanese approach. *Journal of Marketing Practice: Applied Marketing Science*, **2** (4), 53–71.

Ricks, D. A. (1999). *Blunders in International Business*, 3rd edn. Oxford: Blackwell.

Schuh, A. (2000). Global standardization as a success formula for marketing in Central Eastern Europe? *Journal of World Business*, **35** (2), 133–48.

Solberg, C. A. (2002). The perennial issue of adaptation or standardization of international marketing communication: Organizational contingencies and performance. *Journal of International Marketing*, **10** (3), 1–21.

Theodosiou, M. and Leonidou, L. C. (2003). Standardization versus adaptation of international marketing strategy: An integrative assessment of the empirical research. *International Business Review*, **12** (2), 141–71.

Trompenaars, F. and Hampden-Turner, C. (1998). *Riding the Waves of Culture: Understanding Cultural Diversity in Business*, 2nd edn. London: Nicholas Brealey.

Whitelock, J., Roberts, C., and Blakeley, J. (1995). The reality of the Eurobrand: An empirical analysis. *Journal of International Marketing*, **3** (3), 77–95.

international marketing environment

Mohammed Yamin

The MARKETING ENVIRONMENT is commonly defined as the set of actors and forces that influence the success of a company's marketing program. The important observation to be made regarding the marketing environment is that it is simultaneously complex, competitive, and dynamic. This observation is particularly pertinent so far as INTERNATIONAL MARKETING is concerned; it is unlikely that anyone can fully comprehend or understand the environment, and beyond identifying broad and usually ill-defined forces or currents, there can be little in the way of a common environmental diagnosis (MacCrimmon, 1993).

What meaning can we attach to the notion of an international marketing environment? It is clearly not a seamless whole spanning many or all countries. On the other hand, it is not just a collection of different national environments as this would make international marketing almost redundant as a separate field of study. International marketing belongs somewhere between these two poles, and international marketing environments can be viewed in some sense as the linkage between different national environments. This linkage can, in principle, be viewed in two quite different ways: interdependence or integration. Traditional trade theories, for example, implicitly adopt the interdependence view, whereas the notion of GLOBALIZATION that is popular within international business and management studies (including MARKETING) implies an integration view. Globalization is held to be a force that is either dissolving national differences or transcending these differences. Levitt's (1983) view of the globalization of markets is one good example. Another is Badaracco's (1991) view regarding the globalization of knowledge and technology. One can also meaningfully talk of the globalization of competition (Prahalad and Hamel, 1988) or the globalization of business, where this refers to growing integration of business activities in different countries within the multinational corporation (Bartlett and Ghoshall, 2000).

Globalization is driven, essentially, by economic and particularly technological forces reducing the costs of, and barriers to, resource mobility including the mobility of people, money, and (of course) knowledge of all sorts. The same forces have also reduced radically the costs of organizing and managing economic activity across space.

By contrast, political forces, generally speaking, are acting as a break on globalization. Protectionism, which is largely a manifestation of economic nationalism, is still a powerful force and the success of the World Trade Organization (WTO) in removing non-tariff barriers to trade has been limited. In fact, protectionism is more entrenched as it is increasingly exercised by regional blocks rather than by individual countries. For example, the dispute between France and the US relating to the former's restrictions on service imports was enmeshed in the dispute between the European Union (EU) and the US. The tensions within the EU itself also reveal the relevance of political forces.

There is continuing resistance to further integration and some European countries show great reluctance to trade off national for regional sovereignty.

The slogan that marketers "should think globally and act locally" is meant to emphasize the fact that international marketers face a hierarchy of environments. Irrespective of how the linkages between different national marketing environments are construed, the environment of a particular country remains highly relevant to success or failure in that market. ENVIRONMENTAL ANALYSIS should, therefore, concern itself with the international level as well as the national or local levels. International analysis should be used to indicate which countries may be avoided (e.g., on account of their instability or hostility to foreign business) and which countries could potentially be targeted. But the "real" marketing tasks relate to designing a MARKETING MIX for countries that are selected for entry or expansion programs, and clearly require a thorough understanding of the specific conditions of these countries. Furthermore, decisions regarding the feasibility and desirability of standardizing the marketing approach for several countries should be informed by a careful analysis of the relevant markets.

Even ardent advocates of globalization as the basis of marketing strategies (see MARKETING STRATEGY) cannot overlook the significant diversities that still divide national markets. Thus, it is obvious that differences in climate, topography, and other physical conditions will always be with us and will remain a significant influence on buyer behavior (see CONSUMER BUYER BEHAVIOR). For example, it is unlikely that a product (e.g., a washing machine) designed to perform well in the arid climates of Greece or Spain will give an equally satisfactory service in Denmark or Sweden (Baden-Fuller and Stopford, 1991). More generally, the apparent homogeneity in customer preferences across countries, evidenced by their purchase of standardized products and global brands, may in fact mask significant behavioral or attitudinal differences of relevance to international marketers. Research has shown that consumers in different countries and cultures (see CULTURE) show different degrees of INVOLVEMENT with a number of standardized global products (Zaichowsky and Sood, 1989; Sood, 1993). Cultural influences are clearly deeply rooted and very durable, and marketers should be highly skeptical of "evidence" of growing convergence.

See also *international marketing culture*

Bibliography

Badaracco, J. (1991). *The Knowledge Link: How Firms Compete Through Strategic Alliances*. Boston: Harvard Business School Press.

Baden-Fuller, C. and Stopford, J. (1991). Globalization frustrated: The case of white goods. *Strategic Management Journal*, **12**, 493–507.

Bartlett, C. and Ghoshall, S. (2000). *Transnational Management*. London: McGraw-Hill.

Levitt, T. (1983). The globalization of markets. *Harvard Business Review*, **22** (May/June), 41–53.

MacCrimmon, K. (1993). Do firm strategies exist? *Strategic Management Journal*, **14**, 113–31.

Prahalad, C. and Hamel, G. (1988). Creating global strategic capability. In N. Hood and J. Vahne (eds.), *Strategies in Global Competition*. London: Routledge.

Sood, J. (1993). A multi-country approach for multinational communication. *Journal of International Consumer Marketing*, **5** (4), 29–50.

Zaichowsky, J. and Sood, J. (1989). A global look at consumer involvement and use of products. *International Marketing Review*, **6** (1), 20–34.

international marketing organization

Rudolph Sinkovics

Any MARKETING PLANNING will be in danger unless the company is organized to implement these plans. Organizational structures can be seen as a central element of strategy formulation and execution. They determine who does what, provide clarity regarding reporting, information, and decision-making, and also set up the rewards that motivate performance and determine the degree to which activities can be integrated. This is particularly important in the INTERNATIONAL MARKETING context, because IMPLEMENTATION must be carried out by partner institutions located in different countries.

The basic issue regarding international marketing organization revolves around centralization versus decentralization. Some firms need strong coordination at headquarters to provide and supervise the implementation of their international strategy. For others, local country requirements and government pressures may require greater local responsiveness. Thus, the major task for international marketing organization is to balance the opposing needs for centralization and local responsiveness (Bartlett and Ghoshal, 1987; Doz, Bartlett, and Prahalad, 1981).

In deciding on a suitable organization structure, companies traditionally choose between four alternative forms, each of which is based on alternative principles of divisionalization. The first principle is the international division, which is a specialist structure responsible for handling all aspects of a company's activities with foreign markets. These activities can be very diverse. In addition to overseeing relationships with all its international markets and intermediary partners, the international division will be called upon to: be responsible for foreign currency operations; deal with foreign governments as well as its own; handle all documentation pertaining to the supply of products to foreign customers; and work with key business partners such as exhibition contractors (*see* EXHIBITIONS) and advertising agencies (*see* AGENCY). The establishment of a separate international marketing division is potentially problematic in that it creates an artificial distinction between domestic and international activities. However, the argument in favor of this organizational form is that international marketing is so specialized that it warrants this separation.

The second principle of organization is the product division structure. Here, the division is based on a PRODUCT or a suite of related products. These product groups have global responsibilities for marketing. Their product managers are highly specialized, knowledgeable, and fully aware of customer needs in all markets. The product division is popular with firms with several unrelated products/product lines or with firms offering technical products requiring strong after-sales support and service. Divisional structures share the advantage of flexibility, in that the firm can add new product divisions if it enters other or unrelated business areas. However, the product division approach has several

potential limitations. When the domestic market is more important to a product division, international opportunities are likely to be missed (Terpstra and Sarathy, 2000). Area knowledge is commonly found to be weak with product divisions, since each product cannot afford to maintain its own complete international staff. Also, the product-structured approach tends to limit the achievement of company-wide coordination in international markets.

A third organizational principle is structuring by geography. In this case, companies divide their worldwide markets into distinct territories such as North America (i.e., the US and Canada), the Middle East, South America, the European Union (EU), and so on. In this structure, the division is staffed by area specialists, one of whose skills may be knowledge of a foreign language. The regional organization form is used primarily by companies that are highly oriented to marketing with relatively stable technology, such as those in consumer non-durables, pharmaceuticals, and automotive equipment. The growth of regional groupings favors a regional approach to international marketing organization. As nations within a region integrate economically (and politically), it makes sense to treat them as a unit. Also, doing business in specific geographically connected groups of markets requires considerable area knowledge, which a peripatetic product manager can never acquire because of "short-sightedness" in relation to his own (distant) home country. Despite its popularity, the regional organization has drawbacks. Although it insures the best use of the firm's regional expertise, it means less than optimal allocation of product and functional expertise. Duplication of product and functional specialists and also inefficiencies may result, particularly if regional organizations are not coordinating their activities via informal information exchange and cross-country teams.

The fourth divisional structure is known as "functional structure." In this arrangement top executives in marketing, finance, production, etc. enjoy global responsibilities. The functional structure is most suitable for firms with narrow, homogeneous product lines, when product expertise is not a variable (e.g., in oil and gas industries). Further, the functional structure is a good choice if regional variations in operations are not great, thus lessening the need for regional expertise. Since these conditions are not often met, the functional form of international marketing organization is rare.

Overall, one does not frequently encounter a company that adopts one of the organizational structures in the pure form as described here. The need for specialization is balanced with the need to integrate functions and competencies across organizational boundaries. This reasoning gives rise to an organizational development in recent decades in the form of the matrix organization. Companies became frustrated with the shortcomings of unidimensional organizational structures (product, area, function). They therefore moved toward a more complex organizational form that allowed two dimensions to have more or less equal weight in the organizational structure and decision-making. Matrix organizations have a dual rather than a single chain of command. Hence, managers have two bosses. The matrix also involves lateral (dual) decision-making and a chain of command that fosters conflict management and a balance of power. Product and geography are the two dimensions that receive equal emphasis in the matrix organization (Terpstra and Sarathy, 2000). It is therefore organizationally straightforward for local managers to deal directly with headquarter staff responsible for marketing, production, research and development, and so forth. The matrix arrangement has a certain elegance, while representing a pragmatic attempt to add flexibility to relationships between headquarters and local representation. However, there are drawbacks. For example, a principle of the matrix system is that the majority of interactions involve lower-level management and that adequate resources – human, financial, and technical – support these interactions. However, when senior managers are drawn into exchanges, this can lead to factionalism and time-consuming haggling over resource allocations. The matrix often amplifies these differences in perspectives and interests by forcing all issues through the dual chains of command, so that even a minor difference can become the subject of heated disagreement and debate. Dual reporting leads to conflict and confusion (Bartlett, Ghoshal, and Birkinshaw, 2004). In a study of 93 multinationals it was found that

unitary reporting structures still prevailed as dual reporting was perceived as too problematic (Pitts and Daniels, 1984).

Suitable international marketing organizations serve as a means of achieving customer closeness and must prove amenable for fulfilling key tasks of international MARKETING MANAGEMENT. Companies frequently have difficulty combining operational effectiveness with managerial efficiency. As a result, breakdowns in communication occur between distant markets and the strategic center of the company. Organizational designers, therefore, aim to establish structures that are flexible and can be modified according to changing requirements. Furthermore, they incorporate informal elements and coordination mechanisms (e.g., cross-functional teams, communication systems, world boards, company language, etc.) into the structure, to counter-balance inherent rigidities in the formal structure of the organization.

Bibliography

Bartlett, C. A. and Ghoshal, S. B. (1987). Managing across borders: New strategic requirements. *Sloan Management Review*, 28 (4), 7–17.

Bartlett, C. A., Ghoshal, S. B., and Birkinshaw, J. (2004). *Transnational Management: Text, Cases, and Readings in Cross-Border Management*, 4th edn. Boston: McGraw-Hill.

Doz, Y. L., Bartlett, C. A., and Prahalad, C. K. (1981). Global competitive pressures and host country demands: Managing tensions in MNCs. *California Management Review*, 23 (3), 63.

Pitts, R. A. and Daniels, J. D. (1984). Aftermath of the matrix mania. *Columbia Journal of World Business*, 19 (2), 48–54.

Terpstra, V. and Sarathy, R. (2000). *International Marketing*, 8th edn. Fort Worth, TX: Dryden Press.

international marketing research

Michael Greatorex

International marketing research is intended to aid MARKETING decisions involving more than one country. The research can involve global products, large multinational companies active in several countries, or smaller companies interested in new export markets. International marketing research may involve routine yearly forecasting of sales of different products in many established markets, or decisions concerning the introduction of a product successful in one country into another country, or why a product's success varies from country to country. Although the same methods are used as in domestic marketing research, the international marketing research process is complicated by extra problems.

The MARKETING ENVIRONMENT varies from country to country. This is particularly true of the governmental, legal, economic, and cultural environments, and secondary research (see SECONDARY DATA) will have to be carried out on these environments. This immediately multiplies the amount of search for relevant secondary data, and sources outside the domestic country will be needed. The potential for problems with secondary data is greater with international research than for domestic research. The level of information will vary with the informational environment, definitions vary from country to country; indeed, different sources frequently give different values for the same variables, e.g., country A's figure for its imports from country B will differ from country B's figure for its exports to country A. The level of accuracy may be expected to be better in developed countries than in developing countries. Data on national income based on tax returns will be affected by differing tax regimes and attitudes toward tax evasion.

QUALITATIVE RESEARCH becomes important in international marketing research as it is more likely that ignorance of foreign markets means that more exploratory research is needed. It may be difficult to recruit trained personnel with knowledge of both qualitative research methods and the CULTURE and language of the country under study.

Survey research offers two types of problems relating to SAMPLING and QUESTIONNAIRE DESIGN, respectively. Sampling problems include difficulties in population definition and the lack of suitable sampling frames, which make it difficult to relate any sample results to a population. Low levels of telephone penetration or poor postal systems and low literacy levels may make telephone surveys or postal surveys impractical in developing countries. High transport costs in some countries may mean personal interviews are confined to urban areas. On the other hand, personal interviewing may be more economic in lower-wage countries. Response rates depend upon cultural factors such as differing attitudes toward privacy, greater reluctance in some communities to communicate with strangers, and different attitudes toward some products such as food, personal hygiene, and alcohol.

Questionnaire problems begin with language problems. Language varies from country to country and in some countries several languages are spoken in different areas. Some words may have different meanings in different countries using the same language. Direct translation of a questionnaire from one language to another by a bilingual translator is frequently used. A translation needs to be checked by such means as back-translation, whereby the translated questionnaire is translated back to the original language by another translator and comparison of the original questionnaire and the back-translated version is carried out, allowing errors to be identified which can then be rectified. Piloting each language questionnaire in the country in which it is to be used is another check. Other questionnaire problems occur when questions and scales appropriate to one country are inappropriate to other countries. Thus, questions about car parking and out-of-town shopping centers may be inappropriate in countries where there are few cars. Again, items in a scale designed to measure a particular concept and devised in one country may not be appropriate to another country.

See also *international marketing; marketing research*

Bibliography

Jeannet, J.-P. and Hennessey, H. D. (2004). *Global Marketing Strategies*, 4th edn. Boston: Houghton Mifflin Company, ch. 6.

Maheswaran, D. and Shavitt, S. (2000). Issues and new directions in global consumer psychology. *Journal of Consumer Psychology*, **9** (2), 59–66.

Malhotra, N. K. (1999). *Marketing Research: An Applied Approach*, 3rd edn. Englewood Cliffs, NJ: Prentice-Hall.

Moutinho, L. and Evans, M. (1992). *Applied Marketing Research*. Wokingham: Addison-Wesley, ch. 14.

international organizational structure

Mohammed Yamin

The treatment of the structural issues within INTERNATIONAL MARKETING is highly influenced by the dominant paradigm in organizational theory. This holds that the structure of a firm reflects its strategy. In this paradigm, the most forceful statement of which is to be found in Chandler (1962), structure is essentially concerned with the question, "Who does what?" The answer to this question is contingent, largely, on what strategy the firm is pursuing. Strategy, in turn (*see* STRATEGIC MARKETING), is concerned with the question, "What is to be done?," the answer to which is to be sought in environmental imperatives. There is a linear process of causation from environment to strategy to structure: a successful firm develops strategies that "fit" its environment and sets up an organizational structure that insures their effective implementation. Thus, organizational structure defines in broad terms the prerogative and roles of different people or units within the firm. It also sets up an incentive structure of positive and negative rewards to motivate different groups within the firm to identify with, and pursue the goals of, the organization. Finally, an organizational structure creates a coordination or integration mechanism.

For international marketers, the key structure question concerns the appropriate balance between centralization at headquarters and the degree of local autonomy exercised by the subsidiaries. Subsidiaries have minimal input into strategy formulation, which revolves around marketing standardization versus adaptation (*see* INTERNATIONAL PRODUCT ADAPTATION; INTERNATIONAL PRODUCT STANDARDIZATION). Subsidiaries also have little input to decisions relating to organizational "architecture" or organizational "surgery" (Goold and Campbell, 1989). For example, decisions regarding acquisitions, mergers, and the formation of alliances (*see* INTERNATIONAL STRATEGIC ALLIANCES) are made at the center alone. Likewise, decisions relating to the selling off, liquidation, or "downsizing" of particular units or subsidiaries are also usually the prerogatives of headquarters. Headquarters also decide whether international marketing activities are organized on a "separation" or an "integration" basis. The former treats foreign markets separately from the "home" market and all aspects of foreign marketing become the direct responsibility of the international division. The integration approach makes no distinction between domestic and foreign marketing; here the firm adopts a global structure organized around products, functions, or areas. An alternative (but one which is now out of favor; Achrol, 1991) is the matrix organization: this is a dual-authority structure in which subsidiary managers are simultaneously accountable to regional and product managers (*see* INTERNATIONAL MARKETING ORGANIZATION).

The roles of subsidiaries are "residual" in the sense that these roles are specified in terms of the decisions that headquarters do not wish to be heavily involved in. This, in turn, depends on the overall MARKETING STRATEGY being pursued. Firms with a standardization strategy will have a tighter degree of supervision over various MARKETING MIX activities by the subsidiary. In terms of the role typology utilized by Queltch and Hoff (1986), headquarters will have "approving" and "directing" roles. On the other hand, a firm with an adaptation strategy will leave a greater degree of autonomy for subsidiaries and the center will confine itself to "persuading" and "coordinating." In practice, the autonomy enjoyed by subsidiaries is often greater than would be suggested by the range of formal roles assigned to them by the center. This is because effective monitoring and supervision is very expensive and needs information generated or filtered by subsidiaries. Subsidiary managers, particularly of subsidiaries in large and important markets, may in fact be able to largely ignore corporate-level strategies. Effective control of subsidiaries is probably more feasible through an informal or organic socialization process whereby subsidiary managers identify with and adopt the corporate "mission" as their own. This may be easier to achieve if expatriates are employed in key managerial positions within the subsidiary.

The theoretical underpinning for the traditional view of the strategy/structure relationship has been criticized by Hedlund and Rolander (1990). The burden of their argument is the suggestion that structure is not simply an instrument for IMPLEMENTATION but that it influences how the firm "sees" the environment and what range of opportunities is perceived to be within its grasp. In other words, strategy depends on structure. In this view, structure is not only concerned with "who does what" but also acts rather like the "nervous" or "sensing" system of the firm. Hedlund and Rolander (1990) argue that the environment–strategy–structure paradigm ignores the dynamic aspects of strategy that relate to the firm's learning capability. Corporate learning requires a structure that is tolerant of exploration and experimentation by different units. The "brain" functions of the organization cannot, therefore, reside solely at the center. In fact, there is evidence that unless the parent unit or the headquarters has specific "parenting" capabilities, its control of subunits is just as likely to destroy as to create value for the corporation as a whole (Goold and Sommers Luchs, 1996).

In a similar vein, Bartlett and Ghoshal (1989) discuss the drawbacks to the structural setup within which the subsidiaries have implementation roles only. A potential advantage of multinationality is precisely that by operating in a number of diverse market environments (*see* MARKETING ENVIRONMENT), it is possible to gain access to a wider range of ideas, skills, and capabilities. However, this potential is unlikely to be achieved if the roles of subsidiaries are confined to carrying out centrally determined strategy. In fact, Bartlett and Ghoshal (1989) have advocated a "transnational" structure in which subsidiaries, particularly those located in more dynamic markets, have a similar standing to headquarters and participate in strategy formulation. Recent years have witnessed a rapid expansion of research on the strategic role of subsidiaries within multinational companies that has highlighted their key role in the global competitiveness of multinational companies (Birkinshaw, 2001; Subramaniam and Venkatraman, 2001).

Bibliography

Achrol, R. (1991). Evolution of marketing organization: New forms for turbulent environments. *Journal of Marketing*, **55**, 4 (October), 77–93.

Bartlett, C. A. and Ghoshal, S. B. (1989). *Managing Across Borders: The Transnational Solution*. Boston: Harvard Business School Press.

Birkinshaw, J. (2001). Strategy and management in MNE subsidiaries. In A. Rugman and T. Brewer (eds.), *Oxford Handbook on International Business*. Oxford: Oxford University Press.

Chandler, A. (1962). *Strategy and Structure*. Boston: MIT Press.

Goold, M. and Campbell, A. (1989). *Strategies and Styles*. Ashridge Management Center.

Goold, M. and Sommers Luchs, A. (1996). *Managing the Multibusiness Company: Strategic Issues for Diversified Groups*. London: Routledge.

Hedlund, G. and Rolander, D. (1990). Action in heterarchies: New approaches to managing the MNC. In C. Bartlett, Y. Doz, and G. Hedlund (eds.), *Managing the Global Firm*. London: Routledge.

Queltch, J. and Hoff, E. (1986). Customizing global marketing. *Harvard Business Review*, **26** (May/June).

Subramaniam, M. and Venkatraman, N. (2001). Determinants of transnational new product development: Testing the influence of transferring and deploying tacit knowledge. *Strategic Management Journal*, **22**, 359–78.

international pricing policy

Rudolph Sinkovics

PRICING decisions are generally considered to be rather difficult to make. Given that pricing is part of the MARKETING MIX, pricing decisions must be tightly integrated with other aspects of the marketing mix. The complex set of factors that influence pricing decisions, such as the nature and extent of DEMAND, competitors' activities, costs of production and MARKETING, and so on, becomes even more difficult in international markets, where managers are dealing with multiple currencies, additional cost considerations, and longer distribution channels (Cavusgil, 1996). Managers need to carefully balance and weigh off ambiguous considerations between the diverging forces calling for either price standardization or adaptation. Although managers will readily be willing to exploit price differentials for their firm's benefit, as most markets reach saturation, communication technologies such as the Internet lead to more transparency, retail price maintenance disappears, and product life cycles (*see* PRODUCT LIFE CYCLE) become shorter, firms will find it increasingly difficult to establish and maintain international pricing policy

price differences across markets (Stöttinger, 2001).

Against this background, a number of analytic and managerial dimensions have been suggested, which impact on pricing decisions for international markets (Terpstra and Sarathy, 2000; Jeannet and Hennessey, 2004). Dimensions comprise firm-level factors, product-specific factors, market-specific factors, and environmental factors.

At the firm level, it has been suggested that foreign price setting will be a function of the company's cost structure: the level of fixed costs of product development, manufacturing, and marketing. If the company is producing on a large scale and has experience cost effects and/ or scale economies, these will impact on international pricing strategies.

At the product level, the life cycle of the product, the availability of substitutes, or distinct product attributes that necessitate certain quality/service and delivery levels will influence price setting in an international context. Transport is probably the most evident factor that impacts on prices; however, with falling transportation prices, the impact of this factor is confined to situations where shipping speed and quality are of great importance.

Market-specific factors that impact on foreign price setting are, first and foremost, consumers: their ability to buy (income levels) and willingness to buy. However, market-specific costs of product adaptation, marketing and servicing, different distribution channels, and local competition also need to be considered. Furthermore, local government may intervene in transactions, either as active buyers of the products or services or by pressurizing for countertrade agreements, tight price controls, or the setting up of barriers of trade (quotas, tariffs, subsidies, non-tariff barriers). These latter factors can also be considered part of environmental factors, where foreign exchange rates, inflation rates, price controls, and regulations may signal both short-term and long-term considerations for price setting.

The extent to which multinational companies standardize their international pricing strategies depends on the level of similarity between home and host countries in terms of customer characteristics, legal environment, economic conditions, and stage of the product life cycle (Theodosiou and Katsikeas, 2001). Where possible, international pricing decisions will be centralized because the increasing GLOBALIZATION of markets requires greater uniformity of prices across markets, global competition requires coordinated competitive strategies (*see* COMPETITIVE STRATEGY) across market boundaries, and pricing is closely related to production-volume planning as well as global branding (Cavusgil, 1996).

Companies active in international markets have basically three different options in how to set prices for foreign markets (Cavusgil, 1988):

1 the rigid cost-plus pricing approach;
2 the approach of flexible cost-plus pricing; and
3 dynamic incremental pricing.

Cost-plus pricing requires adding up all the costs involved in getting the product to its destination, plus shipping and profit increment. This method is advantageous because it is relatively easy to arrive at a price quote; however, the use of historical accounting costs for price calculation completely ignores demand and competitive conditions in target markets. This is why the flexible cost-plus pricing approach sometimes receives favorable treatment. The strategy sets list prices (*see* LIST PRICE) in the same way as the more rigid system but allows for price variations under special circumstances. For example, discounts (*see* DISCOUNT) may be applied to the final price, depending on the customer, the size of the order, or the strength of local competition. Although this strategy allows a higher degree of freedom to adjust for local conditions, the primary goal is still to maintain profit margins and therefore it too is an essentially static element of the marketing mix (Cavusgil, 1996). The dynamic incremental pricing strategy is based on the idea that fixed costs emerge regardless of whether the company is internationally successful or not. Therefore, it seeks to recover only variable and international marketing and promotion costs in export ventures. This approach is considerably more flexible than cost-plus pricing and allows the company to sell at very competitive prices with the potential of market-share gains (*see* MARKET SHARE).

Other contentious pricing issues involve dumping, i.e., selling products in international markets at prices below those in the home country or even below cost of production, parallel importing, and TRANSFER PRICING. Parallel imports take advantage of price differences between markets by reimporting branded products from low-price into high-price markets. Parallel imports are to blame for the development of gray markets, where trademarked products are distributed through channels unauthorized by the owner of the trademark. TRANSFER PRICING is one of the thorniest problems global companies have to deal with when they venture beyond their home-country borders. The problem is also known as "intra-company pricing" and refers to the pricing of goods and services bought and sold by operating units or divisions of a single company. The prices at which units of the same company sell to each other have a far-reaching effect on the company's success because they influence subsidiary performance, executive compensation, and tax obligations (Cavusgil, 1996). A major motivation for this pricing option is that it provides companies with a mechanism for side-stepping higher tax rates in some countries. Organizations like the World Trade Organization (WTO) or the Organization for Economic Cooperation and Development (OECD) have therefore issued guidelines about how to treat these problematic situations. Company managers who transfer goods and services across their company borders have to respond to questions on how to price such intra-corporate transactions.

Bibliography

Cavusgil, S. T. (1988). Unraveling the mystique of export pricing. *Business Horizons*, 31 (3), 54–63.

Cavusgil, S. T. (1996). Pricing for global markets. *Columbia Journal of World Business*, 31 (4), 66–78.

Jeannet, J.-P. and Hennessey, H. D. (2004). *Global Marketing Strategies*, 6th edn. Boston: Houghton Mifflin.

Stöttinger, B. (2001). Strategic export pricing: A long and winding road. *Journal of International Marketing*, 9 (1), 40–63.

Terpstra, V. and Sarathy, R. (2000). *International Marketing*, 8th edn. Fort Worth, TX: Dryden Press.

Theodosiou, M. and Katsikeas, C. S. (2001). Factors influencing the degree of international pricing strategy standardization of multinational corporations. *Journal of International Marketing*, 9 (3), 1–18.

international product adaptation

Mohammed Yamin

Marketing adaptation is the opposite of standardization and conveys the idea that marketers may tailor their marketing program to the specific conditions of the different countries in which they operate. A distinction is usually made between "mandatory" and "discretionary" adaptation (Hill and Still, 1984; Walters and Toyne, 1989). Mandatory adaptations are those that are dictated by the physical, legal, political, or economic factors in a country. For example, voltage levels and power sockets of electrical equipment need to conform to local requirements; in some countries, safety or anti-pulsion/emission regulation may be particularly restrictive and may make it impossible for the firm to offer a standardized product. In fact, however, research indicates that the majority of adaptations are not mandatory; according to one estimate, more than 70 percent of adaptations made are discretionary (Hill and Still, 1984).

Jain (1989) provides a rigorous examination of factors that affect the balance between program standardization and adaptation and offers a number of specific hypotheses relating to their impact on the degree of standardization. These factors fall into five categories: the nature of the TARGET MARKET; the market position of the firm in different countries; the nature of the product itself; environmental factors; and organizational factors. The observed pattern of standardization seems to confirm Jain's analyses. For example, the nature of the product is a strong predictor of standardization; standardization is more common for industrial as compared to consumer products; and products for which buyer behavior is culturally determined tend to be more adapted than products for which consumer choice is dependent on functional performance (e.g., food products compared to electrical goods).

See also *international product standardization*

Bibliography

Hill, J. and Still, R. (1984). Adapting products to LDC tastes. *Harvard Business Review*, March/April, 92–101.

Jain, S. (1989). Standardization versus adaptation: Some research hypotheses. *Journal of Marketing*, 53 (January), 70–9.

Walters, P. and Toyne, B. (1989). Product modification and standardization in international markets: Strategic options and facilitating policies. *Columbia Journal of World Business*, **29**, 3 (Winter), 37–44.

international product standardization

Mohammed Yamin

There is an inevitable tension between standardization and adaptation within MARKETING, whether domestically or internationally. The fact that customers have different preferences, and given marketing's commitment to CUSTOMER SATISFACTION, implies a pressure toward adaptation or even the customization of the OFFERING to individuals or small groups. However, customization has been (until very recently, at any rate) considered to be prohibitively expensive owing to the existence of economies of scale and other technological and economic constraints suggesting that most people (with the exception of the very rich) must tolerate some degree of standardization or uniformity in what they purchase and consume. The evolution of marketing from "mass" to "target" marketing (*see* TARGET MARKET) reflects this tension; "mass" marketing simply ignores diversity or the desire for variety ("you can have any color as long as it's black"). Target marketing, by contrast, starts by assuming pervasive diversity and searches for groups or segments (*see* MARKET SEGMENTATION) that may have similar preferences for a particular offering. However, the tension between standardization and adaptation is particularly important for the international marketer, as the potential for economic benefits from standardizing across countries could be very substantial, while the diversities may be very great as a result of significant differences in CULTURE and other environmental conditions between countries (*see* INTERNATIONAL MARKETING ENVIRONMENT).

In INTERNATIONAL MARKETING, complete program standardization means offering the same product or product line at identical prices through identical distribution systems and promotional policies to customers in differ-

ent countries. Program standardization is, thus, concerned with the degree to which different elements in the MARKETING MIX are treated in the same or a similar manner by a firm that operates internationally. Process standardization, on the other hand, refers to the uniformity in the approach chosen by a multinational firm in analyzing market potential and the formulation of MARKETING PLANNING for different countries. The vast majority of the literature is concerned, however, with program standardization.

The main attraction of standardization is clearly the scale economies that may result from it, not only in production but also in R&D and product development, and possibly in ADVERTISING and promotional expenditure. Levitt (1983) puts particular emphasis on technology and scale factors in advocating standardization. An uninterrupted production run from one center will allow the firm to move rapidly up the learning curve, thus reducing per unit cost very rapidly. Operating on a large scale will also provide sourcing efficiencies, e.g., purchasing large amounts of raw materials and other inputs gives a multinational the power to bargain with SUPPLIERS. Empirical evidence, however, does not provide much support for Levitt's assertions (Doglus and Wind, 1987; Baden-Fuller and Stopford, 1991). Doglus and Wind have pointed out that economies of scope and flexible manufacturing increasingly make it feasible to make adaptation without incurring increasing costs or diseconomies of scale. Economies of scope arise if it is cheaper to produce a number of different products or product varieties together in one plant than it is to produce each in a separate plant. The basis for economies of scope is a number of interconnected technical developments known as "flexible" manufacturing systems.

In the particular context of mature industries (such as white goods) where basic technological and organizational capabilities have been diffused internationally, standardization strategies face significant difficulties. The leading multinational firms face a greater *variety* of competitive challenges. Competition comes not only from other globally oriented companies with standardized marketing strategies (*see* MARKETING STRATEGY) but also from a variety of nationally based companies capable of fashioning marketing strategies suited to their own national markets. Thus, rather paradoxically, with increasing GLOBALIZATION – in terms of greater mobility of technological and organizational skills – competition for customers may increasingly become locally (nationally) focused. The latter strategy is capable of generating better customer outcomes and satisfaction (Yamin and Altusinik, 2003).

More generally, in spite of much debate between the advocates of standardization and adaptation, little is known regarding the impact of standardization on corporate performance and, until recently, the performance issue had not received any research attention. Samiee and Roth's (1992) work is probably the first systematic investigation of the link between standardization and performance. They found no significant difference in performance between firms that stressed standardization and those that did not.

Bibliography

Baden-Fuller, C. and Stopford, J. (1991). Globalization frustrated: The case of white goods. *Strategic Management Journal*, **12**, 493–507.

Doglus, S. and Wind, Y. (1987). The myth of globalization. *Columbia Journal of World Business*, **22** (4), 19–30.

Levitt, T. (1983). The globalization of markets. *Harvard Business Review*, **22** (May/June), 92–102.

Samiee, S. and Roth, K. (1992). The influence of global market standardization on performance. *Journal of Marketing*, **56** (April), 1–17.

Yamin, M. and Altusinik, R. (2003). A comparison of satisfaction outcomes associated with adapted and non-adapted products. *International Marketing Review*, **20** (6), 604–19.

international strategic alliances

Mohammed Yamin

An alliance is any contractual or cooperative relationship between two organizations for a specific purpose. Relationships between firms can be conceived of in terms of a spectrum at one end of which is "arm's length" exchange. This is purely price-mediated and involves no commitment or promise regarding the future behavior of either party. At the other end of the spectrum is a merger or union between two organizations.

Alliances occupy the mid-range between arm's length exchange and merger. Thus, an alliance involves some degree of long-term commitment between the parties, manifested either through a legally binding contract or through a more informal agreement to cooperate. The duration of the relationship in an alliance is indeterminate but, unlike a merger, it is not permanent. Particular forms of alliances can be very varied and include LICENSING, subcontracting, FRANCHISING, and INTERNATIONAL JOINT VENTURES.

Interfirm alliances have a long history in international business. Until the early 1980s, these alliances were focused on market entry (*see* INTERNATIONAL MARKET ENTRY AND DEVELOPMENT STRATEGIES) into particular markets and were commonly between firms from developed economy markets and firms or government agencies in less developed or centrally planned economies. In such economies, the option of direct investment was often ruled out or was made unattractive by government restrictions regarding foreign ownership and control. To generalize, these "traditional" alliances were a means of exploiting the western or Japanese firms' existing capabilities (most often technological know-how, but also MARKETING and organizational skills), and in this sense were essentially tactical. Any new skills or knowledge generated in the process were typically local market specific and of relatively little value to the rest of the organization.

Recent years have witnessed the rapid growth of various types of interfirm alliances that are motivated very differently (Hergert and Morris, 2002). The recent waves of alliances are commonly between developed economy firms and are focused on global competitiveness rather than on circumventing government-imposed barriers to market entry. In fact, the growth of strategic alliances is strongly linked to a global environment characterized by an increasingly liberal market environment (*see* INTERNATIONAL MARKETING ENVIRONMENT) whereby government restrictions on international business activities are rapidly receding. There is now a vast literature dealing with the determinants, motives, partner selection, collaborative processes, performance, and outcomes of strategic alliances (a representative sample of this literature is collected in Contractor and

Lorange, 2002). One aspect of strategic alliances that has attracted particular attention is the issue of knowledge acquisition and organizational learning associated with interfirm collaborations. The focus on knowledge acquisition is highly apposite since learning and knowledge acquisition are increasingly regarded as central to strategy formation and to competitive performance (Teece, 1998). Furthermore, given the knowledge-intensive environments that most firms face, it is at least arguable that organizational learning inevitably (and increasingly) has a relational or collaborative dimension. In any case, as Inkpen (2000) has observed, "alliances are an ideal platform for learning" irrespective of whether learning is always an explicit motive for alliance formation or not. Thus, understanding the drivers of effective knowledge acquisition in alliances is at least a significant step along the way to understanding alliance performance/outcomes more generally.

The alliance literature has focused on three aspects of knowledge acquisition (Inkpen, 2000). Firstly, there is learning *about* "alliancing." This relates to gaining knowledge/experience useful to future partner selection, alliance structuring, and alliance management through the various phases of its evolution (e.g., Doz, 1996; Pett and Clay, 2001). Secondly, firms may seek *access* to a partner's knowledge and skills without necessarily wishing to "internalize" this knowledge (meaning to integrate this knowledge within their own operational and managerial systems). Hamel (1991) made a forceful argument for knowledge acquisition as opposed to knowledge accessing as the key for gaining from alliances. Most subsequent studies appear to have followed Hamel's lead implicitly and have regarded knowledge acquisition as strategically more important than knowledge accessing. In a recent paper, Grant and Baden-Fuller (2004) depart from this consensus and argue that knowledge accessing provides a more robust explanation of many alliance trends than knowledge acquiring. They argue that alliances are not about extending core knowledge or competence but allow partners to *combine* complementary knowledge to produce products and services that neither could do individually as they lack critical specializations. Interesting examples they give include the alliance between Daimler-

Benz and Swatch to design the "Smart car" and Luciano Pavarotti's collaboration with the Spice Girls. In neither case was one of the parties attempting to acquire the core knowledge or skill of its partner. Broadly, Grant and Baden-Fuller argue that alliances are more about efficient exploitation of existing partner core knowledge bases. The creation and expansion of core competence is more efficiently carried out internally within individual companies. However, it could be argued that Grant and Baden-Fuller operate with an overly "modular" concept of knowledge, where the boundaries of knowledge "pieces" are fairly clearly and discretely identifiable. In more general cases where knowledge bases are less modular and hence the boundaries of core knowledge bases are more fuzzy, there may still be a rationale for alliances as a vehicle for knowledge acquisition.

Thirdly, firms pick up knowledge from a partner that they could employ *outside* the alliance – it is the "private" benefit from the alliance (Khanna, Gulti, and Nohira, 1998). This is in fact what Hamel had in mind by "internalization" of partner knowledge, and, as was pointed out above, it remains the focus of much subsequent research. An influential line of subsequent work has attempted to model knowledge internalization and we now have a fuller understanding of the knowledge acquisition process within alliances. Two broad factors have been emphasized in this context: "accessibility of alliance knowledge" and "partner knowledge acquisition effectiveness." Accessibility of knowledge is a function of inherent knowledge attributes (tacitness and ambiguity make partner knowledge less accessible; Simonin, 1999), relational dimensions such as TRUST and openness, and structural dimensions such as the degree of market or competitive overlap. Partner knowledge acquisition effectiveness is mainly a function of absorptive capacity, which is itself affected by the similarity of the knowledge basis, the existence of prior relationships, and the compatibility of organizational norms and routines.

Bibliography

Contractor, F. and Lorange, P. (eds.) (2002). *Cooperative Strategies in International Business*, vol. 1. Amsterdam: Pergamon.

Doz, Y. (1996). The evolution of cooperation in strategic alliances: Initial conditions or learning processes. *Strategic Management Journal*, 17, Special issue, 55–84.

Grant, R. and Baden-Fuller, C. (2004). A knowledge accessing theory of strategic alliances. *Journal of Management Studies*, 41 (1), 61–85.

Hamel, G. (1991). Competition for competence and inter-partner learning within international strategic alliances. *Strategic Management Journal*, 12, 83–103.

Hergert, M. and Morris, D. (2002). Trends in international collaborative agreements. In F. Contractor and P. Lorange (eds.), *Cooperative Strategies in International Business*, vol. 1. Amsterdam: Pergamon.

Inkpen, A. (2000). Learning through joint ventures: A framework of knowledge acquisition. *Journal of Management Studies*, 37 (7), 1019–43.

Khanna, T., Gulti, R., and Nohira, N. (1998). The dynamics of learning alliances: Competition, corporation and relative scope. *Strategic Management Journal*, 19, 193–210.

Pett, T. L. and Clay, D. C. (2001). A process model of global strategic alliance formation. *Business Process Management Journal*, 7, 349–64.

Simonin, B. (1999). Ambiguity and the process of knowledge transfer in strategic alliances. *Strategic Management Journal*, 20, 595–624.

Teece, D. (1998). Capturing value from knowledge assets: The new economy, markets for knowhow and intangible assets. *California Management Review*, 40 (3), 55–79.

Internet marketing

Dale Littler

The Internet presents an additional powerful channel of distribution of information and sales in both consumer and organizational markets. Although business-to-consumer Internet-based sales have not as yet achieved the original optimistic forecasts, sales by this means are steadily increasing with the greater ownership of personal computers and the MARKETING policies of some marketers that will only sell direct over the Internet (e.g., Easy Jet, Egg Internet bank) or that are promoting this mode of DIRECT SELLING as a convenient alternative to traditional RETAILING. Established "bricks and mortar" retailers are adding credibility to Internet-based retailing by developing it as an additional channel. As consumers gain confidence through experience, it can be expected that Internet-based retailing will increase.

In organizational markets (*see* BUSINESS-TO-BUSINESS MARKETING; ORGANIZATIONAL MARKETING), business-to-business Internet marketing facilitates significant increases in efficiency through the automation of much back-office paperwork. The linking of information systems enables intermediaries to monitor more effectively their inventory levels and the flow of, e.g., foods through the warehouses. Hutt and Speh (2004) suggest that most extra-nets linking business marketing firms to distributors allow the distributor to examine inventory levels at the manufacturer's warehouse. This enables the distributor to customize orders to the availability of inventory. As in consumer markets, the Internet provides as additional channel of distribution for reaching targeted markets.

In general, it is obvious that the Internet is becoming a major method, if not the method of first choice, for many customers to search for information on products and services, thereby considerably empowering them by making it possible to compare and evaluate the features and prices of different products at relatively low cost. This is resulting in, for example, greater price transparency. It is possible to monitor web browsers' viewing behavior, for example through search engines, and in this way generate advertisements and links that appeal specifically to the customers' interpreted requirements.

Some see the Internet as a relatively easy way of collecting MARKETING RESEARCH data, and the use of online surveys, for instance, has been increasing markedly. However, there is likely to be increasing resistance because of the number being despatched, the time involved in completion, and the fatigue generated by the large number of unsolicited email communications sent.

Bibliography

Hutt, M. D. and Speh, T. W. (2004). *Business Marketing Management*, 8th edn. Mason, OH: South-Western-Thomson.

Kotler, P., Armstrong, G., Saunders, J., and Wong, V. (2001). *Principles of Marketing*, 3rd European edn. Harlow: Prentice-Hall, ch. 22.

Robins, J. (2000). The E-Marketing Mix. *Marketing Review*, 1, 249–74.

interpersonal communications

Barbara R. Lewis

Interpersonal communications are the basis of informal channels of MARKETING COMMUNI-CATIONS, sometimes referred to as WORD-OF-MOUTH COMMUNICATIONS, when consumers/buyers pass on information to each other about, for example, products/services or marketing organizations. To understand interpersonal communications requires consideration of personal influence, group influence including reference groups, and opinion leaders.

Personal influence is the change in ATTI-TUDES and/or behavior as a result of interpersonal communications. Personal influence can be initiated by a potential consumer seeking advice and information, or after purchase as a provider of information and opinions. It is a two-way influence, unlike that of the MASS MEDIA, and it may be visual as well as verbal.

The occurrence of personal influence depends on product variables (e.g., visibility, complexity, degree of PERCEIVED RISK, stage in the DIF-FUSION PROCESS), and consumer variables (e.g., life stage, product experience, PERSON-ALITY). Companies try to affect the extent of personal influence in their ADVERTISING and promotion, PERSONAL SELLING, and SALES PROMOTION activities. For example, in their advertising they may simulate personal influence with user stereotypes, testimonials, and group activities; or stimulate it by, e.g., encouraging people to talk about a product.

In the realm of interpersonal communications, not all individuals wield equal influence. Some, opinion leaders, are more influential and others may turn to them for information and advice. Katz and Lazerfeld (1955) believe that people are most influenced by those they are in contact with in everyday life, i.e., by people most like themselves, e.g., doctors for health issues and close friends for the purchase of consumer durables. Research has not been able to clearly identify opinion leader traits, e.g., with respect to DEMOGRAPHICS, personality, LIFESTYLES, or media habits (e.g., Myers and Robertson, 1972). Further, it has not been possible to identify opinion leaders across product categories; opinion leadership is primarily product specific (e.g., King and Summers, 1979).

Group influence is an important aspect of social influence. All groups have values, beliefs, and norms, and expect individual members to share these and conform to them and behave in appropriate ways. Consumers are, therefore, influenced by a number of groups that may be categorized as primary (e.g., family, friends, neighbors, work associates) or secondary, where there has been some deliberate choice in belonging and there is a more formal structure and rules (e.g., political parties, church affiliation, leisure and sporting clubs).

There are pressures on consumers to conform to group beliefs, values, and norms, and there is evidence in the CONSUMER BUYER BEHAVIOR literature that this does occur. The family is the most important source of group influence on an individual, in particular in his/her formative years. However, one of the distinguishing characteristics of western CULTURE is the declining influence of the family.

A specific type of group influence of interest to marketers is reference group influence. Reference groups are groups with which consumers identify and they are used as reference points in determining judgments, beliefs, and behavior. They set standards which are the source of personal behavior norms. They may be membership or aspirant groups. Examples of aspirant groups are personalities whose lifestyles are characterized by luxury products/consumption, or soccer stars who are emulated by small boys (and others), as typified in the purchase of football strips and apparel.

Bearden and Etzel (1982) studied reference group influence and the conspicuousness of a product and its brands, and suggested that reference group influence can be strong or weak for product and/or BRAND. For example, the purchase of a car and the model chosen are both subject to such influence, whereas for satellite television reference group influence prevails with respect to product ownership but not for "brand" choice.

Interpersonal communications are complementary to mass media communications, and consumers use both types depending on the product, stage in the decision-making process (*see* CONSUMER DECISION-MAKING PRO-CESS), and perceptions of risk. Interpersonal communications provide a two-way communication process, are usually seen as more trust-worthy than the mass media, and are harder to selectively ignore or tune out. However, they may also be providing unrealistic or inaccurate information and are, indeed, usually communi-cating evaluations and opinions rather than fac-tual information.

In ORGANIZATIONAL MARKETING inter-personal communications also have a major sig-nificance because of personal interactions in, for example, networks (*see* NETWORK) and confer-ences. Within organizations GATEKEEPERS act as a powerful source of intelligence.

Bibliography

Bearden, W. O. and Etzel, M. J. (1982). Reference group influence on product and brand purchase decisions. *Journal of Consumer Research*, **92** (September), 183–94.

Engel, J. F., Blackwell, R. D., and Miniard, P. W. (1995). *Consumer Behavior*, 8th edn. Fort Worth, TX: Dryden Press.

Hawkins, D. I., Best, R. J., and Coney, K. A. (1995). *Consumer Behavior: Implications for Marketing Strat-egy*, 6th edn. Boston: Irwin.

Katz, E. and Lazerfeld, P. F. (1955). *Personal Influence*. Glencoe, IL: Free Press.

King, C. W. and Summers, J. O. (1979). Overlap of opinion leaders across consumer product categories. *Journal of Marketing Research*, **7** (February), 43–50.

Myers, J. H. and Robertson, T. S. (1972). Dimensions of opinion leadership. *Journal of Marketing Research*, **9** (February), 41–6.

Olkkonen, R., Tikkanen, H., and Alajoutsijarvi, K. (2000). The role of communication in business rela-tionships and networks. *Management Decision*, **38** (6), 403–9.

Schiffman, L. G. and Kanuk, L. Z. (2004). *Consumer Behavior*, 8th edn. Upper Saddle River, NJ: Prentice-Hall, ch. 9.

interpretive research

Mark P. Healey

Interpretive research embraces research para-digms that emphasize interpretation and con-struction/construal of meaning at a micro level. The interpretive paradigm draws heavily on hu-manistic and phenomenological perspectives and is concerned with understanding individual consumer behavior from within the consumer's frame of reference or "meaning frameworks."

Bibliography

Marsden, D. and Littler, D. (1998). Positioning alterna-tive perspectives of consumer behavior. *Journal of Marketing Management*, **14**, 3–28.

interviews

see DEPTH INTERVIEWS; FOCUS GROUPS; SURVEY RESEARCH

involvement

Dale Littler

Involvement refers to "a person's perceived rele-vance of the object based on their inherent needs, values and interests" (Zaichkowsky, 1985). The degree of involvement with a prod-uct category will affect the effort made in, for example, searching for information and evaluat-ing alternatives. Solomon, Bamossy, and Aske-gaard (2002) regard involvement as providing the motivation to process information. There can be seen to be a spectrum of involvement, from none at one end, where inertia (*see* HABIT-UAL BUYING BEHAVIOR) will be the dominant feature, to extreme at the other end, where for example the product will have great significance to the consumer. Involvement may, however, assume several forms:

- *product involvement*: the consumer's degree of interest in purchasing the product;
- *message-response involvement*: the consumer's interest in processing MARKETING COM-MUNICATIONS; and
- *ego involvement*: the importance of the prod-uct to the consumer's SELF-CONCEPT.

Zaichkowsky (1985) developed a scale to meas-ure product involvement.

Laurent and Kapferer (1985) proposed an involvement profile having the following com-ponents:

- the sign value of the product category (rela-tionship to self-concept);
- the pleasure value of the product category;

- the probability of making an inappropriate purchase; and
- the perceived importance of the potential negative consequences of an inappropriate purchase.

Involvement can be related to one or more of these components. This approach highlights the diversity of the involvement construct and can also facilitate segmentation (*see* MARKET SEGMENTATION). Some consumers may find a product has a low sign value, for example, while it could be high for others, thereby enabling marketers to orient their strategies to take account of the different motives of various consumer groups.

Bibliography

Laurent, G. and Kapferer, J.-N. (1985). Measuring consumer involvement profiles. *Journal of Marketing Research*, **22**, 41–53.

Solomon, M. R., Bamossy, G., and Askegaard, S. (2002). *Consumer Behavior: A European Perspective*, 2nd edn. London: Prentice-Hall, ch. 4

Zaichkowsky, J. L. (1985). Measuring the involvement construct in marketing. *Journal of Consumer Research*, **12** (December), 341–52.

joint ventures

see INTERNATIONAL JOINT VENTURES

K

key account

Dominic Wilson

"Account" here refers to a particular stream of transactions between a customer and a supplier with respect to a specified set of offerings (a particular pairing of a customer and a supplier can have more than one account). As some accounts are more important than others, they may be termed "key accounts" because of their implications for either or all parties. Many different factors can make an account "key," such as: the volume or value of the exchanges involved; the knock-on implications of failure in an account (e.g., faulty oil filters can immobilize vast machines); the anticipated flow of repeat business (e.g., from pilot projects); or the reputation of a particular customer (e.g., by appointment to the queen) or supplier (e.g., "Intel inside"). Other customer/supplier accounts may be particularly important because of indirect factors, e.g., a customer may be involved with a supplier in collaborative product development, or in quality improvement measures, or in mutual benchmarking. The importance of "key accounts" should be reflected in the sensitivity with which such accounts are managed, e.g., in the seniority of the account managers and the flexibility allowed in negotiations.

L

latent demand

Dale Littler

Traditionally, latent demand exists where there are no products or services to meet the requirements of customers. It is assumed that customers are aware of what they need. However, it is obvious that DEMAND can be generated by entirely new products that in effect stimulate customers into wanting what previously they had, at least, not been able to articulate. The fact that there are what might be termed unaware wants raises significant issues for innovators, since many MARKETING RESEARCH methodologies are not oriented toward uncovering such latent requirements. Often organizations may have to employ subtle research methods that lead to the development and presentation of different innovative product and service concepts that in some way can be "experienced" (e.g., through a range of computer-generated images or service process) by potential customers/users and their reactions analyzed.

learn-feel-buy model

David Yorke

The learn-feel-buy models (*see* AIDA MODEL; HIERARCHY OF EFFECTS MODEL; INNOVATION-ADOPTION MODEL) in MARKETING COMMUNICATIONS propose that buyers/customers/consumers first learn about a product or service by seeing, reading, and understanding an advertisement or being the recipient of other marketing communications. They not only learn what benefits the product or service may give, but may also develop positive feelings about it, i.e., they are moving through stages of unawareness to AWARENESS, INTEREST, and liking. In turn, this may stimulate the potential customers/consumers to buy the product or service and to develop loyalty toward it in the longer term. This sequence is most appropriate when the buyer/customer has high INVOLVEMENT with a product category with high differentiation, e.g., in the purchase of a car.

See also *buy-feel-learn model; feel-buy-learn model*

learning

see CONSUMER LEARNING

legal system

David Yorke

The legal system is a powerful force in the MARKETING ENVIRONMENT surrounding any organization, both national and international (*see* INTERNATIONAL MARKETING ENVIRONMENT). Legal systems vary from country to country, some being controlled wholly by government, others containing both statute law and common law (case law based on judicial precedent), i.e., judges may modify previous directions to meet changing circumstances. The principal features of any legal system as an element in the marketing environment relate first to the rights of the supplier, i.e., the legal conditions in which marketing activities may be undertaken, and secondly, to the rights of the customer (*see* CONSUMER PROTECTION). Problems may arise when an organization seeks to internationalize its operations, as elements in different legal systems may preclude the use of a standardized marketing plan (*see* MARKETING PLANNING).

licensing

Rudolph Sinkovics

Licensing is a contractual arrangement whereby the licensor (selling firm) allows some elements to be used for a fee by the licensee (buying firm). Elements that can be subjected to licensing are product technology, patents, trademarks, product designs, manufacturing/distribution process, know-how, intellectual property, or anything that is deemed appropriate to generate positional advantages in the market.

In the context of international market entry and market expansion (*see* INTERNATIONAL MARKET ENTRY AND DEVELOPMENT STRATEGIES), licensing is seen as a faster, low-involvement/low-control approach to internationalization, since it does not necessarily entail equity participation (Aulakh, Cavusgil, and Sarkar, 1998), and "control over operations and strategy is granted to the licensee in exchange for a lump-sum payment, a per-unit royalty fee, and a commitment to abide by any terms set out in the licensing contract" (Hill, Hwang, and Kim, 1990: 118). Empirical research reveals that licensors' degree of influence over independent licensees will vary according to the compensation structure of the agreement (Aulakh, Cavusgil, and Sarkar, 1998) and the specific contractual agreement will set the terms and conditions under which the foreign licensor empowers the licensee to exploit the former's assets. A common type of licensing arrangement would permit the licensee to manufacture and market the licensor's product, normally as an exclusive right, for an agreed period of time. Licensors are attracted to licensing because it allows them to deploy production resources in a foreign market without committing financial resources and/or labor to it. While existing theory on internationalization tends to identify technology licensing as a step toward an alternative to wholly owned subsidiaries, recent trends in technology licensing indicate that it is increasingly used as a conscious, proactive component of a firm's global product strategy (Kotabe, Sahay, and Aulakh, 1996).

Licensing can also be seen as a governance mechanism for collaborating with foreign business partners. Due to continuing market GLOBALIZATION and competitive pressures, companies are increasingly choosing partnerships as a way to interact within the dynamic international environment. Herein, licensing can be seen as a partnership that helps firms to leverage their resources and assets to the international business level, while retaining flexibility, reducing costs, and improving the licensor's access to foreign markets (see Cavusgil, 1998). Most international licensing agreements take place between firms from industrialized countries. Similarly, licensing is most frequently deployed in technology-intensive industries such as the pharmaceutical industry or the chemical industry (Atuahene-Gima, 1993; Arora and Fosfuri, 2000; Simonet, 2002), which suggests that licensing is a strategy for technology transfer, establishment of COMPETITIVE ADVANTAGE, and involves more complex arrangements than, e.g., trademarks. Innovating firms are frequently challenged with the strategic decision whether to license their new technology; otherwise competitors may quickly develop their own, possibly better, version of the technology. On the other hand, if competitors are able to rapidly imitate the new technology anyway, by licensing its technology the innovating firm may insure that its version of the technology becomes the dominant design in the industry (Hill, 1992). Despite the importance of licensing in technology sectors, international licensing also occurs in industries that are not necessarily technology-intensive, such as foods, sports, or publishing.

Licensing is a low-involvement/low-commitment approach to international markets; however, certain risks are associated with it. Most importantly, licensees may extract tacit and proprietary knowledge from the licensor and exploit this knowledge unilaterally after the termination of the licensing contract. These risks are similar to those of alliances (*see* INTERNATIONAL STRATEGIC ALLIANCES). Licensors run the risk of losing their proprietary information while increasing their vulnerability to opportunism that results from the open exchange of information (Khanna, Gulati, and Nohria, 1998; Kale, Singh, and Perlmutter, 2000). To this end, licensors need to insure that they are not "generating their future competition in their own backyard" and develop mechanisms to protect themselves from exploitation. A way to achieve this might be to limit the licensee's market and insist on technology feedback or flowback clauses in the licensing agreement. Other risks involved in licensing are related to negative branding/reputation effects, should the licensee not be able or willing to maintain the licensor's desired quality standards or engage in undesired management practices. Furthermore, licensing may not necessarily help to maximize licensors' profits and certain elements of a license agreement may be difficult to enforce.

Consequently, the licensing agreement is an essential contractual element between licensor and licensee, upon which satisfaction and performance of licensing agreements hinge. The licensing agreement specifies the rights that are granted, the consideration payable, and the duration of the terms. Usually, the licensed rights take the form of patents, registered trademarks, registered industrial designs, unpatented technology, trade secrets, know-how, or copyrights. Although no definitive standards exist for license agreements, guidelines, forms, and checklists are available for developing these (Stitt and Baker, 1983; Beamish, 1996).

Bibliography

Arora, A. and Fosfuri, A. (2000). Wholly owned subsidiary versus technology licensing in the worldwide chemical industry. *Journal of International Business Studies*, 31 (4), 555–72.

Atuahene-Gima, K. (1993). International licensing of technology: An empirical study of the differences between licensee and non-licensee firms. *Journal of International Marketing*, 1 (2), 71–87.

Aulakh, P. S., Cavusgil, S. T., and Sarkar, M. B. (1998). Compensation in international licensing agreements. *Journal of International Business Studies*, 29 (2), 409–19.

Beamish, P. (1996). Note on international licensing. *Richard Ivey School of Business Case*, 9A96G008, 1–17.

Cavusgil, S. T. (1998). Executive insights: International partnering – a systematic framework for collaborating with foreign business partners. *Journal of International Marketing*, 6 (1), 91–107.

Hill, C. W. L. (1992). Strategies for exploiting technological innovations: When and when not to license. *Organization Science: A Journal of the Institute of Management Sciences*, 3 (3), 428–41.

Hill, C. W. L., Hwang, P., and Kim, W. C. (1990). An eclectic theory of the choice of international entry mode. *Strategic Management Journal*, 11 (2), 117–28.

Kale, P., Singh, H., and Perlmutter, H. (2000). Learning and protection of proprietary assets in strategic alliances: Building relational capital. *Strategic Management Journal*, 21 (3), 217–37.

Khanna, T., Gulati, R., and Nohria, N. (1998). The dynamics of learning alliances: Competition, cooperation, and relative scope. *Strategic Management Journal*, 19 (3), 193–210.

Kotabe, M., Sahay, A., and Aulakh, P. S. (1996). Emerging role of technology licensing in the development of global product strategy: Conceptual framework and research propositions. *Journal of Marketing*, 60 (1), 73–88.

Simonet, D. (2002). Licensing agreements in the pharmaceutical industry. *International Journal of Medical Marketing*, 2 (4), 329–41.

Stitt, H. J. and Baker, S. R. (1983). *The Licensing and Joint Venture Guide: Determining Your Need, Searching for Technology and Making the Deal in Ontario*. Ontario: Technology Search International.

life cycles

see LIFESTYLES

lifestyles

Margaret K. Hogg and Barbara R. Lewis

Consideration of consumer lifestyles incorporates an awareness of demographic variables and life cycles. Consumer behavior researchers and marketers are interested in trends in consumer DEMOGRAPHICS with respect to: birth rates and age profiles; marriage and divorce rates; number and spacing of children; size and composition of households/families, including the extent of single-person and empty-nest households; incomes and occupation; levels of employment including participation of women in the labor force; and type and location of residence. These all impact on consumer needs (*see* CONSUMER NEEDS AND

MOTIVES), ATTITUDES, and behavior and are often discussed in relation to life cycle and lifestyles.

The term life cycle refers to the progression of stages through which individuals and families proceed during their lives, and consequential financial situation and need for goods and services. The traditional life-cycle stages (*see* FAMILY LIFE CYCLE) were from bachelor stage to newly married, full nest 1, 2, 3, and empty nest 1, 2, solitary survivor in labor force, and solitary survivor retired (see Wells and Gubar, 1966). However, several modernized family life cycles have been put forward (e.g., Murphy and Staples, 1979; Gilly and Enis, 1982) in response to demographic trends such as smaller family sizes, postponement of marriage, and rising divorce rates. Wilkes (1995) argues for seeing these as household rather than family life cycles. He identified three spending patterns: firstly, "a generalized inverted U pattern, with spending rising sharply as households shift from young single to young married, then remaining relatively high, and falling sharply at the older married and/or older single stages"; secondly, "generally increasing expenditure across stages until the last one or two stages"; and thirdly, "generally decreasing expenditures across the life cycle" (Wilkes, 1995: 27).

Consumer lifestyle refers to a consumer's pattern of living, which influences and is reflected by consumption behavior. It is the result of interactive processes between social and personal variables surrounding individuals in childhood and throughout life, e.g., family, reference groups (*see* INTERPERSONAL COMMUNICATIONS), CULTURE. It embodies patterns that develop and emerge from the dynamics of living in a society. Further, economic influences provide constraints and opportunities in the development of lifestyle.

Lifestyle encompasses a person's pattern of living in the world as expressed in terms of activities, interests, and opinions (*see* AIOs) (see, e.g., Wells and Tigert, 1971). Activities refer to how people spend their time: at work, at home, in the community, on special activities, on hobbies, in clubs, on vacation, on sport and entertainment. Interests refer to what they place importance on in their immediate surroundings: family, home, job, community, recreation, fashion, and media. Opinions are in terms of their view of themselves and the world around them, e.g., social issues, politics, business, economics, education, and culture. These variables are considered together with demographics, and the basic premise of lifestyle research is that the more marketers know and understand about customers, the more effectively they can communicate and market to them. It provides a three-dimensional view of customers. The term PSYCHOGRAPHICS is often used interchangeably with lifestyle, but may also include PERSONALITY variables.

One example of lifestyle is the VALS framework (see Solomon, 2002: 181–3; Solomon, Bamossy, and Askegaard, 2002: 514), which is based on some 30–40 demographic and attitudinal characteristics. From this, three broad groups of consumers are identified (in the US population): need driven, outer directed, and inner directed. These are further divided into nine value lifestyle groups: achievers, survivors, sustainers, belongers, emulators, "I am me," experimentals, societally conscious, and integrated – with associated impact on customer needs, attitudes, and behavior.

Another class of lifestyle is ACORN typing (see CACI, 1993), used as an indicator of SOCIAL CLASS. This incorporates GEODEMOGRAPHIC data from the most recent census, including age, sex, marital status, occupation, economic position, education, home ownership, and car ownership, to provide a full and comprehensive picture of socioeconomic status. From these data, and postcode information, ACORN types are developed to profile consumers in terms of their attitudes and behavior with respect to the purchase of products and services, leisure activities, media habits, and financial position.

Bibliography

Arnould, E., Price, L., and Zinkhan, G. (2004). *Consumers*, 2nd edn. Boston: McGraw-Hill Irwin, ch. 11.

CACI (1993). *CACI Information Services*. London.

Engel, J. F., Blackwell, R. D., and Miniard, P. W. (1995). *Consumer Behavior*, 8th edn. Fort Worth, TX: Dryden Press, ch. 13.

Gilly, M. C. and Enis, B. M. (1982). Recycling the family life cycle: A proposal for redefinition. In A. Mitchell (ed.), *Advances in Consumer Research*, vol. 9. Ann Arbor, MI: Association for Consumer Research, pp. 271–6.

Hawkins, D. I., Best, R. J., and Coney, K. A. (1995). *Consumer Behavior: Implications for Marketing Strategy*, 6th edn. Boston: Irwin.

Hoyer, W. D. and MacInnis, D. J. (2001). *Consumer Behavior*, 2nd edn. Boston and New York: Houghton Mifflin, ch. 17.

Loudon, D. L. and Della Bitta, A. J. (1993). *Consumer Behavior*, 4th edn. New York: McGraw-Hill, ch. 7.

Mowen, J. C. and Minor, M. (1998). *Consumer Behavior*, 5th edn. Upper Saddle River, NJ: Prentice-Hall, ch. 7.

Mowen, J. C. and Minor, M. (2001). *Consumer Behavior: A Framework*. Upper Saddle River, NJ: Prentice-Hall, ch. 14.

Murphy, P. E. and Staples, W. A. (1979). A modernized family life cycle. *Journal of Consumer Research* (June), 12–22.

Plummer, J. (1974). The concept and application of life style segmentation. *Journal of Marketing*, 38 (January), 33–7.

Schiele, G. W. (1974). How to reach the young consumer. *Harvard Business Review*, 52 (March/April), 77–86.

Schiffman, L. G. and Kanuk, L. L. (2004). *Consumer Behavior*, 8th edn. Upper Saddle River, NJ: Pearson Educational International, chs. 3, 13.

Solomon, M. R. (2002). *Consumer Behavior: Buying, Having, Being*, 5th edn. Upper Saddle River, NJ: Prentice-Hall, ch. 6.

Solomon, M. R., Bamossy, G., and Askegaard, S. (2002). *Consumer Behavior: A European Perspective*, 2nd edn. Upper Saddle River, NJ: Prentice-Hall, ch. 16.

Wells, W. D. (ed.) (1974). *Lifestyle and Psychographics*. Chicago: American Marketing Association.

Wells, W. D. (1975). Psychographics: A critical review. *Journal of Marketing Research*, 12 (May), 196–213.

Wells, W. D. and Gubar, G. (1966). Life cycle in marketing research. *Journal of Marketing Research* (November), 355–63.

Wells, W. D. and Prensky, D. (1996). *Consumer Behavior*. New York: John Wiley, ch. 6.

Wells, W. D. and Tigert, D. J. (1971). Activities, interests and opinions. *Journal of Advertising Research*, 11, 27–35.

Wilkes, R. E. (1995). Household life-cycle stages, transitions and product expenditures. *Journal of Consumer Research*, 22, 27–43.

linguistic equivalence

see CONSTRUCT EQUIVALENCE

list price

Dominic Wilson

In organizational markets price is often the result of negotiations based on a notional list price, which is then either discounted (e.g., for volume purchases) or augmented (e.g., for customized orders). List prices are often quoted in product catalogues together with stipulated discount levels for specified volumes – a practice referred to by some writers as administered pricing.

logistics

Andrew Newman

The term logistics has origins in the military and in this context refers to the art of movement and supply of troops. In RETAILING this management function is concerned with the process of physical distribution (*see* CHANNELS OF DISTRIBUTION) of merchandise and its stockholding. Logistics plans, implements, and controls the efficient, timely, effective flow and storage of goods, services, and related information from the point of origin to the point of consumption in order to meet customers' requirements (Newman and Cullen, 2002). Logistics management is responsible for the flow of goods from the site of manufacture to the final consumer, and the allocation of financial and human resources to accomplish this function.

Modern retail logistics systems are highly developed, complex, and technologically advanced operations that create significant competitive advantages (*see* COMPETITIVE ADVANTAGE) for retailers. In some sectors, such as food, the efficient and timely movement of products is more critical due to finite delivery times. Efficiency of allocation is of great importance to insure that there is no over- or undersupply, thus avoiding wastage, and that resources are distributed at lowest possible cost. This requires consideration of stockholding, PACKAGING, and transportation costs. Fashion sector logistics is characterized by efficient consumer response (ECR) operations that insure the latest clothing style is in the store when the customer expects it to be. The length of time it takes for merchandise to move through the supply chain from the state of raw fiber to garments purchased can reduce stock-outs and unwanted merchandise on the shelves (Birtwistle, Siddiqui, and Fiorito, 2003).

Bibliography

Birtwistle, G., Siddiqui, N., and Fiorito, S. S. (2003). Quick response: Perceptions of UK fashion retailers. *International Journal of Retail and Distribution Management*, 31 (2), 118–28.

Christopher, M. (1977). *Distribution, Planning and Control: A Corporate Approach*. Farnborough: Gower.

Newman, A. J. and Cullen, P. (2002). *Retailing: Environment and Operations*. London: Thomson Learning.

M

macro environment

Barbara R. Lewis

The environment of an organization (*see* MARKETING ENVIRONMENT) is generally regarded as consisting of a MICRO ENVIRONMENT and a macro environment that is composed of several major elements over which the organization has little, if any, influence. The major forces in the macro environment tend to be viewed as social, economic, legal, political, economic, and technological. It is generally assumed that organizations will identify the major trends and possible future developments in these various components of the macro environment and the possible threats to their existing business and the opportunities for further developments (*see* SWOT ANALYSIS). In this sense, organizations are often depicted as being reactive, although it is clear that they can be active in certain areas, through major technological innovation and attempts at influencing the policy-making and legislative processes. An organization's environmental analysts can be very selective with respect to those aspects of the macro environment on which they focus and in their interpretation of them.

Bibliography

Baker, M. J. (2000). *Marketing Strategy and Management*, 5th edn. Oxford: Macmillan Business, ch. 5.

Dibb, S., Simkin, L., Pride, W. M., and Ferrell, O. C. (2001). *Marketing Concepts and Strategies*, 4th European edn. Boston: Houghton Mifflin, ch. 2.

Jobber, D. (2004). *Principles and Practices of Marketing*, 4th edn. London: McGraw-Hill.

Kotler, P. (2003). *Marketing Management: Analysis, Planning, Implementation and Control*, 11th edn. Englewood Cliffs, NJ: Prentice-Hall.

macro marketing

Barbara R. Lewis

Macro marketing embraces marketing's role in society and can be defined as "the delivery of a standard of living to society." The aggregation of all organizations' marketing activities includes transportation and distribution, and so the efficiency of the system for moving goods from producers to consumers may substantially affect a society's wellbeing. Thus, macro marketing is the aggregate of marketing activities within an economy, or the marketing system within a society, rather than the marketing activities of a single firm.

See also *marketing*

Bibliography

Zikmund, W. G. and d'Amico, M. (1995). *Effective Marketing: Creating and Keeping Customers*. St. Paul, MN: West Publishing, ch. 1, p. 21.

magazines

David Yorke

Magazines are publications that are purchased and read by people as part of their lifestyle (*see* LIFESTYLES). Magazine content may relate to aspects of home life, e.g., cooking, gardening, do-it-yourself; leisure, sporting, and social activities; education (e.g., *The Times Higher Education Supplement*); and employment. Some magazines are industry specific and may be referred to as TRADE JOURNALS (e.g., *Caterer and Hotel Keeper*), and so are bought by organizations as well as individuals; others are associated with professional business groups (e.g., *Investors' Chronicle, Accounting Age*).

The readership of magazines may, therefore, be specific (e.g., *Angling Times*) or much broader (e.g., *Good Housekeeping*); aim at lifestyle groups (e.g., *Men's Health, Cosmopolitan*), and possibly with a mass circulation (e.g., *Radio Times*). Consequently, magazine readers may be profiled with respect to their demographic characteristics (*see* DEMOGRAPHICS), which has implications for MEDIA PLANNING (see ADVERTISING).

Magazines typically provide full-color advertising at a reasonable cost, have a relatively long life and multiple readership, and can provide broad national coverage with, sometimes, flexibility through regional editions. Further, there is proven success of magazines' editorial offers and sales promotions (*see* SALES PROMOTION). One drawback of magazine advertising is the relatively long lead time for copy dates.

mail order

Steve Greenland and Andrew Newman

Mail order is most readily associated with catalogue shopping. Goods are selected from the catalogue assortment and orders mailed or telephoned through to the retailer or a local agent. Mail order has traditionally been directed at the less mobile lower social classes (*see* SOCIAL CLASS), with the attraction of easily obtainable credit terms, and at consumers living in more remote areas, where access to shops is restricted. Customers may purchase merchandise from the comfort of their armchairs, and do not need to travel to the store.

Mail order retailing experienced considerable structural change in the 1990s as agency-oriented operations reorganized around new direct brands (*see* BRAND) and catalogues to capture the growing interest in home shopping. More recently, mail order has been an area of expansion for many of the conventional high street retail chains, such as Next, with Next Directory first launched in 1988. Many well-known high street retailers including Marks and Spencer have success-fully developed catalogues that appeal to upmarket consumers and many others across the spectrum. This growth has helped to revitalize the mail order sector and improve the frequently dowdy and downmarket image associated with this retail distribution channel (*see* RETAIL DISTRIBUTION CHANNELS).

Greenland and McGoldrick (1991) identify over 40 different motives associated with catalogue or mail order shopping, the key dimensions being:

• hassle-free convenience;
• risk reduction;
• added value with credit, promotions, and free gifts;
• recreational experience;
• transaction efficiency;
• decision reassurance.

Thus, the key benefits of the mail order process surround the speedy distribution of goods from the retailer's premises to the agent's home. The mail order agent replaces the conventional store functions by acting as salesperson and merchandiser. Agents are recruited from existing customers and act as salespeople, to sell on the merchandise to their personal customer base. These may be friends, neighbors, or acquaintances (Newman and Cullen, 2002).

The mail order sector is a growth area. However, key issues impacting on the future of this retail distribution channel include the IMAGE of DIRECT MARKETING, merger and acquisition activity, alternative media, and an interactive marketplace (Petsky, 1994). For example, the advent and proliferation of digital television channels are likely to influence the future of mail order shopping.

Bibliography

Greenland, S. J. and McGoldrick, P. J. (1991). From mail order to home shopping: Revitalizing the nonstore channel. *Journal of Marketing Channels*, 1 (1), 59–85.

Newman, A. J. and Cullen, P. (2002). *Retailing: Environment and Operations*. London: Thomson Learning.

Petsky, M. (1994). Critical issues and trends for the future of mail order. *Direct Marketing*, 57 (4), 29–32.

make/buy decision

Dominic Wilson

An important alternative to purchasing goods or services is to supply them from internal sources. Equally, before undertaking internal production of goods or services, it is important to consider whether external purchasing might provide a more efficient or preferable alternative. Make or buy decisions can also apply to internal services such as MARKETING, research, planning, accounting, and DESIGN, which may be better undertaken by external specialists with economies of scale and specialized investments and expertise (Anderson and Weitz, 1986). This issue has many strategic and operational implications beyond the relatively simple aspect of cost control. In-house supplier arrangements appear to offer potential advantages of management control, of cost manipulation (e.g., in TRANSFER PRICING), of acquitting minimum national content requirements where the alternative is international sourcing, of flexible production management, and of using what might otherwise be underutilized assets. But there can also be significant problems of cost control, quality, delivery, and service where the commercial pressures of market forces are (or are perceived to have been) "suspended." Decisions in this area are frequently concerned with political, cultural, personal, historic, and strategic issues rather than with the more routine purchasing concerns.

Bibliography

Anderson, E. and Weitz, B. (1986). Make-or-buy decisions. *Sloan Management Review*, **27** (Spring), 3–19.
Ford, D., Cotton, B., Farmer, D., and Gross, A. (1993). Make-or-buy decisions and their implications. *Industrial Marketing Management*, **22** (August), 207–14.
Venkatesan, R. (1992). Strategic sourcing: To make or not to make. *Harvard Business Review*, **70**, 6 (November/December), 98–107.

margin

Dominic Wilson

Margin refers to the profit earned by a product or service at different stages of the VALUE CHAIN and is usually expressed as a percentage. Margins can be added at each stage of the production and distribution process (where these stages are treated as profit centers) in accordance with the competitive pressures prevailing at each stage. The sum of costs and margins for each stage of the value chain is reflected in the eventual price to the end user (discount notwithstanding). "Margin" is a broad term and is more usually discussed under the slightly more specific variants of GROSS MARGIN and NET MARGIN.

marginal pricing

Dominic Wilson

Marginal pricing is a term used to refer to those occasions when price is calculated to cover only the variable costs of production and/or distribution and little or no CONTRIBUTION is required toward fixed costs and profit margins. Clearly, this is an unusual and uneconomic level for prices and one that could not be sustained for long. Marginal pricing might be used during a temporary fall in DEMAND (e.g., during an economic recession or a price war) to keep assets "ticking over" pending the return of more normal trading conditions. The alternative is to reduce radically (or even suspend) operations, which can lead to even less attractive consequences such as deterioration of skills, reduced customer loyalty, loss of reputation, release of expert staff, and erosion of brands (*see* BRAND). Marginal pricing might also be used to secure what is expected to be a favored position with respect to future sales (as with introductory offers).

market

Fiona Leverick

The term "market" is clearly an important concept in the field of MARKETING, yet while much debate has taken place on what constitutes an appropriate definition of "marketing," less attention has been directed in the marketing literature toward the nature of MARKETS. This is increasingly being recognized as an omission, given that many analytical techniques rely on concepts such as MARKET SHARE and MARKET SEGMENTATION (Curran and Goodfellow, 1990).

The original use of the term "market" referred to a physical location where buyers and sellers came together in order to exchange products and services. Since then, the term has been developed in the field of economics to refer variously to any network of dealings between buyers and sellers of a particular PRODUCT, or to refer to products that are regarded as close substitutes. The latter is often referred to as the substitutability criterion, two products being contained in the same market where the cross-elasticity of DEMAND between the two is greater than a preassigned number (x). However, there is little agreement in the field as to the criterion by which x might be specified.

Elsewhere, the term "market" has been used extensively to describe aggregate demand for a specific product (the "automobile" market) or in a specific physical area (the "European market"). Markets have also been viewed in broader "need" terms (the "transportation" market) and demographic terms (the "female" market; see DEMOGRAPHICS), or any combination of these variables.

In contemporary marketing, however, "market" is most commonly used to refer to the existing or target group of customers for a particular product or service. For example, it may refer to all those customers that have a particular need and who are willing and/or have the ability to satisfy it (Kotler, 2003): "Individuals who, in the past, have purchased a given class of product" (Sissors, 1966). The prevalent view is, then, one of markets as units of analysis with clearly defined boundaries. Yet perspectives offered elsewhere suggest a somewhat more complex understanding of markets. Strategic management literature offers a number of further perspectives. Abell (1980), for example, proposes a three-dimensional concept of markets, with the dimensions being customer group (who is being served with respect to factors such as demographics, user industry, or buyer behavior), customer function (what "need" is being satisfied), and technology (how

the customer function is being satisfied). A "market" is consequently defined by the performance of given functions in given customer groups and includes all the substitutable technologies to perform these functions.

Such definitions recognize that competing SUPPLIERS may define a market in different ways, as may individuals at different levels within the same organization, a recognition shared by Day (1981), who identifies two different perspectives for defining markets, top-down and bottom-up. Top-down, or strategic, definitions reflect the needs of strategists to understand the capacity and competitive potential of the business and specify markets in terms of organizational competitive capabilities and resource transferability. Bottom-up, or operational, definitions reflect the narrower tactical concern of marketing managers and define markets in terms of patterns of customer requirements, usage situations, and "needs," which can be served in many ways.

Another dimension of market definition is apparent in the literature on BUSINESS-TO-BUSINESS MARKETING, where it is recognized that the importance of individual customers is often considerable and the relevance of aggregate markets therefore lessened. Here, the concept of a "market" might refer to only a single customer (see Grönroos, 1989, for further discussion).

A number of authors have also identified a disparity between the way markets are defined in the marketing literature and in practice. Jenkins, Le Cerf, and Cole (1994) elicited definitions of the term "market" from a sample of marketing managers and found that the majority tended to define markets in terms of products or channels (e.g., "the food retail market"), with only a minority of the sample offering definitions in terms of groups of consumers.

It is accepted by some authors at least, then, that the understanding of markets is likely to vary to a greater or lesser extent from marketer to marketer even within a particular organization, significantly from organization to organization with similar offerings (see OFFERING), and radically from sector to sector. Others further assert that "the market," whether defined in terms of existing or potential customers, products, or organizational capabilities, is a volatile concept, where boundaries are arbitrary and seldom clear cut, where definitions are multidimensional, and where perspectives shift with changing individual, corporate, and user views of product offerings and changes in the nature and availability of these offerings (see Curran and Goodfellow, 1990; Jenkins et al., 1994).

Bibliography

Abell, D. F. (1980). *Defining the Business: The Starting Point of Strategic Planning*. Englewood Cliffs, NJ: Prentice-Hall .

Curran, J. G. M. and Goodfellow, J. H. (1990). Theoretical and practical issues in the definition of market boundaries. *European Journal of Marketing*, **24** (1), 16–28.

Day, G. S. (1981). Strategic market analysis and definition: An internal approach. *Strategic Management Journal*, **2**, 281–99.

Grönroos, C. (1989). Defining marketing: A market-oriented approach. *European Journal of Marketing*, **23** (1), 52–60.

Jenkins, M., Le Cerf, E., and Cole, T. (1994). How managers define consumer markets. In M. Jenkins and S. Knox (eds.), *Advances in Consumer Marketing*. London: Kogan Page.

Kotler, P. (2003). *Marketing Management: Analysis, Planning, Implementation and Control*, 11th edn. Englewood Cliffs, NJ: Prentice-Hall.

Sissors, J. (1966). What is a market? *Journal of Marketing*, **30**, 3 (July), 17–21.

market demand

Dale Littler and Fiona Leverick

The term market demand most usually refers to the total demand for a PRODUCT or service over a specific period of time in a specified geographic area in a specified MARKETING ENVIRONMENT and for a specified MARKETING effort. It is used in relation to either individual products or services or product or service categories. Demand may be viewed as potential demand, which is the total possible demand for the product or service based on the amount the maximum number of customers are willing and able to purchase, and the REALIZABLE DEMAND, the actual demand achieved.

See also *demand*

market exchange

see EXCHANGE

market manager

Dale Littler

Market managers are responsible for the MARKETING activities for particular MARKETS or clusters of customers. They may have profit responsibility. A market manager structure is likely to be a feature of organizational markets where companies are marketing to several, perhaps diverse, customer groups with somewhat differing requirements. Thus, a manufacturer of paint will sell not only to consumer markets, but also to professional decorators as well as industrial users, which will comprise possibly several markets (maritime, process plant, etc.).

Such managers can be expected to foster and maintain customer relationships (*see* RELATIONSHIP MARKETING) with key customers, develop an understanding of their requirements, and, increasingly in organizational markets, develop a problem-solving capability and provide a "solutions" package. They will, therefore, have to act as a focus for coordinating all the different activities, both internally and from external parties, involved in providing the appropriate OFFERING. In some instances, managers may be appointed for major or key customers. Such an approach contrasts with the PRODUCT MANAGER structure.

market orientation

Dale Littler

Market orientation in general suggests that organizations are outward looking, collect intelligence on competitors and customers, and disseminate this information throughout the organization (Narver and Slater, 1990). Kohli and Jaworski (1990) argue that market orientation "is the organization-wide *generation* of market intelligence pertaining to current and future customer needs, *dissemination* of the intelligence across departments and organization-wide *responsiveness* to it" (p. 6). Narver and Slater (1990) suggest that interfunctional coordination is an important ingredient: based on the customer and competitor information, it represents the business's coordinated efforts "to create superior value for the buyers" (p. 21). Cadogan and Diamantopoulos (1995) conclude that there is much in common between the perspectives of Narver and Slater and Kohli and Jaworski, and they reconceptualize the concept of market orientation as comprising intelligence generation, intelligence dissemination, and responsiveness activities characterized by a customer and competitor orientation and guided by a coordinating mechanism (p. 55). Market orientation has been regarded as having a significant positive effect on organizational performance (see Harris, 2001).

Bibliography

Cadogan, J. and Diamantopoulos, A. (1995). Narver and Slater, Kohli and Jaworski and the market orientation construct: Integration and internationalization. *Journal of Strategic Marketing*, 3, 1 (March), 41–60.

Harris, L. C. (2001). Market orientation and performance: Objective and subjective empirical evidence from UK companies. *Journal of Management Studies*, 38, 1 (January), 17–43.

Kohli, A. K. and Jaworski, B. J. (1990). Market orientation: The construct, research propositions, and managerial implications. *Journal of Marketing*, 54 (April), 1–18.

Narver, J. C. and Slater, S. F. (1990). The effect of a market orientation on business profitability. *Journal of Marketing*, 54 (October), 20–35.

market penetration

Dale Littler

This is one of the strategies identified in Ansoff's (1965) directional policy matrix (*see* GROWTH VECTOR MATRIX). It is generally regarded as aiming at increasing the firm's MARKET SHARE within its existing markets. This can be achieved in at least one of three ways: increasing purchases by existing customers, winning over the consumers of competitors' offerings (*see* OFFERING), and converting non-users to purchasers of the firm's offerings.

Bibliography

Ansoff, H. I. (1965). *Corporate Strategy: An Analytic Approach to Business Policy for Growth and Expansion*. New York: McGraw-Hill, ch. 6.

market potential

Dale Littler

This is the total DEMAND possible for a product class (*see* PRODUCT) such as cigarettes, automobiles, and digital cameras. It can be calculated by estimating all the possible users multiplied by the amount each individual (organization) is likely to use. The market potential may change over time because of the effects of changes in consumer tastes and preferences, DEMOGRAPHICS, and technology.

market segment

see MARKET SEGMENTATION

market segmentation

Vincent-Wayne Mitchell

Smith (1956) first defined market segmentation in the following terms: "a rational and more precise adjustment of product and marketing effort to consumer or user requirements, it consists of viewing a heterogeneous market (one characterized by divergent demand) as a number of smaller homogeneous markets." If it is assumed, or known, that all consumers in a market have similar needs and wants, then an undifferentiated or total market approach can be adopted by a company using a single MARKETING MIX to satisfy consumers. The Coca-Cola company's early marketing of only one drink, of only one size, is an example of this approach.

If the market has heterogeneous needs, then a TARGET MARKET approach can be adopted. Here, an organization attempts to subdivide the market into clusters of customers with similar requirements and tailor its marketing mix to each cluster. This approach involves additional costs for product modifications and associated administrative, promotional, and inventory costs. In completely heterogeneous markets, where each customer's requirements are different, the only way to satisfy everyone is by offering tailor-made or bespoke products. Nowadays, this is more prevalent in organizational markets (*see* ORGANIZATIONAL MARKETING).

However, in some consumer markets, producers still design their products for individual consumers, e.g., tailor-made clothes and shoes. This type of customized marketing is becoming increasingly possible, even in traditional mass markets, with the use of modern and flexible manufacturing technology, which allows shorter runs of products to be profitable. It should be noted that the idea of market segmentation can be used by profit-making and not-for-profit organizations alike (*see* NOT-FOR-PROFIT MARKETING; SEGMENTATION VARIABLES).

THE PROCESS OF MARKET SEGMENTATION

The first step is usually some form of needs assessment, e.g., BENEFIT SEGMENTATION, in order to decide whether or not groups of buyers seek different product benefits and hence will value different product features. (The starting point is not restricted to benefit segmentation, but must be something that is closely related to the customer's needs.) Since markets are defined in terms of DEMAND or customer needs/requirements, marketers must know how these needs vary by segment in order to design products to meet them. For example, the shoe market is best characterized by identifying customer needs of protection, durability, style, size, price, etc., rather than by the age, sex, or SOCIAL CLASS of the market.

The second step is to describe how the benefit segments differ in their buying loyalties, shopping behaviors, media usage, and sensitivity to various marketing tactics. In this descriptive phase are included all the "normal" segmentation variables discussed by numerous authors. If the benefit segments do not vary significantly on any of these descriptor variables, they will be very difficult to reach and target with tailored marketing mixes. The choice of descriptor variable is not easy, partly because of the enormous number of possible variables that could be used,

and partly because of the often questionable link between the selected base(s) for the segmentation and the descriptor.

A number of authors do not take needs as the starting point for segmentation and argue that, in practice, segmentation may not follow the logical two-step approach. Often descriptor or profile variables, which can be easily measured, are identified first, then the segments so described are examined to see if they show different behavioral responses. This approach of looking for measurable and identifiable variables, then examining their influence on behavior, can be criticized for moving the marketer's attention away from customer requirements and toward implementation issues. Sometimes a product is designed for a particular segment of consumers whose collective need also happens to be accurately characterized by a description of their group association; various clubs and organizations, e.g., the Brownies or football supporters' clubs, etc., might be examples. In these relatively few cases, the two approaches do overlap.

One survey found that the similarity of needs within segments and the feasibility of marketing action were the two most important criteria used to form segments. Stability of the segment over time was third most important, while the difference of needs between segments, and the potential for increased profit and return on investment, were fourth and fifth. The simplicity of assigning customers to segments was least important (Abratt, 1993).

Good market segmentation can result in numerous advantages, including:

1 a closer matching of a company's products with customers' needs, which leads to increased CUSTOMER SATISFACTION and implementation of the MARKETING CONCEPT;
2 checking the basic assumptions and understanding about customers in the market, which can lead to improved communication with customers;
3 identifying new marketing opportunities from segments that have not been hitherto exploited;
4 increased COMPETITIVE ADVANTAGE by viewing a market in different ways from

one's competitors; it also keeps organizations alert to changes in market conditions, competitors' actions, and environmental opportunities and threats;

5   better COMPETITIVE STRATEGY, because companies that do not understand how the market is divided up risk competing head on against larger organizations with superior resources; it can allow a company to dominate a segment – which is not often possible in the total market; and

6   enabling two different pieces of research containing separate data to be combined by means of a common classification, e.g., GEO-DEMOGRAPHICS.

However, a number of disadvantages to target marketing have also been identified:

- efforts toward personalization and individualization of markets can lead to a proliferation of products, which becomes overly burdensome and costly to manage;
- efforts to overly segment markets into too small niches may be viewed cynically by the targeted individual and negatively affect consumer response to marketing efforts;
- narrowly segmenting a market to target may actually prevent a product from developing BRAND LOYALTY.

Some argue that the only way to build a large, sustainable brand-loyal customer base is to build broad brand popularity.

Target marketers have been widely criticized for unethical or stereotypical activities. In addition, not all authors agree that market segmentation is necessarily a profitable strategy, especially when the market is so small that marketing to a portion of it is not profitable; when heavy users make up such a large proportion of the sales volume that they are the only relevant target; or when one brand dominates the market and draws its appeal from all segments of the market. In markets where consumers are willing to accept lower prices in exchange for less-tailored products and where there is a high potential for product and marketing economies by eliminating or fusing market segments, counter-segmentation should be considered (Resnik, Turney, and Mason, 1979).

The question of profitability can be one of the principal limitations of market segmentation. Bonoma and Shapiro (1984) highlight two major cost factors associated with segmentation. The first is the number of segments approached: the more a market is segmented, the more costly it is. Second is that some elements of the marketing mix are more expensive to change than others. The least expensive tactic is tailoring communications. Specialized prices are harder to administer and can have a substantial impact on profits. By far the most expensive change to implement is product change. Bonoma and Shapiro advocate the practical strategy of using the least expensive tools first so long as the segments are responsive to these changes.

In practice, however, Abratt (1993) found that product changes and SALES PROMOTION campaigns were the marketing actions most often used by companies to target different segments, while different ADVERTISING appeals and prices were used less often. Changing the SALES FORCE and distribution systems were used least often. A further limitation is the inability to predict the nature and number of market segments that confront a new product in advance of the product being introduced. If the product has to be altered after introduction to meet the needs of different segments, this can be more expensive for the company and may reduce how well the company capitalizes on its first-mover advantages. Conventional practice is to conduct an attitude and usage study in the test market area (*see* TEST MARKETING) once the product has been introduced. However, from this it is impossible to tell whether the segments that develop existed prior to being exposed to the product and advertisements, etc. One way to overcome this problem is to give written descriptions of concepts to consumers and ask them to indicate the concept's applicability to their situation and the benefits that could be derived therefrom. A final limitation is that segments may not be stable in the longer term, because of changing consumer values, DEMOGRAPHICS, and LIFESTYLES.

TARGET SEGMENT SELECTION

Many authors have written about the criteria used to assess the usefulness of segmentations, but one of the most commonly used sets includes the criteria of measurability, substantiality, accessibility, and actionability (Kotler and Armstrong, 2004). Measurability is the degree to which size and purchasing power of segments can be measured. Substantiality is the degree to which segments are large and/or profitable enough for the organization to pursue. Accessibility is the extent to which segments can be effectively reached and served, and actionability is the degree to which an effective marketing program can be formulated for attracting and serving the segments. Mitchman (1991) adds meaningful to the list, which relates to the similarity of needs within the segments, i.e., when there is low intrasegment variability. Wind (1978) considers other factors, namely, the RE-LIABILITY of the data from which the segments were derived and the temporal stability of resultant segments.

Piercy and Morgan (1993) suggest that little explicit concern has been shown about the difference between strategic and operational aspects of segmentation, and they study the "fit" between segment requirements and company strengths. If the proposed segments do not fit in with the company's long-run objectives or the company does not possess the relevant skills and resources to meet the needs of the segments, then the segmentation is less likely to be successful. Strategic marketing segmentation models may be better judged by such criteria as the ability to create and sustain competitive differentiation and advantage; innovation in how the market is attacked; compatibility with the MISSION STATEMENT; providing a coherent focus for thinking in the organization; and consistency with corporate values and culture. It is important, however, that organizational compatibility does not become the governing criterion for segment selection, since organizations should be able and prepared to adapt to segments identified rather than to target only those which are compatible with existing organizational strengths and weaknesses (see SWOT ANALYSIS).

Finally, some authors have advocated the use of Porter's five forces framework as criteria for determining a segment's structural attractiveness (see COMPETITIVE STRATEGY). A survey of marketing practice found that the ability to reach buyers in the market and the competitive position of their firm in the market were the two most highly rated criteria used by practitioners to select target segments. These were followed by the size of the market, compatibility of market with companies, objectives/resources, profitability, and expected market growth.

See also *organizational segmentation*

Bibliography

Abratt, R. (1993). Market segmentation practices of industrial marketers. *Industrial Marketing Management*, 2 (2), 79–84.

Bonoma, T. V. and Shapiro, B. P. (1984). Evaluating market segmentation approaches. *Industrial Marketing Management*, 13, 257–68.

Green, P. E. (1977). A new approach to market segmentation. *Business Horizons*, 20, 61–73.

Kotler, P. and Armstrong, G. (2004). *Principles of Marketing*, 10th edn. Upper Saddle River, NJ: Prentice-Hall.

Mitchman, R. (1991). *Lifestyle Market Segmentation*. New York: Praeger.

Piercy, N. F. and Morgan, N. A. (1993). Strategic and operational market segmentation: A managerial analysis. *Industrial Marketing Management*, 2 (2), 79–84.

Resnik, A. J., Turney, P. B. B., and Mason, J. B. (1979). Marketers turn to "countersegmentation." *Harvard Business Review*, 57 (September/October), 100–6.

Smith, W. (1956). Product differentiation and market segmentation as marketing strategies. *Journal of Marketing*, 21 (July), 3–8.

Wind, Y. (1978). Issues and advances in segmentation research. *Journal of Marketing Research*, 15 (August), 317–37.

Young, S., Ott, L., and Feigin, B. (1978). Some practical considerations in market segmentation. *Journal of Marketing Research*, 15 (August), 405–12.

market share

Fiona Leverick

This is the ratio of a company's sales of a PRODUCT or service (either by number of units or by value) during a specific time period in a specific market to the total sales of that type of product or service over the same period. It has been pointed out that calculations of market share are likely to vary considerably according to how the total MARKET is defined.

The importance of market share has frequently been noted, with, for example, a connection between market share and profitability identified in a project undertaken by the Marketing Science Institute on the PROFIT IMPACT OF MARKETING STRATEGIES (Buzzell, Gale, and Sultan, 1975). It has been argued that obtaining a high market share can be important in gaining experience (*see* EXPERIENCE CURVE) and thus in lowering costs to remain abreast of competition or even secure a COMPETITIVE ADVANTAGE (*see* COST LEADERSHIP STRATEGY). Such a perspective, however, is increasingly questioned since it can lead to a focus on price as a major competitive weapon when there are clearly other factors (*see* NON-PRICE FACTORS) that affect demand. Other researchers (see, e.g., Jacobson and Aaker, 1985) have suggested that the direct impact of market share on profitability, while not unimportant, is substantially less than is commonly assumed. Jacobson and Aaker express concern that efforts to maintain or increase market share by companies can be myopic, expensive, and detrimental to long-term profitability, and note that one of the premises of niche marketing (*see* MARKET SEGMENTATION) is that the smaller-share competitors can also achieve high returns.

Bibliography

Buzzell, R. D., Gale, B. T., and Sultan, R. G. M. (1975). Market share: A key to profitability. *Harvard Business Review*, 53, 1 (January/February), 97–106.

Jacobson, R. and Aaker, D. A. (1985). Is market share all that it's cracked up to be? *Journal of Marketing*, 49 (Fall), 11–22.

marketing

Fiona Leverick

Marketing was apparently taught as a business subject as far back as 1902, at the University of Wisconsin, although the first textbooks on the subject were not written until several years later (Converse, 1951; Bartels, 1962, 1970). The concept has no single universally agreed definition and perspectives on the nature of marketing have shifted considerably over time. Halbert (1965) has suggested that this is due to marketing having no recognized central theoretical basis such as exists for many other disciplines, the natural sciences in particular.

The development of "marketing" is often seen in terms of at least three "eras" (see, e.g., Webster, 1988; Gilbert and Bailey, 1990). The first of these is most commonly termed the "production" era (Keith, 1960) and is considered to have taken place between 1870 and 1930, when the primary focus of marketing was limited to overcoming constraints on supply rather than paying attention to sales methods or customer requirements. The production era was apparently followed by the "sales" era, between 1930 and 1950, where marketing's responsibility was to sell what the organization produced, with a consequent focus on sales techniques. The shift from the production era to the sales era has been attributed to increased competition in many industrial sectors (Keith, 1960). Finally, the "marketing" era signified a widespread adoption of the "customer orientation" generally held to be part of the modern MARKETING CONCEPT. A number of authors, however, dispute the existence of either the production or the sales eras (see, e.g., Fullerton, 1988), pointing to a number of varied and vigorous marketing efforts by manufacturers during these periods, especially the growth of chain stores (pre-1900), department stores (1850), advertising agencies (by 1900; *see* AGENCY), and supermarkets focusing on self-service and low prices (by 1930 in the US and by 1945 in Europe).

More recent examples of the various definitions of "marketing" include those of the UK's Chartered Institute of Marketing, which views it as the management process that identifies, anticipates, and satisfies customer requirements effectively and at a profit, and the American Marketing Association, which reviewed 25 definitions in 1985 and arrived at its own contribution ("marketing is the process of planning and executing the conception, pricing, promotion and distribution of ideas, goods and services to create exchanges that satisfy individual and organizational objectives"). EXCHANGE is seen by many authors as the central concept underlying marketing.

A number of attempts have been made to categorize definitions of marketing. Crosier (1988), for example, reviewed over 50 definitions, placing them into three broad groups.

The first group consisted of definitions that conceived of marketing as a process (*see* MARKETING PROCESS) connecting a producer with its market via a marketing channel, such as "the primary management function which organizes and directs the aggregate of business activities involved in converting customer purchase power for a specific product or service into effective demand for a specific product or service and in moving the product or service to the final consumer or user so as to achieve company set profit or other objectives" (Rodger, 1971). The second group consisted of definitions that viewed marketing as a concept or philosophy of business, for example, "selling is preoccupied with the seller's need to convert his product into cash; marketing with the idea of satisfying the needs of the consumer by means of the product and the whole cluster of things associated with creating, delivering and finally consuming it" (Levitt, 1960). Crosier's third category of definitions emphasized marketing as an orientation present to some degree in both consumer and producer: the phenomenon that makes the process and the concept possible. However, only one example of such a definition was provided by Crosier, and this was felt by many researchers to be an unconvincing argument in favor of a third category of definitions (*see* MARKETING ORIENTATION).

A number of challenges to the definitions of the scope of marketing outlined by Crosier have emerged. The first of these might be seen as emanating from the field of NOT-FOR-PROFIT MARKETING, where Kotler and Levy's (1969) article extended the scope of marketing to cover activities undertaken for primary aims other than that of profit, including those of organizations such as educational establishments, churches, politicians, national interest groups, or charities, or, indeed, the activities related to INTERNAL MARKETING. Kotler and Levy referred to such not-for-profit marketing as SOCIETAL MARKETING, a term that has more recently come to develop a somewhat different meaning.

A second challenge developed from the area of societal marketing, which has been described by some authors as the "fourth era" of the development of marketing (Bell and Emory, 1971;

Abratt and Sacks, 1989). Societal marketing criticizes traditional marketing definitions for their emphasis on material consumption and short-term consumer gratification, without considering the long-term societal or environmental impact of marketing activities. It is often seen as a response to both the CONSUMERISM movement and wider criticisms of the ills of marketing. Societal marketing does not generally deny that the basic goal of a business enterprise is to insure its long-term profitability and survival; however, it does counsel businesses to be fair to consumers, enabling them to make fully informed and intelligent purchase decisions, and to avoid marketing practices that have negative consequences for society (see Bartels, 1974; Dawson, 1969; Dickinson, Herbst, and O'Shaughnessy, 1986; Elliot, 1990; McGee and Spiro, 1990) (*see* SOCIAL RESPONSIBILITY).

A third challenge has stemmed from those who consider that definitions involving a focus on customer "needs" discourage major product innovations (*see* PRODUCT INNOVATION) in favor of low-risk product changes, given that when consumers are asked to verbalize their needs, they tend to build on the familiar (Kaldor, 1971; Hayes and Abernathy, 1980). A fourth challenge comes from authors like Grönroos (1989) who suggest that existing definitions do not capture the essence of BUSINESS-TO-BUSINESS MARKETING or SERVICES MARKETING, both of which revolve primarily around customer relationships (*see* RELATIONSHIP MARKETING). Grönroos offers an alternative definition of marketing aims as "to establish, develop and commercialize long-term customer relationships, so that the objectives of both parties are met." Finally, marketing could be defined as an academic discipline, with a recognizable body of theory in relation to the study of the issues and processes described above, although, as Halbert (1965) suggests, there might be some disagreement among marketing academics as to the content of such a body of theory.

Bibliography

Abratt, R. and Sacks, D. (1989). Perceptions of the societal marketing concept. *European Journal of Marketing*, 23, 625–33.

Bartels, R. (1962). *The Development of Marketing Thought*. Homewood, IL: Irwin.

Bartels, R. (1970). Influences on development of marketing thought, 1900–1923. In R. Bartels (ed.), *Marketing Theory and Metatheory*. Homewood, IL: Irwin, pp. 108–25.

Bartels, R. (1974). The identity crisis in marketing. *Journal of Marketing*, **38**, 73–6.

Bell, M. L. and Emory, C. W. (1971). The faltering marketing concept. *Journal of Marketing*, **35**, 4 (October), 37–42.

Converse, P. D. (1951). Development of marketing theory: Fifty years of progress. In H. Wales (ed.), *Changing Perspectives in Marketing*. Urbana: University of Illinois Press, pp. 1–31.

Crosier, K. (1988). What exactly is marketing? In M. J. Thomas and N. E. Waite (eds.), *The Marketing Digest*. London: Heinemann, pp. 16–27.

Dawson, M. (1969). The human concept: The new philosophy for business. *Business Horizons*, **12**, 29–38.

Dickinson, R., Herbst, A., and O'Shaughnessy, J. (1986). Marketing concept and customer orientation. *European Journal of Marketing*, **20**, 1018–23.

Elliot, G. R. (1990). The marketing concept: Necessary but sufficient? An environmental view. *European Journal of Marketing*, **24**, 820–30.

Fullerton, R. A. (1988). How modern is modern marketing? Marketing's evolution and the myth of the "production" era. *Journal of Marketing*, **52**, 1 (January), 108–25.

Gilbert, D. and Bailey, N. (1990). The development of marketing: A compendium of historical applications. *Quarterly Review of Marketing*, **15**, 2 (Winter), 6–13.

Grönroos, C. (1989). Defining marketing: A market-oriented approach. *European Journal of Marketing*, **23**, 152–60.

Halbert, M. (1965). *The Meaning and Sources of Marketing Theory*. New York: McGraw-Hill.

Hayes, R. H. and Abernathy, W. J. (1980). Managing our way to economic decline. *Harvard Business Review*, **57** (July/August), 67–77.

Kaldor, A. G. (1971). Imbricative marketing. *Journal of Marketing*, **35**, 2 (April), 19–25.

Keith, R. J. (1960). The marketing revolution. *Journal of Marketing*, **24**, 35–8.

Kotler, P. and Levy, S. (1969). Broadening the concept of marketing. *Journal of Marketing*, **33**, 1 (January), 10–15.

Levitt, T. (1960). Marketing myopia. *Harvard Business Review*, **37** (July/August), 45–56.

McCarthy, E. J. and Perreault, R. (1993). *Basic Marketing*, 11th edn. Homewood, IL: Irwin.

McGee, L. W. and Spiro, R. K. (1990). The marketing concept in perspective. *Business Horizons*, **31**, 340–5.

Rodger, L. W. (1971). *Marketing in a Competitive Economy*. London: Associated Business Programmes.

Runyon, K. E. (1982). *The Practice of Marketing*. Columbus, OH: C. E. Merrill.

Webster, F. E., Jr. (1988). The rediscovery of the marketing concept. *Business Horizons*, **31**, 329–39.

marketing audit

Dominic Wilson

A marketing audit is an analysis, conducted from the perspective of the MARKETING function, of the environment surrounding an organization and its offerings (*see* ENVIRONMENTAL ANALYSIS; OFFERING). The aim of the audit is to examine systematically an organization's operations, offerings, markets, and environment so as to find ways to improve MARKETING PERFORMANCE. This could result, for example, in recommendations that products be adapted to meet new customer requirements, or that old markets be exited, or that fresh investments be considered.

The marketing audit is generally conducted in two interrelated parts: the INTERNAL AUDIT (examining the internal operations and assets of the organization) and the EXTERNAL AUDIT (examining the environment surrounding the organization). This process is similar to the SWOT ANALYSIS recommended for strategic MARKETING PLANNING, where strengths and weaknesses (the "SW" of SWOT) equate to the internal audit, while opportunities and threats (the "OT" of SWOT) correspond to the external audit.

Bibliography

Kotler, P., Gregor, W., and Rodgers, W. (1977). The marketing audit comes of age. *Sloan Management Review*, **18** (Winter), 25–43.

Wilson, A. (1982). *Marketing Audit Checklists*. Maidenhead: McGraw-Hill.

marketing channels

see CHANNELS OF DISTRIBUTION; RETAIL DISTRIBUTION CHANNELS; WHOLESALERS

marketing communications

Barbara R. Lewis

Organizations are involved in a range of marketing communications exchanges; for example, a manufacturer may communicate with its intermediaries, customers (existing and potential), and various publics. Its intermediaries communicate with their customers and various publics. Customers engage in WORD-OF-MOUTH COMMUNICATIONS with other customers and consumers, and each group can provide communication feedback to every other group, especially through the MARKETING RESEARCH activities of organizations.

Marketing communications comprise a mix of techniques or tools known as the COMMUNICATIONS MIX (sometimes referred to as the promotional mix), by which a MESSAGE is delivered from one party in the communications exchange to another.

Schramm (1971) was one of the first to discuss the marketing communications process. This is summarized in Kotler (2003). This model answers the following questions: (1) who (2) says what (3) in what channel (4) to whom (5) with what effect? All communications involve "senders" and "receivers," the "senders" being concerned with messages and channels, i.e., the ways in which messages are carried/delivered to an audience. Marketing communicators require that the message sent is the one that is received, but they are aware of consumers' selective processes (of exposure, attention, distortion, and recall), and intervening variables, referred to as NOISE (i.e., factors over which the communicator has no control, not least of which are messages being sent to target groups simultaneously), which may interfere with the process.

Kotler (2003) refers to the five major tools of the marketing communications mix available to an organization, namely: ADVERTISING, DIRECT MARKETING, SALES PROMOTION, PUBLIC RELATIONS and PUBLICITY, and PERSONAL SELLING. An alternative consideration of the mix is a classification into two broad dimensions: first, whether or not the communications are paid for, and second, whether they are personal, i.e., where there is some direct contact between the sender and the receiver, or impersonal where there is not. Examples include:

- *Paid and personal*: personal selling, TELEMARKETING;
- *Paid and impersonal*: advertising, sales promotion, public relations, DIRECT MAIL, PACKAGING;
- *Non-paid and personal*: social channels, i.e., word-of-mouth communications, INTERPERSONAL COMMUNICATIONS;
- *Non-paid and impersonal*: publicity.

Personal communications tend to be more important when products are expensive, risky, have social significance, or are purchased infrequently, and when buyers seek information, product experiences, and the knowledge of others. Impersonal communications are less insistent than personal channels, and so can easily be avoided or tuned out. Further, they are subject to the consumer psychological processes of selective attention, perception, and retention (*see* CONSUMER PERCEPTIONS; SELECTIVE EXPOSURE). This classification allows for the communication to be initiated by consumers as well as supplier organizations (*see* TWO-STEP FLOW MODEL).

Effective communication/promotion involves a number of activities. These include:

- identifying the target audience and its characteristics, e.g., individuals, groups, families, and businesses, and their socioeconomic profiles, PERSONALITY, perceptions of risk (*see* PERCEIVED RISK), and stages in the buying process, etc.;
- determining the COMMUNICATIONS OBJECTIVES, e.g., to create AWARENESS, knowledge, liking, preference, conviction, or purchase;
- designing the message;
- selecting the communication channels, both personal and impersonal, which will vary between consumer and organizational markets;
- allocating the communications budget and deciding on the promotional mix, which will be influenced by funds available, the nature of the market, and the stage in the PRODUCT LIFE CYCLE, etc.;

- measuring the communications results; and
- managing the marketing communications program.

Bibliography

Kotler, P. (2003). *Marketing Management: Analysis, Planning, Implementation and Control*, 11th edn. Englewood Cliffs, NJ: Prentice-Hall.

Schramm, W. (1971). How communications works. In W. Schramm and D. F. Roberts (eds.), *The Process and Effects of Mass Communications*. Urbana: University of Illinois Press.

marketing concept

Fiona Leverick

The marketing concept has been seen variously as a statement of the philosophy of marketing, an approach to doing business, or a broad umbrella governing business activity. It is viewed by many as synonymous with "marketing" itself, definitions of which as a concept or philosophy of business comprise one of the three types of definitions of marketing identified by Crosier (1988) (see MARKETING).

The marketing concept is generally held to have three major components (see McGee and Spiro, 1990). The first of these is a so-called "customer orientation," whereby an understanding of customer "needs," wants, and behavior is the focal point of all marketing action. The second is a focus on what is usually termed either coordinated activities or integrated effort, with the entire organization sharing the customer orientation by emphasizing the integration of the marketing function with areas such as research, product management, sales, and ADVERTISING. The third is a profit orientation, with attention directed primarily toward profit, as opposed to sales volumes, although clearly a profit focus is not appropriate for all organizations (e.g., NOT-FOR-PROFIT MARKETING). Reflecting these three areas, the marketing concept can be viewed as a customer orientation, supported by an integrated marketing approach, aimed at generating profits (see, e.g., Kotler, 2003). Some have noted a fourth component, a long-term orientation, in order to deflect criticisms of the marketing concept as focused only

on the current, articulable "needs" of consumers.

There has been some concern that the marketing concept as defined above is not broad enough to cover the more recent developments in the scope of marketing. In particular, developments in the area of SOCIETAL MARKETING have led to a number of restatements of the marketing concept to include a focus on consumers' and society's long-term interests (see SOCIAL RESPONSIBILITY). This had led some authors to produce a more "modern" statement of the marketing concept based on the three elements of CUSTOMER SATISFACTION, company profits, and community welfare (Abratt and Sacks, 1989).

Bibliography

Abratt, R. and Sacks, D. (1989). Perceptions of the societal marketing concept. *European Journal of Marketing*, 23, 625–33.

Crosier, K. (1988). What exactly is marketing? In M. J. Thomas and N. E. Waite (eds.), *The Marketing Digest*. London: Heinemann, pp. 16–27.

Kotler, P. (2003). *Marketing Management: Analysis, Planning, Implementation and Control*, 11th edn. Englewood Cliffs, NJ: Prentice-Hall.

McGee, L. W. and Spiro, R. K. (1990). The marketing concept in perspective. *Business Horizons*, 31, 340–5.

marketing control

Dale Littler

It is clear that effective strategic marketing management (see STRATEGIC MARKETING; MARKETING MANAGEMENT) suggests establishing predetermined targets against which actual performance can be assessed. This is the essence of marketing control.

There are at least two major areas where marketing control will be applied: to the MARKETING STRATEGY and to the marketing budget. In the case of marketing strategy, control is viewed as the final phase of the four-stage strategy process (see STRATEGIC PLANNING), and is primarily concerned with insuring that the strategy is developing according to plan so that the established objectives will be realized. If deviations are identified, the implications can be analyzed and appropriate action taken. It may be necessary to adjust expectations or even the strategy where the outcomes differ significantly from expectations and cannot be reconciled with the original strategy. In some instances, the strategy may have to be abandoned where the deviations are such as to make it commercially unviable.

Budgetary control involves monitoring the extent to which the various cost and revenue streams match with those defined in the budget. Assessments are likely to be undertaken regularly (in some cases daily, made possible by the use of computerized data capture and processing systems). Among the variables managers may monitor are: sales/profits and sales/profit variances; MARKET SHARE; and expenses to sales ratios. In addition, it is important to watch more qualitative indicators such as customer ATTITUDES (say, through tracking studies) and complaints.

Firms also need to evaluate periodically the profitability of products, CHANNELS OF DISTRIBUTION, and customers and order sizes, as well as the efficiency of key marketing activities such as ADVERTISING and sales. Firms may employ benchmarking, i.e., compare their costs and efficiencies against the "best practice" elsewhere.

Bibliography

Ward, K. (1999). Controlling marketing. In M. J. Baker (ed.), *The Marketing Book*, 4th edn. Oxford: Butterworth-Heinemann, pp. 455–79.

marketing decision support systems

Michael Greatorex and Vincent-Wayne Mitchell

A marketing decision support system is an information system that allows marketing decision-makers to interact directly with both databases and models (*see* DATABASE). As such, it is an improvement on MARKETING INFORMATION SYSTEMS. A decision support system consists of the computer hardware and communication interface, databases, relevant marketing models and software, and the marketing decision-maker. The aim is to help the decision-maker not only by allowing access to past and current data, but also by providing answers to "what if...?" questions through the incorporation of marketing models deemed appropriate by the decision-maker.

A global information system is an organized collection of computer hardware, software, data, and personnel designed to capture, store, update, manipulate, analyze, and immediately display information about worldwide business activities. Using satellite communications, high-speed microcomputers, electronic data interchanges (*see* ELECTRONIC DATA INTERCHANGE), fiber optics, CD-ROM data storage, fax machines, and other technological advances in interactive media, global information systems are changing the nature of business. For example, at any moment, United Parcel Service (UPS) can track the status of any shipment around the world. Examples of marketing decisions that have been aided by decision support systems include media scheduling (*see* MEDIA SCHEDULE), SALES FORCE management (*see* SALES MANAGEMENT), store location, warehouse location, and competitive bidding.

To be effective, a marketing decision support system should have the following characteristics:

- it should be understood by the managers using it;
- it should be perceived as useful by these users;
- it should be complete on key issues (e.g., on important factors where hard objective data are not available, the system should allow the use of the subjective assessments of the user rather than ignore those factors);
- it should be easy for the manager to interact with and use without the need for an intermediate computer expert;
- it should be flexible and give sensible answers; and
- it should be evolutionary in the sense that it is capable of being extended at a later date.

One of the problems is getting marketing decision-makers to use decision support systems. This will be helped if:

- the potential users are involved in the design of the system;

- the decision-makers specify the decisions where they would like support (probably frequently occurring decisions);
- the marketing models/theories and data-bases being used have the decision-makers' approval; and
- successful use of the system can be demonstrated, probably in the first instance by helping with simple problems.

Bibliography

Malhotra, N. K. and Birks, D. F. (2003). *Marketing Research: An Applied Orientation*, 2nd European edn. Harlow: Pearson Education.

marketing environment

Fiona Leverick

The marketing environment is made up of the actors and forces that directly or indirectly influence the organization's marketing operations and performance. The distinction is often made between the MICRO ENVIRONMENT, which is made up of actors in the company's immediate environment such as SUPPLIERS, market intermediaries, customers, or competitors, and the MACRO ENVIRONMENT, which is made up of wider societal forces (such as legal, cultural, economic, technological, demographic, or political) that affect all of the actors in the micro environment. The company has direct contact with the components of the micro environment and is therefore more likely to be able to influence them.

See also *marketing management*

marketing ethics

David Marsden

Marketing ethics is that branch of knowledge dealing with:

1. the identification and description of the moral issues and controversies surrounding MARKETING;
2. the critical analysis of these moral issues using various ethical theories and frame-works, and on the basis of the strengths and weaknesses of these theories; and
3. the formulation of normative prescriptions (i.e., codes, rules, standards) for judging what is right/good and wrong/bad marketing conduct and behavior.

First, the moral issues surrounding marketing are varied and multiple, covering every topic from PRICING and promotion to BRAND management and INTERNATIONAL MARKETING. Some of the most controversial issues in recent years have included, for example, marketing activities directed primarily at children (e.g., ADVERTISING in schools), the portrayal of women in advertising (e.g., sexist stereotypes), financial mismanagement and accounting fraud (e.g., pensions scandals, Enron), environmentalism (e.g., green marketing), corporate liability (e.g., cigarette companies), and privacy issues (e.g., DATABASE marketing). (For a comprehensive overview of the main marketing moral issues, see Laczniak and Murphy, 1993; Fitzgerald and Corey, 1998; Singhapakdi and Vitell, 1999.)

There are three classical ethical theories that have traditionally been employed to analyze the moral issues surrounding marketing: utilitarianism, deontology, and virtue ethics. Each theory offers a different set of principles by which to judge marketing behavior and conduct.

Very briefly, the utilitarian perspective focuses attention on ends/consequences of a decision or action. As Schlegelmilch (1998) makes clear, "Utilitarianism judges the ethical quality of a decision by its consequences. An action is morally right if it produces the greatest good for the greatest number of people affected by the action." What matters here is the net balance of good and bad, which is typically assessed through a cost/benefit analysis of the consequences for each of the main stakeholders affected by a decision.

In contrast, deontology focuses on the actions/means of a decision and stresses that some moral principles are binding and obligatory regardless of the end results and consequences of an action, even if they are good (Nantel and Weeks, 1996). In particular, deontological marketing ethics is grounded in notions of duty, e.g., promise keeping, honesty (Chonko, 1995).

Finally, virtue ethics focuses on the integrity of the moral actor as being more important than either the moral act or end consequence. As Sorell and Hendry (1994) explain, "Ethics is embedded in the moral character of a person, their motivations, intentions and integrity as defined by their community." This perspective derives from the ideas of the fifth-century BC Greek philosopher Aristotle, who advocated the universal virtues of courage, temperance, and justice.

In terms of deciding which theory and set of principles to adopt when considering moral issues in marketing, most commentators argue against taking a unilateral approach since no one theory, by itself, provides perfect guidance on every issue. Instead, a tripartite approach is advocated since all three theories suggest important factors to keep in mind in making ethical decisions. To meet this end, Trevino and Nelson (1995) offer an integrated, eight-step decision-making framework:

1 gather the facts;
2 define ethical issues;
3 identify affected parties;
4 identify the consequences;
5 identify obligations;
6 consider character and integrity;
7 think creatively about potential actions; and finally
8 check your gut.

Bibliography

Chonko, L. B. (1995). *Ethical Decision-Making in Marketing*. Thousand Oaks, CA: Sage.

Fitzgerald, P. and Corey, R. J. (1998). Moral reflections in marketing. *Journal of Macromarketing*, 18 (2), 104–14.

Laczniak, G. R. and Murphy, P. E. (1993). *Ethical Marketing Decisions*. Upper Saddle River, NJ: Prentice-Hall.

Nantel, J. and Weeks, W. A. (1996). Marketing ethics: Is there more to it than the utilitarian approach? *European Journal of Marketing*, 30 (5), 9–19.

Schlegelmilch, B. (1998). *Marketing Ethics: An International Perspective*. London: Thomson.

Singhapakdi, A. and Vitell, S. J. (1999). International marketing ethics. *Journal of Business Ethics*, 18 (1), 1.

Sorell, T. and Hendry, J. (1994). *Business Ethics*. Oxford: Butterworth-Heinemann.

Trevino, L. K. and Nelson, K. A. (1995). *Managing Business Ethics*. New York: John Wiley.

marketing exchange

see EXCHANGE

marketing financial services

Trevor Watkins

Financial services marketing is a special case of the marketing of services (*see* SERVICE CHARACTERISTICS). The nature of the relationship between supplier and consumer is based on a complex series of interactions, usually over time, which draw on deeply held attitudinal (*see* ATTITUDES) and behavioral beliefs. Understanding buyer behavior (*see* BUYER BEHAVIOR THEORIES) as a basis for effective marketing is therefore difficult for suppliers and the provision of high-quality customer service (*see* SERVICE QUALITY) is a key preoccupation in what has become a very competitive market environment (*see* MARKETING ENVIRONMENT).

In many countries, CONSUMER PROTECTION legislation is used to try to protect consumers from unethical marketing techniques (*see* MARKETING ETHICS), but there are many examples of financial scandals where suppliers have taken advantage of a lack of customer understanding in an unscrupulous way. For example, the misselling of pensions in the UK has led to a number of leading suppliers being fined by industry regulators.

The key features of financial services marketing are:

- The complexity of the price (*see* PRICING) variable. Many financial services are based on long-term investment with an unpredictable return and even basic bank accounts carry a range of add-on costs.
- Regulation of MARKETING COMMUNICATIONS. To protect consumers from misleading claims, there are detailed rules in most countries about what product claims can be made in promotions.
- Complexity of products. Because of regulation, many products such as pensions are bound by a set of rules, which makes them very difficult for buyers to comprehend without expert advice.

- Changes in distribution patterns. As with other sectors, traditional methods of distribution based on face-to-face meetings in branch offices are being replaced by cheaper methods of distribution based on post, telephone, and the Internet.

Many countries have reduced levels of protection for their suppliers, leading to growing levels of internationalization of supply and the growth of global marketing, especially in business-to-business markets (see BUSINESS-TO-BUSINESS MARKETING) where multinationals require their financial service needs to be met on a global scale. To avoid an undue reliance on price-based competition, many retail suppliers are heavily focused on customer service quality as their key competitive weapon. Increasingly, customer service strategies feature a range of contact media rather than the previous norm of face-to-face contact. Building long-term customer relationships (see RELATIONSHIP MARKETING), leading to higher levels of customer retention and hence profitability, is a cornerstone of marketing strategies in the sector.

Financial services are:

- *Intangible*: They possess no physical presence although there are many symbols, such as the appearance of retail premises, which make them visible.
- *Inseparable*: They are processes or experiences and involve cooperation between the supplier and the customer. They are sold, then produced and are hence inseparable from the supplier.
- *Heterogeneous*: Because of the high level of personal INVOLVEMENT of both the supplier and consumer, the experience of use will vary rather than being entirely similar in all cases. Thus, suppliers need to have processes in place to insure consistent quality of provision.
- *Perishable*: If a time-based product such as life insurance is not bought, it perishes and can never be replaced for that time period.
- *A set of financial promises which the supplier undertakes for the customer*: These carry fiduciary responsibilities including the need to operate within current regulations.
- *Two-way information flows*: As provision takes place over time, there is a need for information to flow between the parties and for this process to be managed by the supplier, with the customer being responsible for meeting obligations to inform the supplier of relevant data.

Thus, the marketing of financial services is a complex process based on a number of idiosyncrasies, which make it a special case of the marketing of services.

Bibliography

Burton, D. (1994). *Financial Services and the Consumer*. London: Routledge.

Buttle, F. (ed.) (1996). *Relationship Marketing: Theory and Practice*. London: Paul Chapman.

Chisnall, P. M. (1995). *Consumer Behavior*, 3rd edn. Maidenhead: McGraw-Hill.

Ennew, C., Watkins, T., and Wright, M. (eds.) (1995). *Marketing Financial Services*, 2nd edn. Oxford: Butterworth-Heinemann.

Harrison, T. (2000). *Financial Services Marketing*. Harlow: Pearson Education.

Lovelock, C. H. (1984). *Services Marketing: Text, Cases and Readings*. Englewood Cliffs, NJ: Prentice-Hall.

McGoldrick, P. J. and Greenland, S. J. (1994). *Retailing of Financial Services*. Maidenhead: McGraw-Hill.

marketing information systems

Michael Greatorex

A marketing information system is designed to generate, analyze, store, and distribute information to appropriate marketing decision-makers on a regular basis. The growth in the use of marketing information systems has been facilitated by improvements in computer hardware and software, and contemporary marketing information systems are very much computer driven.

Marketing information systems are designed around individual decision-makers, the decisions they are required to make, and the information needed to make those decisions. The information includes that required both on a regular and on an ad hoc basis. The underlying data may be collected internally or externally. The information is presented in a form requested by the decision-maker. The key task is to specify what information each individual decision-maker requires, when it is required, and in what format. The end result is a series of customized reports that go to the appropriate decision-makers.

Marketing information systems are being superseded by MARKETING DECISION SUP-PORT SYSTEMS, which are more versatile in the way the decision-maker is able to interact with the DATABASE and which, because of the ability to include marketing modeling in marketing decision support systems, permit the decision-maker to ask "what if...?" questions rather than merely retrieve data.

Bibliography

Parasuraman, A., Grewal, D., and Krishman, R. (2004). *Marketing Research*. Boston: Houghton Mifflin.

marketing management

Fiona Leverick

The term "marketing management" is generally used to refer to the management activities undertaken in the practice of MARKETING in organizations. The conventional view of marketing management found in most stand-ard marketing textbooks is of a process whereby the marketing manager uses marketing resources to perform a highly defined and "logical" series of activities and responsibilities (see Baker, 1996; Dibb et al., 1997; Kotler, 2003). Dibb et al. (1997), for instance, see marketing manage-ment as the process of "planning, organizing, implementing and controlling marketing activ-ities to facilitate and expedite exchanges effect-ively and efficiently" (p. 24). The execution of this process defines the marketing manager's areas of responsibility and the nature of his/her work.

The specific activities involved in marketing management will depend to a great extent on the type of MARKETS the business is operating in. The activities involved, for instance, in marketing to consumers and marketing to other businesses may differ significantly (*see* BUSI-NESS-TO-BUSINESS MARKETING; CON-SUMER MARKETING). At a general level, however, standard marketing textbooks fre-quently divide marketing management activities into the four areas of analysis, planning, imple-mentation, and control. Analysis refers to the

gathering and preparation of information about the markets the organization is currently operating in or which it plans to enter, in terms of identifying and evaluating present and emergent customer "needs" and potential opportunities for business expansion. Such an-alysis is often seen as being undertaken by studying both the organization's current MARKETING ENVIRONMENT and identifying future trends.

Planning is most commonly seen as a system-atic process of assessing opportunities and resources (*see* SWOT ANALYSIS), setting marketing objectives, developing a MARKET-ING STRATEGY, and formulating measures for IMPLEMENTATION and control (*see* MARKET-ING PLANNING). In this way, marketing man-agers are required to make decisions on target markets (*see* TARGET MARKET), MARKET POSITIONING, product and service develop-ment (*see* NEW PRODUCT DEVELOPMENT), PRICING, distribution channels (*see* CHAN-NELS OF DISTRIBUTION), physical distribu-tion, communication, and promotion. The result of these activities is often contained in a marketing plan.

Implementation refers to the activities neces-sary to translate the marketing plan into action. It might include organizing marketing resources and developing the internal structure of the marketing unit, coordinating marketing activities, motivating marketing personnel, and effectively communicating within the unit. Bonoma (1985), however, reviewed 17 market-ing textbooks and found implementation to be a generally neglected area of marketing manage-ment, with most emphasis directed toward an-alysis, planning, and control.

Finally, the MARKETING CONTROL process involves the measurement of results and evalu-ating progress according to standards of per-formance such as MARKET SHARE, cost/sales ratios, ADVERTISING/sales ratios, or, more commonly in the case of business-to-business marketing, techniques such as customer PORT-FOLIO ANALYSIS or customer profitability an-alysis. Expected performance standards against which results are judged would commonly be specified as part of the marketing plan. Indeed, analysis, planning, implementation, and control might be seen as a continuous marketing man-agement process in which during planning, guidelines for implementation are set and expected results specified for the control process, and feedback from the control process is used in the development of new plans.

This "textbook" view of marketing management embedded in the work of, for example, Kotler (2003) has, however, been criticized on a number of counts (see Brownlie, 1991 for a summary of criticisms). In particular, the view of the marketing management process driven by "rational" marketing planning has been questioned by authors such as Brownlie (1991) and King (1985), who suggest that such a normative model of marketing management bears little relation to what practicing marketing managers actually do, being based instead on what textbook writers think marketing managers ought to do. According to Brownlie, much marketing management literature overlooks the part played by individual managerial judgment, vision, and experience, qualities seen as especially relevant in the area of marketing as opposed to, say, finance or production, given that the data on which marketing decisions are made are often unreliable and consumers often behave "irrationally" or unexpectedly, making a focus purely on analytical techniques inappropriate.

Whereas marketing management may be reduced to a sole focus on analysis and planning in junior brand management jobs in fast-moving consumer goods sectors, it is questioned whether this is representative across other sectors and levels of responsibility. References are frequently made on this point to the work of authors such as Kotter (1982) and Mintzberg (1973), who have both looked at the nature of managerial work. Kotter, for instance, followed 15 general managers for a month and found that activities such as building networks, developing agendas, executing marketing activities, establishing values and norms, maintaining relationships, working through meetings and dialogues, establishing multiple objectives, spending time with others, and using rewards to secure support and desired behavior were more common in successful organizations than were planning and analysis activities. Mintzberg (1973) found that managers spend a great proportion of their time in oral communication and face-to-face contact rather than in formulating written plans.

A more accurate portrayal of marketing management might also reflect the increasingly wider focus of marketing itself, to include the activities undertaken in SERVICES MARKETING, business-to-business marketing, and NOT-FOR-PROFIT MARKETING, and also marketing activities directed toward parties in the organization's marketing environment other than those individuals and organizations who purchase goods and services, such as stakeholders, publics, or employees (see INTERNAL MARKETING).

Bibliography

Baker, M. J. (1996). *Marketing: An Introductory Text*, 6th edn. Basingstoke: Macmillan.

Bonoma, T. V. (1985). *The Marketing Edge: Making Strategies Work*. New York: Free Press.

Brownlie, D. T. (1991). Putting the management into marketing management. In M. J. Baker (ed.), *Perspectives on Marketing Management*, vol 1. Chichester: John Wiley.

Dibb, S., Simkin, L., Pride, W. M., and Ferrell, O. C. (1997). *Marketing: Concepts and Strategies*, 3rd European edn. London: Houghton Mifflin.

King, S. (1985). Has marketing failed or was it never really tried? *Journal of Marketing Management*, 1, 11–20.

Kotler, P. (2003). *Marketing Management: Analysis, Planning, Implementation and Control*, 11th edn. Englewood Cliffs, NJ: Prentice-Hall.

Kotter, J. (1982). *The General Managers*. New York: Free Press.

Mintzberg, H. (1973). *The Nature of Managerial Work*. New York: Harper and Row.

marketing mix

Fiona Leverick

The term "marketing mix" was first used by Professor Neil Borden of Harvard Business School to describe a list of the important elements or ingredients that make up marketing programs, the idea having been suggested to him by Culliton's (1948) description of a business executive as a "mixer of ingredients" (Borden, 1964). More recently, McCarthy and Perreault (2004) have defined the marketing mix as the controllable variables that an organization can coordinate to satisfy its TARGET MARKET.

The essence of the concept is the idea of a set of controllable marketing variables or a "tool kit" (Shapiro, 1985).

Some diversity of opinion exists as to the components of the marketing mix. Borden's own list is probably the longest, containing merchandising/PRODUCT PLANNING, PRICING, branding (*see* BRAND), CHANNELS OF DISTRIBUTION, PERSONAL SELLING, ADVERTISING, promotion, PACKAGING, display, servicing, physical handling, fact finding and analysis, and market research. The best-known marketing mix is McCarthy's 4Ps, product, price, promotion, and place. However, this has been widely criticized as simplistic and misleading, especially in the areas of BUSINESS-TO-BUSINESS MARKETING, SERVICES MARKETING, and NOT-FOR-PROFIT MARKETING. More recently Kotler (1986) has added politics and PUBLIC RELATIONS, and Booms and Bitner (1981) participants, physical evidence, and process, to McCarthy's 4Ps.

See also *marketing management*

Bibliography

Booms, B. H. and Bitner, M. J. (1981). Marketing strategies and organization structures for service firms. In J. Donnelly and J. R. George (eds.), *Marketing of Services*. Chicago: American Marketing Association, pp. 47–51.

Borden, N. H. (1964). The concept of the marketing mix. *Journal of Advertising Research*, 2–7.

Culliton, J. W. (1948). *The Management of Marketing Costs*. Division of Research, Graduate School of Business Administration, Harvard University.

Kotler, P. (1986). Megamarketing. *Harvard Business Review*, **64**, 2 (March/April), 117–24.

McCarthy, E. J. and Perreault, W. D., Jr. (2004). *Basic Marketing*, 15th edn. New York: Irwin McGraw-Hill/Irwin.

Shapiro, B. P. (1985). Rejuvenating the marketing mix. *Harvard Business Review*, **63** (September/October), 28–34.

marketing organization

Dale Littler

In the early stages, many of the activities now associated with MARKETING would have been undertaken by a number of different functions, often in an uncoordinated manner. Thus, the sales department may have been responsible not only for managing the sales activity, but also for ADVERTISING and rudimentary market research; PRICING may have been shared by accounting, sales, and production; while DESIGN and product development (*see* NEW PRODUCT DEVELOPMENT) may have been the responsibility of research and development. As the importance of marketing became increasingly recognized, it emerged as a distinct corporate activity responsible for at least managing in a more coordinated fashion different activities that were seen to have some bearing on the development of the product and, more generally, on the relationship with the customer. Contemporarily, marketing is widely acknowledged as a core organizational activity, sometimes with representation at board level.

The marketing activity can be structured according to functions, geographic areas, products, and customer types.

In the functional form, marketing is organized in terms of distinct specialisms, such as MARKETING RESEARCH, sales, and product development, that report to a marketing manager or director. However, in organizations with complex PRODUCT PORTFOLIOS that may also operate in several markets, there is clearly a need for marketing responsibility to be shared among several managers, each of whom may have responsibility for particular products and/or market areas. Marketing may also be organized in terms of geographic regions. A naive division may be between overseas and domestic operations. However, companies operating in several countries may have managers for different groups of countries, e.g., Asia Pacific, South America, Europe, or even specific countries. Within countries, there may also be managers for particular areas, such as the south-west or the north-east.

The PRODUCT MANAGER system developed as individual products became increasingly important. Under the general marketing management structure, "assistant" marketing managers were appointed to manage various aspects of the increasingly complex product portfolio. Individual managers, often referred to as brand or product managers, are given responsibility for coordinating all the marketing activities, such as ADVERTISING, marketing research, and product development as well as, in some cases, responsibility for profit, of specific major products or brands.

Alternatively, marketing may be organized according to the customers or markets it serves, this being particularly appropriate where the firm markets to diverse customer groups with significantly differing requirements. Individual managers may be responsible for all the marketing effort for customer groups or markets and even for individual customers where the level of DEMAND merits this. Hanan (1974) has termed this approach "market centering" and argues that it provides the company with a distinct COMPETITIVE ADVANTAGE because of the detailed knowledge of the customer or market that, in theory, the MARKET MANAGER should acquire. Such a structure would appear to support RELATIONSHIP MARKETING.

These approaches to marketing organization are not mutually exclusive, and the marketing activity may be a combination of two or more of these forms. For example, marketing may have functional managers supporting product and market managers. There may, in addition, be managers responsible for geographic regions.

Marketing may have representation at board level and may be expected to be an active participant in the development of overall organizational strategy. It may be a service activity providing marketing advice both to the board and to individual business or operating units. Individual business units or divisions may have individual marketing activities or departments, while marketing may be part of the matrix structure of an organization insuring that marketing contributes to every major activity. Increasingly, it is argued that marketing should be embedded in the culture of an organization and that it should be recognized that all those whose activities in any way have some impact on the customers should be seen as, in effect, part-time marketers.

All decision-makers can have access to customer information, which can be disseminated throughout the organization using computerized information systems (see MARKETING INFORMATION SYSTEMS). It could be argued that this might herald the end of the era of marketing as an important functional activity. Some suggest that marketing in the future may at best be a minimal service activity, advising managers who are responsible for particular relationships on various facets of marketing, much of which may be outsourced to specialist agencies.

Bibliography

Hanan, M. (1974). Recognize your company around its markets. *Harvard Business Review*, November/December.

marketing orientation

Fiona Leverick

A marketing orientation is usually seen as the company orientation necessary in order that the MARKETING CONCEPT may be put into practice. It is often contrasted with the "production orientation" and "sales orientation" associated respectively with the "production era" and "sales era" of the development of marketing thought (see MARKETING).

A number of writers have gone into more detail on the precise nature of a "marketing orientation" in relation to the various activities associated with MARKETING MANAGEMENT. For example, according to McCarthy and Perreault (2004), marketing activities and the product OFFERING are seen as guided primarily by customer "needs"; the role of market research is seen as to determine customer "needs" and how well the company is satisfying them; INNOVATION activity is focused primarily on locating new opportunities, in, for example, products or technologies; PROFIT (as opposed to sales volume) is the critical objective of marketing activity; PACKAGING is designed for customer convenience and as a selling tool (over and above simply the protection of the product); inventory levels are set with customer requirements and costs in mind (rather than at the convenience of the supplier); the focus of ADVERTISING is to promote the needs-satisfying benefits of the product or service; the role of the SALES FORCE, coordinated with the efforts of the rest of the firm, is to help customers to buy only if the product fits their needs; and so on. Somewhat more succinctly, Shapiro (1988) notes three key features of a marketing orientation: information on all important buying influences permeates every corporate function; strategic and tactical decisions are made interfunctionally and interdivisionally; and divisions and functions make well-coordinated decisions and execute them with a sense of commitment.

It has been argued that UK companies in particular have found it difficult to develop a marketing orientation. For example, marketing deficiencies were found in a sample of UK manufacturers involved in BUSINESS-TO-BUSINESS MARKETING (Chartered Institute of Marketing/University of Bradford Management Center, 1995). In recent years, there has been emphasis on MARKET ORIENTATION, which some would argue is a term that more appropriately represents the focus on markets and developments therein.

Bibliography

Chartered Institute of Marketing/University of Bradford Management Center (1995). *Manufacturing: The Marketing Solution*. Oxford: Chartered Institute of Marketing Report.

McCarthy, E. J. and Perreault, R. (2004). *Basic Marketing*, 15th edn. New York: McGraw-Hill/Irwin.

Shapiro, B. P. (1988). What the hell is market-oriented? *Harvard Business Review*, **66** (November/December), 119–25.

Witcher, B. J. (1990). Total marketing: Total quality and the marketing concept. *Quarterly Review of Marketing*, 15, 2 (Winter), 1–6.

marketing performance

Dale Littler

MARKETING PLANNING may involve the definition of targets or performance indicators. Measures commonly employed include product sales, costs, and MARKET SHARE. The company may also monitor the ability to meet customer specifications, delivery times, stock levels, tender success rates, the efficiencies of various operations, and such like. These performance indicators form the basis for exercising MARKETING CONTROL.

marketing planning

Dale Littler

Marketing, like other functions and the organization as a whole, may have a plan that sets out the objectives and the means of achieving them. The plan can be viewed as a blueprint for future action. It will also set out targets against which performance can be monitored (*see* MARKETING CONTROL; MARKETING PERFORMANCE). Doyle (2000) argues that there are four functions of strategic market planning: "facilitating the change process" through the analysis of the business's current and likely future performance in order to assess how well the company as a whole has been in generating shareholder value, CUSTOMER SATISFACTION, and so on, thereby highlighting any need for revisiting the overall goals and direction of the business; "forcing managers to ask the right questions" by focusing "on understanding the needs of customers; evaluating the competition and anticipating their likely strategies, and insuring that the company can communicate a genuine competitve advantage" (p. 185); "motivation and control"; and "balancing the tyranny of accountants" by raising sights above short-term budgeting.

The process of marketing planning, frequently prefaced with the term "strategic," is often depicted as consisting of a number of stages (Leppard and McDonald, 1991) involving: the gathering of information on the company's internal operations and its external environment; the identification of the strengths, weaknesses, opportunities, and threats (*see* SWOT ANALYSIS); the definition of the assumptions regarding the company and its environment; the setting of the marketing objectives in light of the first three stages; the formulation of strategies aimed at achieving these objectives; the devising of programs setting out the timing of activities, costs, and revenues; the definition of responsibilities and the means of monitoring performance. The plan should insure that the organization has in place the rudiments for implementing, monitoring, and controlling the strategy (Bonoma and Crittenden, 1988). The plan might contain specific objectives in terms of: sales, profits, and MARKET SHARE; the PRICING strategy and policies; the communications strategy; and various other elements of the traditional MARKETING MIX necessary for the organization to meet its strategic objectives.

Such marketing plans may be undertaken, *inter alia*, at the level of the product or at the level of the strategic business unit (*see* STRATEGIC BUSINESS UNITS).

In the marketing literature the distinction between corporate, strategic, and marketing planning has become blurred: all are often depicted as involving a similar methodology, for example. However, it is reasonable to assume that corporate planning embraces all of the different activities of the organization, whereas marketing planning should be regarded as focusing on the means by which marketing can play its part in facilitating the attainment of corporate objectives. In this sense, then, (strategic) marketing planning is operational, a stance which appears compatible with that adopted by Greenley (1986).

It could be argued that marketing planning would apply particularly to large firms, which have the resources to direct the extensive analysis that such planning demands, and which operate in stable, and therefore relatively predictable, environments (see Mintzberg, 1973). Given the UNCERTAINTY surrounding many of the assumptions upon which the originally formulated plan may be founded, and the rapid rate of change facing many organizations, the need for revisiting established plans and being sensitive to the need for flexibility may be the hallmarks of effective strategic marketing planning.

Bibliography

Bonoma, T. V. and Crittenden, V. L. (1988). Managing marketing implementation. *Sloan Management Review*, **29** (Winter), 7–14.

Doyle, P. (2000). *Value-Based Marketing*. Chichester: John Wiley.

Leppard, J. W. and McDonald, M. H. B. (1991). Marketing planning and corporate culture: A conceptual framework which examines management attitudes in the context of marketing planning. *Journal of Marketing Management*, **73** (July), 213–36.

Greenley, G. E. (1986). *The Strategic and Operational Planning of Marketing*. Maidenhead: McGraw-Hill, pp. 89–139.

Mintzberg, H. (1973). Strategy making in three modes. *California Management Review*, **16**, 2 (Winter), 44–53.

marketing process

Fiona Leverick

Two levels of understanding of the marketing process are common in the marketing literature. The first refers to the organizational process concerned with directing goods and services from producer to consumer. Indeed, the marketing process is often seen as synonymous with "marketing" itself, with process-related definitions of marketing forming one of the three categories of definition identified by Crosier (1988) (*see* MARKETING). The extent to which the activities involved in the marketing process are specified varies from author to author. The marketing process is often seen as embracing the analysis of market opportunities, undertaking research into and selecting target markets (*see* TARGET MARKET), designing the marketing strategies (*see* MARKETING STRATEGY), devising, planning, implementing, and monitoring marketing programs (see, e.g., Kotler, 2003). In this way, the marketing process is seen as inseparable from structured, normative approaches to MARKETING MANAGEMENT, the activities involved being essentially the same.

A second level of understanding of the marketing process is concerned with the whole marketing system and describes a wider social process that directs an economy's flow of goods and services from producers to consumers in a way that effectively matches supply and demand and accomplishes the objectives of society (see MACRO MARKETING).

Bibliography

Crosier, K. (1988). What exactly is marketing? In M. J. Thomas and N. E. Waite (eds.), *The Marketing Digest*. London: Heinemann, pp. 16–27.

Kotler, P. (2003). *Marketing Management: Analysis, Planning, Implementation and Control*, 11th edn. Englewood Cliffs, NJ: Prentice-Hall.

marketing research

Michael Greatorex

Marketing research is "the function which links the consumer, customer and public to the marketer through information – information used to identify and define marketing opportunities and problems; generate, refine and evaluate marketing actions; monitor marketing performance; and improve understanding of marketing as a process. Marketing research specifies the information required to address these issues; designs the method for collecting information; manages and implements the data collection process; analyzes the results; and communicates the findings and their implications" (American Marketing Association, quoted in Baines and Chansarker, 2002: 4).

Malhotra, who emphasizes the need for information for decision-making, defines marketing research as "the systematic and objective identification, collection, analysis, and dissemination of information for the purpose of assisting management in decision-making related to the identification and solution of problems and opportunities in marketing" (Malhotra, 1999: 10).

Marketing research, therefore, is closely linked with decision-making by marketing managers. O'Dell et al. (1988) suggest a five-stage marketing decision-making process: identify the decision problem; formulate alternative solutions; establish criteria; evaluate the alternative solutions; and resolve the decision. They see change, especially in the environment, as the source of decision problems. If a manager feels that, for example, sales, profits, etc. are not as expected, based on historical or budgeted levels, the question arises as to why. The answer to this question often lies in environmental (in its widest marketing meaning) change. Information concerning the environment may enable changes to be detected or predicted and linked to current or likely marketing problems. Appropriate solutions can be suggested and evaluated when the cause of the problem is known.

Problem solving is the name O'Dell et al. give to their first two stages, the identification of the decision problem and the formulation of alternative solutions, and they suggest the need at these stages is for "environmental data and information." The final three stages, the establishment of criteria, the evaluation of the alternative solutions, and the resolution of the decision-making process, are called decision-making and the authors suggest that the need here is for "actionable data and information." Environmental data

indicate what is, while actionable data are pertinent to what should be done. Environmental data become available and are used prior to and during the formulation of alternative solutions. Actionable data are data sought after the alternative solutions have been formulated and for the specific purpose of evaluating the alternatives. Sometimes environmental and actionable data are collected jointly in a single information-gathering effort, but usually they are gathered separately. Experience has shown that environmental data need not be as precise, relatively, as actionable data. Different methods may be appropriate, depending on the stage in the decision-making process and the type of data required. Thus, SECONDARY DATA, from either external or internal sources, may be satisfactory as environmental data, while a well-designed experiment may be called for to provide actionable data.

Malhotra (1999) suggests two types of marketing research: problem-identification research and problem-solving research. Problem identification is undertaken to help identify problems which are, perhaps, not apparent on the surface and yet exist or are likely to arise in the future. Examples of problem-identification research include research into MARKET POTENTIAL, MARKET SHARE, BRAND or company IMAGE, market characteristics, sales analysis, short-range forecasting, long-range forecasting (see FORECASTING), and business trends. When a problem has been identified, problem-solving research is undertaken to arrive at a solution. Problem-solving research includes segmentation (see MARKET SEGMENTATION) and MARKETING MIX research – what will be the effects of a price change, new PACKAGING, change in SALES PROMOTION or ADVERTISING, change in service levels to retailers, etc.?

Marketing research involves both secondary and PRIMARY DATA. Secondary data are data collected for a purpose other than the problem under consideration. Internal secondary data are available from within the organization from records such as sales records kept for accounting purposes, general management information systems, etc. External secondary data come from governments, trade associations, and marketing research organizations and are accessible from printed publications and, increasingly, from computer databases by way of CD-ROM or computer networks.

Primary data are data collected specifically for the problem under consideration. Two types of data are identified, qualitative and quantitative data. Qualitative data mainly provide insights into the problem by looking at the underlying motives, needs, opinions, etc. of respondents using techniques such as DEPTH INTERVIEWS, FOCUS GROUPS, and PROJECTIVE TECHNIQUES. Quantitative techniques look to provide quantitative data, which sometimes are used in exploratory research but which are usually associated with the decision-making stage. Quantitative techniques also seek to enable results from a sample to be generalized to a population. Techniques include observations (see OBSERVATION), surveys (see SURVEY RESEARCH) using structured questionnaires, and experiments (see EXPERIMENTATION). While much primary research is ad hoc or one-off, an increasing amount is continuous involving the repeated use of the same design or questionnaire, sometimes with different samples, sometimes with the same sample or panel.

The increasing use of electronic capture of data, e.g., at retail store checkouts or in consumer scanner panels or, potentially, in two-way in-home communications associated with cable systems, is capable of providing a continuous flow of data that enables the tracking of key measures that are useful to marketing decision-makers.

The information that marketing research provides becomes part of an organization's marketing information system (see MARKETING INFORMATION SYSTEMS). A marketing information system is one designed to generate, analyze, store, and distribute information to appropriate marketing decision-makers on a regular basis. However, marketing information systems are limited to supplying past and current data in a prescribed, even if customized, form for each manager. Further developments have led to MARKETING DECISION SUPPORT SYSTEMS, which incorporate databases (see DATABASE), marketing modeling, and facilities for the user to communicate easily with the data and models. The easy communication allows improved interaction with databases, and the inclusion of models and databases allows the user to ask "what if . . . ?" questions and so raise analysis to a different level.

Bibliography

Baines, P. and Chansarker, B. (2002). *Introducing Marketing Research.* Chichester: John Wiley.

Malhotra, N. K. (1999). *Marketing Research: An Applied Approach*, 3rd edn. Englewood Cliffs, NJ: Prentice-Hall.

O'Dell, W., Ruppel, A. C., Trent, R. H., and Kehoe, W. J. (1988). *Marketing Decision-Making: Analytical Framework and Cases*, 4th edn. Cincinnati, OH: South-Western Publishing.

marketing strategy

Dale Littler

In essence, marketing strategy embraces the customer targets or segments (see MARKET SEGMENTATION) and the means, in terms of the MARKETING MIX elements, to be employed for these. Foxall (1981), for example, regards marketing strategy as being an indication of how each element of the marketing mix will be used to achieve the marketing objectives. Doyle (2000) believes that marketing strategy embraces the decisions regarding customer targets and how the organization will develop customer preference. Some, such as Kotler (2003), argue that corporate or marketing should heavily influence business strategy, on the grounds that strategy is concerned with the match between the organization and its environment, and that marketing, because of its unique position at the interface between the organization and the environment, must therefore be a prime mover in strategy formulation. It seems reasonable that marketing should be regarded as having a perspective critical to strategic management because it is primarily concerned with operationalizing the MARKETING CONCEPT. However, the other functional activities, such as those concerned with technological development, must also take into account wider environmental considerations; while many activities (finance, manufacturing, LOGISTICS, research and development) all contribute to the development and achievement of wider corporate goals.

Others, such as Greenley (1986), take a more limited view of marketing strategy, arguing that it is operational, i.e., it is oriented toward implementing the overarching strategy of the organization. It is likely that marketing strategy is shaped by and also shapes overall CORPORATE STRATEGY.

Greenley (1993) suggests that marketing strategy has five elements: market POSITIONING and segmentation, involving the selection of segments for each product market; PRODUCT POSITIONING, involving decisions on the number and type of products for each segment; the selection of the marketing mix; market entry – how to enter, reenter, position, or reposition products in each segment; and the timing of strategy and IMPLEMENTATION given that, as Abell (1978) argues, there are only limited periods during which the fit between key requirements of a market and the particular competencies of a firm competing in that market is at an optimum. The marketing strategy is likely to be modified according to different stages of the PRODUCT LIFE CYCLE. Varadarajan and Jayachandran (1999) summarized some of the research themes in marketing strategy as: competitive behavior, INNOVATION, product quality, market pioneering, strategic alliances, MARKET ORIENTATION, and MARKET SHARE.

Bibliography

Abell, D. F. (1978). Strategic windows. *Journal of Marketing*, **42** (3), 22–5.
Doyle, P. (2000). *Value-Based Marketing*. Chichester: John Wiley.
Foxall, G. R. (1981). *Strategic Marketing Management*. London: Croom Helm.
Greenley, G. E. (1986). *The Strategic and Operational Planning of Marketing*. Maidenhead: McGraw-Hill, pp. 89–139.
Greenley, G. (1993). An understanding of marketing strategy. *European Journal of Marketing*, **23** (8), 45–58.
Kotler, P. (2003). *Marketing Management: Analysis, Planning, Implementation and Control*, 11th edn. Englewood Cliffs, NJ: Prentice-Hall.
Varadarajan, P. R. and Jayachandran, S. (1999). Marketing strategy: An assessment of the state of the field and outlook. *Journal of the Academy of Marketing Science*, **27** (2), 120–43.

markets

Barbara R. Lewis

A market comprises all the individuals and organizations who are actual or potential customers for a product or service, and those in a market are involved in market EXCHANGE with companies and others providing goods and services.

Markets have several requirements. First, those in the market for a product or service must need the product; they must also have the ability to purchase the product, i.e., buying power, which can include credit purchase. In addition, they must be willing to use their buying power, and also have the authority to make purchase decisions, e.g., those under 18 years do not have authority in the UK to purchase alcohol.

Markets may be categorized as consumer markets, to include individuals and households who buy or acquire goods and services for personal consumption/use, i.e., for final consumption without further transactions; or organizational markets. Organizational markets comprise: producer or industrial markets, i.e., individuals or organizations buying goods and services for the purpose of manufacturing products; reseller markets (wholesalers and retailers) who buy finished goods and services and resell them; and government markets at local and national level where goods and services are bought to provide citizen services or, more broadly, to carry out government functions, e.g., defense, health, education, and welfare. Institutional markets, such as hospitals and schools, may be in the private as well as the government sector.

Finally, one can consider international markets, which may embrace all the other types of markets.

Maslow's hierarchy of needs

see CONSUMER NEEDS AND MOTIVES

mass media

Dale Littler

Mass media are impersonal channels by which the communicator can communicate directly with the target audience. The major mass media are cinema, TELEVISION, RADIO, POSTERS, NEWSPAPERS, and MAGAZINES. Although the communicator has a high degree of control over the content of the MESSAGE, mass media channels are relatively inflexible in that in general the message cannot be adapted to suit the particular requirements of the audience. They can often be seen to involve the imposition of a message on an audience, and they cannot be adapted to suit specific moods or relevant wants. The use of domestic video recorders enables consumers to be more discerning in their consumption of television ADVERTISING messages, while SELECTIVE EXPOSURE, selective perception (see CONSUMER PERCEPTIONS), and SELECTIVE RETENTION can be powerful filtering processes affecting the effectiveness of mass media communications. Technological developments, such as advertising via the Internet and digital broadcasting, facilitate greater interactivity between the consumer and the communicator.

It may not be possible to aim communications at narrowly defined targets through mass media channels, because by definition these channels tend to have a wide appeal, although the readership of, for example, many magazines and the viewers of certain television programs and cinema films can be specialized. Increasingly, the proliferation of cable, satellite, and terrestrial digital specialist television channels facilitates the targeting of specific clusters of consumers.

See also *communications mix; marketing communications*

matched sampling

Andrew Lindridge

Campbell's (1964) observation that an important cross-cultural/societal methodological problem was falsely attributing behavioral differences to cultural/societal causes raises important issues regarding sample group selection. Van Raaij (1978) suggests that cross-cultural/societal sample groups should be consistent and matched in terms of age, rural–urban residence, sex, and SOCIAL CLASS. Although this limits findings to similarly constituted populations, the internal VALIDITY of the research is greatly enhanced, achieving category equivalence (Cook and Campbell, 1975; Calder, Phillips, and Tybout, 1980) (see CONSTRUCT EQUIVALENCE; EQUIVALENCE). Data drawn from matched samples can therefore be claimed to be more likely due to cultural/societal differences than differences between the sample groups, although previous or existing relationships between the groups should be noted (see GALTON'S PROBLEM).

Determining matched samples, however, may prove difficult depending on each country's self-categorization criteria, the countries being compared, and the researcher's criterion. For example, Pearlin and Kohn (1966), attempting to assess social class positions in Italy and the US, preferred "prestige" to "education" and "income." Thorelli, Becker, and Engledow (1975), however, contradicted this, preferring "education" and "income" in their cross-cultural/societal comparison of consumers. Sample group selection criteria should therefore aim to devise a criterion that is suitable to both cultures, achieved through category.

The use of matched samples, however, is criticized by Scheuch (1968: 190), who argues that "identical sampling procedures as a condition of comparability show little confidence in samples as a tool of inference and constitute a misplaced trust in some of its concrete features." The solution appears to rely upon pursuing matched samples but identifying and recognizing their limitations from a cross-cultural/societal perspective.

Bibliography

Calder, B. J., Phillips, L. W., and Tybout, A. M. (1980). The design, conduct and application of consumer research: Theory vs. effects orientated studies. *Proceedings of the Educators' Conference*, Chicago: American Marketing Association, pp. 307–11.

Campbell, D. (1964). *Distinguishing Differences of Perceptions from Failures of Communication in Cross-Cultural Studies: Epistemology in Anthropology.* New York: Harper and Row.

Cook, T. and Campbell, D. (1975). The design and conduct of experiments and quasi-experiments in field settings. In M. Dunnette and R. McNally (eds.), *Handbook of Industrial and Organizational Psychology*. Chicago: Northwestern University Press, pp. 223–326.

Pearlin, L. and Kohn, M. (1966). Social class, occupation and parental views: A cross-national study. *American Sociological Review*, 31 (4), 466–79.

Scheuch, E. K. (1968). The cross-cultural use of sample surveys: Problems of comparability. In S. Rokkan (ed.), *Comparative Research Across Cultures and Nations*. Paris: Mouton, pp. 176–209.

Thorelli, H. B., Becker, R. S., and Engledow, J. (1975). *The Information-Seekers: An International Study of Consumer Information and Advertising Image*. Cambridge, MA: Ballinger.

Van Raaij, W. F. (1978). Cross-cultural research methodology as a case of construct validity. *Advances in Consumer Research*, 5, 693–701.

measurement and scaling

Rudolph Sinkovics

The majority of questions in MARKETING RESEARCH are designed to measure theoretical concepts (i.e., constructs) or phenomena, which are only indirectly observable. Consequently, the sound assessment of phenomena such as, e.g., BRAND LOYALTY, reputation (*see* CORPORATE REPUTATION), purchase intentions (*see* CONSUMER DECISION-MAKING PROCESS), or ATTITUDES, is vital for marketing researchers and marketing decision-making. Measurement is the standardized process of assigning symbols – such as numbers – to certain characteristics of objects (persons, states, or events) according to pre-specified rules. The assignment of numbers is advantageous, because it helps to summarize responses from samples fairly efficiently and economically. Furthermore, quantified responses in the form of numbers can be easily manipulated by a variety of statistical techniques (Kumar, Aaker, and Day, 1999). Despite this appeal, the assignment of numbers to responses from surveys is not an easy task and is particularly daunting in an international context, where the comparability of measures and scales used is at stake (*see* EQUIVALENCE).

Related to measurement is the process of scaling, which is usually employed in survey-type methodology (*see* SURVEY RESEARCH) and involves the provision of alternative response categories. Scaling is the creation of a continuum on which objects (i.e., respondents to the survey) are located, according to the amount of the measured characteristic that these objects possess. In a questionnaire about viewing preferences of BBC sitcoms, we can ask, "How often do you watch *The Office*?" We can provide respondents with an opportunity to locate themselves on a scale, according to the amount of their actual viewing behavior (e.g., four-step scale, "never," "occasionally," "sometimes," "often"), and quantify responses using numbers (e.g., use "0" to represent "never," "1" to represent "occasionally," etc.).

Quantified response data generally falls into one of four measurement levels, also referred to as "scales of measurement": nominal-scaled data, ordinal-scaled data, interval-scaled data, and ratio-scaled data. Nominal and ordinal-scaled data can be subsumed in the broad group of "non-metric or qualitative data," while interval-scaled and ratio-scaled data build the group of "metric or quantitative data." A clear understanding and purposeful use of measurement scales is important, because linked to the scale choice are certain alternatives regarding interpretation and analysis of the data. Nominal scales, for instance, are simply labels or classifications of qualitative characteristics (e.g., "male," "female" for gender or "PDA," "MP3 player," "Walkman" for portable digital devices) that help to identify groups. Mathematical transformations or statistical analysis beyond descriptive analysis (frequencies, mode as appropriate measure of central tendency) are technically possible but conceptually inappropriate. Ordinal scales are more powerful than nominal scales in that their elements are ordered or ranked (e.g., Pepsi-Cola is preferred to Coca-Cola and Virgin-Cola). Consequently, calculating rank orders, quantiles, or simply the median is appropriate. However, even more appealing for marketing research is the application of metric scales. Interval scales have all the properties of ordinal scales and the differences between scale values can be meaningfully interpreted (e.g., fahrenheit and centigrade scale). Addition, subtraction, and – most importantly – the calculation of mean scores is therefore appropriate for interval scales. Finally, ratio scales (e.g., weight, height, age) possess all the properties of interval scales and – given the equality of intervals and an absolute zero point – the ratios of numbers on these scales have meaningful interpretations. Therefore, all mathematical calculations can be employed. In marketing and business research it is often difficult to collect ratio-level data. However, metric data in the form of interval scales can readily be accomplished when careful QUESTIONNAIRE DESIGN is taking place (Dillman, 2000).

Numbers are equal but some numbers are more "equal" than others. The ways numbers are treated differs substantially and this has considerable implications regarding the use of univariate and multivariate techniques (see UNIVARIATE ANALYSIS; MULTIVARIATE METHODS (ANALYSIS)).

Bibliography

Dillman, D. A. (2000). *Mail and Internet Surveys: The Tailored Design Method*. New York: John Wiley.
Kumar, V., Aaker, D. A., and Day, G. S. (1999). *Essentials of Marketing Research*. New York: John Wiley.

measurement equivalence

see CONSTRUCT EQUIVALENCE

media

see MASS MEDIA

media planning

David Yorke

Media planning is concerned with the selection of the most appropriate media to deliver MARKETING COMMUNICATIONS messages to target audiences. A media plan sets out the media vehicles to be used (specific NEWSPAPERS, MAGAZINES, TELEVISION channels, etc.) and the times and dates when the advertisements will appear. Before making media plans, organizations should have decided on their target markets (*see* TARGET MARKET) and COMMUNICATIONS OBJECTIVES. Media selection may be affected by such factors as the desired REACH, FREQUENCY, IMPACT, and continuity of advertisements. Overall, organizations aim to be cost effective in their choice of media and so choices will be closely related to the relative costs of the available media.

See also *advertising*

Bibliography

Rust, R. T. (1986). *Advertising Media Models: A Practical Guide*. Lexington, MA: Lexington Books.

media schedule

David Yorke

A media schedule is an operational activity which results from MEDIA PLANNING, designed to achieve particular objectives with respect to REACH, FREQUENCY, and IMPACT. The schedule relates to the timing of ADVERTISING expenditures, which depends on the product/service, the stage in its life cycle (*see* PRODUCT LIFE CYCLE), seasonality of purchase, and COMMUNICATIONS OBJECTIVES. For example, a new product will tend to be advertised frequently in a short time period in order to create AWARENESS and knowledge, whereas a less concentrated advertising schedule may be followed for a well-established and successful BRAND. Seasonal products may be advertised near and during their peak sales periods (although advertising can often create unseasonable DEMAND). Products with short life cycles may be advertised intensively.

Macro scheduling relates to choices between schedules over a year or a season (e.g., with respect to tourism services), with allowances for lagged effects and advertising carry-over. Micro scheduling is concerned with allocation over a shorter period of time, and possible advertising timing patterns, namely, concentrated, continuous, or intermittent, which in turn relates to the rate at which new buyers appear in the market, purchase frequency, competitive activity, and forgetting rates.

In making media-scheduling decisions, organizations are inevitably also concerned with the individual media costs of reaching target audiences (see COST PER THOUSAND) and, hence, to achieve a cost-effective mixture of reach and frequency of message exposure.

Bibliography

Crosier, K. (1999). Promotion. In M. J. Baker (ed.), *The Marketing Book*, 4th edn. Oxford: Butterworth-Heinemann, ch. 17.

message

Margaret Bruce and Liz Barnes

Message is central to the communication between the sender (the organization) and the receiver (the various publics) and captures the values that an organization wishes to convey to its various publics. Messages emanating from organizations – products, brands, and corporate identity – are expressions of their "corporate voice," of their heritage and personality, and serve to differentiate and support their POSITIONING in the marketplace. The choice of the company name "Rockwater," for example, was made because "it implied strength and stability. It was substantial, appropriate internationally in the English-speaking offshore industry and did not have negative connotations in other languages. It sounded mature and authoritative and gave the impression that it had always been there" (Lee, 1991).

The message can be conveyed in various forms (or media), such as TELEVISION advertisements, printed leaflets, billboards (see POSTERS), corporate identities, and electronically via multimedia systems, Internet, and so on (see COMMUNICATIONS MIX). Regardless of the form used to convey the message and reach different publics, certain organizational values will be presented and perceptions and opinions of the organization formed by the publics it reaches. Levi advertisements, for example, reinforce the company's heritage and its American birthright, the product's quality and durability, as well as a progressive, youthful, and sexual image.

If the messages coming from an organization fail to match expectations, then the publics may be confused and communication can be made more difficult. For example, Lever's "Persil Power" washing liquid was launched as a safe and effective product. However, after numerous washes it was claimed that the innovative ingredient had a deleterious effect on certain fabrics. After a few months in the marketplace, the product was withdrawn but at significant cost, including a fall in MARKET SHARE of Persil products. Lever had then to build up the public's belief and trust that its existing products were effective and safe. Perrier had faced a similar situation when a potentially harmful ingredient was discovered in its bottled water and the product was withdrawn from the market. Again, the company had to regain the public's trust in the product.

Bibliography

Aaker, D. A. and Myers, J. G. (1987). *Advertising Management*, 3rd edn. Englewood Cliffs, NJ: Prentice-Hall, ch. 11.
Dibb, S., Simkin, L., Pride, W., and Ferrell, O. C. (2000). *Marketing: Concepts and Strategies*, European edn. Boston: Houghton Mifflin.
Lee, S. (1991). The Rockwater story. *Design Management Journal*, Winter, 22–8.

micro environment

Dale Littler

The environment of an organization is generally viewed as comprising two components: the MACRO ENVIRONMENT and the micro environment, which, unlike the former, consists of elements or activities with which the organization interacts directly and over which it can therefore exert influence, if not control. The major aspects of the micro environment are: competitors; SUPPLIERS; CHANNELS OF DISTRIBUTION; CUSTOMERS; and the media (see MASS MEDIA).

Minitab

Michael Greatorex

Minitab is a computer software package used to analyze data, including data obtained in

MARKETING RESEARCH surveys. The components of the package concern data input, data modification, data analysis, presentation of results, and communication with other packages. The range of statistical procedures that can be specified is very large and includes all types of DESCRIPTIVE STATISTICS, HYPOTHESIS TESTING, UNIVARIATE ANALYSIS, BIVARIATE ANALYSIS, and multivariate analysis (*see* MULTIVARIATE METHODS (ANALYSIS)).

Bibliography

Miller, R. B. (1988). *Minitab Handbook for Business and Economics*. Boston: PWS-Kent.

mission statement

Dale Littler

The mission statement is generally presented as the first stage in the STRATEGIC PLANNING process, depicted as consisting of a number of stages, although it may in fact be formulated at any time. The importance of a mission statement in business may have been drawn from the goal statement given to NASA by President John F. Kennedy: "achieving the goal, before the decade is out, of landing a man on the moon and returning him safely to earth." In general, the mission statement should reflect what the organization is striving to do and provide a broad indication of how it intends to fulfill its goal. The general consensus is that it outlines the POSITIONING it wishes to achieve in specified businesses. It may also include "the principal technologies to be mastered, and the competitive competencies that will be employed" (Dickson, 1997: 123).

Greenley (1986) suggests that the mission statement has several aims, including: to provide the purpose for the organization; to express the philosophy that will guide the business; to articulate the vision (*see* VISION STATEMENT) of where the firm will be in the future; to define the business domain, i.e., the customer groups and needs, and the technology to be employed; and to motivate employees by providing them with a clear sense of purpose and direction.

Campbell and Tawadey (1992) devised the Ashridge mission model, which has four elements: purpose ("why the company exists"); strategy ("the commercial rationale," which embraces the business domain in which the firm is aiming to compete and the competitive advantages that it aims to exploit); standards and behaviors ("the policies and behavior patterns that guide how the company operates"); and values ("the beliefs that underpin the organization's management style, its relations to employees and other stakeholders, and its ethics").

Overall, the mission statement might be expected to provide answers to the questions posed by Drucker (1973): What is our business? Who is the customer? What is value to the customer? What will be our business? What should our business be? It is believed that the mission statement should be aspirational and provide a shared sense of purpose, thereby giving a focus for the efforts of all in the organization. It has various audiences, often with different requirements, including customers, shareholders, employees, and SUPPLIERS. To be effective the mission statement has to be widely communicated to, *inter alia*, employees.

However, mission statements may often be general and bland, perhaps for fear of providing competitors with information about future strategies and because they need to appeal to different constituencies. Many contain similar aspirations ("to be the world leader," etc.). They may also reflect what the company has been or is doing, rather than what it intends to do. They may be changed to respond to opportunities or they may be employed as a ploy to distract competitors while, for example, a strategy is being developed and emerges.

Bibliography

Abell, D. (1980). *Defining the Business: The Starting Point of Strategic Planning*. Englewood Cliffs, NJ: Prentice-Hall, ch. 3.

Campbell, A. and Tawadey, K. (eds.) (1992). *Mission and Business Philosophy*. Oxford: Butterworth-Heinemann, ch. 1.

Dickson, P. R. (1997). *Marketing Management*, 2nd edn. New York: Dryden Press.

Drucker, P. (1973). *Management: Tasks, Responsibilities, Practices*. New York: Harper and Row, ch. 7.

Greenley, G. E. (1986). *The Strategic and Operational Planning of Marketing*. Maidenhead: McGraw-Hill.

modified rebuy

Dominic Wilson

Robinson, Faris, and Wind (1967) suggest a division of organizational buying into three categories: NEW TASK, modified rebuy, and STRAIGHT REBUY. The category of modified rebuy refers to those occasions when there are significant differences in the terms of the purchasing contract under review (e.g., changes in price, technical specifications, delivery arrangements, PACKAGING, DESIGN, quality). The significance of these differences might reflect changes in the customer's requirements (e.g., changed specifications or delivery arrangements), or in the customer's competitive position (e.g., entering new markets, developing improved products), or in a supplier's offerings (e.g., increased price, new product features), and will generally require a significant renegotiation of the contract, though not usually a change of supplier.

See also *organizational buying behavior*

Bibliography

Robinson, P. T., Faris, C. W., and Wind, Y. (1967). *Industrial Buying and Creative Marketing*. Boston: Allyn and Bacon.

mood

see AFFECT

multidimensional scaling

Michael Greatorex

Multidimensional scaling is a generic name given to a number of procedures related to attitude (*see* ATTITUDES) and IMAGE research. Its main uses in marketing are in attribute mapping, PRODUCT POSITIONING, and finding ideal BRAND points. Two types of variables form the starting blocks for much multidimensional scaling: perceptions (of attributes, of similarities between brands, etc.) and preferences (e.g., between brands).

Brands are perceived by customers in terms of attributes, e.g., for cars the attributes could be performance, safety, size, style, country of origin, price, etc. Different brands may be perceived in different ways; brands can be represented on maps and some brands will be close together (hence, likely to be competing), while other brands will be apart. It may be possible to discover for individual buyers their ideal positions on these maps and, hence, taken with the product map, predict which brand is likely to be purchased. The ideal point has another interpretation as an indicator of the importance of the dimensions identified. Gaps in the offerings (*see* OFFERING) to customers may be spotted, hence helping with the DESIGN of new products. Dimensions used in the maps indicate the attributes used by respondents to characterize the brands.

Different types of measurement scales include ratio, interval, ordinal, and categorical scales. The latter two scales are known as non-metric scales for obvious reasons. Another scale, known as an ordered metric scale, is used in the commonest type of multidimensional scaling. In an ordered metric scale, all possible intervals between positions on the scale are ranked.

Thus, one technique of multidimensional scaling requires all pairs of brands to be ranked in order of similarity. The brands on offer in a market are listed in pairs and the respondent has to say which pair is the most similar, the next most similar, and so on right down to the least similar. This information is fed into a computer, attribute maps are prepared showing the relative positions of the brands, and a metric measure of the similarities (or differences) between brands is obtained, even though originally the data were merely an ordered metric scale. It may take only two dimensions to map the brands, when it is easy to represent the maps graphically. When three or more dimensions are to be used, several two-dimensional graphs are prepared. The dimensions are not named; they have to be named by the researcher from the grouping of the brands and further knowledge of the brands' attributes. The dimensions identify the attributes used by the respondent to evaluate and compare the brands.

The ideal point can be discovered, based upon the respondent being able to rank the brands in order of preference either overall or on each of several attribute scales according to the program used. The maps, based on similarities data, are produced for each individual. The dimensions that are thrown up may differ from map to map. It is difficult to aggregate maps over individuals; this is unfortunate as it makes it hard to use the knowledge gained about ideal points to discover clusters of respondents with close ideal points. Usually, clustering takes place first; this is followed by obtaining a map to represent each cluster, either for an average individual in each cluster or based on averaging similarities data from each cluster. Ideal points for individuals in the cluster can be mapped in relationship to the positions of the brands on the map.

Bibliography

Green, P. E., Carmone, F. J., and Smith, S. M. (1989). *Multidimensional Scaling: Concepts and Applications*. Boston: Allyn and Bacon.

Johnson, R. A. and Wichern, D. W. (1998). *Applied Multivariate Statistical Analysis*, 4th edn. Upper Saddle River, NJ: Prentice-Hall.

Tull, D. S. and Hawkins, D. I. (1993). *Marketing Research: Measurement and Method*, 6th edn. New York: Macmillan, pp. 426–34.

multivariate methods (analysis)

Michael Greatorex

Multivariate methods of data analysis involve the consideration of relationships between more than two variables and, as such, extend UNIVARIATE ANALYSIS and BIVARIATE ANALYSIS of data. Multivariate methods require the use of computer-based statistical analysis packages such as the STATISTICAL PACKAGE FOR THE SOCIAL SCIENCES (SPSS) and MINITAB.

The best-known methods are multiple regression (*see* REGRESSION AND CORRELATION), which seeks to find the relationship between a dependent variable and several independent variables, PRINCIPAL COMPONENT ANALYSIS and FACTOR ANALYSIS, which are looking for interrelationships within a set of variables, DISCRIMINANT ANALYSIS, which seeks the best combinations of variables to discriminate

between groups of respondents, CLUSTER ANALYSIS, which is a range of grouping techniques, MULTIDIMENSIONAL SCALING, which is used to obtain perceptual maps of how customers perceive brands, and CONJOINT ANALYSIS, which can be used to obtain indirect evaluations of the utilities of product attributes. STRUCTURAL EQUATION MODELS (or latent variable path models) bring together the many parts of the MARKETING RESEARCH effort, and the software, such as LISREL, PROC CALIS, or EQS, used to estimate the parameters of these models can be seen as superseding in a holistic way some of the multivariate methods mentioned above.

Bibliography

Hair, J. F., Anderson, R. E., and Tatham, R. L. (1987). *Multivariate Data Analysis*, 2nd edn. New York: Macmillan, ch. 1.

Johnson, R. A. and Wichern, D. W. (1998). *Applied Multivariate Statistical Analysis*, 4th edn. Upper Saddle River, NJ: Prentice-Hall.

Tull, D. S. and Hawkins, D. I. (1993). *Marketing Research: Measurement and Method*, 6th edn. New York: Macmillan, pp. 686–97.

mystery shopping

Vincent-Wayne Mitchell

In mystery shopping market research interviewers, posing as shoppers, are trained to observe closely all the aspects of customer service during a typical shopping trip, either in a client's own outlets or those of competitors. The researcher goes through the shopping experience, asking the sort of questions an actual customer might ask. The process has many discrete, albeit interlinked, elements, each of which is a "moment of truth" for the customer (a central reason for mystery shoppers using the "sample size of one" – you only get one chance to make a good first impression!).

So why do businesses use mystery shopping instead of CUSTOMER SATISFACTION research? Customer satisfaction is an output, and in order to understand what lies behind outputs, it is necessary to look at inputs and processes, such as customer SERVICE DELIVERY. However, mystery shopping has attracted some criticism largely on account of the sample sizes, the quantitative measures used, and issues of privacy, as well as professional ethics (*see* MARKETING ETHICS). Despite its attraction as being unobtrusive, mystery shopping, like QUALITATIVE RESEARCH, is prone to subjective interpretation and comparatively little is known about its accuracy – the RELIABILITY

and VALIDITY of the technique (Morrison, Coleman, and Preston, 1995).

Bibliography

Morrison, L. J., Coleman, A. M., and Preston, C. C. (1995). Mystery customer research: Cognitive processes affecting accuracy. *Journal of the Market Research Society*, 37, 4 (October).

N

natural environment

Dominic Wilson

The natural environment is one of the elements of the MARKETING ENVIRONMENT. This aspect is concerned with ecological issues such as trends in the availability of raw materials and energy, and increasing measures to protect the natural environment.

See also *environmental analysis*

needs

see CONSUMER NEEDS AND MOTIVES

negotiation

Dominic Wilson

It has been argued that customer/supplier negotiations have traditionally tended to be part of a "zero sum game" and that an advantage for one side (e.g., a discount) was "won" through a disadvantage for the other (Dion and Banting, 1988). This is, of course, an oversimplified view of the complex field of customer/supplier negotiations and there would have been many exceptions to this exaggeratedly aggressive picture of negotiation. Nevertheless, this image seems to have had a powerful influence on the sales negotiation literature, much of which has focused on techniques for manipulating customers into sales agreements which, by definition, they would otherwise have negotiated further or even declined.

A more sophisticated view of marketing negotiation now prevails whereby "win-win" situations are sought in which both supplier and customer gain from negotiation. An example of this mutually beneficial approach is the idea of long-term customer/supplier partnerships, where commitment and TRUST on both sides replace the traditional image of suspicion and hostility.

In reality, different circumstances and personnel will require different negotiating styles, and this has always been the case. The fundamental principle remains that effective negotiation depends not just on skill and techniques, but on understanding the position of all parties involved – a principle that lies at the heart of marketing more generally.

Bibliography

Carlisle, J. and Parker, R. (1990). *Beyond Negotiation*. Chichester: John Wiley.

Dion, P. A. and Banting, P. M. (1988). Industrial supplier–buyer negotiations. *Industrial Marketing Management*, **17**, 1 (February), 43–8.

Fisher, R. and Brown, S. (1988). *Getting Together: Building a Relationship that Gets to Yes*. Boston: Houghton Mifflin.

Lancaster, G. and Jobber, D. (1985). *Sales Technique and Management*. London: Pitman.

Lidstone, J. B. J. (1991). *Manual of Sales Negotiation*. Aldershot: Gower.

McCall, I. and Cousins, J. (1990). *Communication Problem Solving*. Chichester: John Wiley, ch. 6, pp. 89–115.

net margin

Dominic Wilson

Net margin (generally expressed as a percentage) refers to the excess of sales revenues over cumulative costs, after subtracting fixed costs but before taking account of any extraordinary, exceptional, or non-product-related issues.

See also *margin*

network

Judy Zolkiewski

In business-to-business (organizational) markets (*see* BUSINESS-TO-BUSINESS MARKETING; ORGANIZATIONAL MARKETING), emphasis has moved away from a study of single buying units in an organization, where the focus of marketing managers is on the MARKETING MIX, toward a realization that both sides of the buyer/seller interaction need to be considered when trying to understand the dynamics of a market (Håkansson, 1982; Ford, 2002). The study of simple dyadic relationships has developed into studies of an array or portfolio of relationships. Central to this approach has been the recognition of the importance of networks of relationships. It is now readily acknowledged that businesses do not exist in isolation from the other businesses in the same field and that a complex network of relationships and interdependencies exists in a market (Håkansson and Snehota, 1989, 1995; Axelsson and Easton, 1992; Möller and Wilson, 1995; Ford, 2002). Håkansson and Snehota (1989) also suggest that the relationships which an organization has are one of the most valuable (if not the most valuable) resources that an organization possesses. They also note that a firm collects a number of invisible assets from its external relationships, such as knowledge, reputation, and status. Thus, to understand the reality of marketing and purchasing, we need to, at the very least, recognize network positions and effects on simple dyadic relationships.

In the context of business relationships network theory is commonly described as either the industrial network paradigm (Easton and Håkansson, 1996) or ARA (actor resource activity) theory (Håkansson and Johanson, 1992; Håkansson and Snehota, 1995). Here a network is viewed as a set of interactive relationships between firms (actors) surrounding the exchange of a set of goods and/or services.

Networks are both stable and changing, with transactions tending to take place within the framework of long-term relationships, while those relationships are continually changing (perhaps because of competitive activity or partners in the relationship attempting to develop, change, maintain, or even disrupt the relationship) (Johanson and Mattsson, 1988). It should also be noted that both formal and informal cooperation strategies exist within networks and that large numbers of informal cooperation strategies are often in place (Håkansson and Johanson, 1988). Håkansson and Johanson also note that the development of a network is influenced both by its power structure (related to direct and indirect control of resources) and by its interest structure (a combination of the conflicting and common interests of the actors).

Building upon the INTERACTION APPROACH, Håkansson and Johanson (1992) proposed a model of industrial networks, which they believe provides the basis for a study of stability and development in industry and of the actors involved in the process. The model comprises three classes of variables: actors, resources and activities, with *actors* performing *activities* and/or controlling *resources*, the activities being the processes by which activities are changed and resources being the means used by actors to perform activities.

Connected activity links, *activity chains*, are one mechanism for describing a network. Once the activity links have been understood, Håkansson and Snehota (1995) suggest that it is necessary to understand how the relationship between two companies impacts upon the way they utilize resources – how are their resources tied together, and which resources are involved? (Resources include personnel, process plant, other equipment, knowledge, etc.; i.e., they are both tangible and intangible.) They point out that relationships are not just a means of access to resources; they also involve the combination of those resources. They suggest that by looking at the resource ties between the different actors in a network, a resource constellation can be seen, which can be both a valuable asset and a constraining factor. Actor bonds are also an important element in the network and are studied from the perspective of social networks (especially from an organizational sociology perspective).

Håkansson and Snehota (1995) suggest that bonds develop between the organizations (actors) involved in a relationship and that these bonds affect the way that the parties involved view themselves. They also impact upon the perceived identities of the individual actors. For instance, being seen as a "partner" to a powerful or technologically advanced firm has an impact on how other organizations view the actors involved. It is recognized that the bonds between organizations involve the bonds between the individuals in those organizations, but they are not simply a sum of those individual personal relationships.

There is an ongoing debate about the utility of the network concept in strategic management; this includes a vociferous debate about whether or not networks can be managed and, if so, how they can be managed. However, one aspect of network theory that should be recognized as making a useful input to strategic thinking is the concept of network position. Johanson and Mattsson (1988) identify both a micro and a macro position within the overall concept of network position, where the micro position refers to an actor's relationship with another specific individual actor in the network, and the macro position refers to an actor's relations with the whole network (or a specific net within it). Johanson and Mattsson (1992) further develop the concept of position and point out that position provides a means for conceptualizing how individual actors are related to (or embedded in) the environment.

The relationship between strategy models (e.g., Porter, 1979) and the perspective given by the study of networks has been considered by Axelsson (1992). He suggests that there is a dominant perspective in the literature in which the environment dominates, is faceless, and is totally competitive. He believes that networks are an alternative emerging perspective, in which emphasis is placed upon how organizations are embedded in their environment. Additionally, he proposes that networks should be viewed as emergent and cumulative and that it should be recognized that they look different to all actors and for all situations – they are not fixed and actors do not have common goals. He also points out that all relationships between firms are both competitive and cooperative and

it is meaningless to try to reduce them simply to positive or negative relationships. The notion of the tension between competition and cooperation within networks is providing a rich stream of research (see, e.g., Bengtsson and Kock, 2000). In terms of strategy, Axelsson (1992) makes two important points. Firstly, he suggests that by viewing the network creatively, new opportunities can be seen because it will be apparent which actors could be mobilized for different strategies. Secondly, he believes that each step/move should be seen as part of the overall strategic pattern.

Another contentious issue is whether or not networks can be managed. Campbell and Wilson (1996) reflect on the difficulty of this, suggesting that most managers take adversarial standpoints and still view firms as discrete entities. They believe that, at best, such managers may concentrate on developing one or two dyadic relationships, which they perceive will give them a COMPETITIVE ADVANTAGE. They do see some organizations making a success out of managing from a network perspective, and cite the international retailer IKEA as an example of this.

Nonetheless, it is essential to recognize that there are different types of network, even within the same organization, and that different management skills will be needed for each.

With respect to the above debate, the term "network" should not be confused with network marketing, which is closely related to pyramid selling or multilevel marketing schemes (see, e.g., Croft and Woodruffe, 1996). Nor should it be confused with the discussion about governance systems, e.g., the dichotomy between hierarchy and market (Williamson, 1975), bureaucracies and clans (Ouchi, 1980), and hierarchy, market, and network (Thorelli, 1986), which is outside the scope of this discussion. It should also be noted that the study of networks is not limited to marketing and there is an overlap with many other disciplines, such as sociology, institutional economics, and inter-organizational theory.

Bibliography

Axelsson, B. (1992). Corporate strategy models and networks: Diverging perspectives. In B. Axelsson and G. Easton (eds.), *Industrial Networks: A New View of Reality*. London: Routledge.

Axelsson, B. and Easton, G. (eds.) (1992). *Industrial Networks: A New View of Reality*. London: Routledge.

Bengtsson, M. and Kock, S. (2000). Coopetition in business networks to cooperate and compete simultaneously. *Industrial Marketing Management*, **29**, 411–26.

Campbell, A. J. and Wilson, D. T. (1996). Managed networks: Creating strategic advantage. In D. Iacobucci (ed.), *Networks in Marketing*. Thousand Oaks, CA: Sage.

Croft, R. and Woodruffe, H. (1996). Network marketing: The ultimate in international distribution? *Journal of Marketing Management*, **12**, 201–14.

Easton, G. and Håkansson, H. (1996). Markets as networks: Editorial introduction. *International Journal of Research in Marketing*, **13** (5), 407–13.

Ford, D. (ed.) (2002). *Understanding Business Marketing and Purchasing*, 3rd edn. London: Thomson Learning.

Håkansson, H. and Johanson, J. (1988). Formal and informal cooperation strategies in international industrial networks. Reprinted in David Ford (ed.) (1990). *Understanding Business Markets*. San Diego, CA: Academic Press.

Håkansson, H. and Johanson, J. (1992). A model of industrial networks. In B. Axelsson and G. Easton (eds.), *Industrial Networks: A New View of Reality*. London: Routledge.

Håkansson, H. and Snehota, I. (1989). No business is an island: The network concept of business strategy. Reprinted in David Ford (ed.) (1990). *Understanding Business Markets*. San Diego, CA: Academic Press.

Håkansson, H. and Snehota, I. (eds.) (1995). *Developing Relationships in Business Networks*. London: Routledge.

Johanson, J. and Mattsson, L.-G. (1988). Internationalization in industrial systems: A network approach. Reprinted in David Ford (ed.) (1990). *Understanding Business Markets*. San Diego, CA: Academic Press.

Johanson, J. and Mattsson, L.-G. (1992). Network positions and strategic action: An analytical framework. In B. Axelsson and G. Easton (eds.), *Industrial Networks: A New View of Reality*. London: Routledge.

Möller, K. and Wilson, D. T. (eds.) (1995). *Business Marketing: An Interaction and Network Perspective*. Boston: Kluwer.

Ouchi, W. G. (1980). Markets, bureaucracies, and clans. *Administrative Science Quarterly*, **25**, 129–41.

Porter, M. E. (1979). How competitive forces shape strategy. Reprinted in Dale Littler and Dominic Wilson (eds.) (1995). *Marketing Strategy*. Oxford: Butterworth-Heinemann.

Thorelli, H. B. (1986). Networks: Between markets and hierarchies. *Strategic Management Journal*, **7**, 37–51.

Williamson, O. E. (1975). *Markets and Hierarchies: Analysis and Antitrust Implications*. New York: Free Press.

new product development

Margaret Bruce and Liz Barnes

New product development, or NPD, "is the process that transforms technical ideas or market needs and opportunities into a new product that is launched onto the market" (Walsh et al., 1992: 16). New products can make a profound contribution to competitiveness and this is particularly acute in an era of accelerating technological change, general shortening of the PRODUCT LIFE CYCLE, and increasingly intense competition. Fox et al. (1988) identify key drivers for new product development as being the market, technology, process, speed to market, learning, and cost.

The most common representation of the NPD process is as a series of decision stages or activities (Kotler, 2003). Cooper and Kleinschmidt (1986) identify 13 stages of the NPD:

1 screening of new product ideas;
2 preliminary market assessment;
3 preliminary technical assessment;
4 detailed market study/market research;
5 business/financial analysis;
6 physical product development;
7 in-house product testing;
8 customer tests of product;
9 test market/trial sell;
10 trial production;
11 pre-commercialization business activities;
12 production start-up; and
13 market launch.

However, the traditional sequential model of NPD has been criticized for ignoring the interactions that occur between the stages and the interactions between different departments as well as with external agencies, such as CUSTOMERS and SUPPLIERS (Hart, 1995). The uncertainties of NPD are recognized and relate to both market uncertainties and technological uncertainties (*see* UNCERTAINTY). The more radical the NPD, the greater the difficulty in making ex ante assessments of the technical and market opportunities. A considerable amount of research has been devoted to ways to improve the likelihood of new product success. However, there is little agreement as to what constitutes "success," and various indicators have been used, such as different financial measures and different units of analysis, which means that direct comparison of the results of separate studies is not feasible. Nonetheless, some themes have emerged from the different studies that appear to have some bearing on the positive outcome of NPD. These include people factors, such as commitment of senior managers (Maidique and Zirger, 1984); organizational factors, e.g., effective interfunctional cooperation (Pinto and Pinto, 1990); and operational factors, such as the use of market research (Johne and Snelson, 1988). MARKETING has been identified as having a significant role. Rothwell (1977) points to the role of marketing and publicity and of understanding "user needs," and Cooper (1994) notes the value of having a "strong market orientation and customer focus." The constant interaction of R&D, design, production, and marketing from the very early stages of NPD to market launch have been associated with success (e.g., Cooper and Kleinschmidt, 1986). The presence of a PRODUCT CHAMPION has also been acknowledged as a "success" factor. Product development is not always about new products – product modifications, extensions, and style change are also aspects of product development (see PRODUCT MODIFICATION).

To devise, produce, and implement new products and modifications to existing products entails input from different functions, notably marketing, R&D, and production. Their input has to be integrated to insure that products are made that correspond with customer requirements and are made economically and without time delays. Different approaches to the management of product development activities have been identified. "Over the wall" refers to a functionally divided organization wherein product ideas are continually passed back and forth between functions, so that marketing undertakes some development work, then passes this onto R&D, which carries out more development and then passes the ideas back to marketing, and so on. This process can mean that the idea stays in development for a long time. A different approach is that of the "rugby scrum" whereby product development teams are formed with representatives from each function, all of which make an ongoing contribution to the product's development. This organizational approach can

facilitate a quicker time to market than the "over the wall" approach (Walsh et al., 1992).

Different functions may not communicate easily with one another and the interface between R&D and marketing, in particular, has received attention (Gupta, Raj, and Wileman, 1995). A recent study found that effective interface between marketing and design was likely to occur in organizations with a culture of openness, close location of marketing and DESIGN functions, and a multidisciplinary team approach to product development (Davies-Cooper and Jones, 1995). Computer-aided design (CAD), which provides 3D modeling of new product concepts, is used frequently in NPD to improve communication between functions and also in CONCEPT TESTING. Increasingly, with the complexity of INNOVATION, multifunctional teams are needed to pool knowledge and transfer skills. These teams may be formed from collaboration between companies, and collaboration can help to share costs and risks of innovation. Virtual teams can be formed to develop innovations. Information technologies (e.g., CAD) can assist the development of virtual teams, provide access to relevant data and specialized knowledge, and overcome the need for mobility of qualified employees (Prasad and Akhilesh, 2000; Wong and Burton, 2000).

Bibliography

Cooper, R. G. (1994). New products: The factors that drive success. *International Marketing Review*, **11** (1), 60–77.

Cooper, R. G. and Kleinschmidt, E. J. (1986). An investigation into the new product process: Steps, deficiencies and impact. *Journal of Product Innovation Management*, **3** (1), 71–85.

Davies-Cooper, R. and Jones, T. (1995). The interfaces between design and other key functions in product development. In M. Bruce and W. Biemans (eds.), *Product Development: Meeting the Challenge of the Design–Marketing Interface*. Chichester: John Wiley.

Fox, J., Gann, R., Shur, A., von Glahn, L., and Zaas, B. (1988). Process uncertainty: A new dimension for new product development. *Engineering Management Journal*, **10** (3), 19–27.

Gupta, A. K., Raj, S. P., and Wileman, D. (1985). R&D and marketing dialogue in high-tech firms. *Industrial Marketing Management*, **14**, 289.

Hart, S. (1995). Where we've been and where we're going in new product development research. In M. Bruce and

W. Biemans (eds.), *Product Development: Meeting the Challenge of the Design–Marketing Interface*. Chichester: John Wiley, ch. 1.

Johne, F. A. and Snelson, P. (1988). Marketing's role in successful product development. *Journal of Marketing Management*, 3 (3), 256–68.

Kotler, P. (2003). *Marketing Management: Analysis, Planning, Implementation and Control*, 11th edn. Englewood Cliffs, NJ: Prentice-Hall.

Maidique, M. A. and Zirger, B. J. (1984). A study of success and failure in product innovation: The case of the US electronics industry. *IEEE Transactions on Engineering Management*, **EM-31**, 4 (November), 192–203.

Pinto, M. B. and Pinto, J. K. (1990). Project team communication and cross-functional co-operation in new program development. *Journal of Product Innovation Management*, 7, 200–12.

Prasad, K. and Akhilesh, K. B. (2000). Global virtual teams: What impacts their design and performance? *Team Performance Management*, 8 (6), 102–12.

Rothwell, R. (1977). The characteristics of successful innovations and technically progressive firms (with some comments on innovation research). *R&D Management*, 7 (3), 191–206.

Walsh, V., Roy, R., Bruce, M., and Potter, S. (1992). *Winning by Design: Technology, Product Design and International Competitiveness*. Oxford: Blackwell, chs. 1, 5.

Wong, S. and Burton, R. M. (2000). Virtual teams: What are their characteristics and impact on team performance? *Computational and Mathematical Organizational Theory*, 6 (4), 339–60.

new task

Dominic Wilson

Robinson, Faris, and Wind (1967) suggest a division of organizational buying into three categories: new task, MODIFIED REBUY, and STRAIGHT REBUY. Of these categories, new task is the most complex and refers to those occasions when it is necessary to identify new sources for goods or services. This may be because a previous source is no longer satisfactory, or because the requirement itself is new. In principle all stages of the PURCHASING PROCESS will be involved in new task buying, but in practice this will depend on the scale and significance of the purchase in question. Thus, new task purchasing in the defense sector (e.g., for an aircraft carrier) might take years, whereas new

task purchasing for ballpoint pens (e.g., in a bank) might be done very quickly.

See also *organizational buying behavior*

Bibliography

Robinson, P. T., Faris, C. W., and Wind, Y. (1967). *Industrial Buying and Creative Marketing*. Boston: Allyn and Bacon.

newspapers

David Yorke

Newspapers are a communications medium (*see* COMMUNICATIONS MIX), usually using print, but they are also being developed via the Internet. Newspapers can be local, regional, national, or international in terms of readers and distribution, and are usually published daily or weekly. Many newspapers are distributed free at travel to work locations (e.g., at railway stations) or to homes. They are a major ADVERTISING medium, the main advantages for which are mass regular coverage of major target groups (*see* TARGET MARKET); geographic flexibility through regional editions; POSITIONING opportunities; and very short lead times. However, some newspapers have low regional flexibility and limited opportunities for color, which is expensive, and presentation (i.e., creative scope), poor reproduction quality, a short life, and are less intrusive than other media, e.g., TELEVISION. Further, measurement of newspaper "readership" as opposed to "the number of copies sold" is difficult.

noise

David Yorke

Noise occurs when the recipient of a message devises a meaning different from that intended by the communicator. It has a variety of sources and can affect any or all parts of the communications process. A source codes a message into signs (verbal, pictorial, colors) to convey the meaning of the MESSAGE it wishes to communicate. The recipient decodes the coded message. Noise can be a physical disturbance in the medium: faulty printing, interruption of the personal salesperson during presentation of the sales message, distraction while watching or reading the advertisement. Noise can also arise because the source employs signs that are unfamiliar to the receiver, or because for various reasons the recipient screens out the message or perceives the message differently from the sender. In general, the recipient is faced with many competing marketing and other forms of communications and can only give limited, if any, attention to many of these.

See also *consumer perceptions; marketing communications; selective exposure*

Bibliography

Schramm, W. (1971). How communication works. In W. Schramm and D. F. Roberts (eds.), *The Process and Effects of Mass Communication*. Urbana: University of Illinois Press.

non-price factors

Margaret Bruce and Liz Barnes

Products are bought for a variety of reasons relating to cost, convenience, BRAND LOY-ALTY, and quality of the alternatives. Products compete on the basis of price and non-price factors. The non-price factors are those related to the quality and DESIGN of a product, such as reliability, performance, appearance, safety, and maintenance ("intrinsic" non-price factors), and those related to the quality of the service offered by the manufacturer or supplier, such as delivery time, after-sales service, and availability of spare parts ("associative" non-price factors) (Saviotti et al., 1980). Non-price factors such as the environmental impact of the product can influence consumers. Price factors include financial arrangements for purchase or hire, depreciation, running costs, servicing and parts costs as well as the sales price after DISCOUNT. If two products of similar quality are on sale for different prices, the theory is that a rational purchaser will choose the cheaper product. However, this choice will be influenced by brand loyalty, company IMAGE, and ADVERTISING, which affect the consumer's perception of quality and price.

More recently, non-price advantage has been achieved through providing additional convenience or SERVICE QUALITY; for example, efficiencies in the supply chain that lead to new products becoming available quickly can lead to non-price advantage. Spanish retailer Zara has gained significant non-price advantage through its ability to respond quickly to changing trends in fashion (Bruce and Hines, 2002). Several studies have investigated purchasers' decisions to assess the relative importance of price and non-price factors. It is clear that non-price factors affect purchase decisions, but these vary from market to market. Rothwell's (1981) study of agricultural machinery, for example, showed that even where British products were cheaper, farmers were in favor of more expensive, often imported, products on grounds of superior reliability and technical features. Moody (1984) indicated in his study of medical equipment that technical, aesthetic, and ergonomic features were all reasons for doctors' preferences when choosing such products. Non-price advantage is regarded as being increasingly important for COMPETITIVE STRATEGY in the future (Eustace, 2003).

See also *competitive advantage; product differentiation*

Bibliography

Bruce, M. and Hines, T. (2002). *Fashion Marketing: Contemporary Issues*. Oxford: Butterworth-Heinemann.
Eustace, C. (2003). A knew perspective on the knowledge value chain. *Journal of Intellectual Capital*, 4 (4), 588–96.
Moody, S. (1984). The role of industrial design in the development of new science-based production. In R. Langdon (ed.), *Design Policy, vol. 2: Design and Industry*. London: Design Council.
Rothwell, R. (1981). Non-price factors in the export competitiveness of agricultural engineering goods. *Research Policy*, 10, 260.
Saviotti, P., Coombs, R., Gibbons, M., and Stubbs, P. (1980). *Technology and Competitiveness in the Tractor Industry*. A Report of the Department of Industry. Department of Science and Technology Policy, University of Manchester, UK.
Walsh, V., Roy, R., Bruce, M., and Potter, S. (1992). *Winning by Design: Technology, Product Design and International Competitiveness*. Oxford: Blackwell, ch. 2, pp. 64–8.

not-for-profit marketing

Barbara R. Lewis

Not-for-profit marketing is part of "non-business" marketing (together with SOCIAL MARKETING), which relates to marketing activities conducted by individuals and organizations to achieve some goal other than ordinary business goals of PROFIT, MARKET SHARE, or return on investment. Marketing concepts and techniques can be applied to not-for-profit organizations in both the public and private sectors, which include, for example, government agencies, healthcare organizations, educational institutions, religious groups, charities, political parties, and the performing arts.

For example, universities facing increasing costs may use marketing to compete for both students and funds, e.g., defining markets better, improving their communication and promotion, and responding to needs of students and other publics. One of the main characteristics of many not-for-profit organizations is that their support does not (mainly) come directly from those who receive the benefits that the organization produces, e.g., funding for students' education comes from student fees, government sources, endowments, industry sponsorship, and research grant awarding bodies.

Bibliography

Blois, K. J. (1999). Marketing for non-profit organizations. In M. J. Baker (ed.), *The Marketing Book*, 4th edn. London: Heinemann.

observation

Michael Greatorex

Observation is a method of collecting data on a topic of interest by watching and recording behavior, actions, and facts. Informal, unstructured observation is an everyday means of collecting marketing information. However, planned observation is likely to produce better information than casual observation. Observation can in fact be structured or unstructured, with disguised or undisguised observers, in a natural or a contrived setting, using human and/or electronic/mechanical observers.

Observation is used instead of, or in conjunction with, surveys (*see* SURVEY RESEARCH) involving interviews utilizing questionnaires or DEPTH INTERVIEWS. Observation is less suitable than interview techniques for measuring ATTITUDES, needs, motivations (*see* CONSUMER NEEDS AND MOTIVES), opinions, etc., except where the subjects being studied are unable to communicate verbally, e.g., children and animals. Observation is unsuitable for studying events that occur over a long period of time or that are infrequent or unpredictable when an excessive amount of time and money may be required to carry out the research. Observation is suitable for traffic counts, for packaging experiments, for retail audits, etc., where data are more economically gathered through observation than through interviews. Sometimes data are collected by observation and through questionnaires and the results compared.

Structured observation is used when a problem has been defined precisely enough for there to be a specification of the behavior and actions to be studied and the ways in which the actions will be coded and recorded. Unstructured observation is used in exploratory research where the

problem has not been identified and where the observer has less guidance about what to note and record. Structured observation implies prior knowledge of the subject under study, of hypotheses to be tested (*see* HYPOTHESIS TESTING), or inferences to be made. For this latter reason, trained human observers may be preferred to mechanical observers as a human observer can make such inferences in a way that a machine cannot. Perversely, this is a potential weakness of the method, relying as it does on the subjective and possibly biased judgment of the observer.

In disguised observations the participants do not know that they are being observed. Disguised observations are used in order to overcome the tendency for participants to change their behavior if they know that they are being watched. MYSTERY SHOPPING, where observers take on the role of store or bank customers in order to assess the level of service offered by sales staff, is one example of disguised observation. Other examples of disguised observation include the use of two-way mirrors or hidden cameras. Undisguised observations include the measurement of TELEVISION audiences based on a sample of households in which on-set meters record when a television set is in use and to which channel it is tuned.

Sometimes it is possible to study behavior in natural settings. Counting how many people turn right and how many turn left at the top of an escalator in a department store can be done in a natural setting. However, the researcher often wants to control for intervening variables by researching in a laboratory, which is obviously an unnatural setting. As well as controlling intervening variables, laboratory research allows stimuli to be invoked and response measured in situations where occurrences of the stimulating event in real life might be uncommon. This is one way in which laboratory research can be a quick way of obtaining data. Laboratory research also permits easier use of electronic and mechanical devices to record behavior.

Among the electronic and mechanical devices that are used to record behavior are those that record physiological changes in participants when they are subject to stimuli. For example, the galvanometer is used to measure the emotional arousal of subjects exposed to ADVERTISING copy by measuring the changes in electrical resistance caused by the sweating that is brought on by emotional arousal. The eye camera records eye movements of subjects looking at newspaper advertisements (see NEWSPAPERS). Other electronic/mechanical devices include the on-set meters used to measure television audiences and the scanners that are used by panels of shoppers to read the bar codes on their purchases.

Bibliography

Malhotra, N. K. and Birks, D. F. (2000). *Marketing Research: An Applied Orientation*. Harlow: Prentice-Hall, chs. 7–8.

off the page

David Yorke

Off the page is a technique for communication or selling using catalogues (either print or electronic) to which a buyer/customer responds directly in person, in writing, or by telecommunication (see DIRECT MARKETING; INBOUND COMMUNICATIONS). The number of responses may be used as a prima facie measure of the cost effectiveness of the activity, and the names of respondents may be entered onto a DATABASE in order to build a profile of likely future buyers/customers for specific products or services who then may be targeted more precisely.

offering

Dale Littler

Marketing has traditionally differentiated between products and services (see SERVICE CHARACTERISTICS). The PRODUCT has been viewed as consisting of a bundle of tangible and intangible attributes and as having several layers, such as: the core, consisting of the essential benefit(s) to the customer (e.g., providing a convenient, cheap, always available portable means of two-way communication); the tangible product, including the color, taste, DESIGN, BRAND name, and PACKAGING; and the augmented product, such as the back-up service, warranty, and delivery. The "product," then, is a set of benefits, many of which can be seen as involving service, offered to the customer. Firms can be viewed as making an offering of a package of values to customers, rather than selling a pure service or physical product. The customer is, however, not a passive receptor but rather develops his/her own perceptions of the values of the offering (see CONSUMER PERCEPTIONS). In consumer markets the product may be highly symbolic (see SYMBOLIC CONSUMPTION), both to the consumer who employs it as a means, conscious or otherwise, of reflecting what he or she is, i.e., his/her sense of identity (Belk, 1988), and to his/her peers who themselves develop their own meanings of what the product represents about the individual consuming or using it. In some cases, especially in organizational markets, firms will act as "problem solvers" and provide complete systems (the design, development, installation, and implementation of, for example, management information systems).

See also *systems marketing*

Bibliography

Belk, R. W. (1988). Possessions and the extended self. *Journal of Consumer Research*, 15 (September), 139–68.

one-step flow model

Dale Littler

The one-step flow model of communications presents mass communications (see MASS MEDIA), mainly ADVERTISING, as acting directly on each member of the target audience. This model, often called the "hypodermic needle" model of communications (the communication passing directly to individual members of the audience), contrasts markedly with the TWO-STEP FLOW MODEL, which depicts communications as being filtered through intermediaries called opinion leaders (see INTERPERSONAL COMMUNICATIONS). Many individuals are likely to receive information from mass communications, although SELECTIVE EXPOSURE, selective perception (see CONSUMER PERCEPTIONS), and SELECTIVE RETENTION will act as filters. Mass communications may create AWARENESS and even INTEREST, but then further information may be sought or received through interpersonal channels, such as from opinion leaders. In general, all have the potential to pass on information via word-of-mouth (see WORD-OF-MOUTH COMMUNICATIONS), and this may augment impersonal communications (see INDIRECT COMMUNICATIONS) or act to contradict the message they convey.

online consumption

Andrew Newman

Online consumption is the act of purchasing or consuming via a telephone line, which usually necessitates connection to the Internet and the use of a personal computer or digital television and web browser. Some types of online purchasing take place within an intranet or internal network, which is not directly connected to the worldwide web. In general, this manner of consumption differs significantly from the experience created by the physical retail store, which is the classical and more traditional way of buying products and services. The key differences stem from the remote nature of the exchange and interaction that characterizes this type of consumption. Online consumption may therefore not provide the level of emotional gratification associated with conventional store shopping. For example, many of the social and physical dimensions of shopping such as human contact (sales staff) and store ATMOSPHERICS are not available to the remote purchaser. Hence, there may be a tendency for consumers globally to use Internet shopping for convenience or utilitarian items in product areas such as grocery and home entertainment.

Changing social and economic factors are likely to play an important part in the decision of consumers to make more frequent use of online purchasing, and for a wider variety of goods and services. In the financial services sector (see FINANCIAL SERVICES MARKETING; FINANCIAL SERVICES RETAILING), for example, insurance companies and banks frequently offer discounts to encourage the take-up of online purchasing. Young up-and-coming consumers are also more likely to buy online as they have grown up with the technology, mindset, and values that embrace this type of shopping medium (Comor, 2000). Most shoppers online tend to be disproportionately privileged and better educated (Fischer, Bristor, and Gainer, 1996). More recently in the UK, this picture appears to be changing with the advent of government policies, mainly to do with Internet access, which help to offset social exclusion.

See also *electronic commerce*

Bibliography

Comor, E. (2000). Household consumption on the Internet: Income, time and institutional contradictions. *Journal of Economic Issues*, 34 (1), 105–16.
Fischer, E., Bristor, J., and Gainer, B. (1996). Creating or escaping community? An exploratory study of Internet consumers' behaviors. *Advances in Consumer Research*, 23, 178–82.

opinion leaders

see INTERPERSONAL COMMUNICATIONS; WORD-OF-MOUTH COMMUNICATIONS

opportunities

see SWOT ANALYSIS

organizational buying behavior

Judy Zolkiewski and Gillian C. Hopkinson

Organizational buying behavior is, in its simplest terms, the process of how companies or organizations buy goods and services. Understanding organizational buying behavior is central to developing an effective BUSINESS-TO-BUSINESS MARKETING strategy (Turnbull, 1999). However, this understanding can be difficult to achieve because organizational buying behavior is often a complex, dynamic, and intricate process involving a number of phases, a number of individuals, a number of departments, and multiple objectives (Johnston and Lewin, 1996).

Organizations buy a wide range of goods and services that they use as inputs to their own products or as support for their operations, or buy for resale. One of the significant changes in the buying process over the last 20 years has been an increasing professionalism within business-to-business buying, and this raises additional challenges for the business-to-business marketer.

A plethora of models of the organizational buying process has been posited (many of which are reviewed in Turnbull, 1999). The most popular include those of Robinson, Faris, and Wind (1967), Webster and Wind (1972), Sheth (1973), Nielsen (1973), the INTER-ACTION APPROACH (Turnbull and Cunningham, 1981; Håkansson, 1982), Möller (1986), Bunn (1993), and Wilson (1995). Of these models, the Robinson et al. (1967) buy grid model (see PURCHASING PROCESS) is still extensively discussed, especially by American academics, whilst the interaction approach, which considers the relationships involved in the buying process, has attracted much interest outside the US.

The buy grid model includes eight buy phases (identification of need, determination of requirement, specific description of the requirement, search for potential sources, examination of sources, selection of sources, order routine established, and evaluation of performance feedback) and three types of buy class (NEW TASK, MODIFIED REBUY, and STRAIGHT REBUY). Robinson et al. (1967) recognize that the buy phases are used differently or that some phases may even be skipped according to the different buy classes.

Bunn (1993) suggests that many of the earlier models are lacking in supporting empirical evidence. She undertakes an extensive research project from which she develops a taxonomy of

buying decision approaches: casual, routine low priority, simple modified rebuy, judgmental new task, complex modified rebuy, and strategic new task. She argues that these vary according to situational factors (purchase importance, task uncertainty, extensiveness of choice set, and perceived buyer power) and the buying activities undertaken by the buyers (search for information, use of analysis techniques, proactive focus, and procedural control).

The Webster and Wind (1972) model emphasizes the role of the individual in the organizational buying process (and illustrates that the individual's motivation, perception, learning, and experience are all important factors). However, these authors also recognize the importance of the BUYING CENTER and the interaction of the members of the buying center in the decision-making process. They highlight four main areas that influence the buying process:

- the general environment of the firm;
- the organization itself;
- the buying center (interpersonal influences);
- the influence of the individual.

These four levels of influence are often interpreted in a hierarchical fashion, with the general environment of the firm being perceived to have the broadest and most general impact upon organizational buying behavior. Environmental forces are considered to be physical, technological, economic, political, legal, and cultural and are typical of the forces generally recognized as being in the MARKETING ENVIRONMENT.

From the perspective of the early twenty-first century we can see that one of the most pervasive influences on organizational buying behavior from the broader environment is that of technology. The Internet and other associated technological developments can be seen to be changing some of the processes involved in organizational buying, as evidenced, for instance, by the move toward using online auctions and electronic intermediaries, along with trends toward integrated purchasing systems and other forms of e-business (see ELECTRONIC COMMERCE; ELECTRONIC DATA INTERCHANGE). Hutt and Speh (2004) suggest that recent technological changes are resulting in a decline in the importance of the purchasing manager in the purchasing process, along with more intense information searches that are actually taking less time to effect.

Alongside technological developments, the increasing GLOBALIZATION of economic activity can also be recognized to be having an impact upon organizational buying behavior, through the availability of alternatives to the rise of mega-corporations and hypercompetition. Organizational forces include the technology base of the firm, its structure, goals, and task, and the roles within the organization. This would normally include the role of the purchasing department in the firm. Group forces relate to the roles, influence, and interactions of the members in the buying center. Finally, individual forces need to be considered, i.e., the motivations and experiences of the personnel involved in the buying process.

Johnston and Lewin (1996) identify nine constructs that are broadly representative of the earlier models (Robinson et al., 1967; Webster and Wind, 1972; Sheth, 1973; their meta-analysis ignores much of the material published in Europe as it was not presented in journal articles). These constructs are: environmental, organizational, group, participant, purchase, seller, conflict/negotiation, informational, and process or stages.

It can be argued that the above models are problematic because they only describe one side of the buying process, that of the buyer. The interaction approach, for instance, proposes that the interactions of both the buyer and seller need to be taken into account when considering the buying process. These interactions are analyzed by considering:

- the process;
- the participants in that process;
- the environment in which the interaction occurs;
- the atmosphere, which both affects and is affected by the interaction.

Outcomes of the process are seen to be the development of long-term relationships, which are characterized by mutual adaptations involving both parties.

More recently this approach has been developed further to suggest that buying (and sell-

ing) behavior needs to be considered within the whole context of the NETWORK in which the buyer and seller exist. Indeed, the outcome of organizational buying behavior can be seen to culminate in the development of relationships (see RELATIONSHIP MARKETING) rather than simply in a series of transactions. The suggestion, then, is that the strategic management of such firms should focus upon the management of these strategic relationships. The outcomes of such strategies can be seen to include the development of preferred supplier agreements (see SUPPLIERS), partnerships, and even INTERNATIONAL STRATEGIC ALLIANCES. It also has to be remembered that the personnel and organizations involved in these relationships start to develop complex ties, so that consideration has to be given to the social nature of such relationships (Ford, Håkansson, and Johanson, 1986).

Another major aspect of debate surrounding organizational buying behavior is the extent to which it differs from (or is similar to) CONSUMER BUYER BEHAVIOR. The differences in buying behavior are believed to stem from differences in market structure, the centrality and importance of service, the intricate and lengthy purchasing process, the relative significance of environmental factors, differences in DEMAND structure (e.g., DERIVED DEMAND), the impact of NON-PRICE FACTORS (e.g., technical support and speed of delivery), and differences in the MARKETING MIX. Similarities are derived from the fact that both companies and consumers are affected by their previous experiences, need reassurance when the purchase is difficult or complex, make simple repetitive purchases with little or no evaluation, and will make purchases where the main concern is to minimize the time and effort involved (Wilson, 1999; Ford, 2002).

Bibliography

Bunn, M. D. (1993). Taxonomy of buying decision approaches. *Journal of Marketing*, 57 (1), 38–56.

Ford, D. (2002). *The Business Marketing Course*. Chichester: John Wiley.

Ford, D., Håkansson, H., and Johanson, J. (1986). How do companies interact? In D. Ford (ed.) (1997). *Understanding Business Markets: Interaction, Relationships and Networks*, 2nd edn. London: Dryden Press.

Håkansson, H. (ed.) (1982). *International Marketing and Purchasing of Industrial Goods: An Interaction Approach.* Chichester: John Wiley.

Hutt, M. D. and Speh, T. W. (2004). *Business Marketing Management*, 8th edn. Mason, OH: South-Western Thomson.

Johnston, W. J. and Lewin, J. E. (1996). Organizational buying behavior: Toward an integrative framework. *Journal of Business Research*, 35, 1–15.

Möller, K. E. K. (1986). Buying behavior of industrial components: Inductive approach for descriptive model building. In P. W. Turnbull and S. J. Paliwoda (eds.), *Research in International Marketing*. London: Croom Helm.

Nielsen, O. (1973). Models of industrial buyer behavior. Paper presented at the Marketing Workshop, International Institute of Management, Berlin (European Marketing Education Association, May). Cited in Roy W. Hill and Terry J. Hillier (1977). *Organizational Buying Behavior*. London: Macmillan.

Robinson, P. T., Faris, C. W., and Wind, Y. (1967). *Industrial Buying and Creative Marketing*. Boston: Allyn and Bacon.

Sheth, J. N. (1973). A model of industrial buying behavior. *Journal of Marketing*, 37 (4), 50–6.

Turnbull, P. W. (1999). Business-to-business marketing: Organizational buying behavior, relationships and networks. In Michael J. Baker (ed.), *The Marketing Book*, 4th edn. Oxford: Butterworth-Heinemann.

Turnbull, P. W. and Cunningham, M. T. (1981). *International Marketing and Purchasing: A Survey Among Marketing and Purchasing Executives in Five European Countries*. London: Macmillan.

Webster, F. E., Jr. and Wind, Y. (1972). *Organizational Buying Behavior*. Englewood Cliffs, NJ: Prentice-Hall.

Wilson, D. T. (1995). An integrated model of buyer–seller relationships. *Journal of the Academy of Marketing Science*, 23 (4), 335–45.

Wilson, D. T. (1999). *Organizational Marketing*. London: International Thomson Business Press.

organizational marketing

Dominic Wilson

Organizational marketing can be thought of as the activity of marketing between organizations, as opposed to marketing between organizations and individual customers, usually referred to as CONSUMER MARKETING. However, such a simple clarification masks many problems of interpretation and definition. For example, the term "organization" includes many groups that are not primarily concerned with generating PROFIT, such as charities, political parties, military groups, local societies, hospitals, and so on (*see* NOT-FOR-PROFIT MARKETING).

It is worth highlighting two central issues in organizational marketing that have profound implications for marketing and for understanding organizations more generally. The first concerns organizational objectives, the guiding light of marketing activities. With the increasing realization of how widely marketing can be applied to organizational activities, organizational devices can no longer be thought of in quite such straightforward terms as "profit maximization" or "shareholder asset growth." For example, it is clear that, at least in principle, charities are concerned with altruism, that orchestras have cultural objectives, that armies aim at enforcement, and that government agencies are directed at efficient administration – all rather than generating profits. No doubt many of these objectives are also applicable to conventional business organizations and their constituent subunits. It is important to appreciate this multifaceted and overlapping nature of organizational objectives because this kaleidoscope of objectives provides the direction and momentum for marketing activities.

The second issue is the importance of understanding relationships between organizations as continuous evolving interactions rather than as an episodic, atomistic sequence of encounters where "manipulative suppliers" engage with "suspicious customers" (Han, Wilson, and Dant, 1993). Understanding inter-organizational relationships as continuing interactions is important to understanding not only organizations, but also the competitive and strategic dynamics of markets (Håkansson and Snehota, 1989). While the idea of a collaborative interactive relationship is implicit in the idea of marketing as a mutually advantageous exchange, as Chisnall (1995) points out, marketing (more accurately "selling") in business markets has for too long been presented as an antagonistic zero sum game where the customer's gain is the supplier's loss. This raises many conceptual and practical questions, not least of which is the difficulty of reconciling traditional views of organizational relationships as necessarily competitive with the increasing representation of these relationships as fundamentally mutually dependent and collaborative. Competitive behavior is still fundamental, naturally, at both the organizational and the NETWORK levels, but it is not a sufficient perspective on its own to provide useful insight.

Both these issues are inextricably linked also with the role of the manager as an individual, with personal commitments, career objectives, professional ethics, and limited competence, alongside discretionary power, rather than, as seems to have been assumed in much of the marketing literature, as a strictly rational organizational servant routinely enacting corporate executive policies (Pettigrew, 1975). It could be argued, therefore, that not only is organizational marketing an important aspect of marketing, it has also raised issues with profound implications for a better understanding of marketing and of organizations more generally. In line with these developments in the understanding of the role of marketing, organizational marketing can be seen not simply as the marketing of products and services between organizations but more broadly as the management and development of exchange relationships between organizations.

In many respects, organizational markets are more complex and larger than consumer markets, if only because for every consumer market there are usually several upstream organizational markets manufacturing and supplying the products that emerge from the value-added chain (see VALUE CHAIN) to be marketed to consumers. There are also many large and complex organizational markets providing services where conventional payment may not be involved (e.g., churches, charities, schools, hospitals) or where there may be little or no direct connection with consumers at all (e.g., secret services, space agencies, military forces).

Another important distinguishing feature of organizational markets is the nature of DEMAND. Demand in organizational markets is derived from a combination of many factors, depending on the market in question. For example, in industrial markets demand is derived from the requirements of downstream suppliers of various consumer goods and services. In government markets demand may also be a function of political and legislative commitments, economic circumstances, political priorities,

and lobbying. Forecasting this DERIVED DEMAND is, therefore, highly complex and depends on understanding the needs and circumstances not only of immediate organizational customers, but also of subsequent supplier/customer exchanges right down the value chain to the eventual consumer. Inevitably, many organizations are unable to do much more than respond to the anticipated requirements of their immediate customers. One potentially useful approach to this problem of forecasting demand in organizational markets is to build particularly close relationships with selected customers in various key segments. There can, of course, be many other reasons for building such relationships, but the advantage with respect to FORECASTING problems is that such relationships can provide intimate insights not otherwise available into the competitive position of strategic customers, and thus of their markets and customers more broadly.

Much of the theory discussed above seems most obviously appropriate to the more important occasions of organizational marketing – to NEW TASK purchasing and major accounts, to complex customer requirements, and to intensely competitive and fast-changing markets. However, it should not be forgotten that the vast bulk of organizational marketing is concerned with routine activities in relatively familiar circumstances and with few immediate implications for competitive positions or strategic dynamics. On such occasions the application of the processes and principles discussed above remains relevant, but the practice of organizational marketing is more likely to reflect compromises based on experience, work priorities, perceptual and professional limitations, interpersonal tensions, office politics, career games, personal preoccupations (paying the mortgage, schooling the kids, getting a life) – and on common sense.

See also *relationship marketing*

Bibliography

Chisnall, P. M. (1995). *Strategic Business Marketing*, 3rd edn. Englewood Cliffs, NJ: Prentice-Hall.

Håkansson, H. and Snehota, I. (1989). No business is an island: The network concept of business strategy. *Scandinavian Journal of Management*, 43, 187–200.

Han, S.-L., Wilson, D. T., and Dant, S. P. (1993). Buyer–supplier relationships today. *Industrial Marketing Management*, **224** (November), 331–8.

Pettigrew, A. M. (1975). The industrial purchasing decision as a political process. *European Journal of Marketing*, **5** (February), 4–19.

organizational purchasing

see ORGANIZATIONAL BUYING BEHAVIOR

organizational segmentation

Vincent-Wayne Mitchell

The goal of organizational segmentation is to divide a large organizational market (*see* ORGANIZATIONAL MARKETING) into smaller components that are more homogeneous with respect to product needs. Griffith and Pol (1994) argue that segmenting organizational markets is generally a more complex process than segmenting consumer markets, since organizational products often have multiple applications, organizational customers can vary greatly from one to another, and it is sometimes difficult to decide which product differences are important.

Dibb and Simkin (1994) have complained that the selection of SEGMENTATION VARIABLES can be related to the ease of implementation rather than to how valid the segments are in terms of grouping customers with similar requirements. A survey of the variables that organizational marketers use in segmentation suggests that variables are chosen more for convenience and actionability than for grouping purchasers with similar needs. The survey found that geographic segmentation bases were the most often used – by 88 percent of the sample. PSYCHOGRAPHICS, e.g., purchaser risk perceptions (*see* PERCEIVED RISK), were used by only 50 percent of companies, while the most theoretically sound and meaningful base, that of BENEFIT SEGMENTATION, was used by only 38 percent of companies (Abratt, 1993). Bonoma and Shapiro (1984: 259) argue that: "Clearly a benefits-orientated approach is the more attractive in the theoretical sense, but more difficult for management to implement. . . . Often management and researchers face an interesting 'segmentation tension' between the theoretically desirable and the managerially possible."

While it is acknowledged that any starting point for segmentation should be user requirements in the form of needs and benefits, the discussion here focuses on the additional descriptor variables that are only used in organizational markets. These have been grouped into macro variables, based on organizational characteristics, and micro variables, based on decision-making characteristics.

MACRO VARIABLES

These include standard industrial classification (SIC), organizational size, and geographic location. SIC describes an organization's main type of business, e.g., forestry, and is one of the most common variables used to describe business segments. Although this type of information is quite superficial, it is widely available in a standardized and comprehensive form and allows a firm to assess the potential size of a market segment. When using SIC codes, two cautions must be noted. First, all establishments with the same SIC code do not necessarily engage in the same activities. For example, in the grocery store category, large grocery stores sell more than just grocery items. Second, establishments in a given category do not necessarily account for all, or even a large proportion, of the activity in that category.

Organizational size data in terms of total sales volume or number of employees can easily be obtained and related to an organization's need for some products, e.g., insurance and healthcare plans, which can be modified depending on the number of employees in an organization. However, size can be measured in many ways: total size, size by division, size and number of individual branches, sales value, asset value, other types of activity measure, and number of employees, which can sometimes be related tangentially to purchaser requirements. Dickson (1997) describes two "natural" organizational segmentation variables as being the size of the account and growth potential of the account. The so-called "Pareto effect" suggests that in many businesses approximately 80 percent of turnover will be generated by only 20 percent of customers. If an organization has much of its business with a relatively small number of clients, it cannot help but adopt a RELATION-SHIP MARKETING approach. Such individual relationship segmentation makes consideration of other broader segmentation variables some-what redundant, but not all companies are in a position to adopt this relationship approach.

Geographic location can indicate purchaser needs when the industry itself is dependent upon the geography of the area, for example, coal mining and other natural resource indus-tries. Purchasing practices and expectations of companies may also vary by location, e.g., in Central and Eastern Europe. Convenient though it may be to use simple spatial geography to separate complicated purchasing practice or ex-pectations, the variable used to segment the market in this case should be purchasing prac-tice, not geographic location. Using simple geog-raphy as anything other than a descriptor variable can be problematic if further criteria are not specified. For example, which geo-graphic location of the business should be used: the site of the buying office, where the products are received, or where they are used? As Griffith and Pol (1994) point out, the first is of concern to sales management, the second to LOGISTICS managers, and the third to field service people, installation crews, etc.

Micro Variables

These include choice criteria such as productiv-ity and price. This is akin to benefit segmenta-tion. Decision-making unit (*see* BUYING CENTER) characteristics identify the nature of the individuals within the buying center and the benefits they perceive. Different members within an organization may value different attri-butes and benefits. The type of purchasing structure in organizations can also be important, e.g., centralized purchasing is usually associated with purchasing specialists who become experts in buying a range of products.

See also *market segmentation; positioning*

Bibliography

Abratt, R. (1993). Market segmentation practices of in-dustrial marketers. *Industrial Marketing Management*, 2 (2), 79–84.

Bonoma, T. V. and Shapiro, B. P. (1984). *Segmenting the Industrial Market*. Lexington, MA: D. C. Heath.

Dibb, S. and Simkin, L. (1994). Implementation prob-lems in industrial market segmentation. *Industrial Marketing Management*, 2 (3), 55–63.

Dickson, P. R. (1997). *Marketing Management*, 2nd edn. London: Dryden Press/Harcourt Brace College Pub-lishers.

Dickson, P. R. and Ginter, J. L. (1987). Market segmen-tation, product differentiation and marketing strategy. *Journal of Marketing*, 5 (1), 1–10.

Griffith, R. L. and Pol, L. G. (1994). Segmenting indus-trial markets. *Industrial Marketing Management*, 2 (3), 39–46.

Kotler, P. and Armstrong, G. (2004). *Principles of Marketing*, 10th edn. Upper Saddle River, NJ: Pren-tice-Hall.

original equipment manufacturer

Dominic Wilson

An original equipment manufacturer (often ab-breviated to OEM) is the manufacturer of goods and components that are subsequently sold to be included within the products of a customer. Thus, OEM goods tend to be "invisible" to the eventual customer. An example would be the use of OEM diesel engine components in automo-biles, or OEM microprocessors in washing ma-chines.

outbound communications

David Yorke

Communications in DIRECT MARKETING may be either inbound (*see* INBOUND COMMUNI-CATIONS) or outbound. The former are initi-ated by the buyer/customer as a response to a stimulus received from INDIRECT COMMUNI-CATIONS in the media. Outbound communica-tions are initiated by the supplier organization. The two principal techniques are direct marketing and TELEMARKETING. Each is designed to target members of a specific market segment (*see* MARKET SEGMENTATION) and to communicate directly with them with the inten-tion of obtaining a positive response. Evaluation of the cost effectiveness of each of the techniques may be in terms of the number of positive responses, i.e., the volume, or value of sales ultimately generated.

Bibliography

Roberts, M. L. and Berger, P. D. (1989). *Direct Marketing Management*. Englewood Cliffs, NJ: Prentice-Hall.

outsourcing

Dominic Wilson

This refers to the activity of purchasing goods or services from external sources, as opposed to internal sourcing (either by internal production or by purchasing from a subsidiary of the organization). In practice, the term tends to be used in connection with a purchasing decision to change from an internal source to an external source. For example, an organization may decide that in future it will "outsource" part of its distribution operation by purchasing distribution services from an organization specializing in this field. The advantages of "outsourcing" can include cost reduction (external sources may enjoy scale economies), access to specialist expertise, and greater concentration on an organization's "core competence" (by avoiding "peripheral" operations). The potential disadvantages of outsourcing can include reduced control over the operations involved, and so less flexibility in responding to unexpected developments. It is, therefore, important to take into account both the strategic and the operational implications of outsourcing.

There has been a notable increase in the use of outsourcing since the 1980s, for example in UK government, health, and education sectors. It could be argued that this has arisen as a direct consequence of increasing competitive pressures that have forced organizations (often against their cultural predispositions) to outsource "uncompetitive" activities to external specialists and to focus on areas of more sustainable and profitable differentiated competence.

See also *make/buy decision*

own branding

Andrew Newman and Steve Worrall

This is the process whereby a product or service name is developed for or by a retailer for its exclusive use. In some cases the producer of a branded good (*see* BRAND) will produce a similar product for a retailer, giving it a different name as chosen by that retailer. In other cases the retailer may contract to have the product manufactured independently. Examples would include Marks and Spencer's "St. Michael" range and Sainsbury's "Classic Cola."

Own brand goods are usually positioned in the marketplace to compete directly with the manufacturers' brands (often appearing next to them in the store) and may even have a very similar appearance and usage characteristics. In other cases stores may stock only their exclusive brands (e.g., Body Shop, Thornton's Chocolates). In food retailing the continuing development and improvements made to own brands have strengthened these products in the mind of the customer. PACKAGING plays an important part in this strategy and there is often a close match between traditional product brands and retailer own brand designs (e.g., Tesco cereals and Marks and Spencer's wine). In many cases retailer (own) brand sales equal or exceed traditional product brands.

In pursuing such a MARKETING STRATEGY the retailer may be attempting to create consumer loyalty for its retailer brand and take MARKET SHARE from the competitors. This strategy may also raise the retailer's profile in the consumer's mind. The images and "values" of own brand product ranges (*see* IMAGE) have been steadily established coherently in the minds of the consumer via retailer stores, and are now perceived as high-quality alternatives and comparable to the leading manufacturer brands (Burt, 2000). Hence, own branding allows a retailer to gain an advantage over competitors without own brand products, as the perceived quality of own brands increases while still being offered to the customer at a price lower than manufacturers' brands.

By the early 2000s, the balance of power shifted from producer to retailer in many areas of retailing. This has created favorable conditions for long-established and newer retailers to develop their own retailer brands (Newman and Cullen, 2002). In the food sector, the extension of retailer brand names into product and service markets beyond the core product now offered by major grocery chains provides confirmation of the central role that brands play within CORPORATE STRATEGY (Burt, 2000).

Problems with an own brand strategy can include increased pressure on limited store display space, and the possible confusion of customers due to an abundance of very similar products.

Bibliography

Burt, S. (2000). The strategic role of retail brands in British grocery retailing. *European Journal of Marketing*, 34 (8), 875–90.

James, G. and Morgan, N. J. (eds.) (1994). *Adding Value: Brands and Marketing in Food and Drink*. London: Routledge.

Newman, A. J. and Cullen, P. (2002). *Retailing: Environment and Operations*. London: Thomson Learning.

packaging

Margaret Bruce and Liz Barnes

In the past, commodities were typically sold as loose items, the most widely used form of packaging was a paper bag, and packaging had a purely functional role, i.e., to protect the product. Packaging is now more sophisticated and can be made up of a variety of materials such as glass, paper, metal, or plastic. The plethora of competing products from which the prospective buyer has to choose points to packaging's role in product promotion by communicating the product's features, benefits, and IMAGE.

Packaging is often the consumer's first point of contact with the product (Brassington and Pettitt, 2003). Yavas and Kaynak (1981) argue that an effective package design is a promotional tool and should attract the prospective buyer, communicate rapidly and clearly, create a desire for the product, and trigger a sale. Southgate (1994) suggests that creative packaging adds value and helps to achieve BRAND preference. Packaging can, in fact, contribute to overall brand POSITIONING and brand ADVERTISING and communication, and can influence consumers in their choice of product.

The role of packaging in brand communication has become increasingly significant, as spend on MASS MEDIA advertising for brand communication has decreased (Underwood, Klein, and Burke, 2001). It has been found that average consumers inspect only 1.2 products when making a purchase, so packaging can assist in point of sale decisions (Brassington and Pettitt, 2003). A badly designed package may communicate to the consumer that the product it contains is of low value. Conversely, a well-designed package may be perceived as evidence of the care and attention that has gone into the product. A package has to sell the product at the point of sale (*see* POINT OF PURCHASE) and act as the sales tool in self-service environments. Decisions about packaging also have to be considered in business-to-business markets (*see* BUSINESS-TO-BUSINESS MARKETING), for example, bulk packaging and packaging for protection during transportation, etc. (Brassington and Pettitt, 2003).

Bibliography

Brassington, F. and Pettitt, S. (2003). *Principles of Marketing*, 3rd edn. London: Financial Times/Prentice-Hall.

Southgate, P. (1994). *Total Branding by Design*. London: Kogan Page, p. 21.

Underwood, R. L., Klein, N. M., and Burke, R. R. (2001). Packaging communication: Attentional effects of product imagery. *Journal of Product and Brand Management*, **10** (7), 403–22.

Yavas, V. and Kaynak, E. (1981). Packaging: The past, present and the future of a vital marketing function. *Scandinavian Journal of Materials Administration*, **7** (3), 35–53.

Pareto's rule

Dale Littler

The 20/80 rule, based on a principle attributed to the Italian economist and political philosopher Vilfredo Pareto, suggests that the top 20 percent of products/customers account for approximately 80 percent of revenues/profits; or that 20 percent of users account for 80 percent of usage. The major customers or products might then act as a focus of the organization's activities, which begs the question of what to do with the often long tail of products or customers that account for the remainder. For example, effort might be expended into converting these into high-value customers or products. There may also be strategic reasons for retaining the "long tail" customers or products in the PRODUCT MIX.

See also *product deletion*

partnership sourcing

Dominic Wilson

There is considerable evidence to suggest that managing sourcing relationships as partnerships, whether upstream or downstream, can generate a significant COMPETITIVE ADVANTAGE for both partners (Johnston and Lawrence, 1988; CBI, 1991; Han, Wilson, and Dant, 1993; Lamming, 1993). Partnership sourcing refers to the practice of sourcing on an exclusive basis from a single supplier over an extended predetermined period and with extensive customer access to the operations and management systems of the supplier. This provides obvious benefits to the supplier in the guaranteed DEMAND for their offerings (*see* OFFERING) to the customer. Customer benefits include the guarantees of fair prices, appropriate quality, service levels, and continuity of supply, which are underwritten by the customer's access to the supplier's operational systems and accounts. Both organizations benefit from the increasing experience, mutual understanding, and personal relationships that develop as the partnership evolves. Naturally, as with all collaborative relationships, these benefits may become "vulnerabilities" if one of the parties attempts to take advantage of the other. For many organizations the requirement to TRUST their suppliers or customers – perhaps against a sectoral background of relatively antagonistic bargaining – can be a major psychological and cultural barrier to accessing the benefits of partnership sourcing. Partnership sourcing is more relevant to those markets where long-term guarantees of supply continuity are important and it is difficult to switch swiftly between sources, perhaps because of product complexity, scarcity, or high competitive differentiation.

See also *relationship marketing*

Bibliography

Confederation of British Industry (CBI) (1991). *Partnership Sourcing*. London: Confederation of British Industry.

Han, S.-L., Wilson, D. T., and Dant, S. P. (1993). Buyer–supplier relationships today. *Industrial Marketing Management*, **22**, 4 (November), 331–8.

Johnston, R. and Lawrence, P. R. (1988). Beyond vertical integration: The rise of the value-added partnership. *Harvard Business Review*, **66** (July/August), 94–101.

Lamming, R. (1993). *Beyond Partnership*. Englewood Cliffs, NJ: Prentice-Hall.

payback

Dominic Wilson

Payback (or payback period) refers to the time taken to reach the break-even point for the profitability of a particular product or service. Payback is reached when cumulative fixed and variable costs are matched by cumulated sales revenues and so is crucially influenced by PRICING decisions. Many organizations use payback as a key internal measure to prioritize alternative product/service offerings (*see* OFFERING), but there is a danger that this may encourage managers to plan unrealistic or short-term pricing policies.

See also *break-even analysis*

penetration pricing

Dominic Wilson

Penetration pricing is the term used to describe a PRICING strategy whereby an organization uses a low price in marketing a new product so as to develop a large MARKET SHARE very quickly. For example, penetration pricing might be used by a new entrant aiming to develop a substantial competitive position in a market dominated by an established rival. Alternatively, the strategy might be used to launch a new product where the initial barriers to competitive entry were thought to be low and rivals might develop imitative products quickly, or where customer ignorance was expected to be high and low price would be needed to reduce PERCEIVED RISK and encourage trialing behavior (*see* TRIAL).

Following successful entry to a market using a penetration pricing strategy, price levels can subsequently be raised (e.g., where the price had been promoted as a temporary introductory DISCOUNT), although raising prices is often problematic and can generate undesirable market signals. More usually, prices set through a penetration policy are held largely unchanged and become profitable as unit costs decrease in line with the economies of scale made available through growing market share. Scale economies and capital investment requirements in production and distribution can then provide significant barriers to deter new entrants. Thus, the effect of successful penetration pricing is often to accelerate not only the rate of adoption, but also the early stages of the PRODUCT LIFE CYCLE and the emergence of competitive market structures. Alongside these potential advantages, penetration pricing also carries the risks associated with commitment to relatively long-term policies (including reduced competitive flexibility). In short, penetration pricing is likely to be appropriate where there is widespread potential DEMAND for the OFFERING (even with significant levels of perceived risk), where this demand can be accessed quickly by the supplier, where significant scale economies are available, and where rivals could otherwise develop imitative offerings promptly.

See also *adoption process*

perceived risk

Barbara R. Lewis

The concept of perceived risk can be looked on as an extension of the general conceptual framework of the CONSUMER DECISION-MAKING PROCESS, which may be described as problem-solving activity in which a consumer attempts to identify product performance and psychological goals (*see* CONSUMER NEEDS AND MOTIVES) and to match them with products/brands. However, consumer decision-making involves risk in the sense that any action will produce consequences that cannot be anticipated with any-

thing approaching certainty, and some of which are likely to be unpleasant. Consumers cannot conceive of all the possible consequences and those that they are aware of they cannot anticipate with a high degree of certainty.

Consumers may be uncertain with respect to buying goals, their nature, acceptance levels, relative importance, and current levels of goal attainment. They may be uncertain as to which products/brands will best satisfy acceptance levels of buying goals, i.e., the problem of matching goals with purchases. Further, consumers may see adverse consequences if a purchase is made, or not made, and the result is a failure to satisfy buying goals. These consequences relate to performance goals, i.e., functional goals; psychosocial goals; and the time, money, and effort invested to attain the goals. So one can refer to types of risk as:

- *functional risk*, related to the product not performing as expected;
- *physical risk*, the risk to self and others (such as adverse effects on health or security);
- *financial risk*, which is the risk that the product will not be worth the cost of acquiring it (embracing, for example, the price and the effort expended in acquiring it);
- *social risk*, related to the probability of it generating social embarrassment; and
- *psychological risk*, the risk that a poor product choice will affect the purchaser's sense of self-identity.

Roselius (1971) refers to time, hazard, ego, and money losses or risks.

Consumers develop strategies to reduce perceived risk so that they can act with relative ease and confidence in buying situations where information is inadequate and where the consequences of their actions are in some way unknown or incalculable. They either increase certainty (decrease UNCERTAINTY) by information handling, or decrease the amount at stake – i.e., the consequences that would occur. Typically, risk handling is largely concerned with dealing with uncertainty and so can be equated with information handling. In respect of buying goals and needs, consumers generate information needs, and to satisfy them they acquire, process, and transmit information.

Information acquisition may be accidental or sought from marketer-dominated channels, INTERPERSONAL COMMUNICATIONS, or from neutral sources, e.g., consumer reports. Information processing involves evaluation and decisions with respect to use, storage, and forgetting, followed by possible transmission of information to others. Alternatively, to reduce the consequences, consumers can reduce or modify their goals and expectations, avoid or postpone purchases, or purchase and absorb any unresolved risk.

Numerous strategies for reducing risk have been researched (see, e.g., Bauer, 1967; Cox, 1967; Cunningham, 1967) and include:

- BRAND LOYALTY, to economize on effort, substitute habit for deliberate action/decision;
- reliance on ADVERTISING, to give confidence;
- consumer reports, to provide objective information, e.g., evidence of government or private testing;
- personal influence, e.g., word-of-mouth communication (*see* WORD-OF-MOUTH COMMUNICATIONS) with those with experience of the product/brand;
- group influence, usually stronger when the wisdom of one's choice is difficult to assess;
- IMPULSE BUYING, to suppress possible consequences from consciousness and rush through the buying process;
- store used, its image, reputation, and product range (*see* RETAIL IMAGE);
- most or least expensive brand;
- demonstration, e.g., test driving of cars;
- special offers;
- service, to include money-back guarantees and exchanges;
- reliance on well-known brands; and
- endorsements, e.g., testimonials from experts and personalities.

People use different styles in their choice between increasing certainty and decreasing the consequences of purchases, which depend on their buying goals, products under consideration, PERSONALITY, and degree of buying maturity or experience. These may relate to clarifying the purchase situation – typically reacting to ambiguity by seeking new information and increasing understanding; or simplifying – typically avoiding new information and relying on experience of other people.

Bibliography

Bauer, R. A. (1967). Consumer behavior as risk taking. In D. F. Cox (ed.), *Risk Taking and Information Handling in Consumer Behavior*. Division of Research, Harvard Business School.

Cox, D. F. (ed.) (1967). *Risk Taking and Information Handling in Consumer Behavior*. Division of Research, Harvard Business School.

Cunningham, S. M. (1967). The major dimensions of perceived risk. In D. F. Cox (ed.), *Risk Taking and Information Handling in Consumer Behavior*. Division of Research, Harvard Business School.

Dowling, G. R. and Staelin, R. (1994). A model of perceived risk and intended risk handling activity. *Journal of Consumer Research*, 21, 119–34.

Mitchell, V.-W. (1999). Consumer perceived risk: Conceptualizations and models. *European Journal of Marketing*, 33, 163–95.

Roselius, T. (1971). Consumer rankings of risk reduction methods. *Journal of Marketing*, 35 (January), 56–61.

Taylor, J. W. (1974). The role of risk in consumer behavior. *Journal of Marketing*, April, 54–60.

personal influence

see INTERPERSONAL COMMUNICATIONS; WORD-OF-MOUTH COMMUNICATIONS

personal selling

Judy Zolkiewski

Personal selling is one of the main elements of the marketing COMMUNICATIONS MIX and is usually used in combination with the other elements in the communications mix, such as ADVERTISING and SALES PROMOTION. It is perceived to be most effective in the later stages of the buying process (Kotler, 2000). It is a one-to-one (or one-to-a-small group) communication tool in which the seller tries to persuade the buyer to purchase the company's products and/or services. It can take place face to face or over the telephone (*see* TELEMARKETING). Personal selling takes place in a variety of locations, including retail premises, the buyer's home, on location (e.g., show homes), at EXHIBITIONS, and at other organization's premises.

The role of personal selling varies according to the type of product and service that is being sold and also the type of market involved. For instance, it is generally recognized that personal selling has a different role in business markets than it has in consumer markets (*see* ORGANIZATIONAL BUYING BEHAVIOR). Additionally, the more complex the product or service, the more likely that personal selling will be a critical marketing tool. SERVICE CHARACTERISTICS such as intangibility and inseparability also mean that personal selling is important in many service industries. The higher the PERCEIVED RISK associated with a purchase, the more likely it will be that personal selling is a critical element in the MARKETING MIX.

The role of the salesperson includes information provision, persuasion, and negotiation; it can be highly interactive and challenging. The salesperson must deal with questions, impart knowledge about the organization's products and services (sometimes highly complex technical information), understand customers' needs, dispel customers' concerns, and present the human face of the organization that they represent. They may also be involved in tasks such as order taking, market research, and complaint handling.

On a unit cost basis the costs associated with personal selling are considered to be high, even in comparison with advertising. The costs associated with personal selling vary widely across industries, from the costs associated with sales assistants in a shop to those associated with having a salesperson on the road, which include salary, commission, company car, entertainment, accommodation, and meals. Relative spending on personal selling also tends to be much higher in business markets than it does in consumer markets (Kotler, 2000).

Recent trends in marketing such as the move toward relationship management/marketing (*see* RELATIONSHIP MARKETING) and the implementation of KEY ACCOUNT management and global account management by many large organizations suggest that the role of the salesperson is becoming even more critical in developing, maintaining, and enhancing customer relationships

(although it could be argued that this has always been the case in business-to-business markets; *see* BUSINESS-TO-BUSINESS MARKETING). Another important environmental development is the increasing influence upon and use of technology in personal selling. The Internet is providing an alternative mechanism for information dissemination (although not an interactive process). However, it may free up more of a salesperson's time for problem solving and face-to-face discussion. This, in turn, could allow salespeople to become more effective relationship managers. Other technological developments include the widespread introduction of CUSTOMER RELATIONSHIP MANAGEMENT (CRM) systems that are aimed at assisting with the effective management of an organization's customers.

See also *marketing communications; sales management*

Bibliography

Donaldson, B. (1998) *Sales Management Theory and Practice*, 2nd ed. Basingstoke: Macmillan.

Hartley, B. and Starkey, M. W. (eds.) (1996). *The Management of Sales and Customer Relations*. London: International Thomson Business Press.

Kotler, P. (2000). *Marketing Management. The Millennium Edition*. Englewood Cliffs, NJ: Prentice-Hall.

Pickton, D. and Broderick, A. (2001). *Integrated Marketing Communications*. Harlow, Essex. Pearson Education.

personality

Barbara R. Lewis

Personality refers to those characteristics that account for differences among people and are predictive of their behavior. Such differences evolve from heredity, personal experience, and environmental influence. Personality includes intelligence but is usually defined as accounting for non-cognitive behavior, referring chiefly to emotional and social qualities together with drives, sentiments, and interests – characteristics significant in daily living and social interactions. Personality is usually described in terms of traits such as self-confidence, dominance, autonomy, deference, sociability, defensiveness, and adaptability. In understanding personality and its resulting impact on consumer PRODUCT and BRAND choice, media preferences, etc., various frameworks have been considered; these include Horney's classification of compliant, aggressive, and detached people (Horney, 1958), and Reisman's typology of tradition, inner, and other-directed people (Reisman, Glazer, and Denney, 1960). More recent research interest has focused on, for example, the need for cognition (e.g., Haugtvedt, Petty, and Cacioppo, 1992) and the SELF-CONCEPT (e.g., Sirgy, 1982; Arnould, Price, and Zinkham, 2004). Further research investigations have focused on consumer personality and product/brand choice (e.g., Alpert, 1972; Schiffman and Kanuk, 2004).

Bibliography

Alpert, M. I. (1972). Personality and the determinants of product choice. *Journal of Marketing Research*, 9 (February), 89–92.

Arnould, E., Price, L., and Zinkham, G. (2004). *Consumers*, 2nd edn. New York: McGraw-Hill Irwin, ch. 10.

Foxall, G., Goldsmith, R. F., and Brown, S. (1998). *Consumer Psychology for Marketing*. London: Thomson Learning.

Haugtvedt, C., Petty, R. E., and Cacioppo, J. T. (1992). Need for cognition and advertising: Understanding the role of personality variables in consumer research. *Journal of Consumer Psychology*, 1 (3), 239–60.

Horney, K. (1958). *Neurosis and Human Growth*. New York: Norton.

Reisman, D., Glazer, N., and Denney, R. (1960). *The Lonely Crowd*. New Haven, CT: Yale University Press.

Schiffman, L. G. and Kanuk, L. L. (2004). *Consumer Behavior*, 8th edn. Upper Saddle River, NJ: Pearson Educational International, ch. 5.

Sirgy, M. J. (1982). Self-concept in consumer behavior: A critical review. *Journal of Consumer Research*, 9, 287–300.

physical distribution

see CHANNELS OF DISTRIBUTION

PIMS

see PROFIT IMPACT OF MARKETING STRATEGIES

planning style

Dale Littler

Planning is traditionally associated with a process (see STRATEGIC PLANNING; SWOT ANALYSIS), which involves formal analysis of the organization and its environment and the development of appropriate means of meeting the objectives that the organization has established. There are some major advantages of planning *per se*. Quinn (1978) suggests that planning imposes a discipline on managers to look ahead periodically; results in communication of "goals, strategic issues, and resource allocation"; and helps the IMPLEMENTATION of strategic changes. It provides a baseline against which to assess performance, while as Loasby (1967) notes, the major value of formal planning "is in the raising and broadening of important issues that are liable otherwise to be inadequately considered." It can provide a forum for managerial dialogue on the future development of the business.

There are considerable methodological difficulties in researching any relationship between planning *per se* and organizational performance since there are clearly many different approaches to planning; the manner in which planning is implemented can be expected to be a pertinent factor; and there can be extraneous influences affecting the outcome of any planning activity. Overall there is no conclusive evidence to suggest that planning *per se* is positively correlated with higher organizational performance.

One possible pitfall of much planning is to extrapolate into the future without taking account of possible discontinuities. Some would suggest that UNCERTAINTY undermines much formal planning, although this would point to the necessity of engaging in CONTINGENCY PLANNING and of insuring that the plans have scope for flexibility to take account of the unexpected. Mintzberg (1973) suggests that planning is one of three possible strategic modes (see ADAPTIVE STRATEGY; ENTREPRENEURIAL STRATEGY) and is most appropriate for stable environments. For fast-changing environments, Grant (2003: 515) suggests that: "strategic planning processes have become more decentralized, less staff driven, and more informal, while strategic plans themselves have become shorter term, more goal focused, and less specific with regard to actions and resource allocations.... Strategic planning has become less about strategic decision-making and more a mechanism for coordination and performance managing."

Bibliography

Brews, P. J. and Hunt, M. R. (1999). Learning to plan and planning to learn: Resolving the planning school/learning school debate. *Strategic Management Journal*, **20**, 889–913.

Grant, R. M. (2003). Strategic planning in a turbulent environment: Evidence from the oil majors. *Strategic Management Journal*, **24** (June), 491–517.

Loasby, B. J. (1967). Long range formal planning in perspective. *Journal of Management Studies*, **4** (October), 300–8.

Mintzberg, H. (1973). Strategy making in three modes. *California Management Review*, **16**, 2 (Winter), 44–53.

Quinn, J. B. (1978). Strategic change: Logical incrementalism. *Sloan Management Review*, **120** (Fall), 7–21.

Reid, D. M. (1989). Operationalizing strategic planning. *Strategic Management Journal*, **10**, 553–67.

point of purchase

David Yorke

Point of purchase is the place at which the purchase (by an individual or a group) of a product or service is made. This may be, for example, in the home, in a retail store, or at a place of work. In terms of MARKETING COMMUNICATIONS, it is argued that the most effective techniques to be used at the point of purchase are PERSONAL SELLING, SALES PROMOTION, and PACKAGING, as each can have a direct and immediate impact on the decision to purchase. Some ADVERTISING (usually in retail stores) may also be used, although its effectiveness is difficult to measure.

political environment

Dominic Wilson

The political environment is one of the elements of the MARKETING ENVIRONMENT. This aspect is concerned with political developments such as new and proposed legislation at local,

national, regional, and global levels, as well as attempts to influence such regulatory developments through lobbying and disseminating information. It is often argued that organizations can do little to influence their political environment (as with their demographic and cultural environments), but large organizations, or those in marginal political constituencies, have historically been able to exercise considerable political leverage through careful lobbying activities. With the continuing realities of democratic politics, and the availability of sophisticated professional lobbying services, there is no reason to believe that this is likely to change in the future.

See also *environmental analysis*

political marketing

Phil Harris

Political marketing as a concept and practice has its early origins in the US and was first regularly used as a territorial definition within marketing by Kelly (1956). Researchers have subsequently argued that it was first seen as an applied concept in the 1950s and 1960s (Maarek, 1995), and others at the beginning of the twentieth century (McNair, 1996). It is broadly seen to include both political campaigning for elections and referenda and more covert campaigning in support of lobbying, pressure group, and public affairs work. Political marketing was born and has developed as a result of the inevitable consequences of the development of mass electorate, MASS MEDIA, and global government institutions.

Maarek (1995) argues that the main factors responsible for the early development of the phenomenon in the US were the presidential system, tradition of election for all public offices, and rapid expansion of modern mass media. The US also provides good examples of the early usage of typical marketing tools such as the adoption of databases (*see* DATABASE), DIRECT MAIL, political ADVERTISING, and PUBLICITY stunts in political communication (Rothschild, 1978; Newman, 1994, 1999). Political marketing can also be seen in not-for-profit markets (Kotler and Andreason, 1991) (*see* NOT-FOR-PROFIT

MARKETING) and in lobbying and pressure group campaigning within public affairs management (Harris, 2001).

In the UK, political marketing as a phenomenon became established in the 1980s under the party leaderships of Margaret Thatcher and Neil Kinnock, who aimed to integrate all political communications and control the news agenda. It has also been suggested that major political parties have been engaged in marketing-related activities for most of the twentieth century. It has been argued that there is a great increase in focus on packaging and presentation of leaders, partly due to the move of the British Labour Party toward the center ground (Norris, 1997). As in the US, TELEVISION has the most significant impact on political communication, and the factor that dominates all other considerations by party strategists is the battle to dominate the television agenda (Butler and Kavanagh, 1992).

In order to obtain clarity and order in the presentation of the various tools used in political marketing and to illustrate analogies with mainstream marketing, the classic division of MARKETING MIX into promotion, place, price, and product has been adopted.

Promotion plays the crucial role in the political marketing mix. It comprises various elements and techniques such as advertising, PUBLIC RELATIONS, direct mail, and pseudo-events planned to gain publicity and attention. Four influential areas of innovation in technology, computers, television, and direct mail have directly affected the way the campaigns are run (Newman, 1994, 1999). Some of the applications of technological advances include database marketing, fundraising, and polling and enable the candidates to go directly to the voter. Moreover, political marketers are provided with new opportunities because of computer video and Internet development, e.g., with the possibilities of new types of advertising or direct mailing and also with new challenges connected with the development of digital television and reaching target voters.

Televised advertising has become important because it reaches the voters, and at the same time the party or candidates fully control the message (Kaid and Holtz-Bacha, 1995). Contrary to popular belief that political ads are solely concerned with IMAGE (Baines, Harris, and Lewis, 2002), it has been found that most political advertising is concentrated on issues or contains issue-based information. Although there are contradictory theories on the effects of political advertising, most researchers agree that it acts principally to reinforce the existing image (e.g., Kaid and Holtz-Bacha, 1995).

Televised debates are increasingly regarded as the capstone of the election campaign (Maarek, 1995), even though there is no evidence that they can dramatically change the outcome of the campaign (Newman, 1994). Although criticized from the stand that they are mostly based on projecting the right image and not discussing policy differences, debates, like other pseudo-events, are meant to look spontaneous although in fact they are carefully staged and continue to attract the attention of the media as well as gain publicity for the political players.

Several authors stress the growing role of direct mail in the contemporary political marketing mix (e.g., Newman, 1994; Maarek, 1995). Direct mail is used to pre-test the market, personalize and concentrate the MESSAGE, raise funds, promote issues and candidates, and recruit volunteers. Harrop (1990) argues that the real potential of direct mail is that it offers the opportunity to personalize one's basic message so as to convince voters that a party that can campaign so efficiently might actually be up to the job of running the country.

Wring (1997) notes the diminishing role of advertising in favor of free media publicity, which is most frequently connected with public relations designed to attract favorable media attention. Greater importance of free media publicity is also acknowledged by both voting public and media strategists. News management is perhaps the most visible area of contrast between mainstream and political marketing. In political communications staff are deluged on a daily basis by requests from journalists and need to answer highly sensitive questions. Political marketing tends to prescribe negative campaigning, especially in advertising where it is easier to attack than to propound (Maarek, 1995; Scammell, 1995). It might be the consequence of candidate focus in elections and campaigns. Although labeled by some "negative abuse," negative campaigning is not necessarily harmful to political discourse and, in fact, is essential for genuine debate. It insures that policy and politicians' reputations are examined. Media that accept the role of opposition expose flaws and guarantee the transparency of political processes.

Wring (1997) points out that a network at grassroots level is at the heart of a placement strategy. Local electioneering takes the form of traditional activities such as canvassing, leafleting, and "getting the vote out" on polling day. In the marketing era of modern campaigns it is more important to identify and contact potential supporters than to persuade them (Wring, 1997).

Some researchers discount the pricing element of the political marketing mix. Wring (1997) justifies the relevance of price as its constituents comprise voters' feelings of national, economic, and psychological hope or insecurity. Discussing the price aspect of voting behavior, Wring points out two aspects, one resulting from negative campaigning designed to build voters' fear, and the other resulting from the "feelgood factor."

The main differences in views as to what constitutes a political product (e.g., Harrop, 1990; Newman, 1994; Scammell, 1995) have already been presented. Wring (1997) points out three key aspects of the political marketing product: party image, image of leader, and policy commitments (manifesto). Different groups of voters are susceptible to the appeals of these key elements in varying degrees. There is an agreement, however, that the common feature of media election coverage is an increase in using appeals based on promotion of image at the expense of issues. Moreover, there is also growing emphasis of the importance of leader image, which is the reason for the personalization of politics as described by Swanson and Mancini (1996).

Although the debate on the definition and nature of political lobbying continues (Harris and Lock, 1996), growing literature on pressure groups, interest groups, and policy networks (Grant, 1995; Harris and Moss, 2001) offers useful insights and suggests tools to be used in political marketing. Harris, Gardner, and Vetter (1999) find a direct linkage between political marketing and interest lobbying, namely, the need of political parties to raise funds to insure their existence in the electoral marketplace. They claim that the need to run expensive modern political marketing campaigns forces political parties to develop close links with business. However, this area is still largely underresearched for many obvious reasons.

There is also a lack of research in the area of regulation and deregulation, closely connected with the border between lobbying and political marketing. Harris and Lock (1996) argue that governments cannot be treated as a neutral component in the exchange perspective in political marketing. Government politicians play important roles in the process of exchange, and governmental control is a key objective in political processes. Therefore, the regulation of political marketing plays a more important role in this type of exchange than in mainstream marketing settings. These issues gain significance in the context of governmental regulatory involvement in competitive business arenas, and especially in such areas as the deregulation of markets (Harris and Lock, 1996).

Political marketing has been criticized from the ethical stand as undermining democracy because of its ability to promote people with media abilities and the right appearance, and to manipulate and mislead the voter. O'Shaughnessy (1990) argues that the rise of political marketing contributes to the misperception of political processes and the ease with which solutions can be traded and implemented. Egan (1999) suggests that politicians themselves have been uneasy with the concept of marketing, complaining that it damages the political process as it concentrates on image instead of issues.

There is also a strong debate about ethics in conducting political campaigns. Some draw attention to the need to introduce financial regulation, while others point out impracticality and difficulties in enforcing ethical standards in campaigns. Harris and Lock (1996) note widespread concerns about ethics. However, they perceive much of the criticism of political marketing as nostalgia for the "good old days," which are more myth than reality.

Some researchers argue that, given the international exchange of campaign techniques and personnel, the increased complexity of election campaigning has reached its postmodern

Table 1   Political campaign evolution

	Premodern	*Modern*	*Postmodern*
Campaign organization	Local and decentralized	Nationally coordinated	Nationally coordinated but decentralized operations
Preparations	Short term and ad hoc campaign	Long campaign	Permanent campaign
Central coordination	Party leaders	Central headquarters, more specialist consultants, and party officials	More outside consultants, pollsters, and specialist campaign departments
Feedback	Local canvassing	Opinion polls	Opinion polls, focus groups, Internet websites
Media	National and local press Local handbills, posters, and pamphlets Radio leadership speeches	Television broadcasting through major territorial channels	Television narrowcasting through fragmented channels, selective mailshots, selective advertisements
Campaign events	Local public meetings Limited whistlestop leadership tours	Media management Daily press conferences Themed photo opportunities, TV party political broadcasts Billboard wars	Extension of media management to "routine" politics, leadership speeches, policy launches, etc.
Costs	Low budget and local costs	Higher costs for producing TV party political broadcasts	Higher costs for consultants, research, and TV advertisements

Source: Norris (1997: 77).

stage (Norris, 1997). Table 1 illustrates the main changes in campaign evolution. Other researchers believe that the process of Americanization disconnects leaders and voters, oversimplifies and trivializes political discourse, and produces a cynical and disengaged public (Franklin, 1994).

Political marketing has emerged as a major area of research, which has begun to reflect the growing internationalism and professionalism of political campaigning. Research initially focused on image and use of the marketing mix and its adoption. It is now beginning to become a more substantive area of market research and work has more recently investigated segmentation (*see* MARKET SEGMENTATION) of voters, strategy, buyer/consumer behavior, and exchange processes in political lobbying. The subject had its origins in the US but more recently has become established in Europe, with leading theory and research being developed in the UK.

Bibliography

Baines, P., Harris, P., and Lewis, B. (2002). The political marketing planning process: Improving image. *Marketing Intelligence and Planning*, 20.

Butler, D. and Kavanagh, D. (1992). *The British General Election of 1992*. London: Macmillan.

Egan, J. (1999). Political marketing: Lessons from the mainstream. *Journal of Marketing Management*, 15 (6), 495–503.

Franklin, R. (1994). *Packaging Politics*. London: Edward Arnold.

Grant, W. (1995). *Pressure Groups, Politics and Democracy in Britain*. Hemel Hempstead: Harvester Wheatsheaf.

Harris, P. (2001). Machiavelli, political marketing and reinventing government. *European Journal of Marketing*, 35 (9/10).

Harris, P. and Lock, A. (1996). Machiavellian marketing: The development of corporate lobbying in the UK. *Journal of Marketing Management*, **12**, 313–28.

Harris, P. and Moss, D. (2001). In search of public affairs: A function in search of an identity. *Journal of Public Affairs*, **1** (1), 102–12.

Harris, P., Gardner, H., and Vetter, N. (1999). Goods over God. Lobbying and political marketing: A case study of the campaign by the Shopping Hours Reform Council that changed Sunday Trading Laws in the UK. In B. Newman (ed.), *Handbook of Political Marketing*. Thousand Oaks, CA: Sage.

Harris, P., Moss, D., and Vetter, N. (1999). Machiavelli and public affairs: A tale of servants and their princes. *Journal of Communication Management*, **3** (3).

Harrop, M. (1990). Political marketing. *Parliamentary Affairs*, **43**, 277–92.

Jamieson, K. (1992). *Dirty Politics, Deception, Distraction and Democracy*. Oxford: Oxford University Press.

Kaid, L. and Holtz-Bacha, C. (1995). *Political Advertising in Western Democracies*. Thousands Oaks, CA: Sage.

Kavanagh, D. (1995). *Election Campaigning: The New Marketing of Politics*. Oxford: Blackwell.

Kelly, S., Jr. (1956). *Professional Public Relations and Political Power*. Baltimore: Johns Hopkins University Press.

Kotler, P. and Andreason, A. (1991). *Strategic Marketing for Non-Profit Organizations*, 4th edn. Englewood Cliffs, NJ: Prentice-Hall.

Maarek, P. (1995). *Political Marketing and Communication*. London: John Libbey.

McNair, B. (1996). Performance in politics and the politics of performance. In J. L'Etang and M. Pieczka (eds.), *Critical Perspectives in Public Relations*. London: International Thomson.

Newman, B. (1994). *The Marketing of the President: Political Marketing as Campaign Strategy*. London: Sage.

Newman, B. (ed.) (1999). *Handbook of Political Marketing*. Thousand Oaks, CA: Sage.

Norris, P. (1997). Political communications. In P. Dunleavy, A. Gamble, I. Holliday, and G. Peele (eds.), *Developments in British Politics*. London: Macmillan.

O'Shaughnessy, N. (1990). *The Phenomenon of Political Marketing*. London: Macmillan.

Rothschild, M. (1978). Political advertising: A neglected policy issue in marketing. *Journal of Marketing Research*, **15**, 59–71.

Scammell, M. (1995). *Designer Politics: How Elections are Won*. London: Macmillan.

Swanson, D. and Mancini, P. (1996). *Politics, Media and Modern Democracy*. Westport, CT: Praeger.

Wring, D. (1997). Reconciling marketing with political science. *Journal of Marketing Management*, **13** (7), 651–63.

portfolio analysis

Dale Littler

In MARKETING, portfolio analysis is used at both a business and a product level, but the discussion here will be in terms of businesses. The aim is to assess the current mix of businesses in terms of balance of, for example, growing as against maturing businesses. Portfolio analysis techniques generally prescribe the actions to be taken with regard to these businesses, such as invest, abandon, etc.

The most popular framework for portfolio analysis is that proposed by the Boston Consulting Group (*see* BCG MATRIX), which classifies businesses in terms of two major parameters (relative MARKET SHARE and market growth). Other analytical frameworks which employ a composite of variables have subsequently been developed, although essentially they all have the same end in view: of providing an easily employable means of evaluating a mix of businesses and prescribing the courses of action to be adopted.

Two of these, the Shell directional policy matrix and the A. D. Little competitive position–industry maturity matrix, are reviewed in Abell and Hammond (1979) and Hofer and Schendel (1978). The limitations of these approaches are discussed in Day (1977) and Wensley (1981). The market attractiveness–business position matrix based on contributions from General Electric planners and McKinsey and Co. (Aaker, 2001) is based on two parameters: market attractiveness, which is a composite of several factors (e.g., size, growth, government regulations, etc), and the ability to compete, based on an evaluation of the business's competencies and assets compared to those of its competitors. Each business is then positioned according to its strengths (high, medium, low) and the market opportunities (high, medium, low) and a formulaic strategic direction is evident. Thus, where a business has high market attractiveness and a high ability to compete, it would appear wise to invest with a view to further growing the business. A business with low market attractiveness and low ability to compete might be harvested or divested from the portfolio. Some criticisms made are that: there are difficulties in defining the market and the cutoff points to decide between "high, medium, and low"; and these approaches focus on generalized and obvious strategic recommendation. The models are simplistic and deterministic and an overly rigorous application might stifle creative solutions.

Bibliography

Aaker, D. A. (2001). *Strategic Market Management*, 6th edn. New York: John Wiley.

Abell, D. F. and Hammond, S. (1979). *Strategic Market Planning*. Upper Saddle River, NJ: Prentice-Hall, pp. 213–19.

Day, G. (1977). Diagnosing the product portfolio. *Journal of Marketing*, 41 (April), 29–38.

Hofer, C. W. and Schendel, D. (1978). *Strategy Formulation: Analytical Concepts*. St. Paul, MN: West Publishing.

Wensley, R. (1981). Strategic marketing: Betas, boxes or basics. *Journal of Marketing*, 45, 173–82.

positioning

Vincent-Wayne Mitchell

In an attempt to emphasize the non-product aspects of positioning, Ries and Trout (1982) define it as: "not what you do to the product. Positioning is what you do to the mind of the prospect." Ries and Trout focus on the end product of positioning strategies, namely, the "position" the product holds in the minds of consumers. Ideally this IMAGE both reflects what the product is and indicates how it is different from the competition. Slogans like BMW's "The Ultimate Driving Machine" and UPS's "Moving at the Speed of Business" reflect the image these companies would like consumers to have of their products and services. However, psychological positioning must be supported by the reality of the product, otherwise the positioning created by other elements of the MARKETING MIX will be undermined by the use experience and will not be sustainable in the long term.

When developing a positioning strategy, marketers need a good understanding of how their product differs from others. Kotler and Armstrong (2004) suggests that differences should be:

1 important to a sufficient number of buyers;
2 distinctive, i.e., the difference is not offered in the same way, or at all, by competitors;
3 superior to others in achieving the same/more benefit;
4 communicable and visible to buyers;
5 difficult to copy;
6 affordable to the TARGET MARKET;
7 profitable and possible for the company to engineer.

Few products are superior to their competitors on all their attributes. What is required is that they differ on key dimensions that are important to the target customers. Some marketers advocate promoting only one benefit – a unique selling proposition or USP – since buyers tend to remember "number one" messages better than others, particularly in today's overcommunicated society (Reeves, 1960; Ries and Trout, 1982). Others believe that it is possible to employ a double-benefit positioning strategy, e.g., Volvo is positioned on two benefits, safety and durability. One of the main advantages of using benefit or need-based segmentation is that it is the most useful in determining the positioning strategy. If other variables, e.g., age, are used initially, at some stage the marketer needs to return to benefits in order to effect a positioning strategy. When deciding which position to adopt, a company should promote its major strengths, provided that the target market values these strengths.

To overcome the problem that many companies face of how to unlock the psychological grip which large brands have on the market, a company can: strengthen its own position with the message of "because we're number two we try harder"; unlock new unoccupied positions that are valued by consumers; and deposition or reposition the competition, e.g., identify a competitor's weakness through comparative ADVERTISING (Ries and Trout, 1982). A further strategy is the "exclusive club strategy." Since people tend to remember number one, it is important to become number one on something. What counts is to be number one on some valued attribute. However, if the number one position along a meaningful attribute cannot be achieved, a company can promote the idea that it is one of, for example, the Big Three in the industry. The idea was first used by the third largest US car manufacturer Chrysler, although the concept can be extended to any reasonable number (below ten) in any industry where there is some justification for it in the industry's structure.

Occasionally, products will require repositioning because of changing customer tastes and/or poor sales performance. Jobber (2004) identifies four repositioning strategies:

1   Image repositioning, where the product is kept the same in the same market, but its image is altered via changes to the COMMU-NICATIONS MIX. This is akin to what Ries and Trout (1982) view as positioning and is the purest form of repositioning proposed by Jobber, as it focuses solely on changing perceptions in consumers' minds, not the reality of a product.
2   Product repositioning, in which the product is adapted to meet the needs of the target market more closely.
3   Intangible repositioning, which involves a different market segment being targeted with the same product, e.g., Lucozade's attempts to target sporty young adults.
4   Tangible repositioning, when both target market and product are changed.

See also *market segmentation; segmentation variables*

Bibliography

Jobber, D. (2004). *Principles and Practices of Marketing*, 4th edn. London: McGraw-Hill.

Kelly, G. A. (1955). *The Psychology of Personal Constructs*, 2 vols. New York: Norton.

Kotler, P. (2003). *Marketing Management: Analysis, Planning, Implementation and Control*, 11th edn. Englewood Cliffs, NJ: Prentice-Hall.

Kotler, P. and Armstrong, G. (2004). *Principles of Marketing*, 10th edn. Upper Saddle River, NJ: Prentice-Hall.

Marsden, D. and Littler, D. (1995). Product construct systems: A personal construct psychology of market segmentation. Association for Consumer Research Conference, Copenhagen, June.

Reeves, R. (1960). *Reality in Advertising*. New York: Knopf.

Ries, A. and Trout, J. (1982). *Positioning: The Battle for Your Mind*. New York: Warner.

posters

David Yorke

Posters, or street ADVERTISING hoardings, are the principal medium of outdoor advertising, and they are targeted at those people who are thought to pass by them. They are one element in the marketing COMMUNICATIONS MIX and are used, for example, to provide visual support for other media (e.g., TELEVISION) or to achieve long-term exposure.

Posters have public visibility, cover a high percentage of the population, are able to reach the light television viewer, are geographically (i.e., regionally) highly flexible, provide repeated exposure, are relatively low cost (i.e., COST PER THOUSAND reached), and can be changed quickly.

However, they are not suitable for complex advertising (e.g., there are limitations to the length of the MESSAGE that may be communicated), coverage is wasted in terms of the audience reached (i.e., specific targets are not possible), audience selectivity is limited, there may be site control by town planning authorities, and measurement of (sales) effectiveness is virtually impossible.

See also *marketing communications*

postmodern marketing

David Marsden

Postmodern marketing emerged in the 1990s as a radical alternative to mainstream scientific marketing. The principal and fundamental assumptions of postmodern marketing are threefold:

1   a general worldview concerning the changing conditions of modern western societies;

2   a theory of knowledge about these changes; and

3   a set of marketing practices and techniques.

First, postmodern marketing argues that we are living in an age of transition and transformation in which the traditional economic, political, social, and cultural foundations of society are rapidly breaking down and being replaced by new ones. In short, it argues that we are passing through a new era or epoch of world history. For example, the rise of the global economy, the revolution in information communication technologies, and the emergence of a consumer culture are all said to be fragmenting traditional patterns of competition, communication, and consumption (Venkatesh, 1999).

In terms of a theory of knowledge, postmodern marketing argues that the changing conditions of society are impossible to understand without a corresponding change in traditional modes of marketing thought. In other words, the new-looking postmodern world requires nothing short of a new world outlook. In direct contrast to the traditional scientific view of marketing, postmodern marketing denies the possibility of knowing the world – it rejects the belief in an absolute, rock-like, and infallible knowledge of unchanging market reality and standards of consumer behavior (Brown, 1995).

Instead, it argues that all marketing knowledge is incomplete, temporary, uncertain; marketing truths are simply an affair of custom and tradition – they are relative to particular ages, cultures, and language. Since truth is relative, every person is entitled to their own opinion, and postmodern marketing is the celebration of different ways of thinking and speaking about marketing phenomena. In particular, it focuses on generating new forms of marketing knowledge through the study of language, CULTURE, and history (Thomas, 1997).

In terms of marketing practice, postmodernists argue that we are moving toward totally new market conditions for which none of the old marketing strategies (see MARKETING STRATEGY) is suitable. At the center of postmodern marketing practice is the assumption that consumption is a creative source of pleasure,

personal fulfillment, and individual freedom in forming one's self-identity (Firat and Venkatesh, 1995) (see SELF-CONCEPT). This is reflected in such practices as, for example, the marketing of hyper/virtual realities (fantasy worlds) such as themed parks/pubs in which consumers can experience alternative self-identities. The use of DIRECT MARKETING and flexible design/manufacturing technologies is also illustrative of the mass customization of markets, whilst postmodern ADVERTISING techniques such as pastiche (i.e., self-parody) are typical of the fun and play associated with the new consumer culture (for other postmodern marketing practices, see Firat and Shultz, 1997; Patterson, 1998).

Bibliography

Brown, S. (1995). *Postmodern Marketing*. London: Routledge.

Firat, A. F. and Shultz, C. J. (1997). From segmentation to fragmentation: Markets and marketing strategy in the postmodern era. *European Journal of Marketing*, 3 (4), 183–207.

Firat, A. F. and Venkatesh, A. (1995). Liberatory postmodernism and the reenchantment of consumption. *Journal of Consumer Research*, 22 (3), 239–68.

Patterson, M. (1998). Direct marketing in postmodernity: Neo-tribes and direct communications. *Marketing Intelligence and Planning*, 16 (1), 68–74.

Thomas, M. J. (1997). Consumer market research: Does it have validity? Some postmodern thoughts. *Marketing Intelligence and Planning*, 15 (2), 54–9.

Venkatesh, A. (1999). Postmodernism perspectives for macromarketing: An inquiry into the global information and sign system. *Journal of Macromarketing*, 19 (2), 153–69.

potential demand

see MARKET POTENTIAL

predatory pricing

Dominic Wilson

Predatory pricing is where heavy discounting is used as a deliberate attempt to drive out competition with a view to achieving a subsequent monopoly situation where prices can be raised to exploitative levels. Predatory pricing is illegal in many countries, although it can sometimes be difficult to distinguish unambiguously between vigorous discounting (e.g., in "price wars") and more unethical or illegal practices such as dumping and predatory pricing.

pressure groups

see CONSUMERISM

price discrimination

Dominic Wilson

Price discrimination is where different prices are charged to different customers. There are many reasons why it may be necessary to vary the price of a particular product or service, though this practice can sometimes seem inequitable and so may be resisted by CUSTOMERS and consequently avoided by SUPPLIERS. Important variables that can affect costs, and so provide a basis for reasonable price discrimination, include: the costs of distribution to differing markets, the shelf life of the product in different climatic conditions, discounting for volume, the need for incentives to ease supply management, the imposition of local taxes, and the adoption of SKIMMING PRICING or PENETRATION PRICING strategies in new markets. There can also be considerable variation in price sensitivity and DEMAND within the market for a particular OFFERING which may lead to variation in pricing (Shapiro et al., 1991), although the ruthless exploitation of vulnerable demand through inflated prices (profiteering) is both unethical and illegal in many countries.

See also *discount; price elasticity*

Bibliography

Shapiro, B. P., Rangan, V. K., Moriarty, R. T., and Ross, E. B. (1991). Managing customers for profits (not just sales). In R. J. Dolan (ed.), *Strategic Marketing Management*. Boston: Harvard Business School, pp. 307–19.

price elasticity

Dominic Wilson

Price elasticity refers to the effect on demand of changes in price and is similar to the concept of price sensitivity. In elastic (or price-sensitive) markets a small change in price can result in a large change in demand (e.g., interest rates in money markets), whereas in inelastic (or price-insensitive) markets even substantial changes in price tend to have relatively little effect on demand (e.g., luxury goods). Traditionally, inelastic demand has been seen as typical of "basic" needs such as food, health, housing, and education, but it is notable that in all these cases the element of inelasticity refers only to aggregated demand and there can be very considerable price elasticity within subsections of these markets (e.g., respectively, for delicacies, health insurance, mansions, private education).

The elasticity (or price sensitivity) of demand may also be affected by variables such as the availability of product alternatives, variants, and substitutes, or the availability of product prerequisites (e.g., driving lessons, petrol supplies, and spare parts for would-be motorists) (Reibstein and Gatiguan, 1984). The concept of price elasticity continues to be important in many markets and even small price changes can have significant consequences for consumer loyalty (e.g., supermarket groceries, newspapers). The following formula can be used to estimate price elasticity:

$$\text{price elasticity of demand} = \frac{\% \text{ change in demand}}{\% \text{ change in price}}$$

See also *demand*

Bibliography

Hanssens, D. M., Parsons, L. J., and Schultz, R. L. (1990). *Market Response Models: Econometric and Time Series Analysis*. Boston: Kluwer Academic.

Hoch, S. J., Kim, B.-D., Montgomery, A. L., and Rossi, P. E. (1995). Determinants of store-level price elasticity. *Journal of Marketing Research*, 32, 1 (February), 17–29.

Reibstein, D. J. and Gatiguan, H. (1984). Optimal product line pricing: The influence of elasticities and cross elasticities. *Journal of Marketing Research*, 21 (3), 259–67.

price leadership

Dominic Wilson

Where an organization is able to exert considerable influence (whether active or tacit) over rivals' PRICING decisions, then it is said to be the price leader. This influence is often a reflection of a dominant market share (as with IBM in mainframe computer markets during the 1960s and 1970s), but it can result from other factors such as reputation for quality (Barber raincoats) or reputation for value (MFI furniture). Where a group of suppliers together dominate a market in an effective oligopoly (as with petrol retailing, sports shoes, broadcasting), then they may exercise price leadership collectively (though one or two of them may well be more influential than the others), and this might have to be regulated by government or independent administrators to avoid price collusion and unfair practices.

price promotions

David Yorke

Some pricing decisions involve a short-term adjustment to the price of an existing product/service, possibly prompted by disappointing sales caused by an economic downturn, competitors' activities, seasonality, etc. Such adjustments should be made using an estimate of PRICE ELASTICITY, i.e., how much will sales volumes change with a change in price, and what will be the likely CONTRIBUTION margin (*see* MARGIN), i.e., the difference between price and average variable cost? Price promotions need not result in a net profit increase in the short term but may be used to attack competitive offerings (*see* OFFERING) or to defend market position against aggressive competitors' actions. However, price promotions must be used with care. While they might have a beneficial short-term effect, their continuing use may demean the product/service in the mind of the customer/buyer or generate high customer sensitivity to price, resulting in lower profitability for all.

See also *pricing; pricing methods; pricing objectives*

Bibliography

Day, G. S. and Ryans, A. B. (1988). Using price discounts for a competitive advantage. *Industrial Marketing Management*, **17**, 1 (February), 1–14.
Wilcox, J. B., Howell, R. D., Kuzdrall, P., and Britney, R. (1987). Price quality discounts: Some implications for buyers and sellers. *Journal of Marketing*, **51**, 3 (July), 60–70.

price sensitivity

see PRICE ELASTICITY

pricing

Dominic Wilson

At its simplest, price is the value placed on that which is exchanged between a supplier and a customer. However, price is a highly complex and multifaceted issue, reflecting the complexity of EXCHANGE processes. For example, price can be expressed in many different forms – rent, royalties, interest rates, taxes, and gratuities are all forms of "price" – and need not be expressed in monetary terms at all (as in barter, or countertrade). It could be argued that pricing is the most important of the MARKETING MIX elements since the price an organization sets for its offerings (*see* OFFERING) will play a large part in determining an organization's revenues, profitability, and competitiveness. Whereas this is a useful reminder of the significance of pricing, it should also be understood that no single element of the marketing mix can be isolated from the mix as a whole in terms of its effects and significance. Thus the factors, objectives, and strategies relevant to pricing will also be relevant to other aspects of the mix and, indeed, to other functional aspects of the organization's operations.

Management decisions concerning price should reflect PRICING OBJECTIVES that in turn should be consistent with the overall objectives of marketing strategies (*see* MARKETING STRATEGY) and of business and corporate strategies (*see* CORPORATE STRATEGY). Pricing decisions are arrived at, in principle, through pricing methods and can result in prices that are high, low, or neutral with respect to rival offerings, costs, or customer perceptions (*see* CONSUMER PERCEPTIONS). To illustrate the complexity of objectives and strategies in pricing, consider the example of a product that may be priced well above the cost of its production and distribution, though well below that charged by less efficient rivals, and yet still be perceived by potential customers as being poor value (perhaps because of weak promotional strategies or unfamiliar branding). Many organizations will find it necessary to adopt a range of pricing strategies, reflecting differences among the products in their portfolio of offerings and brands, while also attempting to insure a degree of consistency, perceived fairness, and competitiveness in pricing necessary to generate PROFIT and satisfy customers. It is this mix of complex and sometimes conflicting dynamics that makes pricing so difficult and so important.

Much of the specialist literature on pricing refers to consumer products and relatively little attention has been paid to pricing issues in the contexts of organizational markets (Laric, 1980), services markets (Schlissel and Chasin, 1991), or INTERNATIONAL MARKETING (Lancioni, 1989). Nevertheless, there are several well-established and excellent general guides to the theory and practice of pricing (e.g., Gabor, 1988; Winkler, 1989; Nagle and Holden, 1995), while a convenient brief review of the literature is provided by Diamantopoulos (1991).

See also *pricing methods*

Bibliography

Cohen, S. S. and Zysman, J. (1986). Countertrade, offsets, barter, and buybacks. *California Management Review*, 28 (Winter), 41–56.
Diamantopoulos, A. (1991). Pricing: Theory and practice – a literature review. In M. J. Baker (ed.), *Perspectives on Marketing Management*, vol. 1. Chichester: John Wiley.
Gabor, A., (1988). *Pricing: Concepts and Methods for Effective Marketing*, 2nd edn. Aldershot: Gower.
Korth, C. M. (ed.) (1987). *International Countertrade*. New York: Quorum Books.
Lancioni, R. A. (1989). The importance of price in international business development. *European Journal of Marketing*, 23 (1), 145–50.
Laric, M. V. (1980). Pricing strategies in industrial markets. *European Journal of Marketing*, 14 (5/6), 303–21.
Monroe, K. B. (1973). Buyers' subjective perceptions of price. *Journal of Marketing Research*, 10 (February), 70–80.
Nagle, T. T. and Holden, R. K. (1995). *The Strategy and Tactics of Pricing*, 2nd edn. Englewood Cliffs, NJ: Prentice-Hall.
Schlissel, M. R. and Chasin, J. (1991). Pricing of services: An interdisciplinary review. *Service Industries Journal*, 11, 3 (July), 271–86.
Winkler, J. (1989). *Pricing for Results*. London: Heinemann Business.

pricing methods

Dominic Wilson

"Pricing methods" refer to the methods by which prices are decided for any particular product or service. There is an important distinction to be made between price decisions for existing offerings (*see* OFFERING) and those for new offerings. Setting the price for an existing (or "established") product is relatively straightforward as substantial market data are often available (reflecting customer response to previous price levels). However, it should be recognized that not all organizations collect such data rigorously, nor is it always easy to isolate the effect of price variation from shifts in other elements of the MARKETING MIX. It is also the case that even established offerings can experience sudden changes in the market environment (*see* MARKETING ENVIRONMENT) that can undermine the relevance of previous data and so question longstanding pricing policies, e.g., in times of economic recession, at the launch of rival offerings, or when there are dramatic changes in legislation, technology, or consumer expectations.

Nevertheless, the pricing of new products is generally more complex than that of established products as crucial issues such as cost, DEMAND, and competitive response are likely to be relatively unfamiliar. The problems of setting prices for innovative offerings can be so complex that sometimes these decisions are, in effect, intuitive and heuristic (Oxenfeldt, 1973). However, three more rigorous methods have also been identified for determining prices for relatively new products and services: cost-plus pricing, demand-based pricing, and going-rate pricing, each of which is discussed below.

Cost-Plus Pricing

The cost-plus pricing method is an approach which, with deceptive simplicity, sums the costs incurred in producing and distributing a good, adds an appropriate profit margin (or markup) according to company policy, and so generates an appropriate price (also known as markup pricing). A significant variant of this approach is rate of return or target return pricing, which adds in to these calculations the cost of the capital investment involved in production and distribution, aiming to fix a price that will yield a target rate of return on this investment. This variant is more typical of those occasions when substantial investment is required for the development, production, and launch of a new product or service, resulting in particular priority to achieving a prompt return on such investment. The problem with such an approach to pricing is that it makes assumptions about DEMAND and competitive response that can be frail, especially for a new product or service (one might consider the UK Channel Tunnel as an example here). An interesting reversal of this target return approach, which responds to these problems, is that of target costing, favored by some Japanese multinational suppliers of consumer goods. This approach reverses the stream of calculations mentioned above, starting not with the costs but with what is thought to be an appropriate price. The desired profit margin is then deducted, leaving a figure to cover all costs. The issue then is whether or not the offering can be produced and marketed within these costs.

The calculation of these prices is based on the following crude formulae:

cost-plus or markup price = unit cost $(1 - \% \text{ markup})$

where unit cost = variable cost + (fixed cost/forecast unit sales).

target return price = unit cost + ((% target return × capital invested)/forecast unit sales)

While insuring an important priority to cost issues, cost-plus pricing methods have a number of difficulties. First, it can be surprisingly diffi-

cult to allocate all relevant costs to individual product variants, even where a standard cost-accounting system is already in use. Some costs can only be allocated very approximately (e.g., production, inventory, customer service, central administration, R&D, strategic planning, multiple product, or non-specific promotions). Second, this approach takes no account of the discounting and competitive flexibility that provide the necessary discretion for negotiating contracts in organizational markets. Third, the approach takes no direct account either of competitive offerings or of the price sensitivity of demand. And fourthly, costs can vary considerably over time yet it is impractical (and undesirable) constantly to vary price. Nevertheless, the approach is useful for its apparent reasonableness (assuming appropriate margins), its focus on cost control, and its compatibility with existing management accounting systems.

Demand-Based Pricing

The second fundamental approach is that of the demand-based pricing method, which uses a mix of market research, managerial experience, and intuition to arrive at a price that is thought to reflect demand. Here, too, there are problems. First, the assessment (at best) reflects demand prior to the introduction of the new product, which is, presumably, differentiated from previous offerings in some significant way. This problem can be anticipated to some extent through market research techniques (such as FOCUS GROUPS, price recall tests, and buyer response surveys) and by TEST MARKETING. Second, difficult assumptions have to be made about the future response not only of demand but also of competitors. Third, demand is often influenced by qualitative factors such as self-image or risk tolerance, factors that may not easily be quantifiable for pricing decisions. Fourth, demand-based prices in consumer markets can only reflect an aggregate assessment of demand since it would be impractical in most cases to vary prices for each purchase in response to the specific motivations and circumstances of individual customers (an important exception here is pricing by auction). In organizational markets, the individual nature of many supplier–customer relationships makes it possible (even common) to adjust prices in response to specific demand. So consumer prices cannot usually reflect demand directly, even if this could be measured accurately. And fifth, the widespread market and competitive research required by this approach can be costly and time consuming (and may risk leaking news of the product to rivals). Despite these difficulties, the demand-based pricing method is likely to insure that priority is given to the customer's perspective.

GOING-RATE PRICING

A third method of determining prices for new products is one that seeks to minimize competitive disruption by setting prices that are thought to reflect what might be the going rate for a parallel product or service. This is sometimes also referred to as imitative pricing. Relatively few "new" products or services are completely different to anything already on the market and most will compete, in effect, with existing alternatives or substitutes. By setting prices in line with such established offerings, it may be possible to sidestep some of the problems of assessing price sensitivity to new products while also perhaps minimizing immediate competitive response. Prices can subsequently be adjusted to reflect observed demand for whatever differentiating features may be offered by the new product. It may well be sensible to avoid provoking strong competitive responses during the initial, vulnerable, stages of a new product's life cycle (*see* PRODUCT LIFE CYCLE), especially perhaps where the extent of differentiation is not immediately apparent or involves significant changes in customer learning and/or risk perception (*see* CONSUMER LEARNING; PERCEIVED RISK).

The three main methods of pricing discussed above reflect the three principal problems of determining prices for new products – UNCERTAINTY about costs, demand, and competitive response. Cost-based pricing focuses on costs and assumes that demand and competitive response are predictable; demand-based pricing focuses on customer response while paying relatively little attention to cost or rivals; going-rate pricing prioritizes maintaining the competitive status quo over issues of cost or demand. All approaches have difficulties and advantages and all should ideally be considered when making pricing decisions (Gabor, 1988).

HEDONIC PRICING

A fourth method of setting prices is also worth mentioning: hedonic pricing or perceived-value pricing (Kortge and Okonkwo, 1993). This is an interesting approach, originating from the field of economics, which regards products and services as "clusters of desirable attributes" and attempts to allocate a "price" component to each attribute such that the eventual price calculation is the sum of the hedonic price components. For example, a washing machine may merit different price components according to such variables as its spin speed, the time taken by its wash cycles, the availability of economy settings, the strength of its brand, the ease of servicing, its appearance, its power consumption, its eco-friendliness, and so on. Statistical REGRESSION AND CORRELATION analysis of existing washing machines can identify the apparent price that the consumer seems prepared to pay for these attributes in existing washing machines, and so new models can be designed and priced accordingly (Hartman, 1989). This approach presents problems in researching consumer response to genuinely innovative attributes and in its apparent disregard for cost issues, but the concept seems useful, especially perhaps in high-price mature consumer markets such as white goods, cars, furniture, holidays, and housing.

Sensible pricing decisions will, of course, draw on all four pricing methods (Tellis, 1986), though perhaps with a mixture of formal and more intuitive methodologies that will reflect not only the logic of the products/services and their anticipated markets, but also the culture of the organizations involved and the personal preferences (and competence) of individual decision-makers. As with all organizational decision-making processes, it would be foolish to ignore the sociopolitical dynamics and personal interests that are likely to be powerful factors affecting the individual decision-makers involved.

See also *price elasticity; penetration pricing; pricing; skimming pricing*

Bibliography

Cooper, R. and Kaplan, R. S. (1988). Measure cost right: Make the right decisions. *Harvard Business Review*, **66** (September/October), 96–103.

Gabor, A. (1988). *Pricing: Concepts and Methods for Effective Marketing*, 2nd edn. Aldershot: Gower.

Hartman, R. S. (1989). Hedonic methods for evaluating product design and pricing strategies. *Journal of Economics and Business*, **41**, 3 (August), 197–212.

Kortge, G. D. and Okonkwo, P. A. (1993). Perceived-value approach to pricing. *Industrial Marketing Management*, **22**, 2 (May), 133–40.

Nagle, T. T. (1987). *The Strategy and Tactics of Pricing*. Englewood Cliffs, NJ: Prentice-Hall.

Nagle, T. T. (1993). Managing price competition. *Marketing Management*, **2** (Spring), 36–45.

Oxenfeldt, A. R. (1973). A decision-making structure for price decisions. *Journal of Marketing*, **37** (January), 48–53.

Smith, G. E. and Nagle, T. T. (1994). Financial analysis for profit-driven pricing. *Sloan Management Review*, **35**, 3 (Spring), 71–84.

Tellis, G. J. (1986). Beyond the many faces of price: An integration of pricing strategies. *Journal of Marketing*, **50** (October), 146–60.

pricing objectives

Dominic Wilson

An organization might have many objectives in determining its pricing policies. Some of the more typical pricing objectives include: insuring continuity of cash flow (which encourages attention to PAYBACK period); increasing MARKET SHARE (which favors low price strategies such as PENETRATION PRICING); maintaining the competitive status quo (favoring neutral pricing strategies and a focus on non-price competition); and, of course, simply achieving sufficient PROFIT to offset the costs and risks involved in making the OFFERING available. Finally, in times of economic or competitive difficulty, the prime objective of organizations may simply be to survive in the short term, resulting in pricing policies such as MARGINAL PRICING, which would not normally be considered.

It is particularly important that pricing objectives be consistent with the objectives of other elements of the MARKETING MIX, e.g., a product priced to imply quality and prestige (such as a perfume or a liqueur) would seem absurd if promoted and packaged as a commodity product. Equally, the pricing objectives should be consistent with the strategic objectives of the business and the organization as a whole: for example, a supermarket aiming to appeal to a wide range of customers would offer some products such as coffee or beer in several forms (economy, premium, luxury) with different levels of quality, PACKAGING, and price.

See also *pricing; pricing methods*

Bibliography

Marn, M. V. and Rosiello, R. L. (1992). Managing price: Gaining profit. *Harvard Business Review*, **70** (September/October), 84–94.

Oxenfeldt, A. R. (1973). A decision-making structure for price decisions. *Journal of Marketing*, **37** (January), 48–53.

pricing process

Dominic Wilson

In theory, the pricing process can be represented as having several interconnected but distinguishable "stages," though in practice it will rarely be appropriate to go through all of these stages completely except on the most elaborate and important occasions of NEW TASK purchasing (for a concise overview see Corey, 1991). According to this theoretical and idealized model, the pricing process starts with the identification of PRICING OBJECTIVES (derived from STRATEGIC MARKETING objectives), then analyzes the level of DEMAND and price sensitivity in the TARGET MARKET, while also analyzing the relevant cost structure and PROFIT expectations, and evaluating rival offerings (*see* OFFERING), before selecting an appropriate pricing policy (such as PENETRATION PRICING or SKIMMING PRICING), and an actual set of prices for the product range. In effect there are four broad and overlapping phases in this "process":

1 the setting of objectives;
2 the analysis of costs, demand, rival offerings, potential profits, and the development of varying scenarios to test the assumptions involved;
3 the determination of specific prices and the degree of discretion to be associated with each nominal price; and

4 the continuing monitoring and (if necessary) adjustment of the pricing decisions compared to assumptions concerning demand and competitive response.

It would, of course, be sensible to assume that this pricing process was a seamless part of the product development and marketing process rather than a discrete sequence.

See also *price elasticity; pricing; pricing methods*

Bibliography

Corey, E. R. (1991). Pricing: The strategy and process. In R. J. Dolan (ed.), *Strategic Marketing Management*. Boston: Harvard Business School Press, pp. 253–69.

primary data

Michael Greatorex

Primary data are collected specifically to address a particular research issue. Primary data are required when SECONDARY DATA are unavailable or insufficient. They are more likely to be used in the later decision-making stages of a research project. Primary data are collected about such things as the demographic (*see* DEMOGRAPHICS), socioeconomic, psychographic (*see* PSYCHOGRAPHICS), and lifestyle (*see* LIFESTYLES) characteristics of the subjects of research as well as their ATTITUDES, opinions, AWARENESS, knowledge, intentions, motives, and behavior.

See also *primary research*

Bibliography

Churchill, G. A. (1991). *Marketing Research: Methodological Foundations*, 5th edn. Chicago: Dryden Press, pp. 305–14.

primary research

Michael Greatorex

Primary research collects data (*see* PRIMARY DATA) specifically to address a particular research issue. The broad categories of methods of collecting primary data are qualitative (*see* QUALITATIVE RESEARCH) and quantitative, which can be broken down into OBSERVATION, surveys (*see* SURVEY RESEARCH) involving the questioning of respondents, and experiments (*see* EXPERIMENTATION).

Qualitative methods include DEPTH INTERVIEWS, FOCUS GROUPS, and PROJECTIVE TECHNIQUES and are often used in exploratory research. Surveys use structured questionnaires to obtain the desired information, usually from a sample of the population of interest. The questionnaires may be administered personally by an interviewer, in the street or in the home or using the telephone; alternatively, a computer or the postal system may be used. Responses are numerically analyzed using computer statistical packages.

Both qualitative methods and surveys aim to obtain information on respondents' ATTITUDES, opinions, motives, etc., with unstructured (qualitative methods) or structured (surveys) interviews. Qualitative methods are aimed at discovering the hidden or underlying factors that more direct methods may not reveal.

Observation is a method of collecting data on a topic of interest by watching and recording behavior, actions, and facts.

Experimentation is a type of primary MARKETING RESEARCH in which the experimenter systematically manipulates the values of one or more variables (the independent variables), while controlling the values of other variables, to measure the effect of the changes in the independent variables on one or more other variables (the dependent variables).

Primary research may be done on an ad hoc basis, where the data are collected from the respondents once only, or continuously, where data are collected from the same respondents on a regular basis. Examples of continuous research include consumer panels, members of which keep diaries about their purchases, TELEVISION audience measurement, and retail audits. One advantage of continuous research is the opportunity to observe trends.

Bibliography

Churchill, G. A. (1991). *Marketing Research: Methodological Foundations*, 5th edn. Chicago: Dryden Press, ch. 7.

Tull, D. S. and Hawkins, D. I. (1993). *Marketing Research: Measurement and Method*, 6th edn. New York: Macmillan, chs. 6, 7, 8.

Johnson, R. A. and Wichern, D. W. (1998). *Applied Multivariate Statistical Analysis*, 4th edn. Upper Saddle River, NJ: Prentice-Hall.

principal component analysis

Michael Greatorex

Principal component analysis and FACTOR AN-ALYSIS are two closely associated multivariate statistical techniques. Principal component analysis attempts to represent the interrelationships within a set of variables; it tries to reduce the number of variables required to represent a set of observations.

The method first finds the linear function of the variables with the largest variance, so that this newly created artificial (or latent) variable represents as much as possible of the variability in the original data. It then chooses a second linear function, independent of the first principal component, which explains as much as possible of the remaining variability in the original data. This continues until one chooses to stop the process. The idea is to account for the variability in, say, the p variables by m (where m < p) components and, thus, obtain some economy in the representation of the data.

The components may or may not have meaningful interpretations as constructs related to theoretical concepts. Interpreting components offers a challenge to the imagination of the researcher. Thus, a set of 18 variables on consumer ATTITUDES and intentions could be reduced to three components interpreted as measuring views on general economic conditions, personal financial circumstances, and household durable buying intentions.

Component analysis is best carried out using a computer package such as the STATISTICAL PACKAGE FOR THE SOCIAL SCIENCES (SPSS), where it is an optional variation in the factor analysis procedure.

See also *multivariate methods (analysis)*

Bibliography

Hair, J. F., Anderson, R. E., and Tatham, R. L. (1987). *Multivariate Data Analysis*, 2nd edn. New York: Macmillan, ch. 6.

private self

see CULTURE AND SOCIAL IDENTITY

procurement

see PURCHASING

product

Margaret Bruce and Liz Barnes

A product can be an idea, a service, a good, people, events, places, properties, organizations, information, ideas, or a combination of these. For Kotler (2003) a product "is anything that can be offered to market to satisfy a want or need." Obviously, the products of manufacturing firms are tangible, while those of service industries are intangible. A household insurance package is an example of a product that is a service. Such examples indicate the difficulty of clearly distinguishing between a product and a service (*see* SERVICE PRODUCT).

The product is regarded as encompassing a set of benefits and is often referred to as the product (or service) OFFERING. In order to understand the benefits offered, products should be looked at using the whole product model. Products can be viewed as having five levels, starting with the *core benefit*, which is the functional element of the product, i.e., what the consumer is purchasing the product for; for example, the core benefit of a car is the functionality of being able to drive. At the next level we have the *basic product*, where the marketer turns the benefit into a product; for example, to be driven the car must have an engine, wheels, steering wheel, seats, etc. At the third level is the *expected product* comprising attributes normally expected by consumers; for example, when buying a car consumers expect windows, a stereo, an attractive interior, etc. The *augmented product* is the fourth level where the marketer aims to exceed customer expectations, e.g., offering metallic paint, power steering, etc. on a car. In modern markets, competition between products is usually focused on the augmented product. The final level of the product is the *potential product*, which is concerned with the strategic direction of the product, e.g., offering improved BRAND benefits.

Bibliography

Kotler, P. (2003). *Marketing Management: Analysis, Planning, Implementation and Control*, 11th edn. Englewood Cliffs, NJ: Prentice-Hall.

product champion

Margaret Bruce and Liz Barnes

Product champion is a term used to refer to those individuals with a commitment to, or belief in, a new product, which is strong enough to overcome organizational resistance to the new product idea (Maidique, 1980). Product champions are regarded as being key influencers in the NEW PRODUCT DEVELOPMENT process (Hart, 1995). Schon (1963) studied 15 major inventions of the twentieth century and observed that certain highly committed individuals, or champions, were likely to play a role in successfully commercializing these inventions: "no ordinary involvement with a new idea provides the energy to cope with the indifference and resistance that major technical change provokes." Champions of innovations (*see* INNOVATION) "display persistence and courage of heroic quality."

Various studies have associated the existence of a product champion as a differentiating factor between innovations regarded as successful and those regarded as less successful (SPRU, 1972; Roberts and Fusfield, 1981). Roberts and Fusfield (1981) suggest that product champions are critical in new product development, "recognizing, proposing and pushing a new (product) idea." However, the product champion may serve to play a detrimental role precisely because of his/her unshaking commitment to, or belief in, the new product in question in order to overcome resistance to the new idea. This may occur when commitment leads to continued expenditure on a relatively unpromising venture, rather than withdrawing resources before considerable losses are incurred (Leverick and Littler, 1994).

Bibliography

Hart, S. (1995). Where we've been and where we're going in new product development research. In M. Bruce and W. Biemans (eds.), *Product Development: Meeting the Challenge of the Design–Marketing Interface*. Chichester: John Wiley.
Leverick, F. and Littler, D. A (1994). *Marketing in the Process of Managing Ambiguity: The Development of Telepoint in the UK*. Manchester School of Management Working Paper, UMIST.
Maidique, M. A. (1980). Entrepreneurs, champions and technological innovation. *Sloan Management Review*, 3, 299–307.
Najak, P. R. and Ketteringham, J. M. (1985). *Breakthroughs*. London: Mercury Books.
Roberts, E. B. and Fusfield, A. R. (1981). Staffing the innovation technology-based organization. *Sloan Management Review*, 22 (3), 19–34.
Schon, D. A. (1963). Champions of radical new inventions. *Harvard Business Review*, 41 (2), 77–86.
SPRU (1972). *Project SAPPHO: A Study of Success and Failure in Innovation*. SPRU, University of Sussex.

product concept

Margaret Bruce and Liz Barnes

The product concept is a basic outline of the features and values of the PRODUCT. This should be based on the core benefit(s) of the proposition, which is a summary of the advantages the product will offer to the customer. In addition, the proposition should highlight the main features that differentiate it from the competition. The first definition of the product concept will tend to be general, but over time, as a result of market research and management deliberation, it will gradually become more refined. Cross-functional communication is required in order to produce an accurate product concept (Bruce and Biemans, 1995). Examples of product concepts are: a kettle that can be easily filled through the spout and enables the user to boil only small quantities of water at a time; and an ergonomically designed secretarial chair that adapts with ease to different tasks of the secretary and prevents backache. In these cases, more work is required to define some of the basic features outlined, for example, what is a "small volume of water?"

Bibliography

Bruce, M. and Biemans, W. G. (eds.) (1995). *Product Development: Meeting the Challenge of the Design–Marketing Interface*. Chichester: John Wiley.

Littler, D. A. (1984). *Marketing and Product Development*. Oxford: Philip Allan, ch. 7.

product deletion

Margaret Bruce and Liz Barnes

This is the process of eliminating a product that does not perform at a level considered adequate according to certain criteria. Product deletions fall into two categories: product replacement refers to the phasing out of an extant product and replacing it with something new, whereas product elimination means the removal of a product without providing a substitute (Vyas, 1993). Most companies base their decisions to delete weak products on poor sales and profit potential, low compatibility with the firm's business strategies, and unfavorable market outlook (Lambert and Sterling, 1988). A proactive approach to rationalization can maximize an organization's capabilities through maintaining a balanced PRODUCT PORTFOLIO, both in the longer and shorter term, maximizing return on investment, allocating resources efficiently, and understanding what distinguishes "good" and "bad" projects (Kotler, 1964; Cooper and Kleinschmidt, 1986).

The decision to eliminate a product is based on its impact on the overall PRODUCT MIX of the firm, and if a weak product is no longer making a CONTRIBUTION and the resources employed can be more effectively deployed, then it may be deleted. Various approaches to rationalization exist, which are based on different criteria to monitor and evaluate product performance. Such models include those based on "multidimensional" criteria (Kotler, 1964; Hise and McGinnins, 1975) and "product portfolio classification" to develop a matrix to identify weaker-performing products (Wind and Claycamp, 1976). Avolonitis, Hart, and Tzokas (2000) developed a typology of product deletion, which identifies the key factors driving deletion for each category identified in their typology. These range from external forces (e.g., competitive price trends) to slow-moving products (e.g., slow sales due to less demand) to replacement of problem products and outmoded product lines. They recognize the complexity surrounding the decisions to rationalize and so identify financial, strategic, managerial, and changing market needs.

Once the decision to delete has been made, the need to minimize costs and to retain customer goodwill (e.g., providing assurances that spare parts will be available for a certain period) may affect whether the "weak" product is immediately dropped, or phased out gradually. The phase-out approach can either attempt to exploit any strengths left in the product, e.g., by a price reduction to boost sales, or let the product decline with no change in MARKETING STRATEGY.

Bibliography

Avolonitis, G., Hart, S., and Tzokas, N. (2000). An analysis of product deletion scenarios. *Journal of Product Innovation Management*, 17 (1), 41–56.

Cooper, R. G. and Kleinschmidt, E. J. (1986). An investigation into the new product process: Steps, deficiencies and impact. *Journal of Product Innovation Management*, 3 (1), 71–85.

Dibb, S., Simkin, L., Pride, W., and Ferrell, O. C. (2000). *Marketing: Concepts and Strategies*, European edn. Boston: Houghton Mifflin.

Hise, R. and McGinnis, M. (1975). Product elimination: Practices, policies and ethics. *Business Horizons*, 18, 25–32.

Kotler, P. (1964). Phasing out weak products. *Harvard Business Review*, 107–18.

Lambert, D. M. and Sterling, J. U. (1988). Identifying and eliminating weak products. *Business*, July/September, 3–10.

Vyas, N. (1993). Industrial product elimination decisions: Some complex issues. *European Journal of Marketing*, 27 (4), 58–76.

Wind, Y. and Claycamp, H. (1976). Planning product line strategy: A matrix approach. *Journal of Marketing*, 40, 2–9.

product development

see NEW PRODUCT DEVELOPMENT

product differentiation

Dale Littler

Although in some markets, such as commodities, price remains a primary determinant of DEMAND, in general customers will seek an optimum combination of price and non-price variables (*see* NON-PRICE FACTORS), such as technical features, delivery, service support, and BRAND image (Rothwell, 1981). In luxury goods markets price may be regarded as reflecting the status and perceived quality of the product. Businesses may strive to secure a COMPETITIVE ADVANTAGE by developing offerings (*see* OFFERING) providing sets of distinctive values tailored to the requirements of different clusters of customers. In this way, suppliers effectively steepen their demand curves and aim to prevent their products reaching commodity status. Over time, though, because of imitation by competitors, it may be increasingly difficult to implement and sustain effective differentiation. Chamberlain (1956) was among the first to highlight the principle of product differentiation in his exposition of monopolistic (or "imperfect") competition. Porter (1980) later defined differentiation as one of the GENERIC STRATEGIES that businesses can employ. In essence most businesses will strive to be different in a way that attracts customer preference over competitors.

Bibliography

Chamberlain, E. H. (1956). *The Theory of Monopolistic Competition*, 7th edn. Cambridge, MA: Harvard University Press, chs. 2, 5.

Porter, M. (1980). *Competitive Strategy: Techniques for Analyzing Industries and Competitors*. New York: Free Press, ch. 2.

Rothwell, R. (1981). Non-price factors in the export competitiveness of agricultural engineering goods. *Research Policy*, **10**, 260–88.

product innovation

Margaret Bruce and Liz Barnes

Product innovation is often defined as change or the "introduction of something new" or the first successful application of a new product (Cummins et al., 2000). Innovation can be described as being new to the company or new to the world (Johannessen, Olsen, and Lumpkin, 2001). Product innovation occurs when an idea is made into a commercial success. The process of product innovation is concerned with all of the various activities – R&D, MARKETING, production, etc. – involved in converting a new idea or discovery into a novel product for commercial or social use (Walsh et al., 1992; Freeman and Soete, 1997).

Product innovation is similar to NEW PRODUCT DEVELOPMENT (NPD) in that both describe the process of developing an idea to the launch of a product on the market. New products are often interchangeably referred to as product innovations (Johne, 1994). Some researchers suggest that NPD is different to product innovation, as innovation tends to be regarded as something that is fundamentally new, where as NPD is more incremental. In reality, the term can cover a spectrum of different possibilities, ranging from minor adaptations or extensions, such as a new formulation and a new flavor or color of an existing product, to the more technologically advanced, such as a digital camera. Innovations can be categorized in terms of their effects on DEMAND and their perceived degrees of "innovativeness." Robertson and Thomas (1971) define three categories of innovation:

- *Continuous*: This is the least disruptive and is likely to involve a modification to an existing product, rather than the creation of something new.
- *Dynamically continuous*: This can involve the development of something new or alterations to existing products, but not the creation of new consumption patterns.
- *Discontinuous*: The creation of new consumption patterns and the development of previously unknown products.

The new product may entail changes in form, components, materials, PACKAGING, or technology, so that products may have different dimensions of "newness." They may be functionally new or perform an existing function in a new way; be technically new, involving new materials, new ingredients, and sometimes new forms; or have new styles. What really matters is that consumers perceive a product as new, e.g., stylistic innovations such as changes to packaging often are intended to generate a perception of newness (*see* CONSUMER PERCEPTIONS).

See also *discontinuous innovation; innovation*

Bibliography

Cummins, D., Gilmore, A., Carson, D., and O'Donnell, A. (2000). Innovative marketing in SMEs: A conceptual and descriptive framework. *International Journal of Product Development and Innovation Management*, **2**, 3 (September/October), 231–48.

Freeman, C. and Soete, L. (1997). *Economics of Industrial Innovation*, 3rd edn. London: Pinter.

Johannessen, J. A., Olsen, B., and Lumpkin, G. T. (2001). Innovation as newness: What is new, how new and new to whom? *European Journal of Innovation Management*, **4** (1), 20–31.

Johne, A. (1994). Listening to the voice of the market. *International Marketing Review*, **11** (1), 47–59.

Robertson, T. J. and Thomas, S. (1971). *Innovative Behavior and Communication*. New York and London: Holt, Rinehart, and Winston.

Walsh, V., Roy, R., Bruce, M., and Potter, S. (1992). *Winning by Design: Technology, Product, Design and International Competitiveness*. Oxford: Blackwell.

product life cycle

Margaret Bruce and Liz Barnes

This is a representation of a product in the marketplace from market launch to maturity and decline. The product life cycle or PLC is based on the belief that most products go through a similar set of stages over their lives, much like living organisms. Typically, the PLC is represented with a graph of sales over time and is divided into four main stages: introduction, growth, maturity, and decline.

In the introduction stage, sales will be low because people will not know of the product and may be reluctant to try it out because of its novelty. They may be unsure of its features, e.g., its reliability, its "true" costs, and so perceive a risk in its purchase (*see* PERCEIVED RISK). One of the main purposes of ADVERTISING and promotion (*see* MARKETING COMMUNICATIONS) is to create AWARENESS of the product and

stimulate TRIAL; as a consequence, the expenditure for this purpose will be high. Other costs may also be high, such as R&D. Overall, the net losses will intensify in this period.

The growth stage implies increasing sales as people learn of the product and try it out. The perceived risk will reduce as consumers learn of the actual effects of product usage (*see* CONSUMER LEARNING). Advertising and promotion costs, while still high, will reduce as a proportion of total product price. Unit costs will fall as output increases and the product should make profits. Competition will enter the market but, if DEMAND increases, there should be room for competitors. Advertising emphasis will shift from "buy my product" to "buy my brand" (*see* BRAND).

In the mature phase, a fall in sales growth will occur as the market becomes saturated and there is little growth in demand. Demand will consist largely of repeat sales. Competition will intensify, prices will tend to fall, and selling effort will be more aggressive. Profits will then be squeezed.

In the decline period, actual sales will fall with product competition and changing consumer tastes and preferences. Prices and profits will decline. Some firms will delete mature products (*see* PRODUCT DELETION) and reallocate resources to other activities.

As a product moves through its life cycle, marketing strategies (*see* MARKETING STRATEGY) may be adapted; e.g., in the growth stage, it is important to develop BRAND LOYALTY and market position. In the maturity stage, a product may be modified, or new market segments (*see* MARKET SEGMENTATION) may be developed, to stimulate sales. In a period of decline, decisions have to be made about whether to eliminate the weak product, or to reposition it to extend its life.

It is argued (Kotler, 2003) that the PLC can be employed as a planning tool as a basis for timing the development and launch of new products. In other words, PLC can be used to forecast optimum times for the introduction of new products or the removal of outmoded ones, so as to maximize the return to the organization. However, its usefulness as a planning tool is questionable and there is some concern as to whether the concept in itself is valid. Indeed, Dhalla and Yaspeth

(1976) contend that acceptance of the model itself can be a self-fulfilling prophecy in that it may result in the withdrawal of effort and resources when sales cease to grow.

Some products display a "fad" cycle that has no, or a short, maturity phase, e.g., video games; others display one or more recycles between the growth and maturity stage. This can be caused by new technology that extends the uses of the product, e.g., more powerful personal computers. Dhalla and Yaspeth (1976) note that another PLC is that of the growth–decline plateau where the growth phase is followed by a partial decline to a stable volume that is considerably lower than peak sales, e.g., packaged goods.

The four stages of the PLC are not clearly definable, i.e., it is not always clear at what point the introductory phase ends and that of growth begins. The measurement criteria used are not straightforward. A product with an apparently low growth rate may be classed as at "maturity," whereas this level of growth may actually be high for that particular market. If the market situation is not taken into account, then the product may be withdrawn prematurely from that market.

It is important to note that a distinction exists between the life cycles of a product class (e.g., cars, beer), product type (e.g., sports car, lager), and brands (e.g., Nissan Primera, Stella Artois). The PLC of a class can last several decades and within the class life cycle there can be several product-type cycles, while, typically, brands have shorter life cycles. Andrews (1975) notes that a brand or product may be revitalized by refinement, extension (e.g. new flavors or sizes; see BRAND EXTENSION), or new PRICING or PACKAGING. A strategic realignment may open up new markets and product uses and introduce the product to new consumers. This will mean that the product will enter a new growth phase.

Bibliography

Andrews, B. (1975). *Creative Product Development*. London: Longman.
Dhalla, N. K. and Yaspeth, S. (1976). Forget the product life cycle. *Harvard Business Review*, **54** (1), 102–12.
Dibb, S., Simkin, L., Pride, W., and Ferrell, O. C. (2000). *Marketing: Concepts and Strategies*, European edn. Boston: Houghton Mifflin.

Kotler, P. (2003). *Marketing Management: Analysis, Planning, Implementation and Control*, 11th edn. Englewood Cliffs, NJ: Prentice-Hall.
Littler, D. A. (1984). *Marketing and Product Development*. Oxford: Philip Allan.
Moore, W. L. and Pressemier, E. A. (1993). *Product Planning and Management: Designing and Delivering Value*. New York: McGraw-Hill.

product line analysis

Margaret Bruce and Liz Barnes

A product line includes a group of items that are related because of MARKETING, technical, or end-use considerations. A product line consists of the variations of a PRODUCT, for example, the number of different types of refrigerator. A balanced PRODUCT MIX is needed to insure that new products are being developed (*see* NEW PRODUCT DEVELOPMENT) and marketed to replace or augment those products that are in decline. In order to determine which products to "build, maintain, harvest or divest," a company must carry out product line analysis, for example by looking at sales, profits, market attractiveness, and POSITIONING.

Bibliography

Brassington, F. and Pettitt, S. (2003). *Principles of Marketing*, 3rd edn. London: Financial Times/Prentice-Hall.
Dibb, S., Simkin, L., Pride, W., and Ferrell, O. C. (2000). *Marketing: Concepts and Strategies*, European edn. Boston: Houghton Mifflin.
Kotler, P. (2003). *Marketing Management: Analysis, Planning, Implementation and Control*, 11th edn. Englewood Cliffs, NJ: Prentice-Hall.

product manager

Margaret Bruce and Liz Barnes

The product manager is responsible for a PRODUCT, a product line, or several distinct products in a group. A product manager plans the MARKETING activities for the product by coordinating a mix of functions including distribution, promotion, and price (*see* MARKETING MIX). Product managers are regarded as being key in IMPLEMENTATION and control of the marketing plan (Lysonski, Levas, and Lavenka, 1995). The areas for which the product manager may be responsible include PACKAGING, branding (see BRAND), R&D, engineering, and production. He or she has to continually appraise the product's performance in terms of growth targets, MARKET SHARE, working capital targets, and return on assets managed.

Littler (1984) highlights two main criticisms that have been made of the product manager approach for product development. First, a lack of authority commensurate with the responsibilities of the position and, second, the relatively low status of the product manager function, with the result that young and inexperienced recruits may be appointed to the role. It is considered that in companies characterized by downsizing and flattened structures, the role of the product manager is less clearly defined, so that often product management is part of a number of roles that may also include finance, quality, and organizational and risk management (Homes, 2001).

Bibliography

Homes, G. (2001). The hybrid manager. *Industrial and Commercial Training*, 33 (1), 16–26.

Littler, D. A. (1984). *Marketing and Product Development*. Oxford: Philip Allan.

Lysonski, S., Levas, M., and Lavenka, N. (1995). Environmental uncertainty and organizational structure: A product management perspective. *Journal of Product and Brand Management*, 4 (3), 7–18.

product market

Margaret Bruce and Liz Barnes

Two broad categories of products and services exist: consumer and organizational (see CONSUMER MARKETING; ORGANIZATIONAL MARKETING). Consumers buy products to satisfy their personal wants, whereas organizational buyers seek to satisfy the goals of their organizations.

Consumer goods can be divided into different categories: convenience, shopping, specialty, and unsought products. Convenience goods are relatively inexpensive, frequently purchased,

and rapidly consumed items on which buyers exert only minimal purchasing effort, e.g., bread, soft drinks, and newspapers. Shopping products are items that are chosen more carefully than convenience products, e.g., shoes, furniture, and cameras. Specialty products possess one or more unique features and buyers will expend considerable effort to obtain them, e.g., a Gucci watch. Unsought products are bought irregularly to solve a given problem, e.g., emergency car repairs.

Organizational products include raw materials; major equipment; accessory equipment, e.g., tools, calculators; component parts; process materials that are used indirectly in the production of other products, e.g., fiber for products such as computer print ribbon; consumable supplies; and industrial services.

The same item can be a consumer and an industrial product, e.g., when consumers buy envelopes for their homes, they are treated as consumer goods; when a company buys envelopes, they are classified as organizational goods. The ultimate use of the product – for consumers to satisfy their personal wants and for companies to use in the firm's operations – governs the classification.

Bibliography

Brassington, F. and Pettitt, S. (2003). *Principles of Marketing*, 3rd edn. London: Financial Times/Prentice-Hall.

Kotler, P. (2003). *Marketing Management: Analysis, Planning, Implementation and Control*, 11th edn. Englewood Cliffs, NJ: Prentice-Hall.

product mix

Margaret Bruce and Liz Barnes

Product mix refers to the total array of products that a company markets and consists of new, growing, mature, and declining products (see PRODUCT LIFE CYCLE). A product mix may, in turn, consist of one or more product lines. A product line is composed of variations of a basic product, e.g., Cadbury's chocolate bars. The depth of the product mix is measured by the number of different products offered in each product line, and the width of the product mix measures the number of product lines offered by a company. A company selling ice-cream with many flavors, such as Häagen-Dazs, has a narrow product mix but great product depth. Companies such as Unilever have both broad and deep product mixes. A "balanced" product mix or portfolio is required to insure that new products are being developed to replace or augment those in decline or maturity and that there are products with a positive cash flow to finance the development of new products (see NEW PRODUCT DEVELOP-MENT). A company can look at the product mix dimensions to make choices about expansion, e.g., add new product lines, lengthen or deepen the product mix, and so on.

Bibliography

Brassington, F. and Pettitt, S. (2003). *Principles of Marketing*, 3rd edn. London: Financial Times/Prentice-Hall.

Dibb, S., Simkin, L., Pride, W., and Ferrell, O. C. (2000). *Marketing: Concepts and Strategies*, European edn. Boston: Houghton Mifflin.

Kotler, P. (2003). *Marketing Management: Analysis, Planning, Implementation and Control*, 11th edn. Englewood Cliffs, NJ: Prentice-Hall.

product modification

Margaret Bruce and Liz Barnes

Product modification means changing one or more of the product's features and may involve reformulation and repackaging to enhance its customer appeal. Modifications can give a COMPETITIVE ADVANTAGE, e.g., a company may be able to charge a higher price and enhance customer loyalty. Product modification is often used as a way of extending the PRODUCT LIFE CYCLE of a product. Brassington and Pettitt (2003) classify modifications into three distinct types: quality, DESIGN, and performance. Quality modifications relate to the product's dependability and durability; performance modifications relate to the effectiveness, convenience, and safety of products (e.g., washing machines that use less heat and water); and design modifications alter the aesthetic and sensory appeal of the product (such as its taste, texture, sound, and appearance). Such modifications can act to differentiate

products in the marketplace, e.g., BMW cars have an immediately recognizable style.

A number of issues have to be considered before deciding whether or not to keep the product, change it, or eliminate it (see PRODUCT DELETION); for example, what is the customer appeal? The product may have lost its distinctiveness because of the introduction of new products or improvements of its main rivals. By reformulating the product, it may be possible to regain its competitive edge. The company needs to assess the opportunities and threats posed by technological change (see SWOT ANALYSIS). What is the vulnerability of the product to technological innovation and competition? Moreover, the organization should assess the interdependencies of the product and others in the mix (see PRODUCT MIX) and how modification would impact upon the overall cost structure?

Bibliography

Brassington, F. and Pettitt, S. (2003). *Principles of Marketing*, 3rd edn. London: Financial Times/Prentice-Hall.

Dibb, S., Simkin, L., Pride, W., and Ferrell, O. C. (1994). Identifying and eliminating weak products. *Business*, July/September, 3–10.

Littler, D. A. (1984). *Marketing and Product Development*. Oxford: Philip Allan.

product planning

Margaret Bruce and Liz Barnes

The PRODUCT LIFE CYCLE suggests that there is a need to monitor the performance of existing products, to devise appropriate policies for those products, and to develop new products where necessary. All this is the essence of product planning. Littler (1984) points out that product planning entails the creation of procedures to evaluate product performance and to plan the modification, where necessary, of existing products aimed at extending their lives (see PRODUCT MODIFICATION); the deletion of weak products that have reached the terminal stage of their lives (see PRODUCT DELETION); and the development and marketing of new products (see NEW PRODUCT DEVELOPMENT).

The thrust of product planning is to insure that companies have a "balanced" PRODUCT MIX in the sense that there are new products being developed or marketed to replace or augment those in decline or maturity and that there are products with a positive cash flow that can be used to finance the development of new products. In addition, it is important to insure that there is a balanced portfolio of new products (*see* PRODUCT PORTFOLIO) so that those that are highly risky but offer the prospect of a high return are balanced by those that have a low element of risk but also a correspondingly low return.

Companies should periodically review their products and identify those that are satisfying customer requirements and yielding returns and those that are not. Managers have to consider the potential of the market (*see* MARKET POTENTIAL) and company objectives and set performance criteria to review product performance. Action should be taken to modify or delete those products that do not meet the company's performance criteria. Such criteria may include: sales and profit history of the product, relative profitability, future potential, customer appeal, and vulnerability to technological developments and competitors' actions.

As well as considering "weak" products, new product opportunities need to be identified and investment put into new product development. Innovative products (*see* INNOVATION) have to be developed as the differential advantages of existing products are undermined by technological change and competitors' actions. In some sectors, the pace of technological change is so rapid that product life cycles are less than one year old (Cane, 1991). New products generate additional sales and profits. They can add value by offering more perceived customer values and so help to sustain a COMPETITIVE ADVANTAGE. Thus, the development of new products should be a facet of the overall product planning process to insure that new products are available to replace the loss in sales and profits resulting from the maturity and demise of existing products.

Bibliography

Cane, A. (1991). A race that does not lose face. *Financial Times*, May 19.

Littler, D. A. (1984). *Marketing and Product Development*. Oxford: Philip Allan.

product portfolio

Dale Littler

The product portfolio covers all the products that a company markets. The portfolio may consist of several product lines, different individual products, or a blend of both. In theory, an organization will strive to insure that it has products at different stages of the PRODUCT LIFE CYCLE so that, for example, there are new products being introduced to replace those products entering their decline stage (*see* PRODUCT PLANNING). The firm may also strive for a balanced product portfolio in terms of risk and/or cash flow. Frameworks such as the BCG MATRIX, developed for business portfolio analysis, can also be employed in the analysis of product portfolios.

product positioning

Margaret Bruce and Liz Barnes

Product positioning concerns the decisions and activities intended to create and maintain a firm's PRODUCT CONCEPT in the customer's mind. Attempts are made by companies to position new products so that they are seen to possess the features most desired by the TARGET MARKET. Product positioning is linked to MARKET SEGMENTATION, so that effective product positioning helps to serve a specific market segment by creating an appropriate concept in the minds of customers in that segment. A product can be positioned to compete directly with another product, e.g., Pepsi with Coca-Cola, or it can be positioned to avoid competition, e.g., 7UP in relation to other soft-drink products.

Every product offered to a market needs a positioning strategy so that its place in the total market can be communicated to the target market. Alternative bases for constructing a product positioning strategy have been identified. Wind (1982) includes positioning on specific product features, positioning for a specific user category, and positioning against another product. Perceptual maps visually summarize the dimensions or primary needs that customers use to perceive and judge products and they present the relative position of brands in terms of these dimensions. For pain relievers, for example, "effectiveness" and "gentleness" may be used as the dimensions to construct the perceptual maps, and different offerings can be plotted according to these two dimensions. More than two dimensions of primary needs can be used to create perceptual maps; for example, alternative modes of transport can be compared on the basis of "quickness and convenience," "ease of travel," and "psychological comfort." Plotting the perception of the new and existing brands on perceptual maps can help evaluate the brands and assess their competitive position as well as point to new opportunities. Measures of preference are needed that suggest what potential buyers might want in a new product to determine whether or not the product is desirable (Thomas, 1993).

See also *positioning*

Bibliography

Thomas, R. J. (1993). *New Product Development: Managing and Forecasting for Strategic Success*. New York: John Wiley.
Urban, G. L. and Hauser, J. R. (1993). *Design and Marketing of New Products*, 2nd edn. Englewood Cliffs, NJ: Prentice-Hall.
Wind, Y. J. (1982). *Product Policy: Concepts, Methods and Strategy*. Reading, MA: Addison-Wesley.

product/service profit center

David Yorke

The traditional form of financial accountability in an organization is where profit centers are based on products or services, as opposed to customer profit centers. All revenues and direct costs (of manufacturing and distribution) are allocated to specific products/services. Indirect costs (of manufacturing, sales, and promotion) are apportioned in some way, usually by determining how much of each can be attributed to

each product/service. This is called activity-based costing. The product or brand manager (*see* PRODUCT MANAGER) may be held accountable for such profitability and the profit center may also then be used as the basis for future MARKETING PLANNING.

Bibliography

Cooper, R. and Kaplan, R. S. (1988). Measure costs right: Make the right decisions. *Harvard Business Review*, 66, 5 (September/October), 96–103.

profit

Dominic Wilson

Profit is a concept that refers to the financial benefit of engaging in commercial activities. It is usually calculated as the excess of sales revenues over total costs (fixed and variable), but there are many forms of profit and measures are subject to accounting conventions. Profit is an important issue in PRICING as products and services are generally not marketed unless profit is anticipated. However, the profit involved may not necessarily be anticipated exclusively in financial terms (as with charities), or in the short term (as with nuclear power), nor even with respect to the specific product or market in question (through cross-subsidization).

Profit Impact of Marketing Strategies (PIMS)

Dale Littler

Profit Impact of Marketing Strategies (PIMS) was initiated in 1960 by General Electric, developed further by the Marketing Science Institute, and later administered by the Strategic Planning Institute. It is a data bank that provides a source of cross-sectional and time-series data. The DATABASE contains information on a number of environment, strategy, performance, competition, and firm-related variables for approximately 4,000 businesses (or STRATEGIC BUSINESS UNITS) collected from over 500 participating large and small companies, operating in a wide range of industries. It covers markets in North America, Europe, and elsewhere.

The approximate 200 items of data are collected in a standardized format from each business and cover: the environment in which the business is operating, such as the number and size of customers, rates of market growth, the distribution channels it uses (see CHANNELS OF DISTRIBUTION); the business's competitive position in the market, quality, prices, and costs relative to the competition; and annual measures of the business's financial and operating performance. The most publicized use of the PIMS data is in a regression model (see REGRESSION AND CORRELATION), which contains 37 independent variables grouped into seven categories: attractiveness of the business environment; the strength of competitive position; the differentiation of competitive position; the effectiveness of use of investment; discretionary budget allocations; the characteristics of the owning corporation; and the current change in position variables. This explains 80 percent of the variance in the dependent variable, pre-tax return on investment. A similar model has been developed to assess the impact on cash flow.

Schoeffler (1977) summarized the findings and noted that: investment intensity has a negative impact on percentage measures of profitability and cash flow; businesses producing high value added per employee are more profitable than those with low value added; the absolute and relative MARKET SHARE have a positive impact on profit and cash flow; the served market growth rate has a positive impact on dollar measures of profit, no effect on percentage measures of profit, and a negative effect on all measures of cash flow; product and/or SERVICE QUALITY in relation to competitors' offerings (as viewed by the customer) has a favorable impact on all measures of financial performance; a business's extensive actions with regard to new product introduction, R&D, marketing effort, etc. have a positive impact on its performance, but only if the business is in a strong position to begin with; VERTICAL INTEGRATION, for businesses competing in mature and stable markets, has a favorable impact, but the opposite is the case for rapidly changing markets; the effect of cost push factors, such as wage and

salary increases, increases in raw material prices, etc., depends on the ability of the firm to pass on the increase to its customers and/or its ability to absorb these higher costs; with regard to current strategic effort, the direction of change may be opposite to that of the factor itself, so that attempts to increase market share of high-market-share firms have a negative effect on cash flow. The specific contexts of individual businesses, which are not taken into account in the summary data, may, however, have a significant effect on both strategic actions and the consequential performance. Moreover, Marshall and Buzzell (1990) have noted that the PIMS database tends to consist of self-selected businesses and may be unrepresentative because there is some evidence that there is a bias toward market leaders. The tenure of the participating businesses in the PIMS program is positively related to performance, while there may be a tendency for at least some businesses to overstate their market shares.

Bibliography

Abell, D. F. and Hammond, J. S. (1979). *Strategic Marketing Planning*. Englewood Cliffs, NJ: Prentice-Hall, pp. 328–32.

Buzzell, R. D. and Gale, B. T. (1987). *The PIMS Principles*. New York: Free Press.

Johnson, G. and Scholes, K. (1993). *Exploring Corporate Strategy*, 3rd edn. Prentice-Hall, pp. 263–9.

Marshall, C. T. and Buzzell, R. D. (1990). PIMS and the FTC line-of-business data: A comparison. *Strategic Management Journal*, 11, 269–82.

Schoeffler, S. (1977). *Nine Basic Findings on Business Strategy*. Cambridge, MA: The Strategic Planning Institute.

projective techniques

Michael Greatorex

Projective techniques are a group of QUALITATIVE RESEARCH methods which are useful when it is felt that a typical direct questionnaire may not be appropriate in providing the information sought. Projective techniques include word association tests where the respondent is required to give the first word that comes to mind after the interviewer presents a word, e.g., a BRAND name, in a sequence that includes the words of interest along with several neutral words. Two further techniques are sentence completion and story completion where it is felt that respondents will give revealing answers as they relax their conscious defense. Construction techniques require the respondent to construct dialogue, e.g., to fill in a balloon on a cartoon, or to compose a story behind a picture. Third-person techniques allow respondents to project their own ATTITUDES and opinions on to someone else, such as an average person, rather than acknowledge that they are their own attitudes, opinions, etc.

Projective techniques, based on methodologies devised by clinical psychologists, require specialists to conduct and to interpret the responses.

See also *marketing research*

Bibliography

Malhotra, N. K. (2003). *Marketing Research: An Applied Orientation*, 4th edn. Harlow: Prentice-Hall.

Tull, D. S. and Hawkins, D. I. (1993). *Marketing Research: Measurement and Method*, 6th edn. New York: Macmillan, pp. 452–60.

promotion

see MARKETING COMMUNICATIONS; PRICE PROMOTIONS; SALES PROMOTION

psychographics

Vincent-Wayne Mitchell

Psychographics is the general term used to describe the measurement of psychological characteristics of CONSUMERS. While PERSONALITY traits and values are of major concern, many authors also include in this category lifestyle data such as activities, interests, hobbies, and opinions (*see* AIOS; LIFESTYLES). Mitchman (1991) argues that the great diversity of consumer lifestyles arising in the 1980s and 1990s has made MARKET SEGMENTATION more difficult in many markets. The general increasing wealth of western countries, the rise in DEMAND

for more psychological value in products, increasing competition, and the better-tailored MARKETING MIX are factors pushing marketers to develop more precise and effective SEGMENTATION VARIABLES.

Numerous comparisons show that the predictive VALIDITY of psychographic variables is likely to be substantially higher than for demographic variables (e.g., Wilson, 1966; Nelson, 1969; Burger and Schott, 1972; King and Sproles, 1973) (*see* DEMOGRAPHICS). In light of this, psychographics has become more popular over the past two decades. However, there is still no single widely accepted definition. When Wells (1975) published his critical review of the subject, he found no fewer than 32 definitions in 24 articles. Some researchers have used standard personality tests, while others have developed their own scales unique to their purpose. The dominant method of developing psychographic measures has been to use long scales of items/questions that are rated/answered by respondents. The highly structured nature of these questionnaires allows easy administration to relatively large samples of consumers. Once the data are collected, a common set of statistical procedures is used to derive the psychographic segments, which usually involves the use of FACTOR ANALYSIS, CLUSTER ANALYSIS, and DISCRIMINANT ANALYSIS.

An example of a generic psychographic segmentation tool is VALS-2 (Values and Lifestyles). SRI International (of Menlo Park, California) attempted to develop a standard psychographic framework for analyzing US consumers. It identified eight major groups: Strugglers, Makers, Strivers, Believers, Experiencers, Achievers, Fulfilled, Actualizers. It is obvious from the SRI analyses that the categories broadly reflect Maslow's hierarchy of needs, ranging from Strugglers at the bottom, who are powerless, narrowly focused, risk averse, and conservative, to Actualizers at the top, who are optimistic, self-confident, involved, outgoing, and growth oriented (*see* CONSUMER NEEDS AND MOTIVES).

An acclaimed alternative to VALS is LOV (List of Values), which includes segments based on self-respect, security, warm relationships with others, being well respected, self-fulfillment, self-accomplishment, sense of belonging, fun and enjoyment of life (Kahle and Kennedy, 1988). The researchers have claimed that LOV:

1 has greater predictive validity than VALS in consumer behavior trends;
2 is easier to administer; and
3 is better able to diminish communication errors, because it is easier to preserve the exact phrase from a value study and incorporate it into an advertisement.

Global values are a person's most enduring, strongly held, and abstract values that hold in many situations, for example, the idea of freedom. Terminal values are highly desired end states, such as social recognition and pleasure. Instrumental values are the values needed to achieve the desired end states, such as ambition and cheerfulness. Global values are different from domain-specific values, which are relevant only to particular areas of activity such as religion, family, or consumption. Value conflict arises when we do something that is consistent with one value but inconsistent with another equally important value. For example, parents who place equal value on convenience and concern for the environment may experience value conflict if they buy disposable nappies for their babies.

A European value-based segmentation includes: Material Hedonists, Rational Materialists, Empathetic Risk Takers, Self-Actualizers, and Safety-Oriented (Puohiniemi, 1991). Other research on European lifestyles by the RISC organization has identified six "Eurotypes" from 24 Eurotrends, namely: Traditionalists, Homebodies, Rationalists, Pleasurists, Strivers, and Trendsetters. Whereas most lifestyle research provides only a "snapshot" analysis, the RISC approach offers a continuous measurement of sociocultural trends.

Lifestyle and value-based segmentation have been criticized for being too general to be of great use and their international application is limited because lifestyles vary from country to country (Sampson, 1992). Sampson argues that it is possible to understand human social behavior to a limited degree only, by studying values in isolation. This is because values are too general and cannot deal with issues that relate to specific product consumption and brand-choice behavior in different markets. Therefore, while it may be important to understand value change in longer-term strategic MARKETING PLANNING, in the short term, value analysis is of limited worth. Sampson advocates a model that has four psychological traits: outward expressiveness to inward repression, and stereotype masculinity (e.g., strength) to stereotype femininity (e.g., softness). The model has been tested in the US, South Africa, Southeast Asia, Japan, and 17 European countries and claims to be superior to lifestyle and value-based segmentation because people's loves, hates, fears, hopes, aspirations, and hang-ups are more similar than their lifestyles. Trait theorists propose that personality is composed of characteristics that describe and differentiate individuals (Allport, 1937). For example, people might be described as aggressive, easygoing, quiet, moody, shy, or rigid. Personality does not appear to be a good predictor of brand choice, but it may help us understand phenomena such as susceptibility to persuasion, the liking of an ad, or the extent of information processing.

A number of psychographic segmentations have been developed for specific markets. For example, Moschis (1992) has developed a segmentation tool for the 55 years + market. The "gerontographic" clusters include: Healthy Hermits, Ailing Out-Goers, Frail Recluses, and Healthy Indulgers. Pernica (1974) reported that purchasers of stomach remedies can be divided into Severe Sufferers, Active Medicators, Hypochondriacs, and Practicalists.

Despite the usefulness of some psychographic segmentation studies in understanding consumers, the technique is not without its problems. Cost is one major problem, since the time and money involved in developing questionnaires and obtaining, analyzing, and interpreting psychographic and lifestyle data can be significant. It is also difficult to draw firm conclusions based upon the results of any single study, and reported replications of studies, which would allow discernible patterns to be seen, are few (see, e.g., Novak and MacEvoy, 1990). The consumer research literature also contains several critical articles questioning the RELIABILITY (and validity) of psychographic concepts and measures (see Wells, 1975; Lastovicka, 1982).

Bibliography

Allport, G. (1937). *Personality: A Psychological Interpretation*. New York: Holt, Rinehart, and Winston.

Burger, P. C. and Schott, B. (1972). Can private brand buyers be identified? *Journal of Marketing Research*, 9 (May), 219–22.

Kahle, L. and Kennedy, P. (1988). Using the List of Values (LOV) to understand consumers. *Journal of Services Marketing*, 2 (Fall), 49–56.

King, C. W. and Sproles, C. B. (1973). *The Explanatory Efficacy of Selected Types of Consumer Profile Variables in Fashion Change Agent Identification*. Institute Paper No. 425, Krannert Graduate School of Industrial Administration, Purdue University.

Lastovicka, L. (1982). On the validity of life style traits: A review and illustration. *Journal of Marketing Research*, 19 (February), 126–38.

Mitchman, R. (1991). *Lifestyle Market Segmentation*. New York: Praeger.

Moschis, G. (1992). Gerontographics: A scientific approach to analyzing and targeting the mature market. *Journal of Services Marketing*, 63 (Summer), 17–27.

Nelson, A. R. (1969). A national study of psychographics. Paper delivered at the International Marketing Congress, American Marketing Association, June.

Novak, T. P. and MacEvoy, B. (1990). On comparing alternative segmentation schemes: The List of Values (LOV) and Lifestyles (VALS). *Journal of Consumer Research*, 17 (June), 105–9.

Pernica, J. (1974). The second generation of market segmentation studies: An audit of buying motivation. In W. D. Wells (ed.), *Life Style and Psychographics*. Chicago: American Marketing Association, pp. 277–313.

Puohiniemi, M. (1991). Value-based segmentation, social change and consuming orientations. In ESOMAR Seminar on the Growing Individualization of Consumer Life-Styles and Demand: How is Marketing Coping With It? *Helsinki Proceedings*.

Sampson, P. (1992). People are people the world over: The case for psychological market segmentation. *Marketing and Research Today*, November, 236–45.

Wells, W. (1975). Psychographics: A critical review. *Journal of Marketing Research*, 12 (May), 196–213.

Wilson, C. L. (1966). Homemaker living patterns and marketplace behavior: A psychometric approach. In J. S. Wright and J. L. Goldstucker (eds.), *New Ideas for Successful Marketing*. Chicago: American Marketing Association, pp. 305–47.

public relations

David Yorke

Public relations is an element in the marketing COMMUNICATIONS MIX and may be defined as the planned and sustained effort to establish and maintain positive ATTITUDES toward the organization by its target publics. Groups, or publics, at whom public relations activities are aimed, include customers and potential customers, shareholders, employees, competitors, suppliers, and government. The major activities (Doyle, 1998) that may be undertaken by an organization's public relations function or outsourced (*see* OUTSOURCING) to a public relations firm include: achieving a positive IMAGE in the media (*see* MASS MEDIA) through the placing of favorable articles and news stories about the organization; creating and reinforcing the image of the organization by means of the organization's publications such as annual reports, brochures, stationery; sponsoring (*see* SPONSORSHIP) special events in order to create AWARENESS and project the image of the company and its products; lobbying politicians and other influentials (*see* POLITICAL MARKETING); and advising management about key public issues.

See also *publicity*

Bibliography

Doyle, P. (1998). *Marketing Management and Strategy*, 2nd edn. New York: Prentice-Hall, pp. 283–5.

public self

see CULTURE AND SOCIAL IDENTITY

publicity

David Yorke

Publicity is non-personal communications that are not paid for by the source (the marketing organizations) but which provide information about the company and/or its products. Media editors wish to publish information and news stories about organizations and their products, services, etc. to encourage favorable consumer response to the media sources (e.g., sell more newspapers). At the same time, organizations want the information presented in the media to be favorable, so as to stimulate consumer demand for their product/service or create positive ATTITUDES toward the company (e.g., as a result of community involvement). Many organizations will, therefore, prepare publicity material, i.e., company-and product-oriented information and news, which is made available to the media editors (and sometimes directly to consumers and other interested parties), in the hope that this may reach the company's target audience. However, publicity is generally controlled by the MASS MEDIA and, therefore, may be favorable or unfavorable with respect to a company and its products (e.g., in consumer reports).

The main advantage of publicity for the receiver/consumer is its credibility, typically attributed to an independent source.

purchase decisions

see CONSUMER DECISION-MAKING PROCESS

purchase intentions

see CONSUMER DECISION-MAKING PROCESS

purchasing

Dominic Wilson

Purchasing (sometimes also referred to as procurement) is the professional activity of buying goods and services on behalf of organizations. In practice, purchasing tends to be more professionally organized in larger organizations and can be quite informally organized in smaller organizations. The importance of a professional approach to purchasing is now widely recognized as organizations pay increasing attention to issues of cost and quality control where purchasing can make a major contribution. Heinritz (1991) illustrates the importance of professionalism in organizational purchasing at the macroeconomic level by pointing out that the combined purchasing of the largest 100 US corporations amounted to about 10 percent of the entire US economy – clearly it is important to

manage such a vast responsibility in an efficient and professional manner.

At an organizational level, the importance of purchasing can be illustrated by noting that in a typical manufacturing operation there is likely to be about three times as much investment in materials (depending on inventory and production policies) as there is in labor. Thus, equal percentage reductions would return much greater economies in purchasing costs than in labor costs. Nevertheless, much greater managerial attention has generally been paid, historically, to achieving economies in the labor process than in the material side of organizational management. Baily and Farmer (1990) suggest that the importance of purchasing in an organization will significantly increase when the PRODUCT LIFE CYCLE of the organization's output becomes shorter (e.g., computer suppliers), or when the organization's markets become particularly volatile (e.g., television production companies), or when the cost of the organization's purchases form a particularly large proportion of its income (e.g., armed forces). Other factors likely to increase the significance of purchasing could be suggested, including economic recession, increasing competition, the introduction of new technology (reductions of labor costs through automation leave a higher priority on managing purchasing costs), and legislation requiring open tendering (as opposed to routine reordering).

See also *purchasing process*

Bibliography

Baily, P. J. H. and Farmer, D. (1990). *Purchasing Principles and Management*, 6th edn. London: Pitman.
Heinritz, S. (1991). *Purchasing: Principles and Applications*, 8th edn. Englewood Cliffs, NJ: Prentice-Hall.

purchasing process

Dominic Wilson

The purchasing process or buying process in ORGANIZATIONAL MARKETING has been analyzed and modeled as a cycle with various "phases" or "stages." Robinson, Faris, and Wind (1967) not only distinguished three "buy classes" (which they refer to as NEW TASK, MODIFIED REBUY, and STRAIGHT REBUY), but also correlated these buy classes with eight "buy phases" in a buy grid model derived from their empirical research. These eight buy phases are:

1 anticipation and/or recognition of need;
2 determination of features and quantity of required item;
3 specification of purchase requirement;
4 search for potential sources;
5 acquisition and analysis of proposals from potential sources;
6 selection of one (or more) supplier(s);
7 negotiation of purchase arrangements and terms;
8 feedback and evaluation of the flow of purchase (Robinson et al., 1967, cited in Webster and Wind, 1972: 24).

This representation of the purchasing process as a cycle of buy phases is useful for descriptive purposes but it should not be taken literally as a managerial model since it lacks any predictive power or causative explanation of buying decisions (Webster and Wind, 1972). Nor would it be appropriate to regard the buy grid model as necessarily sequential, or serial, or involving all the identified steps and no others. Nevertheless, the buy grid model is not without value. It supports various practical observations and intuitive conclusions, such as what Robinson et al. refer to as "creeping commitment" (the increasing reluctance of customers to consider new suppliers as the purchasing process unfolds), and the different significance of the buy phases in different buy-class situations.

It may be more realistic to envisage an extended purchasing process as continuing beyond the stages of "receipt" and "inspection" through a subsequent stage of "payment" (a stage prone to its own complexities and problems) and then through periodic "review" phases toward eventual rebuy situations (if the supply has proved to be acceptable) or reverting to the new task process (if the supply is no longer acceptable). Purchasing practice can, of course, be very different from the theoretical and full-blown process described here for illustrative purposes. Twelve approximately discernible

stages (which may overlap or be omitted depending on circumstances) might be envisaged in such an extended purchasing process. They are presented below as an illustration in general terms of how the process might be observed for more complex new task purchases:

1 Perception of requirement.
2 Analysis and assessment (including establishment of provisional specifications, probable size and frequency of order, possible costs, MAKE/BUY DECISION, profiles of potential suppliers).
3 Criteria setting (identification and ranking of the most important purchasing criteria).
4 Negotiation (including request for quotations, prototype submission, pilot studies, trials, visits to suppliers' premises and reference sites, pursuit of references, capacity and liquidity assessment).
5 Value engineering (systematic evaluation of the functions of the shortlisted offerings to assess which of the offerings is best able to provide the customer's needs at the lowest net cost, taking into consideration all relevant aspects).
6 Decision (the outcome of the previous stages is considered in the context of broader aspects, where appropriate, and final negotiations may be conducted at senior levels to adjust any residual uncertainties until agreement is struck with one favored supplier).
7 Delivery and receipt (delivery procedures will have been agreed but receiving procedures are often overlooked, can vary considerably, and can often lead to administrative confusion, frustrating delays, deterioration of goods, and problems of disputed payment).
8 Inspection (usually on arrival and before receipt but this may not be practicable because of weather, nature of packaging, type of good/service, or congestion in receiving areas).
9 Storage (preferably only briefly but this will vary according to contract terms, storage life, cost of storage, safety stocks, and so on).
10 Payment.
11 Review (all procurement arrangements should be subject to review, which should

take close account of the views of production management and workers as well as consulting finance (for scrap and obsolescence rates), goods receiving (for delivery performance), quality control, and product engineering (for compatibility with any proposed changes to product design or production systems)).

12   Reassessment of requirement in anticipation of major changes (e.g., in product design, in suppliers, in technology).

See also *organizational buying behavior; purchasing*

Bibliography

Robinson, P. T., Faris, C. W., and Wind, Y. (1967). *Industrial Buying and Creative Marketing.* Boston: Allyn and Bacon.

Webster, F. E., Jr. and Wind, Y. (1972). *Organizational Buying Behavior.* Englewood Cliffs, NJ: Prentice-Hall.

qualitative research

Kalipso Karantinou

Qualitative research and interpretivist methodologies seek to "build" theory as a result of empirical insights, allowing flexibility and variety in the study of complex phenomena in dynamic or changing environments (Carson et al., 2001). Qualitative research techniques are most appropriate in situations calling for exploratory research (Parasuraman, Grewal, and Krishnan, 2004), and when the purpose of the study is to provide insights into, and seek meaning and understanding of, social phenomena (Carson et al., 2001; Malhotra and Birks, 2003). A qualitative study can be conducted before a quantitative study, to provide the basis for the large-scale quantitative investigation; it can follow a quantitative study, in those cases where further analysis of the reasons for certain findings is necessary; or it can be sufficient on its own (Birks, 1994), depending on the research area and the aims of the investigation.

If appropriately conducted, qualitative research is more likely than quantitative tools to lead to serendipitous, broader, and more holistic findings and to new integrations that go beyond initial conceptions (Miles and Huberman, 1994; Carson et al., 2001). According to McCracken (1988: 16), "Qualitative research looks for patterns of interrelationships between many categories rather than the sharply delineated relationship between a limited set of them. This difference can be characterized as a trade-off between the precision of quantitative methods and the complexity capturing ability of qualitative ones." Qualitative researchers aim to construct maps by moving closer to the territory they study, through minimizing the use of such artificial distancing mechanisms as analytical labels and abstract hypotheses (Van Maanen, 1979).

Qualitative research is grounded in a philosophical position, which is broadly "interpretivist," concerned with how the social world is interpreted, understood, experienced, or produced (Mason, 1996). The interpretivist approach includes consideration of multiple realities, different actors' perspectives, and researcher involvement, taking account of the contexts of the phenomena under study. The term *interpret* is important in this approach to research (Carson et al., 2001), taking account of participants' meaning and interpretational systems in order to gain explanation by understanding (Gill and Johnson, 2002).

The methods of data generation in qualitative research are flexible and sensitive to the social context in which data are produced (Mason, 1996). The focus is on identifying key constructs, the relationship between constructs, and the relative strengths of interrelationships between constructs, which can help the researcher build up a richness of understanding and deal with *why* questions (Birks, 1994). Qualitative methods seek to explore the meaning, not the frequency, of certain phenomena in the social world (Van Maanen, 1979). They are characterized by a complexity-capturing ability that makes them particularly appropriate for the study of managerial performance and activities within organizations, which, by their very nature, cannot be adequately studied within neatly arranged compartments in isolated and artificial settings (Carson et al., 2001).

Qualitative data, usually in the form of words rather than numbers, are a source of well-rounded, rich descriptions and explanations of processes in identifiable social contexts, with strong potential for revealing complexity (Miles and Huberman, 1994). Achieving in-depth understanding is based on researcher immersion in the phenomena to be studied (Carson et al., 2001). As a result, qualitative research typically studies relatively few respondents or units (Parasuraman et al., 2004) in depth, as it is more important to work longer, and with greater care, with a few people/cases than more superficially with many of them (McCracken, 1988).

There is a great variety of qualitative methods: in-depth interviews (*see* DEPTH INTERVIEWS), FOCUS GROUPS, participant OBSERVATION, document and visual data analysis, case studies, grounded theory, ethnographic studies, and action research. However, the rules for using qualitative methods are not as clear as with quantitative methods (Birks, 1994). Qualitative research has grown out of a wide range of intellectual and disciplinary traditions and does not represent a unified set of techniques or philosophies (Mason, 1996). This lack of a simple and prescriptive set of principles, however, is considered to be one of its great strengths, as it allows for complexity capturing and in-depth analysis. Much of the success of the methods lies in the experience of the researcher, and in his/her ability to know how to collect the information effectively and interpret the results (Birks, 1994).

A particularly challenging issue associated with qualitative research is analysis of the results. In contrast to quantitative research, there are no specifically and clearly laid down procedures for the analysis of qualitative data, which makes the task of analyzing qualitative data particularly demanding (Miles and Huberman, 1994). The qualitative methods of analysis and explanation building involve understanding complexity, detail, and context and there is more emphasis on holistic forms of analysis and explanation (Mason, 1996). Interpretation to a large extent depends on the individual and thus subjectivity is an inherent part of the qualitative process (Gordon and Langmaid, 1988); all data are mediated by the researchers' and the participants' practices of reasoning (Silverman, 1989). This makes it difficult to guard against unreliable or invalid conclusions (Miles and Huberman, 1994). Qualitative research, therefore, should involve critical self-scrutiny or active reflexivity by the researcher to avoid bias, as researchers cannot be neutral, objective, or detached from the knowledge and evidence they are generating (Mason, 1996).

However, although qualitative research is subjective and dynamic, it is not undisciplined (Gordon and Langmaid, 1988). It should be systematically, strategically, and rigorously conducted, producing social explanations to intellectual puzzles, which are generalizable in some way or which have a wider resonance (Mason, 1996).

See also *marketing research*

Bibliography

Birks, D. F. (1994). Market research. In M. J. Baker (ed.), *The Marketing Book*, 3rd edn. Oxford: Butterworth-Heinemann, pp. 238–67.

Carson, D., Gilmore, A., Perry, C., and Gronhaug, K. (2001). *Qualitative Marketing Research*. London: Sage.

Gill, J. and Johnson, P. (2002). *Research Methods for Managers*, 3rd edn. London: Paul Chapman, ch. 3.

Gordon, W. and Langmaid, R. (1988). *Qualitative Market Research: A Practitioner's and Buyer's Guide*. Aldershot: Gower, ch. 10.

McCracken, G. D. (1988). *The Long Interview*. London: Sage.

Malhotra, N. K. and Birks, D. F. (2003). *Marketing Research: An Applied Approach*, 3rd European edn. Harlow: Prentice-Hall.

Mason, J. (1996). *Qualitative Researching*. London: Sage.

Miles, M. B. and Huberman, M. A. (1994). *Qualitative Data Analysis: An Expanded Sourcebook*, 2nd edn. London: Sage.

Parasuraman, A., Grewal, D., and Krishnan, R. (2004). *Marketing Research*. Boston: Houghton Mifflin, ch. 7.

Silverman, D. (1989). Six rules of qualitative research: A post-romantic argument. *Symbolic Interaction*, **12** (2), 215–30.

Van Maanen, J. (1979). Reclaiming qualitative methods for organizational research: Preface. *Administrative Science Quarterly*, **24** (December), 520–6.

questionnaire design

Michael Greatorex

Questionnaires are associated mainly with SURVEY RESEARCH but are used sometimes as part of experimental research (*see* EXPERIMENTATION). A questionnaire is a formalized set of questions for obtaining information from respondents. A questionnaire can be administered in a face-to-face personal interview, by telephone, by computer, or by post.

Questionnaires are used to measure:

1   behavior, past, present, or intended;
2   knowledge;
3   ATTITUDES and opinions (*see* AIO);
4   demographic (*see* DEMOGRAPHICS) and other characteristics useful for classifying respondents.

The critical concern in questionnaire design is the minimization of measurement error, i.e., minimizing the difference between the information sought by the researcher and that produced by the questionnaire. The factors that need to be considered in questionnaire design include:

1   specification of required information;
2   question content;
3   question wording;
4   response format;
5   question order;
6   physical characteristics; and
7   pilot testing.

Software is available to aid the design of questionnaires and in telephone and computer interviewing to provide the questions and collect the responses as they are made.

The specification of the required information is an essential part of the research process and a necessary prerequisite of good questionnaire design. It is also necessary to consider who the respondents will be and what the interview technique will be – postal, computer, telephone, or personal.

The next consideration is to determine individual question content. Are the data to be produced by a particular question needed? Will a particular question produce the specified data? Are several questions needed rather than one? A common error is to ask two questions in one, resulting in a question that the respondent has difficulty in answering unambiguously. Will the respondent not answer the question because (1) it is outside the competence of the respondent; (2) the respondent has forgotten the answer; (3) the respondent cannot articulate the answer; or (4) the subject is embarrassing

or private and the respondent is unwilling to provide an answer?

The wording of the question is important. Simple, frequently used, and well-understood words are preferred. Leading questions such as "Most people agree that corporal punishment is wrong. Do you?" or "Do you think patriotic Britons should buy Japanese cars?" should be avoided. Questions should give alternatives equal prominence, for instance, a resident of Glasgow might be asked, "Do you prefer to travel by air, train, or road when going to London?"; just asking whether the respondent prefers to travel by air would bias the answers (see Tull and Hawkins, 1993). When using a battery of RATING SCALES, say, Likert scales, the statements should be a positive and negative mixture; indeed, different questionnaires, with the direction of the statements varying, could be prepared and distributed randomly to the respondents.

The response format is a choice between open-ended and closed questions. In open-ended questions the respondent is free to offer any reply using his/her own words. This precludes the influencing of the respondent by the list of response categories. Responses that are different to the researcher's expectations can be forthcoming, making open-ended questions suitable for exploratory research. On the other hand, respondents dislike writing answers on questionnaires and so this reduces the usefulness of self-completion questionnaires; for interviewer-administered questionnaires, the summarization and recording of answers is left to the interviewers, whose abilities and biases may vary. Eventually, responses to open-ended questions have to be coded, which may lead to misinterpretation of responses and certainly adds to cost.

In closed questions a list of possible response categories is provided for respondents to choose and record their choice. Closed or multiple choice questions are easier for the interviewer and the respondent. They increase response rates, reduce interviewer bias, and data analysis is easier. However, multiple choice questions are more difficult to compose as the list of possible answers needs to be complete, a problem whose solution requires preliminary research. The list can bias answers, not only because some response categories may be omitted, but also due to the order in which the categories are listed. For this reason, several questionnaires with different response-category orders may be produced and distributed at random in postal surveys; in computer surveys the order may be easily varied; and in personal interviews several prompt cards with different orders of alternatives may be produced and used at random.

The question sequence can affect replies: the rule is to start with general topics and gradually become more specific. Routes through the questionnaire may need to be devised depending on the responses to early questions: thus, owners of a product may be asked one set of questions, non-owners a different set. Initial questions should be simple and interesting, otherwise respondents may refuse to complete the interview. For the same reason, demographic and classification questions should be left until the end unless they are needed immediately, e.g., to establish whether or not the respondent is qualified to fill a quota in quota sampling.

The physical characteristics should make the questionnaire easy to use, especially when branching questions are used to decide on routes through the questionnaire. Physical appearance is especially important in postal surveys in order to secure the cooperation of the respondent.

Questionnaires should be piloted in order to see if the questions are understood by the respondents and mean the same thing to the respondent as the researcher intended, that the lists of response categories are complete, that the questionnaire is not too long, and that the routes through the questionnaire are appropriate and can be followed by the interviewers or respondents.

Bibliography

Malhotra, N. K. (2003). *Marketing Research: An Applied Orientation*, 4th edn. Harlow: Prentice-Hall.

Tull, D. S. and Hawkins, D. I. (1993). *Marketing Research: Measurement and Method*, 6th edn. New York: Macmillan, ch. 10

R

radio

David Yorke

Radio is a broadcasting medium which depends for its efficacy on the spoken word. The development of commercial, as opposed to government-controlled, radio stations provides ADVERTISING opportunities.

Radio advertising has the advantages of: local and regional flexibility; cheap production and media costs; very short lead times; strength of communication with target audiences; and the ability to reach people who are on the move (e.g., driving) and at work. However, there is limited creative opportunity, and many "listeners" are using the radio as a background while involved in other primary activities (both at work and at home). These elements relate to the IMPACT that radio advertising has in reaching its targets and, in turn, its cost effectiveness.

Bibliography

Crosier, K. (1999). Promotion. In M. J. Baker (ed.), *The Marketing Book*, 4th edn. Oxford: Butterworth-Heinemann, ch. 17.

rating scales

Rudolph Sinkovics

Rating scales allow for the measurement of certain attributes of objects (*see* MEASUREMENT AND SCALING). In MARKETING RESEARCH questionnaires (*see* QUESTIONNAIRE DESIGN) it is often aimed to record information about objects such as individuals, companies, and/or products. However, we are not actually measuring the individuals themselves; rather, we record certain attributes such as individuals' ATTITUDES toward products, beliefs concerning product qualities, willingness and intentions, and so on. Similarly, we measure company attributes such as sales, turnover, profits or product attributes such as IMAGE or BRAND EQUITY. The attribute determines the most powerful scale that can be used for its measurement (Churchill and Iacobucci, 2002) and consequently sets an upper limit for the assignment of numbers to objects. In MARKETING, many of the constructs possess no more than interval-level measurement and some even less. However, by using rating scales for this type of indirect assessment of attributes, we manage to provide a high level of measurement precision and receive useful information which permits nearly all mathematical operations to be performed in subsequent quantitative analysis.

Rating scales require the respondent to provide an estimate of the magnitude of an attitude, belief, importance, or likelihood by placing the object being rated at some point along a numerically valued continuum or in a series of numbered categories (Churchill and Iacobucci, 2002). A continuous rating scale, sometimes also referred to as graphic rating scale or sliding scale, requires the respondent to indicate a rating by placing a mark at the appropriate position on a line that runs from one extreme to the other. A theoretically infinite number of ratings is possible along this straight line. For instance, respondents may be requested to indicate their overall opinion about Amazon.com by placing an "x" mark at an appropriate position on a graphic line ranging from "very good" to "very bad." Quantification of responses is possible by measuring the physical distance between the left extreme position and the right extreme position. Fine distinctions in ratings can be made, but, unless undertaken in an online or computer-based environment, coding is more costly and time consuming. Furthermore, there is some debate over whether respondents will be able to translate their perceptions into measurable physical distances. Consequently, pure or true continuous/graphic rating scales are not widely used in marketing research surveys (Parasuraman, Grewal, and Krishnan, 2004).

Alternatively, itemized rating scales may be used. An itemized rating scale features a set of distinct response categories (typically five) and essentially takes the form of multiple-category questions. Associated with each category is a number or series of descriptors that are ordered and labeled according to, e.g., level of agreement or importance. An example question from a questionnaire can help to illustrate this. The statement "British Airways' food service is . . . " may force respondents to tick a response category from "1 = very bad," "2 = bad," "3 = neither bad nor good," "4 = good," to "5 = very good." While this approach is less refined than a graphic rating scale, it is less costly and time consuming to code. Itemized rating scales are more widely used in marketing research than the graphic type, especially Likert scales and semantic differential scales, which represent special forms of itemized rating scales.

Likert (1932) scales comprise a series of evaluative statements (or items) concerning an attitude object. Respondents are required to record their level of agreement with these statements. Usually five- to seven-point response categories are provided, labeled on a disagree/agree dimension. In a RELATIONSHIP MARKETING survey between manufacturers and distributors, manufacturers may be asked to report their level of agreement on a five-point Likert scale (1 = strongly agree, 5 = strongly disagree) to the following TRUST-related questions: "Our business relationship is characterized by high levels of trust," "We have not developed a strong sense of loyalty to the distributor," etc. The number of items used in the scale may vary from study to study; however, ideally more than five statements should be provided, to allow for appropriate RELIABILITY and VALIDITY tests of the scale. There is a longstanding debate between natural scientists and social scientists on whether Likert scales can in fact be considered metric scales. Practically, marketing researchers treat

these scales as interval scales (therefore assuming arbitrary zero points and equality of intervals) and perform their statistical analysis either on an item-by-item basis, using frequency distributions and arithmetic means, or create summated scores over the series of scale items in order to get an overall assessment of the object studied. In the example given, an overall trust score could be created by summing up the individual item scores and using them in further analysis, e.g., by correlating the trust score with a knowledge-sharing score.

The semantic differential scale is another rating scale, usually with seven points, with end points given labels that have appropriate meaning (e.g., hot/cold, large/small, experienced/inexperienced, slow/fast, etc.). The format originates from Osgood, Suci, and Tannenbaum (1957), who were interested in perceptions of meanings of words and concepts. While similar to the Likert scale in that it consists of a series of items to be rated by respondents, there are some key differences. Striking features of a typical semantic differential scale are (Parasuraman et al., 2004):

1   it consists of a series of bipolar adjectival words or phrases (rather than complete statements) that pertain to the attitude object;
2   each pair of opposite adjectives is separated by a seven-category scale, with neither numerical labels nor verbal labels other than the anchor labels;
3   favorable and unfavorable descriptors positioned on either the right-hand or left-hand side are often reversed and mixed.

Analysis options are similar to the Likert scale and, assuming that we are dealing with interval-type data, can be carried out on an item-by-item basis or by constructing summated measures. Often pictorial profiles are generated, based on semantic differential ratings; this requires consistency in the adjectives and some of the reversed adjectives have to be rescored.

Other types of rating scales include importance scales (a variation of Likert scales, where agreement levels are replaced by importance levels) or staple scales, which are a variation of the semantic differential. Staple scales are defined by ten-point response alternatives, where responses are labeled with bipolar numbers. As with the semantic differential, staple scales assess bidimensional intensity and since they have an even number of categories, they are forced-choice. An advantage is that it is not necessary to develop complete statements or establish bipolar words or phrases. However, staple scales can sometimes create confusion with respondents and are sensitive to the direction of the adjective (negative vs. positive) words.

Bibliography

Churchill, G. A. and Iacobucci, D. (2002). *Marketing Research: Methodological Foundations*. Mason, OH: South-Western.

Likert, R. A. (1932). A technique for the measurement of attitudes. *Archives of Psychology*, **140**, 44–53.

Osgood, C. E., Suci, G. J., and Tannenbaum, P. H. (1957). *The Measurement of Meaning*. Urbana: University of Illinois Press.

Parasuraman, A., Grewal, D., and Krishnan, R. (2004). *Marketing Research*. Boston: Houghton Mifflin.

reach

David Yorke

When organizations are planning their advertising and, in particular, deciding on which media to use (i.e., MEDIA SCHEDULE), they have to consider the desired reach of their advertising, i.e., the number of persons, households, or organizations exposed to a particular media schedule at least once during a specified period of time.

The effective reach is the percentage of the TARGET MARKET exposed to the advertisement for the minimum number of times (frequency) that is judged necessary for the advertisement to be effective.

See also *advertising*

Bibliography

Kotler, P. (2003). *Marketing Management: Analysis, Planning, Implementation and Control*, 11th edn. Englewood Cliffs, NJ: Prentice-Hall.

realizable demand

Dale Littler

The realizable demand is the actual demand that materializes during a specified period given the total marketing effort of the various firms in the market.

See also *market potential*

regionalism

Mohammed Yamin

The global economy and society contains a number of regions which share a degree of commonality in CULTURE, language, political outlook, and, to a lesser degree, economic circumstance. For example, one can mention "the Arab world," "the Indian subcontinent," "Latin America," or north-west Europe. One may expect, all things being equal, that the individual countries within these regions would have reason to engage in extensive trade and economic transactions with one another. In practice, of course, all things are rarely equal and, for example, European colonization introduced a major distortion into the structure of trade relations. Many countries in Asia and Africa, for example, tended to trade mainly with the European colonial powers rather than with one another as the trading infrastructure (transport links, insurance, etc.) tended to discourage this. The UK's pattern of trade was also to some degree distorted away from its neighboring countries in the European continent and toward the Commonwealth.

Since World War II, the demise of European colonialism has been responsible, along with other factors, for restoring the "natural" regional pattern of world trade. The regionalization of international trade has developed most fully in Europe and, in recent years, has also progressed in East Asia and North America. However, it has not progressed so much in other regions, such as the Middle East, as many of these countries are still poor or have economies dominated by one commodity (oil), the demand for which still comes predominantly from the West. The emergence of the "triad" economies in western Europe, the Pacific, and North America is thus a manifestation of the uneven spread of regionalization in these three regions compared with the remainder of the global economy. These three regions have become the natural focus for international business activities; virtually all innovations stem from these regions; the bulk of international merchandise trade is within and between these regions; and in more recent years there has been a growing number of alliances (*see* INTERNATIONAL STRATEGIC ALLIANCES) between firms from these regions (Ohame, 1985).

Recently some analysts have pointed out that economic and business integration is taking place mainly within the triad regions rather than between them (Rugman, 2003). Thus most international investment and trade is within regions and over the last two decades intra-regional trade and investment has grown much faster than inter-regional trade and investment flows. However, this should not necessarily be interpreted as showing that multinational enterprises lack a global horizon. The geographic spread of affiliates and subsidiaries indicates a truly global *reach* for multinational enterprises. Significantly, even though more than 70 percent of foreign investment takes place in a relatively small number of developed countries, the vast majority of foreign affiliates and subsidiaries are in fact in less developed and transitional economies. In the late 1990s, only 14 percent of all affiliates were in developed countries, the remaining 86 percent being in less developed and transitional economies (Yamin and Ghauri, 2004). Multinationals do control an investment and trading *network* that is undoubtedly global (Ietto-Gillies, 2001; UNCTAD 2002; Yamin and Ghauri, 2004). The production of most standardized manufactured goods, in particular, is organized through elaborate networks of geographically dispersed assembly units controlled by multinational companies. The pattern of intra-regional concentration noted by Rugman is thus one facet, albeit a very important one, of a globally configured multinational production system. It is not necessarily correct to conclude, as Rugman does, that "globalization is a myth" (*see* GLOBALIZATION).

From the marketing practitioner's point of view, regionalization is an important element in the emergence of "borderless" economies (Sheth, 1992). Regional integration is beginning to dilute some of the differences between "domestic" and INTERNATIONAL MARKETING. Thus, even for those firms whose marketing horizon is basically local, competition may in fact be international. For those firms whose marketing horizon is already international and global too, regional integration has important implications. The integrated European "single" market, for example, can be viewed as a testing ground for the viability of standardization of the marketing program. Western Europe is probably the most integrated region in the world economy (unless, of course, one regards the US as a region as well as a country). If a company's standardization of the MARKETING MIX does not work within Europe, it is unlikely that it will work beyond Europe.

Bibliography

Ietto-Gillies, G. (2001). *The Multinational Corporation: Fragmentation Amidst Integration*. London: Routledge.

Ohame, K. (1985). *Triad Power: The Coming Shape of Global Competition*. New York: Free Press.

Rugman, A. (2003). Regional strategy and the demise of globalization. *Journal of International Management*, 9 (4), 409–17.

Sheth, J. (1992). Emerging marketing strategies in a changing macroeconomic environment: A commentary. *International Marketing Review*, 9 (1), 57–63.

United Nations Conference on Trade and Development (UNCTAD) (2002). *Trade and Development Report 2002*. Geneva: United Nations.

Yamin, M. and Ghauri, P. (2004). Rethinking the MNE: Emerging market relationships. In B. Parsad and P. Ghauri (eds.), *Global Firms and Emerging Markets in an Age of Anxiety*. London: Praeger.

regression and correlation

Michael Greatorex

The possibility of a relationship between a pair of variables can be investigated in a scatter diagram where each pair of values is plotted as a point on a graph where the axes are used to represent the variables.

Simple correlation measures the strength of a relationship between two variables. If both variables are measured on metric scales, the best measure is the simple product–moment correlation coefficient which ranges from -1 to $+1$. A correlation coefficient numerically equal to 1 indicates a perfect linear relationship, while a value of zero indicates no relationship at all, and values in between indicate the amount of scatter among the points on the scatter diagram. High values of correlation coefficients indicate strong linear relationships, while low values indicate weak relationships. A positive correlation coefficient indicates that high values for one variable are associated with high values for the other; similarly, low values of the two variables occur together; a negative coefficient indicates that high values on one variable are associated with low values of the other variable, and vice versa.

Correlation between pairs of variables measured on ordinal scales can be measured using measures such as Kendall's tau and Spearman's rank correlation coefficient.

Bivariate regression measures the (linear) relationship between a pair of variables; it fits the straight line to the scatter of points that best represents the form of the relationship. One variable (Y) is designated as the dependent variable and the other (X) is the explanatory or independent variable. The relationship is specified as $Y = a + b^{*}X + u$ where u is the error term that accounts for the scatter of points around the straight line $Y = a + b^{*}X$. The "least squares" method is the basis of the procedure for obtaining numerical estimates of the parameters a and b (see Jain, 1994: 166–7).

Multiple regression is an extension of simple regression where more than one independent variable is used to explain variations in the dependent variable.

Regression equations, while usually linear, may be non-linear. The dependent variable could be the sales of beer, the several explanatory variables could be the price of beer, the price of wines and spirits, beer ADVERTISING expenditure, consumers' income, and temperature, with quarterly data for ten years being available for each variable. Relationships are estimated using computer programs, e.g., MINITAB, the STATISTICAL PACKAGE FOR THE SOCIAL SCIENCES (SPSS), etc. Coefficients are estimated, and t-tests and F-tests are used as tests of significance covering individual variables or groups of variables, although in complicated situations

these tests may be approximate only. Regression equations can be built up using step-wise methods based on appropriate test procedures. Regression is probably the most frequently used statistical technique. Fitting a regression equation allows a researcher to see the influence of each independent variable on the dependent variable; in particular some variables may be seen to have little or no effect. Once a regression equation has been obtained, predictions of the dependent variable can easily be obtained given values of the independent variables.

Regression works best when all the variables involved are measured on metric scales, but can be adapted, sometimes with difficulty, for use with other types of measure. For instance, a variable measured on a nominal scale can be replaced by several dummy variables.

Mathematical statisticians have shown that the least squares estimation procedure has optimal properties under certain assumptions. Among the assumptions are that the errors are independent of each other (no auto-correlation), have zero mean and constant variance (no heteroscedasticity), there is no relationship between the dependent variables and the errors, and there is no exact or very strong relationship between the dependent variables (no multicollinearity). In addition, it is advantageous if the errors are normally distributed. The computer packages used in estimation have tests to see if these assumptions hold, and part of the skill of the user is to know what variation of the basic least squares technique is appropriate in circumstances where particular assumptions have been shown to be inapplicable.

Econometricians have developed special estimation techniques for models involving interdependent variables where there are several simultaneous relationships to estimate. For instance, sales may depend upon prices, advertising expenditures, and the weather, but at the same time prices may depend upon sales, competitors' prices, and the cost of production; advertising expenditure might depend upon last year's profits and competitors' advertising expenditure; and so on. To describe this situation, several equations involving some of the same variables are needed. Special econometric estimation techniques are available to fit these equations in computer packages such as Shazaam.

Bibliography

Bryman, A. and Cramer, D. (2001). *Quantitative Data Analysis*. Hove: Routledge.

Jain, D. (1994). Regression analysis for marketing decisions. In R. P. Bagozzi (ed.), *Principles of Marketing Research*. Cambridge, MA: Blackwell, ch. 5.

regulated pricing

Dominic Wilson

Regulated pricing is a convenient term to refer to the practice of setting prices externally, usually through regulatory agencies (e.g., legal fines, wage councils) or political decisions (e.g., prescription charges, income tax). Some prices can be very closely influenced by such external agencies without necessarily being completely determined by them (e.g., interest rates, gas tariffs), while other prices can vary within a range that may be limited by such agencies (e.g., telephone and electricity tariffs). There are also some international regulatory agencies that can have a similar effect on national pricing levels (e.g., OPEC, GATT, EEC).

relationship marketing

Kalipso Karantinou

Retention, loyalty, and relationship development are concepts frequently cited in many different marketing contexts: "the relationship metaphor dominates contemporary marketing thought and practice" (Fournier, 1998: 343). Starting from the proposition that long-term clients tend to be far more profitable than new ones, it is widely argued that companies in all sectors of economic activity should aim to retain their clients and encourage long-term loyalty.

A number of definitions have been proposed for relationship marketing. According to Gummesson (1997: 267), "relationship marketing is marketing seen as relationships, networks and interaction." Grönroos (1994, cited in Tynan, 1997: 696) argued that "relationship marketing is to establish, maintain and enhance relationships with customers and other partners at a profit, so that the objectives of both parties

involved are met. . . . Such relationships are usually, but not necessarily always, long-term." For Christopher, Payne, and Ballantyne (1991: 4, 47), "relationship marketing has emerged as a concept that unites the forces of marketing, customer service and quality to create a new powerful approach to marketing strategy. . . . It is an integrating concept, which insures an external focus, as well as an internal focus, is placed on all the value-adding activities in the business."

The objective of relationship marketing is, therefore, "to turn new customers into regularly purchasing clients, and then to progressively move them through being strong supporters of the company and its products to being active and vocal advocates for the company, generating positive word of mouth and playing an important role as a referral source" (Christopher et al., 1991: 22). "At its best, relationship marketing is characterized by a genuine concern to meet or exceed the expectations of customers and to provide excellent service in an environment of trust and commitment to the relationship" (Buttle, 1996: 13).

One of the central proposed characteristics of relationship marketing, therefore, is that SUPPLIERS and CUSTOMERS create value for each other in a joint effort, and there is more win-win than win-lose involved; the core values of relationship marketing are based on the acceptance that long-term relationships are advantageous to all parties involved (Gummesson, 1997). Relationship marketing thus aims at creating long-term, mutually satisfying, interactive relationships with customers. Although it is sometimes presented as "a bag of smart tricks" that can help a supplier chain a customer, true relationship marketing must be based on a win-win strategy, where both parties voluntarily remain loyal to each other (Gummesson, 1993).

Relationship marketing, however, is not yet clearly defined and there is no single, widely accepted definition (Buttle, 1996; O'Malley and Tynan, 2003). There are several issues and problems of theoretical and practical relevance confronting relationship marketing theory (Hennig-Thurau and Hansen, 2000). What has significantly contributed to the confusion and the lack of conceptual coherence evident in the area is that relationship marketing has been researched across a number of different contexts and from various theoretical viewpoints (e.g., Barnes, 1994; Buttle, 1996; Barnes and Howlett, 1998). This diversity inhibits any possibility of creating a commonly understood definition of relationship marketing and any commonly agreed approach to implementation (O'Malley and Tynan, 2003). As a result, the relationship marketing concept is currently used to cover a very fragmented set of ideas and theoretical frameworks, and the current discussion of relationship marketing has been characterized more by rhetoric than by rigorous examination of what the concept actually involves (Möller and Halinen, 2000).

The literature on business relationships is therefore far from homogeneous or coherent. Rather, there are a number of different theoretical perspectives, as well as a number of disciplinary roots. Möller and Halinen (2000) talk about two types of relationship marketing theory: market-based (more consumer oriented) and network-based (more inter-organizationally oriented), and refer to four disciplinary roots: SERVICES MARKETING; DATABASE marketing; marketing channels; and business MARKETING RESEARCH traditions.

The origins of the concept of business relationships lie in industrial markets where it has been practiced for many years (Payne et al., 1995). Consequently, many of the ideas underpinning the literature on business relationships have been derived from insights gained in industrial markets by the IMP (International/Industrial Marketing and Purchasing) group of researchers (Tynan, 1997). Since its inception in 1976, the major research interests of the IMP Group were the themes of interaction, relationships, and networks (Turnbull, Ford, and Cunningham, 1996). This group of researchers saw the interaction between buying and selling companies as occurring within the context of a relationship. They use relationships as the unit of analysis, suggesting that "the process of interaction between buyer and seller companies within the context of a relationship provides a good way to understand the nature of industrial markets" (Ford, 1990: 2) (see INTERACTION APPROACH; NETWORK).

Another particularly influential research tradition for the development of the business relationships literature was that of services marketing (Gummesson, 1997). Significant contributions that enriched marketing theory were made as the unique characteristics of services were explored and theorized, such as the interactive nature of the exchange; the propensity for the development of relationships (Gummesson, 1987); the significance of SERVICE QUALITY (Lewis, 1999); and INTERNAL MARKETING. Interactions and relationships in services are key: according to services researchers, consumers' experiences with the service and their subsequent degree of satisfaction are mainly an outcome of the interactions and the resulting relationships between the personnel and the consumer (Möller and Halinen, 2000).

In the long and established marketing channels tradition, the focus also is on business relationships and on economic exchange and its efficiency. Relationships are viewed as strongly interdependent and reciprocal. Some of the major issues researched have been the definition of efficient governance forms for different channel relationships and the modeling of their socio-economic nature (Möller and Halinen, 2000) (see CHANNELS OF DISTRIBUTION).

Another area that is associated with relationships is that of database marketing. The development and maintenance of customer databases is an increasingly applied practice in consumer markets, facilitated by the wide availability of the relevant technology (Stone and Woodcock, 1995; Barnes and Howlett, 1998; O'Malley and Tynan, 2003). Rapidly developing information technology has created "a primarily practice-based and consultant-driven literature on managing customer relationships through databases and direct marketing activities...the buzz words 'mass customization' and 'one-to-one marketing' have arrived" (Möller and Halinen, 2000: 33). This has led to the development of a close link between relationship marketing and database marketing. Storage, retrieval, and utilization of broad-ranging information relating to the client can be of particular importance for the initiation, development, and maintenance of relationships. However, the establishment and maintenance of databases is not sufficient on its own and does not constitute an effort to forge true relationships (Barnes and Howlett, 1998). There have even been suggestions that the overt emphasis on technology actually undermines relationship-building efforts (O'Malley and Tynan, 2003) (*see* CUSTOMER RELATIONSHIP MANAGEMENT).

Relationship development and loyalty have been associated with significant benefits for all the parties involved and thus have been given a central role in recent strategy literature (e.g., Grönroos, 1990; Christopher et al., 1991; Payne et al., 1995; Buttle, 1996; Ennew and Binks, 1996; Gummesson, 1997; Tynan, 1997; Hennig-Thurau and Hansen, 2000; Möller and Halinen, 2000; Payne and Holt, 2001). Dwyer, Schurr, and Oh (1987) referred to a number of benefits deriving from buyer–seller relationships for both parties: reduced UNCERTAINTY, managed dependence, exchange efficiency, and social satisfactions from the association, as well as the possibility of significant gains (as a result of effective communication and collaboration in the pursuit of common goals). Furthermore, research findings about the economic value of loyal customers significantly increased the interest in relationship marketing (Diller, 2000). Therefore, from a supplier's point of view, relationships should provide benefits in the form of increased customer retention and reduced transaction costs (Tynan, 1997); loyal customers are believed to cost less to serve (Morgan, Crutchfield, and Lacey, 2000). However, in addition to the benefits derived from reduced acquisition and serving costs, customer loyalty can bring further benefits to the supplier (directly and indirectly, in the short and the long term), which, if taken into consideration, might reveal a more substantial link between relationship quality and performance (Leuthesser, 1997). Customer loyalty is seen as beneficial because of the certainty that loyal customers bring to the business. This is demonstrated by repeat purchase decisions; willingness to try additional products/services; higher tolerance for mistakes; and higher overall degree of TRUST and reliability. It is also considered to bring growth to the business since loyal customers are associated with larger and more frequent purchases and by a tendency to generate positive word-of-mouth (*see* WORD-OF-MOUTH COMMUNICATIONS) (Diller, 2000). Christopher et al. (1991) also referred to the propensity of loyal customers to generate positive word-of-mouth and act overall as strong advocates for the company;

this can substantially enhance a company's reputation and bring long-term benefits. Another benefit to the firm through the development of enduring relationships is that loyal customers are more willing to provide feedback about new products and services, offering insights to unfulfilled needs and opportunities (Morgan et al., 2000). Furthermore, relationship development programs are believed to lead to reduced promotional expenditure through better targeting of efforts, since the organization possesses more detailed customer information (Morgan et al., 2000).

Relationship development is also considered to offer benefits to customers, for example, through reducing transactions costs and improving the supplier's understanding of their requirements (Tynan, 1997). In situations where high sunk costs and switching costs are present, the buyer is expected to be more willing to remain loyal and more interested in maintaining a quality relationship (Dwyer et al., 1987).

Overall, relationship development is regarded as an effective strategy leading to a significant and enduring COMPETITIVE ADVANTAGE; "more and more the quality and strength of customer relationships are considered critical to the survival and profitability of any business" (Payne et al., 1995: 9). However, relationship marketing and customer retention programs have the potential to be a source of sustainable competitive advantage for a firm only if they are unique in a way that is valued by the customer. There is therefore a need for the firm to be aware of the competitors' moves and to insure differentiation in its relationship development and relationship management efforts (Morgan et al., 2000).

However, although loyalty and customer retention could lead to profitability, it is not certain that all customers will be attractive to retain and/or be profitable: different customer segments have different potential profitability and the pattern of profitability may vary depending on a number of considerations (Payne and Holt, 2001). This has important implications for organizations; customer portfolio and account management practices address this issue (*see* CUSTOMER PORTFOLIOS; KEY ACCOUNT).

A number of costs, opportunity costs, and even disadvantages can also, however, be associated with relationship development for both parties. Developing and maintaining relationships is a costly activity for both sides, as there are opportunity and financial costs involved. Turnbull et al. (1996) note that in many cases supplier–customer relationships are very costly, even making a negative contribution to supplier profitability in the early stages. However, the cost of managing relationships tends to decrease over time. Therefore, most cost factors and marketing expenses involved in supplier–customer relationships should be seen as investments and, thus, it is important to keep a long-term perspective when evaluating relationships. Apart from the necessary investments that should be balanced against the benefits derived from long-term relationships, close relationships with customers can have disadvantages as well: suppliers can become overly reliant on long-term customers and show inflexibility and failure to adapt to shifts in market structures or to the changing importance of certain market segments (see MARKET SEGMENTATION). Complacency, inactivity, and carelessness can then creep in (Diller, 2000).

Overall, building relationships is expensive, in terms of both time and effort, and it would thus be a waste if improved relationships did not translate into better performance (Leuthesser, 1997). In that respect, it is important to recognize that relationships are not feasible and appropriate in all cases (Barnes, 1994) and in all sectors. A sector-specific, context-specific investigation is therefore necessary in each case to establish the overall benefits and costs ratio (Steward, 1997) before deciding to adopt and implement relationship marketing.

Furthermore, before deciding on the IMPLE-MENTATION of relationship strategies, the customers' perspective must be approached and understood. Lack of understanding of the customers' perspective – of the expectations that customers have from relationships, or even of whether they want to enter into a relationship in the first place – can largely be responsible for misplaced marketing and relationship development efforts (e.g., Buttle, 1996; Tynan, 1997; Barnes and Howlett, 1998).

Overall, the relational paradigm drives an organization to focus on relationships. Strategically, this involves identifying which relationships are to be pursued and how they are to be managed (O'Malley and Tynan, 2003). In addition to the focal supplier–customer relationship, authors have referred to a range of business relationships, both within the organization and external to the organization. For example, Christopher et al. (1991) identified six relationships, Morgan and Hunt (1994, in O'Malley and Tynan, 2003) four, while Gummesson (1993) talked about 30 relationships.

Bibliography

Barnes, J. G. (1994). Close to the customer: But is it really a relationship? *Journal of Marketing Management*, 10, 561–70.

Barnes, J. G. and Howlett, D. M. (1998). Predictors of equity in relationships between financial service providers and retail customers. *International Journal of Bank Management*, 16 (1), 15–23.

Buttle, F. (ed.) (1996). *Relationship Marketing: Theory and Practice*. London: Paul Chapman.

Christopher, M., Payne, A., and Ballantyne, D. (1991). *Relationship Marketing: Bringing Quality, Customer Service and Marketing Together*. Oxford: Butterworth-Heinemann.

Diller, H. (2000). Fata morgana or realistic goal? Managing relationships with customers. In T. Hennig-Thurau and U. Hansen (eds.), *Relationship Marketing: Gaining Competitive Advantage through Customer Satisfaction and Customer Retention*. Berlin: Springer-Verlag, pp. 29–48.

Dwyer, R. F., Schurr, P. H., and Oh, S. (1987). Developing buyer–seller relationships. *Journal of Marketing*, 51, 11–27.

Ennew, C. T. and Binks, M. R. (1996). The impact of service quality and service characteristics on customer retention: Small businesses and their banks in the UK. *British Journal of Management*, 7, 219–30.

Ford, D. (ed.) (1990). *Understanding Business Markets*. London: Academic Press.

Fournier, S. (1998). Consumers and their brands: Developing relationship theory in consumer behavior. *Journal of Consumer Research*, 24 (March), 343–73.

Grönroos, C. (1990). Relationship approach to marketing in service contexts: The marketing and organizational behavior interface. In A. Payne, M. Christopher, M. Clark, and H. Peck (eds.) (1995). *Relationship Marketing for Competitive Advantage: Winning and Keeping Customers*. Oxford: Butterworth-Heinemann, pp. 82–91.

Gummesson, E. (1987). The new marketing: Developing long-term interactive relationships. *Long Range Planning*, 20 (4), 10–20.

Gummesson, E. (1993). Relationship marketing: A new way of doing business. *European Business Report*, 3Q (Autumn), 52–6.

Gummesson, E. (1997). Relationship marketing as a paradigm shift: Some conclusions from the 30R approach. *Management Decision*, **35** (4), 267–72.

Hennig-Thurau, T. and Hansen, U. (2000). Relationship marketing: Some reflections on the state-of-the-art of the relational concept. In T. Hennig-Thurau and U. Hansen (eds.), *Relationship Marketing: Gaining Competitive Advantage through Customer Satisfaction and Customer Retention*. Berlin: Springer-Verlag, pp. 3–27.

Leuthesser, L. (1997). Supplier relational behavior: An empirical assessment. *Industrial Marketing Management*, **26**, 245–54.

Lewis, B. (1999). Managing service quality. In B. G. Dale (ed.), *Managing Quality*, 3rd edn. Oxford: Blackwell, pp. 181–97.

Möller, K. and Halinen, A. (2000). Relationship marketing theory: Its roots and direction. *Journal of Marketing Management*, **16**, 29–54.

Morgan, R. M., Crutchfield, T. N., and Lacey, R. (2000). Patronage and loyalty strategies: Understanding the behavioral and attitudinal outcomes of customer retention programmes. In T. Hennig-Thurau and U. Hansen (eds.), *Relationship Marketing: Gaining Competitive Advantage through Customer Satisfaction and Customer Retention*. Berlin: Springer-Verlag, pp. 69–83.

O'Malley, L. and Tynan, C. (2003). Relationship marketing. In M. J. Baker (ed.), *The Marketing Book*, 5th edn. London: Butterworth-Heinemann, pp. 32–52.

Payne, A. and Holt, S. (2001). Diagnosing customer value: Integrating the value process and relationship marketing. *British Journal of Management*, **12**, 159–82.

Payne, A., Christopher, M., Clark, M., and Peck, H. (eds.) (1995). *Relationship Marketing for Competitive Advantage: Winning and Keeping Customers*. Oxford: Butterworth-Heinemann.

Steward, K. (1997). Research in a relationship context. In *Marketing Without Borders*, Annual Academy of Marketing Conference Proceedings (Manchester, July), 1505–7.

Stone, M. and Woodcock, N. (1995). *Relationship Marketing*. London: Kogan Page.

Turnbull, P. W., Ford, D., and Cunningham, M. (1996). Interactions, relationships and networks in business markets: An evolving perspective. *Journal of Business and Industrial Marketing*, **11** (3/4), 44–63.

Tynan, C. (1997). A review of the marriage analogy in relationship marketing. *Journal of Marketing Management*, **13**, 695–703.

reliability

Michael Greatorex

Reliability is the extent to which a scale (*see* RATING SCALES), for example in a MARKET-

ING RESEARCH questionnaire (*see* QUESTIONNAIRE DESIGN), produces consistent results if repeated measurements are made. Systematic error (or bias) has no effect on reliability; it is the error that occurs randomly each time something is measured that causes unreliability.

Tests for reliability include test-retest reliability, alternative forms reliability, and internal consistency reliability. In test-retest reliability, the same scale items are presented to the same respondents at different times under conditions that are as similar as possible. In alternative forms reliability, two equivalent forms of a scale are constructed and presented to a respondent in the same questionnaire. Strictly speaking, the respondent should give the same answer but reliability is usually measured in these two approaches by the simple correlation coefficient; the bigger the correlation coefficient, the greater the reliability.

Internal consistency reliability is used to assess the reliability of a summated scale by measuring the intercorrelation among the scores on the individual items. Cronbach's alpha is one well-known measure of internal consistency reliability and measures of less than 0.6 are taken to indicate unsatisfactory internal consistency. The formula for Cronbach's alpha is

$$\alpha = (n/n - 1)^*(1 - \sum s_i^2/s_t^2)$$

where n is the number of scales, s_i^2 is the variance of scale i, and s_t^2 is the variance of the total scale formed by summing the scales. A measure called beta identifies any inconsistent scales used in the total scale. Other tests of internal consistency are available with packages involving STRUCTURAL EQUATION MODELS.

Bibliography

Tull, D. S. and Hawkins, D. I. (1993). *Marketing Research: Measurement and Method*, 6th edn. New York: Macmillan, pp. 314–16.

requirements capture

Margaret Bruce and Liz Barnes

This is a process at the front end of NEW PRODUCT DEVELOPMENT (NPD) where the "needs, preferences and requirements of individuals and groups significant to the product development are researched and identified" (Wootton, Cooper, and Bruce, 1997: 7). There are many factors that may increase risk in NPD, but during its early stages the most likely pressure is the predicament of picking the "wrong" idea and rejecting the "right" one (Bruce et al., 1999). It has been argued that these front-end stages are the "pivotal" step in determining whether a product will succeed or fail (Cooper, 1988). Requirements capture aims to reduce this risk by insuring that the new product incorporates the requirements of as many stakeholders as possible, in order that the "right" idea is progressed.

Despite the importance of the front-end stages, they are often referred to as the "fuzzy front end" as they typically consist of ad hoc decisions and ill-defined processes (Montoya-Weiss and O'Driscoll, 2000), with companies relying on unwritten rules for carrying out activities (Murphy and Kumar, 1997). In fact, in many companies it is often a case of "luck" rather than "good judgment" as to whether an idea makes it into a development process. In order to successfully assess ideas, organizations must define the ideas to a level whereby valid assessments can be made, by understanding the "requirements" needed for the idea, in terms of, for example, product, market, or financial requirements and "trade-offs" between different requirements. It must be ascertained where, from whom, and how requirements are collected and must be perpetuated through all front-end activities (Cooper et al., 1997).

Bibliography

Bruce, M. and Cooper, R. (2000). *Creative Product Design: A Practical Guide to Requirements Capture Management*. Chichester: John Wiley.

Bruce, M., Cooper, R., Morris, B., and Wootton, A. (1999). Managing requirements capture within a global telecommunications company. *R&D Management*, 29 (2), 107–19.

Cooper, R. (1988). Predevelopment activities determine new product success. *Industrial Marketing Management*, 17, 237–47.

Cooper, R., Wootton, A., Bruce, M., and Morris, B. (1997). Focusing on the fuzzy: Design and requirements capture. *European Academy of Design*, Stockholm, April 23–5.

Montoya-Weiss, M. M. and O'Driscoll, T. M. (2000). From experience: Applying performance support technology in the fuzzy front end. *Journal of Product Innovation Management*, 17, 143–61.

Murphy, S. A. and Kumar, V. (1997). The front end of new product development: A Canadian survey. *R&D Management*, 27 (1), 5–15.

Wootton, A. B., Cooper, R., and Bruce, M. (1997). *A Generic Guide to Requirements Capture*. University of Salford and UMIST.

response equivalence

see CONSTRUCT EQUIVALENCE

retail buying

Steve Worrall and Andrew Newman

Retail buying is concerned with the acquisition by retailers of a suitable range of stock from SUPPLIERS for sale within their stores (or, in the case of MAIL ORDER, catalogues). The organization of the function varies widely among retail firms. The retail buying team takes on the role of implementing CORPORATE STRATEGY by offering to the consumer an assortment of goods that is consistent with that strategy. Decisions have to be taken by the buying team concerning the desired quality, price to the consumer, profit levels, and contract terms with suppliers.

The buyer's role is vital in securing a "good" deal that allows the retailer to compete successfully in the marketplace. This may entail purchasing the goods at the lowest possible price, thus allowing greater profits. The buyer needs negotiating skills and an in-depth understanding of the supplier's business. In addition, the buyer should have an understanding, often based on a combination of intuition, experience, and market research, of what the final consumer might buy, often (depending on manufacture and distribution lead times) several months before the goods are available in the high street. In increasingly competitive markets the buyer must also have an eye for something new to offer the consumer.

Buying mistakes can be costly, especially if a chosen product does not sell well or the right price has not been achieved with the manufacturer. This may allow competitors to undercut the retailer's price.

The main responsibilities of the buyer are likely to include product and supplier selection, negotiation, pricing, evaluation of past purchase decisions, market monitoring, and FORECASTING, depending on the size of the organization and the structure of its buying department.

Buying decisions may be taken individually or in committee, again depending on the individual company. It may be that the decision to move into a new line of merchandise would be taken at board level, leaving the individual product decisions to the buying team.

The role of the buyer is becoming increasingly important within the commercial environment and more sophisticated as levels of competition increase and the consumer becomes more knowledgeable about the products available (McGoldrick, 2002).

Bibliography

Ettenson, R. and Wagner, J. (1986). Retailer buyers' salesability judgments: A comparison of information use across three levels of experience. *Journal of Retailing*, 62, 1 (Spring), 41–64.

Fulop, C. (1964). *Buying by Voluntary Chains*. London: George Allen and Unwin.

McGoldrick, P. J. (2002). *Retail Marketing*. London: McGraw-Hill.

Shaw, S. A., Dawson, J. A., and Harris, N. (1994). The characteristics and functions of retail buying groups in the United Kingdom: Results of a survey. *International Review of Retail, Distribution and Consumer Research*, 4 (1), 83–106.

retail distribution channels

Steve Greenland and Andrew Newman

Retail distribution channels include both store and non-store selling media such as MAIL ORDER and catalogue shopping, home shopping, and teleshopping. These represent the end of the manufacturer–wholesaler–retailer distribution channel and serve consumers directly. The effectiveness and efficiency of these channels are critical to the success of a retail business. This is especially so for those operating in the food and fashion sectors. In general, the supply side of retailing has become one of the key drivers in improving profitability for many retailers. Effective management of distribution is important to a retailer's competitive position. Some retailers use distribution strategically to win customers and others make a point of incorporating delivery claims in their communication strategy. In the late 1990s and early 2000s, consumer demand and rapid developments in technology have a significant effect on channel activities (Newman and Cullen, 2002).

In some channels, each activity is performed by independent firms but there is a growing trend toward VERTICAL INTEGRATION, whereby companies are performing more than one level of activity in the channel, e.g., most large grocery retailers, such as Safeway and Aldi, do their own wholesaling and also control physical distribution tasks. Others, such as Marks and Spencer and The Gap, are involved at all levels including product DESIGN, manufacture, and quality testing. Indeed, "Marks and Spencer were the first retailer to be dubbed the manufacturer without factories" (McGoldrick, 2002: 4). Vertical integration enables the retailer to make significant cost savings, enhancing the efficiency of the distribution channel through greater control over the planning and operation of the flow of merchandise to the stores. Many retailers are investing in quick response (QR) delivery systems, which are highly efficient inventory management systems. EPOS and EFTPOS collect information concerning the day's sales at store checkouts and relay the data to enormous, highly efficient, and automated warehouse or distribution centers. Here, stock orders are rapidly made up and dispatched to the stores the same or the following day. The enhanced efficiency minimizes the handling of goods, reducing stock damage and shrinkage, and has eliminated the need for large in-store stock rooms, allowing additional store floor area to be devoted to selling activities, e.g., Next, the high street clothing retailer, has a highly efficient EPOS system and a centralized automated distribution network that have eliminated the need for in-store stock rooms altogether.

Manufacturers' exclusive hold over merchandise production and design matters has gradually been eroded since the 1950s and "[b]ecause of the growing number of regional, national and international retail chains, retailers have more power in the distribution channel than ever before" (Berman and Evans, 1995). The retail multiples' control of the distribution channel stems from their enormous buying power, through which they are able to dictate production terms and prices, driving down manufacturer margins (*see* MARGIN) and further strengthening their own position. Even retailers, which are smaller in terms of asset base, have been able to gain economies of scale, rapid growth, and channel buying power through establishing networks of retail franchises.

O'Reilly (1984) recognized four key economic factors that might reduce the retailers' channel power:

1 Surplus floor space, arising from rapid expansion.
2 Intensification of retail competition.
3 Serious decline in high street property values.
4 The massive scale of retailers' long-term investment in their distribution systems.

Since 1984, with world recession and continued retail property investment in shopping malls and out-of-town shopping centers, all of these factors have begun to take effect to varying degrees. It remains to be seen whether or not this will impact upon the retailers' control and power in the distribution channel.

The store distribution channel produces by far the main retail sales volume. However, new retail formats and technology associated with the distribution of goods, such as home shopping and interactive teleshopping, dictate that the precise level of distribution assigned to each channel will continue to be dynamic until equilibrium between the different retail distribution channels is reached.

See also *high street retailing; retail franchises; television-based home shopping; wholesalers*

Bibliography

Berman, B. and Evans, J. R. (1995). *Retail Management*. Englewood Cliffs, NJ: Prentice-Hall.
Katsikeas, C. S. and Goode, M. M. H. (2000). Sources of power in international marketing channels. *Journal of Marketing Management*, 16 (1–3), 185–203.
McGoldrick, P. J. (2002). *Retail Marketing*. London: McGraw-Hill, p. 4.
Morganosky, M. A. and Cude, B. F. (2000). Consumer response to online grocery shopping. *International Journal of Retail and Distribution Management*, 28 (1), 17–27.
Newman, A. J. and Cullen, P. (2002). *Retailing: Environment and Operations*. London: Thomson Learning.
O'Reilly, A. (1984). Manufacturing versus retailers: The long term winners? *Retail and Distribution Management*, 12 (3), 40–1.
Rosenbloom, B. (1990). *Marketing Channels*. Orlando, FL: Dryden Press.
Williams, L. R. (1994). Understanding distribution channels: An interorganizational study of EDI adoption. *Journal of Business Logistics*, 15 (2), 173–204.

retail environment

see RETAILING

retail franchises

Steve Greenland and Andrew Newman

These are selling rights within a given geographic area for franchising goods and services. The franchising company provides a recognized BRAND name, goods, equipment, and services, such as training in merchandising and management, receiving in return a fee or a percentage of turnover, or both. Facilitating rapid and reduced risk expansion opportunity, franchising has assisted national and international network development for retailers such as Kentucky Fried Chicken, McDonald's, Blockbuster Video, Benetton, and Body Shop. The types of franchise structure can vary according to the products or services provided. In most cases, however, the franchisee is prohibited from selling other products or services from the same retail outlet. A successful retailer with limited capital funds can use a franchise to expand more quickly, by franchising its format (Newman and Cullen, 2002).

Franchising has a long history but emerged as a major element in retailing during the 1980s when it accounted for around 10 percent of the retail market. Within Europe, the main areas of franchise development in retailing have been fast foods, hotels, car hire, and servicing, plus industrial service areas (Quinn and Alexander, 2002). This distribution method is a growth area in the retail sector due to the numerous advantages franchising has to offer both franchiser and franchisee (Baron and Schmidt, 1991). For example, the franchise concept provides retailers with opportunities to expand the brand into add-on services such as travel, utilities (e.g., gas and electric) and financial services products. Other important alliances have emerged between mainstream retailers and MAIL ORDER specialists, such as the joint Tesco–Grattan venture, as retailers seek out partnerships with mail order companies to expand their franchise into home shopping. More recently, a diverse range of retail companies have become aware of the advantages of adopting a franchise strategy for the purposes of international expansion (Quinn and Doherty, 2000).

See also *franchising; retail distribution channels*

Bibliography

Baron, S. and Schmidt, R. A. (1991). Operational aspects of retail franchises. *International Journal of Retail and Distribution Management*, 19 (2), 13–19.

Morgenstein, M. and Strongin, H. (1992). *Modern Retailing*. Englewood Cliffs, NJ: Prentice-Hall.

Newman, A. J. and Cullen, P. (2002). *Retailing: Environment and Operations*. London: Thomson Learning.

Quinn, B. (1998). Toward a framework for the study of franchising as an operating mode for international retail companies. *International Review of Retail, Distribution and Consumer Research*, 8 (4), 445–67.

Quinn, B. and Alexander, N. (2002). International retail franchising: A conceptual framework. *International Journal of Retail and Distribution Management*, 30 (5), 264–76.

Quinn, B. and Doherty, A. M. (2000). Power and control in international retail franchising: Evidence from theory and practice. *International Marketing Review*, 17 (4/5), 354–73.

retail hierarchy

Steve Worrall and Andrew Newman

A retail hierarchy is the organization of stores within a chain according to size or sales per unit of area. The larger stores within the chain (in terms of selling floor space or total sales) would appear higher up the hierarchy than those with lower sales or selling floor space. Larger stores may offer an extended range of goods and services. Two-tier or multilevel store formats can effectively add a new dimension to the portfolio of stores within a retail business or chain, and permit merchandise categories to be split between floors. This in itself is not a new idea and likely stems from the traditional department store layouts found in most city high street locations. So-called "flagship" stores tend to be seen by the retailer as being at the top of the hierarchy and are often situated in prestige locations in major cities.

Bibliography

Lowe, M. (2001). The changing urban hierarchy in England and Wales, 1913–1998. *Regional Studies*, 35, 9 (December), 775–808.

retail image

Andrew Newman and Steve Greenland

Retail image refers to the way in which the retailer is perceived by the public. It has become essential for retailers to develop, maintain, and communicate a compelling, positive image to foster and sustain COMPETITIVE ADVANTAGE. Retail image can thus create a point of difference between one retailer and its major competitor or competitors. A good example of this is the way in which most grocery retailers during the late 1980s and early 1990s chose to trade through a single trading format, the superstore. This strategic choice was a major factor in developing and maintaining a clear image to the customer.

It is, however, difficult to say precisely to what aspects of a retail structure retail image refers, and to what extent the retailer's store(s) feature in defining this image for the customer. As the store environment is the interface between the customer and the retailer, customers' perceptions (*see* CONSUMER PERCEPTIONS) are, by and large, based on what transpires in the store. On the other hand, bad publicity and media reports that stem from outside the store environment create impressions of the retailer for existing and potential customers that read them (Newman and Cullen, 2002).

One of the earliest definitions, specifically in relation to retail stores, was provided by Martineau (1958), who describes retailer image as: "the way in which the store is defined in the shopper's mind, partly by its functional qualities and partly by an aura of psychological attributes." This early store-focused definition illustrates that a customer's image of a retail store is made up of both functional (such as price and merchandise) and psychological (e.g., aesthetically pleasing and inviting or otherwise) attributes. A complete definition of retail image must therefore include a wide variety of factors that guide TARGET MARKET perceptions, so it is possible for customers to mentally position the retailer's store in relation to other similar retail offerings. For example, where a retailer decides to locate is just as important as the internal fittings and fixtures employed to create an appealing shopping environment. Both of these strategic decisions must be aligned to the customer's mental image of the retailer. In another situation, the price of the goods sold in the store can be used to reinforce the retailer's image. This happens when the internal layout of a discount store gives the impression of low value-for-money prices.

Academic research in this field is extensive, yet it has been difficult to establish universal assumptions across the retail sector. Retail image is an area of ongoing development and a wide variety of perspectives have emerged that apply the concept of image to the retail store setting.

See also *image; store design*

Bibliography

Burt, S. (2000). The strategic role of retail brands in British grocery retailing. *European Journal of Marketing*, 34 (8), 875–90.

Louviere, J. J. and Johnson, R. D. (1990). Reliability and validity of the brand-anchored conjoint approach to measuring retailer images. *Journal of Retailing*, 66, 4 (Winter), 359–83.

Martineau, P. (1958). The personality of the retail store. *Harvard Business Review*, 36 (1), 47–55.

McGoldrick, P. J. (2002). *Retail Marketing*. London: McGraw-Hill.

Newman, A. J. and Cullen, P. (2002). *Retailing: Environment and Operations*. London: Thomson Learning.

Porter, S. S. and Claycomb, C. (1997). The influence of brand recognition on retail store image. *Journal of Product and Brand Management*, 6 (6), 373–88.

retail location

Steve Greenland and Andrew Newman

Retail location is one of the most important considerations facing the retailer. "Although a good location is unlikely in itself to compensate for mediocre overall strategy, a poor location can be a deficit that is very difficult to overcome. Even very small physical differences between locations can exert a major influence upon the stores' accessibility and attractiveness to customers" (McGoldrick, 2002: 235). By moving to new locations the retailer can alter its position in the marketplace, and the way customers feel about it. Hence, the location of a store will influence the image of the retailer (*see* RETAIL IMAGE) relative to the competition (Newman and Cullen, 2002).

The location decision is multidimensional in scope, moving from regional analysis, to trade area analysis, to smaller-scale site-specific and premises considerations. Despite their importance to retail success, location decisions "appear, until comparatively recently, to have been taken in a decidedly cavalier fashion and on the basis of obscure rules of thumb, rudimentary calculations, past experience, intuition, and/or entrepreneurial flair" (Brown, 1992). Today, most retailers adopt a far more systematic approach to location. The main techniques used to evaluate retail sites include the following.

Checklists. These provide details of numerous factors, such as geodemographic, competitor, market, and site-specific information, to be considered when evaluating a site's potential.

Analogs. Also known as the same-store approach, this is where other outlets with similar characteristics to the location in question have their key store features and catchment areas described quantitatively. These data are then extrapolated and used to estimate the likely turnover and profitability of the site in question.

Trade area mapping. This is where customer catchment areas for stores or shopping centers are mapped out geographically to identify consumer shopping patterns. Gaps in the marketplace and potentially profitable locations can then be identified.

Mathematical modeling. More systematic approaches to assist the retail planner have been developed using multiple regression techniques and spatial interaction models:

1 Multiple regression involves developing equations, using existing store data, that represent linear relationships between branch performance indicators and location attributes. The regression analysis identifies the key factors in a store's catchment area and site-specific data, concerning factors such as premises size, that determine performance. The regression equation, by incorporating various data from proposed retail sites, can then be used to forecast performance.

2 Spatial interaction or gravity models predict that a retailer's store patronage will exhibit a distance decay relationship with its hinterland, or surrounding area. They work on the principle that a store's sphere of influence will be a function of its size, its distance, and customers' journey times in relation to other outlets in the surrounding area. For example, the Reilly model, an early and basic type of spatial interaction model, predicts that the breaking point or boundary between the trading areas of store A and store B will be equal to:

$$\frac{\text{the distance between store A and Store B}}{1 + \sqrt{\dfrac{\text{size of store A}}{\text{size of store B}}}}$$

Since Reilly's model, more complicated gravity models have been developed which involve a greater number of variables, such as patterns of store distribution, road networks, physical features, center attractiveness values, and population values, and which assess the interaction between more than just two places. They are used to predict a store's catchment areas, which are then used to anticipate retail performance at particular retail locations. The gravity models

can also be used to calculate the probable impact of adding or removing stores from retail distribution networks. In this way store locations can be planned to achieve an optimum pattern of distribution for the retailer.

The most common, and by far the most efficient, way of measuring the catchment area is using purpose-made information system, or a geographic information system (GIS). GEODEMOGRAPHICS is a computer-based information system that combines the DEMOGRAPHICS of the population with accurate geographic data for use in location analysis. This provides a geodemographic picture of the areas around the store or shopping center, marking out the main features and calculating break points.

GIS is a family of systems that draws on census and other market research data to construct digital maps, thus providing retailers with an easy-to-understand visual representation of data. Postcode data can produce maps of customer zones in precise detail, and clustered round socioeconomic and lifestyle groupings (*see* LIFESTYLES). Retailers of all sizes can use this to calculate their markets, or the MARKET POTENTIAL of a particular zone (Newman and Cullen, 2002).

Retail location techniques are used not only to identify sites on which to open new stores, but also to assist in the:

1 closure of non-profitable stores with markets that offer little promise of improvement;

2 downgrading of retail provision at certain outlets and upgrading at others to lower costs and improve the efficiency of the retail distribution network;

3 relocation of stores that are underperforming due to their poor retail location.

These are three key areas of NETWORK rationalization that have become common practices of the major retailers as a result of the current economic and competitive situation (see, e.g., Greenland, 1994). Focusing upon retail location and network planning has therefore become an even more important issue.

See also *retail distribution channels*

Bibliography

Brown, S. (1992). *Retail Location: A Micro-Scale Perspective*. Aldershot: Avebury.

Brown, S. (1993). Retail location theory: Evolution and evaluation. *International Review of Retail, Distribution and Consumer Research*, 3 (2), 185–230.

Clarke, I. and Bennison, D. (1997). Toward a contemporary perspective of retail location. *International Journal of Retail and Distribution Management*, 25 (2/3), 59–70.

Davies, M. and Clarke, I. (1994). A framework for network planning. *International Journal of Retail and Distribution Management*, 22 (6), 6–10.

Greenland, S. J. (1994). Branch location, network strategy and the high street. In P. J. McGoldrick and S. J. Greenland (eds.), *The Retailing of Financial Services*. Maidenhead: McGraw-Hill, pp. 125–53.

McGoldrick, P. J. (2002). *Retail Marketing*. London: McGraw-Hill.

Newman, A. J. and Cullen, P. (2002). *Retailing: Environment and Operations*. London: Thomson Learning.

retail merchandising

Andrew Newman and Steve Greenland

Retail merchandising encompasses primarily the merchandise mix, store space allocation, and the placement of products within it (Rogers, 1985). This is the general definition accepted by many UK retailers. In the US, however, merchandising has a far broader meaning, e.g., "[t]he process of developing, securing, pricing, supporting and communicating the retailer's merchandise offering" (Lewison, 1994). As a consequence, the function of merchandising within different companies varies enormously. McGoldrick (2002) suggests sparing use of the term "[b]ecause of its many different definitions and connotations." In the 2000s, retail organizations tend to adopt a wider, more inclusive definition of merchandising that encapsulates a broad range of activities. This is far closer to the North American model, which takes account of the strategic as well as the systemic issues.

For most UK retail chains the term merchandising is used to describe many aspects of the planning and presenting of stock. It also refers to the intermediate stages through which the products pass from the original source to the end consumer. These stages are: planning, sourcing, buying, arranging, displaying, and space management of products or services. Hence, merchandising is not just about laying out items on shelves; it is also concerned with the planning, sourcing, buying, and arranging of these products and services. It is the coordination of these and other functions that make for a successful retail business.

Merchandising is necessary for most types of products and services (Newman and Cullen, 2002) so that at any point in time a retailer stocks a wide enough variety of merchandise to satisfy the wants and needs of the customers who come into the store on that particular day (Fiorito, May, and Straughn, 1995).

See also *store design*

Bibliography

David, D. K. (1923). Retail merchandising in relation to general business conditions. *Harvard Business Review*, 2 (1), 37–43.

Fiorito, S. S., May E. G., and Straughn, K. (1995). Quick response in retailing: Components and implementation. *International Journal of Retail and Distribution Management*, 23 (5), 12–21.

Lewison, D. (1994). *Retailing*. New York: Macmillan.

McGoldrick, P. J. (2002). *Retail Marketing*. London: McGraw-Hill.

Newman, A. J. and Cullen, P. (2002). *Retailing: Environment and Operations*. London: Thomson Learning.

Rogers, D. (1985). Research tools for better merchandising. *Retail and Distribution Management*, 13 (6), 42–4.

retail positioning

Andrew Newman

Retail positioning aims to provide COMPETITIVE ADVANTAGE by differentiating the retailer from its competitors through a retail OFFERING that appeals to and is readily identifiable by its specific target markets (*see* TARGET MARKET). This process involves identifying potential customers by breaking the consumer population down into groups by such characteristics as gender, age, income, geographic location, and lifestyle (*see* LIFESTYLES; MARKET SEGMENTATION). However, each group must be sufficiently large and within broad categories for each characteristic so that the retailer targets meaningful customer groups. This market segmentation permits retailers to identify a group of customers and match them as precisely as possible to the "retail offering" (Newman and Cullen, 2002).

In the UK fashion sector, for example, the intense competition in the marketplace insures that price inevitably plays a part in the retail positioning of stores. Retail positioning strategy is an integrated activity, which comprises key management decision areas such as merchandising (see RETAIL MERCHANDISING), store format and design (see STORE DESIGN), customer service dimension, and MARKETING COMMUNICATIONS (Walters and Laffy, 1996). The careful integration of these and other activities, such as supply chain management, secure and sustain a retailer's position in the marketplace relative to the competition (see RETAIL IMAGE).

For some discount retailers differentiation is achieved on the basis of price or product alone, and customers have no expectation of service element. Small independent retailers tend to use specialization as a means of setting themselves apart from the larger high street competitors. As larger retailers have become more sophisticated with the help of emerging computer-based technologies, integration of the various elements of the business offers increasing control over the positioning of retail stores. The pursuit of strategy that creates a point of difference, especially in highly competitive sectors such as food, has bred new ways of exceeding customer expectations. These relate to the holding of merchandise and decisions regarding assortment profiles, space allocation, the number and location profile of retail outlets, customer service facilities and products, ADVERTISING promotions and visual merchandising, all of which insure CUSTOMER SATISFACTION and loyalty, with the promise of customer franchise.

Bibliography

Newman, A. J. and Cullen, P. (2002). *Retailing: Environment and Operations*. London: Thomson Learning.

Ring, L. J. (1979). Retail positioning: A multiple discriminant analysis approach. *Journal of Retailing*, **55** (1), 25–37.

Walters, D. and Laffy, D. (1996). *Managing Retail Productivity and Profitability*. London: Macmillan.

retail pricing

Steve Worrall and Andrew Newman

Retail pricing is the process for deciding the price to be charged to the customer for a product or service. This may be a complex activity involving a number of considerations, such as the desired PROFIT level, the price charged by competitors, an understanding of what the market will bear, and promotions being run on a particular product. Within a competitive retail market, customers tend to be relatively price aware, holding a perception of the price competitiveness of the major retailers.

Retailers realize that their particular price position in the market depends on the general level of prices for the products they sell and the degree of customer acceptability and price sensitivity (see PRICE ELASTICITY) in different situations. Retailers also have to take account of various price movements that occur over periods of time in the market. These price movements reflect changes in the underlying supply and demand conditions and include the effects of technical INNOVATION, social change and customer ATTITUDES, and the diffusion of a product (see DIFFUSION PROCESS) or LIFESTYLES among consumers. Long-term price deflation or inflation can affect the general level of prices. Consumers and businesses have become accustomed to continuing changes in the price level, usually upwards. However, product retailers generally face consumers who are demanding lower prices. Thus, while consumers have been increasing their consumption in real terms, many retailers have only seen growth in value of their sales by getting consumers to trade up to perceived higher-quality brands. The greater sophistication of the consumer will continue to exert downward pressure on retail prices. During the downturn in the economic cycle when the economy grows more slowly, consumer caution will move consumers toward the cheaper end of the market. However, as consumer confidence improves, customers become more relaxed about paying higher prices for higher-quality goods (Newman and Cullen, 2002).

A number of pricing options are open to the retailer, depending on whether, for example, MARKET PENETRATION, profit maximization, undercutting the competition, or creating a quality image are the desired goals. For most retailers maximizing sales and/or profitability are the key intentions. In order to achieve this, an understanding of how price will affect demand is required.

Small independent retailers usually have more constraints on their pricing strategy than larger concerns, due to the lack of buying power and the need to aim for higher margins (see MARGIN). Nevertheless, like large multiples, the corner shop must compete effectively where possible. Pricing is one area where smaller retailers are less likely to succeed, so they trade on their specialisms or convenience as an alternative (Newman and Cullen, 2002).

The pricing decision cannot be taken in isolation from other MARKETING MIX decisions. A consistent strategy of merchandise choice (see RETAIL MERCHANDISING), promotion/ADVERTISING, store location (see RETAIL LOCATION), and pricing should be adopted in order to attract and retain customers.

Once decided, the price charged for a good or service tends to be varied from time to time such as at the "end-of-season sale," upon the arrival of updated and improved goods, or as a competitive response to the activities of other retailers. Across many sectors of retailing, the phenomenon of price discounting has come to the fore. This tends to dilute the power of the seasonal "sale" as customers come to expect low prices and adequate levels of service and product quality all year round.

A number of marketing promotions can be offered to the customer based upon the price charged for an item. The device of "two for the price of one" is widely used, as is the "price promise" where a retailer will promise to beat any price available for the same product elsewhere.

See also *pricing*

Bibliography

Betts, E. and McGoldrick, P. J. (1995). The strategy of the retail "sale": Typology, review and synthesis. *International Review of Retail, Distribution and Consumer Research*, 5 (3), 303–32.
Gabor, A. (1988). *Pricing Concepts and Methods for Effective Marketing*, 2nd edn. Aldershot: Gower.
Newman, A. J. and Cullen, P. (2002). *Retailing: Environment and Operations*. London: Thomson Learning.

retail product range

Steve Worrall and Andrew Newman

The retail product range is the assortment of goods and services offered for sale by a retailer. The particular range offered may be tailored closely to the needs of the target customers. The retailer may seldom stock the full range of a manufacturer's goods unless there is the demand for them.

A retail product range is made up of a number of "lines," i.e., closely related products. A product line will have a certain "depth," depending on the number of variants offered. The more variants available in store, the deeper the product range. In addition, the product range has a certain width depending upon the number of product lines stocked. A large supermarket will have a wider range than a specialty store. The product range of a supermarket may be in excess of 30,000 product items.

The retailer needs to decide how deep and wide the range should be. By offering the largest possible range the retailer may be able to extend the appeal to a wide range of customers (see MARKET SEGMENTATION). Conversely, a more focused product range may appeal to selected market segments. In this way the retailer is able to position itself in the marketplace (see RETAIL POSITIONING).

In some areas of the retail sector such as clothing, the provision of a balanced and well-planned variety of merchandise (see RETAIL MERCHANDISING) is more critical. In the case of a fashion retailer this means ordering a suitable range of styles, sizes, and colors for the TARGET MARKET. Providing a well-balanced assortment for consumer types insures CUSTOMER SATISFACTION and repeat business. This is especially important for the catalogue retailers who sell their products remotely (Newman and Cullen, 2002).

Within certain specialist markets, for instance where a great degree of product knowledge is needed, the retailer may benefit from selling only a limited product range. On the other hand, certain so-called "category killer" stores may offer a very wide range of products within a specialist market at a discount to their competitors.

Bibliography

Burt, S. (2000). The strategic role of retail brands in British grocery retailing. *European Journal of Marketing*, 34 (8), 875–91.

Newman, A. J. and Cullen, P. (2002). *Retailing: Environment and Operations*. London: Thomson Learning.

retail promotion

Andrew Newman and Steve Worrall

Retail promotion involves communicating (by the retailer as opposed to the manufacturer) with the organization's target customers (*see* TARGET MARKET). This is typically different to other types of promotion in that the retailer brand (i.e., the store fascia or trading name) is promoted instead of or alongside the products in the store. This may take one or more of several forms, including:

- PERSONAL SELLING: the one-to-one selling of a product to a customer;
- PUBLICITY: non-personal, mass communication with the audience;
- PUBLIC RELATIONS: developing and managing publicity;
- ADVERTISING: paid-for communication; and
- SALES PROMOTION: monetary and other incentives to purchase a particular good or service.

Together these form the COMMUNICATIONS MIX and can be used collectively or individually to create a promotion strategy. The level of emphasis placed on the use of each technique should be decided by the retailer based upon the nature, behavior, and interests of the customer group at which the promotion is aimed as well as the objectives of the promotion, the nature of the product to be promoted, and any wider market considerations. The main measure of promotional effectiveness is the number of extra sales gained that can be attributed to it.

The retailer's promotional activity also takes account of other important groups that have a significant effect on consumer shopping behavior: manufacturers, SUPPLIERS, the community, and staff. A more complex view of promotion considers the retailer's use of promotional activity to generate a favorable public IMAGE among suppliers. Suppliers' attitudes are important in developing supply relationships, particularly where the product brands are important, which can help to lower costs in the long run. The retailer needs to take account of other channel members in developing its promotion strategy, because of the different objectives of the other channel members (*see* CHANNELS OF DISTRIBUTION). There is also the conventional distinction between manufacturer's push and pull strategies in the market. In a push strategy, the supplier promotes the product to the marketing intermediaries who would then push it through the channel of distribution. A manufacturer of an unbranded product would need to use a push strategy and use all forms of promotion to sell to the intermediary.

In general, a retailer promotes itself to the wider community to generate public esteem across a range of issues such as product PRICING and retail development. Promotional campaigns toward the media and public bodies create positive images and reasons for shopping at the company's stores (Newman and Cullen, 2002). The purpose of such communication may be to encourage sales by informing the customer base and stakeholders about new products, new price structures, special offers, or other arrangements, such as philanthropic causes helped by the donation of a proportion of each sale.

In order to be effective, the communicated MESSAGE should be encoded in a manner understood by the target customers. Hence, retail promotions are carefully devised to convey the desired meaning to the customer. This may include straightforward information about a product and/or some element of persuasion to buy. If this meaning is misunderstood, the communication will be lost and the promotion expense wasted. In many societies, the consumer is typically bombarded with numerous commercial communications on a daily basis. Therefore, in order to be noticed, a retail promotion needs to attempt to convey something different. The promotion also needs to be remembered by the consumer, who may require repeat exposure to it. It is clearly important that the promotion itself be targeted at key customer groups, be they existing, new, or potential. It is unlikely that a blanket promotion would appeal to all customer segments.

Inside the store retailers make great use of visual displays (or visual merchandising) to entice customers into the store, and to encourage them to purchase when inside. Visual merchandising uses various displays to increase consumer interest in, and desire for, the products offered for sale. These displays are like the backdrop in a theater because they stimulate lifestyle images (see LIFESTYLES) that support the sale of the products. In this sense, visual merchandising tends to permeate the whole aspect of a retail store and includes the use of fixtures, decorations, signs, and samples of the merchandise to create window and floor displays (see STORE DESIGN). These items also contribute significantly to the visual image and total atmosphere of the store (Newman and Cullen, 2002) (see ATMOSPHERICS). Regulations for conducting such activity are laid down by statute.

Bibliography

Burnett, J. J. (1993). *Promotion Management*. Boston: Houghton Mifflin.

Gedenk, K. and Neslin, S. A. (1999). The role of retail promotion in determining future brand loyalty: Its effect on purchase event feedback. *Journal of Retailing*, 75, 4 (Winter), 433–60.

Newman, A. J. and Cullen, P. (2002). *Retailing: Environment and Operations*. London: Thomson Learning.

retail security

Steve Greenland and Andrew Newman

Retail security concerns several main areas including in-store shoplifting, staff pilferage, premises security regarding shop-breaking, hold-ups, and the personal security of staff members as well as customers. The relative significance and incidence of each varies between different retail activities. General pilfering of stock is referred to as *shrinkage*. This is the difference between the retail value of the goods that the retailers receive (or is supposed to have received) and the actual sales value realized when the goods are sold. Shrinkage is expressed as a percentage of gross sales volume. A retailer can reduce the risk of theft by reducing the accessibility of the merchandise. Shoplifters are also naturally deterred by the risk of being seen and identified. As part of its security management, the retailer can plan the layout of the store so that a small number of strategically placed staff have sufficient lines of sight as to be able to cover the whole store area.

A major advance in retail security has been the development and deployment of electronic article surveillance (EAS). This system uses electronic tags or labels on items. The tag or label is deactivated when the customer pays for the item. A customer must pass by a pedestal or between two pedestals (depending on the system used) when leaving the store. If the tag or label has not been deactivated, the alarm will sound. This system has now improved to the extent that it provides a very cheap means of guarding items (Newman and Cullen, 2002).

Other prevention measures include, *inter alia*, store detectives, electronic merchandise tag systems, closed-circuit television, security mirrors, chain and loop alarms on merchandise, fitting room tags, secure merchandising cabinets, well-lit high-visibility store layouts, strongrooms, security systems, frontage grilles and shutters, external bollards preventing ram raiding, appropriate security procedures and practices, and general staff training on security matters (Cox, 1978; Green, 1986). Activities involving large-volume cash handling and transactions, such as FINANCIAL SERVICES RETAILING, are particularly vulnerable and security is an even greater and growing concern. Risk of violence to both customers and staff members is a real concern and extra security measures and procedures are required. Since financial service activities have become more retail oriented, considerable research has been undertaken to develop more flexible security systems required for the modern open-plan branch formats that have replaced the more traditional branch "bunker" security concepts. More effective staff security training is essential, particularly with the increasing threats of violence and the frequency of hostage taking. The use of high-profile security systems, bullet-proof shop furniture and bandit screens, vacuum tubes transporting cash directly to and from counters to strongrooms, safes, rising security screens, and shutters that seal off the sales area are all common practices. Counseling provision for victims is also desirable to combat any post-raid trauma.

Bibliography

Cox, R. (1978). *Retailing*. Plymouth: Macdonald and Evans.

Green, W. R. (1986). *The Retail Store*. New York: Van Nostrand Reinhold.

Hughes, M. (1994). Retail branch security. In P. J. McGoldrick and S. J. Greenland (eds.), *Retailing of Financial Services*. Maidenhead: McGraw-Hill, pp. 154–62.

Newman, A. J. and Cullen, P. (2002). *Retailing: Environment and Operations*. London: Thomson Learning.

Tonglet, M. (2002). Consumer misbehavior: An exploratory study of shoplifting. *Journal of Consumer Behavior*, 1 (4), 336–55.

Tonglet, M. and Bamfield, J. (1997). Controlling shop crime in Britain: Costs and trends. *International Journal of Retail and Distribution Management*, 25 (8/9), 293–301.

retail service

Andrew Newman and Steve Worrall

RETAILING is a service industry. Many companies have recognized that good customer service can differentiate them from the competition. Providing a good service is desirable in that it may encourage customers to return (*see* SERVICE QUALITY). This may entail enhancing the shopping experience to make it more enjoyable, relaxing, and rewarding. In grocery and other essential forms of retailing, creating a point of difference in the face of increasing competition has driven retailers to generate added value in the form of additional services. These commonly include benefits such as longer opening hours, coffee bar and/or restaurant facilities, personal shopper service with delivery, gift wrapping and packing services. Indeed, service to the customer can be incorporated into every element of retail activity from the selection of goods for sale to the convenience to the customer of store location (*see* RETAIL LOCATION) and opening times.

In order to provide a level of service deemed appropriate, the retailer may engage in extensive staff training, provide a modern and comfortable store environment, and develop policies designed to reduce customer dissatisfaction, such as money-back guarantees and easy exchange of goods. Product retailers have become adept at providing different forms of customer service, the more innovative of which are often copied by competitors. They key is to find elements of service that are valued by consumers.

Although retailing can be seen as a service sector industry (*see* SERVICES SECTOR), both goods and services can be purchased from stores. This makes the boundary between service retailers and other consumer service providers relatively fuzzy. The difference between service providers and service retailers lies very much in the approach to their customers (Newman and Cullen, 2002). For example, financial service providers such as banks and building societies have since the early 1980s begun to see themselves as retailers (*see* FINANCIAL SERVICES RETAILING). New branch store formats and the rearrangement of space allocated to contact staff relative to the customer have altered the shape of the service setting. The current use of self-service within branches (or stores) can be seen as a reduction of customer service, although it is not necessarily viewed negatively by consumers (Bateson, 1985). It is merely the evolution of the retail services OFFERING which now acknowledges the added dimension of the virtual store, and the frequent remoteness of contact for the customer.

Bibliography

Bateson, J. E. G. (1985). Self service consumer: An exploratory study. *Journal of Retailing*, 61 (3), 49–76.

Harris, K. and Baron, S. (2000). Understanding the consumer experience: It's "good to talk." *Journal of Marketing Management*, 16 (1–3), 111–28.

Jones, P. and Pal, J. (1998). Retail services ride the waves. *International Journal of Retail and Distribution Management*, 26 (9), 374–7.

Newman, A. J. and Cullen, P. (2002). *Retailing: Environment and Operations*. London: Thomson Learning.

retail strategy

see RETAILING

retailer patronage

Andrew Newman and Steve Worrall

This is the adoption of an outlet or supplier by a customer, especially on a frequent basis. Understanding the basis for store patronage may allow retailers to develop their MARKETING MIX such that they increase their attractiveness to target customer groups (*see* TARGET MARKET), possibly raising MARKET SHARE and profitability. Larger multiples or department stores regularly record store patronage to insure that an accurate profile of customer requirements and DEMOGRAPHICS is maintained. Data on customer shopping habits may be collected from sales and loyalty information (*see* REWARD/LOYALTY CARDS), which provides a reliable source of customers' actions (*see* DATABASE). Equally important, these sources may be used to track the holding of stock and minimize stock-outs. For the small independent retailer collecting these data may be just a matter of recalling when your regular customers last came in and what they purchased. The continuous analysis of patronage data insures that stockholding is consistent with customer requirements and, where possible, exceeds customer expectations. Food supermarkets make a science of this data-mining practice, factoring in such variables as weather and seasonality into the patronage equation, thereby maximizing the attractiveness of the retail OFFERING to the customer, encouraging loyalty and greater market share (Newman and Cullen, 2002).

The reasons for patronizing a given store are many and varied and include the convenience of store location (*see* RETAIL LOCATION), previous experience with the store, reputation, PRICING, availability and suitability of merchandise, retailer BRAND LOYALTY, and word-of-mouth (*see* WORD-OF-MOUTH COMMUNICATIONS).

In addition to patronizing a certain store, the consumer may develop loyalty toward a certain product BRAND or specific product. These two examples of shopping behavior should not be confused. It is also important to note that ethical issues (*see* MARKETING ETHICS) are strong determinants of store patronage. That is to say, customers shop where they feel comfortable with the policies and ideals held by a particular retail organization (Newman and Cullen, 2002).

See also *retailing*

Bibliography

Berman, B. and Evans, J. R. (1995). *Retail Management: A Strategic Approach*, 6th edn. Englewood Cliffs, NJ: Prentice-Hall.

Erdem, O. and Oumlil, A. B. (1999). Consumer values and the importance of store attributes. *International Journal of Retail and Distribution Management*, 27 (4/5), 137–45.

Newman, A. J. and Cullen, P. (2002). *Retailing: Environment and Operations*. London: Thomson Learning.

Walters, D. (1994). *Retailing Management: Analysis, Planning and Control*. Basingstoke: Macmillan, ch. 10.

retailers

see RETAILING

retailing

Steve Worrall and Andrew Newman

Retailing embraces those activities concerned with selling goods or services to the final consumer or another person acting on his/her behalf. Retailing permeates our daily lives, comes from a very old tradition, and is thus rooted in the social fabric. We are aware of those retailers we consider favorites – we buy products and services from their shops, their websites, and their catalogues. Retailers fulfill the important economic role of making these products and services accessible to consumers, and we rely on them to supply us with hundreds of products and services each year (Newman and Cullen, 2002).

Retailing need not take place exclusively in a shop setting. Home shopping via a printed catalogue and MAIL ORDER is a firmly established phenomenon. Less widely adopted is television-based shopping (*see* TELEVISION-BASED HOME SHOPPING) through a fiber optic cable or satellite dish, although this area continues to grow. The future is likely to see wider use of computer-based shopping "online" with the availability of fast ESDN and broadband telephone lines. Advances in website design, in particular improved secure sockets layer (SSL) security arrangements, have encouraged the more frequent use of Internet shopping. Retailers, particularly those in the grocery sector, offer a range of food and non-food purchases direct from transactional websites. One of the most successful of these in the UK is www.Tesco.com. This website offers most of the advantages of a store shop, with carriage-to-customer arrangements in small refrigerated vehicles on a seven-day basis.

Retailing takes place in many forms. The typical examples include everyday shopping for clothing and food, etc. However, retailing is also the method by which we acquire mortgages or investment policies from banks and building societies. It is also the medium through which dental treatment is received and paid for; airline or concert tickets are booked over the telephone, through an agent, or online; soft drinks are bought from vending machines, and so on.

Although highly visible to the consumer on the high street, website, or through catalogues and home shopping systems, the retail industry is heavily involved in a wide range of activities. These include storage, distribution, and selling a product or service at a price that is competitive, of a quality that is appropriate, at a time that is convenient, and at the greatest possible convenience to the customer. In order to fulfill this role, the most successful retailers have become highly effective in a number of management disciplines, including personnel management, financial control and accounting, LOGISTICS, strategy development, distribution, and MARKETING. In some cases retailers have also become involved in manufacturing.

For a store-based retailer, siting the outlet at the best possible location (*see* RETAIL LOCATION) is a primary concern. In order to achieve high visibility, and thus achieve passing trade, the best store site is likely to be in the high street of a town or in a shopping mall. The better locations tend to command higher rents, leaving the retailer faced with a trade-off between higher operating costs and potentially higher sales. For some stores, notably larger supermarkets and DIY outlets, an "out-of-town" site may be more appropriate given the importance of car-borne trade and the need for large car parking lots. Other retailers may choose to locate in a "retail park," which tend to include electrical goods superstores, furniture stores, and car accessory retailers.

Retail companies should also develop a strong understanding of their customer profile. By targeting different segments (*see* MARKET SEGMENTATION) of the population, retailers are able to tailor their offerings closely to the needs of customers. Some retailers may aim themselves at the affluent, fashion-conscious section of society, whereas others appeal to the less well off or the price conscious.

By understanding their customers' socioeconomic background, LIFESTYLES, and beliefs, retailers are able to develop marketing strategies (*see* MARKETING STRATEGY) in order to serve their target customers more profitably. Such strategies entail manipulating the various elements of the MARKETING MIX to provide an image and service appropriate to the customer. Therefore, merchandise would be selected, pricing levels decided, store interiors designed, and MARKETING COMMUNICATIONS developed (ADVERTISING, promotions, etc.) to appeal to the target customer.

Retailers' performance in the marketplace is heavily influenced by the forces within the business environment (*see* MARKETING ENVIRONMENT). These consist of economic, political, sociocultural, demographic, technological, and physical influences (Kotler, 2003). In recent years, increasing competition and recessionary forces affecting many retail sectors have, in part, led to cost-cutting, price reductions, and lowered profits. Other forces include the growing internationalization of retailing, with a number of operators expanding overseas as international trade becomes less restricted. Other issues such as 24-hour opening, EPOS and scanning services, legislation affecting part-time workers, minimum wage, and possible planning restrictions on out-of-town sites are likely to continue to impinge on retail activity.

Retail companies are typically organized into chains of stores and may own several hundred outlets across the country, all trading under the same "fascia." Other forms of organization include:

- franchise agreements (*see* RETAIL FRAN-CHISES), where a trader pays a proportion of his/her profits to the parent retailer in exchange for trading under that retailer's name (e.g., Benetton);
- concessions involving a retailer trading from a small store sited within a larger store;
- market traders who pay a local authority for the use of a market stall site; and
- independent retailers who may own one or two stores (e.g., the traditional corner shop, butcher, or baker).

Non-store retailing through the medium of a printed catalogue is also a highly competitive business. In recent years, the quality of such publications has increased dramatically and the manner of trading has vastly improved, with better customer service through telephone ordering, credit and debit card payment facilities, easier exchange policies, and quick postal or vehicle delivery. This has been largely due to the innovative practices of companies such as Next Directory, Cotton Traders, and the Marks and Spencer catalogue. Sales agents are still used by some catalogue retailers although recruiting, motivating, and retaining such staff has proved difficult.

Bibliography

Ghosh, A. (1990). *Retail Management*. Chicago: Dryden Press.

Kotler, P. (2003). *Marketing Management: Analysis, Planning, Implementation and Control*, 11th edn. Englewood Cliffs, NJ: Prentice-Hall.

Liebmann, H.-P., Foscht, T., and Angerer, T. (2003). Innovations in retailing: Gradual or radical innovations of business models. *European Retail Digest*, 37 (March), 55–61.

Morgenstein, M. and Strongin, H. (1992). *Modern Retailing, Management Principles and Practices*, 3rd edn. Englewood Cliffs, NJ: Prentice-Hall.

Newman, A. J. and Cullen, P. (2002). *Retailing: Environment and Operations*. London: Thomson Learning.

Silverstein, M. J. and Fiske, N. (2003). Luxury for the masses. *Harvard Business Review*, **81**, 4 (April), 48–58.

reward/loyalty cards

Andrew Newman

This refers to the concept adopted by many supermarkets and other types of retailers that offers discounts and/or money off in exchange for frequent or continuous store purchases. Typically, a reward card scheme uses some form of membership card which is presented at the point of sale so as to record the value of the purchase and/or the value of the rewards earned (Wright and Sparks, 1999). Such cards use various technology (e.g., magnetic strip, laminated plastic, smart chip) to offer a range of benefits such as discounts and money back in exchange for customer loyalty. In essence, this is a method of rewarding customers for their loyalty to the brand with a tangible gift, rather than relying on the quality systems and continuity of merchandise and/or the service element. There are many types of loyalty card issued by retailers and various communities such as shopping or town centers. For example, research by Worthington and Hallsworth (1999) has produced evidence of some 60 types of card in total.

The reward or benefit concept is by no means new and has undergone several revivals and design changes, ranging from the "green shield stamps" of the 1970s to Tesco's introduction of its Club Card in February 1995. Regardless of the format type, the basic "tie-in" concept tends to remain similar with regular changes of emphasis. For example, collectable cigarette coupons in the 1960s and 1970s encouraged BRAND LOYALTY by offering increased gift value the more coupons a smoker collected. More recently, frequent flyer reward cards, such as British Airways Air Miles and KLM's Flying Dutchman program, offer free points (miles) with each flight. Regular flyers can build up points, which can then be exchanged when swiped against the cost of an airline seat. Cards may also permit entry to high-status executive airport lounges.

Supermarkets and food giants have been highly successful at developing the reward card concept as a strategic tool in the battle to gain MARKET SHARE. This is based on the idea that consumers are motivated by the chance of accruing *points* or bonuses that may be used against the cost of their weekly shop, or when making special purchases. Retailers strategically target "on sale" or slow-moving merchandise with higher points to reduce wastage or holding stock out of season. A by-product of this, data mining, has been used by supermarkets to great advantage in the move to gain a better knowledge of their customers' purchasing patterns. For example, merchandising and promotional initiatives can differ from one location to the next, as can the behavior of consumers' differing reactions to particular offers and methods of ADVERTISING. Through analysis of a retail organization's existing loyalty card DATABASE, tactical decisions at corporate level can lead to the fine tuning of the retail OFFERING to specific geographic markets (Byrom, 2001).

Bibliography

Byrom, J. (2001). The role of loyalty card data within local marketing initiatives. *International Journal of Retail and Distribution Management*, 29 (7), 333–41.

Worthington, S. and Hallsworth, A. (1999). Cards in context: The comparative development of local loyalty schemes. *International Journal of Retail and Distribution Management*, 27 (10), 420–8.

Wright, C. and Sparks, L. (1999). Loyalty saturation in retailing: Exploring the end of retail loyalty cards? *International Journal of Retail and Distribution Management*, 27 (10), 429–39.

risk reduction

see PERCEIVED RISK

S

sales call cycle

Dale Littler

SALES FORCE management (*see* SALES MAN-AGEMENT) usually involves defining the number of calls that a salesperson would be expected to make to particular customers. Customers may be classified according to their importance in terms of sales volume, profitability, reputation, and growth potential, and the number of calls during a period specified according to the importance of the account. The number of hours that sales representatives are expected to spend with customers may be an additional or alternative target. A distinction may be made between servicing existing customers and prospecting for new accounts. The latter can involve a significant amount of time in cultivating the relationship with the potential customer, assessing their requirements, and negotiating mutually acceptable terms and conditions for any sales order. Companies may expect sales representatives to spend a proportion of their time seeking new accounts, and establish a target for the number of unsuccessful calls to be made to a prospect.

Some flexibility is required in establishing a sales call cycle in order to allow the sales representative the discretion to deal with, for example, unexpected demands of customers. The use of computers and modems means that sales personnel have in effect a mobile office that enables them to communicate rapidly with their company base, thereby significantly enhancing not only their productivity but also their ability to respond speedily to customer/client issues raised while away from the base.

Bibliography

Dalrymple, D. J. and Cron, W. L. (1995). *Sales Management: Concepts and Cases.* New York: John Wiley, chs. 5, 11.

sales force

David Yorke

In many, although not all, organizations, the sales force is the principal means of obtaining orders. This will be achieved by PERSONAL SELLING, either by visiting customers or by TELEMARKETING (telephone selling) on a planned basis. Each member of the sales force may have a territory or group of customers, which is organized geographically, by product/service type, by customer type, or by some combination of these (*see* SALES TERRITORY). Sales targets (by volume or value) may be set, but, in addition, members of the sales force may have other defined activities such as customer service (e.g., problem solving and training), attendance at EXHIBITIONS, and collecting overdue accounts.

A feature of SALES MANAGEMENT, in its planning and control of the sales force, is to balance sales potential with workload. For instance, in the case of sales territory, two territories may contain an equal potential, in terms of actual and likely potential customers and their demand for certain products/services, but the geographic spread of the customers may be totally different, with one territory needing much more travel. If salespersons' remuneration is to be equitable, the workload, however measured, must be perceived to be similar. Much will depend on the job definition of the sales force as laid down by sales management in the quest to satisfy both customer needs and its own corporate objectives.

Bibliography

Cravens, D. W. and LaForge, R. W. (1983). Salesforce deployment analysis. *Industrial Marketing Management,* **12** (July), 179–92.

Dalrymple, D. J. and Cron, W. L. (1995). *Sales Management: Concepts and Cases*. New York: John Wiley, ch. 24.
Wilson, M. T. (1983). *Managing a Sales Force*, 2nd edn. Aldershot: Gower.

sales management

David Yorke

Sales management is responsible for the organization and performance of the SALES FORCE. More specifically, this will include: defining the task of the sales force, organization into sales territories, planning sales call cycles (*see* SALES CALL CYCLE), recruiting and training of personnel, setting objectives, establishing budgets, motivation of personnel, and performance evaluation against objectives. From the evaluation, sales management can determine strengths and weaknesses and initiate any changes in line with corporate objectives and support.

Bibliography

Adams, T. (1988). *Successful Sales Management*. London: Heinemann.
Churchill, G. A., Jr., Ford, N. M., and Walker, O. C., Jr. (1985). *Sales Force Management: Planning, Implementation and Control*. Homewood, IL: Irwin.
Wilson, D. (1999). *Organizational Marketing*. London: International Thomson Business Press.

sales promotion

David Yorke

Sales promotion is a part of the marketing COMMUNICATIONS MIX and is an activity and/or material that acts as a direct inducement, offering added value and incentive for a product to resellers, salespersons, or end customers.

Sales promotions are designed to stimulate dealer or trade purchases and, in consumer markets, to get customers to try a new BRAND; encourage favorable opinions; match competitors' actions; increase sales frequency and amounts, and so on. Most sales promotions are short term and tend to be used more intensively in the marketing of fast-moving consumer goods, where brand switching and perceived homogeneity of the offerings prevails. They are relatively easier to isolate and evaluate than other elements in the communications mix.

Trade promotions include buying allowances, free goods, cooperative ADVERTISING, dealer sales contests, and display materials. Consumer promotions include samples, COUPONS, price promotions, redeemable vouchers for gifts, contests, combination offers, trading stamps, and clubs (e.g., Tesco Club Card). Promotions may also be targeted at the sales force, e.g., contests and prizes.

Bibliography

Blattberg, R. C. and Nelsin, S. A. (1990). *Sales Promotion: Concepts, Methods and Strategies*. Englewood Cliffs, NJ: Prentice-Hall.
Peattie, S. and Peattie, K. (1999). Sales promotion. In M. J. Baker (ed.), *The Marketing Book*, 4th edn. Oxford: Butterworth-Heinemann, ch. 18.

sales territory

David Yorke

A SALES FORCE needs, typically, to be structured in order to achieve its objectives effectively. It can be structured entirely geographically, by product type, by customer type, or by some combination of these. Whichever form is used, each salesperson will be allocated a territory, ranging from a few square kilometers/miles to the whole country or, indeed, a number of countries. The simplest form of sales territory is one where all customers are visited or telephoned by one person responsible for all products/services. Where the product range is wide and/or where customer types with differing needs can be readily identified, territories will tend to occupy more than one salesperson and, in the former case, customers may be visited/telephoned by more than one person.

There is a need to balance the costs of implementing different structures with the benefits/problems as perceived by individual customers. A particular feature will be the frequency with which each customer needs to be contacted, thus necessitating the planning of sales call cycles (*see*

SALES CALL CYCLE) within each territory. Such sales call cycles will also attempt to balance workload with potential, for each territory.

Bibliography

Dalrymple, D. J. and Cron, W. L. (1995). *Sales Management: Concepts and Cases*. New York: John Wiley.

sampling

Michael Greatorex

Census or Sample?

Research is usually undertaken to obtain information about the characteristics or parameters of a population. A population comprises all the individuals or cases or elements that make up the universe of interest in the MARKETING RESEARCH problem being studied. Information about the population may be obtained by taking a census or a sample. A census involves taking measurements from each and every member of the population and population parameters can be computed directly from the measurements obtained. A sample is a subgroup of the population chosen to be representative of the population as a whole. Measurements are taken from each member of the sample; sample characteristics, or statistics, are computed for the sample; and these statistics are used to make inferences or test hypotheses (*see* HYPOTHESIS TESTING) about population parameters and characteristics.

Should a census of the whole population be carried out, or should a sample representative of the population be taken? Common sense suggests that, when possible, a census of the whole population is better but there are compelling reasons for taking samples. These include cost, time, population size, population variability, cost of errors and accuracy required, and the destructive nature of some measurements.

The Sampling Process

A requirement of the sampling process is that the sample should be representative of the population and so permit, if other factors are also satisfactory, accurate estimates of the population parameters and characteristics. The steps in the sampling process are: definition of the population; specification of the sampling frame; selection of the type of sample; determination of the sample size; and implementation of the sampling plan.

Defining the population is often not simple, especially in industrial marketing research (*see* INDUSTRIAL MARKETING). The population may be all organizations in a specified industry, but defining an industry precisely may be difficult. Many organizations operate in several establishments at different sites, so is the population to comprise organizations or establishments? Who is to provide the information? Industrial marketing researchers are aware that buying decisions in organizations are often made by formal decision-making units made up of changing personnel (*see* BUYING CENTER; ORGANIZATIONAL BUYING BEHAVIOR). Will one individual be able to answer for the whole group? If so, which individual should be approached? Or should several individuals be questioned so that interactions within the group and with suppliers' personnel can be studied?

The sampling frame is a list of the population. Examples of frames include the electoral roll, telephone directories, membership lists of professional organizations, and trade directories listing organizations by activity, geographic location, etc.

Any discrepancy between the population and the sampling frame will lead to sampling frame error. For example, electoral rolls are often incomplete even at the time of compilation due to the ineligibility of some members of the population to vote (e.g., those under 18 years of age) and the failure to register by some people. Internal migration, deaths, etc. cause the rolls to become out of date quickly. The electoral roll may not be an appropriate list of the specified population, e.g., the purchase of home owners in a particular area.

A frame is not needed for non-probability samples; rather, the sample is chosen on the basis of convenience or by referral in sampling methods such as quota sampling, purposive sampling, snowballing, etc.

There are several considerations to bear in mind when selecting the type of sample. The most important consideration is whether or not to use a probability or a non-probability sample. Probability samples are of various types but involve the use of a frame listing the entire population of interest and the selection of individuals for the sample in such a way that the chance of each individual in the population being chosen for the sample is known. In non-probability samples, methods other than chance selection procedures are used. Probability samples are difficult to select and expensive and time consuming to use but are preferred by statisticians as rules and formulae derived by mathematicians can be used to allow results from the sample to be related to the population. Non-probability samples are quicker and cheaper to implement and are often preferred by practicing market researchers.

The sample size depends on a number of factors such as the importance of the decision and the level of accuracy desired, the number of variables, the variability of the data, the extent of the decomposition of the sample in order to study segments, and finally, a factor often overlooked by statisticians, the resources available to the researcher.

The sampling plan involves the implementation of the preceding decisions and leads to the actual selection of the sample. The elements selected for the sample are contacted and measurements taken. This involves a substantial amount of office and fieldwork. Data, concerning all the cases in the sample, are collected together and analyzed. The results are interpreted and suggestions for action or further research are made in a report submitted to the client.

PROBABILITY SAMPLES

In probability samples, the probabilities of the individual elements in the population being selected for the sample are known.

Simple random samples. In simple random sampling, all of the individual elements in the population have an equal chance of being selected for the sample. A frame or list of the entire population of interest is essential. All of the elements in the frame are given numbers and the numbers of the elements who are to make up the sample are selected at random, by drawing from a hat, by using tables of random numbers, or by a com-

puter using a random number generator. In telephone sampling, the numbers are selected and dialed automatically using a technique called random digit dialing.

It is important to note that an interviewer standing on the street and subjectively selecting people as they walk past will not obtain a random sample. Such samples should not be called random or probability samples and could better be described by a non-technical term such as haphazard samples.

Systematic samples. This is very close to simple random sampling. A list of individuals or items in the population is available. The sampling fraction (ratio of the desired sample size to the size of the population) is determined, say, 1 in 20; then a number is chosen at random in the range 1 to 20, say, 8; then the 8th item in the list and every subsequent 20th item, i.e., the 8th, 28th, 48th, 68th, etc. individual is selected for the sample. This is a random sample for, at the outset of the process, every individual in the population has an equal chance of selection. A possible danger occurs if there is a cyclical pattern to the list that leads to the sample being unrepresentative of the population, but this danger is usually slight. One advantage of systematic sampling over simple random sampling is that the mechanism of selecting the individuals for the sample is simpler – the random selection is done only once – and the effort required is less. Another possible advantage is that a fully detailed frame is not required. For instance, if every 20th customer passing a store is intercepted and interviewed, a systematic random sample of people passing by the store can be obtained without knowing the full sampling frame. Thus, for some populations, systematic sampling can be used in shopping mall surveys (*see* SURVEY RESEARCH).

Stratified samples. The population is divided into strata (the equivalent marketing term is segments; *see* MARKET SEGMENTATION) such that every element of the population is in precisely one of the strata. Stratified sampling is most suitable when there is much similarity between the elements within each stratum but differences between elements in different strata. A probabilistic sample, usually a simple random sample, is selected from each stratum, thus insuring that each stratum is adequately represented. Stratified sampling differs from quota sampling in that the sample elements are selected probabilistically rather than by judgment or convenience, as is the case with quota sampling.

Stratified samples can be of two kinds, with either uniform or variable sampling fractions. In the former, the sizes of the samples drawn from the strata are proportionate to the sizes of the populations in each stratum, thus using uniform sampling fractions for each stratum. The latter method, when the sampling fractions of the different strata vary, can be used to increase the efficiency of the sampling by reducing the sampling error of the estimate of the sample mean. Maximum efficiency is obtained when the sampling fractions of the different strata are proportionate to the variance within each stratum. Thus, small sampling fractions occur when there is little within-strata variation; larger sampling fractions are taken in strata where there is more variability. This makes sense, as when the elements within a stratum are very similar, only a small sample needs be taken to get an accurate measure, while larger samples are required to get similar accuracy for strata containing much variability.

Stratified random sampling with variable sampling fractions requires some estimates for the different strata, e.g., the variances, within each stratum, of the variable of interest. It may be possible to base such estimates on information from previous surveys or on the results of pilot surveys.

Cluster samples. (Also referred to as multistage sampling and area sampling.) The population is divided into groups; again, every member of the population belongs to precisely one group. Cluster sampling works best when each group is similar and typical of the population as a whole. A random sample of the groups is selected, and within each selected group a random sample of individuals is selected. The idea can be extended to more than two stages, but at each stage it is essential that each selection is by use of a probability sampling method.

Often the division into groups is done geographically to reduce interviewing costs by having samples of individuals living close together. Thus, if the basic frame is the electoral roll, a number of parliamentary constituencies are chosen at random, then within the chosen constituencies a number of wards are chosen at random, then within the chosen wards a number of individuals are chosen at random. However, while this reduces interviewing costs, it is likely that the clusters differ from one another and thus it is possible that the clusters selected at the first stage are not typical of the population as a whole.

NON-PROBABILITY SAMPLES

Convenience samples. Individuals are chosen because they are handy for the researcher. For example, students make up many convenience samples in research carried out by university marketing lecturers, retailers interview their customers, magazines invite their readers to use tear-out questionnaires, etc. It becomes difficult to generalize the results to any sensible population and there is the danger that the sample is untypical of a population, should the researcher have actually specified a population in the first place.

Purposive samples. Individuals are selected with some purpose in mind, e.g., in research concerning a new computer, university lecturers may be selected because they are (supposed to be) intelligent, articulate, opinion leaders, etc., whose opinions might be more useful than the views of a purely random sample of the population.

Judgment samples. Individuals are chosen to get a sample that, in the judgment of the researcher, is typical of the population. Thus, examples of judgment samples are: (1) the stores selected for testing new product PACKAGING; (2) constituencies selected for opinion polling; and (3) individuals to take part in focus group sessions (*see* FOCUS GROUPS). Experience has shown that biases inevitably enter into judgment and that the samples may be non-typical of population.

Snowball samples. Initial respondents are selected and after being interviewed, these respondents are asked to suggest other individuals who belong to the target population. These respondents in turn are asked for suggestions and the sample snowballs. This method has use in industrial buyer–seller research where buyer–seller relationships are being studied; buyers are asked to nominate sellers, who nominate other buyers, who nominate other sellers, and so on. It is useful when the researcher has initial difficulty in identifying members of the target population and without such a method may have many unproductive interviews.

Quota samples.   The researcher first of all selects variables to be used as control variables so that the selected sample matches the population for these variables. Typical control variables in consumer research are demographic variables such as age, sex, income, geographic location, etc. (*see* DEMOGRAPHICS). From knowledge of the composition of the population in terms of the control variables, the researcher gives interviewers quotas of respondents with the specified characteristics. The choice of the individuals is left to the interviewer as long as his/her sample matches his/her quota on the specified variables.

Unfortunately, there is no guarantee of fulfilling the hope that because the sample is typical of the population for the control variables, it will be typical for all variables. For one thing, it may not be possible to use a key control variable, e.g., education level, owing to practical difficulties. For another, the choice of respondents by interviewers may be biased, e.g., interviewers may avoid poorly dressed people, or foreigners who may have difficulties with the language, or people whose location makes interviewing difficult.

Quota sampling is a popular sampling method with market researchers because it attempts to provide representative samples at a low cost. It is like stratified sampling in that samples are chosen from all groups in the population. It can be like area (cluster) sampling in that sample members can be located close together to minimize interviewers' traveling costs. However, at the final step, individuals are not selected probabilistically but according to the judgment of the interviewers. Attempts can be made subsequent to the polling to validate the sample by comparing sample characteristics with known population characteristics other than those used in quota specification. If the sample differs from the population on these characteristics, it indicates bias in the subjective selection procedure.

QUOTA VS. PROBABILITY SAMPLES

Arguments for probability samples

1   Formulae are available so that estimates of population parameters can be made based on data from the sample. Thus, the sample mean and sampling errors can be calculated and used in formulae for CONFIDENCE INTERVALS. The distributions of some statistics are known, enabling hypotheses to be tested. None of this is possible with quota samples. (Note, the formulae, e.g., for the sampling error, differ according to the type of probability sample used. The formulae for simple random sampling are well known; equivalent formulae for stratified, cluster, etc. samples are more complicated but can be seen in textbooks on sampling.)
2   It is difficult to insure quota samples are representative owing to interviewer selection bias within quotas and/or with respect to variables not used to define quotas.
3   It is difficult to check fieldwork in quota samples.

Arguments for quota samples

1   Quota samples are economical and quick because they are independent of frames, involve no callbacks, and suffer from less non-response.
2   With proper controls, quota samples can be representative.
3   Because of non-response, so-called random samples are not random anyway, hence the use of formulae that assume samples are random is questionable.

Bibliography

Malhotra, N. K. and Birks, D. F. (2000). *Marketing Research: An Applied Orientation*, 3rd European edn. Harlow: Prentice-Hall, chs. 13, 14.

scenario building

David Yorke and Dale Littler

Differing assumptions on the future performance of environmental factors (*see* MARKETING

ENVIRONMENT) may lead to different predictions or forecasts. These may then be used to construct a range of possible future situations or scenarios, which are often difficult to quantify but may involve complex relationships. Scenarios may then be regarded as "plausible descriptions of alternative futures" within which a strategic plan can be "tested" or for which different strategic plans can be developed and evaluated as part of an exercise in "mental experimentation" (De Wit and Meyer, 2004). Scenarios may be formally constructed at different levels – global, national, regional, or local – and may be based on the probability of certain "events" occurring. They may also be totally unstructured when individuals, who are constantly scanning the environment in an informal way through conversations and the monitoring of the media and other sources of information, meet to exchange views. Depending on the product or service, the future time span will vary. Scenario building and the probability of each scenario occurring may be important in deciding on future strategies.

Bibliography

Beck, P. W. (1982). Corporate planning for an uncertain future. *Long Range Planning*, **15** (4), 12–21.

De Wit, B. and Meyer, R. (2004). *Strategy: Process, Content, Context*, 3rd edn. London: Thomson, pp. 125–6.

Wilson, I. (2000). From scenario thinking to strategic action. *Technological Forecasting and Social Change*, **65**, 23–9.

secondary data

Michael Greatorex

Secondary data are already available data that have been collected for some purpose other than the problem at hand. The development of commercially available databases (*see* DATABASE) and the use of computers, giving access to the Internet, has seen a large increase in the use of secondary data. While secondary data are used in all stages of the MARKETING RESEARCH process, they are used mainly in the initial exploratory stages.

Secondary data come from sources internal to the company such as accounting and sales records, and from external sources such as government, industry, and marketing research sources. In addition, libraries have access to books, reports, and articles on a wide range of topics.

The advantage of secondary data is that they can be obtained quickly and, usually, inexpensively. However, secondary data on the required topic may not be available. Secondary data that are available in the general area under study may not fit precisely the requirements of a particular problem. For instance, the geographic area for which the data are available may not coincide with the area for which the data are required. The definitions of the variables may differ; e.g., secondary data on unemployment may be of the numbers of people claiming unemployment benefit, which may be different from the numbers available for work. Government data based on the governmental administration process may contain unquantifiable biases, e.g., national income data based on tax returns will be affected by tax evasion. Definitions used in the collection of secondary data may change over time. Secondary data may be published annually when quarterly or monthly data are required. Secondary data may be out of date by the time they are published, e.g., input–output tables.

Internal sources of secondary data include accounting records and sales reports. Sales invoices form the bases of internal accounting records of much of the internal secondary data of interest to marketers. These data when reanalyzed can give a picture of sales over time by product, by customer, or by SALES TERRITORY. Marketing expenditures on such variables as the SALES FORCE, ADVERTISING, promotion, distribution, NEW PRODUCT DEVELOPMENT, and marketing research can also be determined from internal accounting records. Reports by salespersons on customers and MARKET POTENTIAL are another internal source of marketing data. The trend toward developing MARKETING INFORMATION SYSTEMS means that a coordinated effort is taking place to collect internal information and make it available on a regular basis to marketing decision-makers.

External sources of information include the growing services from computerized commercial database providers who gather together data from a wide variety of secondary sources. The majority of these provide numerical data but bibliographical databases provide references to articles, reports, and books based upon abstracts and key words. The best-known bibliographical database for marketers is ABI/Inform.

The government and its agencies and associates collect and make available data on a wide range of business and economic topics of interest to marketers. Topics include national income data, production, imports and exports, price data, agriculture, travel and tourism, consumer confidence, and so on. UK government publications include the *Annual Abstract of Statistics*, the *Monthly Digest*, *Economic Trends*, the *National Income Blue Book*, the *Business Monitor* series, which gives production systems for many different products, and the *Family Expenditure Survey*: some of these data are available from the ESRC archives.

Many trade associations collect data about their industries, including size of markets, and distribute this information to members.

Marketing research organizations collect information for sale to customers or on behalf of syndicates of clients. Examples of surveys of the flow of products at the retail level in the UK are Nielsen's Retail Audits, which measure sales of a large number of brands through retailers, which in turn allows trends in brand shares in total or through different types of outlets or in different regions to be observed and reported to clients. Electronic point-of-sale scanner equipment (*see* EFTPOS), which is improving the amount of such data and the speed with which they can be gathered, is revolutionizing the provision and use of this kind of data. An example of a survey of consumers in the UK is the Target Group Index (TGI), a large annual survey based on diaries kept by a panel which provides information on who buys what product and prefers which brand. One example of a survey of interest to advertisers in the UK is the National Readership Survey, which measures the readership of leading NEWSPAPERS and MAGAZINES, together with a lot of classification information, and is used by media owners to sell, and advertisers and advertising agencies to buy, press ADVERTISING. Similarly, data are collected on TELEVISION audiences for the BBC and ITV companies and for advertisers and their agents.

A number of marketing research companies collect data on specific products, industries, or markets in order to sell to many clients. In the UK, Market Intelligence (Mintel), Retail Business, and Keynotes publish monthly reports on different markets.

The amount of secondary data available is great. The examples mentioned above are just a few of the sources of secondary data. The problem is to track down what is available on the topic of interest.

Bibliography

Tull, D. S. and Hawkins, D. I. (1993). *Marketing Research: Measurement and Methods*. New York: Macmillan, ch. 4.
Webb, J. R. (2002). *Understanding and Designing Marketing Research*, 2nd edn. London: Thomson Learning, ch. 3.

segment

see MARKET SEGMENTATION

segmentation

see GEODEMOGRAPHICS; MARKET SEGMENTATION; ORGANIZATIONAL SEGMENTATION; POSITIONING; PSYCHOGRAPHICS; SEGMENTATION VARIABLES

segmentation variables

Vincent-Wayne Mitchell

The segmentation model requires a selection of a basis for segmentation (the dependent variables) as well as descriptors (the independent variables) of the various segments. Descriptor variables are used to understand more about identified market segments and include: reference group influences (*see* INTERPERSONAL COMMUNICATIONS), where people live, where and when they shop, their media habits, what social backgrounds they come from, and so on. One of the main reasons for using descriptor variables to profile segments is that readership and viewership data on NEWSPAPERS, MAGAZINES, and TELEVISION programs tend to be expressed in this way.

Segmentation variables fall into two broad groups: customer characteristics, which include geographic and demographic variables (*see* DEMOGRAPHICS), and consumer responses to a particular product, such as benefits sought, usage occasions, brand loyalties (Kotler, 2003) (*see* BRAND LOYALTY).

CUSTOMER CHARACTERISTICS

These include demographic and geographic variables. Demographic variables are most prevalent because consumers can be placed into categories that are easily understood, easily interpreted, relatively easily gathered, widely available from government sources, and easily transferable from one study to another. Demographics are often the best descriptors of identified segments. They include: age; sex; family size; type of residence, whether it be an apartment or semi-detached house; income; occupation; education, e.g., secondary, graduate, postgraduate; religion; ethnic origin, e.g., African, Asian, Caribbean, European; nationality; and socioeconomic grouping (SEG). In the UK, one SEG that is commonly used is the A, B, C1, C2, D, E categorization, where A refers to those at the top of their professions such as judges, directors, etc., and E to those on a subsistence level, e.g., state pensioners.

Some markets can easily be segmented by age, e.g., the holiday market has 18–30 holidays and holidays for the over-fifties. However, it is important for marketers to realize that their target can be psychologically, rather than chronologically, young. Age stereotypes need to be guarded against. One can have a 70-year-old who is housebound and another who still actively engages in voluntary work. Another popular descriptor is the FAMILY LIFE CYCLE.

Geographic segmentation is used when consumer patterns and preferences vary by geographic location. This can involve looking at the postcode, city, town, village, whether it is coastal or inland, county, region, e.g., television region, country, continent, climate, or population density. For example, a franchise restaurant organization may only locate in cities with a population greater than 100,000 people, while other companies may choose to locate in cities with fewer than 100,000 people to avoid well-entrenched competitors. Unlike population density, market density refers to the number of potential customers within a unit of land (such as a square kilometer). Unfortunately, many of the measurable geographic variables are not closely related to needs. Only those that are related to local climate or terrain and natural resources can truly be said to have a direct influence on consumers' needs. For example, the market for snow tires is greater in certain mountainous parts of the US than in Florida; and differences in hobbies such as mountain climbing, surfing, and other recreational activities can clearly be seen to be related to geography.

One major advancement in segmentation in the last two decades has been GEODEMOGRAPHICS. This identifies groups of consumers by combining a large number of demographic and geographic variables together. Its advantage is that it is able not only to characterize consumers, but also to identify (to postcode level) where consumers are located. This helps enormously in market measurement and market accessibility.

CUSTOMER RESPONSE CHARACTERISTICS

These are the second major category of segmentation variables. Basic demographic variables such as age and sex can determine needs in certain markets, e.g., denim jeans, perfume, and jewelry, but they can result in market segments within which there is considerable variation in consumers' needs and outlook. The use of any variable as a base for market segmentation is ultimately related to the extent to which it can be correlated with product purchase or use. Therein lies the fundamental limitation of using customer demographic characteristics, since they are usually only indirectly related to behavior. Although highly reliable in measurement terms, there is evidence that demographic data have generally failed to explain consumption behavior. Much more important are customer response variables such as benefits sought, usage patterns, and price sensitivity.

One of the best ways to segment a market is via its needs or benefits perceived (*see* BENEFIT SEGMENTATION). Volume of consumption can be one way of segmenting markets, e.g., into non-users, light users, and heavy users of a product. Each user category can have different informational needs. For example, an advertisement to a non-user might give more information about the product class in general, while a regular user might be told the merits of one product versus another. Research has found that often 20 percent of consumers can account for between 70 percent and 80 percent of total consumption, something known as the Pareto effect (*see* PARETO'S RULE). Heavy users of products often have common demographics, PSYCHOGRAPHICS, and media habits as well as needs that make them suitable for targeting with tailored marketing activities.

Another response characteristic is loyalty status. Brand-loyal consumers are of greater value to marketers since it is estimated to cost five times more to attract a new customer than to retain an existing one. Kotler (2003) identifies four categories of loyalty status: hardcore loyals, who buy one brand all the time; softcore loyals, who buy two or three brands regularly; shifting loyals, who shift from favoring one brand to another; and switchers, who show no loyalty to any brand. By studying softcore loyals a company can pinpoint which brands are most competitive with its own, and by analyzing motives of customers who are shifting away from its brands a company can learn about its marketing weaknesses. Sometimes what appears to be a brand-loyal purchase pattern may reflect habit, indifference, low price, or the non-availability of alternatives. Following this line of argument, Dickson (1997) describes several types of brand loyalty that relate to the reasons for being loyal. These include: emotional loyalty, e.g., to a hospital that saves a child's life; identity loyalty, which is an expression of the self that bolsters the self-esteem, e.g., Porsche cars; differentiated loyalty, which is based on the perceived superiority of features and attributes of a particular appliance; contract loyalty, when the consumer believes that continued loyalty will earn him/her special treatment and that a social contract exists, e.g., loyalty schemes in petrol and grocery retailing; switching-cost loyalty, when the effort involved in considering alternatives and adapting to new alternatives is not worth the expected return, e.g., loyalty to a particular computer system; familiarity loyalty, the result of

top-of-the-mind brand awareness, e.g., Coca-Cola; and convenience loyalty, which is based on buying convenience, e.g., the most convenient snack at a counter.

Image segmentation involves the consumer's self-image or SELF-CONCEPT and its relationship to the IMAGE of the product, e.g., perfumes that try to differentiate themselves from one another by having their own distinctive image. While image-oriented features can be difficult to create in new brands, once established in the consumer's mind they can generate many years of consumer loyalty. Landon (1974) discusses two forms of self-concept: one is the regular concept, i.e., how we see ourselves; the other is the ideal concept, i.e., how we would like ourselves to be seen. One criticism of the use of self-image research is the difficulty in identifying cause and effect. If one considers self-image in relation to a product already purchased by the consumer, the consumer's self-image may have already been altered by the purchase of the product. In addition, there is the problem of the non-availability of products that exactly match a person's self-image.

Purchase occasion can influence the needs for a particular product. For example, products may be bought as gifts or as self-purchases. In purchase-occasion segmentation, consumers are grouped based on the reasons or times they purchase products. Consumers can also be divided by their attitudes toward risk (*see* PERCEIVED RISK) or their willingness to purchase new products. Dickson (1997) examines how time pressure can affect the purchase of new products and, therefore, be used as a possible segmentation variable. He argues that while the "wealthy" may have more money to buy innovative products, many do not have the time to invest in learning how to use them. The real INNOVATORS, then, are likely to be consumers who have more leisure time to devote to their interests. One can observe an interesting role reversal where teenagers teach their parents how to use selected products, particularly electronic equipment. In addition, at any given time, people are at different stages of readiness to purchase a product: some are unaware of the product, some are aware, some are informed, some are interested, some have a desire to buy, and some have an intention. Consumers can also be categorized by their degree of enthusiasm for a product, e.g., enthusiastic, positive, indifferent, negative, or hostile, as well as by their price sensitivity, e.g., during economic recession segments tend to be more price sensitive.

Finally, buyers may differ in their search behavior and the way they can be "contacted" by marketers. They use different retail outlets, different shopping styles, are exposed to different media, and are sensitive to different creative advertisements. It is suggested that in mature markets it may be effective to segment by this contact sensitivity (Dickinson, 1997). CACI, the company which originally created the ACORN system of classification (see LIFESTYLES), has devised a profiling system known as "e-types," which permits the behavioral segmentation of the population according to its relationship with the Internet. Seven types of behavioral groupings have been identified. Contact segmentation may also be less obvious to competitors and, therefore, more difficult to imitate.

See also *market segmentation*

Bibliography

Cook, V. J. and Mindak, W. A. (1984). A search for constants: The "heavy user" revisited. *Journal of Marketing*, 48 (4), 79–81.
Dickson, P. R. (1997). *Marketing Management*, 2nd edn. London: Dryden Press/Harcourt Brace College Publishers.
Kotler, P. (2003). *Marketing Management: Analysis, Planning, Implementation and Control*, 11th edn. Englewood Cliffs, NJ: Prentice-Hall.
Landon, E. L. (1974). Self-concept, ideal self-concept, and consumer purchase intentions. *Journal of Consumer Research*, 1 (September), 44–51.
Mitchman, R. (1991). *Lifestyle Market Segmentation*. New York: Praeger.
Murphy, P. E. and Staples, W. A. (1979). A modernized family life cycle. *Journal of Consumer Research*, 6 (June), 12–22.
Sheth, J. (1977). *What is Multivariate Analysis? Multivariate Methods for Market and Survey Research*. Chicago: American Marketing Association.
Twedt, D. W. (1974). How important to marketing strategy is the "heavy user?" *Journal of Marketing*, 38 (January), 70–6.
Wells, W. C. and Gubar, G. (1966). Life cycle concept in marketing research. *Journal of Marketing Research*, 3 (November), 355–63.
Yankelovich, D. (1964). New criteria for market segmentation. *Harvard Business Review*, 42 (March/April), 83–90.

selective exposure

David Yorke

In response to MARKETING COMMUNICATIONS and, in particular, ADVERTISING, consumers are selective in their exposure, perceptions, selection, and retention (see CONSUMER PERCEPTIONS). Consumers are potentially exposed, on a daily basis, to many thousands of communications messages (see MESSAGE). However, they are aware of only a small proportion of these, and selective exposure and perception depends on variables such as congruence with beliefs and ATTITUDES, needs and values, personal characteristics, and PERSONALITY. Rogers and Shoemaker (1971) argue that selective exposure and perception "act as particularly tight shutters on the windows of our minds in the case of innovation messages, because such ideas are new"(p. 105).

Bibliography

Ries, A. and Trout, J. (1986). *Positioning: The Battle for Your Mind*. New York: McGraw-Hill.
Rogers, E. M. and Shoemaker, F. F. (1971). *Communication of Innovations: A Cross-Cultural Approach*. New York: Free Press.
Schramm, W. (1971). How communication works. In W. Schramm and D. F. Roberts (eds.), *The Process and Effects of Mass Communication*. Urbana: University of Illinois Press.

selective perception

see CONSUMER PERCEPTIONS

selective retention

David Yorke

Retention of a positive MESSAGE in the mind of a buyer/customer/consumer is a prime objective of MARKETING COMMUNICATIONS.

However, before a message is received it is, first of all, subject to SELECTIVE EXPOSURE. Should it overcome this problem, the message still may not have enough impact to compete with others to be stored in the receiver's limited memory. Organizations rely heavily on the expertise of an AGENCY to develop creative and memorable messages for their products and services.

Bibliography

Ries, A. and Trout, J. (1986). *Positioning: The Battle for Your Mind*. New York: McGraw-Hill.
Schramm, W. (1971). How communication works. In W. Schramm and D. F. Roberts (eds.), *The Process and Effects of Mass Communication*. Urbana: University of Illinois Press.

self-concept

Emma Banister

The self-concept provides a means to seek understanding of the actions and motivations of consumers. There is considerable agreement about the *general* definition of the self, but disagreement about its scope. Possibly the most widely quoted definition of the self-concept within the marketing literature is Rosenberg's (1979: 7). He considered it to denote the "totality of the individual's thoughts and feelings having reference to himself as an object." Along similar lines is the definition offered by Grubb and Grathwohl (1967: 24), who give an idea of the value of the self to the consumer, and its influence on consumer behavior (*see* CONSUMER BUYER BEHAVIOR): "The self represents a totality which becomes a principal value around which life revolves, something to be safeguarded and, if possible, to be made still more valuable." Ross (1971: 39–40) considers it to encompass the "attitude one holds about or toward one's person (self), this attitude consisting of cognitive components (knowledge, belief), affective components (evaluations), and behavioral-motivational components (predisposition or tendencies to respond)." Researchers tend to agree that the self-concept represents "the perception of oneself" (Sirgy, 1982: 288) and incorporates such considerations as ATTITUDES,

feelings, perceptions, and evaluations of oneself (Grubb and Grathwohl, 1967). It is also generally agreed that the self-concept is valued highly by the consumer, and warrants considerable attempts to protect and enhance it (Sirgy, 1982).

Confusion has arisen with regard to whether the self-concept is a single-self construct or variable (e.g., the actual self or the real self) or whether the self-concept is actually multidimensional. Multidimensional perspectives are generally agreed to include:

1 the "actual self" – how a person perceives their self;
2 the "ideal self" – how a person would like to perceive their self;
3 the "social self" – how a person will present his/her self to others (Sirgy, 1982).

These definitions are important because they recognize that the self is not necessarily stable over time and across contexts. Postmodernism (*see* POSTMODERN MARKETING) has led many consumer researchers to question the very notion of the self, with recent theories emphasizing the need to incorporate multiple selves into our understanding, in order to appreciate its relational nature (Gergen, 1991). Kleine, Kleine, and Kernan (1993: 210) argue for a multilayered or multidimensional self: "The significance of a product to consumers depends on *which* of their ideas it enables and the *importance* of that identity – what it contributes to their overall sense of self." The theory of possible selves incorporates this view of the self as a dynamic structure involving a multiplicity of selves (Cantor et al., 1986) or end states. These "possible" selves provide consumers with the goals, aspirations, motives, fears, and threats and self-relevant information that individuals need to organize and give direction to their lives (Markus and Nurius, 1986). An appreciation of the interaction between different "selves" can be used to aid our understanding of consumer behavior and enhance our ability to provide appropriate marketing responses.

Bibliography

Cantor, N., Markus, H., Niedenthal, P., and Nurius, P. (1986). On motivation and the self-concept. In R. M. Sorrentino and E. T. Higgins (eds.), *Handbook of Mo-*

tivation and Cognition: Foundations of Social Behavior. Chichester: John Wiley, ch. 4.

Gergen, K. J. (1991). *The Saturated Self: Dilemmas of Identity in Contemporary Life.* New York: Basic Books.

Grubb, E. L. and Grathwohl, H. L. (1967). Consumer self-concept, symbolism and market behavior: A theoretical approach. *Journal of Marketing*, **31**, 22–7.

Kleine, R. E., Kleine, S. S., and Kernan, J. B. (1993). Mundane consumption and the self: A social-identity perspective. *Journal of Consumer Psychology*, **2** (3), 209–35.

Markus, H. and Nurius, P. (1986). Possible selves. *American Psychologist*, **41** (9), 954–69.

Rosenberg, M. (1979). *Conceiving the Self.* New York: Basic Books.

Ross, I. (1971). Self-concept and brand preference. *Journal of Business*, **44**, 38–50.

Sirgy, M. J. (1982). Self-concept in consumer behavior: A critical review. *Journal of Consumer Research*, **9** (December), 287–300.

self-regulation

see CODES OF PRACTICE

service characteristics

Barbara R. Lewis

A number of generic characteristics of services distinguish them from products, namely: intangibility, inseparability, heterogeneity, and perishability.

INTANGIBILITY

Services are generally characterized as intangible although tangible elements may prevail (*see* SERVICE PRODUCT). Services may be seen as "performances" rather than products (e.g., entertainment, professional services, education), and are consumed rather than possessed (e.g., legal, hairdressing). They cannot be seen, touched, or used prior to consumption and often the results of use cannot be seen (e.g., medical treatment, insurance policies, education). This leads to problems for both service providers, e.g., patenting is not possible, promotion is difficult, and quality standards (*see* SERVICE QUALITY) are difficult to set and adhere to, and for the consumer, e.g., testing prior to purchase is not available.

One should also note that with the growth of digital products and the digitization of both goods and services (e.g., music, newspapers, education, banking) there is increasing intangibility as a characteristic of both goods and services (see Laroche, Bergeron, and Goutaland, 2001). Laroche et al. also note that intangibility, as perceived by consumers, comprises inaccessibility to the senses (physical intangibility) and also mental intangibility. This has implications for marketers with respect to consumer decision-making (difficulty of evaluation), PERCEIVED RISK, and promotion (*see* CONSUMER DECISION-MAKING PROCESS; SALES PROMOTION).

INSEPARABILITY OF PRODUCTION AND CONSUMPTION

For most services, creating or performing the service (production) may occur at the same time as partial or full consumption of it (e.g., entertainment, hairdressing). Further, services may be sold before they are produced and consumed (travel services, university education). In addition, many services cannot be separated from the person of the service provider (e.g., lawyer, real estate agent), and the service provider is often present when consumption takes place (e.g., hairdresser, advice services). In general the role of service providers' personnel (both customer-contact and "backroom" employees) has implications for human resource management issues. Customers may be involved in the production of a service (e.g., dentist, hairdresser, a meal in a restaurant) and affect the SERVICE PROCESS and the consumer's perceptions of service quality (*see* CONSUMER PERCEPTIONS). In many instances, inseparability of production and consumption implies that direct sale is the only channel of distribution (*see* SERVICE DISTRIBUTION).

HETEROGENEITY

Heterogeneity of services refers to the variability or lack of standardization or uniformity in the "assembly," "production," and delivery of services. Service standards may not be precise because of a lack of mass production (in most services), owing to the characteristics of the SERVICE PRODUCT, e.g., haircuts, football team performance, professional services.

There will also be variability with respect to the SERVICE ENVIRONMENT, i.e., the mix of physical facilities involved, and the involvement of people (both service personnel and customers) in the production and delivery process.

Lovelock, Vandermerwe, and Lewis (1999) also refer to variation with respect to customization and judgment in service delivery. This is the extent to which the service is customized to meet consumer needs (high for professional services, healthcare, education, restaurants), and the extent to which customer-contact personnel exercise judgment in meeting individual customers' demands.

PERISHABILITY

Services are perishable and so cannot be stored. Perishability is manifested in various ways. If theater seats and hotel rooms are not sold and occupied, then their capacity is wasted. "No-shows" and vacant appointments with dentists and other service professionals represent an element of lost capacity although the provider may be able to use the time for some other, more peripheral, purpose. Under-enrolment in a class is also wasted capacity and revenue – although it might improve the quality of service provided to those in the class. Potential perishability is exacerbated by fluctuating demand, which service providers may be able to manage (e.g., with respect to utilities) or which may present problems (e.g., with respect to transport, accommodation, theater seats). Excess demand may lead to delays, unmet demand, and dissatisfied customers.

Service providers manage their supply and demand in a number of ways (see, e.g., Sasser, 1976; Lovelock et al., 1999). Demand may be managed by:

- differential pricing and price incentives at non-peak times (see SERVICE PRICE);
- developing and promoting non-peak demand (see SERVICE PROMOTION);
- developing complementary services for consumers while they are waiting;
- creating reservation systems to reduce waiting;
- using technology/computers in service delivery.

Alternatively, service companies aim to manage supply through a combination of:

- part-time employees;
- increased customer participation (to reduce labor input);
- shared capacity and services;
- multiple jobs for employees;
- a substitution of machines for labor;
- attempts to maximize efficiency.

Integral to managing demand and supply in capacity-constrained services is yield management. Using yield management models, companies find the best balance at a particular point in time among the prices charged, the segments sold to, and the capacity used. The goal of yield management is to produce the best possible financial return from a limited available capacity.

A further issue that emerges in relation to varying demand and capacity relates to customer queuing and queuing systems. Companies can develop strategies to manage customer behavior whilst queuing, minimize the perceived length of the wait, and promote efficient and effective reservation systems – linked to yield management strategies (see Lovelock et al., 1999: ch. 13).

Bibliography

Grönroos, C. (2000). *Service Management and Marketing: A Customer Relationship Management Approach*, 2nd edn. Chichester: John Wiley.

Ingold, A., McMahon-Beattie, U., and Yeoman, I. (eds.) (2000). *Yield Management: Strategies for the Service Industries*. London: Continuum.

Keims, S. (2000). Yield management: An overview. In A. Ingold, U. McMahon-Beattie, and I. Yeoman (eds.), *Yield Management: Strategies for the Service Industries*. London: Continuum, pp. 3–11.

Keims, S. E. and Chase, R. B. (1998). The strategic levers of yield management. *Journal of Service Research*, 1, 2 (November), 156–66.

Laroche, M., Bergeron, J., and Goutaland, C. (2001). A three-dimensional scale of intangibility. *Journal of Service Research*, 4 (1), 26–38.

Lovelock, C. H. (1983). Classifying services to gain strategic marketing insights. *Journal of Marketing*, 47 (Summer), 9–20.

Lovelock, C. H., Vandermerwe, S., and Lewis, B. (1999). *Services Marketing: A European Perspective*. Upper Saddle River, NJ: Prentice-Hall, chs. 1, 13.

Maister, D. H. (1985). The psychology of waiting lines. In J. A. Czepiel, M. R. Solomon, and C. F. Surprenant (eds.), *The Service Encounter*. Lexington, MA: Lexington Books.

Palmer, A. (2001). *Principles of Services Marketing*, 3rd edn. Maidenhead: McGraw-Hill, ch. 13.

Sasser, W. E. (1976). Match supply and demand in service industries. *Harvard Business Review*, **48** (November/December), 133–40.

Zeithaml, V. A. and Bitner, M. J. (2003). *Services Marketing: Integrating Customer Focus Across the Firm*, 3rd edn. New York: McGraw-Hill, ch. 14.

service delivery

Barbara R. Lewis

The consumer may be actively involved in the production and delivery process, e.g., in applying for a loan, providing information for tax returns, using salad bars in restaurants, and explaining symptoms to a healthcare professional. The organization may have to "manage" the customer input, e.g., to tell him/her how to use equipment in a gym, to clear the table in McDonald's, and "how to behave" in Disney-World. This will facilitate and enhance the service encounter (*see* SERVICE ENCOUNTERS). Customers' participation in service delivery may provide them with some control in the service delivery process, allow more customization and a faster service, and may lead to lower prices.

Technology is typically central to service delivery, and also integral to the SERVICE PRODUCT, SERVICE PROCESS, and SERVICE ENVIRONMENT: technological advances have made major contributions to facilitating customer–company exchanges and to increasing levels of service. For example, mechanization and computerization can increase speed, efficiency, and accuracy of service (e.g., in stocktaking, ordering and distribution, operations, reservations systems, management and MARKETING INFORMATION SYSTEMS, and security systems), but can also depersonalize service. Depersonalized service can free employees for other activities that may detract from customer contact and lead to less customer loyalty; or it may allow employees time to concentrate on developing interactions and relationships to maintain customer loyalty. Ultimately, technology will not replace people in the provision of service(s), and "high-tech" and "high-touch" go hand in hand – better personal service with enhanced technological efficiency.

See also *service distribution*

Bibliography

Kelley, S. W., Donnelly, J. H., and Skinner, S. J. (1990). Customer participation in service production and delivery. *Journal of Retailing*, **66**, 3 (Fall), 315–35.

Rodie, A. R. and Kleine, S. S. (2000). Customer participation in service production and delivery. In T. A. Swartz and D. Iacobucci (eds.), *Handbook of Services Marketing and Management*. Thousand Oaks, CA: Sage.

Zeithaml, V. A. and Bitner, M. J. (2003). *Services Marketing: Integrating Customer Focus Across the Firm*, 3rd edn. New York: McGraw-Hill, chs. 12, 13.

service design

Barbara R. Lewis

Design management is relevant in the context of the SERVICE PRODUCT and also relates to other elements of the MARKETING MIX, in particular the extended marketing mix for the services sector (Booms and Bitner, 1981). A particular aspect of service design is service blueprinting, which is basically a flowchart of the SERVICE PROCESS, in which all the elements or activities, their sequencing, and interactions can be visualized (Shostack, 1984, 1987, 1992; Kingmann-Brundage, 1989).

Bibliography

Booms, B. H. and Bitner, M. J. (1981). Marketing strategies and organizational structures for service firms. In J. H. Donnelly and W. R. George (eds.), *Marketing of Services*. Chicago: American Marketing Association, pp. 47–51.

Edvardsson, B. and Olsson, J. (1996). Key concepts for new service development. *Service Industries Journal*, **16** (2), 140–64.

Kingmann-Brundage, J. (1989). Blueprinting for the bottom line. *Proceedings of the Annual Services Marketing Conference*. Chicago: American Marketing Association.

Lovelock, C. H., Vandermerwe, S., and Lewis, B. (1999). *Services Marketing: A European Perspective*. Upper Saddle River, NJ: Prentice-Hall, ch. 8.

Shostack, G. L. (1984). Designing services that deliver. *Harvard Business Review*, **62** (January/February), 133–9.

Shostack, G. L. (1987). Service positioning through structural change. *Journal of Marketing*, **51** (January), 34–43.

Shostack, G. L. (1992). Understanding services through blueprinting. In T. A. Swartz, D. E. Bowen, and S. W. Brown (eds.), *Advances in Services Marketing and Management*, vol. 1. Greenwich, CT: JAI Press, pp. 75–90.

Zeithaml, V. A. and Bitner, M. J. (2003). *Services Marketing: Integrating Customer Focus Across the Firm*, 3rd edn. New York: McGraw-Hill, ch. 8.

service distribution

Barbara R. Lewis

Service distribution channels comprise service firms, their intermediaries, and their customers. Typically, there are high levels of direct sale due to the inseparability of services and the provider organizations, e.g., business and professional services, utilities, personal services, together with the existence of intermediaries, e.g., agents for tourism, insurance, employment, and retailers. Quasi-retail outlets are also used to sell services, e.g., banks, building societies, launderettes, hotels, real estate agents.

In addition, one needs to consider the ways in which the customer is involved in service distribution (*see* SERVICE DELIVERY). Sometimes the customer travels to the service-providing organization, e.g., theater, airplane, hotel; at other times the provider comes to the customer, e.g., business and household cleaning services. Various services may have both types of distribution, e.g., taxi services, hairdressing, beauty services, professional business services. A third scenario may involve no direct personal interaction, e.g., television and radio services, and other remote service operations.

A recent trend in service distribution is the growth of FRANCHISING: this happens when standardization is possible and includes industries such as fast food, hotel chains, car rental, dry cleaning, and employment services. Technology and the Internet also have increasing impact on services distribution, e.g., in financial services with delivery from remote locations, the use of software packages to facilitate "best deals" for buying insurance and mortgages, and reservation systems for tourism and hospitality organizations, professional services, healthcare, etc.

Bibliography

Csipak, J. J., Chebat, C., and Ventakesan, V. (1995). Channel structure, consumer involvement and perceived service quality: An empirical study of the distribution of a service. *Journal of Marketing Management*, 11 (1), 227–41.

Kasper, H., van Helsdinger, P., and de Vries, W. (1999). *Services Marketing: An International Perspective*. Chichester: John Wiley, ch. 13.

Lovelock, C. H., Vandermerwe, S., and Lewis, B. (1999). *Services Marketing: A European Perspective*. Upper Saddle River, NJ: Prentice-Hall, ch. 9.

Palmer, A. (2001). *Principles of Services Marketing*, 3rd edn. Maidenhead: McGraw-Hill, ch. 9.

Rosenbloom, B. B. and Behrens-Urich, G. (1998). *Marketing Channels*, 6th edn. New York: Dryden Press.

service encounters

Barbara R. Lewis

The extent of direct interaction between a service provider and its customers in the SERVICE DELIVERY process is referred to as service encounters or "moments of truth" or "critical incidents" (Carlzon, 1987; Czepiel, Solomon, and Surprenant, 1985).

A service encounter is any direct interaction between a service provider and customers and may take varying forms. For example, a bank customer wishing to make account inquiries may choose between an interaction with an ATM or over the Internet, or with a bank employee by telephone, letter, or face to face in a branch. Every time the customer comes into contact with any aspect of the bank and its employees there is an opportunity to form an impression and evaluation of the bank and its service(s). Service encounters, in particular those involving employees, have a high impact on consumers and the quality of the encounter is an essential element in the overall quality of service experienced by the customer (*see* SERVICE QUALITY).

Service encounters also have an impact on employees in relation to their motivation, performance, job satisfaction, and rewards. Perspectives and research relating to service encounters are reported by Bitner (1990), Bitner, Booms, and Tetreault (1990), and Bitner, Booms, and Mohr (1994).

Further, one can witness the extent to which technology is impacting on and improving service encounters for both customers and employees. Meuter et al.'s (2000) work on self-service technologies highlights the utility of technology-oriented service encounters from the perspective of consumers, and the satisfaction that these can engender (*see* CUSTOMER SATISFACTION). The increase in the customer–technology interface has implications in many industries, e.g., over half of retail banking transactions are now conducted without the interpersonal assistance of service employees.

In addition, Bitner, Brown, and Meuter (2000) have examined the ability of technology to effectively customize service offerings, recover from service failure (*see* SERVICE FAILURE(S); SERVICE RECOVERY), and delight customers.

Managing service encounters entails consideration of the varying levels of customer contact and the ensuing service operations (*see* SERVICE PROCESS) and delivery systems.

Bibliography

Bitner, M. J. (1990). Evaluating service encounters: The effects of physical surroundings and employee responses. *Journal of Marketing*, **54**, 2 (April), 69–82.

Bitner, M. J., Booms, B. H., and Mohr, L. A. (1994). Critical service encounters: The employees' view. *Journal of Marketing*, **58** (4), 95–106.

Bitner, M. J., Booms, B. H., and Tetreault, M. S. (1990). The service encounter: Diagnosing favorable and unfavorable incidents. *Journal of Marketing*, **54**, 1 (January), 71–84.

Bitner, M. J., Brown, S. W., and Meuter, M. L. (2000). Technology infusion in service encounters. *Journal of the Academy of Marketing Science*, **28** (1), 138–49.

Carlzon, J. (1987). *Moments of Truth*. Cambridge, MA: Ballinger.

Czepiel, J. A., Solomon, M. R., and Surprenant, C. F. (eds.) (1985). *The Service Encounter: Managing Employee–Customer Interaction in Service Businesses*. Lexington, MA: Lexington Books.

Lovelock, C. H., Vandermerwe, S., and Lewis, B. (1999). *Services Marketing: A European Perspective*. Upper Saddle River, NJ: Prentice-Hall, ch. 3.

Meuter, M. L., Ostrom, A. L., Roundtree, R. I., and Bitner, M. J. (2000). Self-service technologies: Understanding customer satisfaction with technology-based service encounters. *Journal of Marketing*, **64** (July), 50–64.

Palmer, A. (2001). *Principles of Services Marketing*, 3rd edn. Maidenhead: McGraw-Hill, ch. 3.

Shostack, G. L. (1985). Planning the service encounter. In J. A. Czepiel, M. R. Solomon, and C. F. Surprenant (eds.), *The Service Encounter: Managing Employee–Customer Interaction in Service Businesses*. Lexington, MA: Lexington Books, pp. 243–53.

service environment

Barbara R. Lewis

The service environment (or physical evidence) plays a key role in almost all service production and delivery (*see* SERVICE DELIVERY); exceptions would comprise remote services such as communications and utilities. The service environment includes consideration of the physical environment (both physical design and access aspects, and emotional or atmospheric impact), and also facilitating goods and tangible clues, all of which influence consumers' (and employees') judgments of a services marketing organization. The physical design comprises aspects of space, color, furnishings, temperature, noise, music, decor, layout, and employee dress, and provides an atmosphere within which the consumer buys and consumes services. Access includes hours, availability, convenience of location, and privacy. Closely integrated with these are facilitating goods (e.g., cars used by a rental company) and tangible clues (e.g., wrappings for dry cleaning, report folders of accountants) utilized by service organizations to create awareness of and interest in their offerings and to differentiate themselves from competitors. Sometimes the tangible aspects are essential to the provision of the service (e.g., aircraft), and at other times are much more peripheral and/or of no independent value (e.g., the "freebies" in hotel bathrooms, report folders, check books).

The service environment has been a major focus of research for Bitner (1990, 1992, 2000), who introduced the concept of "servicescapes," which may involve customers only (e.g., in self-service), employees only (as in remote services), or customer–employee interactions, as in most service delivery. She discusses the effects of physical settings on both customer expectations, perceptions, and satisfactions, and on employee motivation and ability to work. Perceptions of the environment lead to emotions, beliefs, and, in turn, behavior. For example, the office decor, furniture, and clothes of a lawyer lead to consumer beliefs about his/her success, cost, and trustworthiness, and to employee opinions about the desirability of the organization and lawyer as employers. Further, pleasurable environments lead to positive customer evaluations of a service and a desire to spend more time and money there, whereas unpleasant servicescapes lead to avoidance.

Bibliography

Bitner, M. J. (1990). Evaluating service encounters: The effects of physical surroundings and employee responses. *Journal of Marketing*, **54**, 2 (April), 69–82.

Bitner, M. J. (1992). Servicescapes: The impact of physical surroundings on customers and employees. *Journal of Marketing*, **56** (April), 57–71.

Bitner, M. J. (2000). The servicescape. In T. A. Swartz and D. Iaobucci (eds.), *Handbook of Services Marketing and Management*. Thousand Oaks, CA: Sage.

Sherry, J. F., Jr. (ed.) (1998). *Servicescapes: The Concept of Place in Contemporary Markets*. Chicago: NTC/Contemporary Publishing.

Zeithaml, V. A. and Bitner, M. J. (2003). *Services Marketing: Integrating Customer Focus Across the Firm*, 3rd edn. New York: McGraw-Hill, ch. 10.

service failure(s)

Barbara R. Lewis

Organizations should strive for zero defects in their SERVICE DELIVERY, to get things right the first time. However, all service organizations will, from time to time, find themselves in situations where failures occur in their encounters with customers (*see* SERVICE ENCOUNTERS) with respect to one or more dimensions of SERVICE QUALITY (*see* SERVICE QUALITY DIMENSIONS). For example, problems do occur (bad weather may delay an airline flight or employees may be sick and absent), and mistakes will happen (e.g., a dirty rental car, a lost suitcase). Further, a service failure may not

only relate to a flawed outcome: it can occur if the service fails to live up to the customer's own expectations (Michel, 2001).

Service failures may be classified with respect to: problems in the service organization (e.g., with regard to employees, equipment, and systems); those that may be customer induced; and those that are a result of the actions of other organizations. The consequences of service failure include dissatisfaction, decline in consumer confidence, negative word-of-mouth (*see* WORD-OF-MOUTH COMMUNICATIONS), and the inability to retain customers. Armistead, Clark, and Stanley (1993) also include the increased costs of putting services right, providing compensation, and recruiting new customers to replace lost ones. In addition, there is evidence that service failure can lead to a decline in employee morale and service performance (Bitner, Booms, and Mohr, 1994).

Bibliography

Armistead, C. G., Clark, G., and Stanley, P. (1993). Managing service recovery. In P. Kunst and J. Lemmink (eds.), *Managing Service Quality*. London: Paul Chapman, pp. 93–105.

Bitner, M. J., Booms, B. M., and Mohr, L. A. (1994). Critical service encounters: The employees' viewpoint. *Journal of Marketing*, **58** (4), 95–106.

Grönroos, C. (2000). *Service Management and Marketing: A Customer Relationship Management Approach*, 2nd edn. Chichester: John Wiley, ch. 5.

Michel, S. (2001). Analyzing service failures and recoveries: A process approach. *International Journal of Service Industry Management*, **12** (1), 20–33.

service guarantees

Barbara R. Lewis

In the provision and delivery of services and service, as customers' expectations and company standards rise, organizations become competitive in the promises they make to customers. There is now increasing evidence of service guarantees with respect to services, delivery, and aspects of performance in both the public and private sectors; for example, a hotel chain that offers cash compensation or free accommodation if difficulties are not resolved in 30 minutes; a pizza delivery that becomes free after a certain time delay; telecommunications promises with respect to waiting periods for telephone installations and repair of faults; and the mail services' compensation for late/lost delivery and damaged items. In the public sector there is increasing evidence of service charters and standards, and in financial services CODES OF PRACTICE in which customers are advised of their rights.

Some aspects of service and CUSTOMER SATISFACTION cannot be guaranteed, e.g., unconditional on-time arrival of planes, and so promises and guarantees have to be realistic (Hart, 1988). A good service guarantee should be unconditional, easy to understand and communicate, easy to invoke, and easy to collect on. It should also be meaningful, especially with respect to payout, which should be a function of the cost of the service, seriousness of failure, and perception of what is fair, e.g., 15-minute lunch service in a restaurant or a free meal.

Ideally a service guarantee should get everyone in a company to focus on good service and to examine SERVICE DELIVERY systems for possible failure points. However, inevitably, failures may occur and some customers will become dissatisfied (see SERVICE FAILURE(S)).

Bibliography

Hart, C. W. L. (1988). The power of unconditional service guarantees. *Harvard Business Review*, July/August, 54–62.

Zeithaml, V. A. and Bitner, M. J. (2003). *Services Marketing: Integrating Customer Focus Across the Firm*, 3rd edn. New York: McGraw-Hill, ch. 7.

service personnel

see INTERNAL MARKETING

service price

Barbara R. Lewis

The price of a service is not always readily known or available to the consumer. For example, the consumer may not know the price prior to production and delivery (e.g., dentist, professional services) as the requirement for the service is not fully known at the onset. Even if the consumer has a fair indication of the amount of service required (e.g., painting a house), the price may depend on the skills required from the person of the service provider and, in turn, the time involved. So the price may then relate to time and speed of delivery and in turn necessitate quotations or estimates to provide information to the consumer prior to production commencing.

Pricing of services is further complicated by the use of various terminologies to reflect how much the consumer pays. Examples include:

- Admissions – e.g., to a theater. Consumers do not all pay the same price, which depends on variables such as the place, event, seat location, age of customer, number of customers, time of day, and season.
- Charges – e.g., hairdresser, which depend on the skills of the people involved in delivery.
- Commission – e.g., estate agent, which depends on the amount of business being considered, i.e., value of property.
- Fares – e.g., transport. These vary with respect to the company, distance traveled, age of passenger, number of passengers, seat, location, time, and seasonality.
- Fees – e.g., professional services, which may be a function of an hourly rate, fee for the job, or some more complex method.
- Interest – e.g., financial services organizations. This is a charge for the use of money and is a function of the amount borrowed, company policy, and in turn the prevailing interest rate in the economy.
- Taxes – levied by both local and central governments for citizen and community services. Tax levels will depend on consumers' income, type and location of home, and government policies; and typically the consumer has no choice with respect to taxation levels.
- Salaries and wages – for employment. Levels depend on employee skills, length of service, labor union influence, employee performance, etc.

In setting prices, many service providers take account of the fact that price is one mechanism for balancing fluctuations in supply and demand

and may participate in one or more types of PRICING tactics:

- flexible or differential pricing to build demand at non-peak times, to even out fluctuations in demand, and to decrease perishability;
- DISCOUNTS – e.g., promotional pricing;
- diversionary – e.g., a basic meal in a restaurant at a low price but with expensive "extras";
- guaranteed pricing – e.g., estate agents who only charge when a sale is made, and employment agencies who only charge client fees when employee recruitment is completed.

A key aspect of pricing strategies is yield management (see SERVICE CHARACTERISTICS), which involves varying prices for the same service in response to the price sensitivity of different segments at different times. It is concerned with maximizing the revenue yield that can be derived from available capacity at any given time.

Bibliography

Kasper, H., van Helsdinger, P., and de Vries, W. (1999). *Services Marketing: An International Perspective.* Chichester: John Wiley, ch. 14.

Lovelock, C. H., Vandermerwe, S., and Lewis, B. (1999). *Services Marketing: A European Perspective.* Upper Saddle River, NJ: Prentice-Hall, ch. 10.

Palmer, A. (2001). *Principles of Services Marketing,* 3rd edn. Maidenhead: McGraw-Hill, ch. 10.

Zeithaml, V. A. and Bitner, M. J. (2003). *Services Marketing: Integrating Customer Focus Across the Firm,* 3rd edn. New York: McGraw-Hill, ch. 16.

service process

Barbara R. Lewis

Service processes may be classified as "people" (e.g., hairdressing, healthcare, education) or "possession" (e.g., laundry, cleaning services, gardening, insurance, banking) processes – with tangible or intangible actions (see Lovelock, Vandermerwe, and Lewis, 1999). This leads to a number of challenges and tasks with respect to service production and delivery.

The process of service production and delivery is generally concerned with operations management issues. Operations management is,

additionally, problematic in services due to problems in managing supply and demand and the variability of services (see SERVICE CHARACTERISTICS) and the role of employees in production and delivery (see INTERNAL MARKETING), and the incumbent issue of lack of traditional quality standards and control (see SERVICE QUALITY).

Nevertheless, service organizations set standards and develop delivery systems which operate efficiently and effectively, and which are responsive and reliable, ranging from systems for car hire pick-up, procedures for providing loans and mortgages, preparing and serving restaurant meals, and integrated reservations systems in the tourism industry.

Silvestro et al. (1992) classify service process/delivery on a continuum ranging from mass services to professional services. Mass services have many customer interactions, limited contact time and customization, a product orientation, and with value added in the back office (e.g., fast food). In contrast, professional services are characterized by few transactions, highly customized services, a process orientation, relatively long provider–customer contact time, and with most value added in the front office. Setting standards and designing systems and processes involves consideration of the service being offered, the extent of organization–customer interaction, the degree of customization, the impact of advanced computer technology (see SERVICE DELIVERY), and employee-related issues.

Research focused on the service process, and the need for dynamic models, is reported by Grönroos (1992) and Boulding et al. (1992).

Bibliography

Boulding, W., Katra, A., Staelin, R., and Zeithaml, V. A. (1992). A dynamic process model of service quality: From expectations to behavioral intentions. *Journal of Marketing Research,* 30, 7–27.

Chase, R. B. and Hayes, R. H. (1992). Applying operations strategy to service firms. In T. A. Swartz, D. E. Bowen, and S. W. Brown (eds.), *Advances in Services Marketing and Management.* London: JAI Press, pp. 53–74.

Chase, R. B. and Haynes, R. M. (2000). Service operations: A field guide. In T. A. Swartz and D. Iacobucci (eds.), *Handbook of Services Marketing and Management.* Thousand Oaks, CA: Sage, 455–71.

Grönroos, C. (1992). Toward a third phase in services quality research: Challenges and future directions. In *Frontiers in Services Conference*, September. Chicago: American Marketing Association.

Grönroos, C. (2000). *Service Management and Marketing: A Customer Relationship Management Approach*, 2nd edn. Chichester: John Wiley, ch. 9.

Lovelock, C. H., Vandermerwe, S., and Lewis, B. (1999). *Services Marketing: A European Perspective*. Upper Saddle River, NJ: Prentice-Hall, ch. 2.

Silvestro, R., Fitzgerald, L., Johnston, R., and Voss, C. (1992). Toward a classification of service processes. *International Journal of Service Industry Management*, 3 (3), 62–75.

service product

Barbara R. Lewis

A service or service product may be defined as "an activity of more or less intangible nature that normally, but not necessarily, takes place in inter-action between the customer and service employees and/or physical resources or goods and/or systems of the service provider, which are provided as solutions to customer problems" (Shostack, 1984). Shostack highlights the fact that the distinction between services and products is not clear cut, that there are few pure services and products. For example, a car is a physical object and an airline provides a service, but transport is common to both. Shostack (1977, 1982) provides molecular models that combine product and service elements, and she also offers a continuum of market offerings of products and services with respect to their tangibility (*see* SERVICE CHARACTERISTICS), i.e., tangible elements (see figure 1).

A further view is provided by Grönroos (1987, 2000), who develops a concept of the service product – the service OFFERING – which is geared to the concept of perceived SERVICE QUALITY. First, there is the basic or core

service package, such as a hotel, which includes facilitating services that are required to assist consumption of the service (e.g., reception), together with supporting services that are not required but which enhance the service and differentiate it from competition (e.g., restaurants and bars, leisure and conference facilities). All this is what the customer receives. In addition, one needs to consider how the service is delivered or received, which is dependent on the augmented service offering. This includes the accessibility of the service, the extent of customer participation, and interactions/communications between the service provider (its personnel, systems, technology, and environment) and the consumer.

In addition, Lovelock, Vandermerwe, and Lewis (1999) highlight core products and supplementary services, which include facilitating services (information, order taking, billing, and payment) and enhancing services (consultation, hospitality, safekeeping, and exception).

Bibliography

Grönroos, C. (1987). Developing the service offering: A source of competitive advantage. September, Helsinki: Swedish School of Economics and Business Administration.

Grönroos, C. (2000). *Service Management and Marketing: A Customer Relationship Management Approach*, 2nd edn. Chichester: John Wiley, ch. 7.

Lovelock, C. H., Vandermerwe, S., and Lewis, B. (1999). *Services Marketing: A European Perspective*. Upper Saddle River, NJ: Prentice-Hall, ch. 8.

Palmer, A. (2001). *Principles of Services Marketing*, 3rd edn. Maidenhead: McGraw-Hill, ch. 2.

Shostack, G. L. (1977). Breaking free from product marketing. *Journal of Marketing*, 41 (April), 73–80.

Shostack, G. L. (1982). How to design a service. *European Journal of Marketing*, 16 (1), 49–63.

Shostack, G. L. (1984). Designing services that deliver. *Harvard Business Review*, 62 (January/February), 133–9.

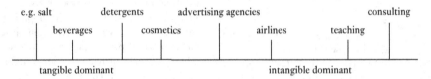

Figure 1   The service produce (Shostack, 1977, 1982)

service promotion

Barbara R. Lewis

The communication and promotion of services presents problems for providers due to the features of services (*see* SERVICE CHARACTERISTICS), in particular intangibility (services cannot usually be presented as physical entities), and variability in their production and delivery, owing to the presence and participation of service personnel. In ADVERTISING services, organizations may try to create tangible clues; capitalize on WORD-OF-MOUTH COMMUNICATIONS, e.g., feature satisfied customers and persuade them to tell others about the service; demonstrate employees in work roles and situations; and "promise what is possible" (George and Berry, 1981). The last aspect is critical with respect to consumers' perceptions of SERVICE QUALITY: it is essential for organizations to be able to follow through on what they say or claim about their services, employees, and delivery. They should only promise what can be delivered a very high proportion of the time, in order to foster realistic consumer expectations. A key means of promotion in the services sector is PERSONAL SELLING, due to the high levels of interaction and personal contact between the service organization's employees and its customers.

Bibliography

George, W. R. and Berry, L. L. (1981). Guidelines for the advertising of services. *Business Horizons*, July/August, 52–6.

Grönroos, C. (2000). *Service Management and Marketing: A Customer Relationship Management Approach*, 2nd edn. Chichester: John Wiley, ch. 9.

Kasper, H., van Helsdinger, P., and de Vries, W. (1999). *Services Marketing: An International Perspective*. Chichester: John Wiley, ch. 12.

Lovelock, C. H., Vandermerwe, S., and Lewis, B. (1999). *Services Marketing: A European Perspective*. Upper Saddle River, NJ: Prentice-Hall, ch. 11.

Mittal, B. (1999). The advertising of services: Meeting the challenge of intangibility. *Journal of Service Research*, 2 (1), 98–116.

Palmer, A. (2001). *Principles of Services Marketing*, 3rd edn. Maidenhead: McGraw-Hill, ch. 11.

Zeithaml, V. A. and Bitner, M. J. (2003). *Services Marketing: Integrating Customer Focus Across the Firm*, 3rd edn. New York: McGraw-Hill, ch. 15.

service quality

Barbara R. Lewis

Service quality is critical for all organizations in the SERVICES SECTOR, and for the manufacturing sector in relation to customer service – before, during, and after sales. The provision and delivery of services and service involve a variety of interactions between an organization and its customers (*see* SERVICE ENCOUNTERS) and, in particular, the organization's personnel are instrumental in the creation and provision of service quality. The concept of service quality is wide and includes service to the customer (providing what is required and being "nice" to the customer), delivery/operations, employees' relationships with customers, and internal relationships between employees and management. In developing service quality strategies and programs, organizations are managing products and services, systems, environment, and people, which brings together marketing, operations management, and human resource management; and service quality programs are increasingly integral to total quality management initiatives within companies.

The need for service quality is driven by customers, employees, technological developments, and a changing business environment.

Customers, be they individuals, households, or organizations, are increasingly aware of alternatives on offer, in relation to services and provider organizations, and also of rising standards of service(s). Consequently, their expectations of service and quality rise and they become more critical of the quality of service they experience. In addition, knowledge of the costs and benefits of keeping customers relative to attracting new ones draws companies' attention to looking after present customers, responding to their needs and problems, and developing long-term relationships (*see* RELATIONSHIP MARKETING).

Advances in technology include management information systems, MARKETING INFORMATION SYSTEMS, and the development of the Internet for accessing information, interaction with service providers, and for shopping. These advances provide a major contribution to facilitate customer–company exchanges and increasing levels of service.

Looking after employees is also an opportunity for an organization. As companies become larger, they may also become anonymous and bureaucratic. Communications may deteriorate and relationships (between customers and customer-contact personnel, between customer-contact staff and backroom staff, and between staff and management) may suffer. Further, in a recession climate, cost-cutting exercises and re-organizations can impact on staff morale, motivation, and performance. However, companies are realizing that commitment to employees brings rewards (see INTERNAL MARKETING).

The business environment is increasingly complex and competitive as a result of economic conditions and legislative activity. For example, in financial services, laws resulting in deregulation have increased competition and brought retailers into the industry, thus providing more choice for the consumer. In air travel, deregulation has brought not only competition but also problems of survival. In a competitive environment companies react by emphasizing operations and financial efficiency and/or more focused product and market strategies. Additionally, they can focus on service quality in their corporate and marketing strategies (see CORPORATE STRATEGY; MARKETING STRATEGY). Superior service quality may be seen as a mechanism to achieve differentiation and a COMPETITIVE ADVANTAGE, and so become integral to the overall direction and strategy of an organization.

With a focus on service quality an organization can expect a number of benefits, including the following.

Customer loyalty through satisfaction. Cronin, Brady, and Hult (2000) note the relationship between perceived service quality and overall satisfaction and perceived customer value as determinants of repatronage and customer loyalty. Looking after present customers can also lead to attraction of new customers from positive WORD-OF-MOUTH COMMUNICATIONS. Customer retention is more cost effective than trying to attract new customers. Cost savings also accrue from "getting things right the first time" (see CUSTOMER SATISFACTION).

Increased opportunities for cross-selling. Comprehensive and up-to-date product knowledge and sales techniques among employees, combined with developing relationships and rapport with customers, enables staff to identify customer needs and suggest relevant products/services.

Employee benefits. These may be seen in terms of increased job satisfaction, employee morale, and commitment to the company, and successful employer–employee relationships and increased staff loyalty, which contribute to reducing the rate of staff turnover and the associated costs of recruitment, selection, and training activities. Committed and competent employees will also make fewer mistakes (and in turn lead to fewer customer complaints), and so contribute to further costs savings.

Enhanced corporate image. In addition, good service enhances corporate image and may provide insulation from price competition: some customers may pay a premium for reliable service. Overall, successful service leads to reduced costs (of mistakes, operating, advertising, and promotion) and increased productivity, sales, MARKET SHARE, profitability, and business performance.

SERVICE QUALITY PROGRAMS

Service quality initiatives are high priorities in many organizations with expenditure seen as long-term investment for future growth and profitability. The development of service quality programs requires, firstly, an awareness and understanding of the interactions between an organization and its customers and employees and, in turn, the areas for potential service quality shortfalls (see SERVICE QUALITY GAPS). Programs typically involve a number of stages:

- Identifying the key components of service quality (see SERVICE QUALITY DIMENSIONS) from internal (employees) and external customer research – their needs and expectations from the company. These relate to the products/services being offered (see SERVICE PRODUCT), delivery systems (see SERVICE DELIVERY; SERVICE PROCESS), delivery environment (see SERVICE ENVIRONMENT), technology, and employees, which are highly interdependent.
- Measuring the importance of service quality dimensions (see SERVICE QUALITY MEASUREMENT).

- Translating customer and employee needs into appropriate product/service specifications.
- Setting measurable standards and systems for service delivery to include a suitable delivery environment.
- Making the best use of technology in products/services, systems, and environment.
- Developing personnel policies to include recruitment, selection, training, rewards, and recognition.
- Managing the delivery process. This includes paying attention to potential failure points and developing service guarantees and procedures for service recovery (see SERVICE FAILURE(S); service guarantees; service recovery).
- Monitoring service quality initiatives, i.e., developing systems to research and evaluate customer satisfaction and dissatisfaction and employee performance.

In order for an organization to be successful with its service quality program, there needs to be management commitment to service quality and the creation of an appropriate culture. The organizational culture may require changes to achieve employee orientation to the company and everyone's orientation to the external customer. This change starts at the top: the service quality process begins with senior management commitment to employees and customers, ideally with strong and visible leaders.

Bibliography

Berry, L. L. (1999). *Discovering the Soul of Service*. New York: Free Press.

Berry, L. L. and Parasuraman, A. (1991). *Marketing Services: Competing Through Quality*. New York: Free Press.

Cronin, J. J., Jr., Brady, M. K., and Hult, G. T. M. (2000). Assessing the effects of quality, value and customer satisfaction on consumer behavioral intentions in service environments. *Journal of Retailing*, **76** (2), 193–218.

Grönroos, C. (1984). A service quality model and its marketing implications. *European Journal of Marketing*, **18** (4), 36–43.

Grönroos, C. (2000). *Service Management and Marketing: A Customer Relationship Management Approach*, 2nd edn. Chichester: John Wiley, ch. 6.

Heskett, J. L., Sasser, W. E., and Hart, C. W. L. (1990). *Service Breakthroughs: Changing the Rules of the Game*. New York: Free Press.

Heskett, J. L., Sasser, W. E., and Schlesinger, L. A. (1997). *The Service Profit Chain: How Leading Companies Link Profit and Growth to Loyalty, Satisfaction and Value*. New York: Free Press.

Kasper, H., van Helsdinger, P., and de Vries, W. (1999). *Services Marketing: An International Perspective*. Chichester: John Wiley, ch. 5.

Lovelock, C. (2001). *Services Marketing: People, Technology, Strategy*, 4th edn. Upper Saddle River, NJ: Prentice-Hall.

Lovelock, C. H., Vandermerwe, S., and Lewis, B. (1999). *Services Marketing: A European Perspective*. Upper Saddle River, NJ: Prentice-Hall, ch. 12.

Palmer, A. (2001). *Principles of Services Marketing*, 3rd edn. Maidenhead: McGraw-Hill, ch. 8.

Zeithaml, V. A. and Bitner, M. J. (2003). *Services Marketing: Integrating Customer Focus Across the Firm*, 3rd edn. New York: McGraw-Hill, ch. 3.

Zeithaml, V. A., Parasuraman, A., and Berry, L. L. (1990). *Delivering Service Quality: Balancing Customer Perceptions and Expectations*. New York: Free Press.

service quality dimensions

Barbara R. Lewis

The dimensions of service quality relate to the products/services being offered, delivery systems, delivery environment, technology, and employees (*see* SERVICE QUALITY), and have been widely conceptualized and researched. Lehtinen and Lehtinen (1982) referred to process quality, as judged by consumers during a service, and output quality judged after a service is performed. They also made a distinction between physical quality (products or support), interactive quality (where the dimensions of quality originate in the interaction between the customer and the service organization), and corporate quality (Lehtinen and Lehtinen, 1991).

Grönroos (1984) discussed the technical (outcome) quality of service encounters, i.e., what is received by the customer, and the functional quality of the process, i.e., the way in which the service is delivered. Functional aspects include the attitudes, behavior, appearance and personality, service-mindedness, accessibility, and approachability of customer-contact personnel. In addition, there exists the "corporate image" dimension of quality, which is the result of how customers perceive an organization and is built up by the technical and functional quality of its services. This model was later incorporated with one from manufacturing that incorporates design, production, delivery, and relational dimensions (Gummesson and Grönroos, 1987).

LeBlanc and Nguyen (1988) suggested that corporate IMAGE, internal organization, physical support of the SERVICE PRODUCT, systems, staff–customer interaction, and degree of CUSTOMER SATISFACTION all contribute to service quality. Further, Edvardsson, Gustavsson, and Riddle (1989) presented four aspects of quality which affect customers' perceptions:

- Technical quality – to include skills of service personnel and the design of the service system.
- Integrative quality – the ease with which different portions of the service delivery system work together.
- Functional quality – to include all aspects of the manner in which the service is delivered to the customer, to include style, environment, and availability.
- Outcome quality – whether or not the actual service product meets both service standards or specifications and customer needs/expectations.

The most widely reported set of service quality determinants is that proposed by Parasuraman, Zeithaml, and Berry (1985, 1988). They suggested that the criteria used by consumers that are important in molding their expectations and perceptions of service fit ten dimensions:

- *Tangibles*: physical evidence.
- *Reliability*: getting it right the first time, honoring promises.
- *Responsiveness*: willingness, readiness to provide service.
- *Communication*: keeping customers informed in a language they can understand.
- *Credibility*: honesty, trustworthiness.
- *Security*: physical, financial, and confidentiality.
- *Competence*: possession of required skills and knowledge of all employees, e.g., to carry out instructions.

- *Courtesy*: politeness, respect, friendliness.
- *Understanding/knowing the customer*, e.g., his/her needs and requirements.
- *Access*: ease of approach and contact, e.g., opening hours, queues, phones.

Subsequent factor analysis and testing by Parasuraman, Berry, and Zeithaml (1990) condensed these ten determinants into five categories (tangibles, reliability, responsiveness, assurance, and empathy) to which Grönroos (1988) added a sixth dimension – recovery (*see* SERVICE RECOVERY).

In addition, there is the contribution of Johnston et al. (1990) and Silvestro and Johnston (1990), investigating quality in UK organizations. They identified 15 dimensions of service quality which they categorized as: hygiene factors, expected by the customer and where failure to deliver will cause dissatisfaction (e.g., cleanliness in restaurant, train arrival on time); enhancing factors, which lead to customer satisfaction but where failure to deliver will not necessarily cause dissatisfaction (e.g., bank clerk addressing one by name); and dual threshold factors, where failure to deliver will cause dissatisfaction, and delivery above a certain level will enhance customers' perceptions of service and lead to satisfaction (e.g., a full explanation of a mortgage service).

More recently, Zeithaml, Parasuraman, and Malhotra (2000) researched the delivery of service quality over the Internet and found 11 dimensions of e-service quality: access, ease of navigation, efficiency, flexibility, reliability, personalization, security/privacy, responsiveness, assurance/trust, site aesthetics, and price/knowledge. Personal service was not considered critical in e-service quality except when problems occurred or when consumers had to make complex decisions.

There are a number of criticisms of the service quality dimensions that were the focus of the groundbreaking research and appeared in the early literature (see, e.g., Buttle, 1996). These relate to dimensionality (SERVQUAL dimensions are not universal), discriminant VALIDITY is questionable, item intercorrelations are evident, and there is frequently a process orientation – i.e., the outcome of encounters is under-represented due to focus on the process of service

delivery (*see* SERVICE QUALITY MEASURE-
MENT for further discussion).

Bibliography

Buttle, F. (1996). SERVQUAL: Review, critique, research agenda. *European Journal of Marketing*, **30** (1),
8–32.

Edvardsson, B., Gustavsson, B. O., and Riddle, D. I.
(1989). *An Expanded Model of the Service Encounter
with Emphasis on Cultural Context*. Research Report
89: 4, University of Karlstad, Sweden: Services Research Center.

Grönroos, C. (1984). *Strategic Management and Marketing
in the Service Sector*. Bromley: Chartwell-Bratt.

Grönroos, C. (1988). Service quality: The six criteria of
good perceived service quality. *Review of Business*, **93**
(Winter), 10–13.

Grönroos, C. (2000). *Service Management and Marketing:
A Customer Relationship Management Approach*, 2nd
edn. Chichester: John Wiley, ch. 4.

Gummesson, E. and Grönroos, C. (1987). *Quality of
Products and Services: A Tentative Synthesis Between
Two Models*. Research Report 87: 3. University of
Karlstad, Sweden: Services Research Center.

Johnston, R., Silvestro, R., Fitzgerald, L., and Voss, C.
(1990). Developing the determinants of service quality.
In E. Langeard and P. Eiglier (eds.), *Marketing, Operations and Human Resources Insights into Service*. First
International Research Seminar on Services Management. Aix-en-Provence, France: IAE, pp. 373–400.

LeBlanc, G. and Nguyen, N. (1988). Customers' perceptions of service quality in financial institutions. *International Journal of Bank Marketing*, **6** (4), 7–18.

Lehtinen, U. and Lehtinen, J. R. (1982). *Service Quality:
A Study of Quality Dimensions*. Working paper. Helsinki: Service Management Institute.

Lehtinen, U. and Lehtinen, J. R. (1991). Two approaches
to service quality dimensions. *Service Industries Journal*, **11** (3), 287–303.

Parasuraman, A., Berry, L. L., and Zeithaml, V. A.
(1990). Guidelines for conducting service quality research. *Marketing Research*, December, 34–44.

Parasuraman, A., Zeithaml, V. A., and Berry, L. L.
(1985). A conceptual model of service quality and its
implications for future research. *Journal of Marketing*,
49 (Fall), 41–50.

Parasuraman, A., Zeithaml, V. A., and Berry, L. L.
(1988). SERVQUAL: A multiple item scale for measuring consumer perceptions of service quality. *Journal
of Retailing*, **64**, 1 (Spring), 14–40.

Silvestro, R. and Johnston, R. (1990). *The Determinants of
Service Quality: Hygiene and Enhancing Factors*. Cov-
entry: Warwick Business School.

Zeithaml, V. A., Parasuraman, A., and Malhotra, A.
(2000). *A Conceptual Framework for Understanding
E-Service Quality: Implications for Future Research and
Managerial Practice*. Report 00–115. Cambridge, MA:
Marketing Science Institute.

service quality gaps

Barbara R. Lewis

Service quality is variously defined, but essentially it is to do with meeting customers' needs
and requirements and with how well the service
delivered matches customers' expectations. The
term "expectations" as used in the service quality context differs from the way it is used in the
consumer satisfaction literature (*see* CUSTOMER
SATISFACTION), where expectations are seen as
"predictors" (probabilities) made by a consumer
about what is likely to happen during an
impending transaction. In relation to service
quality, expectations are seen as desires/wants,
i.e., what one feels a service provider should
offer (rather than what it would offer), and are
formed on the basis of previous experience of a
company and its MARKETING MIX, competitors, and WORD-OF-MOUTH COMMUNICA-
TIONS. Consequently, quality becomes a
consumer judgment and results from comparisons by consumers of expectations of service
with their perceptions of actual service delivered (see Grönroos, 1984; Berry, Zeithaml,
and Parasuraman, 1985, 1988). If there is a
shortfall, then a service quality gap exists which
providers would wish to close. However, one
needs to bear in mind that higher levels of performance lead to higher expectations. Further,
to find expectations greater than performance
implies that perceived quality is less than satisfactory, but that is not to say that service is of low
quality. Quality is relative to initial expectations
– one of the issues to be taken into account when
measuring service quality.

The concept of service quality gaps has been
developed from the extensive research by Berry
and colleagues (Parasuraman, Zeithaml, and
Berry, 1985; Zeithaml, Berry, and Parasuraman,
1988). They defined service quality to be a function of the gap between consumers' expectations
of the service and their perceptions of the actual
service delivery of an organization, and suggested that this gap is influenced by four other

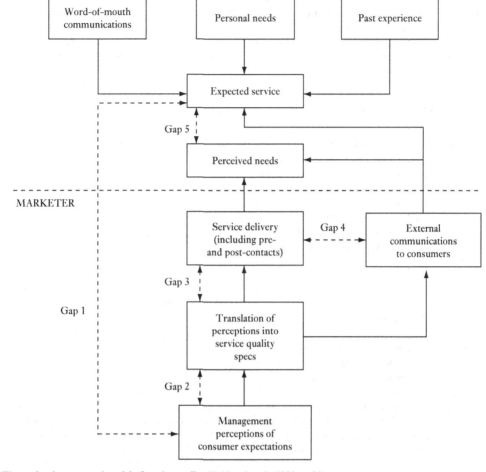

Figure 1   A conceptual model of service quality (Zeithaml et al., 1988, p. 36)

gaps that may occur in an organization (see figure 1).

GAP 1: CONSUMER EXPECTATIONS – MANAGEMENT PERCEPTIONS OF CONSUMER EXPECTATIONS

Managers' perceptions of customers' expectations may be different from actual customer needs and desires, i.e., managers do not necessarily know what customers (both internal and external) want and expect from a company. This may be remedied by market research activities (e.g., interviews, surveys, FOCUS GROUPS, complaint monitoring), and better communication between management and personnel throughout the organization.

GAP 2: MANAGEMENT PERCEPTIONS OF CONSUMER EXPECTATIONS – SERVICE SPECIFICATIONS ACTUALLY SET

Even if customer needs are known, they may not be translated into appropriate service specifications, owing to a lack of resources, organizational constraints, or absence of management commitment to a service culture and service quality. The need for management commitment and resources for service quality cannot be overstated.

GAP 3: SERVICE QUALITY SPECIFICATIONS – ACTUAL SERVICE DELIVERY

This is referred to as the service performance gap and occurs when the service that is delivered is different from management's specifications for service due to variations in the performance of personnel – employees not being able or willing to perform at a desired level. Solutions are central to human resources management (*see* INTERNAL MARKETING).

GAP 4: ACTUAL SERVICE DELIVERY – EXTERNAL COMMUNICATIONS ABOUT THE SERVICE

What is said about the service in external communications is different from the service that is delivered, i.e., ADVERTISING and promotion can influence consumers' expectations and perceptions of service. Therefore, it is important not to promise more than can be delivered (or expectations increase and perceptions decrease), or to fail to present relevant information (*see* SERVICE GUARANTEES). Success in this area requires appropriate and timely information/communication, both internally and to external customers.

Gaps 1 to 4 together contribute to consumers' expectations and perceptions of actual service (Gap 5). Service providers need to identify the gaps prevalent in their organization, determine the factors responsible for them, and develop appropriate solutions.

Zeithaml, Parasuraman, and Malhotra (2000), researching the delivery of service quality over the Internet, identified service quality gaps that may occur when companies interact with their customers through the Internet:

- *an information gap*: owing to insufficient or incorrect information about website features desired by customers;
- *a design gap*: to include aspects of site design and functioning of the website;
- *a communications gap*: to include inaccurate or inflated promises.

The combined effect of these gaps leads to a fourth, fulfillment, gap, which relates to stock availability, the reordering process, and delivery: this may occur as a result of deficiencies in the design and operation of the website.

However, the gaps notion has been the subject of increasing scrutiny and criticism in recent years (e.g., Iacobucci, Grayson, and Ostrom,

1994; Buttle, 1996). Buttle (1996) argues that there is no evidence that customers assess service quality in terms of perceptions–expectations gaps. Further, the use of inferred difference scores (i.e., objective P–E) has been questioned on the basis that inferred scores do not reflect subjective interpretations, e.g., of expectancy disconfirmation (Peter, Churchill, and Brown, 1993).

See also *service quality; service quality measurement*

Bibliography

Berry, L. L., Parasuraman, A., and Zeithaml, V. A. (1988). The service-quality puzzle. *Business Horizons*, July/August, 35–43.
Berry, L. L., Zeithaml, V. A., and Parasuraman, A. (1985). Quality counts in services too. *Business Horizons*, **28**, 3 (May/June), 44–52.
Buttle, F. (1996). SERVQUAL: Review, critique, research agenda. *European Journal of Marketing*, **30** (1), 8–32.
Grönroos, C. (1984). A service quality model and its marketing implications. *European Journal of Marketing*, **18** (4), 36–44.
Grönroos, C. (2000). *Service Management and Marketing: A Customer Relationship Management Approach*, 2nd edn. Chichester: John Wiley, ch. 5.
Iacobucci, D., Grayson, K. A., and Ostrom, A. L. (1994). The calculus of service quality and customer satisfaction: Theoretical and empirical differentiation and integration. In T. A. Swartz, D. E. Bowen, and S. W. Brown (eds.), *Advances in Services Marketing and Management*. Greenwich, CT: JAI Press, pp. 1–67.
Parasuraman, A., Zeithaml, V. A., and Berry, L. L. (1985). A conceptual model of service quality and its implications for future research. *Journal of Marketing*, **49** (Fall), 41–50.
Peter, J. P., Churchill, G. A., Jr., and Brown, T. J. (1993). Caution in the use of difference scores in consumer research. *Journal of Consumer Research*, **19**, 655–62.
Zeithaml, V. A., Berry, L. L., and Parasuraman, A. (1988). Communication and control processes in the delivery of service quality. *Journal of Marketing*, **52** (April), 35–8.
Zeithaml, V. A., Parasuraman, A., and Malhotra, A. (2000). *A Conceptual Framework for Understanding E-Service Quality: Implications for Future Research and Managerial Practice*. Report 00–115. Cambridge, MA: Marketing Science Institute.

service quality measurement

Barbara R. Lewis

In measuring service quality, organizations may often compare consumer expectations of service(s) with their perceptions of actual service delivered, rather than just assessing CUSTOMER SATISFACTION with a particular service outcome. Quality service is believed to exist when perceptions exceed expectations.

Researchers have developed increasingly sophisticated mechanisms to assess levels of consumers' expectations and perceptions with respect to SERVICE QUALITY DIMENSIONS. Many use RATING SCALES that are similar to, or are adapted from, the SERVQUAL instrument. Such scales allow researchers and organizations not only to measure performance against customers' expectations, but also to track service quality trends over time, compare branches/outlets of an organization, measure performance against competition (competitor mapping), measure the relative importance of service quality dimensions, compare service performance with customer service priorities, and categorize customers (see Parasuraman, Berry, and Zeithaml, 1990). The relative importance of key service quality dimensions may also be established from rankings, points allocations, trade-off analysis, and by competitor mapping.

There are various methodological problems associated with measuring service dimensions, relating to the dimensions themselves, variations in customer expectations, and the nature of the measurement tools.

DIMENSIONS

Companies need to be aware that some elements of service(s) are easier to evaluate than others (Parasuraman, Zeithaml, and Berry, 1985, 1988). For example, tangibles and credibility are known in advance, but most elements are experience criteria and can only be evaluated during or after consumption. Some, such as competence and security, may be difficult or impossible to evaluate, even after purchase and consumption. In general, consumers rely on experience properties when evaluating services.

VARIATIONS IN CUSTOMER EXPECTATIONS

Customer expectations are usually reasonable but vary depending on circumstances and experience, and will rise over time; and experience with one service provider may influence customer expectations of other providers. In addition, consumers have zones of tolerance (Parasuraman, Berry, and Zeithaml, 1991a), the difference between desired and adequate expectations. The desired level of service expectation is what they hope to receive, a blend of what "can" and "should" be, which is a function of past experience. The adequate level is what is acceptable, based on an assessment of what the service "will" be – the "predicted" service – and depends on the alternatives that are available. Tolerance zones vary between individuals and companies, with service aspects, and with experience, and tend to be smaller for outcome features than for process dimensions. In addition, if options are limited, tolerance zones may be higher than if many alternatives are available and it is easy to switch service providers. Further, expectations are higher in emergency situations and when something was not right the first time.

In addition, it is necessary to realize that as customers are increasingly aware of the alternatives on offer and rising standards of service, expectations may change over time. Higher levels of performance lead to higher expectations. Also, over time the dimensions of service may change, as may the relative importance of such factors. In addition, research and measurement usually focus on routine service situations: organizations also need to consider non-routine SERVICE ENCOUNTERS that may have a major impact on consumer (and employee) evaluations and satisfactions, e.g., SERVICE RECOVERY situations (*see* SERVICE FAILURE(S)).

MEASUREMENT TOOLS

A host of researchers have used SERVQUAL or similar instruments to assess the dimensions of service quality. Of particular interest are those researchers who have debated SERVQUAL and related methodologies (e.g., Smith, 1995; Buttle, 1996). Buttle (1996) provides a review of a number of the problems associated with the measurement of service quality generally, and SERVQUAL specifically. Overall, areas of concern have focused on conceptual/theoretical, operational, and interpretive issues, to include, for example:

- The relative focus on the process and outcome of service delivery.
- The measurement of expectations: what is being measured – ideal, desired, or adequate expectations and level of service performance?
- The timing of measurement: before, during, or after a particular service encounter.
- The scaling techniques incorporated and associated importance weightings (or not) of service quality dimensions.
- The disconfirmation paradigm: should service quality measurement be based on an assessment of performance minus expectations, or is performance only a better description of service quality? Several authors argue for "performance only" measures of service quality, due to conceptual concerns over the measurement and predictive VALIDITY of expectations, and operational concerns over respondent fatigue (e.g., Cronin and Taylor, 1992, 1994). Cronin and Taylor (1992) and Brady, Cronin, and Brand (2002) found that a performance-only based measurement of service quality (SERVPERF) may be an improved means of measuring the construct, as opposed to the gap-based SERVQUAL scale. Grönroos (2001) has also noted that "perceived" service quality should not be measured *per se*, but that the success of an organization's quality efforts should be measured via the assessment of customer satisfaction.
- The dimensionality of SERVQUAL and its applicability to all service industries, situations, and cultures. Increasingly, the research evidence does not replicate the SERVQUAL dimensions: they would appear to be specific to the context – both industry and CULTURE. Further, cultural differences in attitude and behavior include the cultural context of a rating scale assessment and consumer willingness to respond, and if necessary criticize companies and service. Babakus and Boller (1992) were among

the first to suggest that the dimensionality of SERVQUAL may depend on the services under study, and Ioannou, Lewis, and Cui (2003) incorporated the potential impact of cultural setting on the dimensionality of service quality.

- Changes in attributes and importance, expectations and perceptions over time. Cottam and Lewis (2001) considered the extent to which consumer expectations (both ideal and predicted), perceptions, and satisfaction may change during the course of extended service delivery and consumption.

In light of the current debate and available research evidence it is clear that there remains a considerable challenge for both academics and practitioners to refine the methods used to identify and measure appropriate dimensions of service quality.

See also *service quality; service quality gaps*

Bibliography

Babakus, E. and Boller, G. W. (1992). An empirical assessment of the SERVQUAL scale. *Journal of Business Research*, **24** (May), 253–68.

Brady, M. K., Cronin, J. J., and Brand, R. R. (2002). Performance-only measurement of service quality: A replication and extension. *Journal of Business Research*, **55**, 17–31.

Buttle, F. (1996). SERVQUAL: Review, critique, research agenda. *European Journal of Marketing*, **30** (1), 8–32.

Cottam, A. M. and Lewis, B. R. (2001). *The Measurement of Expectations: Timing and Relevance Issues in Services Consumption*. Manchester: School of Management, UMIST.

Cronin, J. J. and Taylor, S. A. (1992). Measuring service quality: A re-examination and extension. *Journal of Marketing*, **56**, 3 (July), 55–68.

Cronin, J. J. and Taylor, S. A. (1994). SERVPERF versus SERVQUAL: Reconciling performance-based and perceptions-minus-expectations measurement of service quality. *Journal of Marketing*, **58** (January), 125–31.

Grönroos, C. (2000). *Service Management and Marketing: A Customer Relationship Management Approach*, 2nd edn. Chichester: John Wiley, ch. 4.

Grönroos, C. (2001). The perceived service quality concept: A mistake? *Managing Service Quality*, **11** (3), 150–2.

Ioannou, M., Lewis, B. R., and Cui, C. C. (2003). Service quality in the Cypriot banking sector: Determinants and gaps. *Journal of Business and Society*.

Lewis, B. R. (1993). Service quality measurement. *Marketing Intelligence and Planning*, 11 (4), 4–12.

Lewis, B. R., Orledge, J., and Mitchell, V. (1994). Service quality: Students' assessments of banks and building societies. *International Journal of Bank Marketing*, 12 (4), 3–12.

Parasuraman, A., Berry, L. L., and Zeithaml, V. A. (1990). Guidelines for conducting service quality research. *Marketing Research*, December, 34–44.

Parasuraman, A., Berry, L. L., and Zeithaml, V. A. (1991a). Understanding consumer expectations of service. *Sloan Management Review*, 32 (3), 39–48.

Parasuraman, A., Berry, L. L., and Zeithaml, V. A. (1991b). Refinement and re-assessment of the SERVQUAL scale. *Journal of Retailing*, 67, 4 (Winter), 420–50.

Parasuraman, A., Zeithaml, V. A., and Berry, L. L. (1985). A conceptual model of service quality and its implications for future research. *Journal of Marketing*, 49 (Fall), 41–50.

Parasuraman, A., Zeithaml, V. A., and Berry, L. L. (1988). SERVQUAL: A multiple item scale for measuring consumer perceptions of service quality. *Journal of Retailing*, 64, 1 (Spring), 14–40.

Parasuraman, A., Zeithaml, V. A., and Berry, L. L. (1993). More on improving service quality. *Journal of Retailing*, 69 (1), 140–7.

Smith, A. M. (1995). Measuring service quality: Is SERVQUAL now redundant? *Journal of Marketing Management*, 11 (1/3), 257–76.

service recovery

Barbara R. Lewis

Service organizations typically strive for zero defects in their SERVICE DELIVERY, i.e., 100 percent CUSTOMER SATISFACTION, to get things right the first time. So they develop their systems and personnel policies accordingly. But when problems occur and mistakes happen, the challenge for service providers is to recover the problem or mistake and get it right the second time – to turn frustrated customers into loyal ones.

The actions that a service provider takes to respond to SERVICE FAILURE(s) are referred to as service recovery, i.e., "the specifications taken to insure that the customer receives a reasonable level of service after problems have occurred to disrupt normal service." Service recovery may also be defined as "a thought-out, planned, process/strategy of returning an aggrieved/dissatisfied customer to a state of satisfaction with a company after a service or product has failed to live up to expectations" (Hart, Heskett, and Sasser, 1990), i.e., making a special effort to put things right when something is wrong. This includes focus on critical SERVICE ENCOUNTERS and anticipating and preventing possible failure points. It also includes identifying service problems, making it easy for customers to complain (e.g., toll-free telephone numbers), conducting research (e.g., phoning customers to check on services delivered), tracking and analyzing failures, offering rewards for improvement suggestions, and measuring performance against standards (e.g., pizza delivery).

When problems do occur, companies have to expedite service recovery to meet customers' recovery expectations, which may be even higher than initial expectations. It is increasingly accepted that companies should first believe the customer, acknowledge the problem, take responsibility, and avoid defensiveness. They should also apologize, then fix the problem and recompense explicit and hidden costs if appropriate. Service recovery is "emotional and physical repair." Organizations need to deal with the customer first and then with the problem (Hart et al., 1990).

Service recovery strategies should be flexible, and integral to this is the role of front-line employees and the extent to which they have been empowered (see Bowen and Lawler, 1992) to respond to the customer (*see* INTERNAL MARKETING). Employees should have the authority, responsibility, and incentives/rewards to identify, care about, and solve customer problems and complaints. They should be allowed to use their judgment and their creative and communications skills to develop solutions to satisfy customers.

A recent stream of research focuses on consumers' evaluation of satisfaction with complaint handling in terms of perceived justice (see Blodgett, Hill, and Tax, 1997; Smith and Bolton, 1998; Tax and Brown, 1998; Tax, Brown, and Chandrashekaran, 1998; Smith, Bolton, and Wagner, 1999; Mattila, 2001; Michel, 2001). Perceived justice comprises three dimensions:

- *Distributive justice*: the perceived fairness of the outcome. What did the offending firm offer the customer to recover from the service failure?
- *Interactive justice*: this refers to the perceived fairness of the manner in which the customer is treated during the complaint-handling process.
- *Procedural justice*: the perceived fairness of the process used to rectify a service failure.

In order to recover effectively from service failure, an organization must provide a fair outcome, with a sincere apology, while taking the blame and acting swiftly to recover from the failure. Further, interactions between the justice dimensions mean that failure to deliver on one of them can impact negatively on the total success of the recovery.

The service recovery paradox (i.e., customers more satisfied following a recovered service failure than if things had "gone right first time"; Johnston, 1995) illustrates the managerial significance of understanding consumer reactions to recovery efforts, and of having effective recovery mechanisms in place (e.g., employee empowerment). Based on social exchange, social justice, and equity theories, Smith et al. (1999) have also demonstrated that satisfaction is maximized following service failure where the recovery resources received by customers "match the type of failure they experience in amounts commensurate with the magnitude of failure that occurs." For example, failures resulting in the loss of social/psychological resources (e.g., esteem) are best recovered with efforts designed to redress customer justice perceptions by offering social resources (e.g., an apology).

Overall, successful service recovery has economic benefits in terms of customer retention and loyalty. It costs less to retain customers than to replace them. There is also increasing evidence of customers who complain and who then receive a satisfactory response subsequently being more loyal to an organization, more likely to buy other services/products, and more likely to engage in positive WORD-OF-MOUTH COMMUNICATIONS. It is also a means to identify organizational problems with respect to all the dimensions of service quality and to improve overall customer awareness and service.

See also *service quality*

Bibliography

Blodgett, J. G., Hill, D. J., and Tax, S. S. (1997). The effects of distributive justice, procedural justice and interactional justice on post-complaint behavior. *Journal of Retailing*, **73** (2), 185–210.

Bowen, D. E. and Lawler, L. L. (1992). Empowerment: Why, what, how and when. *Sloan Management Review*, Spring, 31–9.

Grönroos, C. (2000). *Service Management and Marketing: A Customer Relationship Management Approach*, 2nd edn. Chichester: John Wiley, ch. 5.

Hart, C. W., Heskett, J. L., and Sasser, W. E., Jr. (1990). The profitable art of service recovery. *Harvard Business Review*, **90**, 4 (July/August), 148–56.

Johnston, R. (1995). Service failure and recovery: Impact, attitudes and process. In T. A. Swartz, D. E. Bowen, and S. W. Brown (eds.), *Advances in Services Marketing and Management*, vol. 4. Greenwich, CT: JAI Press, pp. 211–28.

Lovelock, C. H., Vandermerwe, S., and Lewis, B. (1999). *Services Marketing: A European Perspective*. Upper Saddle River, NJ: Prentice-Hall, ch. 7.

Mattila, A. S. (2001). The effectiveness of service recovery in a multi-industry setting. *Journal of Services Marketing*, **15** (7), 583–96.

Michel, S. (2001). Analyzing service failures and recoveries: A process approach. *International Journal of Service Industry Management*, **12** (1), 20–33.

Smith, A. K. and Bolton, R. N. (1998). An experimental investigation of customer reactions to service failure and recovery encounters: Paradox or peril? *Journal of Service Research*, August, 65–81.

Smith, A. K., Bolton, R. N., and Wagner, J. (1999). A model of customer satisfaction with service encounters involving failure and recovery. *Journal of Marketing Research*, **36**, 356–63.

Tax, S. S. and Brown, S. W. (1998). Recovering and learning from service failure. *Sloan Management Review*, Fall, 75–88.

Tax, S. S., Brown, S. W., and Chandrashekaran, M. (1998). Customer evaluation of service complaint handling experiences. *Journal of Marketing*, **62** (April), 60–76.

Zeithaml, V. A. and Bitner, M. J. (2003). *Services Marketing: Integrating Customer Focus Across the Firm*, 3rd edn. New York: McGraw-Hill, ch. 7.

services marketing

Barbara R. Lewis

Services marketing has evolved as a discipline for a number of reasons, in particular an increasing acknowledgment that all organizations participate in MARKETING MANAGEMENT, and the growth of service industries in developed economies.

The MARKETING CONCEPT is based on market EXCHANGE between buyers and sellers. All organizations have "products" and "markets" and are involved in market exchange, and so they need to be marketing oriented and adopt the marketing concept. This includes public and private sector organizations, and profit and not-for-profit organizations, where organizational objectives may relate to social or community orientation (*see* NOT-FOR-PROFIT MARKETING). Further, organizations may have more than one market, e.g., charities and hospitals (see figure 1).

Charities are involved in exchanges with "donors" who contribute money, material goods, or their time/commitment in return, typically, for "intangible" personal rewards, and also with "clients" who are recipients of help and benefits and who may, for example, be producing products that the charity can sell. Similarly hospitals, which are in the "business" of providing healthcare to patients, are involved in numerous marketing exchanges with patients, employees, trustees, government, suppliers, etc. The concept of multiple customer markets was first developed by Christopher, Payne, and Ballantyne (1991).

Charities and hospitals are examples of organizations/businesses that comprise the SERVICES SECTOR of an economy. As services have become increasingly critical within developed economies, so has the attention to marketing management within the sector, owing largely to the characteristics of services (*see* SERVICE CHARACTERISTICS) and the ensuing implications for managing the MARKETING MIX.

Services are typically characterized by intangibility, heterogeneity, inseparability, and perishability. Further, the notion of the service encounter (*see* SERVICE ENCOUNTERS) is particular to the services sector and is concerned with interactions between services and their providing organizations, personnel, and consumers, and with technology. Service characteristics and service encounters are central to understanding marketing management in the services sector, and have implications for the marketing mix, which includes product, price, place, and promotion (*see* SERVICE DISTRIBUTION; SERVICE PRICE; SERVICE PRODUCT; SERVICE PROMOTION). In addition, Booms and Bitner

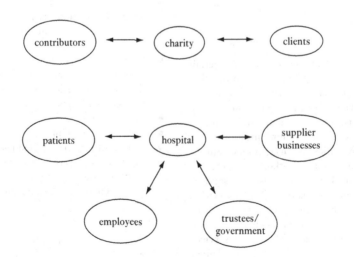

Figure 1   Services marketing

(1981) were the first to offer an extended marketing mix for the services sector to include physical evidence, process, and people (*see* IN-TERNAL MARKETING; SERVICE ENVIRON-MENT; SERVICE PROCESS).

Bibliography

Booms, B. H. and Bitner, M. J. (1981). Marketing strategies and organization structures for service firms. In J. H. Donnelly and W. R. George (eds.), *Marketing of Services*. Chicago: American Marketing Association, pp. 47–51.

Christopher, M., Payne, A. F. T., and Ballantyne, D. (1991). *Relationship Marketing: Bringing Quality, Customer Service and Marketing Together*. Oxford: Butterworth-Heinemann.

Kasper, H., van Helsdinger, P., and de Vries, W. (1999). *Services Marketing: An International Perspective*. Chichester: John Wiley, chs. 1–3.

Kotler, P. (1979). Strategies for introducing marketing into non-profit organizations. *Journal of Marketing*, 43 (January), 37–44.

Kotler, P. and Andreasen, A. R. (1996). *Strategic Marketing for Non-Profit Organizations*, 5th edn. Upper Saddle River, NJ: Prentice-Hall.

Kotler, P., Roberto, N., and Lee, N. (2002). *Social Marketing: Improving the Quality of Life*, 2nd edn. Thousand Oaks, CA: Sage.

Lovelock, C. H., Vandermerwe, S., and Lewis, B. (1999). *Services Marketing: A European Perspective*. Upper Saddle River, NJ: Prentice-Hall, ch. 1.

services sector

Barbara R. Lewis

The services sector of an economy is generally considered to include all industries other than those involved in manufacturing, and so covers: financial services; tourism and hospitality; healthcare; leisure, sport, and entertainment; professional services; communications and transport; information services; public utilities; government and local authority; education; charities; personal services; household services; industrial and business services, and so on. The sector embraces both profit and not-for-profit organizations (*see* NOT-FOR-PROFIT MAR-KETING), and includes public sector services. In addition, one can consider the service element in manufacturing industries, e.g., service support provided by computer manufacturers – before and after sales, advisory, technical and maintenance services, etc.

The services sector in developed economies is characterized by continuing growth with respect to output and consumption, employment, and its role in export trade. Many factors contribute to this growth resulting from demographic, social, economic, political, and legal changes, and impact variously on the demand for particular services. The determinants of services industry expansion include:

- demographic trends, in particular increasing life expectancy and an expanding retired population (with demand for nursing homes, medicines, etc.);
- an increasing percentage of women in the labor force (requiring child-minding services, house cleaning, etc.);
- more leisure time associated with employment conditions and changing LIFESTYLES (impacting on demand for recreation and tourism, etc.);
- increasing affluence, wealthier societies, and improving quality of life (impact on entertainment, meals outside the home, etc.);
- increasing numbers of new products and greater product complexity (requiring repairs and maintenance and advice services);
- greater complexity of life (requiring personal services, e.g., financial);
- greater concern about ecology and resource scarcity;
- breakthroughs in computers and information technology and in communications to facilitate provision of information, exchanges, and consumer behavior;
- development of new towns and regions;
- international mobility and travel;
- GLOBALIZATION of business;
- the size of governments and the development of the European Union and other world economic/trade collaborations.

Bibliography

Lovelock, C., Vandermerwe, S., and Lewis, B. (1999). *Services Marketing: A European Perspective*. Upper Saddle River, NJ: Prentice-Hall, ch. 1.

SERVQUAL

Barbara R. Lewis

Parasuraman's five major dimensions of SER-VICE QUALITY (tangibles, reliability, responsiveness, assurance, and empathy) form the basis for the SERVQUAL questionnaire (Parasuraman, Zeithaml, and Berry, 1988).

This has 22 pairs of Likert-type scales. The first 22 items are designed to measure customer expectations of service for a service industry and the following 22 to measure the perceived level of service provided by a particular organization in that industry. For example:

Service Expectations (E): "Customers should be able to trust bank employees."

"Banks should have up-to-date equipment."

Strongly Agree						Strongly Disagree
1	2	3	4	5	6	7

Service Perceptions (P): "I can trust the employees of my bank."

"My bank has up-to-date equipment."

Strongly Agree						Strongly Disagree
1	2	3	4	5	6	7

A quality perception or gap (Q) is calculated by subtracting the expectations scale values (E) from the performance scale values (P): i.e., $Q = P - E$. The scale was offered as one with good RELIABILITY and VALIDITY, which may be used to: track service quality trends and improve service; categorize customers; compare branches/outlets of an organization; and compare an organization with its competitors. Even so, it is limited to current and past customers as respondents need knowledge and experience of the company.

There has been considerable debate over the use and generalizability of SERVQUAL, which led to various modifications by the original authors (see Parasuraman, Berry, and Zeithaml, 1991; Parasuraman, Zeithaml, and Berry, 1993, 1994a, 1994b; Zeithaml, Berry, and Parasuraman, 1996).

See also *service quality dimensions; service quality measurement*

Bibliography

Grönroos, C. (2000). *Service Management and Marketing: A Customer Relationship Management Approach*, 2nd edn. Chichester: John Wiley, ch. 4.

Parasuraman, A., Berry, L. L., and Zeithaml, V. A. (1991). Refinement and re-assessment of the SERVQUAL scale. *Journal of Retailing*, **67**, 4 (Winter), 420–50.

Parasuraman, A., Zeithaml, V. A., and Berry, L. L. (1988). SERVQUAL: A multiple item scale for measuring consumer perceptions of service quality. *Journal of Retailing*, **64**, 1 (Spring), 14–40.

Parasuraman, A., Zeithaml, V. A., and Berry, L. L. (1993). More on improving service quality. *Journal of Retailing*, **69** (1), 140–7.

Parasuraman, A., Zeithaml, V. A., and Berry, L. L. (1994a). Alternative scales for measuring service quality: A comparative assessment based on psychometric and diagnostic criteria. *Journal of Retailing*, **70** (3), 201–30.

Parasuraman, A., Zeithaml, V. A., and Berry, L. L. (1994b). Reassessment of expectations as a comparison standard in measuring service quality: Implications for further research. *Journal of Marketing*, **58** (January), 111–24.

Zeithaml, V. A., Berry, L. L., and Parasuraman, A. (1996). The behavioral consequences of service quality. *Journal of Marketing*, **60**, 31–46.

shape

David Yorke

Shape is a variable in the DESIGN of PACKAGING and is used in conjunction with different types of packaging materials, e.g., plastic, card, metals. The shape can communicate the nature of a product to the potential customer/consumer/user, e.g., angular packaging may convey an image of strength/power, rounded packaging often conveys softness. The shape of the packaging may have symbolic significance in certain cultures. However, the shape of packaging should not be too unorthodox as problems may result for resellers in stacking and shelf display, thus reducing turnover/profitability per cubic meter.

shopper typologies

Steve Worrall and Andrew Newman

Shopper typologies involve a classification that identifies shoppers based upon their purchase behavior, motives (*see* CONSUMER NEEDS AND MOTIVES), and ATTITUDES. The sciences of DEMOGRAPHICS and PSYCHOGRAPHICS offer measures now widely used to define these shopper groupings. In addition, common lifestyle patterns among consumers can aid the classification process (*see* LIFESTYLES).

A number of shopper groupings have been proposed:

- *The convenience shopper*, who tends to be short on disposable time and with a higher-than-average income. Such time scarcity may influence shopping behavior in terms of time available, preferred locations of stores, and opening hours.
- *The leisure shopper*, for whom discretionary time is relatively high and the consumer seeks to fill it with shopping activity. This may include a high number of shopping trips for both purchase and browsing activity, often as a form of leisure activity.
- *The price-conscious shopper*, who may range from the relatively logical "economic shopper" to the more price-prone "special deal" shopper. For such consumers, PRICING is a relatively important consideration and one that may influence the choice of product and outlet more than in other cases.
- *The store-loyal consumer* is seen as one who regularly patronizes a particular retailer when seeking certain goods and who may therefore restrict his/her consideration of competing stores. The reasons for such behavior may include repeated good service and/or a perception that the retailer in question is consistently able to meet his/her needs.

Other shopper types may include the economic consumer, the personalizing consumer, the ethical consumer, and the apathetic consumer (Stone, 1954). Commercial research and market intelligence sources (Mintel, 1998) suggest that younger, less affluent women are shopping addicts, time-rich consumers but relatively cash poor when it comes to actually spending money.

To attract older shoppers with greater spending power, retailers frequently employ older sales staff and sell classic merchandise styles from an unthreatening shopping environment.

Bibliography

Karande, K. and Ganesh, J. (2000). Who shops at factory outlets and why? An exploratory study. *Journal of Marketing Theory and Practice*, 8, 4 (Fall), pp. 29–43.

Mintel (1998). *Consumer Shopping Habits*. Mintel International Group.

Schiffman, L. G. and Kanuk, L. L. (2004). *Consumer Behavior*, 8th edn. Upper Saddle River, NJ: Pearson Educational International.

Stone, G. P. (1954). City shoppers and urban identification: Observations on the social psychology of city life. *American Journal of Sociology*, 60, 36–45, cited in P. J. McGoldrick (2002), *Retail Marketing*. London: McGraw-Hill.

shopping centers

Andrew Newman and Steve Greenland

Shopping centers are generally more planned than the traditional HIGH STREET RETAILING central shopping areas and have more pedestrian activity. Guy (1994) confines the term to "shopping developments of at least 50,000 sq. ft. gross retail area that include at least three retail units." Bolen (1988) describes a shopping center or mall as: "A group of stores with balanced tenancy – enough of one kind of store to attract traffic but not too many stores of any one type. A shopping center or mall should have adequate parking and a good store visibility from the parking area along with two or more large stores to draw the customer."

Encapsulating all the above points, McGoldrick (2002) favors the International Council for Shopping Centers classification. This describes a shopping center as "a group of retail and other commercial establishments that is planned, developed, owned and managed as a single property." This description suggests that a shopping center has far more control over its tenant mix, which is a crucial success factor as it insures continuity over the retail provision and facilities.

Hence, for the customer, there is a concentration of retail outlets such as fashion and food, and a consistent overall design, level of maintenance and security. The latter is a particularly important factor and influences customer patronage and typologies (*see* RETAILER PATRONAGE; SHOPPER TYPOLOGIES).

There are essentially four specific types of shopping center, which may be classified as follows: regional shopping center $(30,000m^2+)$; intermediate shopping centers $(10,000-20,000\,m^2)$; retail parks $(5,000-20,000\,m^2)$; and speciality centers $(1,000m^2)$.

Bibliography

Bolen, W. H. (1988). *Contemporary Retailing*. Englewood Cliffs, NJ: Prentice-Hall.

Frasquet, M., Gil, I., and Mollá, A. (2001). Shopping-center selection modeling: A segmentation approach. *International Review of Retail, Distribution and Consumer Research*, **11** (1), 23–38.

Guy, C. (1994). *The Retail Development Process*. London: Routledge.

McGoldrick, P. J. (2002). *Retail Marketing*. London: McGraw-Hill.

Prendergast, G., Marr, N., and Jarratt, B. (1998). Retailers' views of shopping centers: A comparison of tenants and non-tenants. *International Journal of Retail and Distribution Management*, **26** (4/5), 162–72.

single/multiple sourcing

Dominic Wilson

Traditionally, the ideal in purchasing has been to use multiple sources for goods and services where the strategic consequences of source failure (e.g., in terms of halting production or compromising safety) outweighed the scale economies and operational convenience of single sourcing (Segal, 1989). The use of multiple sourcing to increase the customer's negotiating power was also seen as an important benefit. In practice, even where alternative SUPPLIERS were approved, they were not always used, perhaps because of inertia, pressure of work, the strength of established relationships, or perceived switching costs. It is important to recognize that in practical terms changing suppliers can be disruptive, time consuming, resource intensive, costly, and even career threatening for

purchasing staff if they make mistakes. To justify change, clear benefits have to be identified to overcome systemic inertia, accumulated personal commitment, alternative work priorities, and switching costs. Most of these factors operate to the advantage of existing suppliers and it takes management determination to maintain a thorough approach to multiple sourcing strategies.

See also *purchasing process*

Bibliography

Paliwoda, S. J. and Bonaccorsi, A. J. (1994). Trends in procurement strategies within the European aircraft industry. *Industrial Marketing Management*, **23**, 3 (July), 235–44.

Segal, M. N. (1989). Implications of single v. multiple buying sources. *Industrial Marketing Management*, **18**, 3 (August), 163–78.

skimming pricing

Dominic Wilson

Skimming pricing is the use of high prices (often reflecting large profit margins) for the initial marketing of new products. Such new products will be adopted initially by the least price-sensitive parts of the market. Once demand in these niches falls off, subsequent incremental price reductions may be used to devolve the product to increasingly price-sensitive market areas until DEMAND is replete. Thus, the objective of skimming is to maximize short-term profitability. Skimming pricing contrasts with PENETRATION PRICING in that it adopts a relatively high price compared to the relatively low price of penetration policies.

Skimming policies might be adopted where there is little prospect of a long-term market for offerings (e.g., novelty items, fads, seasonal items), or where organizations perceive only a short-term sustainable differentiation in their offerings due to copying (e.g., fashion markets), or where premium pricing is based on strong brands and consumer loyalty (e.g., luxury goods), or by organizations placing a high priority on short PAYBACK periods as a key corporate measure (e.g., where capital costs are high), or by organizations simply seeking to capitalize on the unique benefits of their product (e.g., the sale of distinctive vehicle registrations). The advantages of successful skimming pricing include rapid cost recovery (thereby reducing investment risk) and less commitment to long-term policies to insure break-even (thereby allowing a more flexible response to market developments and some insurance against FORECASTING errors). However, skimming strategies can be difficult to manage since an organization may have to defend its offering (e.g., by patent or branding) from any credible imitators or pirates that might be attracted by the high profits associated with skimming, but it must also insure that the corporate IMAGE is not tarnished, nor potential demand alienated, by any appearance of profiteering.

See also *pricing; pricing methods*

Bibliography

Dean, J. (1950). Pricing policies for new products. *Harvard Business Review*, **28**, 6 (November/December), 45–53.

social change

see DEMOGRAPHICS

social class

Margaret K. Hogg and Barbara R. Lewis

Social class refers to the stratification of members of a society into a hierarchy. Every known human society is stratified, i.e., the hierarchical evaluation of people in different social positions is inherent in human social organizations. Within societies, different occupations, trades, and professions have a more immediate impact on a community and may attract social prestige and authority. Early definitions of social class focused on reputation; for example, Warner, Meeker, and Eells (1949) defined social class in terms of how people in a community view one another and place their associates in the social structure, putting an emphasis on status/reputation and participation in the community.

More recently, various "objective" criteria have been used to define and measure social class, e.g., occupation, income level and source, wealth, house type, area of residence, and educational level. Consequently, various categorizations of social class have been developed, e.g., those referring to typologies such as upper, middle, and lower class, and the A, B, C1, C2, D, E system developed in the UK by the Joint Industry Committee for National Readership Surveys, based on the occupation of the head of the household. Current typologies are, however, specifically related to LIFESTYLES, e.g. ACORN types.

Levy (1964, 1966) discussed social class in terms of variations that are a combination of a consumer's values, interpersonal attitudes, self-perceptions, and daily life. Such differences find expression in consumer behavior (*see* CONSUMER BUYER BEHAVIOR) in a number of ways: products and services bought (accumulation of certain products and services can serve as a symbol of class position); use of and reaction to the media, e.g., critical or accepting response to advertisements, questioning of claims; spending, saving, and investment (Martineau, 1958a); stores used (Martineau, 1958b); reaction to INNOVATION; entertainment and leisure; CONSUMERISM; use of credit cards and facilities – in this case Mathews and Slocum (1969) considered instalment versus convenience usage of credit cards, and products and services which are acceptable to charge.

Social classes are considered to be relatively permanent and homogeneous. However, the concept of a hierarchy of social class suggests vertical mobility, both upwards and downwards. This may be a function of educational mobility (witness the emergence of a "meritocracy," professional and business leaders who have achieved prominence through intelligence and hard work) and changes in employment and income (witness the disappearing divisions between white-collar and blue-collar consumption habits as economic income levels). However, fundamental social values and ATTITUDES may not change as suddenly as behavior with increased spending power.

Further, one needs to be aware of the concept of "over/underprivilege" within social classes (see Coleman, 1960, 1983). This is the notion of looking at DISCRETIONARY INCOME within social class groups such that certain luxury products and services are targeted at the "overprivileged" across all social classes.

Bibliography

Arnould, E., Price, L., and Zinkhan, G. (2004). *Consumers*, 2nd edn. Boston: McGraw-Hill Irwin, ch. 12.

Coleman, R. P. (1960). The significance of social stratification in selling. In M. L. Bell (ed.), *Marketing: A Maturing Discipline*. Chicago: American Marketing Association, 171–84.

Coleman, R. P. (1983). The continuing significance of social class to marketing. *Journal of Consumer Research*, **10** (December), 265–80. Reprinted in H. H. Kassarjian and T. S. Robertson (eds.) (1991). *Perspectives in Consumer Behavior*, 4th edn. London: Prentice-Hall International, pp. 487–510.

Engel, J. F., Blackwell, R. D., and Miniard, P. W. (1995). *Consumer Behavior*, 8th edn. Fort Worth, TX: Dryden Press, ch. 19.

Hawkins, D. I., Best, R. J., and Coney, K. A. (1995). *Consumer Behavior: Implications for Marketing Strategy*, 6th edn. Boston: Irwin.

Hoyer, W. D. and MacInnis, D. J. (2001). *Consumer Behavior*, 2nd edn. Boston and New York: Houghton Mifflin, ch. 14.

Levy, S. J. (1964). Symbolism and lifestyle. In S. A. Greyser (ed.), *Toward Scientific Marketing*. Chicago: American Marketing Association, pp. 140–50.

Levy, S. J. (1966). Social class and consumer behavior. In J. W. Newman (ed.), *On Knowing the Consumer*. New York: John Wiley, pp. 146–60.

Martineau, P. (1958a). Social classes and spending behavior. *Journal of Marketing*, **23** (October), 121–30.

Martineau, P. (1958b). The personality of the retail store. *Harvard Business Review*, **36** (January/February), 47–55.

Mathews, H. L. and Slocum, J. W. (1969). Social class and the commercial bank credit card usage. *Journal of Marketing*, **33** (January), 71–8.

Mowen, J. C. and Minor, M. (1998). *Consumer Behavior*, 5th edn. Upper Saddle River, NJ: Prentice-Hall, ch. 18.

Mowen, J. C. and Minor, M. (2001). *Consumer Behavior: A Framework*. Upper Saddle River, NJ: Prentice-Hall, ch. 14.

Rich, S. U. and Jain, S. C. (1968). Social class and life cycle as predictors of shopping behavior. *Journal of Marketing Research*, **5** (February), 41–9.

Schiffman, L. G. and Kanuk, L. Z. (2004). *Consumer Behavior*, 8th edn. Upper Saddle River, NJ: Prentice-Hall, ch. 11.

Solomon, M. R. (2002). *Consumer Behavior: Buying, Having, Being*, 5th edn. Upper Saddle River, NJ: Prentice-Hall, ch. 13.

Solomon, M. R., Bamossy, G., and Askegaard, S. (2002). *Consumer Behavior: A European Perspective*, 2nd edn. Upper Saddle River, NJ: Prentice-Hall, ch. 12.

Warner, W. L., Meeker, M., and Eells, K. (1949). *Social Class in America*. Chicago: Scientific Research Associates.

social identity

see CULTURE AND SOCIAL IDENTITY

social marketing

Barbara R. Lewis

Social marketing is part of "non-business" marketing (together with NOT-FOR-PROFIT MARKETING), which relates to marketing activities conducted by individuals and organizations to achieve some goal other than ordinary business goals of PROFIT, MARKET SHARE, and return on investment.

Social marketing is concerned with the development of programs designed to influence the acceptability of social ideas, and may be defined to be a set of activities to create, maintain, and/or alter attitudes and/or behavior toward a social idea or cause, independently of a sponsoring organization or person. The purpose may be to trigger one-time behavior from people (e.g., contribute to a foundation for AIDS research); to change behavior (e.g., to discourage cigarette smoking, drug or alcohol abuse, unsafe sexual practice, to recycle more newspapers, plastics, etc.); or to change ATTITUDES and beliefs (e.g., toward birth control and family planning or toward pollution control). Adkins (1999) has argued that social marketing is generally less sophisticated than that conducted for profit, due to the former's misinterpretation of the MARKETING CONCEPT as synonymous with ADVERTISING. She further argues that the increased adoption of customer-oriented techniques and strategies will increase the efficiency of social marketers.

Bibliography

Adkins, S. (1999). *Cause-Related Marketing: Who Cares Wins*. Oxford: Butterworth-Heinemann.

Christy, R. (1995). The broader application of marketing. In G. Oliver (ed.), *Marketing Today*, 4th edn. Hemel Hempstead: Prentice-Hall, ch. 24, pp. 500–27.

Kotler, P. (2003). *Marketing Management: Analysis, Planning, Implementation and Control*, 11th edn. Englewood Cliffs, NJ: Prentice-Hall.

social responsibility

David Marsden

In 1960 Davis described social responsibility as business "decisions and actions taken for reasons at least partially beyond the firm's direct economic or technical interests." The various lines of academic inquiry and the different conceptions of the meaning of the term social responsibility, however, have resulted in a spectrum of definitions. For example, one of the most popular versions today is termed corporate social responsibility (CSR), defined as "categories or levels of economic, legal, ethical and discretionary activities of a business entity as adapted to the values and expectations of society" (Joyner and Payne, 2002). In short, CSR posits that by being socially responsible, marketing can achieve greater profits as well as a higher quality of life for the whole society, and as such, it is closely associated with SOCIETAL MARKETING. This can be accomplished by companies being proactive, consumer oriented, and by considering consumers' wellbeing as the highest priority. Moreover, CSR encourages marketing to consider its obligations and duties to its various stakeholders – the people affected by an organization's policies and practices. As Smith (2001: 142) makes clear, "Fulfillment of these obligations is intended to minimize any harm and maximize the long-run beneficial impact of the firm on society." One way companies can do this is by reaching out and catering not only to the mainstream core markets, but also to those that contain consumers who do not have access to full equal opportunities, such as the poor, the elderly and frail, the undereducated, certain minorities, and those who are particularly vulnerable (Coskun, 1992). Charitable contributions (Thorne-McAlister and Ferrell, 2002) and green/sustainable marketing (van Dam and Apeldoorn, 1996) are also expressions of CSR programs in that they both attempt to "communicate proactively the company's raison d'être to opinion leaders and the general public" (Orgrizek, 2002).

Bibliography

Coskun, S. A. (1992). *Social Responsibility in Marketing*. Greenwood, CT: JAI Press.

Davis, K. (1960). Can business afford to ignore its social responsibilities? *California Management Review*, 2 (3), 70–6.

Joyner, B. E. and Payne, D. (2002). Evolution and implementation: A study of values, business ethics and corporate social responsibility. *Journal of Business Ethics*, 41 (4/3), 297–311.

Orgrizek, M. (2002). The effect of corporate social responsibility on the branding of financial services. *Journal of Financial Services Marketing*, 6 (3), 215–28.

Smith, N. C. (2001). Changes in corporate practices in response to public interest advocacy and actions. In P. N. Bloom and G. T. Gundlach (eds.), *Handbook of Marketing and Society*. Thousand Oaks, CA: Sage, pp. 140–61.

Thorne-McAlister, D. and Ferrell, L. (2002). The role of strategic philanthropy in marketing strategy. *European Journal of Marketing*, 36 (5/6), 689–705.

Van Dam, Y. K. and Apeldoorn, A. C. (1996). Sustainable marketing. *Journal of Macro Marketing*, 16 (2), 45–56.

societal marketing

David Marsden

The societal marketing concept (*see* MARKETING CONCEPT) was first proposed in the early 1970s as an alternative to the traditional MARKETING MANAGEMENT concept (Kotler, 1972). Although largely ignored at first, in the 1990s it received a lot of academic attention in response to major changes in consumer AWARENESS and ATTITUDES to social-environment issues inherent in MARKETING. The main distinguishing feature of societal marketing is the emphasis it attaches to the moral responsibility of marketing in meeting the needs of customers profitably.

According to Kotler and Armstrong (2004), for example, societal marketing refers to an organization that "makes marketing decisions by considering consumers' wants, the company's requirements, consumers' long-run interests, and society's long-run interests." In short, societal marketing requires companies to include social and ethical considerations into their marketing practices.

Crane and Desmond (2002) point out that from a societal marketing perspective, products are categorized in terms of their short-and long-term benefits:

1 *Deficient products*: neither short-term nor long-term consumer benefits;
2 *Salutary products*: low short-term but high long-term benefits;
3 *Pleasing products*: high short-term but harmful long-term benefits; and
4 *Desirable products*: high short-term and long-term benefits.

Cigarettes would be an example of pleasing products because they provide short-term benefits but are detrimental in the long run.

In practice, societal marketing necessitates close dialogue and communication between the business and its environment as well as a commitment to the community "in the form of feedback mechanisms, consultations and negotiations between competitors, consumers and government" (Abratt and Sacks, 1988: 26). For example, it has been found that many firms are now starting to integrate their communication activities that have a social dimension with their economic marketing strategies (Handelman and Arnold, 1999).

A variation of the societal marketing concept is corporate societal marketing (CSM), defined as "marketing initiatives that have at least one non-economic objective related to social welfare and use the resources of the company and/or one of its partners" (Drumwright and Murphy, 2001: 164). Corporate philanthropy, cause-related marketing, and green/sustainable marketing are also expressions of the corporate societal marketing concept (*see* SOCIAL RESPONSIBILITY). It has been argued that the benefits of CSM include PRODUCT DIFFERENTIATION, increased customer loyalty,

enhanced company IMAGE, strengthened employee commitment, and higher BRAND awareness and credibility (Hoeffler and Keller, 2002).

Bibliography

Abratt, R. and Sacks, D. (1988). Perceptions of the societal marketing concept. *European Journal of Marketing*, **23** (6), 25–33.

Bloom, P. N. and Gundlach, G. T. (eds.) (2001). *Handbook of Marketing and Society*. Thousand Oaks, CA: Sage.

Crane, A. and Desmond, J. (2002). Societal marketing and morality. *European Journal of Marketing*, **36** (5/6), 548–69.

Drumwright, M. and Murphy, P. E. (2001). Corporate societal marketing. In P. N. Bloom and G. T. Gundlach (eds.), *Handbook of Marketing and Society*. Thousand Oaks, CA: Sage, pp. 162–83.

Handelman, J. M. and Arnold, S. J. (1999). The role of marketing actions with a social dimension: Appeals to the institutional environment. *Journal of Marketing*, **63**, 33–48.

Hoeffler, S. and Keller, K. L. (2002). Building brand equity through corporate societal marketing. *Journal of Public Policy and Marketing*, **21** (1), 78–89.

Kotler, P. (1972). What consumerism means for marketers. *Harvard Business Review*, **50**, 48–57.

Kotler, P. and Armstrong, G. (2004). *Principles of Marketing*, 10th edn. Upper Saddle River, NJ: Prentice-Hall.

source effect

David Yorke

The source of a MARKETING COMMUNICATIONS message is the sender of information, be it a manufacturer, distributor, other organization, salesperson, or another customer. The IMPACT of the MESSAGE depends on a number of factors, including the source effect. This has two dimensions, credibility and incongruity.

Credibility comprises dimensions of knowledge and expertness, trustworthiness and likeability. High-credibility sources may add persuasiveness to the communication: e.g., doctors testifying to the benefits of a drug, or a well-known personality endorsing products. Such sources reinforce images or cause attitude change more easily than low-credibility sources, although some people may more easily identify with and be persuaded by sources that they perceive as being similar to themselves.

Source incongruity arises when receivers hold a positive attitude toward the source (e.g., a celebrity) and a negative attitude toward the message (with respect to the product/brand), or vice versa. This is something that organizations would wish to avoid. Over time, there is evidence that the message may become dissociated from its original source.

Bibliography

Bauer, R. A. (1965). A revised model of source effect. Presidential address of the Division of Consumer Psychology. American Psychological Association Annual Meeting.
McGuire, W. J. (1969). The nature of attitude and attitude change. In G. Lindzey and E. Aronson (eds.), *Handbook of Social Psychology*. Reading, MA: Addison-Wesley.

specifiers

Dominic Wilson

Specifiers are members of the decision-making unit (*see* BUYING CENTER) and are those individuals involved in the technical specification of purchasing requirements. Examples might include design engineers, production engineers, operators, and administrators – in short, anyone with sufficient expertise or experience to be able to recommend the technical parameters of a purchase requirement.

See also *purchasing process*

sponsorship

David Yorke

Sponsorship is an element of the marketing COMMUNICATIONS MIX and is considered to be the provision of assistance, financial or in kind, to an activity by a commercial organization, for the purpose of achieving commercial objectives.

Reasons for, or objectives of, sponsorship are interrelated and include: keeping the com-

pany name before the public; building or altering perceptions of the organization and, therefore, goodwill; portraying a socially concerned and community-involved company; identifying with a TARGET MARKET and, therefore, promoting products and brands; countering adverse PUBLICITY; aiding with recruitment; and helping sales forces with prospects.

Typically, sponsorship is associated with the arts, sports, and community activities, and so companies are seen to be supporting these "events" and would, therefore, claim such support to be an objective of their sponsorship.

Sponsorship monies might finance part of the cost of a community or cultural or sporting event, or assume responsibility for the production of a TELEVISION or RADIO program. Thus, the sponsoring organization aims to establish high visibility and the credibility of being associated with the development and success of the venture.

A recent development with sponsorship is corporate hospitality, in particular at sporting and cultural events.

A major problem with sponsorship is measurement of its cost effectiveness.

See also *marketing communications*

Bibliography

Meenaghan, T. (1991). The role of sponsorship in the marketing communications mix. *International Journal of Advertising*, **10** (1).

SPSS

see STATISTICAL PACKAGE FOR THE SOCIAL SCIENCES

Statistical Package for the Social Sciences

Michael Greatorex

The Statistical Package for the Social Sciences (SPSS) is a popular package of computer software used to analyze data, including data obtained in MARKETING RESEARCH surveys (*see* SURVEY RESEARCH). The components of the package concern data input, data modification, data analysis, presentation of results, and communication with other packages. The range of statistical procedures that can be specified is very large and includes all types of DESCRIPTIVE STATISTICS, HYPOTHESIS TESTING, UNIVARIATE ANALYSIS, BIVARIATE ANALYSIS, and multivariate analysis (*see* MULTIVARIATE METHODS (ANALYSIS)). Different versions of SPSS are available: SPSS-X is for mainframe computers, while SPSS/PC+ and SPSS for WINDOWS are for personal computers, with SPSS for WINDOWS being the most user-friendly.

Bibliography

Bryman, A. and Cramer, D. (2001). *Quantitative Data Analysis with SPSS Release 10 for Windows.* London: Routledge.

statistical sources

David Yorke

In order to monitor and, if possible, forecast environmental change (*see* MARKETING ENVIRONMENT), access to information, in the form of statistics, is vital. In most cases, statistics are presented historically, which means that the user has to make assumptions before extrapolating them into the future. Problems arise, however, in the credibility and comparability of statistics. Government statistics, particularly those in the developed world, have high credibility, but other sources may need careful investigation to discover how the information has been collected. A major problem exists when making international comparisons in that the basis for presentation of information may be different for individual reporting countries.

Bibliography

Central Statistical Office. *Guide to Official Statistics* (annual). London: HMSO.
United Nations Yearbook (annual). New York: United Nations.
United States Bureau of the Census. *Statistical Abstract of the United States* (annual). Austin, TX: Reference Press.

statistical tests

Michael Greatorex

There are many statistical significance tests. The approach to take in a particular set of circumstances depends upon the type of data, the number of samples, whether samples are independent or matched (*see* MATCHED SAMPLING), the type of probability sample, the size of the samples, and whether or not some population characteristics are known (*see* SAMPLING). A list of some common tests and the conditions of their use is given in table 1.

In addition, hypotheses (*see* HYPOTHESIS TESTING) concerning the relationships between variables measured on interval scales are studied using REGRESSION AND CORRELATION. Relationships between variables measured on ordinal scales are studied using Spearman's rank correlation coefficient or Kendall's tau.

There are many more test statistics that are available and can be used according to the circumstances. Some are in direct competition with the ones listed in table 1, others are for circumstances not mentioned.

It is easy to carry out such tests using computer packages such as SPSS (*see* STATISTICAL PACKAGE FOR THE SOCIAL SCIENCES), SAS, and MINITAB. However, care must be taken not to misuse these packages by using tests in inappropriate circumstances, e.g., when data are not from probability samples, and when tests that require interval data are used with data that are only ordinal.

Bibliography

Tull, D. S. and Hawkins, D. I. (1993). *Marketing Research: Measurement and Methods,* 6th edn. New York: Macmillan.

store choice

Steve Worrall and Andrew Newman

This is the decision made by the consumer as to which store to visit. In a highly competitive marketplace, an understanding of why the consumer chooses a particular store is of great importance. Getting the consumer to cross the

Table 1   Common statistical tests

Type of data	No. of samples	Independent samples?	Other conditions	Statistical technique
Interval	1	N.R.	σ known Z test	
Interval	1	N.R.	σ unknown	t test
Ordinal	1	N.R.		Kolmogorov-Smirnov 1 sample test
Nominal	1	N.R.	small sample	Binomial test
Nominal	1	N.R.	large sample	Z test
Interval	2	Yes	σ's known	Z test
Interval	2	Yes	σ's unknown	t test (either pooled or unpooled variance formula)
Interval	2	No	σ's unknown	t test (one sample test of differences)
Ordinal	2	Yes		Mann-Whitney test K-S 2 sample test
Ordinal	2	No		Sign test, Wilcoxon matched pairs test
Nominal	2	Yes		Fisher's Exact test, Z test, Chisquared test
Nominal	2	No		McNemar test
Interval	2+	Yes		1-way ANOVA
Interval	2+	No		t tests (as above) of all pairs
Ordinal	2+	Yes		Kruskal Wallis 1-way ANOVA
Ordinal	2+	No		Friedman 2-way ANOVA
Nominal	2+	Yes		Chi-squared test
Nominal	2+	No		Cochran Q test

σ is the population standard deviation

threshold and enter a store naturally opens up a number of selling opportunities.

Store IMAGE studies have elicited a large number of reasons as to why consumers choose as they do. The choice factors and the strength of their effects naturally vary from one consumer to another and from one time period to another. Many factors are likely to influence store choice, including CONSUMER PERCEPTIONS of the price and quality of the merchandise, the internal environment of the store (*see* ATMOSPHERICS; STORE DESIGN), the helpfulness of staff, ease of access, the product range, and the "image" held by the customer of the outlet or chain.

Given such differences, it is difficult to generalize about the store choice of consumers. The individual retailer is likely to develop an intuitive approach to this question based upon previous experience.

Bibliography

Erdem, O. and Oumlil, A. B. (1999). Consumer values and the importance of store attributes. *International Journal of Retail and Distribution Management*, **27** (4/5), 137–45.

Van Kenhove, P., De Wulf, K., and van Waterschoot, W. (1999). The impact of task definition on store-attribute saliences and store choice. *Journal of Retailing*, **75**, 1 (Spring), 125–38.

store design

Steve Greenland and Andrew Newman

The store has traditionally occupied a central role in RETAILING as the direct point of contact between retailer and consumers. It is the place where the retailer can meet the customer's requirements and insure continued business. The store is also an important extension of the retailer's image (*see* RETAIL IMAGE), and an indicator of such things as price, quality, and merchandise range. This helps the retailer position itself (*see* RETAIL POSITIONING) and creates important differences between competitors. However, the major function of the store is to provide a basic storage and display for the merchandise OFFERING, whether it is products or services or both. For most retailers this physical space is crucial to the business operation and is constantly manipulated to facilitate the customer (Newman and Cullen, 2002).

The store is also the main retail distribution channel (*see* RETAIL DISTRIBUTION CHANNELS) and is perhaps the most powerful medium for communicating with customers; consequently, store design is extremely important. It encompasses the entire store environment including aspects such as layout, ambience, ATMOSPHERICS, visual aspects of RETAIL MERCHANDISING, and RETAIL SECURITY. Retailers may think of their stores as a theater with a well-trained cast (the sales staff) and walls and floors representing the stage. In this context, lighting, fixtures, and visual communications such as signs represent the sets, and the merchandise represents the show. Similar to the role that props play in the theater, the store's design and all its components should work in harmony to support the merchandise (Levy and Weitz, 1998).

The significance of store design as a competitive weapon and selling tool is frequently overlooked. When implemented properly, however, the design of a retail outlet can influence how successful it is at:

1 Initially, visually attracting customers to the retailer.
2 Communicating the desired corporate, store, and product images, differentiating them from those of other retailers.
3 Creating the most effective balance between products and functions.
4 Selling, promoting, and ADVERTISING products and services, as well as the retailer.
5 Encouraging the customer to browse around the store and maximize the time spent in it, thereby maximizing the chance of impulse purchase (*see* IMPULSE PURCHASING).

6 Supporting and giving "environmental substance" to media campaigns.
7 Providing an ergonomically sound environment, freeing more staff time for sales-oriented activities.
8 Facilitating efficient and quality SERVICE DELIVERY.
9 Developing customer/staff relationships.
10 Giving user satisfaction, for both staff and customers, aesthetically, emotionally, and in terms of functionality.
11 Enabling the rapid implementation of any future environment alterations or refurbishment.
12 Providing an acceptable design life cycle.
13 Preventing robbery/fraud.
14 Imbuing staff and customers with confidence in their safety and security (Greenland, 1994).

Many larger retailers with expansive store networks adopt a centrally controlled, uniform approach to store design. A fully researched, standardized design concept is implemented across the network, projecting a uniform corporate image and enabling considerable equipment/store furniture cost savings to be made through economies of scale and the use of key suppliers. Stores represent the retailers' front-line physical contact with consumers; accordingly, their design is one of the most important components of retailer image. Store atmospherics and some of the more subtle aspects of its design impact particularly upon customer perceptions and attitudes concerning the retailer. Store design is even more significant in services retailing where there are fewer tangible cues to influence customer perceptions (*see* SERVICE CHARACTERISTICS). Here the outlet environment becomes a key transmitter of the institution's image. FINANCIAL SERVICES RETAILING is a prime example.

Within stores, the most effective balance between products is developed through research into the space elasticity exhibited by products. Space elasticity is the ratio of the relative change in unit sales to relative change in shelf space (Curhan, 1973). Different products reveal different degrees of space elasticity: e.g., unresponsive products such as salt do not exhibit any significant increase in sales when allocated shelf space is increased; other products do, however (McGoldrick, 2002). Store layouts, presentation techniques, and the positioning of goods within stores also affect their sales. By emphasizing an item to consumers, the retailer enhances the chance of impulse purchase. These are generally termed point-of-purchase displays or merchandising (in its abbreviated form POP). Store layout patterns and efforts to control the direction and speed of consumers through the store also have similar objectives (Greenland, 1994). Store design is becoming an increasingly scientific subject.

Bibliography

Curhan, R. C. (1973). Shelf space allocation and profit maximization in mass retailing. *Journal of Marketing*, 37 (3), 54–60.

Greenland, S. J. (1994). The branch environment. In P. J. McGoldrick and S. J. Greenland (eds.), *Retailing of Financial Services*. Maidenhead: McGraw-Hill, pp. 163–96.

Levy, M. and Weitz, B. A. (1998). *Retailing Management*, 3rd edn. Boston: McGraw-Hill.

McGoldrick, P. J. (2002). *Retail Marketing*. London: McGraw-Hill.

Newman, A. J. and Cullen, P. (2002). *Retailing: Environment and Operations*. London: Thomson Learning.

Turley, L. W. and Chebat, J.-C. (2002). Linking retail strategy, atmospheric design and shopping behavior. *Journal of Marketing Management*, 18 (1/2), 125–45.

straight rebuy

Dominic Wilson

Robinson, Faris, and Wind (1967) suggest a simple division of organizational purchasing into three categories: NEW TASK, MODIFIED REBUY, and straight rebuy. This categorization of organizational purchasing is now widely accepted. The most straightforward of these three categories is that of straight rebuy where an existing contract for goods or services from a particular supplier is renewed with little or no change in price, specifications, delivery arrangements, etc. With no significant change involved, straight rebuys can often be managed routinely through standard operating procedures and at a junior level. There can, however, be a danger of overlooking small but significant changes (e.g.,

in technical specification or delivery arrangements) when an organization has become habituated to treating particular routine contracts as "straightforward."

See also *organizational buying behavior*

Bibliography

Robinson, P. T., Faris, C. W., and Wind, Y. (1967). *Industrial Buying and Creative Marketing*. Boston: Allyn and Bacon.

strategic business units

Dale Littler

The term strategic business unit (SBU) allegedly originated in the General Electric Company in the US, when it analyzed its diversified corporate structure with the assistance of the McKinsey Corporation (McKiernan, 1992: 2). There are several approaches an organization can adopt in describing its strategic business units: in terms of, for example, segments, geographic markets, or products. They have certain major features: they are discrete units with clearly identifiable costs and revenues (they are, therefore, profit centers), which are either a single business or a collection of related businesses; they have an external market; they have a manager responsible for the SBU; and they have their own competitors. They have (or should have) a clear strategy. CORPORATE STRATEGY may be concerned with allocating the total resources among the different SBUs so as to meet overall organizational STRATEGIC OBJECTIVES, and various analytical frameworks have been proposed to facilitate the process (*see* BCG MATRIX; PRODUCT PORTFOLIO).

However, it has been argued by Prahalad and Hamel (1990) that SBUs can be dysfunctional in that the SBU manager may adopt a narrow business, as opposed to an organizational, perspective so that skill, knowledge, and other capabilities tend not to be shared and organizationally exploited, to perhaps the long-term detriment of the firm's overall competitiveness. They propose that organizations instead build on their core competencies.

Bibliography

Aaker, D. A. (2001). *Strategic Market Management*, 6th edn. New York: John Wiley, p. 8.
McKiernan, P. (1992). *Strategies of Growth*. London: Routledge.
Prahalad, C. K. and Hamel, G. (1990). The core competence of the corporation. *Harvard Business Review*, 68, 3 (May/June), 79–91.

strategic control

Dale Littler

Strategic control is a periodic assessment of the effectiveness of the CORPORATE STRATEGY, business strategy, or MARKETING STRATEGY. The concern will be to insure that STRATEGIC OBJECTIVES are being achieved as planned. More broadly, the aim might be to assess the current strategy in light of, *inter alia*, competitors' performance and the demonstrated ability of the company to capitalize on opportunities. Such assessments may be part of an annual STRATEGIC PLANNING cycle with the results feeding into the next annual cycle. Alternatively, especially in sectors that are experiencing rapid rates of change, they may be undertaken more regularly.

Effective strategic control will involve assessing whether or not, amongst other things, the organization is effectively capitalizing on opportunities and will highlight the importance of taking remedial action where there are significant deviations from plan or there is inadequate performance relative to competitors. It is desirable that companies occasionally undertake a critical review of their marketing effectiveness. This may involve setting performance standards (e.g., reducing the number of customer complaints; increasing sales by a specified percentage; increasing product awareness; achieving a certain objective within an agreed budget). Detailed, timely information at an operational level needs to be obtained on the various marketing activities in order to compare actual with desired performance. Discrepancies may lead to action to improve performance through, for example, higher incentives or improving the procedures and techniques employed, or may even lead to changes in performance standards

where these are recognized in hindsight as being unrealistic. In exercising marketing control, the marketing manager is faced with several challenges: it may be difficult to secure the requisite information or it may only be obtained at significant costs; there may be environmental and other changes that render effective control problematic; and there can be time delays between marketing activities and their effects, as well as extraneous influences, that make assessment of effectiveness problematic.

Bibliography

Bungay, S. and Goold, M. (1991). Creating a strategic control system. *Long Range Planning*, 24 (June), 32–9.
Bureau, J. R. (1995). Controlling marketing. In M. J. Baker (ed.), *The Marketing Book*. Oxford: Butterworth-Heinemann.

strategic decisions

Dale Littler

Ansoff (1965) draws the distinction between three types of decisions: operational, administrative, and strategic. He argues that strategic decisions are primarily concerned with external rather than internal issues of the firm and "specifically with the selection of the product mix which the firm will produce and the markets to which it will sell." Operational decisions, on the other hand, are day-to-day decisions concerned with managing efficiently current operations; while administrative decisions are involved with organizational structure and with the acquisition and development of resources. Some of the key strategic decisions are, Ansoff suggests, those concerned with objectives and goals; diversification strategy; expansion strategy; finance strategy; growth strategy; and the timing of growth.

Various features of strategic decisions have been identified to distinguish them from tactical decisions (Weitz and Wensley, 1983). In particular, they tend to be important (i.e., they are concerned with doing the right thing rather than doing things right); have major resource implications; be taken at the highest levels in the organization; have a longer-term impact on the total organization; have less detail, generally being described in broad statements; be typically complex, unstructured, and lacking parallels, whereas tactical decisions are more structured and repeatable; be focused on the environment of the organization, such as competitive activity; and demand creativity and innovation in devising appropriate responses.

Johnson and Scholes (1999) note that strategic decisions are concerned with the scope of an organization's activities, such as how diversified it should be and whether or not it should enter international markets; achieving some advantage for the organization (see COMPETITIVE ADVANTAGE); insuring that the organization's activities are compatible with its resources; and matching the organization to its environment (see MARKETING ENVIRONMENT). The latter may involve adjustments in its activities to insure that the organization remains competitive as its environment changes. Organizations can, however, take strategic decisions (such as investing in some radical technological development) that can shape the environment, rather than being merely responsive to their environment.

The distinction between tactical and strategic decisions may not be as clear cut as is often suggested. Tactical decisions, such as short-term responses to competitors' activities, can have significant long-term, and therefore strategic, repercussions.

Bibliography

Ansoff, H. I. (1965). *Corporate Strategy: An Analytic Approach to Business Policy for Growth and Expansion.* New York: McGraw-Hill, ch. 1.

Johnson, G. and Scholes, K. (1999). *Exploring Corporate Strategy*, 5th edn. Upper Saddle River, NJ: Prentice-Hall, ch. 1.

Weitz, B. A. and Wensley, R. (eds.) (1983). *Strategic Marketing.* Boston: Kent.

strategic marketing

Dale Littler

The essence of strategic marketing is to insure that the organization's marketing adapts to adjustments or exploits opportunities in its environment (see MARKETING ENVIRONMENT) and that it develops or obtains the marketing resources to do so effectively. STRATEGIC PLANNING may be employed as a means of structuring a process for identifying environmental threats and opportunities, the organization's vulnerabilities, and its differential capabilities and competencies that may provide the basis for future product and market development (see SWOT ANALYSIS). However, entrepreneurial or opportunistic organizational behavior may be more the hallmark of much strategic marketing.

strategic objectives

Dale Littler

Organizations are expected to have objectives, often regarded as part of the strategic plan (see STRATEGIC PLANNING), that act as foci for organizational activities. Such objectives should, according to Quinn (1980), be clear and "state what is to be achieved and when results are to be accomplished, but they do not state how the results are to be achieved." They will often be expressed in quantitative terms.

Objectives tend to be shaped by a variety of influences, although the need to satisfy financial stakeholders is understandably likely to be very strong. However, other constituencies, such as employees, consumers, and various pressure groups, may also have some effect. Moreover, as has been noted by many, the separation of ownership from control means that the aspirations of managers can be a significant intervening factor in shaping objectives.

The objectives that emerge will, as Cyert and March (1963) among others have noted, be a balance between the somewhat differing, and on occasions conflicting, requirements of the various organizational constituencies.

Major strategic objectives are likely to be financial: growth in revenue and profitability; growth in earnings per share; or increases in shareholder value. There may also be other objectives expressed in terms of, for example, MARKET SHARE. In addition, organizations may establish objectives in terms of, for instance, CUSTOMER SATISFACTION levels, or "concern about the environment." However, it could be argued that these may be factors that need to be taken into account in order to achieve the overarching financial targets (to ignore issues of customer satisfaction, for example, may be regarded as having a deleterious impact on the long-term financial health of the organization). They can be seen in essence to be secondary objectives to the primary requirement of insuring that financial objectives are satisfied.

Not all firms emphasize financial objectives, let alone the continued growth in them. The owners of small firms may, for example, be more concerned with maintaining their independence. Many non-profit organizations, such as charities, might be expected to have altruistic concerns, but nevertheless they are increasingly interpreting themselves as businesses with the need to generate selected levels of revenue at targeted margins in order to meet their overall mission. In such cases, though, the financial targets may be defined either in concert with, or subsequent to, the non-financial objectives.

In some cases the purpose of the organization may be difficult to articulate, so that clear objectives may not emerge. This would be the case in, for example, large bureaucratic bodies, particularly those operating in the public sector. For these, Lindblom (1968) argued that policy making is a process of incremental steps, often with objectives emerging over time. As with any objectives, they are likely to be adjusted and even redefined in light of changing circumstances and through acquisition of additional information.

The articulation of strategic objectives provides one benchmark against which the performance of the organization can be evaluated, and if, for example, the organization fails to achieve these, appropriate action may need to be taken, including the redefinition of the strategic objectives.

See also *strategic control*

Bibliography

Cyert, R. M. and March, J. G. (1963). *A Behavioral Theory of the Firm*. Englewood Cliffs, NJ: Prentice-Hall.

Lindblom, C. E. (1968). *The Policy Making Process*. Englewood Cliffs, NJ: Prentice-Hall.

Quinn, J. B. (1980). *Strategies for Change: Logical Incrementalism*. Homewood, IL: Irwin, ch. 1.

strategic planning

Dale Littler

Strategic planning is generally regarded as a structured approach to the formulation of corporate or business strategy (*see* CORPORATE STRATEGY) involving a sequence of stages that embrace: the definition of the STRATEGIC OBJECTIVES and often, in addition, the MISSION STATEMENT or vision (*see* VISION STATEMENT); a SWOT ANALYSIS; the identification and evaluation of the strategic options; and the selection of those likely to yield the optimum return. Increasingly, attention has been directed to the implementation of strategy. Consideration must also be directed to STRATEGIC CONTROL. There may be iterations between these various stages.

In the post-World War II period, strategic planning was adopted by and became routine in many organizations (e.g., Ross and Silverblatt, 1987), generally because, paradoxically, it was viewed as a means of coping with environmental uncertainties (*see* UNCERTAINTY). Often planning departments were established that were concerned with, *inter alia*, the formulation of strategic plans, generally on an annual basis. There were possibly at least two consequences: first, planners and planning became divorced from IMPLEMENTATION, with the result that elaborate plans were written that may have had only a marginal impact on decision-making. Second, the routine strategic planning could result in the extrapolation from previous plans, without taking account of existing or potential environmental discontinuities.

Mintzberg (1990) criticized the structured approach to strategic planning, which he termed the "design school." He argued that this is based on three premises: strategy formulation precedes implementation; the process of strategy formulation consists of conscious thought involving senior managers, and more especially the chief executive; and the process and the strategy produced is explicit, simple, and unique. He suggested that the "design school" approach to strategic management can apply only in a minority of cases where the environment is stable; and that thinking and acting are likely to be intertwined, while strategies will tend to be the fruits of experimental trial and error rather than of detached analytical thinking.

Kotler (1994) has argued that strategic plans become obsolete quickly because of intense competition and the rapid dissemination of information using the latest technology. He believes that companies are forced to move from strategic planning to "strategic improvising," and they do this by empowering front-line people to make more of the decisions, subject, of course, to certain parameters.

Bibliography

Kotler, P. (1994). Reconceptualizing marketing: An interview with Philip Kotler. *European Management Journal*, **12**, 4 (December).

Mintzberg, H. (1990). The design school: Reconsidering the basic premises of strategic management. *Strategic Management Journal*, **11**, 3 (March/April), 171–95.

Ross, J. E. and Silverblatt, R. (1987). Developing the strategic plan. *Industrial Marketing Management*, **16**, 103–8.

strategic styles

Dale Littler

It has been suggested that organizations can be categorized according to their broad strategic style. For example, Mintzberg (1973) suggests that there are three main approaches to (or modes of) strategy making: the adaptive; entrepreneurial; and planning (*see* ADAPTIVE STRATEGY; ENTREPRENEURIAL STRATEGY; PLANNING STYLE). Goold and Campbell (1987) in a study of 16 major diversified companies classified them according to how the "center" (i.e., the headquarters) controlled and measured performance. They identified three major types: strategic planners, where the "center" makes crucial decisions for subsidiaries; strategic controllers, in which the center's role is to review the plans formulated by subsidiaries; and the financial controllers, in which the strategic decisions are made by the subsidiaries, with the center judging performance by numbers.

Littler and Leverick (1994), in an analysis of the strategies employed by firms entering the mobile communications sector, identified four major styles, all of which exhibited, to differing degrees, opportunistic behavior: the "visionaries," who had a clear view on how they wanted the market to develop; the "calculated gamblers," attracted by the potential of high profits while minimizing downside risk; the "incrementalists," who saw entry into the market as a natural extension of the current portfolio of product interests; and the "bureaucrats," who entered the market after a detailed analysis and the use of formal planning procedures. They also identified three major styles of strategic management followed by these companies after they had entered the mobile communications market: the "ad hoc," with an emphasis on operational management rather than on longer-term strategic issues; the "lodestar," which emphasized the articulation of clear targets but which lacked detail on the means by which these were to be achieved (*see* UMBRELLA STRATEGY); and the "conformists," who were bureaucratic, relying on formal strategic planning and analyses. There have been many other attempts to identify strategic styles. There is an issue of whether or not the classification of strategic style has anything other than academic utility, unless of course strategic style can in some way be associated with measures of performance. There are, however, formidable methodological issues that would raise questions about the VALIDITY of any identified relationships.

Bibliography

Goold, M. and Campbell, A. (1987). *Strategies and Styles: The Role of the Center in Managing Diversified Corporations*. Oxford: Blackwell.

Littler, D. and Leverick, F. (1994). Marketing planning in new technology sectors. In J. Saunders (ed.), *The Marketing Initiative*. Prentice-Hall, 72–91.

Mintzberg, H. (1973). Strategy making in three modes. *California Management Review*, **16**, 2 (Winter), 44–53.

strategy

Dale Littler

Strategy is derived from the Greek *strategia*, meaning generalship. Clausewitz (1976) wrote the classic military strategy. The widespread use of the term in business occurred after World War II, although businesses, in particular the Pennsylvania railroad, employed strategy in the nineteenth century. Zinkham and Pereira (1994) suggest that the notion of strategy was first introduced to the management literature in 1944 by von Neumann and Morgenstern in their classic work on the theory of games, which essentially focused on situations of conflict. Following on from this, there was a series of major contributions on strategy such as those of Selznick (1957) and Chandler (1962).

Ansoff's comprehensive text *Corporate Strategy*, published in 1965, firmly established strategy in the management lexicon. The military connotations of strategy undoubtedly appeared apt given the traditional perspectives of competition in which firms were seen as "fighting for market share" (*see* MARKET SHARE), engaging in "price wars," and embarking on ADVERTIS-ING "campaigns." The military analogy was extended to MARKETING (Kotler and Singh, 1980; James, 1985). However, Liddell-Hart (1967) was critical of the view, put forward by Clausewitz, that: "The destruction of the enemy's main forces on the battlefield constitutes the only true aim in war." He suggested that: "The 'object' in war is a better state of peace, even if only from your own point of view." Contemporary management theory is much more likely to identify a spectrum of strategies, ranging from the extreme "competitive" (*see* COMPETITIVE STRATEGY) through to various forms of cooperation. Indeed, many companies now regard strategic alliances (*see* INTERNATIONAL STRATEGIC ALLIANCES), which may be formed for some markets with firms that are competitors in others, as strengthening their competitive position.

There are many definitions of strategy, but in general it is regarded as embodying the joint selection of the product-market arenas in which the firm is competing or will compete and the key policies defining how it will compete (Rumelt, Schendel, and Teece, 1991). The Walker, Boyd, and Larreche definition (1992) suggested that an effective strategy would embrace: what is to be attained; which product markets should be the focus; and how resources and activities will be allocated to each product market to meet environmental opportunities and threats. Johnson and Scholes (1999) define strategy as: "the *direction* and *scope* of an organization over the *long term*: which achieves *advantage* for the organization through its configuration of *resources* within a changing *environment*, to meet the needs of *markets* and to fulfill *stakeholder* expectations" (p. 10). In general, a strategy encompasses the goals, regarded as a general statement of aim or purpose, and objectives, and the means by which these are to be achieved. It can apply at several levels: the organizational or corporate; the business (*see* STRATEGIC BUSINESS UNITS); and the product. Strategy may also be associated with certain activities. Thus, for example, there is reference to PRICING strategies and NEW PRODUCT DEVELOPMENT strategies. There is much debate about whether or not strategy can be clearly formulated in advance of being applied. However, as Mintzberg (1990) argues, managers may often define strategy in terms of past actions, rather than in terms of intentions. Moreover, a consciously conceived strategy may not be easily realized because of the intervention of, *inter alia*, UNCERTAINTY. Strategy may evolve as a consequence of a series of incremental decisions, informed by the feedback from previous decisions, actions of those responsible for implementation, and changes in the context within which the strategy is being formed.

See also *strategic decisions; strategic planning*

Bibliography

Ansoff, H. I. (1965). *Corporate Strategy: An Analytic Approach to Business Policy for Growth and Expansion*. New York: McGraw-Hill.

Chandler, A. D., Jr. (1962). *Strategy and Structure*. Cambridge, MA: MIT Press.

Clausewitz, C. von (1976). *On War*, trans. M. Howard and P. Paret. Princeton, NJ: Princeton University Press.

James, B. G. (1985). *Business Wargames*. Harmondsworth: Penguin.

Johnson, G. and Scholes, K. (1999). *Exploring Corporate Strategy*, 5th edn. Upper Saddle River, NJ: Prentice-Hall.

Kotler, P. and Singh, R. (1980). Marketing warfare in the 1980s. *Journal of Business Strategy*, 13, 30–41.

Liddell-Hart, B. H. (1967). *Strategy*. New York: Praeger.

Mintzberg, H. (1990). The design school: Reconsidering the basic premises of strategic management. *Strategic Management Journal*, 11 (3), 171–95.

Rumelt, R., Schendel, D., and Teece, D. (1991). Strategic management and economics. *Strategic Management Journal*, **12**, 5–29.

Selznick, P. (1957). *Leadership in Administration*. New York: Harper and Row.

Von Neumann, J. and Morgenstern, O. (1994). *Theory of Games and Economic Behavior*. Princeton, NJ: Princeton University Press.

Walker, O. C., Boyd, H., and Larreche, J. (1992). *Marketing Strategy: Planning and Implementation*. Homewood, IL: Irwin.

Zinkham, G. M. and Pereira, A. (1994). An overview of marketing strategy and planning. *International Journal of Research in Marketing*, **11**, 185–218.

structural equation models

Michael Greatorex

Structural equation models bring together research methods in a holistic way. Hypothetical relationships between variables are represented in a network of causal and functional paths. The variables may be latent constructs related to directly measurable variables in a way that is part of the specification of the structural equation model. The computation procedures are such that the empirical estimation of the relationships between the latent variables and their specified manifest variables and the estimation of the specified relationships between the latent variables are carried out jointly, using a common objective, rather than as separate activities each using a separate objective. Some multivariate methods (*see* MULTIVARIATE METHODS (ANALYSIS)) can be seen as special cases of structural equation modeling.

Structural equation models can be used throughout MARKETING RESEARCH, for instance studying the links between ADVERTISING, ATTITUDES toward brands, intentions, and purchasing. They have also been used to test for RELIABILITY and VALIDITY in a number of studies.

Structural equation modeling using latent variables is becoming a popular tool in marketing research, being seen as a comprehensive tool capable of replacing older and more elementary multivariate methods. To assist this development, computer programs have been developed. Among the well-known programs are LISREL, now incorporated in the STATISTICAL PACKAGE FOR THE SOCIAL SCIENCES (SPSS), and the PROC CALIS procedure in SAS and EQS, now available in a PC version.

Bibliography

Bagozzi, R. P. (1980). *Causal Models in Marketing*. New York: John Wiley.

Bagozzi, R. P. (1994). Structural equation models in marketing research: Basic principles. In R. P. Bagozzi (ed.), *Principles of Marketing Research*. Cambridge, MA: Blackwell, ch. 9.

suppliers

Dominic Wilson

It is an axiom of MARKETING that suppliers are customers too (Kotler and Levy, 1973). A graphic illustration of this point is provided by the Mandarin pictograms for "buy" and for "sell," which are virtually identical, the difference being in intonation. It is self-evident that any marketing transaction requires a "supplier" as well as a "customer," but the logical extension of this into "supplier strategies" as well as "customer strategies" has been given much less attention in the marketing literature until relatively recently. Now there is widespread recognition of the importance of fostering long-term relationships with suitable suppliers, and there is considerable research into such crucial issues as understanding MARKETING STRATEGY in terms of a network of suppliers (Håkansson and Snehota, 1989); the management of customer/supplier relationships (Han, Wilson, and Dant, 1993); and the advantages and disadvantages of long-term "partnerships" between customers and suppliers (Lamming, 1993; Matthyssens and van den Bulte, 1994). Rather less attention has been given to the costs and problems involved in collaborative relationships between suppliers and customers, and to the situations when such relationships may be less appropriate (i.e., when the risks of providing a supplier with privileged access may exceed the potential benefits).

See also *relationship marketing*

Bibliography

Kotler, P. and Levy, S. J. (1973). Buying is marketing too. *Journal of Marketing*, **37**, 1 (January), 54–9.

Håkansson, H. and Snehota, I. (1989). No business is an island: The network concept of business strategy. *Scandinavian Journal of Management*, **43**, 187–200.

Han, S.-L., Wilson, D. T., and Dant, S. P. (1993). Buyer–supplier relationships today. *Industrial Marketing Management*, **22**, 4 (November), 331–8.

Lamming, R. (1993). *Beyond Partnership*. Englewood Cliffs, NJ: Prentice-Hall.

Matthyssens, P. and van den Bulte, C. (1994). Getting closer and nicer: Partnerships in the supply chain. *Long Range Planning*, **27**, 1 (February), 72–83.

survey research

Michael Greatorex

Survey research is one of the four main sources of PRIMARY DATA, the others being OBSERVATION, QUALITATIVE RESEARCH, and EXPERIMENTATION. Surveys can provide information on past and intended behavior, ATTITUDES, beliefs, opinions, and personal characteristics. While the data provided by surveys are basically descriptive, appropriate analysis of the survey data can provide evidence of association between variables.

Surveys involve asking people (respondents) questions, either verbal or written. The term sample survey indicates that survey data have been collected from a sample of a population. Data are collected with the aid of questionnaires through the mail or by means of computers, or administered to individuals or groups in face-to-face interviews in the home or in the street or using the telephone.

In *cross-sectional studies*, data are collected at a single point in time from a cross-section of the population. Typical analysis of cross-sectional surveys involves attempting to measure characteristics of the population as a whole and/or breaking down the sample into subgroups and seeing if behavior, opinions, etc. vary between the groups.

In *longitudinal studies*, respondents are studied at different moments in time in order to examine trends and changes, if any, over time.

TYPES OF SURVEYS

Surveys usually involve the use of structured interviews with the interviewer or respondent following the wording and order provided on a questionnaire. Survey methods are usually classified by mode of administration, the three main modes being personal, telephone, and postal interviewing.

Personal interviews. Personal interviews usually take place either in the home of the respondent or in a public place such as the street or a shopping mall.

In face-to-face interviews in the home, it is the interviewer's job to contact the respondent, often selected by the research director using some form of probability sampling (*see* SAMPLING), pose the questions, and record the answers. Lengthy interviews are possible and the interviewer can use physical stimuli as part of the interviewing process. The respondent is able to seek clarification of confusing questions or terms and the interviewer is able to observe the respondent, for instance, to see if the questions have been understood. In-home, or door-to-door, interviewing is expensive and its use is declining.

Street or shopping mall intercept interviews are the commonest type of personal interview. Interviewers intercept passers-by and either question them on the spot or take them to a nearby facility to conduct the interview. It is possible to get a random sample of passers-by by selecting every *n*th passer-by. However, it is unlikely that the population of interest will pass by the places where interviewers are located. For this reason mall intercept surveys are rarely statistically representative of the required populations and rely on quota sampling procedures to insure some amount of representativeness. They are cheaper than door-to-door interviews and it takes less time to complete an intercept survey.

In direct computer interviewing, the computer presents the questions to a respondent on a screen and the respondent uses a keyboard or a mouse to answer. These may be used in shopping malls or at conferences and trade shows. For some surveys, respondents are selected by interviewers as in other types of personal interviewing research; in other surveys the computer is placed in a prominent place and interested passers-by select themselves as respondents. As well as freeing the interviewer from posing the questions and recording the answers and reducing data inputting time and expenses, this method has an extra advantage in that interviewer bias is low.

Telephone interviews. Telephone interviewers, stationed at a central location, present their questions using the telephone to interviewees over a wide area. Computer-assisted telephone interviewing (CATI) is growing quickly. As in other computer-assisted interviewing methods, the questionnaire is programmed into the computer. The interviewer reads the questions from the screen and records the answers directly into the computer. The computer can be programmed to make the calls, for instance using random digit dialing, and subsequent recalls can be made when initial calls are unanswered.

Flexibility is the main advantage of computer-presented questionnaires. The questions can be varied according to earlier answers, e.g., buyers of a BRAND may be asked one set of questions and non-buyers a different set. Also, order problems caused in some closed questions where possible answers are presented to respondents can be averted by the computer varying the answers from respondent to respondent.

Low cost and the speed with which a survey can be carried out are two other advantages of telephone interviews. Interim results and updates are easy to obtain as the data are recorded immediately. Interviewer bias is low, respondents can feel that their anonymity has been maintained, and sensitive questions can be posed with less embarrassment than in face-to-face interviews. On the other hand, it is difficult to use physical stimuli as part of the interview, although the use of fax machines can ease this problem. The fact that not every household has a telephone, that some numbers are ex-directory, and that an individual member of a large household has a smaller chance of being chosen than a member of a small household, means that a sample may not be truly representative of a specified population.

Postal surveys.   Questionnaires (*see* QUESTIONNAIRE DESIGN) are delivered to the respondents who return completed questionnaires by post to the researcher. Postal interviews are widely used. They allow a large sample to be contacted very cheaply and the absence of an interviewer cuts out interviewer bias. On the other hand, complex questionnaires are unsuitable and the questionnaire has to be carefully constructed. The major disadvantages of postal surveys are the high level of non-response and the length of time allowed for respondents to reply.

Non-response is a problem for all types of surveys but especially so for postal surveys. Non-response can be reduced in the first place through pre-notification, by offering monetary inducements including a free entry to a prize draw, by use of reply-paid envelopes, by making the questionnaire interesting, etc. Follow-up contacts can be used to increase the overall response rate.

The critical issue concerning non-response is the extent to which the respondents and non-respondents are alike on the important variables. Among the ways of assessing this is to make comparisons of successive waves of respondents and to subsample intensively non-respondents for comparison with the original respondents. Unless care is taken to assess the effects of non-response on representativeness of the sample obtained, results from postal surveys should be treated cautiously.

CONCLUSION

Two problems of interviewing include the responses to sensitive questions and biases caused by interviewer effects. Since face-to-face interviews and, to a lesser extent, telephone interviews involve social interaction between interviewer and respondent, it is possible that respondents will answer sensitive questions with socially acceptable, rather than truthful, answers. Postal and computer surveys, which do not suffer from this social interaction, may yield more accurate answers to sensitive questions.

Interviewers may vary the way that they pose the questions, by changing the wording or simply altering their tone of voice or body language, from interview to interview, with the result that each respondent has a slightly different interview, a disadvantage in survey research.

The interviewer's age, sex, appearance, SOCIAL CLASS, etc. may affect the answers as respondents seek to give answers that they believe will be acceptable to the interviewer. The recording of answers to open-ended questions may be biased by the interviewer's opinions. These interviewer effects will be most pronounced in personal interviews, least pronounced in computer and postal interviews, with telephone interviews somewhere in between.

Bibliography

Malhotra, N. K. and Birks, D. F. (2000). *Marketing Research: An Applied Orientation*, 3rd European edn. Harlow: Prentice-Hall, ch. 8.

Tull, D. S. and Hawkins, D. I. (1993). *Marketing Research: Measurement and Method*, 6th edn. New York: Macmillan, pp. 134–42, 163–97.

SWOT analysis

Dale Littler

As part of the STRATEGIC PLANNING process, it is generally prescribed that organizations undertake an INTERNAL AUDIT, aimed at identifying their major skills, technologies, competencies, and resources, and existing and possible future vulnerabilities, and an ENVIRONMENTAL ANALYSIS aimed at identifying, amongst other things, existing and future societal (e.g., demographic), technological, legal, and economic developments. The major purpose is to identify the strengths and weaknesses of the organization, and the major opportunities and threats opened up by what is happening and likely to happen in its environment; hence, SWOT. The purpose of the strategic planning exercise, then, is to build on the strengths, and where possible overcome or avoid the weaknesses, by exploiting opportunities in the environment as well as defending the organization against possible threats, or even converting so-called threats into opportunities.

In the positivist tradition, this analysis is presented as though objective data about the organization and its environment (*see* MARKETING ENVIRONMENT) are present to be discovered, ignoring the fact that individuals have their own values, prejudices, and motives that can affect their interpretation of, for instance, the environment and the capabilities of the organization. Those involved in the analysis are subject to a range of cognitive biases (Hill and Jones, 1995) that include prior hypothesis bias, where decision-makers have existing strong beliefs that affect their perception and interpretation; representativeness, or the tendency to generalize from a small sample or even a single anecdote; and groupthink, where decision-makers act uniformly without questioning underlying assumptions, often under the leadership of one or more strong personalities. The power plays within organizations can also affect the interpretation of both the competencies of the organization and what is happening in the environment. Attribution for past failures (and successes) may be affected by existing attempts to secure position and resources.

Bibliography

Hill, C. W. L. and Jones, G. R. (1995). *Strategic Management Theory*, 3rd edn. Boston: Houghton Mifflin, pp. 19–21.

Littler, D. and Leverick, F. (1994). Marketing planning in new technology sectors. In J. Saunders (ed.), *The Marketing Initiative*. Englewood Cliffs, NJ: Prentice-Hall, pp. 72–91.

symbolic consumption

Emma Banister

Symbolic consumption refers to the tendency for consumers to focus on meanings beyond the tangible, physical characteristics of material objects (Levy, 1959). Thus products function as social tools, "serving as a means of communication between the individual and his significant references" (Grubb and Grathwohl, 1967: 24). In order for consumer products and brands to function as communication symbols, meanings must be socially shared and continuously produced and reproduced during social interactions (Dittmar, 1992).

Bibliography

Dittmar, H. (1992). *The Social Psychology of Material Possessions*. Hemel Hempstead: Harvester Press.

Grubb, E. L. and Grathwohl, H. L. (1967). Consumer self-concept, symbolism and market behavior: A theoretical approach. *Journal of Marketing*, 31, 22–7.

Levy, S. J. (1959). Symbols for sale. *Harvard Business Review*, 37 (4), 117–24.

symbolic interactionism

Emma Banister

Symbolic interactionism is a sociological theory reflecting the means by which individuals understand their world. The theory is primarily identified with the work of Herbert Blumer and George Herbert Mead and the University of Chicago (Blumer, 1969, 1980). The individual is recognized as an actor. Actions toward others and objects are based on the particular meanings these others and objects hold for them. The importance of social interaction with others and the interpretive process by which individuals deal with the things they encounter is emphasized (Blumer, 1969).

Bibliography

Blumer, H. (1969). *Symbolic Interactionism: Perspective and Method*. Englewood Cliffs, NJ: Prentice-Hall.

Blumer, H. (1980). Mead and Blumer: The convergent methodological perspectives of social behaviorism and symbolic interactionism. *American Sociological Review*, 45 (June), 409–19.

systems marketing

Dale Littler

Especially in organizational markets (*see* ORGANIZATIONAL MARKETING), a COMPETITIVE ADVANTAGE may be secured by developing the capability to provide what might be termed "total solutions" to customer "problems" or requirements. For example, suppliers of computerized businesses systems will design, develop, and implement, including the training of users, a management information system to meet the information requirements of customers; or process plant contractors might be involved in the design, construction, and commissioning of chemical plant. These suppliers may have all the resources in house to provide the total "package," or they may, as appropriate, subcontract to others. In some cases there are firms, such as consultant engineers, that act as coordinators based on their skills in planning and managing the various activities required.

In many markets, such as defense or where complex plant and equipment is required, there is a tradition of providing "systems." The purchaser often solicits tenders from what are termed prime contractors, who are responsible for the project management involving assembling the different activities, often requiring other suppliers, and insuring effective implementation of, for example, the installation. These prime contractors provide a "turn-key" operation, so called because the customer simply turns one key to obtain what is sought.

target market

Fiona Leverick

This is a group of potential users or consumers which is the focus of the business's marketing effort for a particular product or service, usually identified by means of MARKET SEGMENTATION. In theory marketers segment the market, and from this analysis they identify appropriate market targets based on, *inter alia*, the potential they offer and the ability of the business to meet their requirements; they then position the offerings to appeal to the target market(s).

See also *positioning*

targeting

see MARKET SEGMENTATION; POSITIONING

technological environment

David Yorke

The technological environment is one of the elements of the MARKETING ENVIRONMENT. This aspect is concerned with developments and trends in technology, not only in terms of customer offerings, but also with respect to the technology of production and distribution. For example, there have been important developments in aspects of technology relevant to marketing itself, such as the use of relational databases (*see* DATABASE), bar-code scanning, ELECTRONIC DATA INTERCHANGE, personal mobile communications, computerized animation, interactive multimedia systems, and tele-

phone shopping. Technological innovation both in processes and in products/services can provide a powerful means of securing a COMPETITIVE ADVANTAGE, and firms need to have means of sensing and assessing the implications for themselves of developments in technology.

See also *environmental analysis*

telemarketing

David Yorke and Mark P. Healey

Telemarketing (or telephone selling) systematically uses a DATABASE of actual and potential customers to define and sell to customers with a high probability of purchase. Telemarketing is a form of DIRECT MARKETING in which customers are contacted directly via the telephone by a representative of an organization to actualize or stimulate sales, to build relationships, or gather information (outbound telemarketing). Organizations also use inbound telemarketing in the form of freephone numbers to receive orders, inquiries, feedback, and complaints from customers. Increased usage of telemarketing is evident in many markets, e.g., the US and UK, although in some markets (e.g., Germany) restrictions on unsolicited calling may limit the adoption of this form of direct marketing. Greater efficiency is achieved by: avoiding expensive sales visits; widening the range of possible contacts, particularly for smaller organizations; and responding more quickly to customer requests or complaints. Disadvantages, if not managed properly, are: a possible breakdown in coordination between the inside and outside SALES FORCE, if both are used; too much harassment of customers; the creation of the impression that it is a cost-cutting and less personal substitute for a field sales force; and lack of coordination of customer selling and service.

Bibliography

Kotler, P., Armstrong, G., Saunders, J., and Wong, V. (2001). *Principles of Marketing*, 3rd European edn. Harlow: Prentice-Hall, ch. 22.

Moncrief, W. C., Shannon, S., Lamb, C. W., Jr., and Cravens, D. W. (1989). Examining the roles of telemarketing in selling strategy. *Journal of Personal Selling and Sales Management*, Fall, 1–12.

teleshopping

see TELEVISION-BASED HOME SHOPPING

television

David Yorke

Television is a communications medium (*see* MASS MEDIA) combining sound and visibility with animation. Its availability is widespread in developed countries, enhanced by the development and growth of cable networks and satellite channels. Television is a major ADVERTISING medium, its main advantages being: national or selective coverage; intrusiveness; an ability to build AWARENESS quickly; a family medium; a capacity to stimulate INTERPERSONAL COMMUNICATIONS; and availability of accurate audience audit/market research data. However, television areas may be too large for potential advertisers, although the increasing fragmentation of the market with the proliferation of channels, some aimed at specialized interests, facilitates more specific targeting; geographic coverage may be restricted; potential targets may be light viewers; and the attention of the viewer may not be guaranteed owing to choice of channels, fast forwarding of video recorders during commercial breaks, the adoption of personal video recorders that make it easier to skip commercials, and channel switching during commercial breaks. The development of interactive television permits the capture of audience reactions both to programs and to advertisements

and promotions. Consumers are able to respond directly to promotions, thereby permitting real-time measurement of effectiveness. For terrestrial and much satellite television, although measures of REACH and FREQUENCY are known, the cost effectiveness of television advertising is difficult to evaluate.

television-based home shopping

Steve Greenland and Andrew Newman

Television-based home shopping involves the purchase of products advertised on television programs and commercial breaks by telephoning orders through to the advertised number. This may be undertaken at the press of a button with the advent of digital satellite and cable television. Digital television considerably improves a retailer's chances of launching interactive television shopping, and can provide hundreds of channels of output and interactive services. Home shopping, educational activities such as home tutoring, and regional information services are likely to be the most popular interactive services in the future (Newman and Cullen, 2002). Earlier predictions by Whitford (1994) discussed the advantages afforded to the retailer by the home shopping channel, namely, wide audience REACH, the equivalent of free ADVERTISING, instant market feedback, high short-term volume of sales, and immediate results. The increasing number of television channels, introduced via cable and satellite television networks, is thus likely to increase the proportion of retail sales generated by this retail distribution channel.

More recent research undertaken in the UK market by Jupiter MMXI suggests that over half of UK homes will use digital television by 2005. However, the same research indicates that consumers tend to purchase lower-cost impulse purchases (*see* IMPULSE PURCHASING) such as CDs and takeaway food from interactive television (McGoldrick, 2002). As people become more familiar with interactive services and expect to access online activities from the comfort of the home, this retail channel may well expand or converge with PC shopping and mobile phone services. Ultimately, the digital format will be the sole television system in the UK as the government switches off analogue television services around the year 2010 (Newman and Cullen, 2002).

See also *retail distribution channels*

Bibliography

Levy, M. and Weitz, B. A. (1998). *Retailing Management*, 3rd edn. Boston: McGraw-Hill.
McGoldrick, P. J. (2002). *Retail Marketing*. London: McGraw-Hill.
Newman, A. J. and Cullen, P. (2002). *Retailing: Environment and Operations*. London: Thomson Learning.
Solomon, B. (1994). TV shopping comes of age. *Management Review*, 83 (9), 22–7.
Wade, N. and McKechnie, S. A. (1999). The impact of digital television: Will it change our shopping habits? *Journal of Marketing Communications*, 5, 71–84.
Whitford, D. (1994). TV or not TV, Inc. *INO*, 16 (6), 63–8.

tender

see BIDDING

test marketing

Margaret Bruce and Liz Barnes

Test marketing involves the marketing of the product using the proposed MARKETING STRATEGY in a limited area that is representative of the total market. It strives to reduce the risk of a full-scale product launch by securing customer reaction to the new product and the proposed means of marketing it within a limited market area. The ratio of the marketing effort for the test region to that agreed for the total market must be approximately the same as the ratio of the size of the test market to the total market in order to give a reasonably accurate forecast of the possible total market response.

Test marketing will generally be employed to predict the results of a full national launch of a new product. It is also a means of testing the implementation and management of the launch.

Test marketing can also be used to assess the impact of any changes to the MARKETING MIX.

Although test marketing may be expensive, it will incur a lower cost than a full national launch, while information received during the test may be used to modify or even significantly alter the marketing program before a full national launch.

There are a number of advantages of test marketing, such as the detection of possible weaknesses with the marketing mix and the ability to experiment with alternative marketing mixes in different test areas to assess BRAND awareness, BRAND LOYALTY, and repeat purchases that may result from variations in the marketing mix. Test marketing can also be used to gain information about buyers, dealers, and MARKET POTENTIAL.

However, test marketing can alert competitors of an impending product launch. They may decide to develop a rival product that benefits from observations made of the test marketing exercise. Test marketing in any case gives competitors time to develop and launch their own product. In addition to competition, other conditions may also change, resulting in, for example, lost opportunities flowing from the decision not to market fully earlier.

Another risk is that other companies marketing products, which in some way compete with the new product, may take actions to disrupt the test market. They may increase ADVERTISING and promotion, introduce special offers, or temporarily cut prices. Meaningful conclusions on the performance of the new product will consequently be difficult to make.

The decision to test market is then a result of a careful balancing of the opportunity costs against the benefits of lowering risk and possibly improving the full market launch. For example, high-risk products such as those that create a new product category will require more testing than minor-risk products such as product modifications.

STAGES IN PLANNING A TEST MARKET

There are several stages involved in planning a test market exercise.

● *Establish aims*: In general, the aim will be to predict the sales that are likely to be obtained if the product was marketed in the total market. Moreover, since it is in effect a re-hearsal of the national launch, the company will also be interested in evaluating the operation of the test marketing exercise.

- *Select of a test market representative of the total market*: For many products, the area selected should be a microcosm of the national market in terms of demographic structure, number and size of retailing outlets, employment, and socioeconomic factors. This may be difficult to guarantee, and some approximations will have to be made. Where specialized market segments (*see* MARKET SEGMENTATION) form the target, and/or where television advertising is not a component of the marketing program, more limited areas, including towns or areas of cities, may be selected.

- *Decide on the duration of the test*: In general, companies will strive to obtain an indication of the "equilibrium" MARKET SHARE, while at the same time having as short a test market period as possible so as not to give competitors time to develop and market competitive products before the test marketer decides to go national. In order to gain a realistic insight into the acceptability of the product, marketers may wish to observe at least one repeat purchase cycle – particularly in the case of convenience products, where it is the extent to which customers will purchase the product again (and again!) that is relevant. In deciding on the duration of the test, the following should be borne in mind: initial demand for a new product will inevitably involve much trial and experimentation; many of the initial users will, for various reasons, often not re-purchase; and eventually sales will fall to some reasonably stable level that reflects the degree of repeat purchasing behavior.

- *Decide on the marketing research to be undertaken*: Careful consideration should be paid to the sorts of information that need to be collected before, during, and after the test marketing prior to the start of the test. Companies may decide to measure retail sales achieved during the test marketing, the awareness of an attitude toward the advertising, the level of distribution, the sales per outlet, and so on.

The test market data may not, however, be a true indicator of the results to be obtained from a full national launch. There are a number of reasons why this might be the case:

- The test market may not be fully representative of the national market.
- There may be "learning effects" as a result of experience gained from the test market.
- The environment may change between the test marketing and the full launch; e.g., new competition may emerge, and economic conditions may alter. Competition may have disrupted the test marketing by engaging in exceptional marketing activity (such as severe price cutting and dramatic promotional offers).

Test marketing was typically carried out by selecting a television region for the test market, but the advent of satellite channels makes it more difficult to isolate the test market. Managing other variables in the test area is also increasingly difficult, for example, competitor spoiling, timing, area selection, and cost. These issues have resulted in the virtual disappearance of traditional area and store testing in favor of simulated test marketing, which takes place under laboratory conditions. Despite criticism that these tests are not reflective of "real life," research has found them to be accurate and a more efficient way of controlling the negative variables of test marketing.

Test marketing is a key stage of the NEW PRODUCT DEVELOPMENT process and can result in the product having further development before launch.

Bibliography

Dibb, S., Simkin, L., Pride, W., and Ferrell, O. C. (2000). *Marketing: Concepts and Strategies*, European edn. Boston: Houghton Mifflin.

Kotler, P. (2003). *Marketing Management: Analysis, Planning, Implementation and Control*, 11th edn. Englewood Cliffs, NJ: Prentice-Hall.

Littler, D. A. (1984). *Marketing and Product Development*. Oxford: Philip Allan.

Urban, G. L. and Hauser, J. R. (1993). *Design and Marketing of New Products*, 2nd edn. Englewood Cliffs, NJ: Prentice-Hall.

Wilson, A. (2003). *Marketing Research: An Integrated Approach*. Harlow: Financial Times/Prentice-Hall.

threats

see SWOT ANALYSIS

trade journals

Dale Littler

Trade journals are a range of journals that are aimed at specific industries, e.g., footwear, and at "trades" (e.g., *The Caterer*). They provide a conduit to a clearly defined target audience for both ADVERTISING and PUBLICITY. It is suggested (e.g., by Martilla, 1971) that they comprise a medium that may be a valuable source of information to opinion leaders or GATEKEEPERS in organizational markets (*see* ORGANIZATIONAL BUYING BEHAVIOR).

Bibliography

Martilla, J. A. (1971). Word of mouth communication in the industrial adoption process. *Journal of Marketing Research*, 8 (May), 173–8.

transaction

Fiona Leverick

This is the transfer of ownership or use of a product or service from one party to another in return for a payment of some kind. For a transaction to occur, a number of conditions would usually have to be satisfied: the existence of two things of value that are being transferred between the parties involved in the transaction, agreed-upon conditions, a time of agreement, and a place of agreement. A transaction can be seen as being distinguishable from a transfer, the latter describing a situation where one party gives to another but receives nothing in return.

transfer pricing

Dominic Wilson

Transfer pricing refers to the pricing of internal movements (or "transfers") of goods and services between cost centers within an organiza-

tion and is an important aspect of cost control (Ward, 1993). Transfer pricing is a necessary aspect of management accounting but can be unethical or even illegal where it is used to evade corporate taxation, perhaps in the movement of goods between organizational subsidiaries operating within different taxation regimes.

Bibliography

Crow, S. and Sauls, E. (1994). Setting the right transfer price. *Management Accounting*, **76**, 6 (December), 41–7.
Ward, K. (1993). Gaining a marketing advantage through the strategic use of transfer pricing. *Journal of Marketing Management*, **9** (July), 245–53.

trial

David Yorke and Dale Littler

A trial is an element in the CONATIVE STAGE of the INNOVATION-ADOPTION MODEL of MARKETING COMMUNICATIONS. In order to reduce the PERCEIVED RISK, the potential purchaser may wish to undertake a physical or vicarious trial of the INNOVATION before actually fully committing to it. A vicarious trial may involve, for instance, visualizing how the innovation might perform given observations of how others use it. In the case of industrial innovations, trial may involve adoption for the production of a small proportion of the output, or the loan by the innovation's developer of the innovation for use *in situ* in the potential adoptor's production facility. Trialability, or the ability to use the innovation at a reduced risk, is considered an important feature of innovations facilitating their diffusion (*see* DIFFUSION PROCESS).

Bibliography

Rogers, E. M. (1995). *Diffusion of Innovations*, 4th edn. New York: Free Press.

trust

Dale Littler

Trust is viewed as an important influence affecting the effectiveness of inter-organizational relationships (*see* CUSTOMER RELATIONSHIP MANAGEMENT; INTERNATIONAL STRATEGIC ALLIANCES; RELATIONSHIP MARKETING) because, in order to make commitments through investment in joint projects, sharing information, or engaging in other forms of partnership (*see* LICENSING), organizations need to be assured that partners will not engage in opportunistic behavior. Indeed, "Relationship marketing is built on the foundation of trust" (Berry, 1995: 242). Opportunistic behavior can be ameliorated by formal contracts and social controls (Parkhe, 1993), but not eliminated. Blois (1999) explores different definitions of trust and suggests that "if you trust somebody, then you are accepting that while it is a *theoretical possibility*, you do not believe it is a *realistic probability* that they will act in a manner that would disadvantage you" (p. 204). He suggests that trust is specific, person-embodied, and as such the focus is on truthworthiness rather than on trust; furthermore, it implies an expectation that, given unexpected events, the other party will deal with them in a way that does not disadvantage the relationship. Trust can be developed over time as organizations obtain experience of the behavior of those with whom they have been in contact, or in the case of strategic alliances by, *inter alia*, the allocation of non-recoverable resources.

Bibliography

Berry, L . L. (1995). Relationship marketing of services: Growing interest, emerging perspectives. *Journal of the Academy of Marketing Science*, **23**, 4 (Fall), 236–45.

Blois, K. J. (1999). Trust in business to business relationships: An evaluation of its status. *Journal of Management Studies*, **36**, 2 (March), 197–215.

Parkhe, A. (1993). Strategic alliance structuring: A game theoretic and transaction cost examination of interfirm co-operation. *Academy of Management Journal*, **36**, 4 (August), 794–829.

via opinion leaders to customers, or opinion "followers." Opinion leaders are portrayed as direct receivers of information from impersonal mass media sources (*see* INDIRECT COMMUNICATIONS), and they interpret, legitimize, and transmit this information to customers, i.e., they are intermediaries.

This theory assumes that mass media influence on mass opinion is not direct, i.e., that the mass media alone cannot influence the sales of products; that mass media communications are mediated by opinion leaders; that opinion leaders are more exposed to mass media than those they influence; and that opinion leaders may alter communications messages (i.e., they are GATEKEEPERS).

However, this is not an accurate portrayal of the flow of information and influence. Modifications to the theory accept that: mass media and interpersonal channels of communications (*see* INTERPERSONAL COMMUNICATIONS) are complementary, not competitive, i.e., that mass media may inform both opinion leaders and followers; opinion leadership is not a dichotomous trait, i.e., that interpersonal communications can be initiated by both leaders and followers, e.g., receivers are not passive and may request information/advice from opinion leaders, or seek it directly from the mass media; and information and advice may be sought from a diverse range of personal sources, e.g., friends, relations, work colleagues, that might not prima facie be categorized as "opinion leaders" as traditionally identified in the literature.

Bibliography

Lazarsfeld, P. F., Berelson, B., and Goudet, H. (1948). *The People's Choice*, 2nd edn. New York: Columbia Press.

Schiffman, L. G. and Kanuk, L. Z. (2004). *Consumer Behavior*, 8th edn. Upper Saddle River, NJ: Prentice-Hall, p. 513.'

two-step flow model

Barbara R. Lewis

The two-step flow model is concerned with the flow of MARKETING COMMUNICATIONS from the MASS MEDIA, in particular ADVERTISING,

types of measure

Michael Greatorex

Measurement involves assigning numbers to characteristics of objects or events in such a way that the numbers reflect reality. Essentially, there are four different types of measurement scales: nominal (or categorical), ordinal, interval, and ratio. As we move from categorical to ratio, so the arithmetic powers of the measures increase. The selection of the appropriate descriptive statistical measure (*see* DESCRIPTIVE STATISTICS) and/or test statistic depends upon, among other things, the type(s) of scales used to measure the variables of interest.

Nominal measurement scales use numbers to categorize objects or events. Thus, for a variable called gender, the number 1 can be used as a label for males, the number 2 as the label for females. Again for a variable such as occupation, doctors can be labeled 1, teachers 2, students 3, market researchers 4, and so on. The numbers are being used as shorthand to identify categories, and the numbers are replaceable by fuller descriptions or labels at any time. There is no suggestion that males precede females just because in everyday arithmetic 1 comes before 2, or that one female is worth two males because 2 is twice 1, or that adding a doctor to a teacher gives a student just because 1 plus 2 equals 3. The well-known rules of arithmetic do not apply to these numbers for obvious reasons.

Ordinal scales use numbers to rank items in order. As with nominal scales, cases are given the same number as other cases that share the same characteristic, but the order of the given numbers reflects the order in reality. Thus, respondents may be asked about their level of agreement or disagreement with a statement. For such a variable, respondents who "agree strongly" may be given the number 1, those "agreeing" given 2, those "neither agreeing nor disagreeing" given 3, those "disagreeing" given 4, while those "disagreeing strongly" are given 5. The numbers reflect the relative position of the responses but not their magnitude. There is no suggestion that the difference between the categories "agreeing" and "agreeing strongly" is necessarily the same as the difference between the categories "neither agreeing nor disagreeing" and "agreeing," despite the fact that, in other circumstances, the differences between 2 and 1 and between 3 and 2 are the same.

Much MARKETING RESEARCH involving the use of questionnaires (*see* QUESTIONNAIRE DESIGN) to measure the ATTITUDES, opinions, preferences, etc. of consumers is based on ordinal measurement scales. Ordinal measures are better than nominal measures in that with ordinal scales the order of the numbers reflects a real-life order of the categories, while nominal measures are used when such real-life ordering is not possible.

Interval measurement scales have the property that equal distances on the scale represent equal differences in the characteristic being measured. Thus, temperature can be measured on interval scales, the difference between 10 and 15 degrees is the same as the difference between 25 and 30 degrees. An improved form of interval scale, the *ratio scale*, has the additional property that it is possible to compute and compare ratios. Thus, the difference in price between 1 and 2 is the same as the difference between 8 and 9, but also the ratio of 10 to 5 is the same as the ratio of 6 to 3. Many variables can be measured on scales with these properties; examples are height, weight, incomes, revenues, sales, prices, profits, ages, etc. Such scales have all the properties of nominal and ordinal scales, indeed it is possible to convert ratio/interval scales into ordinal scales, which themselves can be converted to nominal scales, in each case with some loss of information.

The first question to be asked when a statistician begins to analyze a set of data is what type of scale is used to measure each variable. Only then can a decision be made as to which statistics and tests are appropriate.

Bibliography

Malhotra, N. K. and Birks, D. F. (2000). *Marketing Research: An Applied Orientation*, 3rd European edn. Harlow: Prentice-Hall.

U

umbrella strategy

Dale Littler

An organization is said to have an umbrella strategy when there is a clear definition of strategic goals, and even the general strategic direction, by the chief executive (or senior management), but the detail of how these goals are to be achieved has yet to be decided. Within these established boundaries, the various actors (such as functional managers) have the flexibility, often through a process of iteration and consensus building that will involve senior management, to develop the substance of the strategy, i.e., the means by which the strategic goals are to be realized. The strategy has also been termed "deliberately emergent" (Mintzberg and Waters, 1985) as the leadership purposefully allows others the flexibility to devise strategic content.

See also *emergent strategy*

Bibliography

Mintzberg, H. and Waters, J. A. (1985). Of strategies, deliberate and emergent. *Strategic Management Journal*, 63 (July/September), 257–72.

uncertainty

Dale Littler

Uncertainty has traditionally been defined in terms of its difference from risk, the classic distinction between the two being made by Knight (1921). He suggested that "risk" applies to those instances where the outcome(s) can be measured, i.e., where some value (or probability) can be ascribed to the possibility of some particular event occurring. Uncertainty, on the other hand, applies when it is not possible to do this. Hague (1971) adopts a slightly different terminology, distinguishing between "insurable" and "non-insurable" risk. The former, he suggests, refers to situations where it is possible to assess the likelihood of a particular occurrence based on statistical analysis by experts such as actuaries. "Non-insurable risk" applies when it is difficult to predict the outcome, which is the case, so Hague contends, in most business investment decisions. Shackle (1970) suggested that uncertainty exists when "there can be no knowing for certain what will be the consequences of action" (p. 21).

Some, e.g., Freeman (1984), have argued that in the case of technological INNOVATION, where there is generally considerable uncertainty about the outcome, uncertainty can be an aggregation of at least three different types: market, technological, and general business uncertainty. Market uncertainty arises from the difficulties in predicting competitors' actions and the market reaction at different prices. Technological uncertainty occurs because of the difficulties involved in predicting whether or not the initial technical specifications will be achieved at a cost that will enable the company to set a price acceptable to customers and at the same time make a satisfactory return. In many cases, product development (*see* NEW PRODUCT DEVELOPMENT) may be attended by increasing costs of development as unforeseen technical hurdles arise, demanding, sometimes, novel technical solutions. Finally, general business uncertainty surrounds all major investment decisions, and stems from the possibility of random events.

Uncertainty can have a profound impact on decision-making, and especially that related to significant changes. It undermines many of the assumptions surrounding the "design school" of strategy formation (Mintzberg, 1990) (*see* IM-PLEMENTATION), and suggests the need for flexibility and CONTINGENCY PLANNING.

In general, uncertainty is not awarded a central role in much traditional academic marketing and yet it has powerful and insidious implications for MARKETING MANAGEMENT. It requires a mindset that acknowledges that any planning needs to provide considerable scope for changes in the assumptions on which it is founded. Careful monitoring of the MAR-KETING ENVIRONMENT, and in particular of possible changes in consumer tastes and preferences that can affect the DEMAND for the organization's offerings, is desirable. The developments in information and communications technologies facilitate real-time information gathering and its widespread dissemination to a wide range of decision-makers.

Bibliography

Freeman, C. (1984). *The Economics of Industrial Innovation*, 2nd edn. London: Frances Pinter.

Hague, D. C. (1971). *Managerial Economics*. Harlow: Longman, ch. 7.

Knight, F. H. (1921). *Risk, Uncertainty and Profit*, 2nd edn. Boston: Houghton Mifflin.

Mintzberg, H. (1990). The design school: Reconsidering the basic premises of strategic management. *Strategic Management Journal*, 11, 3 (March/April), 171–95.

Shackle, G. L. S. (1970). *Expectation, Enterprise and Profit*. London: Allen and Unwin.

univariate analysis

Michael Greatorex

Univariate analysis is concerned with the quantitative analysis of data where each variable is analyzed in isolation. The preliminary analysis of a survey (*see* SURVEY RESEARCH) often begins with a univariate analysis of the data. Data for a series of variables, one variable at a time, for the whole of a sample, can be summarized into a frequency distribution for each variable with a suitable accompanying GRAPHICAL REPRE-SENTATION, such as a pie diagram, bar chart, histogram, ogive, etc. Alternatively, DESCRIP-TIVE STATISTICS such as measures of average, variation, skewness, and kurtosis may be calculated for each variable.

Point estimates of population characteristics, such as population proportions or population means and totals, can be made, and CONFI-DENCE INTERVALS based on the normal or t-distributions are easily computed. Hypothesis tests (*see* HYPOTHESIS TESTING) concerning population parameters for each variable, such as population proportions, population average, or standard deviation, are well known and include the z-test and t-test for interval data, the binomial test and one sample chi-square test for nominal data, and the Kolmogorov–Smirnov test for ordinal data.

Bibliography

Tull, D. S. and Hawkins, D. I. (1993). *Marketing Research: Measurement and Method*, 6th edn. New York: Macmillan, ch. 18.

users

Dominic Wilson

Users are members of the decision-making unit (*see* BUYING CENTER) and are those individuals working in an organization who are directly involved in the use of the goods and services purchased by the organization. For example, a welder could be a user of his/her organization's welding machinery, protective clothing, canteen, first-aid station, training courses, pension scheme, etc. It is important to involve users in the PURCHASING PROCESS to insure that whatever is eventually purchased will be practicable, acceptable, and readily integrated in organizational systems. Users can be influential in the early stages of the purchasing process where they may initiate a purchasing process through identifying a particular need and specifying what is necessary to meet that need. They can (and should) also be involved in later trials and quality monitoring.

See also *organizational buying behavior*

utility

Barbara R. Lewis

Businesses, in providing products and services through their production and marketing activities, create a number of kinds of economic utility to consumers. These economic utilities (of form, task, time, place, and possession) enable an organization to provide consumer satisfaction (*see* CUSTOMER SATISFACTION).

Form utility is created by converting raw materials into finished goods that meet consumer needs, e.g., producing a tennis racket. Task utility is provided when someone performs a task for someone else, e.g., a bank handling financial transactions. But just producing tennis rackets or handling bank accounts does not result in consumer satisfaction; the product (or service) must be something that consumers want or there is no need to be satisfied, and, therefore, there is limited utility. Consumers will not be satisfied until possession, time, and place utilities are also provided.

Possession utility means facilitating the transfer of ownership or use of a product/service to the consumer. Thus, the consumer obtains a good or service and has the right to use or consume it; customers usually exchange money or something else of value for possession utility (*see* EXCHANGE).

Time utility is created by having goods/services available when consumers want them, and relates to opening hours of retail outlets, 24-hour telephone lines for banking and/or advice services, etc.

Place utility is created by making goods/services available where consumers want them, e.g., moving products from warehouses or producers to a location where consumers want to buy them, and having services available where consumers want to consume them.

validity

Michael Greatorex and Mark P. Healey

A scale or a measure is valid if it measures what it is intended to measure. Validity is established by considering the following criteria: face validity, RELIABILITY, criterion validity, and construct validity.

Face or content validity is the degree to which a measure captures the characteristics of a concept one desires to measure. It is a subjective assessment of the correspondence between the theoretical concepts under study and the measurements being constructed.

High *reliability* is essential for validity but does not insure validity. A measure may be reliable but not valid when errors are consistent or systematic.

Criterion validity considers whether or not the scale performs as expected in relation to other variables, the criterion variables. The criterion variables may be selected attitudinal, behavioral, socioeconomic, or psychographic variables. Concurrent validity is assessed when the scale being evaluated and the criterion variables are measured at the same time. Predictive validity is assessed when the data on the scales are collected at one point in time and used to predict values of the criterion variables that are measured at a later point in time.

Construct validity involves understanding the concepts that the constructs are measuring and their interrelationships. Is a constructed measure highly positively correlated with other measures of the same construct (convergent validity), not correlated with theoretically unrelated constructs (discriminant validity), or correlated in an expected way with different but related constructs (nomological validity)? A construct is valid if it behaves as expected in relation to other constructs.

In the case of QUALITATIVE RESEARCH, natural validity, for example, concerns the extent to which findings and conclusions are influenced by situational reflexivity (is the study focus unmodified by researchers' actions?) and is important due to the demands placed on naturalism by idiographic research. Theoretical validity refers to the "presence of a more abstract explanation of described actions and interpreted meanings" (Miles and Huberman, 1994: 279). Appreciating the different forms and concerns of "validity" may be particularly important where researchers and practitioners are increasingly relying on both quantitative and qualitative data, and (comparatively) evaluating and reconciling the outputs of each form of research is of increasing importance.

Bibliography

Miles, M. B. and Huberman, A. M. (1994). *Qualitative Data Analysis: An Expanded Sourcebook*. London: Sage.
Tull, D. S. and Hawkins, D. I. (1993). *Marketing Research: Measurement and Method*, 6th edn. New York: Macmillan.

VALS

see LIFESTYLES; PSYCHOGRAPHICS

value added

Dominic Wilson

The notion of value added refers to the principle that value is added cumulatively to a product or service by successive participants in the VALUE CHAIN. Thus, value added at any particular stage of the chain can be estimated as: value of output less cost of input (not including labor). Value-added analysis can provide a useful input to internal productivity calculations (e.g., value added per person or per work group) and can also, of course, be an important basis for taxation.

For the purposes of PRICING decisions it is important to assess value in terms of the user at the next stage in the value chain. In other words, in a competitive market, value should be determined by the "customer perspective." The concept is also particularly useful in competitive analysis where organizations can examine their own activities to insure that they only engage in operations where they are able to add significant value, leaving other aspects of their activities (e.g., distribution, DESIGN) to specialist subcontractors.

value chain

Dale Littler

The value chain embraces the various activities aimed at creating value for the customer and the MARGIN that the firm obtains. It was first articulated by Porter (1985). The value activities can be divided into two main categories: support activities, which include firm infrastructure, human resource management, technology development and procurement, and the primary activities of inbound LOGISTICS, operations, outbound logistics, MARKETING and sales, and service. It provides a framework for analyzing not only how the organization currently provides value, but also how value can be enhanced. Organizations may strive to secure synergies with, e.g., SUPPLIERS by, for instance, developing inbound logistics systems that provide mutual benefits. Accounting data are often not in a form that permits the easy application of this kind of analysis while securing information on other organizations' value chains (and especially competitors') is very problematic (Hergert and Morris, 1989). In general, therefore, although it is an interesting concept, its practical usefulness remains to be demonstrated.

Bibliography

Hergert, M. and Morris, D. (1989). Accounting Data for Value Chain Analysis. *Strategic Management Journal*, **10**, 175–88.
Porter, M. E. (1985). *Competitive Advantage: Creating and Sustaining Superior Performance*. New York: Free Press.

vertical integration

Dale Littler

This is regarded as a growth strategy (*see* GROWTH VECTOR MATRIX), although it can be employed to defend the organization against powerful competitors, SUPPLIERS, and CUSTOMERS (*see* COMPETITIVE STRATEGY). It generally involves the acquisition of suppliers and/or customers, thereby providing, *inter alia*, security of supply or of access to the market. Companies may engage in backward vertical integration, involving the acquisition of suppliers, or forward vertical integration, i.e., taking control of customers. There are also vertically integrated systems in which there may not be complete ownership, but in which cooperation is founded on, e.g., agreements or minority stakes by the various parties in each other. Such systems may be effectively coordinated or administered by one dominant organization

See also *horizontal integration*

viral marketing

Mark P. Healey

Viral marketing is the term applied to an Internet-based promotional strategy that encourages users to transfer to others a fixed MARKETING COMMUNICATIONS message, usually without the volition of either sender or recipient. The MESSAGE is usually transmitted via electronic mail from one user to the recipients of this user's messages. In this way, the communications message achieves mass exposure at great speed, with little incremental effort on the part of the marketer. The classic example of viral marketing is Microsoft's attachment of a simple promotional message to all messages sent via hotmail.com, its free electronic mail service. Each time a user sends a message, he/she inevitably perpetuates the original message by increasing its exposure to a new audience, and this effect is continued when new users subscribe to the service, creating exponential growth.

Although the term carries clear negative connotations owing to its semantic association with both its biological and computational namesakes, it has been termed the worldwide web equivalent of WORD-OF-MOUTH COMMUNICATIONS. However, this is not an apt analogy, as it suggests that the endorsement passed on by a user is volitional. This is not so in the case of viral marketing; rather, the message is forced by necessity upon both sender and recipient by the source of the virus (i.e., the promoting organization). Most viral marketing programs involve giving away free goods or services (e.g., software, information) based on the rationale that the interest generated from this will stimulate profitable sales on other offerings, will facilitate the collection of valuable information (email addresses, e-commerce sales opportunities; *see* ELECTRONIC COMMERCE), or will help generate ADVERTISING revenue.

vision statement

Dale Littler

The vision statement is a relatively recent introduction to the lexicon of strategic management and is generally regarded as encapsulating the desired-for future for the organization, usually as expressed by the chief executive or senior management group. It can therefore provide a guide for the development of the strategy. Collins and Porras (1996) suggest that a business vision should contain: core values that are the guiding principles of the organization; the core purpose, the organization's rationale for existing, which extends beyond its current offerings; and ambitious goals that provide a major challenge. The distinction between vision and mission (*see* MISSION STATEMENT) is somewhat blurred. For some, though, vision is regarded as an element in the mission statement.

Bibliography

Collins, J. C. and Porras, J. L. (1996). Building your company's vision. *Harvard Business Review*, September/October, 65–77.

Hamel, G. and Prahalad, C. K. (1994). Competing for the future. *Harvard Business Review*, **72**, 4 (July/August), 122–8.

W

wealth

David Yorke

A person's purchasing power derives from DIS-POSABLE INCOME and DISCRETIONARY INCOME, resulting from employment, investments, credit, and other means. An increasingly important source is that of wealth, i.e., the ownership of assets such as property, savings, shares, etc. which themselves yield an income and which help to create a lifestyle (*see* LIFESTYLES). In some countries, especially the US and the UK, through mortgaging or increasing the mortgage on their home property, consumers have taken advantage of the inflation in home valuations to release equity which can then be employed for consumption. However, as a consequence, consumer debt levels have risen.

The second half of the twentieth century witnessed an increase in wealth among large numbers of people in economically developed countries, but as the populations of such countries age, and the state is unable or unwilling to support those in retirement, the income from wealth may not be spent in the short term but may be reinvested for the future. Unquestionably, the increase in the proportion of people of pensionable age that is occurring in many developed economies, as well as the reducing proportion of those of working age and the possible resistance to significant tax increases, suggests that the state will not be able to provide high levels of pension support. This highlights, therefore, the importance to many of preserving their wealth as a means of income for retirement.

Bibliography

Central Statistical Office. *Family Spending* (annual). London: HMSO.

United States Bureau of the Census. *Statistical Abstract of the United States* (annual). Austin, TX: Reference Press.

wheel of retailing

Steve Worrall and Andrew Newman

There are a number of theories that attempt to explain the evolution of retail enterprises, and the *wheel of retailing* is probably the most well known of these (Newman and Cullen, 2002). Wheel theory is one of the oldest methods of explaining the patterns of competitive development and change in RETAILING, suggesting that entrants to a new retail market will begin trading as cut-price, low-overhead, low-margin, and low-status operations (McNair, 1958). Over time, these traders will increase their overheads by offering additional services and product lines, perhaps in better locations, smarter premises, and with more sophisticated MARKETING COMMUNICATIONS. These retailers are then more vulnerable to new low-cost entrants to the market who may be able to undercut the original retailer's prices. The retail cycle will then have come full circle.

The wheel theory is a generalization that may not hold true in all cases. Many academics have warned of the dangers of generalizing the wheel theories too widely (McGoldrick, 2002). For example, retailers entering new markets may be tempted to copy the trading format of established retailers, which may require sophisticated trading patterns from the start. In other cases, such as in times of recession, retailers may attempt to cut costs and even reduce some services, thus moving in the opposite direction to that suggested by the wheel theory (Kaynak, 1979).

Bibliography

Brown, S. (1990). The wheel of retailing: Past and future. *Journal of Retailing*, **66**, 2 (Summer), 143–9.

Brown, S. (1995). Postmodernism, the wheel of retailing and will to power. *International Review of Retail, Distribution and Consumer Research*, **5** (3), 387–415.

Kaynak, E. (1979). A refined approach to the wheel of retailing. *European Journal of Marketing*, **13** (7), 237–45.

McGoldrick, P. J. (2002). *Retail Marketing*. London: McGraw-Hill.

McNair, M. P. (1958). Significant trends and developments in the postwar period. In A. B. Smith (ed.), *Competitive Distribution in a Free High-Level Economy and its Implications for the University*. Pittsburgh, PA: University of Pittsburgh Press, 1–25.

Newman, A. J. and Cullen, P. (2002). *Retailing: Environment and Operations*. London: Thomson Learning.

wholesalers

Andrew Newman and Steve Greenland

Wholesalers form the part of the marketing channel (*see* CHANNELS OF DISTRIBUTION) between producers/manufacturers and the retailer. Wholesalers buy and sell in large quantities direct to the retailer and generally do not sell goods direct to the public. Particularly for the smaller retailer, the wholesaler is an indispensable part of their supply process. The main function is to provide a halfway house between manufacturers and retailers. Manufacturers are widely dispersed and undertake the dedicated large-scale production of goods. However, many thousands of retailers need a convenient means of selecting relatively small amounts of the various products to build the appropriate product assortments for their stores. The wholesaler provides a gathering point for many different products and performs a bulk-breaking service for the retailer so that it can make up its required assortment of products. The wholesaler thus provides warehousing services where this process takes place. These services include: storage of items until the retailers require them; picking of items from stock to make the retailer's assortment; consolidation of the items into a load for distribution to the retailer; and transport of the consolidated load to the retailer's store. Wholesalers also take ownership of the goods and so assume some of the producer's risks of non-saleability caused by damage, obsolescence, or lack of customer demand. This arrangement also speeds up the process of payment to the producer.

Wholesalers may sometimes be referred to as *cash and carry* depots. This service still provides storage facilities, but retailers may carry out the other functions themselves (Newman and Cullen, 2002).

See also *retail distribution channels*

Bibliography

Carr, N. G. (2000). Hypermediation: Commerce as clickstream. *Harvard Business Review*, **78**, 1 (January/February), 46–8.

Lewison, D. (1994). *Retailing*. New York: Macmillan.

Newman, A. J. and Cullen, P. (2002). *Retailing: Environment and Operations*. London: Thomson Learning.

word-of-mouth communications

David Yorke

Word-of-mouth communication is a non-commercial form of marketing communication (*see* MARKETING COMMUNICATIONS) where the sender of the MESSAGE is assisted by intermediaries in attempting to reach the target buyer/customer/consumer. Opinion leaders may benefit an organization with positive word-of-mouth communications, but there is a danger that word-of-mouth may be detrimental to the organization and its products or services as a result of poor experiences of the intermediary. Word-of-mouth communications may or may not be solicited; they are often regarded as being more reliable because of the perception that the communicator does not have a vested interest in the subject of the communications; and intermediaries with negative experience(s) can be particularly active and effective.

See also *interpersonal communications; two-step flow model*

Index

Note: Headwords are in **bold** type